INTERACTIONAL LINGUISTICS: STUDYING LANGUAGE IN SOCIAL INTERACTION

The first textbook dedicated to interactional linguistics, focusing on linguistic analyses of conversational phenomena, this introduction provides an overview of the theory and methodology of interactional linguistics. Reviewing recent findings on linguistic practices used in turn construction and turn taking, repair, action formation and ascription, sequence and topic organization, the book examines the way linguistic units of varying size – sentences, clauses, phrases, clause combinations, particles – are mobilized for the implementation of specific actions in talk-in-interaction. A final chapter discusses the implications of an interactional perspective for our understanding of language as well as its variation, diversity, and universality. Supplementary online chapters explore additional topics such as the linguistic organization of preference, stance, footing, and storytelling, as well as the use of prosody and phonetics, and further practices with language. Featuring summary boxes and transcripts from recordings of everyday conversation, this is an essential resource for advanced undergraduate and postgraduate courses on language in social interaction.

ELIZABETH COUPER-KUHLEN is Distinguished Professor (Emerita) at the University of Helsinki, Finland. She has published widely on prosody and grammar in interaction; in addition to numerous journal articles, she has authored, co-authored, and co-edited many volumes on interactional linguistics, including *Prosody in Conversation* (with Margret Selting, 1996) and *Studies in Interactional Linguistics* (with Margret Selting, 2001).

MARGRET SELTING is Professor of Linguistics and Communication Theory at the University of Potsdam, Germany. She has published extensively on prosody and grammar in interaction, including *Prosody in Conversation* (with Elizabeth Couper-Kuhlen, 1996), *Studies in Interactional Linguistics* (with Elizabeth Couper-Kuhlen, 2001), and *Problems of Understanding* (1987).

INTERACTIONAL LINGUISTICS: STUDYING LANGUAGE IN SOCIAL INTERACTION

ELIZABETH COUPER-KUHLEN AND MARGRET SELTING

CAMBRIDGE
UNIVERSITY PRESS

University Printing House, Cambridge CB2 8BS, United Kingdom

One Liberty Plaza, 20th Floor, New York, NY 10006, USA

477 Williamstown Road, Port Melbourne, VIC 3207, Australia

314–321, 3rd Floor, Plot 3, Splendor Forum, Jasola District Centre, New Delhi – 110025, India

79 Anson Road, #06–04/06, Singapore 079906

Cambridge University Press is part of the University of Cambridge.

It furthers the University's mission by disseminating knowledge in the pursuit of education, learning, and research at the highest international levels of excellence.

www.cambridge.org
Information on this title: www.cambridge.org/9781107032804
DOI: 10.1017/9781139507318

© Elizabeth Couper-Kuhlen and Margret Selting, 2018

This publication is in copyright. Subject to statutory exception and to the provisions of relevant collective licensing agreements, no reproduction of any part may take place without the written permission of Cambridge University Press.

First published 2018

Printed in the United Kingdom by TJ International Ltd., Padstow, Cornwall

A catalogue record for this publication is available from the British Library.

Library of Congress Cataloging-in-Publication Data
Names: Couper-Kuhlen, Elizabeth, author. | Selting, Margret.
Title: Interactional linguistics : an introduction to language in social interaction / Elizabeth Couper-Kuhlen, Margret Selting.
Description: Cambridge, United Kingdom ; New York : Cambridge University Press, 2017.
Identifiers: LCCN 2017026501 | ISBN 9781107032804 (hardback)
Subjects: LCSH: Discourse analysis – Social aspects. | Conversation analysis. | Intercultural communication. | Grammar, Comparative and general – Syntax. | Pragmatics.
Classification: LCC P302.84 .C69 2017 | DDC 401/.41–dc23
LC record available at https://lccn.loc.gov/2017026501

ISBN 978-1-107-03280-4 Hardback
ISBN 978-1-107-61603-5 Paperback

Additional resources for this publication at www.cambridge.org/interactional.

Cambridge University Press has no responsibility for the persistence or accuracy of URLs for external or third-party internet websites referred to in this publication and does not guarantee that any content on such websites is, or will remain, accurate or appropriate.

Contents

Preface   *page* xiii

Introduction   1

Chapter 1. What is Interactional Linguistics?   3
  1. Roots of Interactional Linguistics   4
    1.1 Conversation Analysis   5
    1.2 Contextualization Theory   8
    1.3 Linguistic Anthropology   10
  2. Development of Interactional Linguistics   12
  3. Premises and Goals of Interactional Linguistic Research   14
  4. Principles of Interactional Linguistic Work   18
    4.1 Naturally Occurring Data   18
    4.2 Context-sensitive Analysis   22
    4.3 Online Perspective   22
    4.4 Categories Empirically Grounded   23
    4.5 Claims Warranted through Participant Orientation   25

Online-Chapter A. Motivating an Interactional Linguistic Perspective
        (Available at: www.cambridge.org/interactional)
  1. Implementing Social Action with Language
  2. Using Language to Implement Social Action
  3. Alternative Ways of Saying the Same Thing

Part I. How is Interaction Conducted with Linguistic Resources?   27
  Preface   27

Chapter 2. Turn Construction and Turn Taking   31
  1. TCU Construction   34
    1.1 Projection   39
    1.2 The Roles of Syntax and Prosody   47
    1.3 Pauses and Break-offs within TCUs   54
    1.4 Inserts/Parentheticals   56
    1.5 Compound TCUs   59

Contents

- 2. Multi-unit Turns — 61
  - 2.1 Lexico-semantic and Pragmatic Projection — 61
  - 2.2 Action/Activity Type-specific Projection — 63
  - 2.3 Prosodic Projection — 65
- 3. The Organization of Turn Taking — 69
  - 3.1 Opening the Transition Relevance Space in English and German — 70
  - 3.2 Turn Yielding — 72
  - 3.3 Turn Holding — 88
- 4. Turn Expansion — 94
  - 4.1 Conceptions of Incrementing — 95
  - 4.2 Cross-linguistic Turn Expansion — 97
- 5. "Deviant" Turn Taking — 103
  - 5.1 Turn Overlap and Turn Competition — 103
  - 5.2 Stopping and Abandoning Turns — 108
- 6. Conclusion — 110

Chapter 3. Repair — 112
- 1. Introduction — 112
  - 1.1 Basic Terminology — 113
  - 1.2 Repair as a Vehicle for Other Actions — 115
  - 1.3 Repair as a Universal Practice — 116
- 2. Self-initiation of Repair — 116
  - 2.1 Pre-positioned Self-initiation — 118
  - 2.2 Post-positioned Self-initiation — 123
  - 2.3 Repair Operations — 128
  - 2.4 Conclusion for Self-initiation of Repair — 138
- 3. Other-initiation of Repair — 138
  - 3.1 Conceptualizing Other-initiated Repair — 140
  - 3.2 Types of Other-initiated Repair — 146
  - 3.3 Conclusion for Other-initiation of Repair — 196
- 4. Other-correction — 201
  - 4.1 Producing a Correct Version — 204
  - 4.2 Explicitly Correcting an Item — 205
  - 4.3 Explicitly Correcting an Entire Verbal Representation — 206
  - 4.4 Conclusion for Other-correction — 207
- 5. Conclusion — 208

Chapter 4. Action Formation and Ascription — 210
- 1. Preliminaries — 210
  - 1.1 Action and Action Type — 211
  - 1.2 Social Actions and Speech Acts — 213

		1.3	Sequence Type and Project	215
		1.4	Turn Design and Practices	216
		1.5	"Top-down" versus "Bottom-up" Analysis	216
	2.	Questions and their Responses		217
		2.1	Recognizing Questions	219
		2.2	Question-word Interrogatives	220
		2.3	Polar Interrogatives	224
		2.4	B-event Statements	227
		2.5	Questioning and the Epistemic Gradient	230
		2.6	Responding to Question-word Interrogatives	232
		2.7	Responding to Polar Interrogatives and B-event Statements	238
	3.	Offers, Requests, and their Responses		249
		3.1	The Linguistic Design of Offers	249
		3.2	The Linguistic Design of Requests	253
		3.3	Requests Masquerading As Offers	257
		3.4	Responding to Offers and Requests	259
	4.	News Deliveries, Informings, and their Responses		266
		4.1	News Deliveries Distinguished from Informings	268
		4.2	The Linguistic Design of News Deliveries	270
		4.3	The Linguistic Design of Informings	273
		4.4	Responding to News and Informings	275
	5.	Assessments, Compliments, Self-deprecations, and their Responses		283
		5.1	Assessing Actions in First Position	287
		5.2	The Linguistic Design of Assessments	288
		5.3	Epistemic Primacy in First Assessments	289
		5.4	The Linguistic Design of Compliments and Self-deprecations	292
		5.5	Responding to Assessments	294
		5.6	Responding to Compliments and Self-deprecations	307
	6.	Conclusion		311

Online-Chapter B. Preference and Other Asymmetric Alternatives
(Available at: www.cambridge.org/interactional)
  1. Preference as a Property of Initiating Action Type
     1.1 Linguistic Resources for Projecting Response Preference
     1.2 Linguistic Resources for Reversing and Relaxing Projected Response Preference
  2. Preference as a Property of Responsive Turn Design
     2.1 Linguistic Resources for Designing "Plus" Responses
     2.2 Linguistic Resources for Designing "Minus" Responses

3. Type Conformity
    3.1 Linguistic Resources for Yes-no Interrogative-type Conformity in English
    3.2 Linguistic Resources for Yes-no Interrogative-type Conformity in Finnish
4. Conclusion

Chapter 5. Topic and Sequence — 312
1. Distinguishing Topicality from Sequentiality — 312
2. Topic Management — 314
    2.1 Topicality — 314
    2.2 Some Linguistic Resources for Managing Topic — 316
3. Sequence Organization — 328
    3.1 Sequence and Sequential Structure — 328
    3.2 Some Linguistic Resources for Marking Sequence Beginnings — 330
    3.3 Some Linguistic Resources for Initiating Sequence Closings — 335
    3.4 Some Linguistic Resources for Marking Misplaced Sequences — 342
    3.5 Some Linguistic Resources for Returning to a Prior Non-adjacent Sequence — 345
4. Conclusion — 354

Online-Chapter C. Stance and Footing
        (Available at: www.cambridge.org/interactional)
1. On the Notions of Stance and Footing
2. Epistemic Stance
    2.1 Conveying Epistemic Stance in English
    2.2 Conveying Epistemic Stance in Other Languages
3. Deontic Stance
    3.1 Conveying Deontic Stance in English
    3.2 Conveying Deontic Stance in Other Languages
4. Affective Stance
    4.1 Affective Displays and their Situatedness
    4.2 Some Affective Displays and How they are Accomplished Linguistically
5. Footing in Reported Speech and Thought
    5.1 Direct Reported Speech and Thought as a Shift in Footing
    5.2 Linguistic Devices for Reporting Speech and Thought
6. Conclusion

Online-Chapter D. A "Big Package": Storytelling
        (Available at: www.cambridge.org/interactional)

1. Story Prefacing
2. Telling the Story Itself
   2.1 Distinguishing Background from Foreground Information
   2.2 Dramatization through the Use of Narrative Present Tense
   2.3 The Combination of Syntax and Prosody for Dramatization
   2.4 The Construction of Reported Speech and Thought
   2.5 Contextualizing the Climax of the Story
   2.6 Story Completion
3. Responses to Storytelling
   3.1 Responses in Mid-telling
   3.2 Responses After the Climax and/or at the End of Telling
   3.3 Responses as Context-sensitive Objects
   3.4 Affiliative and Non-affiliative Responses to Complaint Stories
   3.5 Affect Display Sequences at Story Climaxes
4. Conclusion

Part II. How are Linguistic Resources Deployed in Interaction?   355

    Preface   355

Chapter 6. Sentences, Clauses, and Phrases   359
1. Analyzing Sentences, Clauses, and Phrases in Talk-in-interaction   359
   1.1 An Eye-opener   361
   1.2 Conceptualizing Sentences, Clauses, and Phrases Interactionally   362
   1.3 Sentences, Clauses, and Phrases As Emergent Constructions   364
   1.4 Cross-linguistic Evidence for the Interactional Relevance of the Clause   365
   1.5 Packaging of Sentences, Clauses, and Phrases   371
2. Internal Organization of Clauses   374
   2.1 Word Order   375
   2.2 Pivots   381
   2.3 Finiteness versus Non-finiteness   389
3. Extensions of Clauses   393
   3.1 Initial Extensions: Left Dislocation and Other Pre-positionings   394
   3.2 Final Extensions: Right Dislocation and Other Post-positionings   402
4. Other Clausal Variants   410
   4.1 "Argument Omission" Constructions in English   411
   4.2 "Dense" Constructions in German   412

5.	Phrases	416
	5.1 The Flexibility and Projectability of Phrases	416
	5.2 Building Actions with Phrases	419
6.	Conclusion	423

Chapter 7. Clause Combinations — 426

1.	Introduction	426
2.	Paratactic Clause Combinations	429
	2.1 Agenda-invoking with "And"	435
	2.2 Resuming a Topic with "But"	436
	2.3 Building Subsequent Versions with "Or"	438
	2.4 Accounting for "How I Know This" or "Why I Say This" with Reason Combinations	440
	2.5 Taking Exception to Something Just Said with Adversative Combinations	443
	2.6 Conceding and "Show Concessions" with Concessive Combinations	445
	2.7 Projecting Failure with First Verb Combinations	447
3.	Hypotactic Clause Combinations	449
	3.1 Designing versus Adding on Accounts with "Because"	454
	3.2 Verb-first Forms in Conditional Clauses	457
	3.3 Freestanding "If" Clauses	458
	3.4 "Although" as a Concessive Marker	460
4.	Subordinate Clause Combinations	462
	4.1 Complement Clauses	462
	4.2 Relative Clauses	469
5.	Other Clausal Combinations	475
	5.1 Pseudoclefts	476
	5.2 Extraposition	482
	5.3 Other Projector Constructions	487
6.	Practices of Clause Combining: Co-construction, Incrementation, Projector Frames	489
7.	Conclusion	492

Chapter 8. One-word Constructions: Particles — 493

1.	Introduction	493
2.	Particles	495
	2.1 Freestanding Particles	497
	2.2 Turn-initial Particles	514
	2.3 Turn-final Particles	527

   3. Conclusion   537

Online-Chapter E. Prosody and Phonetics
          (Available at: www.cambridge.org/interactional)
1. On the Interactional Relevance of Prosodic and Phonetic Resources
2. Prosodic-phonological Units
3. Pitch and Loudness
   - 3.1 Pitch and Loudness in Turn Construction and Turn Taking
   - 3.2 Pitch and Loudness in the Other-initiation of Repair
   - 3.3 Pitch and Loudness in Action Construction and Sequence Organization
   - 3.4 Pitch and Loudness in Displaying Stance and Footing
4. Duration, Pause, and Syllable Timing
   - 4.1 Duration, Pause, and Syllable Timing in Multi-unit Turn Construction and Organization
   - 4.2 Duration, Pause, and Syllable Timing in Turn Projection
   - 4.3 Duration, Pause, and Syllable Timing in Turn Transition
   - 4.4 Duration, Pause, and Syllable Timing in Self-repair
5. Articulation
   - 5.1 Articulation in Turn Holding and Turn Yielding
   - 5.2 Articulation in Self-repair
   - 5.3 Articulation in Marking Stance
6. Phonation and Phonatory Settings
7. Airstream Mechanisms
8. Breathing
9. The Interplay of Prosodic and Phonetic Resources
10. Conclusion

Online-Chapter F. Further Practices with Language
          (Available at: www.cambridge.org/interactional)
1. Referring to Person and Place
   - 1.1 Reference as an Interactional Achievement
   - 1.2 Person Reference
   - 1.3 Place Reference
2. Addressing an Interlocutor
   - 2.1 Ensuring Recipiency in Multi-party Talk
   - 2.2 Prefacing a Turn with an Address Term in Two-party Talk
   - 2.3 Concluding a Turn with an Address Term in Two-party Talk
   - 2.4 Pivoting from One Unit to Another with an Address Term
3. Repeating and Repetitions
   - 3.1 Repetition for Registering Receipt of a Prior Turn

     3.2 Repetition for Articulating the Target of a Next Action
     3.3 Repetition for Confirming an Allusion
     3.4 Repetition for Quoting as Opposed to Mimicking
          an Interlocutor
  4. Listing and Lists
     4.1 The Three-partedness of Lists
     4.2 The Embedding of Lists in their Sequential Context
     4.3 Lexico-semantic and Syntactic Properties of Lists
     4.4 The Prosody of Lists
     4.5 The Multimodal Organization of Lists in Swedish
     4.6 Lists as an Interactional Resource
  5. Preliminaries and Preliminaries to Preliminaries
     5.1 Type-specific Pre-expansions
     5.2 Pre-pre-expansions
     5.3 Generic Pre-expansion
  6. "My Side" Tellings and Reportings
     6.1 "My Side" Tellings
     6.2 Reportings
  7. Formulating and Formulations
     7.1 Formulations as an Explicating Practice
     7.2 Extreme Case Formulations as a Rhetorical Practice
  8. Conclusion

Conclusion   539

Chapter 9. Implications for Language Theory   541
  1. Language in an Interactional Linguistic Perspective   541
  2. Design Features of Language   542
  3. Language Variation and Interaction   546
  4. Language Diversity and Interaction   548
  5. Language Universals and Interaction   551

Bibliography   556
Appendix: Transcription Systems   606
Index   611

Preface

Putting this book together has been a long and arduous journey, but we have had help along the way from many friends and colleagues around the world. Our special thanks go to Peter Auer (University of Freiburg), Dagmar Barth-Weingarten (University of Potsdam), Auli Hakulinen (University of Helsinki), Kobin Kendrick (MPI Nijmegen), Maxi Kupetz (University of Potsdam), Marja-Leena Sorjonen (University of Helsinki), and Sandra A. Thompson (University of California Santa Barbara) – all of whom have spent precious time talking through the issues with us and reading pre-versions of the chapters. We have profited tremendously from their input and hope that the final version will do justice to their concerns. All remaining errors are our own.

Our deepest appreciation goes as well to Helen Barton (CUP), who has been ever so accommodating and supportive in helping us adapt our output to Cambridge University Press standards. The end result is as much to her credit as to ours. For reasons of space some chapters had to be "extraposed" as online chapters; in the Table of Contents they appear in their original position.

We are grateful to the VolkswagenStiftung, who generously funded the writing of this volume with an *opus magnum* grant ("Interactional Linguistics", AZ.: 86 281) to Margret Selting.

We dedicate our book to instructors and students alike, who will hopefully be as excited as we were to discover the extraordinary power of studying everyday language through a social interactional lens.

Helsinki and Potsdam, September 2016
Elizabeth Couper-Kuhlen and Margret Selting

Introduction

1

What is Interactional Linguistics?

Throughout much of the twentieth century, modern linguistics suffered from a written language bias (Linell 2005): the general thinking about language, as well as the descriptive concepts and categories developed for linguistic research, were tailored to language as it appears in writing. Interactional Linguistics, by contrast, grew out of an interest in spoken language and a desire to see it studied in its natural habitat: in social interaction. Interactional linguists took seriously the observation that "some of the most fundamental features of natural language are shaped in accordance with their home environment in co-present interaction, as adaptations to it, or as part of its very warp and weft" (Schegloff 1996b:54). They pursued this observation to its logical conclusion: namely, that as a consequence language must be *analyzed* in the home environment of co-present interaction. The idea was to apply the same empirical methods that had been so successful in revealing the structure and organization of everyday conversation, the methods of ethnomethodological Conversation Analysis, to explore the structure and organization of language as used in social interaction. From the cumulative results of such exploration, it was hoped, a new theory of language would emerge.[1]

Naturally, in order to explore language in its home environment, Interactional Linguistics needed and continues to need an appreciation of the structure and organization of interaction. For this, it is heavily indebted to Conversation Analysis, whose practitioners over the years have laid bare the structural underpinnings of coordinated interaction in social contexts. However, as the "founder" of Conversation Analysis, Harvey Sacks, explained early on, he was not interested in ordinary conversation because he had any "large interest in language," but rather simply because it was easy to record and because these recordings could be listened to again and again (Sacks 1984:26). Conversation analysts are primarily interested in understanding how

---

[1] The name of the new approach was modeled on one of its inspirations: Gumperz' (1982) "Interactional Sociolinguistics", the original "home" of Contextualization Theory and one of the donor fields of Interactional Linguistics (see below).

interaction works, in uncovering the mechanisms of, for example, how turns at talk are coordinated, how actions are constructed and recognized, and how they are made to cohere in sequences of interaction. Interactional linguists, by contrast, do have a "large interest" in language, because they believe that turns, actions, and sequences are accomplished and made interpretable by the systematic use of linguistic resources; consequently, they make the linguistic forms deployed by ordinary speakers in everyday and institutional encounters the focus of their attention.

1. Roots of Interactional Linguistics

The origin of interactional linguistic thinking, i.e., of conceptualizing linguistic structure as a resource for social interaction, can be traced back to functional theories of language. As early as the 1930s, Bühler (1982 [1934]) described the verbal sign (*sprachliches Zeichen*) as being used for three functions: as a *symbol* for the representation of objects and facts, as a *symptom* for expressions by the sender or speaker, and as a *signal* for appeals to the receiver or hearer. The forms of language were thus described with respect to their functions. In the Anglo-Saxon world, it was seminal work by M. A. K. Halliday (1978) that propagated a functional view of language. For Halliday, three macro-functions of language can be identified that reflect what we need language to do: to refer to the categories of experience (experiential function), to take on a role in the interpersonal situation (interpersonal function), and to embody these in the form of text or discourse (textual function) (Kress 1976:29). These functions are said to be manifest as grammatical structure in the language system (Halliday 1985).

At roughly the same time but in another part of the world, a different kind of functionalism was being developed by linguists such as Givón (1979), Chafe (1980), Du Bois (1980), and Hopper and Thompson (1980, 1984). Known as "West Coast functionalism" or "discourse functional syntax", this approach to grammar grew out of a close inspection of naturally produced (typically narrative) discourse. The idea was to observe grammar in actual use and to locate motivations for the patterns observed in the cognitive and communicative demands of producing coherent discourse. When discourse functional linguists began expanding their database to include conversation, they found themselves dealing with grammar in interaction (Fox 1987; Ford 1993; Ford and Thompson 1996). At this point, a branch of discourse functional linguistics began to do interactional linguistic research.

> The ground for interactional linguistic inquiry was prepared by functional linguists on both sides of the Atlantic, who sought motivations for linguistic structure in the way language is used. While Hallidayean systemic functional linguists developed an abstract model of grammar that reflects language functions, discourse functional linguists observed the use of grammar in real discourse and attributed the attested patterns to cognitive and communicative functions. All functionalists agree that linguistic form is shaped and motivated by function. As will emerge in the following chapters, this is also one of the basic tenets of Interactional Linguistics.

Interactional Linguistics was initially conceived as a Conversation Analysis-informed approach to the study of language (Linguistics) and languages (Linguistic Anthropology). Because this approach was radically empirical with a focus squarely on language use, contextual factors were considered to be as important as referential meaning (see Contextualization Theory below). From the beginning there was a natural confluence of interest between these fields and Interactional Linguistics – and more recently, with the availability of video technology, bodily-visual behavior is increasingly being incorporated. In the following sections we introduce the most important donor fields for the development of Interactional Linguistics: Conversation Analysis, Contextualization Theory, and Linguistic Anthropology.

1.1 Conversation Analysis

Conversation Analysis (CA) emerged as a constructionist approach in sociology.[2] On the basis of ethnomethodological thinking (see Garfinkel 1967), CA describes everyday social interaction as an ordered and orderly phenomenon, as a locus of social order. The assumption is that there is "order at all points" (Sacks 1984:22), that participants methodically produce social meaning with and for each other, thereby collaboratively constructing social reality (Berger and Luckmann 1966). In essence, the organization of natural conversation is conceived of as revealing the basic mechanisms of the organization of human social interaction at large.

In contrast to other approaches in sociology, psychology, and linguistics, ethnomethodology and CA view actors in interaction as fundamentally social beings. These actors do not simply follow their own intentions and pursue their own plans, but from the start they take into account their co-participants' assumed expectations and stances (on the philosophical underpinning of this view of human nature as fundamentally intersubjective see the work of George Herbert Mead and Alfred Schütz). As participants in natural interaction ordinarily need to cooperate in order to achieve

---

[2] On the roots and context in which CA developed see Heritage (1984b) and Maynard (2013a). For a recent introduction see Sidnell (2010) and Sidnell and Stivers (2013).

their goals, they constantly demonstrate to each other what they are doing, ensuring and/or restoring mutual understanding. Since this order is methodically produced and "publicly" available, it can be observed and reconstructed by social scientists.

In this, participants' actions are conceived of as reflexively related to their contexts: on the one hand, the actions being performed are adapted to and shaped by the context in which they occur; on the other hand, this very context is constituted and renewed by the actions being performed in it. In brief, actions are thus conceived of as both *context-shaped* and *context-renewing* (Heritage 1984b:242). Actions, however, seldom come out of the blue and almost never come alone. Instead they are reconstructed as interactional accomplishments in social interaction, collaboratively achieved and (often overtly) co-constructed. Most importantly, participants produce actions that follow one another in orderly ways to form recognizable sequences of actions. Sequential contexts are, thus, among the most important kinds of context studied in CA.

CA is careful to avoid using predetermined categories and notions, ones imported from commonsense conceptions about reality or from social theory. Instead, "analysts need to discover participants' orientations rather than imposing their own" (Maynard 2013a:19). CA aims at reconstructing the underlying expectations that are observably oriented to in the production and interpretation of actions in talk-in-interaction. Levinson describes the aim of CA as follows:

> ... what conversation analysts are trying to model are the procedures and expectations actually employed by participants in producing and understanding conversation. In addition, for each conversational device we should like, by way of explanation, to elucidate the interactional problems that it is specifically designed to resolve – that is, to provide *functional* explanations, or expositions of rational design, for the existence of the device in question. (1983:319)

Against the background of participants' expectations that the structures they encounter in talk (utterances, turns, sequences) will conform to the norm, structures that depart from these norms are accountable: they give rise to special inferences. As Levinson says: "Conversationalists are [...] not so much constrained by rules or sanctions, as caught in a web of inferences" (1983:321, n. 16). For example, answering a question may pass as ordinary and expected behavior, but not answering the same question may lead co-interlocutors to make inferences – for example, that the recipient is deaf, that s/he lacks the necessary knowledge, that s/he wishes to avoid answering, or that s/he is in general unwilling to cooperate, depending on the particulars of the situation.

Even though CA is not focused on the analysis of language per se, most actions are performed through the use of language, or more precisely through spoken language. CA uses the term *talk-in-interaction* as a cover term for all kinds of naturally occurring speech exchanges in which participants directly interact with one another (see Schegloff 1998 for a discussion).

CA has developed a set of methodological tools for the radically empirical investigation of data from social interaction, in both everyday and institutional contexts. These tools are also instrumental for studying language in an interactional linguistic perspective. They include:

i. the audio or video recording of naturally occurring talk;
ii. the transcription of these data using a notation system designed to represent the features of spoken talk-in-interaction as faithfully as possible;
iii. the noticing and/or observing of relevant phenomena with an "analytic mentality" devoid of premature theories or hypotheses;
iv. the compilation of data collections consisting of multiple instances of the phenomenon selected for analysis, or the selection of single cases for in-depth analysis;
v. rigorous methodology for data analysis aiming at the reconstruction of members' methods of sense-making; and
vi. strict standards for the validation of claims, enabling analysts to warrant their analytic interpretations with reference to the observable orientation of the participants themselves, using what Sacks et al. (1974) called "next turn proof procedure" (see also, e.g., Schegloff 1996b).

As noted above, being a field of sociological inquiry, CA is primarily interested in social organization through language, not necessarily in language in its own right. Conversation analysts have long focused on an account of the sequential organization of conversation, although they have also occasionally investigated its linguistic detail (as, e.g., in some of the work by Jefferson, Schegloff, Drew, Heritage, and Lerner). In much early CA work, the interpretation of turn transition as, for example, overlap or interruption, or the interpretation of an utterance as, for example, a question or an assessment, was taken for granted, without asking how these interpretations were suggested and the actions thus made recognizable as such. Recently, however, more and more important work on linguistic structures and their use in interaction has come from practitioners of CA.

Increasingly, studies by researchers with a background in linguistics have stressed that sequential interaction is organized through the use of linguistic structures. Thus, participants have been shown to orient to the interplay of syntactic, prosodic, and pragmatic cues in the organization of turn taking (Chapter 2); the organization of repair has been shown to be closely tied up with syntax (Chapter 3); and grammar has been shown to differentiate various types of initiating and responsive actions (Chapter 4). In other words, it has been demonstrated on numerous occasions that sequential structures are organized with linguistic means. From this it can only be concluded that linguistic structures are of paramount importance for the conduct of interaction. This is the insight that has led to the development of Interactional Linguistics.

Recently, our understanding of interaction has been deepened through groundbreaking work by CA practitioners on *grammatical preference, sequence organization, repair, person reference*, and *epistemics*, in both everyday and institutional contexts. Practitioners of CA and Interactional Linguistics increasingly collaborate, exploring hitherto neglected aspects of interaction, including, for example, *forms of responding*, means for indexing *epistemic and deontic rights*, and ways of *building actions*. Sidnell and Stivers' (2013) *Handbook of Conversation Analysis* gives an up-to-date overview of some of this CA work.

> CA provides a unique way of thinking about talk-in-interaction, a rigorous methodology, and a wealth of excellent research on the sequential structure of interaction. Interactional Linguistics can build on this body of knowledge, underpinning CA findings with more detailed linguistic analysis. It can reveal how linguistic (and other) resources are systematically and methodically deployed as practices to implement and make actions interpretable in their sequential environments.

1.2 Contextualization Theory

Contextualization Theory has its origins in linguistics, more specifically sociolinguistics, transformed through Gumperz' work (1982) into interpretive or interactional sociolinguistics. Its ideas go back to the observation that the *way* something is said in interaction is often as important, if not more important, than the content of what is said. In bilingual situations, it was observed that language choice and code-switching were not only triggered by extralinguistic contextual features (situational code-switching), but also deployed constructively to suggest the degree of formality of the situation or to imply interactional meanings ("metaphorical code-switching") (see Blom and Gumperz 1972).

Contextualization Theory, developed by Cook-Gumperz and Gumperz (1976) and Gumperz (1982), argues that besides the verbal component of spoken interaction, prosody and other non-verbal components such as tone of voice, gaze, facial expression, etc. serve as "contextualization devices" cueing schematic frames for the interpretation of the spoken message. Contextualization cues afford contexts, or interpretive constructs, for the understanding of verbal utterances. Moreover, they are language-specific. In inter- or cross-cultural communication, their inappropriate use may lead to serious misunderstandings whose origins are hard to uncover.

In cases of a mismatch between the verbal message and its prosodic or non-verbal rendering, the interpretations suggested by non-verbal contextualization often override the verbal message.

Especially in the community of German conversation analysts working within language and linguistic departments, Gumperz' work was seen as a bridge between the sequential analysis of action in interaction and linguistics. Aspects of prosody and non-verbal communication could be thought of as contextualization devices, making actions recognizable within the sequential structures so masterfully described by conversation analysts. The theoretical and analytic gap between CA-style sequential analysis and the question of how participants are able to interpret actions in the first place was nicely bridged by Gumperz' notion of contextualization (see also Auer 1992b).

This approach was a mind-opener for the study of prosody in conversation (Couper-Kuhlen and Selting 1996a). Yet soon research on reported speech showed that, in addition to prosody, other vocal parameters need to be incorporated into the analysis in order to capture, for example, the layering of "voices" in participants' reporting of speech and thought. From this recognition it was only a small step to realizing that, besides vocal parameters, all linguistic structures can serve as contextualization cues, in that their systematic use contributes to making actions and activities interpretable. This was how the research program of Interactional Linguistics came into being.

Recently, the study of the contextualization of talk has been enriched through the explosion of interest in multimodality and embodiment (see, e.g., Stivers and Sidnell 2005; Streeck et al. 2011). Research on the multimodality of interaction has made it evident that, in addition to verbal and vocal resources, we must also attend to the visible embodiment of talk (Fox 2001b), as well as to how cues from all semiotic systems are used in co-occurrence with objects in the material world (C. Goodwin 2000, 2007a).

In order to account comprehensively for the organization of talk, we need to describe how interlocutors use verbal, vocal, and visible resources in the service of performing actions and activities in social interaction. The systematic use of these resources constitutes practices designed to implement and make actions and activities recognizable. For Interactional Linguistics this means that we need to take all communicative modes, or channels, into account in order to appreciate the specific contribution of language to the management of social interaction (see Sidnell 2006; Enfield 2009).

1.3 Linguistic Anthropology

Linguistic Anthropology was originally concerned primarily with the documentation of the grammars of aboriginal languages (Duranti 1997, 2004). Working on indigenous languages in North America, Sapir and Whorf introduced the notion of linguistic relativity, hypothesizing that culture, through language, influences the way we think (Whorf 1956).[3] With the appearance of Gumperz and Hymes' research (1964, 1972), however, a new paradigm emerged focusing more on communicative events and their contextual variation within and across speech communities, using ethnographic methods. It is this paradigm, with its emphasis on the actual use of language in social interaction, that has been influential for Interactional Linguistics.

During the 1980s, anthropological researchers began to look at language as used in specific speech communities, subcultural groups, professional circles, business contexts, etc., in order to investigate the ways members of these groups and institutions interact in their daily encounters (see Schieffelin and Ochs 1986; Moerman 1988; Maynard 1989; Hanks 1990). The goal was to uncover particular means of collaboratively constructing social relations and social reality through talk. Groundbreaking work was done by, for example, M. H. Goodwin (1990), who investigated girls' ways of playing, negotiating, and fighting out their social relations in a black urban community (see also M. H. Goodwin 2002, 2006, 2007). Studies in this branch of Linguistic Anthropology have dealt with language in its socio-cultural embeddedness, often as a tool for socialization (see, e.g., Ochs 1996; Aronsson and Cekaite 2011). Drew and Heritage (1992) called attention to the relevance of studying talk at work and interaction in institutional settings, a line of research that has been pursued *inter alia* in work on media, political, and medical interaction (see, e.g., Heritage 1985, 2010a; Heritage and Clayman 2010). Nowadays, researchers use mobile recording devices to collect data in all kinds of everyday contexts, as well as social and cultural institutions, in their own and others' cultures, in order to study language use in these contexts. Linguistic Anthropology thrives today through the work of Ochs, M. H. Goodwin, Haviland, and others, and is currently being renewed by Sidnell, Enfield, and many others (see Enfield et al. 2014 for a recent overview).

The study of the relation between language and culturally diverse social orders has given rise to the hypothesis that ways of conducting conversation impinge differently on language, and that languages contribute differently to the social order constructed through them. This hypothesis has been borne out by interactional linguistic studies. For instance, research by Auer (1996a) on projection and turn

---

[3] For a more recent re-examination of this hypothesis see Gumperz and Levinson (1996).

completion in German, as well as by Tanaka (1999, 2000a) on the organization of turn taking in Japanese, has revealed that there are fundamental differences between English, German, and Japanese in terms of turn transition and the projection of possible completion. These differences are due to the different syntactic organization of the languages in question, which impinges on the practices of turn taking (Chapter 2). Further differences have been shown to exist, for instance, in the practices of turn incrementation in English, German, and Japanese (Couper-Kuhlen and Ono 2007a) and of self-repair in these and other languages (Fox et al. 1996; Fox et al. 2010; Chapter 3). Even speaker-recipient interaction during the production of turn-constructional units and turns has been argued to be different owing to the language-specific organization of clauses in English as compared to, for example, Japanese (Clancy et al. 1996). Research on typologically different languages thus suggests that common tasks in interaction are dealt with in ways that are shaped by the linguistic resources a language provides (Couper-Kuhlen and Selting 2001). A cross-linguistic and cross-cultural perspective is thus crucial to the interactional linguistic enterprise.

Linguistic anthropologists have always paid attention to the use of language in displaying affectivity and emotion in interaction (see, e.g., Ochs and Schieffelin 1989; Goodwin and Goodwin 2000; M. H. Goodwin 2006; M. H. Goodwin et al. 2012). Recently, interest in this body of work has blossomed and yielded a range of new studies (see, e.g., Peräkylä and Sorjonen 2012 for a collection of articles on emotion in interaction; also Couper-Kuhlen 2009a; Selting 2010, 2012; and Reber 2012).

In parallel to the studies of language use in interaction in specific cultural and institutional contexts, a group of linguistic anthropologists at the Max Planck Institute for Psycholinguistics (Nijmegen, Netherlands) began work with an explicit focus on comparative studies of language in interaction (see Enfield and Levinson 2006; Sidnell 2009; Sidnell and Enfield 2012). This group has carried out investigations, for example, of person reference (Enfield and Stivers 2007; Online-Chapter F §1), of timing in turn taking (Stivers et al. 2009; Chapter 2), of question-response sequences (Stivers et al. 2010; Chapter 4), and of other-initiation of repair (Enfield et al. 2013; Dingemanse et al. 2015; Chapter 3) – all in a wide variety of unrelated languages.[4] With this work, Linguistic Anthropology has developed rigorous standards and procedures for comparative socio-cultural research on language use (Enfield and Levinson 2006; Sidnell 2009). These standards and procedures are also relevant for Interactional Linguistics.

---

[4] A comparative study of recruitment practices for enlisting someone's assistance in a variety of unrelated languages is currently nearing completion (see Floyd et al. Forthcoming).

> Linguistic Anthropology has contributed in several major ways to the development of Interactional Linguistics: it has encouraged the inclusion of data from a wide variety of languages, (sub)cultures, and contexts; it has revealed that the practices of organizing talk-in-interaction (may) vary with language type; it has developed new ways of thinking about and analyzing affectivity, or emotion displays, in interaction; and it has established a methodology for the socio-cultural comparison of linguistic practices in social interaction. Linguistic Anthropology encourages interactional linguists to see opportunities for, and merits in, investigating the trade-off between interaction universals on the one hand and language (type)-specific practices on the other.

2. Development of Interactional Linguistics

At least three different strands of independent research contributed to the development of Interactional Linguistics during the 1980s and 1990s. In Europe, phoneticians at the University of York in Great Britain were focusing on the phonetics of conversation (starting with, e.g., French and Local 1983 and Local et al. 1986). In Germany, research at this time was concerned with the study of prosody and syntax in conversation (e.g., Auer 1992a, 1993, 1997, 1998; Couper-Kuhlen and Selting 1996a). And in the United States, research on discourse functional syntax (e.g., Chafe 1979; Hopper 1979; Hopper and Thompson 1980, 1984; Du Bois 1985, 1987) and grammar and interaction (Ford et al. 1996; Ochs et al. 1996) began to concentrate on the role of grammar in the organization of conversation. All three approaches had in common that they investigated linguistic structures on the basis of natural data from conversational interaction, demonstrating that participants use these structures systematically in the conduct of conversation. All harked back to ethnomethodology for their theoretical premises, and to the methodology and descriptive findings of CA (Sacks et al. 1974), in particular with respect to the fundamental sequential organization of talk-in-interaction. These three approaches have now, for all practical purposes, merged into one.

Internationally, the term *Interactional Linguistics* was first proposed by Couper-Kuhlen and Selting in a series of articles (Selting and Couper-Kuhlen 2000, 2001b; Couper-Kuhlen and Selting 2001) and an edited volume (Selting and Couper-Kuhlen 2001a), aiming to encompass the study not only of grammar but of all aspects of language as systematically deployed in talk-in-interaction. It was intended as a cover term for the growing body of research that at that time was accumulating under labels such as "phonology of conversation", "grammar and interaction", "contextualization of language", and "prosody in talk-in-interaction" (e.g., Schegloff 1998:236). The term has since been adopted by many researchers around the world for the study of the linguistic organization of talk-in-interaction in diverse languages (Fox et al. 2013:727–8). The body of work incorporated here includes investigations of linguistic structures and constructions by a number of these researchers both in single languages and in a cross-linguistic perspective.

Originally, Interactional Linguistics advocated a rather orthodox version of CA methodology for the investigation of language in interaction (Wootton 1989; Selting and Couper-Kuhlen 2001b). This methodology involved adopting the "analytic mentality" of a curious observer who brings along no preconceived beliefs or ideas about what will be found, but merely engages in "unmotivated looking" at how participants behave in social interaction. Since the architecture of conversation affords participants a public means of achieving mutual understanding (Heritage 1984b), analysts can come to appreciate participants' own (ethno-)methods simply by careful observation. Early interactional linguistic thinking suggested that because systematic language use is one of participants' primary methods, linguists could focus their sights specifically on the linguistic forms and on what participants demonstrably show these forms to be doing.

Yet in practice, over the years, Interactional Linguistics has undergone subtle changes. Perhaps inevitably, it now means different things to different people. For some, it continues to refer to the data-driven, inductive search for ways in which interaction shapes language and language shapes interaction. For others, however, it can mean the use of conversational data as input for various kinds of quantitative and statistical analyses of language, or the use of conversational extracts to illustrate linguistic patterns whose existence has been determined on other grounds. Thus, what the term *Interactional Linguistics* is understood to cover has enlarged significantly over the past decade.

But also, what the defining features of the Interactional Linguistics enterprise are understood to be has changed. This has come about in part because Interactional Linguistics is no longer practiced only by linguists. Of course there are still numerous prominent linguistic scholars, of both theoretical and applied persuasions, whose names are associated with the endeavor today. However, there are also any number of non-linguists, including phoneticians, conversation analysts, sociologists, discursive psychologists, linguistic anthropologists, social scientists, speech scientists, communication scientists, and embodied interactionists, who also pay special attention to language as used in social interaction. Thus, the denotation of the term *Interactional Linguistics* has undergone significant expansion, because the investigation of language as a resource for the conduct of social interaction is not confined to linguistics alone but cuts across a broad range of disciplines and allegiances.

To be sure, not all the non-linguists implicitly referred to in the paragraph above would necessarily feel comfortable calling themselves Interactional Linguists (with upper-case letters). Yet in a generic sense, researchers who study in one way or another the interplay of language with social interaction are engaged – for all practical purposes – in an interactional linguistic (lower case) enterprise. We believe that this disciplinary diversity should be embraced and celebrated: it constitutes one of the greatest strengths of the field and accounts for its extraordinary richness.

The interactional linguistic enterprise, when broadly conceived, encompasses not only multiple disciplines but also diverse methodologies. To begin with, the field of CA has itself broadened its methodological toolbox, as reflected in the quantitative underpinnings of work by, for example, Heritage, Clayman, Stivers, and others (Clayman and Heritage 2002; Stivers 2005, 2007; Heritage et al. 2007). Moreover, large-scale cross-linguistic projects have been carried out using statistical measures of coded categories in relation to, for example, transition timing, question type, and other-initiation of repair in order to explore the common and divergent aspects of language use in interaction (Stivers et al. 2009, 2010; Dingemanse and Enfield 2015). The success of these endeavors suggests that the interactional linguistic enterprise depends less on orthodox methodology than on certain essential principles such as, first, the use of naturally occurring data from social interaction and, second, an interactional perspective on the analysis and description of the data. As with disciplinary diversity, we believe that methodological heterogeneity must be embraced. Ultimately, the pay-off of a broadly conceived interactional linguistic endeavor will offset any adverse effects from heterogeneity.

> The term *Interactional Linguistics* was introduced early in this century as a cover term for research endeavors such as phonology of conversation, grammar and interaction, contextualization of language, and prosody in talk-in-interaction – all attempts to explore the workings of language as systematically deployed in social interaction. Originally conceived as a sub-field of linguistics, Interactional Linguistics has since broadened in scope: it is no longer practiced exclusively by linguists but also by scholars from diverse disciplines who are united in an interest in language as used in social interaction. Interactional linguistics now also encompasses diverse methodologies, ranging from orthodox conversation analytic, qualitative procedures to interaction-informed, quantitative ones. This encompassing embrace of diverse practitioners and methodologies is one of the strengths of the interactional linguistic enterprise.

3. Premises and Goals of Interactional Linguistic Research

The most important premise of interactional linguistic research is that linguistic categories and structures are designed for service in the organization of social interaction and must be described and explained accordingly. For this, descriptions of linguistic structure are combined with CA-informed analyses of sequential organization. Where relevant for an account of particular actions or interaction sequences, interactional linguistic analyses should also be combined with multimodal analysis, for example, gaze, facial expression, gesture, body posture, etc.

The goal of Interactional Linguistics has been described as an appreciation of how interaction is shaped by language and, in turn, how language shapes interaction (Couper-Kuhlen and Selting 2001). To pursue this goal, researchers take one of two possible points of departure: (i) they start from social interaction and ask how actions and courses of action are implemented with linguistic resources and made interpretable as such for co-participants; or (ii) they start from linguistic resources and ask how the structures of language are mobilized for the conduct of social interaction. The assumption is, on the one hand, that the use of linguistic structures is motivated by sequential context (context dependence), but on the other, that it also actively creates that context (context renewal). Investigations can be carried out on the basis of a single language or a comparison of two or more languages.

Interactional linguistic methodology establishes a link between the sequential analysis of naturally occurring talk in everyday and institutional interaction as practiced in CA, and a linguistic analysis of the rhetorical, lexico-semantic, morpho-syntactic, segmental-phonetic, and vocal-prosodic means mobilized in such sequences. Most practitioners employ the analytic framework of modern descriptive linguistics (but see also Laury et al. 2014). When data from face-to-face interactions are examined, not only verbal and vocal, i.e., phonetic-prosodic, but also visible resources are taken into account if they are relevant for the conduct of conversation.[5] Among researchers in Interactional Linguistics there is a distinct preference for qualitative studies; however, the value of quantitative measures for categories whose prior relevance has been established qualitatively is not to be underestimated.

Each of the two starting points mentioned above has its own merits and drawbacks. Starting from social interaction yields an analysis of the linguistic (and other) forms that are deployed as resources for the enactment of particular social actions. Yet it does not in itself lead to generalizations regarding these linguistic resources beyond these actions and contexts. Starting from linguistic resources requires investigating a particular resource and its use in diverse sequential contexts; this then allows generalizations across a diversity of sequential contexts but runs the risk of culminating in an unmotivated list of observations. In fact, most

---

[5] We use the term *linguistic* on a general level to refer to verbal and prosodic forms including variable aspects of voice quality, and the term *non-linguistic* to refer to forms of visible behavior such as gaze, facial expression, body posture and movement, etc. When more precision is needed, we use *verbal* to denote everything expressed with segmental-phonetic sounds and conventionalized lexical items, *vocal* to denote prosodic and voice quality effects, and *visible/visual* to refer to gaze, facial expression, body posture and movement, etc.

investigations starting from linguistic resources choose to restrict the object of study to some sequential context. The drawback, however, is again that we cannot make generalizations about the resource beyond the particular context studied.

In effect then, studies of language in social interaction, no matter what the starting point, are always studies of the sequentially specific deployment of linguistic resources conceived of as practices in particular sequential contexts. Analysts often fare best by moving back and forth between the analysis of form and the analysis of function. It is only after we have compiled a large body of research on the situated deployment of resources within various sequential contexts that we can expect to be able to come up with generalizations across sequential contexts. For this, the detailed study of participants' situated use of linguistic resources and the warranting of analytic categories as participants' categories (see below) is indispensable.

> Interactional Linguistics pursues three objectives: (i) it aims at a *functional description* of linguistic structures as interactional resources mobilized in practices designed for the accomplishment of recurrent tasks in social interaction; (ii) it aims at *cross-linguistic analysis and comparison* of these practices in order to determine both how interactional exigencies shape language structure and use in social interaction, and how language and language type impinge on the details of the organization of social interaction; (iii) it aims at drawing *general linguistic* conclusions for a theory of language in social interaction which explains how language is organized and practiced in social interaction. The goal of Interactional Linguistics is a realistic reconstruction of the linguistic structures and practices that participants themselves deploy and orient to in the conduct of social interaction.

It could be argued that a separate field of inquiry called Interactional Linguistics is not necessary, because its purview lies within CA. However, at least two sets of arguments speak in favor of actively continuing to develop and articulate the approach advocated here.

i. Conceptions of language and linguistics

Most non-interactional approaches to linguistics share what Linell (2005) calls the "written language bias"; examples, if used at all, are typically constructed ones. Non-interactional conceptions of language and linguistics conceive of language use as the mere application (*performance*) of knowledge concerning an abstract linguistic system (*competence*). However, since the seminal work by C. Goodwin (1981, 1995), interactionally oriented linguists have shown that linguistic units such as sentences, clauses, phrases, etc., when used in interaction, are situated accomplishments, actively produced and reproduced in real time, in a context-sensitive fashion. They are both context-dependent and context-constitutive, and must be treated as fundamentally flexible entities that are adapted to the local exigencies and contingencies of interaction. Linguistic units can be constructed collaboratively and are therefore distributed across speakers (Lerner 1991). In consequence, these units must be conceived of as emergent in use (Hopper 1988, 1998), being interactively achieved in talk. This is only one example of how language as used in interaction cannot be adequately conceptualized as the simple application of an abstract and context-free system. As the following chapters will show, there are many others.

In order to describe language as used in interaction, it needs to be carefully examined in its natural habitat, in a radically empirical fashion and on the basis of fundamentally constructionist and interactionist premises. This will show how linguistic resources and practices are adapted to and designed for carrying out routine tasks in the management of interaction. The context of language use, especially its sequential interactional context, must be an integral part of linguistic theory and practice (see also Duranti and Goodwin 1992). An interactional linguistic description of language as used in social interaction will lead to a more realistic and therefore improved basis for, among others, grammars of spoken language; courses on language awareness, language teaching, and intercultural communication; speech analysis and synthesis programs in computerized interactive dialog systems; and counseling and training programs in rhetoric and communication skills.

ii. Relationship to CA

Although they overlap in many respects and build on each other's results, CA and Interactional Linguistics have partly different goals and objectives: both are interdisciplinary endeavors but CA is grounded in sociology, Interactional Linguistics in linguistics. CA is primarily interested in sequential and social order; on occasion it is also concerned with explaining the "macro"-sociological phenomena that are reproduced through everyday and institutional practices in social interaction (see Schegloff 1987d). Often this ensues without close attention to the details of linguistic structure. By contrast, linguists working in an interactional perspective are concerned with reconstructing the phonetic-phonological, morphological, syntactic, and semantic details of sequences of social interaction. Interactional Linguistics is primarily interested in the use of language and linguistic structures in social interaction. In the long run, it seeks to contribute to changing the way we think about language within linguistics, applied linguistics, and language pedagogy. The interactional perspective has already led to the development of new approaches in sub-areas of linguistics: among these "interactional semantics" (Deppermann, esp. 2007, 2011a; Norén and Linell 2007), "interactional stylistics"

(Selting, e.g., 1999a, 2008, 2009), and "interactional dialectology and sociolinguistics" (Gilles 2005).

Nevertheless, although CA and Interactional Linguistics have different interests, there is in general much common ground. We do not need to draw a sharp boundary between studies stemming primarily from CA and those stemming primarily from Interactional Linguistics. Rather than trying to define borders, the field of Interactional Linguistics should be looked upon as an interdisciplinary space in which conversation analysts and linguists with common interests can meet to study talk-in-interaction. Ultimately, the question of how far we need to attend to linguistic or social/sociological categories does not depend on the discipline or on possible boundaries between them, but on the object to be investigated and the research questions to be pursued. (For an overview of research on CA and Interactional Linguistics, see also Fox et al. 2013.)

> A field of Interactional Linguistics separate from CA is needed, for one, to actively counter non-interactional conceptions of language in linguistic disciplines, which continue to view language use as the "performance" of an underlying linguistic "competence". Second, a separate field is needed because Interactional Linguistics has interests and aims that are different from those of CA: while CA is primarily interested in social order and aims to account for its normative organization, Interactional Linguistics is primarily interested in language and aims to account for its practices in social interaction. Yet there is much overlap between the two fields. Rather than drawing boundaries between them, it is more productive to think of them as intersecting, affording a meeting space for those with a common interest both in language and in social interaction.

4. Principles of Interactional Linguistic Work

In this section we revisit and update the original principles of interactional linguistic work, first applied to the analysis of prosody in conversation (Couper-Kuhlen and Selting 1996a)[6] but later extended to the study of all aspects of language as used in social interaction (Selting and Couper-Kuhlen 2001a). It also includes some practical advice for how to do interactional linguistic work.

4.1 Naturally Occurring Data

As noted above, Interactional Linguistics was introduced as a strictly empirical, data-driven approach to the investigation of language as used in social interaction.

---

[6] See also Local and Walker (2005) for an extension of these principles to phonetics in general.

4. Principles of Interactional Linguistic Work

The *data* typically come from telephone or face-to-face interaction in everyday, private, or institutional contexts, between two or more participants who are conversing with one another directly. They are recorded, transcribed, and analyzed making full use of modern technological instrumentation and support systems.

4.1.1 Choice of Data

Interactional linguistic work often begins with data from informal, everyday conversation, since this is phylogenetically as well as ontogenetically the primary use of language in interaction. Institutional talk, it has been pointed out, is distinct from ordinary talk because of its orientation to specific institutional goals. Consequently, there may be constraints placed on what is a possible contribution to institutional talk, and inferences may differ from those normally made in ordinary conversation (Drew and Heritage 1992). Nevertheless, there have been revealing studies on linguistic aspects of institutional interaction (see, e.g., Heritage et al.'s (2007) report on the use of *some* versus *any* in doctor–patient interaction, or Heritage and Roth's (1995) study of questions in the news interview), and institutional data offer a rich field of investigation for interactional linguists. In choosing whether to examine everyday or institutional interaction, much will thus depend on questions of data accessibility, as well as on the research question to be pursued.

While most of our analyses are based on focused interaction, i.e., interaction in which the participants' main objectives are carried out through talk, it is not unusual for studies to include non-focused interaction. Yet this has far-reaching consequences. When, say, participants are mainly concerned with cooking a complicated meal or with operating on a patient, the organization of these activities may take precedence over that of talk. In consequence, the principles of contiguity and conditional relevance may be relaxed (Stivers and Rossano 2010; Hoey 2015); verbal, prosodic-phonetic, and visual cues may be used in a different way than in focused interaction. In consequence, interactional linguists typically keep their analyses of focused and non-focused interaction separate. At a later stage, if desired, the two sets of data can be compared and the different ways in which language is used in them described and accounted for.

Some of the data-related issues relevant for students of Interactional Linguistics are as follows:

i. What kind of data basis do we need for what kind of investigation?

A good deal of earlier work in CA and Interactional Linguistics is based on recorded data from telephone conversations. At a time when video equipment was still large and heavy, filmed recordings were expensive and difficult to obtain; consequently, telephone conversations were considered ideal due to their accessibility. They were also easier to handle: since the participants interacted only via the auditory channel, audio recordings captured for the researcher all that was available to the participants themselves. There was no need to worry about the visual channel.

Meanwhile, however, video recording has become easy. Video material of face-to-face interactions is increasingly available and providing access to the wider range of semiotic resources used by participants. Most recently, in order to obtain best-quality data for both video and acoustic-phonetic analysis, researchers have begun to combine (multi-camera) video recording with separate high-quality audio recordings (see, e.g., Peräkylä and Ruusuvuori 2006; Selting 2010; on the problems resulting from the observer paradox in data collection see Labov 1972). Yet on occasion, restricting data collection to the audio channel may be unavoidable: for instance, some institutions dealing with sensitive personal data may be willing to allow audio but not video recording. Increasing attention is also being paid to various forms of mediated internet communication at the interface between speech and writing (chat, social networking). In principle, thus, the choice of data must be carefully considered and justified with regard to the research question.

ii. How large should our database be in order to yield reliable results?

The smaller the database, the greater the risk of basing one's analysis on coincidental instances, or of paying too much attention to marginal or unusual forms of the phenomenon under consideration. The larger the database, the more clearly frequency patterns will emerge. Nevertheless, students may wish to start with the careful analysis of single cases in order to get a first grip on the phenomenon in question and to develop hypotheses that can then be used in the analysis of a larger database. In general, the size of the corpus will depend on the material available, the research question, and the goals of the investigation.

iii. Do we wish to include data from technically mediated interaction in the new media?

Technically mediated forms of virtual co-present interaction between participants, for example, in internet chatrooms (see, e.g., Neuage 2004; Beißwenger 2007), blur the traditional boundaries between spoken and written communication. What are the consequences of including such data in our investigations? The challenges are significant, in part because the turn-taking system of everyday conversation is distorted by technological constraints. Yet at least one interactional linguistic research study has suggested that the organization of, for example, repair in computer-mediated interaction is not abandoned, but instead simply adapted to meet the specific affordances of the new medium (Schönfeldt and Golato 2003).

4.1.2 Transcription

Transcription is a hotly debated issue. At least four different approaches are currently being pursued:

i. Jeffersonian transcription

Researchers working with data from CA corpora use the system originally developed by Gail Jefferson (see Sacks et al. 1974) and successively revised over the past decades (see, e.g., Atkinson and Heritage 1984; Jefferson 2004a; Schegloff 2007a:265–9; Hepburn and Bolden 2013).[7]

ii. Du Bois transcription

Researchers working with data from the Santa Barbara corpus of spoken American English use the transcription system devised by Du Bois et al. (1993).

iii. Minimal orthographic transcription plus enhanced lines as needed

Walker (2004a:45), for instance, advocates "unadorned orthographic transcriptions" as "relatively simple presentation transcriptions" for the analysis of the sequential organization of talk. These are then "enhanced" for the investigation of the object under analysis – for example, for the study of fine phonetic detail.

iv. GAT transcription

Researchers working in the German research context and/or with German data use the GAT system. GAT is an acronym for **G**esprächs**A**nalytisches **T**ranskriptionssystem (literally: conversation analytic transcription system), a system that takes CA transcription as its basis but is designed to allow for a more precise representation of prosodic and phonetic parameters. The first version of the GAT system (Selting et al. 1998) has recently been revised as GAT2 (Selting et al. 2009) and is now also available in English (Couper-Kuhlen and Barth-Weingarten 2011) and Portuguese (Schröder et al. 2016).

As transcription is an important means of constituting the object of research, and as it necessarily presupposes theory (see Ochs 1979; also Edwards and Lampert 1993; Selting 2001b), students must carefully consider the choice of transcription system for their own work (see also Mondada 2013). Overviews of the transcription systems underlying the data presented here are included in an appendix to this book.[8]

---

[7] For a critical discussion see Couper-Kuhlen and Selting (1996b:39–45) and Walker (2004a:39–44).

[8] Our policy in citing data from the literature in this book has been to retain the transcription used in the original source but to adapt Jeffersonian "eye dialect" to standard orthography. For an explanation of the glossing abbreviations in the translation of examples see the Leipzig Glossing Rules: https://www.eva.mpg.de/lingua/resources/glossing-rules.php. Glossing abbreviations cited in the transcripts are only explained when relevant for the discussion.

4.2 Context-sensitive Analysis

In an interactional linguistic perspective, data are analyzed as an integral part of the sequential conversational context in which they occur. Utterances are assumed to be designed in a *context-sensitive* fashion, i.e., built to fit the particular location and occasion of their use. This means that, for instance, syntactic categories and units must be analyzed as occurring in turn-constructional units (TCUs) and turns. However, TCUs and turns are constructed in order to accomplish actions, and actions build sequences and larger trajectories of interaction. Linguistic structures, thus, must also be analyzed with reference to action and sequence. In sum, there are multiple kinds of context to be considered: turn, action, sequence, project, etc., all of which are relevant for the organization of interaction and for the analysis of language structure within it.

4.3 Online Perspective

The term *online perspective* refers to a progression in the analysis that follows the real-time production and processing of talk by the participants. Originally this was understood to mean turn by turn, or TCU by TCU. Yet as current research is showing, there are smaller stretches of talk that are also interactively relevant, so that an online perspective requires considerations below the level of TCU (Iwasaki 2009, 2013).

Analyzing data from an online perspective means reconstructing structures both as *emergent* in real time and as *interactional achievements*. The production of a sentence or clause, for example, is the result of the speaker and the recipient coordinating their respective actions in real time (C. Goodwin 1981). Linguistic constructional schemata or formats are deployed systematically as practices to manage interaction and achieve mutual understanding. The construction and completion of these structures is always the product of ongoing talk-in-interaction which both (or all) parties are involved in as they deal with the *contingencies* of situated interaction. In Schegloff's words: "Good analysis retains a sense of the actual as an achievement from among possibilities: it retains a lively sense of the contingency of real things" (1982:89).

How much detail should interactional linguistic studies go into? With respect to this question, Schegloff's (2000d) notion of "(levels of) granularity" is helpful. Depending on the research question, a more general description with a lower degree of resolution/detailing may be called for. On other occasions, more "zooming in" to higher degrees of resolution/detailing may be appropriate (see also Imo 2009). The limit is likely to be reached with whatever it is that regulates progressivity for the participants. Yet this may depend on what is going on in the interaction: under certain circumstances, sensitivity to segments even smaller than the word has been observed to be relevant (e.g., in some types of self-repair: Jefferson 1974). Thus, the granularity of analysis needs to remain flexible and adapted to the research goals.

4.4 Categories Empirically Grounded

Categories must be inductively developed, i.e., grounded in the data itself. This imperative pertains both to the analysis of interaction and to the analysis of language as used within interaction. Yet special vigilance is called for from interactional linguists, who must be wary of taking the relevance of traditional linguistic categories for granted. *Sentences*, for example, have been shown to have different properties in interaction from those traditionally attributed to them by grammarians based on isolated examples and/or written texts. The notions of *sentence*, *clause*, *phrase*, etc., are discussed in the following chapters not because they have a long and important tradition in grammar and linguistics, but because they have been shown to be what participants in interaction orient to in the conduct of conversation (Sacks et al. 1974; Schegloff 1979; Selting 1995b; Thompson and Couper-Kuhlen 2005).

In fact, interactional linguistic studies have begun to question the relevance of many traditional grammatical and prosodic units for participants. Fox et al. (1996), for instance, cast doubt on the verb phrase as a relevant unit for self-repair in English. Selting (1997a) denies the relevance of the notion of "ellipsis" for spoken talk-in-interaction (see also Thompson et al. 2015). Walker (2004a) questions the assumption that segmentation into intonation phrases and placement of accented syllables is necessarily meaningful for the analysis of English conversation (see also Barth-Weingarten 2016). Ford et al. (2013) raise similar questions with respect to the relevance of, for example, the grammatical category *noun phrase* for responding to content questions. They more generally call into question "the usefulness of uncritically adopting *a priori* grammatical units" (p. 18) and argue in favor of conceiving of grammatical categories such as noun phrases as epiphenomena of the practices and actions they are used to perform (see also Hopper 2004:153).

Our standpoint here will be somewhat more moderate than in the above-mentioned studies: we will use the technical terminology of traditional linguistic analysis where it seems an appropriate way of describing what we find participants doing. This is, however, not necessarily to claim that such category notions are themselves meaningful to participants; rather, we assume that participants tacitly orient to the *practices* captured by these notions.

Sacks et al. (1974) stressed that through the sequential organization of interaction participants display to each other their understanding of prior turns in next turns. They also pointed out that this mutual display of understanding can be used by analysts as a "search procedure" in order to discover "what a turn's talk is occupied with" (pp. 728–9). Building on this, Wootton (1989) has singled out five types of evidence that can be drawn on in order to discover what a turn at talk is doing. These types of evidence can also be appealed to in discovering interactionally relevant language forms and functions (see also Couper-Kuhlen and Selting 1996b:31–8; Selting and Couper-Kuhlen 2001b:278):

i. Relationship to prior turns

Evidence for the interactional relevance of a linguistic phenomenon can be found in the relationship of a turn featuring this phenomenon to just prior turns. For instance, a turn built with a phrase can be shown to stand in a different relationship to the prior turn than a turn built with a clause (Chapter 6).

ii. Co-occurring evidence within the turn

The interactional relevance of a linguistic phenomenon can be corroborated through co-occurring evidence within the turn or in neighboring turns. For example, "dense" syntactic constructions (Günthner 2011c) as found in many story climaxes frequently co-occur with extreme formulations (see also Pomerantz 1986) and marked, salient prosody (Selting 1996b; Online-Chapter D §2). Alternatively, prosodic configurations may have verbal formulations in their vicinity that shed light on their function (see, e.g., Reber 2012:149–50).

iii. Discriminability

The interactional relevance of a linguistic phenomenon may be discoverable through a comparison of the action it is used to perform with the action performed by other forms in the same or similar contexts. In response to news deliveries and informings, for instance, a comparison of English "do you?" to "you do?" reveals that these responses lead to different participant interpretations, suggesting that two distinct interactionally relevant categories are involved (Thompson et al. 2015).

iv. Treatment in subsequent talk

The function or interactional meaning of a linguistic phenomenon may be discoverable through an analysis of the treatment that the turn featuring the phenomenon receives in subsequent talk. If question words are used to initiate repair with both falling and rising final pitch, the way the repair operation is accomplished in next turn will help determine what work falling and rising final pitch accomplish in this sequential environment (Chapter 3).

v. Deviant case analysis

At first sight, deviant cases appear to be exceptions; they are other-than-expected usages of the phenomenon in question. However, on closer analysis, deviant cases can often be shown to be treated *as* deviant, thus providing evidence that participants orient to non-deviant usage as the expected norm. The deviant cases can then be seen as noticeable departures from the norm, giving rise to special interpretations and inferences. For instance, if phrasal forms are established as the norm for responding to information-seeking question-word or content questions, then the use of a clausal form instead can be said to trigger inferences that go beyond the simple provision of information (Chapter 4).

4.5 Claims Warranted through Participant Orientation

Interactional linguistic claims can be validated by showing that and how participants observably orient to the phenomenon under analysis. To give an example: the analysis of a phrasal response as being the norm for responding to an information-seeking question-word question can be validated by showing that recipients do not delay in producing it, do not initiate repair on it, and in general give no indication that it is in any way problematic for them, while a clausal response is often produced with delay and leads to an expanded sequence dealing with its implications. The strongest kind of warrant for an interactional linguistic claim comes by way of speakers' explicitly problematizing the use of the phenomenon in question or the inferences it gives rise to.

Thus, all the types of evidence for claiming the interactional relevance of a phenomenon listed in §4.4 above can at the same time serve to warrant such a claim. For instance, the category of sentence or clause can be warranted by showing that speakers and recipients orient to it by timing their follow-up TCU and actions accordingly, by waiting for or even pursuing its completion, and/or by interpreting its break-off or abandonment as a source of inferences. It is thus crucial in interactional linguistic research to show participant orientation to the phenomenon under analysis, i.e., that it functions according to an interactional logic that can be reconstructed from the data. This, of course, does not mean that participants are necessarily aware of the logic or its relevance, or that they have a category name or conscious knowledge of or about it.

Warranting claims in terms of the methods discussed above has an advantage over other methods of validation: having recourse to the empirical data themselves frees researchers from having to rely on introspective and subjective judgments and/or statistical calculations of validity, whose relevance for participants is unproven. The outcome of warranting claims as proposed here is an empirically realistic and interactionally relevant account of how the structure of language interacts with the organization of conversation. See Online-Chapter A for analysis of a concrete example that helps to motivate an interactional linguistic perspective (available at www.cambridge.org/interactional).[9]

> Interactional Linguistics is a strictly empirical approach to the study of spoken language in talk-in-interaction. It takes a doubly empirical stance: it advocates empirical data from natural interaction as its object of study, and it seeks empirical evidence from the same data for the validation of its analyses. It uses naturally occurring data, conducts context-sensitive analyses in an online perspective, and strives to ground its categories empirically as well as to warrant its claims through participant observation. Its aim is the reconstruction of linguistic phenomena as interactionally relevant categories that real-life participants in social interaction can be shown to orient to. Since language in talk-in-interaction is normally used in a "semiotically rich framework of interaction" (Fox et al. 2013:739), interactional linguistic studies must also be relatable to analyses of the visible organization of interaction.

---

[9] For a discussion of the challenges facing Interactional Linguistics, and among them the methodological strategies it pursues, see also Fox et al. (2013:736ff.).

Part I

How is Interaction Conducted with Linguistic Resources?

Preface

We start from the assumption that social interaction in informal conversation between family members and friends is organized in fundamentally similar ways in the languages and cultures of the world (Stivers et al. 2009). For our examination of how interaction is conducted with linguistic (and other) resources, we can thus rely on the descriptive categories developed in conversation analytic studies of talk-in-interaction. These serve as a *tertium comparationis* (basis of comparison) and can be underpinned with detailed studies of the linguistic (and other) resources deployed to realize them. This is what practitioners of Interactional Linguistics have been doing since about the middle of the 1990s, for English and other languages.

In this part of the book we begin with interaction and ask how it is conducted with linguistic (and other) resources, comparing as far as possible the organizational details of talk in different languages. We start with the most basic mechanisms of conversation: turn construction and turn taking (Chapter 2) and repair (Chapter 3). We then turn to action formation and ascription (Chapter 4), followed by topic management and sequence organization (Chapter 5). In addition, in Online-Chapter B we deal with preference, and in Online-Chapter C we examine the display of stance and footing. In Online-Chapter D we discuss an interactional linguistic perspective on storytelling as a "big package".[1]

Prior to embarking on these topics, however, a clarification of terminology is in order.

If we assume that participants' construction and co-construction of actions is what interaction is primarily about, what, then, is an *action*? Do all utterances in talk-in-interaction perform actions? If not, what other categories do we need? (For more detail on actions and action formation see Chapter 4.) Conversation Analysis distinguishes *actions* from the *practices* that are used to accomplish them

---

[1] These chapters can be downloaded from www.cambridge.org/interactional.

(Schegloff 1997a). The action of initiating repair, for instance, is ordinarily associated with the use of questioning items such as *huh?*, *who?*, etc. and certain forms of repeats. When such formats are deployed for initiating repair, this is described as a practice.

As Schegloff points out, practices associated with, for instance, the initiation of repair can also be used for other purposes. For instance, *huh?* or *hm?* may also be used for pursuing a response or promoting a telling (1997a:508ff.). *Excuse me?* may also be used as a ritual marker of remedy (e.g., in cases of sneezing) (p. 513). This means that the analyst must carry out a situated analysis of each occurrence. It also motivates the distinction between a *practice*, where the items are recurrently deployed in initiating repair, and the items themselves, i.e., *forms* or *formats* consisting of the particles *huh* and *hm* or the expression *Excuse me*, here all with rising final pitch, which may also be deployed for other purposes. (On methods for studying practices see Heritage 2010b.)

When we speak of practices in the following sections, we thus conceive of them as a link between linguistic (and other) resources (forms or formats) on the one hand and actions on the other, in such a way that the action is accomplished and its recognition enabled by the deployment of the practice. The practice itself is constituted by the recurrent use of particular forms or formats in particular sequential contexts.

To summarize, these are the terms we will be using in the chapters to follow:

i. *Actions*. This term refers to the "'main job' that the turn is performing [...] what the response must deal with in order to count as an adequate next turn" (Levinson 2013b:107; emphasis omitted). Actions in talk-in-interaction include, for example, initiating and executing repair, asking, answering, assessing, agreeing or disagreeing, inviting, promising, offering, requesting, delivering news, informing, contesting, teasing, complaining, confirming allusions, fishing for information, and so forth. Such actions are conceived of as the interpreted effects of situated practices in their sequential contexts (see Levinson 2013b).

ii. *Sequences*. This term refers to ordered courses of events. In this book, it mostly refers to courses of action that are implemented by adjacency pairs such as question-answer, first assessment-second assessment, request-compliance/refusal, invitation-acceptance/rejection, and their expansions (see Schegloff 2007a).

iii. *Activities*. This term is used to refer to larger action complexes, "big packages" such as storytellings, argumentations, descriptions, including what is called "genres" or "kommunikative Gattungen" in the German research context (see Günthner 2000a).

iv. *Practices*. This term describes the recurrent ways in which linguistic (and other) resources are used for particular purposes, for instance, in constructing turns, organizing turn taking, initiating repair, *try-marking* a referring term (Sacks and Schegloff 1979), etc.[2]

v. *Resources*. This term refers to substance-based linguistic (and other) forms or entities that can be described with respect to their structure and use. Resources include *single* forms of different sizes, including *verbal* forms such as phones and other sound objects, morphs, words, phrases, clauses, sentences, and recurrent larger discourse units, and *non-verbal* forms such as prosodies, gaze, facial/bodily gestures, and bodily position and movement;[3] as well as *combinations* of forms in (construction) formats, for example, the format *what is X* for initiating repair or syntactic constructions such as *left dislocation* or *right dislocation*, etc.

In the following chapters we compile and summarize some of the most important research that has been done on central linguistic practices and actions in talk-in-interaction. Our stocktaking will show that, in many cases, (further) work on phonetic-prosodic and/or visible dimensions is still needed. For the most part, we will cite data as well as summarize descriptions from our colleagues' work in the field. When citing other researchers' work, we have left the transcriptions in their original form, making only minor adjustments where necessary. An overview of relevant transcription systems is given in the appendix.

---

[2] Online-Chapter F, which can be downloaded from www.cambridge.org/interactional, discusses specific practices with linguistic resources such as referring, repeating, listing, reporting, formulating, etc.

[3] Non-verbal forms are considered here to the extent that they accompany language and interface with it systematically in the communication process.

2
Turn Construction and Turn Taking

In contrast to monologues or institutionally regulated interaction, it is the *local* management and negotiation of turn exchange that is crucial for the organization of conversation. In conversation the issue of who takes a turn at what point in time is not predetermined, but is negotiated between the participants at the moment when it becomes relevant in the interaction. In general, there is a normative orientation to a next speaker taking the turn "on time", i.e., not too early and not too late, with minimal overlap and minimal gap, after the prior speaker has ended his or her turn. Taking over the floor too early or too late can give rise to inferences concerning possible reasons for noticeably deviating from normative expectations. But how is it possible for turn taking to work so smoothly?

The basic mechanism of turn taking was reconstructed in the seminal paper by Sacks et al. (1974). According to their model, turn taking is organized in two components:

i. a turn-constructional component, dealing with the construction of basic units called "turn-constructional units" (TCUs); and
ii. a turn-allocation component, dealing with the distribution of turns at the end of each TCU for the next such unit.

The system is described as abstract, i.e., *context-free*, and at the same time adaptable to all kinds of contingencies, thus *context-sensitive*, *locally managed*, and *party-administered* (for an overview see also Levinson 1983 and Sidnell 2010).

In order to explain how smooth turn taking is possible, Sacks et al. assume that TCUs are *projectable*, i.e., their first possible completion point can be predicted by the recipient in advance of its occurrence. Such a possible completion point is referred to as a "transition-relevance place" (TRP) (Sacks et al. 1974:703). It is here that the rules of the turn-allocation component become relevant and result either in the transfer of speakership or in a continuation by the same speaker. According to this model, then, the continuation of the same speaker after a first TRP is an interactional achievement resulting from the fact that other participants have refrained from taking the turn themselves.

Turn-allocation techniques are grouped according to whether (a) the next turn is allocated by a current speaker selecting the next speaker; or (b) a next turn is allocated by self-selection (pp. 703–4). A set of rules applies at the TRP of an initial TCU. Thus, (1a) if the turn is constructed in such a way that the current speaker selects the next, the speaker selected has the right and obligation to take the next turn to speak. If, however, (1b) the turn is not constructed in such a way that the current speaker selects the next, next speakers may, but need not, select themselves, with the first starter acquiring rights to the turn. If (1c) no next speaker self-selects, the current speaker may, but need not, continue. If the rules of turn allocation (1a–c) at the TRP of an initial TCU are applied in such a way that the current speaker continues, they (2) re-apply recursively at each following TRP until a transfer of speakership ensues (Sacks et al. 1974:704).

> Conversation Analysis offers an account of turn construction and turn taking that concentrates on sequential organization. The model developed by Sacks et al. (1974) can explain the basic mechanisms of turn taking in everyday conversation, as well as the import of different kinds of overlap and of silence or pause in talk-in-interaction (see also Levinson 1983:298ff.).

Various aspects of this model have been taken up by interactional linguists interested in investigating how linguistic structures are involved in the projection and recognizability of TCUs and TRPs. Initially, this research focused on the interplay of syntax and prosody for unit construction and turn organization. More recently, studies have also pointed to the relevance of visible cues (e.g., Mondada 2006, 2007). Furthermore, while many researchers have used the notion of "unit", more recently this notion has been questioned in several respects:

i. it has been pointed out that by foregrounding the task of identifying and describing units, we background the fact that in reality their precise shape is subject to contingencies (see Ford 2004);
ii. in naturally occurring conversational interaction we often find not only discrete and easily identifiable units that can be described with the help of fixed clusters of parameters, but also many fuzzy units that can only be captured with reference to varying phonetic parameters that may or may not cluster (see Auer 2010; Barth-Weingarten 2013a); and
iii. participants in conversation arguably orient not only to units in the sense of TCUs but also to other entities such as "interactional units" (Ford and Thompson 1996), "action-units" (Steensig and Heinemann 2013), "response-slots" (Raymond 2013), and larger units such as in storytelling (Li 2010).

Some of these issues will be discussed in the following sections.

Finally, comparative, quantitative studies of turn taking have investigated the issue of cultural variation and possible universals in the organization of turn taking in conversation.

Anthropological linguists have often wondered whether the turn-taking system as described by Sacks et al. (1974), and in particular the timing of turn taking, is subject to cultural variation. They refer primarily to informal observation according to which, for instance, Nordic cultures allow for relatively long silences between turns (see Stivers et al. 2009:10591 for references), or members of New York Jewish communities prefer a conversational style with faster turn taking and more cooperative overlap than West Coast communities (see Tannen 1984:30).

Stivers et al. (2009) have investigated this issue quantitatively on the basis of a sampling of polar question-response sequences (i.e., questions making a yes/no answer relevant next) from natural conversations in ten languages belonging to different language types and representing a variety of geographical locations and cultural settings. The authors measured response timing, i.e., the amount of space between the end of a question and the beginning of the answer. Their results show that in all languages overlapping talk is avoided and silence is minimized between turns. In addition, they find that the same factors are likely to lead to delays in answering, namely: (i) dispreferred responses, i.e., producing something other than an answer, (ii) disconfirmations, (iii) vocal-only responses, and (iv) non-gazing questions, i.e., questions asked without the questioner gazing at his or her addressee. There are, however, small differences across the languages in the average length of the gap between turns. According to the authors' calculations, these have a range of 250 milliseconds, or a quarter of a second, approximately the time it takes to produce a single syllable. These differences are not explainable by linguistic kinship, but may instead be related to culturally specific variation in "interactional pace" or "overall tempo of social life". Thus, subjectively noticeable delays may vary in absolute duration depending on the language involved (2009:10590).

> According to the cross-linguistic study by Stivers et al. (2009), turn taking in informal conversation is universally organized so as to minimize gap and overlap in languages all over the world, with only small local variations; delayed responses are explainable by reference to the same factors in all languages. Thus, the description of turn taking as reconstructed by Sacks et al. (1974) seems to capture well the universal mechanism that organizes human turn-taking conduct in informal conversation.

1. TCU Construction

How are TCUs built and made recognizable for the recipient? In the following, we will show that turn organization is not just a sequentially managed mechanism, but one that relies heavily on linguistic resources deployed in specific sequential (and multimodal) contexts.

It will become clear that, across languages, the basic units and types of resources used in the construction of TCUs and turns are very similar, presumably because the tasks to be managed are the same. At the same time, different languages and language types will be shown to have different resources at their disposal for the projection and organization of turn taking. This has repercussions for the fine-grained organization of interaction.

Let us start by trying to differentiate TCUs and turns.[1]

From what we have seen so far, *turns* can be defined as utterances that speakers produce when they occupy the floor. Upon turn completion, transition to the next speaker becomes relevant. Turns can be composed of one single utterance or several utterances; they are then *single-unit* or *multi-unit turns*. Sacks et al. term the utterances which single-unit or multi-unit turns are composed of *TCUs*. They caution, however, against conceiving of turns and TCUs as the product of a single speaker, a product that recipients only need to recognize. Rather, "the turn as a unit is interactively determined" (1974:726–7).

Sacks et al. imply that there is a relation between TCUs and syntactic units (sentences, clauses, phrases, single words). They give, among others, the following examples of turns composed of (2.1) single words, (2.2) single phrases, and (2.3) single clauses (1974:702–3, n. 12; adapted):

(2.1) One-word turn
```
1        Desk:    What is your last name   [Loraine.
2   ->   Caller:                           [Dinnis.
3   ->   Desk:    What?
4   ->   Caller:  Dinnis.
```

(2.2) One-phrase turn
```
1        A:  Oh I have the- I have one class in the e:vening.
2   ->   B:  On Mondays?
3        A:  Y- uh::: Wednesdays.=
4        B:  =Uh- Wednesdays,=
5        A:  =En it's like a Mickey Mouse course.
```

---

[1] For a brief overview of the construction of TCUs and TRPs see also Clayman (2013a); on turn design as tailored to forming actions in their sequential context and addressing particular recipients see Drew (2013a). For an account of turn design at turn beginnings see Deppermann (2013).

(2.3)　　　One-clause turn
```
1  -> A:  Uh you been down here before [haven't you.
2     B:                               [Yeh.
3  -> A:  Where the sidewalk is?
4     B:  Yeah,
5  -> A:  Where it ends,
6  -> B:  Goes [all the way up there?
7  -> A:       [They come up to the:re,
8     A:  Yeah
```

Despite referring only to the syntactic categories or units mentioned above, Sacks et al. were well aware that other dimensions also play an important role in TCU construction. For instance, they pointed out that whether a single word is a TCU itself or only the beginning of a TCU depends on intonation (1974:721–2). But even syntax and intonation, or prosody and phonetics more generally, do not suffice to fully capture all the relevant ingredients of a TCU. Building on work by Charles and Marjorie Goodwin (e.g., Goodwin and Goodwin 1987; C. Goodwin 1996), Hayashi (2005a:47) has recently described turns at talk as "*multimodal packages for the production of action (and collaborative action) that make use of a range of different modalities, e.g., grammatical structure, sequential organization, organization of gaze and gesture, spatial-orientational frameworks, etc., in conjunction with each other*" (our italics). With reference to data from Japanese conversation, Hayashi documents the ways in which participants make use of diverse semiotic resources to assemble, parse, and project the interactional trajectory of activities in progress in concert with one another, through practices that include visible projection, gestural co-construction, and gestural tying. He thus proposes a conceptualization of the turn as *embodied* action (2005a:47–8).[2]

> Although we concentrate primarily on linguistic resources in this book, the deployment of language for the organization of TCUs and turns in getting actions accomplished in face-to-face interaction is always embedded in a variety of concurrent multimodal practices.

If turns are built to accomplish actions and TCUs are merely parts of such turns, do we really need to trouble ourselves with TCUs at all? Why not go straight for the analysis of actions and the turns that implement them?

---

[2] A multimodal conception of units and turns at talk is also advocated by Iwasaki (2009) (see below). For an analysis of the multimodal construction of single units in talk-in-interaction see also Bolden (2003). On gaze in conversation see Rossano (2013).

Is there evidence that TCUs are relevant for participants in conversation? Several points can be made here.

i. TCUs are cooperatively achieved objects.

In contrast to written sentences in texts, spoken utterances need to be adaptable to the emerging and ever-changing trajectory of the interaction. If, say, I start a TCU and then become aware that you are frowning, I may change the course of what I first intended to say to something that I presume you will like better. This manoeuver may mean that I have to change the syntactic structure of my TCU, the result being a pivot construction (see Chapter 6) or an expanded TCU (see §4 below), as the case may be. Such a thought experiment shows that producing TCUs is not simply equivalent to carrying out the intention of a single speaker but is rather the result of interaction between the interlocutors. In short, it is a cooperative achievement.

This point has been masterly shown by C. Goodwin (esp. 1979, 1981), who demonstrated that the construction and completion of a sentence as a single TCU is a truly interactional accomplishment. Consider the following example, where the gaze of the speaker is notated above the utterance:

(2.4)   "I gave up smoking" (Goodwin 1981:160) (layout adapted)

```
1   John:   ..,,..........    Don,,        Don_____
                               [            [
            I gave, I gave u p smoking  ci garettes::.=
2   Don:    =Yeah,
3   John:   ......Beth_____  ,,.......  Ann_____
                               [            [
            I- uh: one-one week ago toda: y. actually,
```

(Transcription for verbal and vocal behavior: *italics* for emphasis/accentuation, "-" for cut-off, "." for falling contour, "," for falling-rising contour; for gaze: a line shows that the party is gazing toward another, a series of dots "....." indicates one party bringing its gaze to the other, a series of commas ",," denotes a withdrawal of gaze (ibid.:52).)

Goodwin's point here is that the sentence *I gave up smoking cigarettes one week ago today actually* is the result of talk addressed to three different addressees in succession. At the beginning of the utterance, during the section *I gave up smoking cigarettes*, the speaker John is gazing at Don; during the section *one week ago* he is gazing at Beth, and finally, for the section *actually*, he directs his gaze to Ann. In each case John's words are designed for the person to whom he is gazing. Since John has not seen Don for some time, he can assume that Don has not heard the news he is announcing in the first part of his sentence: *I gave up smoking cigarettes*. However, as Don does not seem to be paying attention, John now shifts his gaze to

Beth, his wife, who already knows that he has given up smoking. For her, thus, he transforms the news of his giving up smoking into a reminder that today is the anniversary of that event: *one week ago today*. But John is not successful in securing Beth's gaze either, so he now turns his gaze to Ann and adds a new section to his utterance: the word *actually*. This item transforms the reminder of the anniversary into a report about it, thus accommodating to Ann as an unknowing recipient. Goodwin's example shows strikingly the process by which a single sentence emerges as coherent even though the speaker accommodates his TCU to meet changing interactional needs during its production. The fact that, when reorganizing their talk, speakers orient to the production and completion of such grammatical and prosodic units supports the assumption that these units are relevant for participants. (For more detail on sentences and clauses in interaction see Chapter 6.)

ii. TCUs are flexible units allowing projection and expansion.

If TCUs are contingent and interactionally achieved, they are also expandable, stoppable, and hence flexibly adaptable to the local exigencies of the interaction, which by its very nature is always negotiable (Sacks et al. 1974:726–7; see also Ford et al. 1996:428). In particular, sentential and phrasal constructions, when used to build TCUs, allow projection and expansions of their length. With respect to sentential TCUs, Sacks et al. say: "In the course of its construction, any sentential unit will rapidly (in conversation) reveal projectable directions and conclusions, which its further course can modify, but will further define" (1974:709). It is because of the expandability of sentential and other unit types that Sacks et al. do not speak of the ends of sentential, clausal, etc. constructions, but of "'possible completion points' of sentences, clauses, phrases and one-word constructions, [. . .] and multiples thereof" (p. 721).[3] This terminology reflects the conception of the TCU as a fundamentally flexible and expandable unit.

iii. Participants orient to the completion of TCUs.

When speakers stop midway, leave pauses, and/or initiate self-repair in the course of the production of TCUs, in particular sentential or clausal ones, participants orient to the projected TCU and its completion. Evidence for this comes from two observations: first, *speakers* themselves show an orientation to the completion of their TCUs by continuing and completing them after "disturbances" of progressivity. Second, on such occasions *recipients* also show an orientation to the TCU under construction by typically waiting for speakers to continue and

---

[3] In a footnote, Sacks et al. point to the relevance of linguists' contributions for understanding methods of projection: "How projection of unit-types is accomplished [. . .], is an important question on which linguists can make major contributions" (1974:703).

complete their projected TCU. There is thus a normative orientation on the part of both speaker and recipient to projected units and their completion in talk-in-interaction.

This point has been aptly shown by Schegloff (1979). He investigates the relevance of self-initiated same-turn (self) repair to a "syntax-for-conversation" and shows – *inter alia* – the effects of repair on the syntactic form of sentences. He notes various ways in which the practices of repair can change the syntax of sentences, for instance by expanding phrases, changing the structure underway, converting an independent clause into a subordinate one, converting a question into an assertion, etc. (pp. 263–6). It becomes quite clear from this study that units of the length and structure of clauses and sentences – in addition to others – are relevant to participants in organizing their talk-in-interaction.

iv. Recipient responses can become relevant within the boundaries of single TCUs.

Occasionally, there are specific kinds of response that are made relevant within the boundaries of a single TCU: apart from the coordination of recipient gaze (see C. Goodwin 1979, 1986a; M. H. Goodwin 1980; also Rossano 2013), in-speech laughter may make the recipient's joining in relevant as a demonstration of understanding and affiliation even before the end of the TCU in progress (Lerner 1996a; Sidnell 2010:160). Tasks such as pursuing and displaying referent recognition as well as inviting and conveying assessments are in many cases relevant within the course of a single TCU (Sidnell 2010:160–7). This suggests again that TCUs are not formal monoliths but rather "living" entities that are oriented to by participants in interaction.

v. Participants can share in the construction of TCUs.

In collaborative completions, a TCU is begun by one speaker and completed by another speaker or by both speakers simultaneously, as in lines 17 and 18 of the following example:

```
(2.5)      "Madeline" (Sidnell 2010:168) (adapted)
14      Marsha:     oh- you mean for living in: Madeline?
15      Madeline:   ye:ah
16                  (0.3)
17  ->  Marsha:     ·hh It's just (0.8)
18  ->  Madeline:   no:t possible.=h[uh?
19      Marsha:                     [ye:ah we- Gi:na tri:ed that at one
20                  ti:[me.=but-]
```

The collaborative completion of sentences and/or clauses, as in lines 17–18 here, reveals that syntactic structures are interactionally shared (Lerner 1991, 1996a,

2004). The fact that participants are able to collaboratively complete TCUs at all attests to the interactional relevance both of projection and of single units in talk-in-interaction. Without projection, this kind of interaction between speaker and recipient would not be possible at all within the bounds of a single TCU (see also Ono and Thompson 1995 and, for more detail, Sidnell 2010:167–71).[4]

> TCUs are interactionally achieved, flexible, and adaptable units in turns at talk that are oriented to as relevant by the participants. Yet they are not ends in themselves. They are the epiphenomena of turn construction, which itself delivers action (see Selting 2000).

We now examine the most important properties of TCUs.

1.1 Projection

Projection means that the earlier part of a structure foreshadows its later trajectory and thus makes its completion predictable. Projection presupposes knowledge of linguistic and other holistic structures (*gestalts*) that, once begun, have recognizable trajectories and possible completions. Both speakers and recipients in everyday interaction normally assume that they can rely on their language's devices for projecting as mutually shared knowledge.

The notion of projection is an apt one for explaining the smooth transition of speakership in talk-in-interaction. How can would-be speakers otherwise know when the moment for a next turn onset has come? If they wait for the prior speaker to end the turn and possibly even its expansion, then their own onset will be too late. If they come in too early, they may be heard as overly eager or impatient. It is projection that allows next speakers to anticipate the point of possible completion of the current turn and thus predict the correct moment for beginning their own turn. Projection is relevant not only for final TCUs in turns, but for the construction of units in general. When we talk about the construction and projection of units, these units can always be TCUs in both single-unit and multi-unit turns.

Projection operates within different domains and on various levels of organization. Schegloff (2013) draws a distinction between *macro-projection* and *micro-projection*. Macro-projection operates in the domain of the overall structural organization of both TCUs and turns: "what sort of TCU this is and where in it we now are; and if a multi-unit turn, what sort of multi-unit turn this is, what shape or trajectory such a project

---

[4] Yet, as Sidnell makes clear, turns, and even TCUs, are not the minimal units of interaction: "Rather, [...] recipients monitor a turn word by word (perhaps sound by sound) so as to find not only that it is now beginning, now continuing, now reaching completion but also where, in the course of its production, they may be called upon to respond either with talk (as in the case of a designedly incomplete utterance) or something else (e.g., laughter, gaze, display of recognition, etc.)" (2010:172).

takes, and where in that shape or trajectory we now are" (2013:42). Micro-projection operates locally in the domain of the linguistic organization of TCUs: "what kind of construction this is, and what it makes relevant next; what kind of word and what that projects for next word; what kind of sound and what that projects for what might follow" (2013:42). Both kinds of projection are interdependent: macro-projections are realized through local progression within the projected TCU or the projected multi-unit turn, while micro-projections of, for example, next words or next sounds are tailored and interpreted by reference to the overall structural organization of the TCU in progress (2013:43). In another perspective, Auer distinguishes between projections on different levels: action projection, sequential projection (adjacency pairs and other formats), content-based projection, syntactic projection, and phonological projection (2005a:10ff.). Languages may differ in the domains in which they facilitate projection.[5]

Research has shown that projectability can vary cross-linguistically. There are languages whose structures provide for *early projection*, which means that the syntactic structure can be used to project possible completion points early in the unit. Clauses and sentences in languages such as English and German allow for early projection. By contrast, languages such as Japanese, for example, have been said to operate with *delayed projection*,[6] meaning that the moment at which recipients can predict possible completion points comes much later in the current unit. In these languages recipients have less time to anticipate possible completion points in ongoing turns.

In the following sections we examine these two types of projection more closely.

1.1.1 Early Projection in English and German

In languages such as English and German, speakers rely on syntax for the projection of sentences or clauses as holistic structures. This is possible because the order of constituents is rather rigid: in English, this is Subject-Verb-Object (where relevant), i.e., SV(O). Core constituents are typically expressed.[7] The grammatical subject at the beginning of clauses in conversational units is often short (e.g., a pronoun) and is typically followed by a verb or verb complex, for instance, auxiliary + verb. These two constituents at the beginning of TCUs present the core information needed to recognize the action being implemented by the emerging TCU. Hence, TCU beginnings are important: elements that shape the TCU and its interpretation are quite regularly placed here (Hayashi 2004a; also Schegloff 1987a:71–2; Thompson and Couper-Kuhlen 2005).

---

[5] Auer (2014b) discusses general parameters that determine the projection potential of a language: (1) rigid versus loose serialization restrictions (word order), (2) serialization in modifier/modified structures, (3) serialization and government, and (4) split constructions (2014b:20–2). On levels of organization involved in projection in general and the resources deployed to achieve this projectability in Japanese see Hayashi (2004a:1340–3).

[6] We use the terminology *delayed projection languages* for Japanese and Korean as this is well established in the literature (Tanaka 1999, 2000a). However, we do not mean to imply that these languages are in any way deficient compared to *early projection languages*. In this respect the term *late projection* might be more appropriate.

[7] See Thompson (2002) for a more nuanced view of this statement.

Speakers of English know, for instance, that a structure like *I will give*, when begun in the context of a teacher–student counseling session, will normally need objects like *you* and *some examples* in order to reach completion. More generally, they know that clauses with the verb *give* require both direct and indirect objects. As a consequence, once the interlocutor is heard beginning a clause with *I will give*, it can be predicted that the clause will not reach completion before the obligatory objects have been produced. So the syntax of sentences and clauses in English can be used as a projection device.

In German, word order, or rather constituent order, varies with clause type. Main clauses normatively have the finite verb occupying the second slot, i.e., following the subject or other topicalized constituent in first position. In clauses with complex verb forms or separable verb prefixes, the non-finite part of the verb occupies a slot later in the clause according to the rules of normative German grammar. In subordinate clauses, the finite verb is placed toward the end of the clause, normatively in final position. This creates what has been called the German "sentence brace" (*Satzklammer*) (Auer 1996a; Table 2.1).[8]

Table 2.1 *The German sentence brace*

			Main clause structures:		
(1)	die	**waren**	gestern	in der Stadt.	
	SUBJ	VERB$_{fin}$	ADV	ADV	
	they	*were*	*yesterday*	*in town*	
(2)	die	**sind**	gestern	in der Stadt	**gewesen**.
	SUBJ	VERB$_{fin}$	ADV	ADV	VERB$_{non-fin}$
	they	*have*	*yesterday*	*in town*	*been*
(3)	die	**hängen**	da	immer	**rum**.
	SUBJ	VERB$_{fin}$	ADV	ADV	VERB$_{non-fin}$
	they	*hang*	*there*	*always*	*around*
			Subordinate clause structure:		
(4)	...**dass**	die	gestern	in der Stadt	**gewesen** **sind**.
	COMPL	SUBJ	ADV	ADV	VERB$_{non-fin}$ VERB$_{fin}$
	...that	*they*	*yesterday*	*in town*	*been* *have*

Note: The abbreviations denote the following categories: SUBJ = subject, VERB$_{fin}$ = finite verb, VERB$_{non-fin}$ = non-finite verb, ADV = adverb/adverbial, COMPL = complementizer.

---

[8] In conversational German, however, the finite verb does not always occur in final position in structures of types (2) through (4) (see Chapter 6).

German grammar thus prescribes patterns that both enable early projection and provide a clear indication of possible completion: for structures like (1), speakers and recipients can rely on the knowledge that the use of a finite form of a verb such as *sein* "to be" in the second slot makes a continuation of the clause expectable, for instance with an adverbial. In structures like (2) and (3), the production of the first part of the verb complex in second position makes a continuation of the unit expectable – and indicates that the structure is not complete until the production of the non-finite part(s) of the verb. Similarly, in structures like (4), the production of a complementizer at the beginning of the clause makes a continuation of the clause expectable – and indicates that the structure will not be complete until a finite verb is produced. Furthermore, obligatory objects projected by the verb are case marked; sentences and clauses are not complete before these verb projections have been fulfilled and marked through morphological case. So, even if in (subordinate or other) clauses the main verb is in final position, an early case-marked dative object like *dem Kind* ("to the child") projects a final verb that may take such an object, virtually binding the syntactic projection together via morpho-syntactic structuration.[9] Thus, the grammar of German, like that of English, provides for the early projection of clausal units and their possible completions; but unlike English, German gives a precise indication of when the clausal structure will be potentially complete.[10]

1.1.2 Delayed Projection in Japanese

While early projection in languages like English and German has been extensively studied, less research has been done on languages with different grammatical structuration. Of these, Japanese is the one that has come to be understood best.[11] Japanese has been described as a language providing for delayed projection. There are several features of the grammatical structure in Japanese that contribute to this kind of projectability.[12]

First, Japanese is a so-called *verb-final* or *predicate-final* language, the normative order of its constituents being Subject-Object-Verb (SOV). Furthermore, it is an agglutinating language with (normatively) post-positioned case markers and subordinate clause markers; main clauses follow their complement clauses (see Fox et al. 1996:196ff.). There is a normative orientation to the placement of the verb or other predicate in final position in clausal and sentential TCUs (see Tanaka 1999, 2000a). For example:

---

[9] We are grateful to Peter Auer for bringing to our attention the relevance of case marking in German as opposed to the lack of case marking in Japanese.
[10] For more detail on projection in German see, e.g., Auer (2005a, 2009).
[11] For Korean see, e.g., Kim (1999a, 2001).
[12] For more general discussions of the characteristics of conversational Japanese see Maynard (1989: Chapter 3); Fox et al. (1996); Tanaka (1999, 2000a); and Hayashi (2003: Chapter 2).

(2.6) "I think that it was so" (Fox et al. 1996:196) (adapted)
```
T:  Soo  yatta    to         omou.
    so   be-past  quotative  think
```
((I)) think that ((it was)) so

(*Note*: items given in double parentheses (( )) in the translation are not expressed in the Japanese original.)

Verbs, auxiliaries, and other predicates carry important information about the action being implemented in the ongoing TCU. This information tends to be delivered relatively late in the Japanese TCU. Moreover, Hayashi cites the case of yes-no questions in Japanese, which are typically constructed by placing the question particle *ka* (or a variant thereof) at the end of a clause (2004a:1345):[13]

(2.7) "Did you buy this, Mr. Y.?" (Hayashi 2004a:1345) (adapted)
```
Shoko:  kore::   (.)     yamamoto san ga  katta     n desu  ka:?
        this             Yamamoto  TL  SP  bought  N  CP    Q
```
Did ((you)) buy this ((yourself)), Mr. Yamamoto?

This means that in Japanese the grammatical format of the TCU as an interrogative clause, and thus the social action implemented by it, is only made explicit at the end of the TCU. More generally, as Tanaka puts it, "turns in Japanese do not necessarily project from their beginnings what their ultimate shape and type will be" (2000a:29).

Second, even though there is a strict orientation to positioning the predicate finally, the ordering of constituents preceding the final predicate is fairly flexible and thus hardly predictable (Tanaka 2000a:11ff; Hayashi 2004a:1344.). Furthermore, the addition of postpositional particles and other grammatical elements can change the structure and meaning of an emerging utterance. Tanaka gives the following example to demonstrate how what occurs after a verb expression can alter its meaning:

(2.8) "Fever was gone" (Tanaka 2000a:14–15)
((Telephone conversation, slightly simplified; K is explaining to Y that her baby first developed a fever and then a rash.))
```
1   K:  Moo        netsu    ga   moo-      sagatta*    to
        already    fever    NOM  already   fell        QUOT:that
```

---

[13] In this example the following transcription symbols and glosses are used: ? = rising intonation, TL = title marker, SP = subject particle, N = nominalizer, CP = form of the copula verb *be*, Q = question particle; items in (()) are inferred but unexpressed elements.

```
2            omot         tara          [ne:=
             thought      CONJ:when     [FP

3     Y:                                ['N
                                        [yeah
                                        [Yeah

4     K:     =>deta<=
             came out
             ((the rashes)) came out

5     Y:     =↑Ha::
             Oh
             Oh::
```

Gloss of lines 1–2: "When ((I)) thought that already the fever was already gone, you know"

As Tanaka explains, K's utterance up to the asterisk constitutes a complete sentence "in an analytic sense", i.e., it contains a subject and a verb:

```
(a)          Moo          netsu        ga           moo-         sagatta*
             already      fever        NOM          already      fell
             already the fever was already gone
```

The addition of the quotative particle *to* ("that") transforms the sentence into a clause that is being commented on:

```
(b)          Moo          netsu        ga           moo-         sagatta*      to
             already      fever        NOM          already      fell          QUOT:that
             that already the fever was already gone
```

Next, the new predicate *omot-* ("thought") embeds the prior construction as a subordinate clause under it:

```
(c)          Moo          netsu        ga           moo-         sagatta*      to       omot
             already      fever        NOM          already      fell          that     thought
             ((I)) thought that already the fever was already gone
```

Finally, the conjunctive particle *tara* ("when") further transforms the new structure into the first part of a potential complex sentence, *when X, Y*, which now projects a clause Y.

```
(d)          Moo          netsu        ga           moo-         sagatta*      to       omot       tara
             already      fever        NOM          already      fell          that     thought    when
             When ((I)) thought that already the fever was already gone
```

The post-positional structure of Japanese, in conjunction with its flexible word order, thus results in the incremental transformability and revisability of TCUs, and therefore also turns. As the relation of constituents to the verb is not fixed via case marking, the addition of elements after an initial verbal expression can modify the structure and meaning of the unit preceding it, as well as change the social action performed by the emergent TCU (Tanaka 2000a:17). The structuring of TCUs has consequences for the behavior of recipients in Japanese conversation: as they cannot be certain whether the production of a verb or a part of the verbal complex is indeed intended as an incipient turn ending or will be embedded into something else, recipients need to "wait and see" what ensues (p. 14).

Third, in Japanese, syntactic elements such as core arguments can be left unexpressed if they are identifiable from the context (Hayashi 2004a:1344). This results in a prevalence of unexpressed syntactic constituents, a property which further contributes to the limited projective force of TCU beginnings. The presence of some constituent at the beginning of a TCU provides very little information about how the unit will develop, except that some kind of predicate may be produced toward the end of the TCU in progress (2004a:1344). Consequently, Japanese turns have been said to be produced in a "bit-by-bit fashion" (Hayashi 2003:207), with limited means for predicting what will come next.[14]

Japanese recipients have been said to respond differently given this organization of the turn: earlier accounts have claimed that they are led to provide more recipiency tokens and to chunk their utterances into smaller parts than do conversational recipients in languages such as English or German (see also Schegloff et al. 1996:32; Sidnell 2007b:236). This has even been interpreted as creating a culturally specific and emotively involved interactional style (Maynard 1989; Clancy et al. 1996). More recent analyses have stressed the interdependence of linguistic and interactional structuring and suggested that participants hold off coming in, in order to see how the turn develops (Tanaka 2000a:14).

Iwasaki (2009) contests the latter view – although her work could be said to complement prior research rather nicely. While the research reported so far describes projection in the domain of what Schegloff (2013:42) calls macro-projection in the TCU, Iwasaki's analysis operates in the domain of micro-projection (see above). She investigates the collaboration of participants

---

[14] Other consequences are, as Tanaka (2000a:7–8) points out, the absence of clause-level recycling in self-repair, the preference for co-participants to collaboratively complete only terminal items, and the vulnerability of post-predicate components to overlap by the next speaker.

within TCUs. Her work shows that speakers create "interactive turn spaces" inside TCUs: they use predominantly vocal and visible practices to make a recipient's display of recognition, understanding, and/or affiliation locally relevant as the TCU is being produced.[15] Figure 2.1 schematizes such an interactive turn space (see next page).

Iwasaki concludes that what has been discussed in the literature as the "delayed projectability" of turns and a "wait-and-see" strategy for next-turn incomings in Japanese is misconceived. She argues instead that recipients make projections and seek to co-participate prior to TRPs, and that speakers encourage this by creating opportunities for "micro-collaboration" (2009:231; see also Iwasaki 2011).

We can conclude that while syntactic macro-projection in Japanese may be delayed in comparison to languages such as English, there is vocal-visible micro-projection and collaboration within TCUs. In addition, as shown by Hayashi (2004a), Japanese speakers have other means of projection, among them the use of the distal demonstrative *are* (see §2.1 below), although such forms of projection are not built into basic clausal structure.

> While early projection languages such as English and German provide for syntactic macro-projection in clauses, delayed projection languages such as Japanese do not facilitate it. However, Japanese makes extensive use of vocal-visible micro-projection for the organization of collaboration within TCUs, perhaps more so than in languages with so-called early projection.
>
> Whether a language has early or delayed/late projection appears to depend on the interplay of the following parameters: (i) early or late positioning of the finite verb, (ii) more fixed versus less fixed word order or serialization of constituents, (iii) degree of bonding between the verb and the objects it projects, for example, via morphological case marking, (iv) the possibility, or not, of leaving constituents unexpressed. Further work on other languages in interaction is needed to corroborate the relevance of these parameters.

So far, we have considered only the role of syntax for TCU construction and projection. Yet other devices, in particular phonetic/prosodic ones, must also be considered when addressing the question of how unit ends are made recognizable prior to actual turn completion (see also Fox et al. 2013:732). What is the role of which device?

---

[15] For Korean, another agglutinating SOV language, Kim (1999a) shows how phrasal unit boundaries *within a turn* serve as a place where the speaker can invite the recipient to respond by, e.g., acknowledging the speaker's point so far, displaying her/his understanding, or collaboratively co-constructing and completing the turn. (See also Kim 2001.)

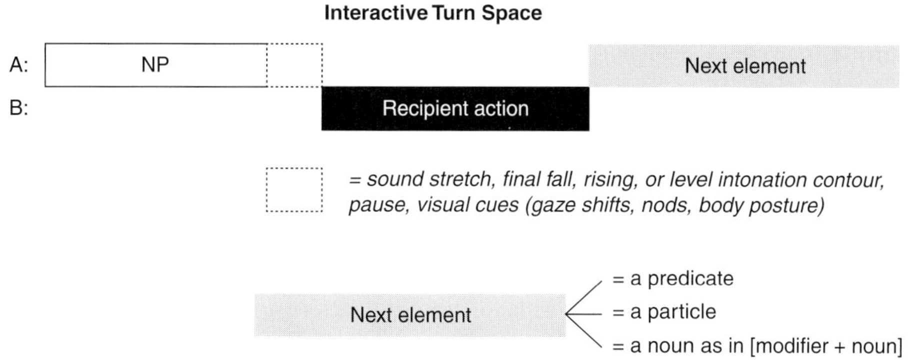

1. TCU Construction 47

Interactive Turn Space

A: | NP | | | Next element |
B: | | Recipient action | |

▭ = sound stretch, final fall, rising, or level intonation contour, pause, visual cues (gaze shifts, nods, body posture)

Next element ⟵ = a predicate
= a particle
= a noun as in [modifier + noun]

Figure 2.1 Unit segmentation and recipient's collaborative action in an interactive turn space (Iwasaki 2009:228)
Note: NP = noun phrase.

1.2 The Roles of Syntax and Prosody

Researchers interested in language and social interaction have become increasingly aware that more is at stake in TCU construction than the choice of words or syntactic structures. Consequently, interactional linguists have taken a closer look at the role of prosody and phonetics and their interplay with other resources. But as with syntax, this role has turned out to vary cross-linguistically.

1.2.1 Syntax and Prosody in Languages with Early Projection

Research on prosodic, phonetic, and syntactic detail in talk-in-interaction has shown that in order to explain the mechanisms of TCU construction and projection in languages such as English and German, the Sacks et al. (1974) model needs some revision. There have been two different suggestions: Selting's (2000) proposal for a revised understanding of the turn-constructional component, and Ford et al.'s (1996) proposal of "Complex TRPs".

i. Suggestion 1: revise the description of turn construction

Working on the basis of German data, Selting (1996a) conceives of TCUs as flexible entities constructed in their local sequential context through an interplay of syntax and prosody. Syntax is used as a resource for more far-reaching projection (Schegloff's macro-projection; see above), while this syntactic projection is locally contextualized through prosody. Syntactic and prosodic units are described as flexible schemata that participants adapt to the exigencies of the situation. In the projection of TCUs, both play individual and complementary roles (p. 384; see also Selting 1995a). TCUs are conceptualized as having at once possibly complete syntactic and possibly complete prosodic trajectories.

To see this, consider the following example from a conversation between three young university teachers: Lea, Eli, and Cis are talking about the possible motives of their students for keeping quiet rather than protesting. Eli has suggested that students nowadays are narcissistic and apolitical, whereupon Lea has claimed that her students are searching for new forms to express their criticism of current life styles but have not yet found them. After this Eli backs down from her prior assessment and continues the conversation as shown in the extract in Figure 2.2 (see next page).

In this extract, it is predominantly pitch that is deployed to "package" TCUs prosodically; minor loudness and tempo changes etc. that normally co-occur are not notated separately here. Figure 2.2 presents Eli's talk and pitch trajectories iconically (note that lines of transcript are not co-extensive with TCUs). The pitch can be inspected with respect both to how it moves throughout the units and to how it interplays with the beginning of new syntactic clauses to display them as continuing or set off from prior ones. Continuing pitch moves on without creating a melodic break (prosodic integration), whereas non-continuing pitch shows disjunctions (e.g., upsteps or downsteps) that make melodic breaks hearable at the beginning of new syntactic clauses (prosodic independence).

Now the same extract is presented in a transcription showing the transcriber's interpretation of what constitutes individual TCUs within Eli's turn (in this case, new TCUs begin in a new numbered line of transcription).

(2.9)   "Didn't think about it" (Selting 2000:493) (adapted)

```
822 Eli: <<p> ich `WEISS es nich;>
              I    know it  not
         I don't know
823           (ca. 2.0)
824 Eli: ich ´hAb mir keine ge`DANken darüber gemacht;
         I    have myself no  thoughts about it  made
         I didn't think about it
825 Lea: `´hm,
826 Eli: <u> zu`mAl ich auch `ÜBERwiegend studenten hab die:?((swallows))
             since  I   also  overwhelmingly students have who
         since I mostly have students who
              <c> die also schon `!ÄL!ter sind;
                  who thus already older are
              who are already older
```

1. TCU Construction 49

k4: 824–833

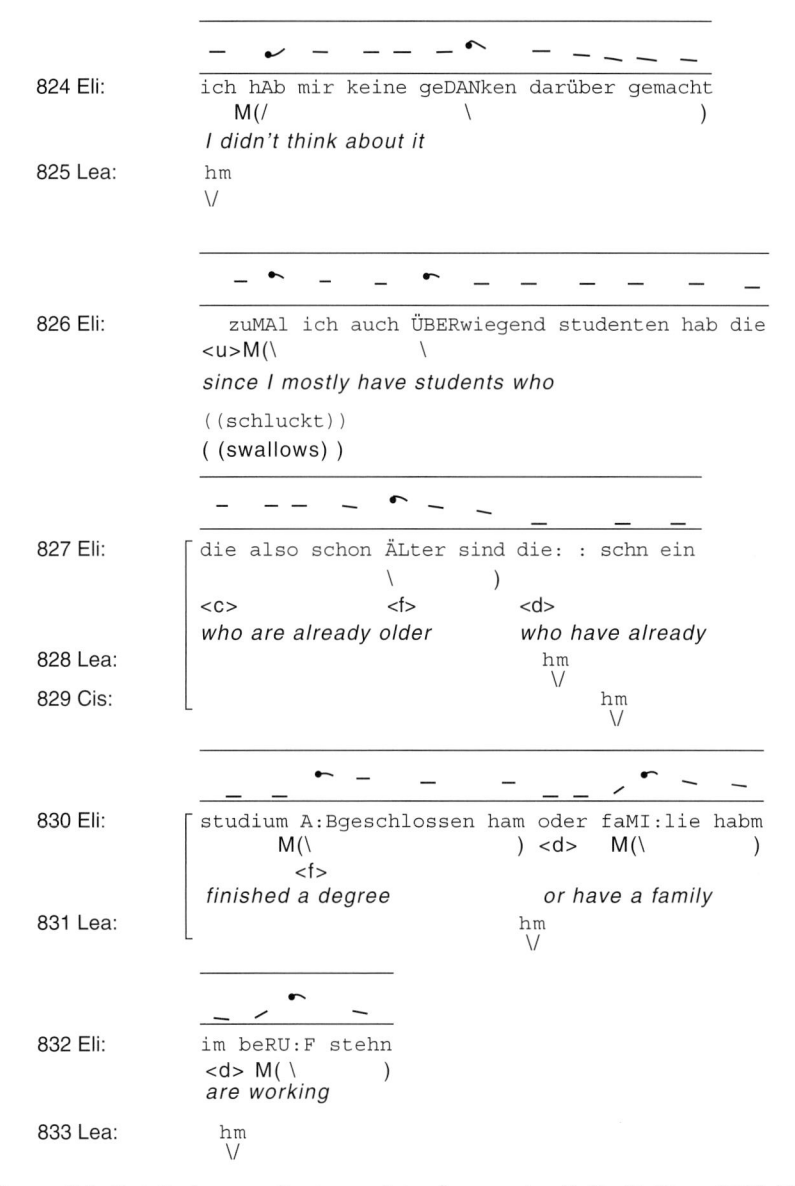

```
824 Eli:   ich hAb mir keine geDANken darüber gemacht
             M(/              \                    )
           I didn't think about it
825 Lea:   hm
           \/

826 Eli:      zuMA1 ich auch ÜBERwiegend studenten hab die
           <u>M(\            \
           since I mostly have students who
           ((schluckt))
           ((swallows))

827 Eli:   ⎡die also schon ÄLter sind die:: schn ein
           ⎢              \         )
           ⎢   <c>          <f>      <d>
           ⎢who are already older   who have already
828 Lea:   ⎢                         hm
           ⎢                         \/
829 Cis:   ⎣                                  hm
                                              \/

830 Eli:   ⎡studium A:Bgeschlossen ham oder faMI:lie habm
           ⎢        M(\            )  <d>   M(\       )
           ⎢           <f>
           ⎢finished a degree           or have a family
831 Lea:   ⎣                            hm
                                        \/

832 Eli:   im beRU:F stehn
           <d> M( \      )
           are working
833 Lea:   hm
           \/
```

Figure 2.2 Detailed prosodic transcript of example (2.9) (Selting 2000:496) (adapted)

```
827         <d> di[e::  [schn ein   studium  `!A:B!geschlossen ha[m;
                who         already one degree finished            have
            who have already finished a degree
828 Lea:            [`´hm,                                              [`´hm,
829 Cis:                 [`´hm,
830 Eli:    <d> oder: fa`MI:lie habm;
                or     family    have
            or have a family
831         <d> im be`RU:F stehn;
                in employment are
            or are working
832 Lea:    `´hm,
```

(Transcription symbols used here: <u> local upstep in pitch, <d> local downstep in pitch, <c> continuing pitch, <p> piano loudness; for more detail on the pitch contours see Figure 2.2 from Selting (2000:496) as reproduced above.)

In line 826, we can observe a complex syntactic unit that consists of two different clauses packaged into a single prosodic unit or intonation phrase. Here, the subordinate clause *zumAl ich auch ÜBERwiegend studenten hab* ("since I also mostly have students") is followed by a relative clause *die also schon !ÄL!ter sind;* ("who are already older") that is added as a prosodically integrated continuation, i.e., without a prosodic break.[16] In other words, the simple continuation of a prior syntactic unit without a prosodic break prevents the continuation from being heard as a new TCU.

By contrast, each of the lines 827–831 is set off from the preceding one by a prosodic break that in this case comprises a downstep in pitch in relation to the end of the preceding unit, as indicated by "<d>" in the transcription. This leads to the interpretation that each of these lines adds a new detail to further explain Eli's account, launched in line 826, for the information given in line 824. In other words, starting a syntactic continuation with a prosodic break, and thus packaging an expansion into a separate prosodic unit or intonation phrase,[17] indicates that it is a new TCU.[18]

What this example shows is that syntactic units can be continued both by prosodically independent and by prosodically integrated expansions. The simple

---

[16] Eli's cut-off with a glottal stop (" ? ") at the end of the first mention of the relative pronoun *die:* does not amount to a prosodic break between TCUs; instead, it makes turn holding interpretable. This analysis is supported by the fact that she first swallows and then repeats the relative pronoun with continuing pitch and loudness when resuming the projected relative clause.

[17] The following are criteria for recognizing intonation phrases in German: a coherent/cohesive intonation contour, at least one prosodically prominent syllable (accent, focus accent), some recognizable final pitch movement, final lengthening, final loudness diminuendo, final creaky voice (glottalization), pitch step up or down at the beginning of the next unit, fast anacrustic syllables at the beginning of the next unit, (micro-)pause (Selting et al. 2009:370; for more detail see Online-Chapter E).

[18] In particular, line 830 could in principle have been formatted as a prosodically integrated continuation of line 827. Here, however, its production with a prosodic break exposes it as a separate TCU.

continuation of a prior syntactic unit without a prosodic break prevents the continuation from being heard as a new TCU.[19]

For Selting, then, a TCU is conceptualized "as the smallest interactionally relevant complete linguistic unit, in a given context, that is constructed with syntactic and prosodic resources within their semantic, pragmatic, activity type-specific, and sequential conversational context" (2000:477). Since not all TCUs thus defined end in TRPs, Selting separates TCUs from TRPs: a TCU ends in a TRP unless extra work is done to postpone the TRP to the end of a larger unit.[20] This accounts for the observation that in longer multi-unit turns, such as in storytelling, not every (mid-story) TCU ends in a TRP;[21] in this case, the speaker's projection of telling a story postpones the TRP to the possible end of the story.

> Single TCUs are made recognizable in their local sequential context through the interplay of syntactic and prosodic devices. They are displayed as internally cohesive units, and they are delimited from neighboring units. Nevertheless, they are flexible, expandable, and adaptable to the exigencies of the interaction, and they cannot be determined with reference to either syntax or prosody alone. Hence, their actual completion can only be attested retrospectively. For recipients, the recognition of a TCU is a result of context-sensitive inferences.

ii. Suggestion 2: identify complex TRPs as a practice for TCU and turn construction

Ford and Thompson (1996) investigate quantitatively the comparative power of syntactic, intonational, and pragmatic or action completion for the projection of turn completion in English. They operationalize syntactic completion as the occurrence of possible syntactic completion points within or at the actual end of units; intonational completion as the occurrence of final intonation in the form of falling-to-low or rising-to-high pitch; and pragmatic completion as "a complete conversational action within its specific sequential context" (1996:150).[22] They conclude that syntax is the least reliable resource for turn completion. Instead, they suggest that "intonation and pragmatic completion points select from among the syntactic completion points to form [...] 'Complex Transition Relevance Places'" (p. 154). For Ford and Thompson, TCUs are thus formed when syntactic, intonational, and

---

[19] See also Local (1992) on the use of pitch and loudness for continuing versus restarting a turn in English.
[20] In the above example, all TCUs also end in TRPs. The recipients' delivery of recipiency tokens after most of the TCUs, with the exception of lines 822 and 830, attests to their interpretation of these points as TRPs.
[21] On the deployment of glottalization in German conversation for designing a turn-internal TCU as a new action – as opposed to linking TCU-initial vowels for continuing an action in progress – see Szczepek Reed (2014).
[22] Since pragmatic completion was defined as requiring final intonation, the three notions are not completely independent one of another.

pragmatic completion points converge (1996:172). It is these points of convergence that participants orient to in taking and yielding turns.

Ford et al. (1996:431) move away from the notion of "unit" entirely. They advocate focusing instead on the range of practices participants use to construct co-participation in conversation, syntax being only one of these (see also Auer 1996a). With reference to the following example they argue that although the utterance in the arrowed line could – out of context – be possibly complete syntactically at an earlier point, in the given context it is only possibly complete after the complement of the verb *go*:

```
(2.10)    "I gotta go to the john" (Ford et al. 1996:429–30) (adapted)
1     Pam:  .hh Oh yeah you've gotta tell Mike tha:t. Uh cuz they
2           [want that on fi:lm.
3     Car:  [Oh: no: here we go ag(h)[(h)ain o(h)o(h)o.hh=
4     Cur:                            [Huh huh huh huh
5     Gar:  =I [don't thin[k it's that funny.
6     Car:     [ O  h  :  [ :,
7  -> Pam:                [I gotta go to t'the joh:[n before I hear that
8  -> Car:                                         [You'll like it, you'll
9     Pam:  [again.
10    Car:  [really like it.
```

In this context, the first possible syntactic completion point in line 7 would be after *I gotta go*. Yet after this there are several more possible completion points, namely after *t'the joh:n*, and then again after *before I hear that again* where the turn finally ends. In contrast to *I gotta go*, which is delivered with non-terminal pitch, the intonation of *to t'the joh:n* does project possible completion. At this point the utterance so far is also pragmatically a possibly complete action, and in fact Pam begins to move away from the picnic table here. Moreover, Carney now comes in. However, in overlap Pam retrospectively continues her prior unit by adding on the adverbial phrase *before I hear that again*. Ford et al.'s argument is that trying to determine whether Pam's turn has one TCU or two misses the point: what counts is that she has deployed practices allowing her to talk past a projection of possible completion. They conclude that analysts must account for what people are doing when they draw on syntactic, pragmatic, prosodic, and gestural practices to display and revise their understanding of whose turn it is to talk (1996:450). (See also §4 below and Online-Chapter E §2.)

In other words, although the construction of TCUs and turns can and should be described systematically, such descriptions must not become mechanistic. When we analyze unit construction, we must always keep in mind the contingency inherent in interaction (Ford 2004). Contingency is a core feature of interaction, evident not only in the collaborative production of talk but also in the simultaneous production of trajectories in various modalities (sound, gesture, grammar, etc.).[23] Our reconstruction of how TCUs and turns are built must incorporate this contingency.[24]

> For languages with early projection it is widely accepted now that an account of turn and TCU construction needs to consider the interplay of syntax and prosody (at least) in the given action and activity-related sequential context, with attention paid to participants' practices of projecting and negotiating completion, and with due acknowledgment of the role of contingency.

1.2.2 Syntax and Prosody in Languages with Delayed Projection

Recall that the syntactic configuration of languages such as Japanese and Korean leads to the projection of possible completion late in the ongoing unit. Imminent turn completion is normally marked by the use of final particles (Tanaka 2000a:25). In these cases, prosody does not seem to play an important role. It is only in the case of *iikiri* (truncated turn shapes) that prosody appears to compensate for the absence of final particles. Tanaka gives the following example:

(2.11)   "Tummy alright" (Tanaka 2000a:26)
((Telephone conversation; Y's daughter Yurika has previously been suffering from an upset stomach.))

```
1 A: Yurika chan onaka no hoo daijoo ↑bu
     ((name))   tummy  P  as for all right
     Is Yurika's tummy alright?

2 Y: 'N  daibun  mata naotte kita.    ((falling intonation))
     yeah a lot again getting better
     Yeah, ((it))'s getting a lot better again

3 A: ↑Ah ↓soo
     oh  right
     Oh, is ((that)) right
```

As Tanaka explains, none of the turns in this fragment of talk end with utterance-final elements. Yet the final item in line 1, the predicate *daijoo ↑bu*, has a last mora,

---

[23] Ford's argument is reminiscent of Schegloff's celebration of contingency in interaction: "Contingency – interactional contingency – is not a blemish on the smooth surface of discourse, or of talk-in-interaction more generally. It is endemic to it. It is its glory. It is what allows talk-in-interaction the flexibility and robustness to serve as the enabling mechanism for the institutions of social life" (Schegloff 1991:22).
[24] On methods of turn construction and projection in other languages with early projection see, for instance, Steensig (2001) for Danish and Turkish and J. Lindström (2006) for Swedish. On multimodal practices of projection see also, e.g., Mondada (2006) and Streeck (2009).

i.e., the short syllable-like phonological unit *bu*, that is spoken with clearly rising final intonation. Line 2 is said to finish with distinct falling intonation, while in line 3, the prosody is said to be particularly pronounced since the rising tone of ↑*Ah* makes a sharp contrast with the falling tone of ↓*soo* (2000a:27). Such prosodic patterns are described as variants of a "marked prosodic contour." Tanaka argues that a marked final prosodic contour displays "early" completion of the unit, implying that it will undergo no further transformation through utterance-final elements (2000a:28).

> In Japanese, marked prosody plays a role as an alternative to final particles: it can be deployed to signal the end of truncated TCUs and turns. While it is final particles that typically indicate turn completion, with truncated turn shapes marked prosody can override the expectation of an utterance-final particle and make turn completion locally recognizable (Tanaka 2000a:31).

1.3 Pauses and Break-offs within TCUs

TCUs can have internal breaks and pauses, with the parts before and after the breaks being interpreted as belonging to the same TCU. How do participants know whether a speaker's words after a break or pause are continuing the TCU or beginning something new? Research has shown that prosodic and phonetic cues are deployed to contextualize TCU-internal pauses – yet to partly different effect, depending on whether the language allows early or delayed projection. In languages with early projection, unit-internal pauses are regularly analyzed as *holding pauses* for planning the continuation of talk, whereas in languages with delayed projection they are analyzed as contributing to the creation of "interstitial interactive turn spaces" (Iwasaki 2009) that delimit the bit-by-bit production of TCUs (see Fox et al. 1996; Hayashi 2003).

1.3.1 Unit-internal Practices in Languages with Early Projection

Local and Kelly (1986) were the first to inquire, on the basis of English data, how pausing affects "stretches of talk": in some cases it leads to internal cohesion within a stretch and in others to delimitation from surrounding stretches. To distinguish these two situations, they find that it is necessary to analyze sound production around the pauses. They examine pauses after so-called "conjunctionals" (*well*, *but*, *so*, and *uh*) in two different locations:

i. conjunctional + pause + more talk from the same speaker ("intra-utterance" pause), as in:

(2.12) "So I left" (Local and Kelly 1986:193) (adapted)

```
Lottie: S:o: uh:⁷(.)⁷I left?, en then I (0.2) *e::u well I stopped on
        the way to ↓ea:t °'n then°
```

and

ii. conjunctional + pause + "clean" speaker transition ("trail-off"), as in:

(2.13) "Wear it for Christmas" (Local and Kelly 1986:194) (adapted)

```
Lottie: Yeh I'll see what she says a↓bout it ↓you kno:w an' uh
        (.)
Emma:   ↑Yeah ↓wear it for ↑Christ↓mas again God you hate to just
        wear it once
```

The pause after *uh* in (i) they describe as a "holding" silence, implying that the speaker maintains a claim to the turn, while the pause after *uh* in (ii) is called a "trail-off" silence, implying that it is a place for legitimate turn transition (1986:195).[25] A unit-internal holding pause is initiated by glottal closure, held until the beginning of the next word. Regularly, the initial sounds of the next word are assimilated to those immediately before the pause. A holding pause thus projects that the speaker will continue to talk. A trail-off silence, by contrast, has no glottal closure and is normally accompanied by an audible outbreath. In this case, the conjunctional shows loudness diminuendo and a slowing down of tempo; its vowel is noticeably centralized, lax, and creaky.[26] Local and Kelly (1986:200) conclude that the phonetic features of trail-off break talk and yield the floor, while those for holding break talk but project that more will come.[27] In other languages other cues may be used in these two situations.[28]

In English, unit-internal pauses are marked by glottal holding with subsequent phonetic assimilation, while unit-external pauses trail off without glottal closure (see also Online-Chapter E §4). Silences within TCUs are typically analyzed as pauses for planning the continuation of the unit.

---

[25] Notice that this categorization is supported by what participants do next.
[26] See also Walker (2012) for a refined description of the vocal and visible resources deployed with trail-off conjunctions in English.
[27] In Finnish, too, glottal stops are reportedly deployed as turn-holding cues when associated with incomplete syntax and prosody (Ogden 2001:145–9; see below).
[28] In German, unit-internal pauses or hitches are contextualized by continuing the prosodic (pitch and loudness) parameters from before the pause or hitch; glottal closure does not seem to be used as systematically as in English (Selting 1995a).

1.3.2 Unit-internal Practices in Languages with Delayed Projection

In languages with delayed projection, prosody is also used for the contextualization of processes within TCUs, yet arguably to other ends. In both Japanese and Korean, there is evidence that prosody is systematically deployed to mark unit-internal loci for participant cooperation. Thus, although the practices are similar to those in languages with early projection, they appear to be used more frequently and to be more tailored to the elicitation of recipient responses.

According to Hayashi, it is speakers' silences, sound stretches, laugh tokens, and recognizable word searches in locations before a possible turn completion that afford opportunities for recipients to collaboratively complete the turn in Japanese (1999:483). Iwasaki notes that interstitial interactive turn spaces in Japanese (see above) are created by visible cues as well as by sound stretches and pauses; they invite recipients' micro-collaboration (2009:228). Finally, in Korean, continuing intonation and pauses are said to be frequently used at phrasal boundaries within units to invite recipients to acknowledge and display their understanding of the turn so far (Kim 1999a:425). These practices (pause, sound stretch) look similar to ones found in languages such as English and German, although they may not be used as frequently there. This is no doubt a question for further research.

> In languages with delayed projection, speakers regularly use phonetic resources at clausal and phrasal unit boundaries within TCUs to create interstitial spaces where recipients can signal understanding, acknowledge the speaker's point so far, and/or negotiate micro-collaboration. Due to the bit-by-bit production of units and the absence of early projection, the need for micro-cooperation may be more prevalent here than in languages with early projection. Yet the ways in which prosodic and phonetic cues are deployed unit-internally in Japanese and Korean are reminiscent of TCU and turn-holding prosody for more to come in languages with early projection. Such practices may thus be universal, with their loci, frequency, and interactional relevance varying across languages and language types.

1.4 Inserts/Parentheticals

Internal expansions within TCUs may be occasioned, among other things, by a speaker's same-turn self-repair, but also by inserts of different kinds. Repair is dealt with in Chapter 3; here we will be concerned with *parenthetical* inserts.

In general, parenthetical inserts (sometimes also called parentheses)[29] result from the insertion of material into an ongoing but recognizably incomplete TCU

---

[29] For recent work on parentheses in spoken English see, e.g., Wichmann (2000:93–100, 2001) and the references given below; on parentheses in spoken German see, e.g., Betten (1976) and the references given below.

or turn: a speaker begins a unit of talk but then halts the production of that unit to insert something before resuming the suspended unit of talk. Parentheticals may be placed either within an ongoing TCU or between TCUs in an ongoing multi-unit turn. Here we deal with research on parentheticals within an ongoing TCU. These may consist of various types of linguistic entities such as complete clauses (side-remarks or explanations), lists of illustrative examples, address terms, discourse markers, response cries, etc. The defining criterion is that the material be inserted into a TCU that has been begun but is as yet incomplete.

It is not always easy to determine whether a given item in a clausal unit is an integral part of that unit or an insert. For instance, it may not be obvious whether an expression such as *I think* in a clause such as *I saw her I think on Sunday* is a hedging expression integrated into the clause or an insert set apart from the clause. Parenthetical inserts are often claimed to be set off via prosody: they are said to be produced with faster speech rate, softer volume, and lower pitch than the surrounding unit – but this does not hold true in all cases.

1.4.1 Parenthetical Sequences within Ongoing Units

In order to capture "true parentheticals", some researchers have restricted their analysis to parentheticals that are demonstrably treated as inserts by recipients. This means they consider only inserts that (are designed to) receive a response from recipients. Mazeland (2007), for instance, analyzes the interactional management of parenthetical sequences within the boundaries of ongoing units in Dutch conversation. Here is one of his examples from a business phone call by a print shop owner to his customer Inez (the reference is to Leendert, an employee of the print shop):

```
(2.14)     "Red color disappointing" (Mazeland 2007:1817) (adapted)
1  Caller:   ik hoor van Leendert wel: (uhruh) ((coughs))
             I heard from Leendert though
2             want ik zit-    >ben niet,< thuis nouh,
              because I am-   am not at home now,
3             ·h[h           [(°onderweg.°)]
                              (on my way.)
4  Inez:      [jah, da ho[or ik. HhH!    ]
              yes, I can hear this. hhh ((laughing))
5  Caller:   [maar:] e:h >dat 't rood wel wat< tegenviel,
             but u:h that the red ((color)) was actually a little disappointing,
6  Inez:     [HhH!]
7            (0.4)
8            o:h.
```

At the beginning of his turn, the caller projects the report of what he has heard from Leendert, but then in line 2, before his projected unit is complete, he accounts for the fact that he himself is not the source of the bad news he is about to deliver (see line 5) by explaining his current situation (lines 2–3). The customer Inez now responds to this side remark (line 4) before the caller resumes his turn in line 5.

Mazeland analyzes the parenthetical insert as a new TCU begun and inserted into an as yet incomplete host TCU. By placing the parenthetical at a point at which the host TCU is still incomplete, the new TCU is made recognizable as initiating a subsidiary activity, supportive of and subordinate to the action already underway. The recipient can respond within the space it defines.

Parentheticals are overwhelmingly started at two positions: (a) within clausal or phrasal constructions, and (b) within compound TCUs such as those organized by an *if-then* construction (see §1.5 below).[30] In the example given above, the parenthetical is started after a main clause and before the projected beginning of the complement clause with *dat* ("that").[31] The placement of parenthetical inserts is related to their grammatical construction type: syntactically incorporable parentheticals – i.e., appositives and additions to relative clauses – often occur after a nominal phrase within an as yet incomplete clause, whereas grammatically independent parentheticals – i.e., those providing characterizations with "that is ..." or accounts with "because" – more often occur after the first clause of a compound TCU (2007:1837) (see below).

1.4.2 The Prosody of Parentheticals

Besides syntax, prosody is deployed to make parentheticals recognizable.[32] Mazeland (2007) found only about half of his pre-inserts ending with falling-rising pitch; most often his speakers do not leave silences before inserting a parenthetical but move right into the insert. Mazeland did find, however, that the parenthetical insert itself is realized as a separate intonation unit, often characterized by a notably lower pitch level. It is often less modulated, i.e., has a narrower pitch range than the surrounding host, and is slower in tempo. In the majority of cases, the parenthetical ends with rising pitch (p. 1842). The return to the host construction seems to vary depending on whether it is done in the form of a continuation, in the form of a resumption, or in the form of a redesign (p. 1853).

---

[30] On parentheticals inserted into compound TCUs see also Schegloff (2007a:241–2).
[31] For German, Auer (2005b), with reference to work by Stoltenburg (2002), specifies that "there are canonical syntactic environments for prototypical parentheses (parenthesis niches). In German, they exclude break-off within a phrase, and highly favor (if not require) placement before or immediately after the left sentence brace", i.e., the finite verb in most cases (Auer 2005b:98). See also Stoltenburg (2007).
[32] For Dutch data, Mazeland does not find as uniform a situation as Local (1992) has described for English data. On the prosodic and non-verbal demarcation (via gesture and gaze) of parenthetical inserts within host sentences in a corpus of Austrian German TV discussions see Schönherr (1993, 1997).

Rising pitch at the end of the parenthetical may be used not only to mark the end of the parenthetical, but also to invite a response from the recipient: the recipient can then react in an interstitial within-turn response space whose opening boundary is the first possible completion point of the inserted TCU and whose foreseeable closing boundary is the speaker's projected return to the host. In general, the recipient only attends minimally to the action performed in the parenthetical, acknowledging it, confirming it, or simply registering it (Mazeland 2007:1848). Recipients thus display their understanding of the subsidiary character of a parenthetical insert and facilitate the speaker's return to the host.

Mazeland's study shows that participants make methodic use of a variety of sequential, syntactic, and prosodic resources for coordinating the insertion of a subsidiary parenthetical sequence into an ongoing TCU. Every aspect of production is precisely designed to accomplish the co-construction of the insert sequence as a successful subsidiary action to the action the host is designed to achieve.

Speakers may embed parentheticals, grammatically complete units themselves, inside ongoing TCUs in order to clarify, specify, detail, or secure understanding. Preferred positions for the insertion of parentheticals in Dutch and German are, for instance, between grammatical constituents of the clause, preferably toward the beginning of a TCU, or between the two clauses of a compound TCU – places of specifiable incompleteness where speakers have maximum grammatical control over the trajectory of the emerging host TCU. In order to make the start of a parenthetical insertion and the return to the host TCU recognizable, speakers frequently make use of prosodic devices. In both English and Dutch talk-in-interaction, parentheticals are often (but by no means always) realized with lower pitch register and faster tempo than their host clauses. They tend to have their own pitch contours, often rising at the end of the insert. Post-insert continuations of the projected TCU typically continue the pre-insert construction with matched prosody. In face-to-face interaction, these prosodic cues may be supplemented by visible cues. Some, but not all, parentheticals are designed to elicit a response from the recipient and thus lead to the formation of a parenthetical sequence within a TCU.[33]

1.5 Compound TCUs

Speakers can also deploy what has been called a "compound turn-constructional unit format" to build a TCU (Lerner 1991, 1996a). In Lerner's words, a compound

---

[33] On parentheticals in other languages see, e.g., Duvallon and Routarinne (2005) for Finnish, and Mondada and Zay (1999) for French.

TCU is constituted by "[a]ny turn unit which in the course of its construction projects a [preliminary component + final component] turn format (i.e., a compound turn format)" (1991:444). Compound TCUs may be built, for instance, with two clauses, say, *if X, Y; when X, Y;* or *X said →Y* clause, as well as with constructions such as *instead of X →Y* clause. In languages with early projection such as English, the beginning of the first component of these compound TCU formats regularly makes the second component relevant. The following example contains a compound TCU in line 1:

(2.15)   "If..." (Lerner 1991:443) (adapted)
```
1      Vic:    If you're into one I'll take one too.=
2      Mike:   =Yeh.
```

As Lerner explains, the two components of the compound TCU *if X* and *then Y* (in the example the word *then* is left unsaid) are oriented to by participants "as sequential components of a single turn-constructional format" (1991:442). The first component is conceived of as a preliminary component ending in a completion which is not a TRP; it projects a second component, and the form it will take, which completes the TCU and thus ends in a TRP. Since there may be multiple preliminary components, after preliminary component completion recipients must inspect the next component for whether it is an instance of the projected final component.

Even though the parts of these compound formats may be realized as prosodically integrated in a single TCU, they are often delivered in two separate prosodic units, displaying what Lerner calls "semi-permeability": after the completion of the first part, recipients may come in for anticipatory completions. Thus, the compound TCU format can be used as a resource for constructing a turn collaboratively (see especially Lerner 1996a). Here is an example where this happens:

(2.16)   "When..." (Lerner 1996a:241) (adapted)
```
1      Dan:      when the group reconvenes in two weeks=
2  ->  Roger:    =they're gonna issue strait jackets
```

Lerner concludes that "compound TCUs project the form of the final component and indicate a place for recipient entry" (1996a:254).[34]

---

[34] On differences between English and Japanese in the organization of compound TCUs see Lerner and Takagi (1999). They find that the onset of co-construction varies as a result of the different ways of constructing compound TCUs in the two languages.

> Compound TCUs may be built by producing the first part of a syntactically compound sentence or other construction with a preliminary component, thus projecting the occurrence of a fitted second part as final component. Even though the components may be packaged in separate prosodic units, with the completion of the preliminary component providing for possible recipient incomings, the syntactic projection is strong enough to project a "semi-permeable" compound TCU that extends up to the completion of its final component.

2. Multi-unit Turns

Recall that according to the rules of turn taking reconstructed by Sacks et al. (1974), the continuation of the turn by the same speaker after a first TCU is an interactional achievement (see also Schegloff 1982). Multi-unit turns can be the result of recipients' refraining from taking a turn, thus affording the current speaker an opportunity to continue. If, however, speakers intend from the start to produce a longer turn, for instance, in order to formulate an argument or to tell a story, they can make use of techniques to negotiate permission for a multi-unit turn beforehand. (See also Online-Chapter D.)

Other than to negotiate permission for a "big package," there are various ways in which speakers can secure the turn for more than a single (possibly compound) TCU. Among these are, for instance, lexico-semantic or pragmatic projection, action type or activity type-specific projection, and prosodic projection of more to come (see also Selting 2000:504). At least some of these techniques vary cross-linguistically. The use of syntactically complex sentences was dealt with in §1.5 above for the projection of compound TCUs; this same device can also serve to project multi-unit turns. In the following, we will deal with other practices for projecting multi-unit turns.

2.1 Lexico-semantic and Pragmatic Projection

Lexical items, in particular so-called discourse markers, can be deployed to convey that a speaker intends to continue the turn after an initial TCU.[35] For instance, Schegloff (1982) mentions the use of a list-initiating marker such as "first of all" (p. 75). Here are more examples of such markers in German and English:

erstmal – und dann	"(at) first – and then"
erstens – zweitens	"firstly – secondly"
einerseits – andererseits	"on (the) one hand – on the other hand"

---

[35] The borderlines between syntactic compounding, lexico-syntactic constructions, and semantic-pragmatic projection are often fuzzy.

Furthermore, "first verbs" (Sacks 1992b) such as *wanted* and *thought* have been identified as a means for projecting multi-unit turns. By "first verbs" Sacks refers to a class of verbs that, when used in a first clause, imply that another clause will follow. In his words: "when somebody says 'I thought X,' by and large, they're saying 'I thought X and now it turns out I find it's wrong'" (1992b:181). A TCU built with a first verb projects further talk that has to do with the failure of the event mentioned in the first clause. (See also Chapter 7 §2.)

Finally, the deployment of negative items at turn beginning can pragmatically project a continuation. Ford (2001b) has studied turns beginning with *no* or other markers of negation expressing disaffiliation or disagreement with prior talk in American English conversation. She finds that such turn-initial units are regularly followed by an elaboration of some sort, providing, for example, an explanation or an alternative; where such elaboration is lacking, participants treat the talk as problematic (2001b:51). In this sense, it could be said that the action of negating what a prior speaker has said pragmatically projects the speaker's own elaboration.

> With all these practices for projection, it is not so much lexico-syntactic knowledge that is relevant, but pragmatic knowledge about likely trajectories and action sequences. Participants know that the use of a given (first) item is a projective device making expectable a continuation in the turn to follow. In languages with early projection, such projective devices tend to come early in the first TCU of the multi-unit turn.

Are there similar practices in languages with delayed projection? Hayashi (2004a) points to the use of the distal demonstrative pronoun *are* ("that one", "that thing") in Japanese as a means for projecting subsequent elaboration in the turn. Here is one of his examples:

(2.17)   "Gas pipes" (Hayashi 2004a:1339)
((Akira, an employee at a gas company, is explaining to his friends that the material used for underground gas pipes is changing from metal to plastic.))

```
1 ->Akira:  sono:   saikin      are           na  n   desu   yo
            uhm     recently    that.one      CP  N   CP     FP
            Uh:m, recently, ((it))'s been are (=that thing).
2           °ano:::° (0.7)   GAsu  kan    aru       ja  nai  desu  ka:.
            uhm              gas   pipe   exist     CP  not  CP    Q
            °Uh:::m° (0.7) You know there are gas pipes, right?
3           (.) >are  zenbu  ima<  purasuchikku  ni   naritsutsu     aru
                that   all   now   plastic       PT   is.becoming    exist
            (.) They've all been changing to plastic pipes now=
4           n  desu  yo.=  DONdon.=       =TEtsu    kara.
            N  CP    FP    MIM (steadily)  metal    from
            =one after another=from metal.
```

In this example the speaker Akira first produces an initial TCU, a "semantically light sentence" with the cataphoric *are* embedded in it (line 1) and then provides the substance of what he is talking about in a subsequent TCU (line 3). The use of *are* projects at least one more TCU in which its referent will be elaborated. As Hayashi explains, this kind of early "action-projecting" can compensate for "delayed projectability" in Japanese turn construction (2004a:1337).

The practice described by Hayashi is very similar to what Kim (1999a) observes for topic-initial utterances in Korean conversation: these are often designed with proforms or zero anaphora, i.e., "informationally light reference forms", which are then elaborated on in subsequent talk. Kim's account for the logic of such a practice is that it allows speakers of Korean, an SOV language, to get to the verb and hence to the upshot of the utterance quickly, providing the details only later (Kim 1999a:440; see also Kim 2001:365).

> A common strategy to compensate for "delayed projectability" in languages such as Japanese and Korean is the production of an initial TCU with semantically light, cataphoric items that forward the upshot of the turn while at the same time projecting elaboration in a subsequent TCU.

As Hayashi notes (2004a:1376), there is a striking similarity between the practices described above and the use of what C. Goodwin has dubbed "prospective indexicals" in English, i.e., cataphoric devices with variables like *something*, *what*, or *this* as in, for instance, *Guess what* or *Listen to this*, etc. (C. Goodwin 1996:384). Yet it remains to be seen whether these are one and the same practice differing merely in terms of frequency of use, or whether they are different practices altogether.

2.2 Action/Activity Type-specific Projection

Another kind of projection is specific to the kind of action or activity underway, for example, "big projects" to be realized in multi-unit turns. In order to secure the turn for a multi-unit story (Sacks 1974; Jefferson 1978, etc.), for instance, would-be tellers may initiate a pre-sequence by saying *I want to tell you something* (Schegloff 2007a:41) (see also Sidnell 2010:174ff.). Practices for this are dealt with in more detail in Online-Chapter D. Here, we will give some examples of other kinds of action type-specific projections of multi-unit turns.

Multi-unit turn projection can also be achieved by constructing a contribution as contrasting with something before. Ford (2000) provides evidence showing that, in many contexts, the speaker's production of contrast to something previously said makes relevant a subsequent explanation or solution. [Contrast + explanation] and [contrast + solution] constitute schemata, i.e., recurrent and expectable rhetorical patterns, that are used for performing action sequences (2000:306). The contrast, which involves opposing or incompatible positions, may include concession, antithesis, or disagreement; it is made explicit by devices such as antonymy (in nouns, adjectives, and prepositions), negation, comparatives, conjunctions, adverbs suggesting contrast, temporal oppositions, or prosodic highlighting via contrastive stress or pitch, etc. (2000:289). Alternatively, contrast may remain implicit but be inferable based on the positions expressed in prior talk.

Here is an example of a [contrast + explanation] sequence of turns in which two participants are talking about R's new job:

(2.18)   "First pay check" (Ford 2000:293) (adapted)
```
1     A:    Did you get your (.) first pay check from it?
2           (.)
3     A:    [At least?
4->   R:    [NO: I won't get that for a couple of weeks yet.=
5     A:    =Oh,
6           (.)
7     A:    [Well
8     R: -> ['Cause it takes a long time.
```

After the question (line 1), A pursues a positive answer from R (line 3). Instead, however, R produces a negation and a response that sets up an explicit contrast with the content of A's question (line 4). This is followed by an explanation, here an account prefaced by the conjunction *because*. (See also Chapter 7 §3.1.)

As Ford shows, speakers regularly treat explanations or solutions as relevant and expected after the expression of contrast. In cases where explanations or solutions are withheld, recipients orient to this as noticeable, waiting for them through delays of their own next turns, or pursuing them in further talk. In sum, the production of a TCU that is in contrast to some prior TCU is treated as needing explanation or resolution in subsequent talk. In this sense, the expression of contrast can be said – in most cases – to project a continuation of the turn and action providing an explanation or solution for the problematic state of affairs.

Concessive sequences involve yet another kind of action-specific projection of a multi-unit turn. Couper-Kuhlen and Thompson (2000) describe conversational concession as a three-part interactional sequence in which a first speaker claims something or makes some point (X) and a second speaker acknowledges, or concedes, the validity of this claim (X') but goes on to make a potentially contrasting and/or incompatible claim (Y) (2000:381–2). The constitutive parts of the basic pattern, X, X', and Y, may be realized by linguistic units of varying sizes; the relations between them can be either explicit or inferable in the situational context.

Here is an example in which two interactants, currently in New York City, are lamenting the advent of Starbucks coffee shops (see also Chapter 7 §1):

(2.19) "Charles and Steve" (Couper-Kuhlen and Thompson 2000:385–6) (adapted)

```
1   X    Charles:   but even the privately owned places here- HERE,
2   X               are so CHAracterless,
3                   (-) I mean by and large.
4   X'   Steve:     (--) OUTside [of the village they are.
5        Charles:               [you know.
6   Y    Steve:     there's [some in the village that are nice.
7        Charles:           [outside of the village, yeah.
```

Charles is critical of the fact that even privately owned coffeehouses in NYC are *characterless*, thus making an initial point (X) in lines 1–2. When Steve does not respond immediately, Charles downgrades his claim slightly in line 3. In line 4, Steve now concedes that Charles' claim is partially true, agreeing with it as far as the coffeehouses *outside* Greenwich Village are concerned (X'), but in line 6 he goes on to counter that *there's some in the village that are nice*, a partially contrastive claim (Y). This method of accomplishing concession allows the second speaker to partially agree with the first speaker before conveying disagreement.

The concessive schema forms a recurrent rhetorical pattern allowing speakers, on production of the concessive move (X'), to strongly project a next move, i.e., a countering and disagreeing point (Y). The projection can be reinforced either lexico-semantically or through implicative prosody. (For more detail on concession in spoken English see Barth-Weingarten 2003.)

> The studies just mentioned describe two different rhetorical patterns used in building multi-unit turns: one in which an initial expression of contrast projects more talk giving an account, explanation, or solution to the potential problem, and one in which an initial expression of partial agreement projects more talk conveying a contrast or counter-claim. In both cases a multi-unit turn results from the negotiation of common ground.

2.3 Prosodic Projection

The projection devices dealt with so far are all based on verbal resources. Most of them are designed to achieve rather far-reaching projection – for a multi-unit turn with as many internal TCUs as the accomplishment of that project requires. Yet in addition to verbal means of projection, speakers can also make use of prosodic resources.

For one, in English, "high onset" in a turn after the opening section of a telephone call, where the reason for the call can be expected, has been shown to project something like "This is going to take long, there are more units to come" (Couper-Kuhlen 2001). ("Onset" refers to the first accented syllable in an intonation phrase; "high" here means higher than in a prior TCU by the same speaker. See also Online-Chapter E §3.3.) Here is an example from a radio phone-in program recorded during the 1991 Gulf War:

(2.20)   "Franklin" (Couper-Kuhlen 2001:37) (adapted)
```
1      Leo:         FRANKlin.
2                   uh YOU'RE next on the giant sixty eight kay en bee ar,
3                   from san rafaEL.
4      Franklin:    helLO.
5      Leo:         hi FRANKlin-
6      Franklin:    HI.
7 ->                uh ↑FIRST i wanna say that uh-
8                   i'm one of the PROtesters and; (.)
9                   i wanna say RIGHT up front that;
10                  uhm (.) I support; (.)
11                  the SOLDiers OVer there.
```

Line 7 is the place where, after caller identification and an exchange of greetings, the caller can be expected to say why he is calling. Notice that Franklin immediately launches into something that looks like a "preliminary" (see also Online-Chapter F §5): *uh first I wanna say that* ... (line 7). And indeed he formats this line with extra high pitch on *first*, indicating that he is going to say more, i.e., produce a multi-unit turn. The moderator orients to this by withholding any talk of his own, although he would conceivably have had an opportunity to come in, for instance, toward the end of line 8.

Lack of high onset in similarly positioned turns results in the moderator *not* treating the talk as presenting the reason for the call but as doing something ancillary to it requiring prior ratification. Here is an example:

(2.21)   "Mike" (Couper-Kuhlen 2001:40, 43) (adapted)
```
1      Leo:     MIKE on the line from walnut CREEK,
2               you're on the GIant sixty eight KAY en bee ar;
3               HI mike.
4      Mike:    oh HI there.
```

```
5 ->              I have a little something to say about the: uh PROtests that
                  are taking place,
6     Leo:       oKAY,
7     Mike:      uhm ↑I kind of feel that uh- (.)
8                if PEOple- (.)
9                i think there're a lot of REAsonable people out there;
10               who WANT to uh- (.)
11               support PEACE;
                 ((turn continues))
```

Here, Mike does not use high onset at the place where his reason for the call is to be expected (line 5). Accordingly, the moderator does not take Mike's unit as beginning a multi-unit turn; instead, he ratifies Mike's announcement in line 6 as if it were an independent action, although it ends in slightly rising (i.e., continuing) intonation. Interestingly, after the moderator's ratification, Mike does deploy high onset in his next TCU (line 7), which is now treated as launching the reason for his call. This thus corroborates the analysis that the use of high onset in such a sequential context projects a multi-unit turn where the action being carried out will be the reason for the call.

But it is not only at the beginning of turns and TCUs that prosody is used to project the further development of talk to come. Couper-Kuhlen and Thompson (2000) describe contrastive stress placement and a fall-rise final pitch movement (what they call "implicative prosody") in the conceding turn of a concessive sequence as a way of projecting an upcoming counter-claim by the same speaker (see also §2.2 above). This is exemplified in the next example, where Wendy has been teased about making a clue, to which she has responded with *Stop it. Don't make fun of me* in a playful, childlike voice:

```
(2.22)    "A little proud" (Couper-Kuhlen and Thompson 2000:401) (adapted)
1                    Wendy:    [but don't make FUN of me:     ]
2     X              Marci:    [you look pretty PROUD of your] self Wendy.
3     X'+Y-impl      Wendy:    WE:LL,
4     X'+Y-impl                I'm a ↑`LITTLE ´proud,=
5     Y-hypoth                 =except if you [think it's STUpid. heh
6                    Kevin:                   [ha
7     Y-hypoth       Wendy:    [then [I'll feel BA:D.
8                    Kevin:    [ha   [ha ha ha
```

After Marci's initial assertion that Wendy looks pretty proud of herself (line 2), Wendy concedes that this is partially true, i.e., that she feels *a little proud* (line 4).

But at the same time her contrastive accent on *little* instead of *proud*, as well as her use of falling-rising pitch spread over the focus accent and the following unaccented syllable, suggest something more to come, in this sequential context a potentially contrastive claim. The counter-claim is produced as a hypothetical: should the others think her clue stupid, she would feel bad. So, in the context of a concessive sequence, contrastive stress placement as well as fall-rise pitch beginning in the focus-accented syllable of a partially agreeing turn may be deployed to project at least one more unit delivering an explicit (or implied) contrasting claim.

Accent placement and final pitch have also been shown to be decisive for the projection of more to come in other multi-unit turn types, for instance in what Barth-Weingarten (2009) has called "parallel-opposition constructions". These involve an opposition between two TCUs that are constructed with parallel syntax. Here is an example: it takes place during a conversation about a long-distance flight to Australia where it has become clear before that the couple planning the trip (co-present) will not need to keep money for buying food and drink during their stop-over. Rory now explains:

(2.23) "Drink and food" (Barth-Weingarten 2009:2273) (adapted)
```
9    Rory:    =you mIght want a ˇDRINK, hh
10            you wOn't want any FOO:D;
```

In constructions like these, parallel syntactic structures are used in the exposition of a topic to contrast two states of affairs. Syntactically and lexico-semantically, the first part does not project continuation. But it regularly displays prosodic features that hold the turn and project more to come. In the example above, for instance, Rory ends the first component with a falling-rising pitch movement on *drink* projecting turn continuation (Barth-Weingarten 2009:2273). The bundle of prosodic features deployed to project continuation at the end of the first TCU in a parallel-opposition construction include the following: narrow focus[36] and continuing intonation, in combination with, for example, the avoidance of boundary signals such as final lengthening, pauses, or breaks in rhythm and tempo (2009:2290). All in all, Barth-Weingarten shows that in the absence of other projection devices, prosody is deployed as a turn-holding cue at the end of a first clause in order to secure the floor, in this case for the completion of the biclausal construction.

---

[36] Narrow focus is achieved by placing the main or focal accent of a TCU such that only a specific part of the utterance is presented as being foregrounded, not the entire TCU. One special case of narrow focus is contrastive focus, in other frameworks often termed contrastive stress.

> In the initiation of multi-unit turns in various situational and sequential contexts in English, prosodic formatting (especially high pitch at the beginning of something to be presented as new, together with increased volume and other prosodic-phonetic features) can be relevant for projecting that more same-speaker talk will follow. In addition, accent placement (narrow or contrastive focus) and fall-rise final pitch ("continuing intonation"), as well as the avoidance of final phonetic features indexing turn completion (such as final lengthening, pauses, etc.), have been shown, in particular action sequences, to project more talk by the same speaker. Whether these kinds of prosodic projection are also deployed in other languages and language types is still an open question.[37]

3. The Organization of Turn Taking

As a TCU reaches its projected end, participants need to address the allocation of the next TCU or turn, i.e., they need to manage and possibly negotiate whether transition to a next speaker is relevant or not. They do this through the use of linguistic (and multimodal) cues anchored in the practices of projection and turn construction within sequentially organized social interaction, as outlined by Sacks et al. (1974) and detailed in the previous sections. With such cues, speakers suggest particular interpretations; these, however, are always open to negotiation and subject to unforeseeable contingencies in the interaction.[38]

The projectability of TCUs and turns in different languages has been dealt with in prior sections. In this section, we focus on local (micro-)projection: the allocation of next TCUs at imminent TCU completion. Practices deployed for this interactional task have been relatively well described for languages such as English and German, but little research has been carried out for other languages. Nevertheless, it has become clear that speakers of different languages and language types make use of different practices.

For instance, English and German use accentuation, i.e., making stressable syllables prominent in utterances, in order to mark the semantic or information focus and to open the "transition relevance space" (Sacks et al. 1974:706, n. 15; Schegloff 1987b, 1988a, and see below; see also Sidnell 2010:47–51). These languages belong to the

---

[37] For "local" practices of turn holding in German see Selting (2000:508), and for Finnish see Ogden and Routarinne (2005).

[38] It is important to point out here that, in contrast to signal-based models such as Duncan and Fiske's (1977), the description of prosodic cues we propose must be thought of as locally contextualizing the workings of the turn-taking mechanism described by Sacks et al. (1974) and based on opportunity assignment rules. According to this conception, the interactional meaning of prosodic cues does not rely on the cues themselves, or their combination, but results from their deployment at particular locations in emerging TCUs. For instance, as we will argue in this section, based on the prior projection of possible syntactic, lexico-semantic, and pragmatic completion, in and following the possible final accent of the TCU, final falling pitch, possibly in combination with other phonetic parameters, can be deployed to make turn yielding locally interpretable. But as turns ending with these cues only suggest turn yielding and do not make it mandatory, they do not organize turn taking per se. Instead, they locally contextualize the rules of the turn-taking mechanism as reconstructed by Sacks et al. (See below. For an overview of practices of turn allocation and turn sharing see also Hayashi 2013.)

group of so-called "accent-timed languages", which afford the structural possibility of reducing and compressing unaccented syllables in order to create accentuation-based rhythm, also relevant for the organization of turn transition. In other languages, such as French, Turkish, or Finnish, there is no semantically relevant (possible) final accent that might open the *transition relevance space*. Instead, we are likely to find phrase-final and utterance-final accents that have phonological, delimitative functions rather than semantic-pragmatic ones. These languages belong to the group of so-called "syllable-timed languages", in which syllables tend to be produced with equal length and may create syllable-based rhythms. For Finnish, creaky voice has been shown to be relevant for turn yielding (Ogden 2001, 2004; see below). In Japanese, which has been described as a "mora-timed language", it is morae that are produced with equal length. Japanese makes use of final particles and other final elements to signal the end of TCUs and turns; prosody has been described as relevant for the completion of truncated turns only (Tanaka 2000a; see above). These preliminary remarks are meant to indicate how different the linguistic resources are that different languages and language types mobilize for the organization of turn transition.

We will start by presenting the structures relevant for opening the transition relevance space in English and German. Thereafter, we describe the practices deployed in turn yielding, i.e., projecting and contextualizing a transition relevance point at TCU completion, as well as in turn holding, i.e., postponing the TRP until the end of a later unit.[39]

3.1 Opening the Transition Relevance Space in English and German

As the developing grammatical structure of an utterance is often compatible with alternative points of possible completion, it is useful – and usual – for speakers to give an indication as to which of the syntactically possible completions is to be a completion point in this instance, and which is not. In order to account for the practices relevant to this task we can draw on a distinction made by Sacks et al. (1974: 705–6) with respect to the notion of TRP. They explain that what they term more generally a "transition-relevance place" can – according to the aspects of transition under analysis – be specified as both "space" and "point" (p. 706, n. 15). For the organization of turn taking as described here, both transition relevance *spaces* and transition relevance *points* need to be distinguished. As we will argue, particular linguistic and prosodic-phonetic phenomena (e.g., accented syllables near the

---

[39] Recently, it has emerged that turn construction and turn taking are not only organized with verbal and vocal resources, but that visible resources also play an important role. Building on earlier work by C. and M. H. Goodwin (e.g., C. Goodwin 1979, 1981, 2000; Goodwin and Goodwin 1987; see §1 above) and Streeck and Hartge (1992), it is especially Mondada (e.g., 2006, 2007) who has investigated multimodal resources in the organization of turn taking. On multimodal practices for securing recipiency in workplace meetings see also Ford and Stickle (2012).

projected possible completion of TCUs) open the transition relevance *space*, i.e., the stretch of time in which possible transition to next speaker is relevant. In this space, however, transition can also be prevented. The practices of turn yielding and turn holding deployed in the transition relevance *space* determine whether the projected imminent completion of the TCU is designed to be an actual transition relevance *point* yielding the turn or whether it is designed not to be that, thus holding the turn and postponing the transition relevance point until later.

Schegloff argues that pitch peaks and raised amplitude in syllables shortly before the end of a turn are deployed to project that the next grammatically possible completion is the intended and designed turn completion in American English. Such pitch peaks thus open the transition relevance space (Schegloff 1987b:107; 1988a:144–5). According to Schegloff, it is after these pitch peaks that early starters place the beginning of their turns, and that speakers increase the tempo of their talk in order to effect a *rush-through* (see below and Online-Chapter E §4). Thus, on the one hand, speakers place their syntactically and semantically relevant pitch peaks so as to project TRPs (Schegloff 1998:240–1), and on the other hand, they suppress such pitch peaks when they wish to prevent recipients from interpreting imminent possible completion points as actual completion points (see also Schegloff 1998:237–43).

Here is an example of the practice Schegloff is describing:

```
(2.24)      "Played basketball" (Schegloff 1998:239; part of example (1)) (adapted)
1      Ava:   I'm so:: ti:red. I just played ba:sketball today since the
2 ->          first time since  I was a freshman in hi:ghsch[ool.]
3 ->   Bee:                                                 [Ba::]sk(h)et=
4             b(h)a(h)ll? (h) [('Whe(h)re.)
5      Ava:                   [Yeah for like an hour and a ha:[lf.]
6      Bee:                                                   ['hh] Where
7 ->   Bee:   did you play ba:sk[etball.]
8 ->   Ava:                     [(The) gy]:m:
```

In lines 2 and 7 of this extract, each speaker is building a TCU with a pitch peak toward the end (indicated by underlining of the respective syllable). In lines 3 and 8, the next speaker starts her turn shortly after these pitch peaks.

Yet other researchers have come to different conclusions. For instance, on the basis of actually occurring turn transitions in American English conversations, Fox (2001a) is unable to confirm the hypothesis that "last" accents are phonetically more prominent than "non-last" accents (2001a:287). After comparing various phonetic parameters normally held to distinguish between pitch-accented syllables that project upcoming turn completion and those that do not, she finds that only duration makes a statistically significant difference (2001a:287).[40]

The relevance of the final prominent syllable of a TCU (regardless of whether this TCU turns out to be the final one in the turn or not) for the organization of TCU completion and allocation of the next TCU is well established in research on English and German. The pitch peaks Schegloff identifies correspond to the syllables where other researchers and phoneticians have found that the phonetic features of turn yielding and turn holding begin (see Local et al. 1986; Selting 1996a, 2000; Wells and Peppé 1996; Wells and Macfarlane 1998).[41] As TCUs are flexible and can always be expanded, Selting conceives of the final accented syllable as the "possible last accent" of a TCU (Selting 1996a:379ff.; see also 1995a:195ff., 2000).

In English and German, the (possible) final accent of a TCU opens up the transition relevance space of the turn. The transition relevance space is where participants orient to practices for turn yielding, projecting an imminent transition relevant point, or turn holding, postponing the TRP beyond the completion of the current TCU.[42]

3.2 Turn Yielding

Speaker transition at the end of turns is organized according to the rules of turn allocation as outlined by Sacks et al. (1974) (see above). In the case of turn yielding, it is the techniques of current speaker selecting next or simply current speaker relinquishing the turn that are relevant.

Sacks et al. (1974:716–18) list the following techniques for allocating the turn to a next speaker:

i. The production of an "addressed question". The party to whom the question is addressed is expected to speak next. Alternatively, other types of first pair parts will select a specific next speaker if accompanied by an explicit address term and/or gaze-directional addressing.

---

[40] Using experimental methodology, de Ruiter et al. (2006) also find pitch and amplitude irrelevant for turn transition (but see Online-Chapter D §3).

[41] Some researchers do not look at the final prominent syllable in isolation but see it as the final part of an intonation contour. For instance, Ford and Thompson (1996:171) maintain: "Projecting when a new turn could start must centrally involve the perception of intonation units and pitch peaks within intonation units." (See also Selting 1996a, 2000.)

[42] According to Sacks et al. (1974), the system of turn taking favors turn yielding at the end of TCUs as the unmarked case. This prediction is borne out by the fact that, prosodically and phonetically, turn yielding seems indeed to be the simple and unmarked option. In comparison to this, turn holding seems to be the more complex option involving marked contextualization (see below).

ii. The initiation of repair with devices such as *what?*, *who?*, or the repetition of parts of the prior turn with what they call "question intonation" (p. 717). This selects the prior speaker as next speaker.
iii. The addition of a "tag question" such as *You know?*, *Don't you agree?*, etc., as a "generally available 'exit technique' for a turn" (p. 718). Tag questions are also used as "re-completers" after current speakers have yielded their turn but no next speaker has taken over.[43]
iv. Addressing a turn (and the action performed by it) to a concerned addressee. Addressees can be "concerned" with respect to social identity, epistemic knowledge, relevance, or the like.[44]

Although explicit techniques such as addressed questions may be effective means of selecting the next speaker, they are not the most frequent practices. Tacit practices such as directing gaze to a possible next speaker are more common.[45]

3.2.1 Turn Yielding in English (Regional) Conversation

Pioneering work has been done on turn yielding in English by phoneticians in York under the rubric of "Phonology for Conversation". They have investigated the general phonetic resources involved in marking the end of a turn, with special attention to features such as pitch, loudness, duration, tempo, voice quality, etc. On the assumption that these resources vary regionally, they have examined materials from the Northern English variety spoken in Tyneside (Local et al. 1986), the Northern Irish variety of Ulster (Wells and Peppé 1996), the English variety of the West Midlands (Wells and Macfarlane 1998), and the ethnic style of London Jamaican (Local et al. 1985).

Wells and Peppé give a table to summarize the regionally specific phonetic features associated with turn endings "in the clear", i.e., not in overlap, in London Jamaican, Tyneside, and Ulster English (1996:124): see Table 2.2. In this table, the term "last ictus" refers to the last accented syllable of the unit.

Evidence for the relevance of these clusters of features for the participants is gained from sequential analysis of the data. For example, Local et al. (1986:

---

[43] Other techniques for prolonging the turn in "post-possible completion" include: expansions to the TCU (see §4 below); address terms, courtesy terms, and the like; and "post-completion stance markers" such as "nodding, facial expressions (e.g., smiles and grimaces), shrugs, posture shifts, disclaimers ("I dunno"), laugh tokens, coughs, exhalations and sighs, in-breaths" (Schegloff 1996b:92). Some of these devices may also be used for tacit addressing.
[44] This is what Lerner (2003:190) refers to as designating certain participants as "response-eligible recipients".
[45] For examples see Sacks et al. (1974:716–18), Sidnell (2010:45–6), and Hayashi (2013). For more detail, especially on the use of gaze and address terms for selecting next speakers, see Lerner (2003); also C. Goodwin (1979, 1980).

Table 2.2 *Phonetic features associated with turn delimitation (Wells and Peppé 1996:124)*

Feature	London Jamaican	Tyneside	Ulster
Pitch	narrow fall on last syllable, start no higher than previous syllable; no greater pitch movement earlier	step up at end of turn; ends higher, and is no narrower, than any earlier step up	bowl-shape pattern; drop may precede final rise; following syllables level or slight fall; earlier peak usually not higher than final peak
Tempo		slowing over last two feet approx.	slowing over last two feet approx.
Loudness	resurgence on last syllable	swell on last ictus	swell on last ictus
Duration		extra on last ictus	extra on last ictus
Other	creaky voice on last syllable	centralized vowel quality on last ictus	

425–33) observe five kinds of evidence to warrant their analysis of turn delimitation in Tyneside English:

i. Stretches of talk that display these phonetic features are designed as complete. The speaker never retrospectively indicates that his or her turn was anything other than complete.
ii. Other participants in the conversation treat such stretches of talk as complete. They begin their next turns without delay.
iii. Other participants do not routinely begin their turns at syntactic completion points where these phonetic features are absent.
iv. If other speakers do begin their talk at points where these features are absent, this talk is designed to be heard as non-competitive: it has the phonetic features "piano" (loudness) and "low" (pitch).
v. If another participant does not take the turn after turn endings displaying these features, speakers indicate that their turn was complete, that they wish to stop talking, and that the failure by co-participants to take over is "noticeable". For this, speakers may re-complete their turn with, for example, tag questions or increments (see §4 below).

After comparing the results of research on delimitative systems in the varieties of English studied, Wells and Peppé (1996) conclude that "native" varieties, i.e., Tyneside, Ulster, and probably Southern British English, differ only at the level of phonetic exponency: they share the place at which the particular cluster of phonetic features realizes turn delimitation, but each variety makes use of a different cluster of features. *Pitch* features are those that show the greatest differences (p. 127).[46]

In later work, Wells and Macfarlane (1998) highlight the role of what they call "TRP-projecting accents" in the West Midlands of England or, more precisely, accents projecting an imminent transition relevance point. They identify two types of TRP-projecting accents in the West Midlands variety of British English. Type 1 is realized with a mid-low accented syllable, lower than before, followed by pitch that rises to mid, with the accented syllable also being louder and longer than in surrounding syllables (1998:285–6). Here is an example of a Type 1 TRP-projecting accent on the word *Ga:rdening*:

(2.25)   "Gardening calendar" (Wells and Macfarlane 1998:285)

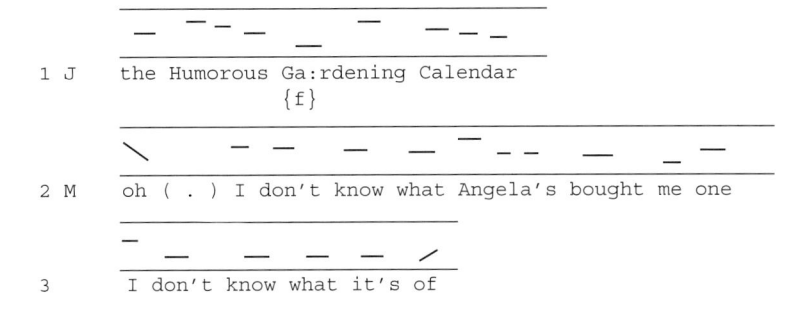

```
1 J    the Humorous Ga:rdening Calendar
                    {f}

2 M    oh ( . ) I don't know what Angela's bought me one

3      I don't know what it's of
```

Type 2 is realized with a mid-high accented syllable, higher than before, followed by pitch that falls to mid-low, with the accented syllable at least in some cases being louder and longer than surrounding syllables (1998:286ff.). In the following example a Type 2 TRP-projecting accent is located on the word *Gloucestershire*:

(2.26)   "Gloucestershire" (Wells and Macfarlane 1998:287)

```
1 J    well yes 'sgot Gloucestershire in

2 M    yes
```

---

[46] A significantly different system has been observed in the ethnic style of London Jamaican. Local et al. (1985) show that in London Jamaican turn delimitation is marked by features of pitch, loudness, and rhythm invariably centering on the last syllable of the turn, not the ictus syllable of the last foot of the turn. In London Jamaican, dynamic pitch movement is not used for marking semantic focus, as in other varieties of English, but for turn delimitation, as in languages such as French or Turkish (1985:316–17). On the prosodic features of the ethnic style of Turkish German see Kern and Selting (2006a, 2006b), Kern and Simsek (2006), Simsek (2012), and Kern (2013).

Wells and Marfarlane (1998:288) make two observations suggesting that it is indeed the occurrence of the accent that projects an upcoming TRP: first, next speakers often come in in overlap with the post-accentual syllables; second, turn-competitive overlap, in which a next speaker tries to usurp the turn prematurely (see below), is routinely started before the occurrence of the TRP-projecting accent. In contrast to TRP-projecting accents, non-TRP-projecting accents, even when they occur in final position in an utterance, are done differently: they are realized with low pitch on the accented syllable followed by rising pitch in the post-accentual syllables. In these cases, the accented syllable is not noticeably louder or longer than surrounding syllables (1998:289; see below). According to this analysis, the issue of whether or how participants can anticipate the final accent does not arise. The listener only needs to recognize the final TRP-projecting accent when it occurs, and this recognition can be achieved on the basis of the phonetic properties of the accent itself, without recourse to features earlier in the TCU or turn (1998:290). But of course the location of TRP-projecting accents is constrained by the interplay of syntactic and semantic principles: the accent needs to be placed such that it expresses the semantic focus of the TCU in accordance with the rules of syntax. Based on this research we must conclude that when in the sequential context a pragmatically and semantically plausible accent is produced with the phonetic features described above, it will be recognized as a TRP-projecting accent.

Altogether, the York studies on turn delimitation and turn yielding show that both segmental-phonetic and prosodic features are involved in the organization of this task – especially pitch, loudness, duration, tempo, rhythm, and certain phonatory (and articulatory) events such as creaky voice – but that the precise combination of features is different in different varieties of English. Yet there are divergences in the studies themselves.

Local et al.'s earlier work (1985, 1986) looked for phonetic exponents of turn delimitation but carefully avoided the use of traditional phonetic or phonological categories such as "intonation unit" or "accent". Wells and Macfarlane's (1998) later work on TRP-projecting accents, however, integrates the description of individual parameters with the more holistic notion of "accent," thus striking a compromise between a strictly parametric description and a more integrative approach to intonation. Local et al. looked primarily at the phonetic characteristics of the two last feet of the TCU or turn, including post-accentual syllables. Wells and Macfarlane, however, insist that "it is the occurrence of the accent itself that projects an upcoming TRP, and not just the phonetic characteristics of the post-accentual syllables" (1998:288). Thus, the studies reveal slight differences in the analysis of the details of turn yielding.

And the discussion continues. More recently, Local and Walker (2012) have argued that in Southern British English it is *non-pitch* phonetic features that play the most important role in projecting either more to come from the same speaker or turn transition to the next speaker at points of possible syntactic completion. According to this study, features projecting turn yielding include durational lengthening, no reduction of consonants and vowels, articulatory breaks (i.e., absence of articulatory anticipation), discontinuation of voicing, pausing (i.e., no production of talk in maximally close proximity to a preceding point of possible turn completion), and the release of plosives and audible outbreaths. What is often conceived of as "final" pitch, the study suggests, may only be heard as projecting finality in the absence of other features projecting more talk to come by the same speaker (2012: 273–4) (see also Online-Chapter E §9).

> Although there is agreement that a number of prosodic and phonetic features are involved in the design of turn yielding in English, research results differ in descriptive detail. Is it clusters of phonetic features from the domains of pitch, loudness, duration, tempo, assimilation, voice quality, etc. in the last two feet of a TCU, with regional variation in pitch, that foreshadow imminent turn yielding? Or is it TRP-projecting (versus non-TRP-projecting) accents? Is pitch always relevant for turn yielding? Or is it relevant only in the absence of other phonetic features projecting turn continuation? Only future research can resolve this puzzle.

3.2.2 Timing of Next-turn Onset in English Conversation

If all goes well in conversational interaction, we do not normally attend to transition timing. But sometimes we do get the impression that our interlocutor has come in too quickly or not quickly enough, i.e., reluctantly. When this happens, we look for accounts: why did our interlocutor take over so quickly or so slowly? Couper-Kuhlen (1993) has argued that our impressions of early and late turn transition in conversation are not a question of absolute time as measured in seconds or milliseconds, but of experienced time. She suggests that what is relevant for participants in English conversation is rhythm-based timing. For the organization especially of turn transition and of action sequences, she argues, rhythm plays an important, albeit subtle, role.

Rhythm in English conversational talk is based on "accent-timing": it is created when a succession of three prominent accented syllables occur at regular, i.e., perceptually isochronous, intervals of time.[47] Rhythmic patterns can be created by

---

[47] Also in German (another so-called accent-timed language), it is the regular production of *accented* syllables that leads to the perception of rhythmic patterns (see Kohler 1995:116ff.). By contrast, in languages such as

the same speaker or by different speakers across turn boundaries.[48] The occurrence of prominent accented syllables at regular intervals is said to create rhythmic beats or pulses; the rhythmic unit starting with the accented syllable and including any following unaccented syllables up to the next accented syllable is called a "foot" or a "cadence". For the perception of rhythm in English conversation, Couper-Kuhlen found that the intervals between rhythmic beats do not need to have the same absolute duration; in some circumstances, they can diverge by as much as 30 percent and still be perceived as regular (Couper-Kuhlen 1993:78).

As for the timing of turn transition and turn taking, Couper-Kuhlen distinguishes between the *unmarked* onset of a next turn and several *marked* alternatives (pp. 126ff.). In the unmarked case, a next speaker times the beginning of his or her turn so as to preserve the rhythm and tempo of the prior speaker's talk. This means that the first accented syllable of the new speaker's turn must come on the next pulse following the last two rhythmic beats of the prior speaker's turn. In order to achieve this coordination, the next speaker's new turn may need to be minimally overlapped, to be latched, or to be minimally separated from the end of the prior turn, depending on how far apart in time the prior rhythmic beats have been produced. The following schema represents this structure (ó stands for a prosodically prominent, accented syllable; ^ for a projected rhythmic pulse; and (..) denotes optional unstressed or rhythmically weak syllables):

(2.27)   Rhythmic coordination (schema adapted from Couper-Kuhlen 1993:127)

```
                                    TRP
        A:   ó   (..)   ó   (..)   ó   [(..)
                         ^           ^  [         ^
        B:                              [(..)   ó
```

(2.28) is an example of a rhythmically coordinated question-answer sequence taken from a telephone call between the caller John and the studio moderator DJ on a radio phone-in program. In the rhythmic transcription, slashes delimit rhythmic cadences; when the slashes are aligned with one another, the timing is regular.

The DJ's question has two accented syllables, on *do* and *John*, timed so as to create a potential rhythmic interval (lines 2 and 3). The caller John now responds in a rhythmically coordinated fashion by placing his own accented syllables – *uh*, *off*, and *pres-* – at equal temporal intervals so as to coincide with the projected pulses.

French or Spanish (so-called syllable-timed languages), it is the duration and timing of the *syllables* that is relevant for the production and perception of rhythm. Informal observation suggests that Italian and Finnish are positioned somewhere between the extremes of accent-timing and syllable-timing. In yet other languages such as Japanese, it is the duration of the morae that seems to be relevant. Couper-Kuhlen's model may thus be transferable to other accent-timed languages, but probably not to languages with other kinds of rhythm.

[48] For background on previous research and the methodology of rhythmic analysis, as well as studies on timing and rhythm in English, German, and Italian conversation, see Auer et al. (1999).

(2.28)   "Off sick" (Couper-Kuhlen and Auer 1991:14) (adapted)
```
1   DJ:   what d'you
2                /DO in life  /
3                /JOHN?       /
4   J:         /UH well I'm  /
5                /OFF sick at /
6                /PRESent,
```

In consequence, John's answer is presented in a well-timed fashion and the sequence as a whole comes off cohesively.

In cases of marked transition timing, the first accented syllable of a next turn does *not* coincide with the next pulse following a prior turn's possible completion. Couper-Kuhlen differentiates between various kinds of marked onsets. Here we consider two of these: (i) anticipated and early onsets, and (ii) delayed and late onsets.

i. Anticipated and early onsets

Here the onset of the new turn is timed such that it occurs *after* the last beat of the prior possibly complete turn but *before* the projected next beat. The following example from a radio phone-in program shows an anticipated beat in line 8:

(2.29)   "Decorating the kitchen" (Couper-Kuhlen 1993:263) (adapted)
```
1    C:    we're
2                /DECorating the      /
3                /KITCHen actually,   /
4    D:         /PARdon?
5    C:                        we're /
6                /DECorating the      /
7                /KITCHen.=
8 -> D:   /=ARE you,
9                /WHAT, this time of the /
10               /NIGHT,
```

After Dave's repair initiation (line 4) and Corinne's verbatim repeat of her news (lines 5–7), Dave begins his next turn with latching and an accented syllable that anticipates the beat set up by prior talk (line 8). However, his subsequent accented syllables coincide with the rhythmic pulse (lines 9–10). The premature timing of Dave's accent on *are* thus creates a temporary syncopation in the rhythm of the sequence, but does not disturb it overall. The anticipated beat suggests that the speaker is hastening to take the turn. As Couper-Kuhlen writes: "Dave may be anxious to demonstrate that he is not slow to understand" (1993:264).

ii. Delayed and late onsets

In these cases, the first accented syllable of the new turn is placed *after* the last beat of the prior possibly complete turn and *after* the projected pulse for the next turn. Here is an example where the two speakers produce their own turns with rhythmic timing of the accented syllables, but they do not establish a common rhythm across the speaker transition. After DJ's question, Gary misses the projected next beat and his answer sets in late. As a result, there is no rhythmic cohesion between the speakers in the construction of this sequence.

(2.30)   "Part-time student" (Couper-Kuhlen and Auer 1991:11) (adapted)
```
1   DJ:         /WHEREabouts in    /
2               /BOLton do you     /
3               /WORK.
4   G:    (0.5) eh - I
5                         /DON'T; I'm unem-  /
6                         /PLOYED - well a   /
7                         /STUdent;          /
8                         /PART-time.
```

DJ's question (lines 1–3) appears to make an unwarranted assumption about Gary, one that he must repair in his answer. Gary's failure to pick up the rhythm established by DJ in his response (lines 4–8) can be seen as indicative of his trouble with DJ's question.

In the exchange of turns at talk in everyday conversation we normally orient to a fundamental rhythmicity. Within most kinds of sequences, the establishment or maintenance of a shared rhythm is the preferred option, producing the tacit understanding of "interaction proceeding smoothly" or "no special notice needed". The destruction or breaking down of a shared rhythm within a sequence is a marked, often dispreferred option, producing a tacit understanding that "we have a problem" or "this needs notice", depending on the situation (Couper-Kuhlen 1993:267).

> In English conversation, a previously established rhythmic beat in talk projects the moment in time at which the next turn can be expected to set in; deviations from this expectation give rise to inferences. In consequence, a rhythm-based analysis offers advantages for our description of turn taking: it provides a measuring device, a *metric*, with respect to which turn onsets can be judged as well-timed or ill-timed. Furthermore, it can account for why some pauses between turns are barely noticeable, while others are interpreted as salient and significant silences; for why some kinds of overlap are merely temporal coincidences, while others are perceived as competitive interruptions; as well as why some topic changes appear to be achieved smoothly as negotiated and cohesive transitions, while others come off as abrupt and non-cohesive disruptions (Couper-Kuhlen 1993:131, 219). (For more detail on context-sensitive timing norms in English conversation see Couper-Kuhlen 1993; also 2009b.)

3.2.3 Turn Yielding in German

Turn yielding in Standard Northern German has been described as indexed by the production of a possible final accent, opening the transition relevance space, and the choice of non-turn-holding prosody for this accent (spreading to any following unaccented syllables). Selting (1995a, 1996a, 2000) finds that speakers of spoken Standard Northern German do not use specific pitch contours for turn yielding; instead, it is the choice of non-turn-holding pitch and other prosodic features that implies turn yielding at the projected end of the TCU.

Possible last accents are identified on the basis of prior syntactic and/or lexico-semantic projections of the TCU or turn in their sequential context. With only few exceptions, it is lexically determined word stresses that are selected for accentuation in TCUs. Syllables are heard as accented due to their more prominent pitch movements, loudness, and/or length in comparison to surrounding unaccented syllables. Normally, unaccented syllables following last accented syllables are softer and/or decrease in volume. They often prolong the pitch direction begun in the accented syllable, most often continuing a falling or rising pitch movement, or reversing its direction as in falling-rising or rising-falling pitch movements. It is through the design of the possible last accent of a TCU that turn yielding versus turn holding is accomplished.

For turn yielding, speakers can deploy, for example, pitch *peaks* on the accentual syllable that are higher than before, followed by falling or falling-rising pitch on the post-accentual syllables; or pitch *valleys* on the accentual syllable that are lower than before, followed by rising or rising-falling pitch on the post-accentual syllables, depending on the action they are performing,[49] and in interplay with the style of interaction they are establishing. Neither the direction of the pitch movement, i.e., rising versus falling, nor the extent of the pitch movement, i.e., the depth of the fall or the height of the rise, seem to be relevant for the design and interpretation of turn yielding (see Selting 1996a:372). But the various forms of falling and rising pitch that may be used for turn yielding are in sharp contrast to the pitch and other devices deployed for turn holding; the latter is indexed by level or slightly rising pitch, and increased tempo as in rush-throughs, etc. (see §3.3 below). In Selting's analysis, turn yielding is thus the unmarked case; it ensues when speakers refrain from signaling turn holding at possible completion points.

---

[49] In certain contexts, for instance, speakers distinguish informings from certain kinds of questions through the choice of falling versus rising final pitch; or they differentiate between different types of repair initiation by selecting falling versus rising final pitch, etc.

The following example illustrates designed turn yielding with a pitch peak in the accented syllable followed by mid-falling final pitch in the post-accentual syllables. The interlocutors are talking about working part-time in addition to studying. Ida's TCUs (lines 475 and 476), in response to Nat's prior question about whether she works every night, end with a pitch peak on the accented syllable followed by mid-falling pitch in the post-accentual syllables:

(2.31)   "Ida and Nat" (Selting 1995a:189) (adapted)
```
474      Ida:    n:Ee das:
                 no that
475              <<all>aber ´dAs> wär ja un`MÖGlich; (-)
                        but that would be PART impossible
476->            ´dAs würde man überhaupt nich `SCHAFfen;
                 that would one   not at all        manage
                 you wouldn't be able to manage that
477      Nat:    `nEe:;
                 no
478              ?ich `Arbeite `AU;=
                 I work too
479              =deswegen `FRAG ich;
                 that's why ask   I
                 that's why I ask
```

The pitch peak and mid-falling final pitch at the end of line 475 occurs in a TCU in which Ida formulates a first rejection of Nat's assumption that she might work every night. Even though this might be a possible turn completion, a brief gap ensues and Ida continues with an account of her rejection, an expectable continuation in this context (see Ford et al. 2004).[50] In line 476 the turn ends with pitch and loudness similar to that in the prior TCU. After Ida's account (line 476), Nat takes over without delay to express her affiliation by confirming Ida's position from her own point of view. So here, pitch peaks in accented syllables followed by mid-falling pitch in post-accentual syllables are deployed for designed turn yielding, although the first one does not lead to actual turn transition.

The same is true for pitch valleys in accented syllables followed by rising pitch in post-accentual syllables: they are deployed for designed turn yielding, but may

---

[50] The TCU completion in line 475 is not designed to be turn-holding; Ida's continuation in line 476 is produced just because Nat does not happen to take over at the end of the TCU in line 475.

end up in turn-internal as well as in turn-final TCUs. The following example illustrates rising pitch at the end of a turn. The participants are talking about a big white scar that is clearly visible on Ida's arm; Ida has been telling Nat about the accident that left her with this scar.

(2.32)   "Big white scar" (Selting 1995a:191) (adapted)
166   Nat: <<l,p,all_i> a das muss>_i ja ziemlich `TIEF gewesen sein.=
                    a that must PART pretty deep been have
              =ne,>
              you know
              oh that must have gone pretty deep, you know
              (2.0)
167-> Nat: <l,p,all_i> wenn da so>_i ne ´FETTschicht zu ´sEhen is,>=
                    if there such a layer of fatty tissue to see is
              if you can see such a layer of fatty tissue
168   Ida: =ja `MUSS wohl ((lau[ghs for ca. 4 secs.))
              yea must PART
169   Nat: [((joins in laughing))
       Ida: bis `Unter die siebm `HAUTschichten gegangen sein;
              till under the seven layers of skin gone   have
              yeah must have gone till under the seven layers of skin
              (4.0)
170   Nat: <<p> `´hn,>

When Ida does not respond verbally to Nat's remark that the cut in Ida's arm must have been pretty deep (line 166), a silence ensues. In line 167, Nat takes the floor again and continues her prior syntactic clause with a *wenn* clause ("if" clause), adding on the condition that led to her prior observation concerning Ida's scar. This TCU *re*-completes Nat's turn. It ends on the accented *FETTschicht* "layer of fatty tissue", which has a pitch valley lower than before, followed by mid-rising pitch on the post-accentual syllables. Here, then, final mid-rising pitch is deployed at the end of the *re*-completion of a turn. Ida takes over immediately with an agreement (line 168).[51]

According to Selting, non-turn-holding final accents in non-turn-final TCUs and non-turn-holding final accents in turn-final TCUs do not have different prosodic-phonetic features. Possible turn-final accents can only be identified

---

[51] Apart from such cases, pitch valleys in accented syllables followed by final rising pitch in post-accentual syllables may, of course, be deployed for a range of other actions, for instance questions, but also invitations, offers, informings, etc. In fact, virtually anything seems to be contextualizable with final rising pitch, indexing it as try-marked. For examples see Selting (1995a: §2.3).

negatively: they exhibit no features of turn holding (see below). The recipient estimates whether a given accent might be the possible last accent "by tacitly 'calculating' the position of the accent in relation to the progress of the emerging possible sentence or other syntactic construction so far" (1996a:383–4), within the given semantic, pragmatic, and sequential context. For this, s/he makes use of syntactic projections as described above (§1.1). According to this hypothesis, participants orient to syntax for more far-reaching projections, and to prosody for local contextualization in order to infer the imminent approach of a TCU or turn ending.

> Turn yielding in Northern Standard German talk-in-interaction is not marked by any specific pitch movement. Various kinds of pitch trajectories may be used in final accented syllables and post-accentual syllables at the ends of TCUs and turns, depending on the action being carried out – with the exception of level or slightly rising pitch, which is reserved for turn holding. Prosodically, then, turn yielding is the unmarked option; it is signaled through the absence of cues for turn holding. This confirms Sacks et al.'s (1974) description of turn yielding as the unmarked option in the organization of turn taking.[52]

As in the case of English, the final pitch movements deployed for the realization of turn completion in German can vary regionally. See Gilles (2005) for a study of *Abschlusskonturen* ("completion contours") in eight selected regional varieties of German.[53]

3.2.4 Turn Yielding in Japanese

As explained above, the verb-final ordering of constituents and the agglutinating morphological structure of Japanese result in turns in this language having "delayed projectability" (see §1.1 above). How, then, is turn yielding accomplished? Tanaka (2004) explains that in most cases turn completion is indicated by the presence of one or more utterance-final elements (e.g., final verb suffixes, nominalizers, copulas, final particles, question particles). In these cases the final prosody is said to be "unremarkable" (2004:89–91).

---

[52] Ford (2001a:75) finds a similar organization for American English. In a footnote she presents her informal observations: "Even though speakers seem to be able to package units with contours indicating 'non-completion,' there is a great variety of rising and falling final contours on utterances which are treated as finished by interactants; that is, units after which a next speaker unproblematically begins a next turn."

[53] For parallel practices from prosody and gesture in the organization of turn taking in German conversations see Bohle (2007: esp. 277).

Evidence for the importance of utterance-final elements comes from the fact that would-be next speakers regularly come in at their onset, while they bypass points of syntactic completion before them.

Consider, for instance, the following case from a multi-party conversation (utterance-final elements are in bold; "FP" is the gloss for "final particle", "COP" for "copula"):

(2.33)   "Tokyo 7" (Tanaka 2000a:20) (adapted)

```
1  W:  'N: soo [ne
       yeah so [FP
       Yeah isn't it?
2  G:            [Sore wa   aru  deshoo [: ne
                 [that  TOP exist COP    [ FP
                 [That's quite plausible, isn't it
3  W:                             [Soo na n de [shoo ne
                                  [so  COP N  c [OP     FP
                                  [That's probably right, isn't it?
4  G:                                         ['N ...
                                               [yeah ...
                                               [Yeah ...
```

Here we find next speakers starting up shortly after the onset of utterance-final elements in the prior turn.

Yet there is another class of turns that do not end with utterance-final elements (see also §1.2 above). These "truncated turns" are found predominantly in informal interaction; their use can even bring about the informality or intimacy of a setting or relationship (Tanaka 2004:69). In these cases, speakers regularly deploy "marked" prosodic features to convey that their turn is being brought to completion although it lacks utterance-final elements.

Tanaka identifies five types of truncated turns whose endings are summarized in Table 2.3 (2004:90); types 1, 2, and 3 are the most prevalent.

Remarkably, even though the degree of projectability of the upcoming TRP is relatively weak, types 1–4 are rarely overlapped by next-turn beginnings (2004:92); the latter come after short pauses. This suggests that Japanese recipients indeed wait either for the onset of utterance-final objects or for the production of utterance-final marked prosodic features as cues to turn completion.

Table 2.3 *Types of truncated turns: clusters of prosodic features and their receipt*

Feature	Types of truncated turns				
	Type 1: final lengthening	Type 2: penultimate lengthening	Type 3: glottal stop	Type 4: turn compression	Type 5: partial repeats
locus of prominence	final mora (final syllable = 1 mora)	penultimate mora (final syllable = 2 moras)	end of final word	final word or stretch of talk approaching end of turn	final word or stretch of talk approaching end of turn
loudness	resurgence of loudness	resurgence of loudness			decaying
duration	extra on final mora	extra on penultimate mora	isochronous moras	compressed in time	often compressed in time
pitch	often tends to fall on last mora, but variable	often rising-falling on last syllable, but variable	tends to fall toward end of turn	tends to fall toward end of turn	falling, sometimes in double cascading waves
recipient conduct	next-turn beginning following short pause	next-turn beginning following short pause	next-turn beginning following short pause	next-turn beginning following short pause	contiguous or overlapped next-turn beginning

> With limited syntactic projectability of TRPs, Japanese turn yielding is accomplished locally either through the use of utterance-final elements such as particles, copulas, nominalizers, and the like, or – alternatively, in truncated turns without such elements – through the use of marked prosodic features. Rather than a single specific cluster, at least five different clusters of marked prosodic features have been identified as cues to turn yielding in Japanese.

3.2.5 Turn Yielding in Finnish

Creaky voice has occasionally been mentioned as occurring at the end of turns in English. For Finnish conversation, however, Ogden (2001) claims that creaky voice is a systematic turn-yielding device in association with syntactic, pragmatic, and prosodic completion. In a later paper (2004), he identifies non-modal voice quality (NMVQ) more generally as instrumental in the projection of transition relevance in Finnish. NMVQ in turn-final position encompasses creak, breathiness, whisper, voicelessness, and exhalation; at least one of these features, Ogden claims, will mark a turn as transition-ready (2004:35). If several of these features are used at once, they will occur in the order mentioned.

Here is an example where creak, whisper, and exhalation mark transition relevance:

```
(2.34)    "Voix bulgares" (Ogden 2004:38) (adapted)
69                                  {C-}{W--}
   P:   onks   sulle tuttu    täm{mö}{nen}h
        is-QCLI 2SG-ALL familiar this-kind
        have you heard of them
70 C:   ei o,
        NEG be
        no
```

Next speakers orient to a current speaker's change to NMVQ by coming in not before, but rather just after it starts. This is what we see happening here in line 70.

On occasion, next speakers may take the turn without the current speaker having switched to NMVQ, but they then make their incoming talk recognizable as a competitive incoming or as a collaborative completion (2004:36). This shows an orientation to the use of NMVQ as a normative practice for marking an upcoming TRP.

> Turn yielding has been described differently for different languages. In all languages, speakers deploy the interplay of syntactic and prosodic-phonetic structures within local semantic, pragmatic, and sequential contexts to project and/or suggest turn yielding. In English and German as early projection languages, syntactic projection is locally reinforced by prosodic and phonetic devices, with (possible) final accents opening the transition relevance space and projecting either turn yielding, resulting in a transition relevance point, or turn holding, resulting in the postponement of the TRP to later.
> The precise coordination of syntax, prosody, and phonetics in the organization of turn yielding in these languages, however, still needs more research. Thus, it does not seem to be entirely clear *how* the (possible) final accent is made recognizable. Does it exhibit distinctive and thus locally recognizable phonetic properties – as Wells and Macfarlane (1998) claim? Or is the possible last accent inferred from the interplay of projecting syntax and contextualizing prosody in the given semantic, pragmatic, and sequential context – as other researchers suggest (Fox 2001a:306, 308–9; Selting 1996a)?[54] For languages such as French, Italian, or Spanish, research is scarce indeed. In Japanese as a delayed projection language, turn completion is displayed locally, as a rule by one or more turn-final elements or, in truncated turns, by marked prosody. The investigation of voice quality in the organization of turn transition, as described for Finnish, has only just begun.

3.3 Turn Holding

In Sacks et al.'s (1974) simplest systematics for the organization of turn taking, the production of more than one TCU by a current speaker is the outcome of (a) current speaker not selecting a next speaker to take over, and (b) potential next speakers refraining from self-selecting at the TRP; under these conditions, current speaker may continue the turn and produce another TCU (see rule (1c) in Sacks et al. (1974:704)). Yet current speakers can also do extra work at the end of a first TCU in order to continue speaking right away. In other words, they can designedly hold the turn for the production of another TCU. The resources deployed for this purpose are verbal, prosodic-phonetic, and non-verbal/visible in nature.

The verbal practices for turn holding include the addition of conjunctions as well as other "delaying devices" to the end of a TCU. These are some of the same practices as those used for continuing after pauses within TCUs (see §1.3 above); they suggest at the possible completion of TCUs that continuation is designed. *Conjunctionals*[55] such as *and, or, well, but, so,* etc. in English, or *und* ("and"), *oder* ("or"), *weil* ("because"), and the like in German, may be appended to the end of

---

[54] Recent psycholinguistic research suggests that next speakers use the emerging lexico-syntactic structure of the current turn for planning their upcoming turn well in advance of the TRP, but that they wait for prosodic cues indicating turn completion before launching its execution (Levinson and Torreira 2015).
[55] We purposely use Jefferson's term here, as this group contains not only conjunctions (*and, but*) but also conjunct adverbials (*so*) and so-called discourse markers (*well*).

TCUs in order to suggest that despite the completion of the TCU, the current turn could be continued (see also Raymond 2004). Depending on the prosodic formatting of the conjunctional, it may be a *trail-off*, projecting continuation only weakly, if at all (Local and Kelly 1986), or constituting the beginning of a new TCU.[56]

While the use of conjunctionals often suggests what kind of continuation will follow, the use of "delay devices" leaves the kind of continuation projected open. As "delay devices" at the end of TCUs speakers produce items such as *uh* and *uhm* in English, or *äh*, *ähm*, etc. in German, i.e., sound objects that are often called *hesitation tokens* (produced and transcribed differently in different languages). These tokens, frequently delivered with lengthening and more or less level pitch, serve to project more to come by the current speaker but do not indicate what this will be. Depending on whether they are prosodically integrated into the prior TCU or not, such tokens may be used to project the continuation of the current TCU or to project a subsequent TCU in the current turn (see also §1.3 above).

Prosodic and phonetic devices for turn holding include primarily tempo-related practices such as *rush-through* and *abrupt-join*, as well as primarily pitch-related practices such as the use of level pitch and non-TRP-projecting accents (see below), in addition to the practice of holding a glottal stop (holding pause). Silences formatted as holding pauses at the end of TCUs are organized just like those within TCUs; they are used to suggest that despite the possible completion of the TCU, the current turn is in fact not yet complete but will be continued. The practice thus works to transform what could be a pause at the end of a TCU into a turn-internal pause, bypassing possible turn completion. As holding pauses have been dealt with above (§1.3), we will not go into further detail here. Instead we will concentrate on tempo-related and pitch-related practices that are specifically designed to achieve turn holding at the end of a TCU. Turn-holding prosodic features are often begun on or just after the beginning of the designed-to-be-last accent of a TCU: their deployment prevents the hearing of the imminent TCU completion as a transition relevance point, postponing it instead to later.

Among the non-verbal/visible devices for turn holding are, for example, gazing away from the recipient (Kendon 1990:71).[57] These will not be dealt with here.

3.3.1 Turn Holding through Tempo-related Devices

Schegloff (1982) was the first to describe the phenomenon he called "rush-through" as a current speaker's temporal device to hold the turn: in his words, just as the possible completion point of a TCU is being reached, the speaker "speeds up the pace of talk, withholds a dropping pitch or the intake of breath, and phrases the talk to

---

[56] After the first word of this new TCU the speaker may leave a pause before continuing (see Selting 1995a:182ff; Schegloff 1996b:93.).
[57] On body posture as a turn-holding device in the construction of larger units such as storytelling in Mandarin Chinese conversations see Li (2013).

bridge what would otherwise be the juncture at the end of a unit" (1982:76); see also Online-Chapter E §4.1. Here is one of Schegloff's examples:

(2.35)   "Nothing else to do" (Schegloff 1987a:78) (adapted)
```
1 A: Maybe if you come down I'll take the car down.
2 B: Well I'k y'know I- I don't wanna make anything definite because I-
3    y'know I just I just thinking today all day riding on the trains heh hh
                                    →
4 A: Well there's nothing else t'do=I w's thinking
5    [of taking the car anyway*
6 B: [that I would go into the ssss::-* I would go into the city but I don't know.
```

The arrow above line 4 indicates "a sharp speed up in the pacing of the talk" (here also indicated by lighter gray shading), while the arc indicates "that the phrasing is built so as to carry over what would otherwise be a possible completion point" (Schegloff 1987a:78) (here also indicated by darker gray shading).

More recently, Walker (2010) has investigated the phonetics of rush-throughs in English talk-in-interaction. He finds that the articulation rate is doubled in the last foot of the first TCU and that there is "close juncture" between the two units, involving various kinds of articulatory and phonatory assimilation (2010:69). Rush-throughs are thus accomplished with phonetic as well as prosodic (temporal) means. (See also Online-Chapter E §4.)

> A rush-through is a speaker's technique to quickly get past a TCU's possible completion point and into a next unit, thereby preventing another participant from taking the turn. It is used ad hoc and late in the unit, without the speaker having planned beforehand to say more (Schegloff 1987a:78). Both temporal and articulatory/phonatory processes are involved in the conjoining of the two units.

Another temporal practice for turn holding has been dubbed an "abrupt-join" (Local and Walker 2004); see also Online-Chapter E §4.1. Like rush-throughs, abrupt-joins pre-empt turn transition at possible TCU completion points by quickly adding another TCU to the speaker's turn. However, in contrast to rush-throughs, which have uniquely "integrative" features (assimilations and the like), abrupt-joins have a number of "disjunctive" features (2004:1376). Here is an extract from one of Local and Walker's examples ("▶" indicates the position at which the next unit is added):

(2.36)   "How're you feeling" (Local and Walker 2004:1377–8) (adapted)
((The extract here begins after Jane and Ilene have closed topical talk and are moving into the closing section of their call.))
```
16   Ile:   o[kay
17   Jan:    [I've got to ru(h)un
```

```
18              (.)
19    Ile:     alright
20    Jan:     .hh okay▶how're you feeling
21    Ile:     oh I feel fine
22              (1.0)
23    Ile:     absolutely fine
24    Jan:     you do
```

This example illustrates the sequential environment in which abrupt-joins are typically found. When Jane heads into closing with the figurative expression *I've got to run* (line 17) (see also Drew and Holt 1998), Ilene seconds this with *alright*. Jane now pursues closing by producing a second closing component *.hh okay*. But then instead of yielding the turn to Ilene for the delivery of a terminal component such as *bye*, Jane suddenly moves out of closing to proffer further topical talk: *how're you feeling* (line 20). This new unit creates an abrupt and disjunctive shift in the course of ongoing talk (Local and Walker 2004:1379).

Phonetically, abrupt-joins involve a local "speeding up" on the last syllable of the first unit and close temporal proximity between the two units. But in contrast to rush-throughs, there is an audible pitch step-up and increased loudness on the first stressed syllable of the second unit, marking the new unit as beginning something new (2004:1388) (see also Online-Chapter E §3). Local and Walker describe abrupt-joins as a local means to unilaterally re-direct sequence or topic closure in an ad hoc fashion; they are not pre-planned.

> Speakers use abrupt-joins in managing issues of sequence and topic closure or change. Like rush-throughs, abrupt-joins are local, ad hoc devices that capitalize on speeding up at the end of one TCU and starting the next unit early, but they mark the two units so joined as disjunct rather than conjunct. Abrupt-joins allow speakers to effect a unilateral shift in the projected development of talk to a new action and/or topic. With both rush-throughs and abrupt-joins, speakers can build a multi-unit turn without having planned it in advance.

Rush-throughs and abrupt-joins have been identified as tempo-related devices for turn holding in English.[58] Scattered research as well as informal observation suggests that they are also found in other languages, but more systematic research is still needed.[59]

---

[58] As Local and Walker (2012) make clear, there are also non-time-related phonetic features at the end of possibly complete syntactic "pieces" that play a role in turn holding, among these articulatory and phonatory assimilation, and the reduction of consonants and vowels (Local and Walker 2012:255).

[59] Cf., e.g., Selting (1995a:98–104) on "*Durchhecheln*" (rush-through) in German, and Zhang (2012) on "latching/rush-through" in Mandarin Chinese conversation.

3.3.2 Turn Holding through Pitch-related Devices in English and German

For the regional variety spoken in the West Midlands of England, Wells and Macfarlane (1998) identify a non-TRP-projecting accent, realized with low pitch in the accented syllable followed by rising pitch in the post-accentual syllables. The accented syllable does not have noticeable lengthening or loudness compared to surrounding syllables (1998:289). Line 1 in the following example shows a case in point (the accented syllable is on *left*):

(2.37)   "Several left" (Wells and Macfarlane 1998:290)

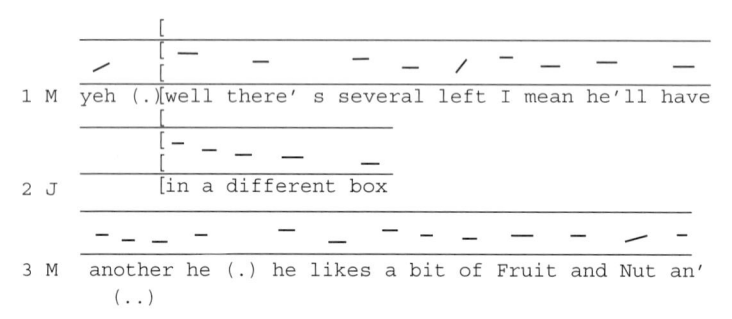

```
                [
              [ —    —    —    — / —    —    —
            /  [
1 M  yeh (.)[well there's several left I mean he'll have
                [
              [ — —  —
              [           —
2 J          [in a different box

    — _  _   —    —  _  — — _  — — _  /  —
3 M  another he (.) he likes a bit of Fruit and Nut an'
     (..)
```

The non-TRP-projecting accent on *left* (line 1) projects turn continuation, and indeed the speaker goes on without a pause or other prosodic break. Evidence for the non-TRP-projecting nature of such accents is that they are usually followed by smooth continuation; that next speakers do not come in until after a substantial pause; and that if there is an immediate incoming, it is treated as turn-competitive (Wells and Macfarlane 1998:290).

For spoken Northern Standard German, the use of level or slightly rising final pitch starting from and continuing after the final accented syllable of a TCU has been identified as turn holding (Selting 1995a, 2000). See the following example:

(2.38)   "Finish this now" (Selting 2000:509) (adapted)

422	Nat:	<<l> aber `KUNST is aber nich kein gutes `Angebot hier.=
		but there's not much offered in art here
		=oder,
		is there
423		(0.5)
424	Ida:	`Es `GE:HT.
		it's all right
425		`NEE:; (0.3)
		no
426		`NICH so `sOnderlich `gUt.
		not so very good
427	Nat:	hm-
428		(1.0)

```
429->  Ida:    <<f>⁻A:>ber ich mach das jetzt hier zu↑⁻ENde⁻ (0.7)
               but I'm going to finish this now here
430->          ⁻wEil: eine ausbildung ↑⁻BRAUCH der mensch⁻ (1.4)
               because everyone needs an education
431            <<all> aso> s `hAb ich mir jetzt so ge`SA:GT.
               or so I've said to myself now
432            (0.2)
433->  Ida:    und: (0.2) ich `KÜMmer mich da nich ↑⁻wEiter drum⁻ (0.7)
               and           I'm not going to worry about it any more
434->          <<all> ich ⁻mAch> das hier zu↑⁻ENde⁻ (0.7)
               I'm going to finish this here
435            un mal `sEhn was `DANN kommt.
               and I'll see what happens then
436            (1.0)
437    Nat:    in `wElchem semester ↑`BIS du denn;
               what semester are you in anyway
```

This example shows that, even when a turn could be considered complete on syntactic, semantic, and discourse-pragmatic grounds, a pitch step-up to level on the final accented syllable followed by level or slightly rising unaccented syllables serves as a turn-holding device. This is what happens in the example above at the ends of lines 429, 430, 433, and 434.[60] Each of the units in these lines can be heard as holding the turn for a same-speaker continuation. This technique does not rely on prior projection; instead, it is implemented locally, beginning on the last accented syllable and continuing to the end of the unit. Furthermore, it has only local scope, projecting simple continuation – be it another TCU or something else. It is thus a local contextualization means for holding the floor.[61]

---

[60] For a more iconic impression of the pitch deployed in lines 433 and 434 see the following representation (from Couper-Kuhlen and Selting 1996b:35):

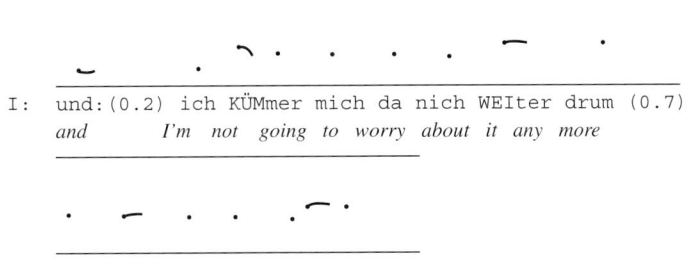

```
I:    und:(0.2) ich KÜMmer mich da nich WEIter drum (0.7)
      and        I'm not going to worry about it any more
```

```
I:    ich MACH das hier zuENde (0.7)
      I'm going to finish this here
```

[61] For more detail on this example see Selting (2000:509–10). Selting (2004a) investigates similar contours in the Berlin vernacular, and Selting (2007) discusses the use of level final pitch for turn holding in list construction.

> To accomplish turn holding at the end of possibly complete turns in English and German, interlocutors deploy the resources of tempo and pitch (complemented by other phonetic devices). Tempo-related practices include rush-throughs and abrupt-joins; pitch-related practices include non-TRP-projecting accents (in West Midlands English) and the use of final level or slightly rising pitch (in Standard Northern German). These are local devices for projecting turn continuation, with turn-holding intonation starting on the possible last accent of a TCU. Rush-throughs and abrupt-joins are used ad hoc, on the spot, at the end of possibly complete TCUs, to pre-empt turn transition. Much work remains to be done on turn-holding practices in other languages and language families.[62]

4. Turn Expansion

On occasion, after a speaker yields the turn at a point of possible completion, the recipient does not take the floor. Instead, the speaker – often after a gap – continues speaking. This will be referred to as turn expansion.

There may be various reasons for a recipient not to take the turn after a speaker's designed-to-be-complete turn ending. For instance, the recipient's attention may have been distracted due to some contingency, or the recipient may be delaying the onset of a dispreferred response, etc. In the face of this, the current speaker may wish to *re*-complete the turn and provide another point of possible completion, or to add elements making it easier for the recipient to respond. Turn expansions after prior TRPs are one way to provide material for negotiating turn transition after a previous failure to achieve it.

Turn expansion, thus, occurs at or near a TRP when some complication or trouble arises in turn taking (see also Luke et al. 2012:158). The following example from Schegloff shows that speakers have two possibilities for dealing with such complications:

(2.39)   "When I get home" (Schegloff 1996b:90) (adapted)
```
1  Ava:   I'll give you a call tomo[rrow.]
2  Bee:                           [Yeh: ] 'n [I'll be ho:me tomor]row.
3  Ava:                                      [When I-I get home. ]
4  Ava:   I don't kno-w- I could be home by- hh three, I could be home
          by two I don't know.
```

Ava's utterance *I'll give you a call tomorrow* reaches a point of possible completion at the end of line 1. This unit is grammatically complete and is also heard as prosodically complete (as indicated by the period at its end). Bee comes in in (terminal) overlap, thus taking the turn a bit early, but in a perfectly legitimate

---

[62] For findings on prosodic turn holding in eight regional varieties of German see Gilles (2005). On turn holding in Finnish see Ogden (2001) and Ogden and Routarinne (2005).

fashion. However, just after Bee has started speaking, Ava continues her turn from line 1 by adding *When I-I get home* (line 3). This continuation is what is called an *increment*: it grammatically extends the prior unit, which now ends up as *I'll give you a call tomorrow when I-I get home.* The new, expanded unit is again grammatically and prosodically complete (note the period at its end), thus providing another point of possible completion. Yet once again, Ava continues her turn by adding *I don't kno-w- I could be home by- hh three*, etc. Ava's further talk, however, cannot be construed as a grammatical continuation of the prior (expanded) TCU: it is not analyzable as an increment, but as the construction of a new TCU (see also Ono and Couper-Kuhlen 2007:506).

4.1 Conceptions of Incrementing

The first systematic analyses of this phenomenon were carried out by Auer (1991, 1992a, 1996a, 2005a, 2006a), with reference to data from German interaction. He presented a classification of "expansions" following prior possible completion points in sentences and clauses and pointed out that they can be packaged as prosodically integrated or prosodically independent/exposed with respect to the prior unit.

It was Schegloff, however, who coined the term "increment" with reference to "grammatically structured extensions of ... the talk" (1996b:90) occupying post-possible completion position. Schegloff does not refer to prosody or phonetics, but the transcription of his examples suggests that what he calls increments are added on in a prosodically independent format, i.e., in their own intonation phrase. In a later unpublished paper, Schegloff (2000a) specifies that increments are expansions of *hosts*; he describes them as appearing in three distinct positions: *next-beat, post-gap*, and *post-other-talk* (see also Walker 2001:20ff. and Luke et al. 2012:158).

With reference to linguistic structure, Ford et al. (2002:16) describe increments as "nonmain-clause continuations after a possible point of turn completion", i.e., after a TRP. They distinguish two types:

i. *Extensions.* These are hearable as syntactically and semantically coherent with the prior possibly complete turn (2002:16). Here is one of their examples:

(2.40) Extension (Ford et al. 2002:16)
```
1        Bill said that he was at least goin' eighty miles an hour.
2 ->     with the two of 'em on it.
```

ii. *Free constituents.* These are "unattached noun phrases" and other constituents that do not belong syntactically to the prior unit but are semantically dependent on it (2002:17). This is one of their examples:

(2.41)   Free constituent (Ford et al. 2002:17)
```
1    Curt:    °(Oh Christ) °fifteen thousand dollars wouldn't touch a Co:rd;
2             (0.7)
3    Curt:    That guy was (dreaming).
4 ->          fifteen thousand dollars [for an original Co:rd,
5    Gary:                             [Figured he'd impress him,
```

Ford et al. find that both types of increments emerge in environments where *recipiency* is at issue, that is, where speakers face problems pursuing uptake from a recipient (2002:18). Yet the two types of increments deal with such problems in distinct and iconic ways. Extensions, as integrated continuations of syntactic structures, function as action continuations; they produce new points of possible completion and thus create renewed opportunities for recipient uptake (2002:30). By contrast, unattached noun phrases are resources for accomplishing separate, new actions: they display a stance toward the prior unit that affords a model for how the recipient might respond (2002:33).

Ford et al. define their increments primarily with reference to syntax, taking their investigation to provide evidence for the interactional relevance of the notion of syntactic constituent (2002:33). They do voice the expectation that the two types they identify might also be prosodically packaged in different ways (2002:32). Yet in their transcriptions, the types of increments are rendered prosodically in a similar fashion.

Recall now the different organization of word or constituent order in English and German, as described in §1.1 above. The possible completion point of most clauses and sentences in German is marked by a strong boundary at the right of the sentence brace (*Satzklammer*). This entails that, while TCUs in English can be expanded freely, expansions in German are more difficult, because any clausal elements that come later are somehow "misplaced": they should have come earlier. Auer thus points out that the notion of incrementing as developed for English does not capture what happens in a wider variety of languages (2007b:657). Moreover, he argues that syntactic types of turn expansion need to be differentiated prosodically (2007b:652).

> There are different conceptions of what increments are and how best to describe them.[63] These conceptions pay differing attention to syntax and prosody, and they seem to be at least partly biased by the languages their descriptions are based on. There is thus a need for systematic cross-linguistic comparison of turn expansion in different languages.

---

[63] Recently, Sidnell (2012) has extended the notion of increment by looking at turn continuations not only by the same speaker but also by another speaker.

4. Turn Expansion

4.2 Cross-linguistic Turn Expansion

Building on prior work by Auer (1991, 1992a, 1996a) and Vorreiter (2003), Couper-Kuhlen and Ono (2007b) present a typology of turn expansion that systematically includes syntax and prosody and provides a cross-linguistic perspective.

4.2.1 A Typology of Turn Expansion

The authors first locate different ways of continuing a turn at talk on a "continuum of 'relatedness' to the prior unit" (Figure 2.3).

Maximal dependence		Minimal dependence
TCU continuation	Free constituents	New TCUs

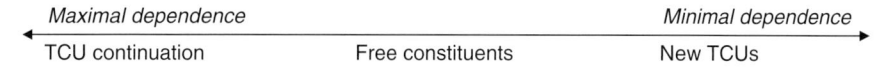

Figure 2.3 Continuing a turn at talk – syntactic and semantic dependence on prior unit (adapted from Couper-Kuhlen and Ono 2007b:515)

While new TCUs contain material that is syntactically and semantically independent from the prior talk and constitutes a new action, TCU continuations comprise material which is syntactically and semantically dependent on the host and continues its action. Free constituents fall somewhere in between these two extremes; they are syntactically not dependent on the prior unit, but often semantically and pragmatically so, and they often initiate a new action (2007b:515).

TCU continuations are then further classified as shown in Figure 2.4.

The authors illustrate the different types of TCU continuation, as well as free constituents, in conversational data from English, German, and Japanese, and argue that speakers rely differently on these types depending on their language. In the following, we will give examples from English and later discuss cross-linguistic variation. (TCU continuations are printed in bold.)

i. Non-add-on

This category comprises, for example, "right dislocations" (see Geluykens 1992) and other elements that follow a clearly marked closure and thus appear to be out of place (Couper-Kuhlen and Ono 2007b:517). The continuation may or may not repair some item in the prior talk. This is the only kind of continuation that follows its host without a prosodic break. In the following example, Mum is initiating a new topic.

(2.42)   "Cyd Arnold" (Couper-Kuhlen and Ono 2007b:517–18) (adapted)
((Underlining marks the constituent that is replaceable.))
10->   Mum: ↑Cyd rang this evening **Cyd Arnold**

Although she has referred to *Cyd* at the beginning of her turn, Mum appears to secure recognition by adding the full name *Cyd Arnold* after a possible completion

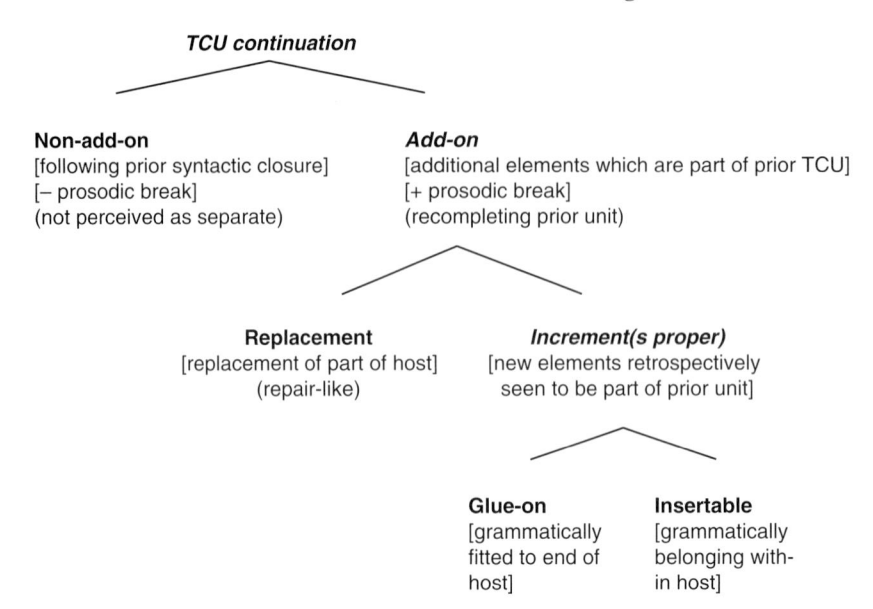

```
                          TCU continuation
                      _____/_____

    Non-add-on                         Add-on
    [following prior syntactic closure] [additional elements which are part of prior TCU]
    [– prosodic break]                 [+ prosodic break]
    (not perceived as separate)        (recompleting prior unit)
                                     _____/_____

                           Replacement              Increment(s) proper
                           [replacement of part of host]  [new elements retrospectively
                           (repair-like)                   seen to be part of prior unit]
                                                    _____/\_____

                                             Glue-on          Insertable
                                             [grammatically   [grammatically
                                             fitted to end of belonging with-
                                             host]            in host]
```

Figure 2.4 Types of TCU continuation (adapted from Couper-Kuhlen and Ono 2007b:515–16)

of her turn. As she adds this expansion within the same prosodic unit – there is no pause or other prosodic break separating the expansion from its host – it is analyzed as a *non-add-on*.

ii. Replacement

With this kind of continuation, one or more items in the host is replaced or repaired. The new item is added on after a prosodic break.

(2.43)   "North Cadbury Court" (2007b:519) (adapted)
((Underlining marks the constituent that is replaceable.))

```
 8 ->   Les:   And em.t.hh (0.2) it was in a beautiful ol:d (0.2)
 9             cou↓:rt. (0.2) uh: (.)
10 ->          North Cadbury Court which used to be a very old
               monastery
```

At the beginning of Les' story, Mum does not signal recognition of the place characterization *a beautiful old court* (lines 8–9), although Les appears to be waiting for her to do so. Now Les adds the specification *North Cadbury Court which used to be a very old monastery* (line 10). This phrase replaces the first one Les used: in other words, she is now heard as saying *it was in North Cadbury Court which used to be a very old monastery*. Replacement continuations are typically produced, as here, after a prosodic break.

iii. Glue-on

Glue-ons correspond most closely to Schegloff's increments (see above). Here is an example:

(2.44)   "Hard studying" (2007b:521) (adapted)
```
1 ->  Gor:    .t O:kay. .h I: sh- I shall leave you. .h
2 =>          to get on with your hard studying.
3 =>          that I know I interrupted. .hhhhhh
4 =>          rather [rudely
5     Dan:           [(Oh yes.)
```

Each continuation in Gordon's turn is fitted grammatically to the prior possibly complete turn, although it is delivered in a new prosodic unit. With each continuation Gordon re-completes the turn after there is no response from his interlocutor Dana.

Glue-ons can be quite diverse syntactically; when they are core arguments, they lead retrospectively to a syntactic re-structuring of the host (Couper-Kuhlen and Ono 2007b:524).

iv. Insertable

Insertables are produced after a clear prosodic break. The added elements could have been part of the prior host construction; they often sound out of place.

(2.45)   "Or not" (2007b:524) (adapted)
((@ marks the syntactic slot where the "displaced" material might be said to belong.))
```
1 ->  Gor:    .tch Are you gonna drive in @.
2             Cuz I n- I know there was some rumor about it,
3             (0.5)
4 =>  Gor:    .hhhh Or not.
```

After completing his TCU at line 1, Gordon delivers an add-on in line 2. When Dana still does not respond (line 3), Gordon produces an inbreath and then the phrase *Or not.* (line 4). Normatively speaking, this phrase belongs at the end of line 1 and for this reason is called an insertable. Insertables are rare in English, but frequent in German and Japanese.

v. Free constituent

For continuations classified as *free constituents*, it is not the syntactic structure that is dependent on the prior unit, but its interpretation. Free constituents are backward oriented because they display a stance toward what has been said (see

Ford et al. 2002), yet they do not extend the syntax or the action of the previous unit.

(2.46)   "House on her own" (2007b:526) (adapted)
```
1      Les:   Katherine's got to sleep,
2             in:: the house up in York alo:ne this weeken[:d.
3      Tre:                                              [Oh really?
4      Les:   And she's no-t too-oo ha-ppy about it=
5 ->   Tre:   =No:.
6             (0.3)
7 =>   Tre:   House on her ow:n. [°Oh G]od.°
```

Trevor's phrase *House on her ow:n.* (line 7) is not syntactically dependent on his prior acknowledgment (line 5) of Lesley's report of her daughter's uneasiness about sleeping in the York house all alone over the weekend. But it would not be interpretable without it.

4.2.2 Cross-linguistic Variation

Languages differ with respect to the frequencies with which these types of continuations are used in talk-in-interaction. Couper-Kuhlen and Ono's observations are summarized in Table 2.4 (2007b:546).

While glue-ons and replacements are the most frequent in English, in German it is insertables and non-add-ons. Japanese frequencies are more like those in German than in English.

This difference in distribution is arguably related to the different linguistic structurings in the respective languages. As will be recalled from §1.1 above, German syntax is characteristically organized around the sentence brace (*Satzklammer*), which provides for a clear and strong syntactic boundary to the right. Although very different in other respects, Japanese has final particles, which

Table 2.4 *Summary of preferences for TCU continuation*

TCU continuation type	English	German	Japanese
Non-add-on	Infrequent	Frequent	Frequent
Replacement	Frequent	Frequent	Frequent
Glue-on	Most frequent	Non-clausal: Infrequent Clausal: Frequent	Infrequent (only clausal)
Insertable	Infrequent	Most frequent	Very frequent
Free constituent	Frequent	Frequent	Frequent

also constitute a clear right-hand boundary; later items are heard as out of place (2007b:547). The strong final boundary in German and Japanese discourages glue-ons (with the exception of clausal increments), but enhances other types of increments. Couper-Kuhlen and Ono argue that these preferences are related to the right- versus left-headedness of phrases in the languages concerned (see Figure 2.5).

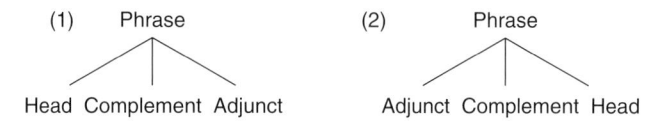

```
(1)      Phrase                    (2)      Phrase
        /  |  \                           /  |  \
   Head Complement Adjunct        Adjunct Complement Head
```

Figure 2.5 Left-headed and right-headed phrases (adapted from Couper-Kuhlen and Ono 2007b:547)

English is left-headed, as in (1) in Figure 2.5. Syntactic constructions emerge with time; optional elements can be added freely. German and Japanese are right-headed, as in (2). In this case, the production of the head gives a strong indication of completion. Optional elements that are added later on appear out of place (2007b:547).

> Research on TCU continuations and their cross-linguistic variation shows that grammar and interaction are closely intertwined. On the one hand, interactional exigencies require that it should be possible to talk beyond a point of possible (syntactic) completion: languages are thus called on to provide the resources for this practice. On the other hand, language-specific grammar provides for, and constrains the preferences for, different types of continuation (Couper-Kuhlen and Ono 2007b:549).[64]

4.2.3 Some Observations on the Phonetics and Prosody of Increments in English and Korean

Investigation of the phonetics of hosts and increments (in Schegloff's (1996b) sense: see above) shows that, in addition to grammatical fittedness, there is also close phonetic fittedness (Walker 2004b). On the basis of audio recordings of face-to-face and telephone conversations in British and American English, Walker reports that all hosts are displayed as complete intonational phrases, and that a range of phonetic parameters are involved in achieving an increment's coherence

---

[64] On right dislocations used as increments in French conversation and their emergent character see Pekarek Doehler (2011a); see also Chapter 6 §3. For recent studies of increments in other languages see *Discourse Processes* 49, 3–4 (2012), e.g., Krekoski (2012) and Ono et al. (2012) for Japanese; Luke (2012) and Zhang (2012) for Chinese (see also Luke and Zhang 2007). For more references on the languages mentioned, as well as on Korean, Finnish, and Navajo, see Luke et al. (2012:159).

with its host, including pitch (contour and range), loudness, articulation rate, and certain articulatory characteristics (2004b:159). However, these phonetic parameters are deployed as *relational* devices, not as constitutive of increments in an absolute sense. This means that there are no phonetic features specific to increments as such, independent of their hosts. It is rather that the phonetic features of the host are taken up and matched in the production of the increment in order to show the syntagmatic relationship between the two (2004b:159). Walker concludes that grammatical fittedness entails phonetic fittedness: both display that a stretch of talk is a continuation of a prior utterance and not something new.[65]

As for predicate-final and syllable-timed Korean, Kim argues that when post-predicate elements are produced after a host TCU, they "inherit" its syllabic and prosodic composition (2007:596). In many of his examples, the number of syllables in the post-predicate increment matches the number of syllables in the host TCU. Here is an example, where each underlined part represents a syllable and each pair of asterisks surrounds a rhythmic beat:

(2.47)   "It is America, the style" (Kim 2007:596) (adapted)
```
[*mi*   *kwuk*  *i*    *ya,* ] "It is America,"  ((host TCU))
[*su*   *tha*   *il*   *i.*  ] "The style."      ((post-predicate element))
```

This indicates that a syllable-timed language may make use of parallel syllabic rhythmic structure between the host TCU and an increment in order to display the cohesive syntagmatic relationship between the two. Kim suggests that by re-doing the prosody of the final component of the host, the post-predicate increment reenacts it, prompting the recipient to respond (2007:598).

> Increments in Schegloff's sense are not only grammatically cohesive with the host; they are also phonetically cohesive, displaying (in English) at their outset various forms of matching and assimilation to the end of the prior unit, and (in Korean) a form of syllabic and prosodic "inheritance" from the host. In both languages, increments are done prosodically-phonetically in a way that marks their syntagmatic relationship to the host.

4.2.4 Future Perspectives in the Study of Turn Expansion

There is still much work to be done on turn expansion. In their summary of the main findings in current research, Luke et al. (2012:160) criticize the lack of systematicity so far. It is the "oddities" in conversational data that seem to have captured analysts' imagination – departures from how utterances are normatively supposed

---

[65] See also Local (1992) on continuing and restarting stretches of talk.

to be built. Moreover, they argue that too much attention has focused on the relevance of increments for turn transition, thus possibly neglecting other issues they may be designed to address, such as achieving a particular kind of closing, adding on a complaint, handling imminent disagreement, etc. (2012:160).

In a critical appraisal of the notion of turn expansion, Auer points out that a full typology may also need a non-verbal component (2007b:657). One study that goes in this direction is that by Ford et al. (2012). The authors are interested in the coordination of *bodily-visual practices* (BVPs) with verbal (i.e., lexico-grammatical) material in positions at or near a place of possible turn completion. Assuming that each modality has its own temporal organization, they identify several different types of coordination between verbal turns and BVPs, including cases where the BVP is launched in the space where a verbal increment would otherwise be located (2012:195–6). Most of the BVPs in their data were deployed by speakers to index something that *could* be verbalized, but in fact was not. This suggests that the use of BVPs at or in the vicinity of TRPs may be the result of a choice to perform a turn-extending action without words (2012:210).

5. "Deviant" Turn Taking

On occasion, participants choose to take the turn even though the current speaker is nowhere near a TRP. The following sections deal with some practices that may result, among others, in deviations from the orderly organization of turn taking as described so far.

5.1 Turn Overlap and Turn Competition

Sacks et al. (1974) define overlap in terms of placement: it occurs at the TRP. But Jefferson gives us detailed studies of different kinds of overlap (1983, 1987). Taken together, her studies make the following distinctions[66] (for recent accounts of overlap onset see Schegloff 2000b and Drew 2009):[67]

i. *transitional* overlap: onset at the TRP (majority of cases), with three subtypes:

— *unmarked-next-position onset*, i.e., both recipient and prior speaker start up talk after a tiny pause following the prior speaker's TRP ("byproduct overlap");

---

[66] Our account here is based on Wells and Macfarlane (1998), who summarize and illustrate Jefferson's distinctions.
[67] On the use of visible resources such as gestures, changes of bodily posture, movements, object manipulations, and gaze in the management of overlap see Mondada and Oloff (2011).

- *latched onset*, i.e., both recipient and prior speaker start up talk immediately after the prior speaker's TRP (another type of "byproduct overlap");
- *terminal onset*, i.e., the next speaker overlaps the final sound segments of the prior speaker's turn;

ii. *interjacent* overlap: onset before a TRP, with subtypes:

- *progressional onset*: incoming of a recipient following "hitches" by current speaker, i.e., breaks in fluency such as "hesitations" or "stutters";
- *recognitional onset*: incoming upon recognition of the gist of what the current speaker is saying, again with two subtypes:
  . *item-targeted onset*;
  . *thrust-projective onset*; and

iii. *blind spot onset*: the recipient's incoming talk starts just slightly after the previous speaker has continued the turn after a TRP and a pause (Wells and Macfarlane 1998:276ff., with reference to Jefferson 1986:165–7).

Overwhelmingly, overlap is found at TRPs (Sidnell 2010:52). The majority of cases in conversation can be accounted for by the three types of overlap shown above, referred to by Sidnell as turn-terminal ("transitional terminal onset" in Jefferson's terms), turn-initial ("blind spot onset"), and recognitional (see 2010:53). Normally, these types of overlap are not treated as problematic by participants. Schegloff (2000b:5–6) notes further instances of non-competitive, non-problematic overlapped talk: overlapping continuers such as *uh-huh* and *mm-hm* and context-fitted assessment terms; cases of "conditional access to the turn" such as for participation in word searches or in collaborative utterance construction; and choral speaking as in laughing, collective greeting, leave-taking, congratulations, etc. Typically, competitive overlapped talk gets repeated, so that it is eventually produced *in the clear*. "Post-overlap" hitches like *uhm* or the stuttering start-up of post-overlap talk are very common, as if speakers were "defending the beginning of a turn against further incursion" (Sidnell 2010:55).[68]

Overlap as a "normal" occurrence in talk-in-interaction, one that does not generally give rise to inferences, must be distinguished from *interruption*. Schegloff (1987a:85, n. 5) reserves the term "interruption" for "starts by a second speaker while another is speaking and is not near possible completion."[69] Levinson (1983) mentions cases of "violative interruption", where either one of the speakers drops out, or one or both of the speakers engage in "a competitive allocation

---

[68] For more detail on the conversation analytic approach to overlap see, e.g., Jefferson (1983, 1984a, 1984b, 1986, 2004b) and Schegloff (2000b).
[69] A recent study by Vatanen (2014) on Finnish and Estonian, however, finds that, especially in assertion and assessment sequences, recipients can mark agreement from an epistemically independent position by coming in at recognition points well before the TRP. Such incomings are not treated as interruptive.

system". In the latter case, the speaker who upgrades the most, for example, with an increase in volume, a slowing down of tempo, a lengthening of vowels, etc., wins out (1983:300–1).

Sidnell points out that most instances of overlapped talk are not interruptive (2010: 53–4). Interruptive overlaps, he argues, involve "competing trajectories of talk" (p. 54) and possibly even disaffiliation. Here is the example he uses to illustrate this:

(2.48) "Unwanted call" (Sidnell 2010:53)
```
        ((Ring))
1  Cld:  °hh He:llo::¿
2  Clr:  Hello:,=my name is Naomi=from con:quest research?
3        one of [Cana
4  Cld:         [No::. I'm sorry.
5  Clr:  °No problem°
        ((Hang up))
```

The overlap in line 4 does not occur anywhere near a TRP. Yet the called party can infer that the caller is about to say "one of Canada's leading telemarketing research firms" or the like. Sidnell argues that the called party's incoming (line 4) is interruptive because it stops an unwanted trajectory of talk (2010:53). Yet apart from the early incoming and a declining of participation plus an apology, there does not appear to be any audible sign of competition for the floor, for example, through an escalation of loudness/volume or pitch. This incoming is thus not *designed* as a turn-competitive incoming in the sense of French and Local (1983) (see below), although it interrupts the trajectory of talk.

Schegloff (2000b) reconstructs an "overlap resolution device" for the management of competitive overlap in ordinary conversation. According to this device, when two co-participants both lay a claim to the turn, it seems to be especially increased volume, deployed by one or both speakers from the second overlapping syllable onwards, that constitutes the overlapping talk as a "competitive production" (2000b:21). Schegloff's data are predominantly from American English.

French and Local (1983) also claim that prosody is constitutive for how overlapping talk is treated in conversation; see also Online-Chapter E §3.1.[70] Their data come from overlapping talk in British English, subject to a positional constraint: they examine only cases where a speaker comes in clearly prior to a TRP and is understood to be claiming the floor "right now" (1983:18). According to their account, it is in particular the pitch height, tempo, and loudness of the incoming speech that constitute the incoming as competitive or non-competitive for the

---

[70] For a quantitative corroboration of the main points of this study for speakers of American English see Kurtić et al. (2009); for a very similar picture with reference to German conversation see Selting (1995a:208–29).

current turn. Incomings that are treated as directly turn-competitive are routinely done with high pitch <h> and increased loudness <f>; those that are treated as non-competitive lack these features.[71]

Here is an example of a competitive incoming: K has delivered a longish contribution, after which F has responded with *m::* (line 7), before N then takes the turn. After producing *oh yeah I mean it* (line 8), K comes back in again (line 9).[72]

(2.49)   Competitive incoming (French and Local 1983:19) (adapted)

```
1      K:    I was - I was gonna ask about those (0.5) cos (.) in terms of
2            your stuff about hints in the first thing because it seems to
3            me that something like.hhhhh Fionna's not letting me have the
4            scissors.hhhh is as much a threat to Fionna (0.7) as it is a
5            heh hint h to-is a - is a hint to her father
6            (1.6)
7      F:    m::
8 ->   N:    oh yeah I mean it ['s some sort of-/
                             [<      dim      >
                             [<      accel    >
9 ->   K:                    [y'know I mean and / this is
                             [<      high     >
                             [<      forte    >
             your thing ab[out the / two edged (0.4) way that these things
10     N:               [nyeah /
11     K:    work=
12     N:    =nyeah (0.4) nyeah
```

Immediately upon registering K's incoming (line 9), formatted with <h + f>, N begins to produce the continuation of the current turn with decreasing loudness and increasing tempo and then eventually breaks off (line 8). That is, N defers to the competitive incoming by "retreating" to quieter and faster speaking before ultimately yielding the floor to K.

Here is an example of a non-competitive incoming: K produces a longish turn which N first acknowledges with *m::* before coming in prior to K's completion with *well exactly yeah* (line 5). This incoming is produced with normal loudness and tempo, but with low pitch; it thus lacks the prosodic features associated with turn competition. K continues his turn undisturbed, without any change in prosody, as if nothing out of the ordinary had happened.

---

[71] The combination of <h + f> means that the incoming speech is higher and louder than the incomer's speech norms elsewhere (French and Local 1983:23).
[72] In the following two transcripts, dim = diminuendo, i.e., becoming quieter; accel = accelerando, i.e., speeding up; high = higher pitch; forte = increased loudness; low = low pitch.

(2.50)   Non-competitive incoming (French and Local 1983:20) (adapted)
```
1     K:    it would be interesting you know (0.3) to know what kind of
2           categories you're gonna play around with if you're gonna
            (0.4)
3     N:    m::=
4 ->  K:    =achieve both [instances at the same / time
5 ->  N:                  [well exactly yeah /
                          [<        low        >
6     E:    .h in fact there's possible evidence in the data that - that
7           Fionna's the next speaker
8           (.)
9     D:    m::
```

The authors conclude that the feature combination <h + f> constitutes incoming overlapping talk as turn-competitive, a non-legitimate interruption or attempt to take the floor immediately and urgently. In contrast to this, non-competitive incoming speech as well as turn holders' overlapped (legitimate) turn continuations in fights for the floor are constituted as such with other prosodic signals.[73]

Altogether, French and Local's (1983) findings for English as well as Selting's (1995a) findings for German can be summarized as in Figure 2.6.

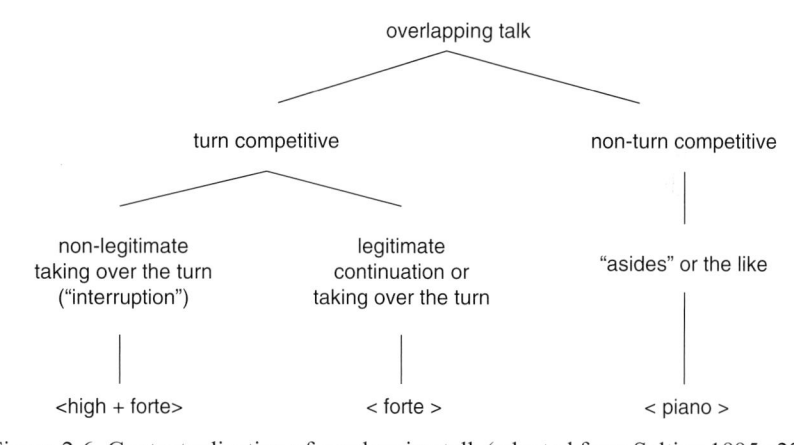

Figure 2.6 Contextualization of overlapping talk (adapted from Selting 1995a:228)

---

[73] French and Local (1983:24ff.) provide four kinds of evidence for their analysis: (i) the features <h + f> are maintained only as long as there is overlap; (ii) current turn occupants often counter the incomer's interruption with prosodic adaptations of their own talk: either they fight for their turn with slower tempo and increasing loudness, or they trail off and relinquish their turn with decreased loudness; (iii) overlapping talk that lacks the features <h + f> is not treated as competitive by the turn holder; (iv) turn holders who treat the turn as legitimately theirs continue only with greater loudness.

> The combination of the prosodic features high pitch <h> and increased loudness <f> is thus a powerful resource that can be used independently of action, activity type, or sequential unfolding in order to constitute an incoming at a non-TRP as competing for the floor now and not later (French and Local 1983:36).

But of course would-be next speakers not only come in well before TRPs. Wells and Macfarlane (1998) complement French and Local's study by looking at overlapping talk at or around TRPs. They find that instances of transitional onset, i.e., cases where the incoming begins on or after the last major accent, are not turn-competitive: they lack <h + f> (1998:279). Moreover, turn-competitive prosody is also lacking in cases of progressional onset, when a next speaker comes in at points of dysfluency or hesitation (1998:279).[74]

But not all the issues concerning overlapped talk have been settled yet. More recently, in a large-scale quantitative analysis of resources for turn competition in overlapping talk in American English meetings, Kurtić et al. (2013) come to the conclusion that, contrary to what has been assumed so far, turn-competitive overlap can also be found around the TRP (see esp. p. 737). Furthermore, they report that, apart from positioning, recycling plays a major role in indicating turn competition, recycling being used by overlappers as well as those overlapped to fight for the floor.

> Not all interruptions need to be designed as such in order to be effective. But in ordinary English and German conversation, for an overlap to be treated as an interruption, it seems to be both its position and its prosodic features that are relevant. Among the latter, high pitch and increased loudness, or <h + f>, are most important.

5.2 Stopping and Abandoning Turns

Sometimes we need to break off our talk, either to begin anew or to leave things open. In cases when we prematurely discontinue the construction of a TCU, we need to make this recognizable for our recipients. The unfinished unit left behind will be called a *fragment* here. In many cases, whether a stretch of speech is a complete unit or only a fragment of one is interpretable only in the sequential context. How, then, is stopping or abandoning a turn made recognizable?

---

[74] For an example of competitive collaborative completion see Local (2005:276–8). On the use of prosodic resources in children's turn taking, especially in overlapping speech, see Wells and Corrin (2004).

In general, just as for the construction and interpretation of complete units, projection plays an important role – although this time it is a question of projections that remain unfulfilled (Selting 2001a:252).[75]

But in addition to not fulfilling the projections created at the outset of a turn, something that is only interpretable in retrospect, speakers frequently deploy practices to make their "breaking" and/or abandoning of talk immediately recognizable. In German conversation, these practices include:

i. cutting off speech in order to begin a new unit or to change a unit underway; and
ii. trailing off, i.e., dropping out of the role of speaker, relinquishing the unfinished unit, and yielding the floor to the recipient(s).

In both cases, a turn is discontinued and a fragment is left behind (2001a:253).

These practices correspond to what Jasperson (2002) found when studying the phonetics of "cut-offs" in American English. He identified two types of cut-off, described as "closure cut-off" and "pulmonic cut-off", that are deployed for different purposes.

Closure cut-offs stop the projected occurrence of the next sound (2002:274; see also Schegloff 1979:273 and Online-Chapter E §4.4).[76] Even though closure cut-off is frequently used to initiate same-turn self-repair, due to its phonetic characteristics it is recognizable independently of the actual operation of repair. This means that it can be a generalized resource for stopping a turn prematurely (Jasperson 2002:275).

Pulmonic cut-offs do not block the flow of air by cutting it off. Instead, they remove the source of the airflow by preventing the chest cavity from generating further pulmonic pressure (2002:275). They initiate the abandonment of units in progress. Pulmonic cut-off appears to correspond to the practice of "trail-off", which has been identified as occurring in turn yielding.

> Distinct phonetic resources are deployed to make the stopping versus the abandoning of a turn recognizable for recipients: stopping is achieved by oral or glottal closure cut-off, abandoning by pulmonic trail-off.

As we have seen above (§1.3), deploying closure cut-off does not automatically create a fragment as such; instead, it indicates TCU and turn holding for projected continuation. In retrospect, however, if and when the continuation is not realized, the prior piece becomes recognizable as a fragment.

---

[75] Just like TCUs and turns, fragments are not produced for their own sake: "fragments of units, as well as units themselves, are epiphenomena of the participants' practices of constructing, organizing and making recognizable turns at talk" (Selting 2001a:254).

[76] Closure cut-offs are produced with an oral and/or glottal closure that blocks the egressive flow of air during speech (Jasperson 2002:271).

6. Conclusion

This chapter has shown that there is an interdependence between language structure and social interaction. The organization of turn taking in interaction is an interactional accomplishment that shapes and is shaped by the linguistic resources deployed to manage it.

On the one hand, interactional tasks – here, in particular, turn construction and turn taking – have resulted in languages developing resources for participants to use in the conduct of interaction. All languages need resources, for example, for building TCUs and turns, for projecting TCU and turn completion, for making break-offs and inserts within TCUs recognizable, for organizing turn yielding and turn holding, for distinguishing non-competitive overlap from turn-competitive interruptions, and for making the stopping versus abandoning of turns recognizable. The informal structures found in conversational language use result from practices adapted to the conduct and negotiation of spontaneous interaction between co-present participants. Thus, the interactional tasks of turn construction and turn taking shape the linguistic structures recurrently and routinely deployed to implement them.

On the other hand, languages and language types all over the world have developed different kinds of resources and structures. We have seen some of these differences with respect to early and delayed projection. The ways in which languages organize the construction of sentences, clauses, and phrases affect the ways in which interactional tasks are accomplished, here especially the practices of turn projection and turn yielding. And, as we have seen, this may in turn affect the ways in which speakers and recipients cooperate in constructing TCUs and taking turns.

This chapter has also shown that there are vast areas of unexplored territory. Some languages as used in interaction are relatively well understood, while research on others has not even started. More research, and more systematic research, on the use of other languages in social interaction is needed in order to better appreciate the interdependence between linguistic structure and social interaction.

At a number of points in our exposition it has become clear that visible resources are deployed in concurrence with verbal and vocal resources and also play an important role in the organization of turn transition. Future research will need to integrate more systematically the description of verbal, vocal, and visible resources to the extent that they are relevant for the dual tasks of turn construction and turn taking. Following C. Goodwin's early example, recent research in this domain has also begun to explore the organization of these tasks in special settings and contexts such as in institutional and media talk, as well as at workplace meetings.

6. Conclusion

Turn construction and turn taking are not ends in themselves. We do not conduct our daily interactions merely in order to accomplish these tasks. Rather, turn construction and turn taking are byproducts of the actions we carry out in talk-in-interaction and of the ways we construct and maintain social relations – in socializing with our families and friends, in doing our work at home or in the office/on the factory floor, and in living our daily lives. Through the manipulation of turn construction and turn taking we construct different ways of doing interaction, creating, for instance, more or less competitive styles of interaction. This shows that the mechanisms of turn construction and turn taking are intricately related to the construction of social reality.

3

Repair

1. Introduction

Interaction normally proceeds apace, that is, it is not held up or halted for any particular reason: this is known as progressivity. But sometimes progressivity is compromised: due to our own or the other's lapse of attention we may fail to produce the next word or to hear what the other said. Or our tongue may slip and we come out with the wrong word. Spoken talk-in-interaction – once it is produced – is out there, for others to hear: there is no eraser. Occasions on which we wish to revise something we have just said, or do not hear or understand something that our interlocutor says, are typical and omnipresent in interaction. As Schegloff et al. (1977) have shown, the ways in which we remedy such everyday trouble in talk-in-interaction are highly organized: taken together they are known as the practices of "repair". Yet not every "objective" mistake or error is repaired, and what gets repaired need not be a "real" mistake at all (see Schegloff 2007a:100).

Repair is important for the maintenance of intersubjectivity: it enables speakers to accomplish, sustain, and defend mutual understanding in talk (Sidnell 2010:136). Schegloff et al. (1977) conceive of the repair system as a "self-righting mechanism" that allows talk-in-interaction to keep itself going in the face of problems (see Schegloff 1992:1337ff.). Like the turn-taking mechanism, the repair mechanism is conceived of as being both *context-free*, i.e., so general that its basic organization will be relevant everywhere, and *context-sensitive*, i.e., adaptable to the particularities of specific contexts, situations, and languages.[1]

---

[1] We will limit the current presentation largely to research on repair in ordinary conversation, focusing on English and German but including other languages where possible. Research on repair in special (institutional) contexts such as, for instance, in the classroom, or in adult-child or native-non-native interaction, will not be dealt with here. For a recent overview of research on repair see also Hayashi et al. (2013).

1. Introduction

We will argue that repair is not only a sequential self-righting mechanism but also one that allows participants, for whatever purpose or contingency, to negotiate both the trouble source and the repair, often in a preferred order.

1.1 Basic Terminology

Most conversation analysts use the term *repair* to refer to "practices for dealing with problems or troubles in speaking, hearing, and understanding the talk in conversation" (Schegloff 2000c:207). Repair halts the progressivity of interaction so that participants can address, handle, and potentially resolve problems in producing talk themselves, or in hearing or understanding a co-participant's talk. All repairs, however small, break the continuity of talk and constitute a digression from the action being carried out. Repair is conceived of as an action that is implemented through an orderly organization of practices (2000c:207).

There is an abundance of work dealing with repair. In the following we present an overview of research in Conversation Analysis (CA) and Interactional Linguistics, in particular on linguistic aspects of repair practices.[2]

Ever since Jefferson's first study on error correction (1974) and Schegloff et al.'s seminal paper on the preference for self-correction (1974), the repair process has been conceptualized as involving the ordered accomplishment of a series of steps, including:

i. *Initiation of repair*, i.e., identifying and locating a problem, either by *self* (the producer of the *repairable* or *trouble source*), or by *other*. These are known as *self-initiation* and *other-initiation* of repair, respectively. Speakers have been shown to deploy special techniques or *formats* in order to make the initiation of repair and/or the trouble source recognizable for the recipient (see below).
ii. *Repair* (or *correction*) of the repairable, i.e., solving the problem, either by *self* (the producer of the repairable), or by *other*. Also called the *repair operation* or the *repair proper*, this is known as either *self-repair* or *other-repair*, respectively.

Combining these options, four types of repair can be distinguished (post hoc): *self-initiated self-repair, self-initiated other-repair, other-initiated self-repair*, and *other-initiated other-repair*.

The repair *outcome* is a solution or an abandonment of the problem (Schegloff 2000c:207). Often the outcome is not made explicit but is implied by the resumption of topical talk.

---

[2] For more extensive overviews, especially of the sequential aspects of repair, see Schegloff (2007a:100ff.); Sidnell (2010: Chapter 7); Kitzinger (2013); see also Levinson (1983: Chapter 6).

Repair is typically initiated at particular positions, so-called *opportunity spaces*, in or after the turn-constructional unit (TCU)/turn with the trouble source:

T1	in the same turn/TCU, either prior to or immediately following the repairable;
T1–2	in the transition space following the transition-relevance place of the turn;
T2	in next turn;
T3	in the turn following next turn ("third-position repair" as well as "third-turn repair"; see Schegloff 1997b);[3]
T4	in a later turn ("fourth-position repair"; Schegloff 1992, 2000c:209ff.).

Particular types of repair initiation and repair are designed to be deployed in these locations: position T1 for the self-initiation of repair; T1–2 for a belated self-initiation of repair; T2 for the other-initiation of repair or for other-repair; T3 for self-repair after other-initiation at T2, or for repair of a misunderstanding which has become apparent at T2; T4 for dealing with the trouble later. As almost all other-initiations of repair occur in next turn after the trouble-source turn, these have also been referred to as "next-turn repair initiations". Self-initiations of repair occur in all the other positions (see Schegloff 2000c:207–8).

The sequential organization and the participation framework among interlocutors can vary with different types of repair. While *self*-initiated repair is ordinarily executed within the same turn, *other*-initiated repair ordinarily involves a recipient initiating repair and the speaker of the trouble-source turn dealing with it next, thus creating a *repair sequence*. The action, or actions, of repair can replace or defer whatever else was due next (Schegloff 2000c:208). Since repair is a powerful action type that can be initiated anywhere in conversation, interactional logic requires it to be restricted to the "repair initiation opportunity space" (Schegloff et al. 1977). This means, in Schegloff's words, that "virtually all repair *initiations* occur within the [...] limited space around their self-declared *trouble-source*, and [...] virtually all *repairs* (i.e., *solutions*) occur within a very narrowly circumscribed space from their repair *initiations*" (2000c:208).

Repair operates on an item or an issue that is implied to be repairable. The term is thus more general than *correction*. While *correction* usually denotes the remedy of an error of some kind, *repair* also includes re-formulations or specifications by the speaker in order to improve the recipient design of a prior turn, or to check a recipient's understanding of what has been said. The outcome of repair need not be a modification of prior talk: it may also be a repetition or confirmation of it. Schegloff highlights the interruption of progressivity as a criterion for repair: "Whatever the response – whether modification/correction or confirmation/

---

[3] This is also one position in which misunderstandings can be addressed. On some sources of misunderstandings in talk-in-interaction, in particular related to problematic reference and problematic sequential implicativeness, see Schegloff (1987c).

repetition/affirmation – the ongoing trajectory of the interaction has been stopped to deal with possible trouble, and that marks this interlude of talk-in-interaction as repair" (2000c:209).[4] In consequence, the boundaries between repair and, for example, the negotiation or display of disagreement may be fuzzy. As the organizational practices for correction and repair are the same, we will follow CA practice and speak of *repair* in both cases.

Schegloff et al. (1977) identify *preference* structures in the operation of repair: self-initiation is preferred over other-initiation, and self-repair is preferred over other-repair. These preferences are based both on frequency of occurrence and on the turn formats involved. Thus, participants in everyday conversation typically give speakers every structural opportunity possible to carry out self-initiation and self-repair. Other-initiation of repair is often delayed or only implied, giving the speaker of the trouble source another opportunity to carry out self-repair. Moreover, other-initiation of repair and other-repair are often realized in turn shapes characteristic of dispreferred actions (see Online-Chapter B).

Recently, Sidnell and Barnes (2013) have argued that preference structures for repair are related to epistemic relations. Analyzing cases in which descriptions are being given, they observe that participants display sensitivity to the distribution of epistemic rights (see also Online-Chapter C §1) in repairing: a subsequent speaker is only treated as entitled to *replace*, and possibly also correct, a first description if the talk describes something within his or her own epistemic domain. If this is not the case, i.e., if the prior speaker is describing something in his/her own epistemic domain, a subsequent speaker is treated as entitled only to identify a possible problem, for example, through an other-initiation of repair, but not to replace or correct it (see also Haakana and Kurhila 2009).

1.2 Repair as a Vehicle for Other Actions

Repair can be initiated for a variety of reasons, for example, in order to correct an error, to prevent some misunderstanding, to improve the recipient design of a turn, to request the recipient's gaze (C. Goodwin 1981), etc. But repair can also be initiated as a vehicle or instrument for achieving something else: for instance, self-initiated self-repair can be used to present a turn as dispreferred or to allude to something left unsaid; other-initiation of repair can be used as a pre-rejection or a pre-disagreement; other-repair or correction can be used to instruct, admonish, complain, accuse, ridicule, display doubt, challenge, reject, reveal another's ignorance, etc. (see Jefferson 1987:88; Schegloff 1997a:505, 2007a:102ff.; Sidnell

---

[4] As a contrasting case, "correction which does not constitute repair" (Schegloff 2000c:209) refers to Jefferson's analysis of "embedded correction" (1982, 1987; see below).

2010:114). Usages of repair to achieve some other action, as interesting as they are, cannot be dealt with systematically in this chapter.[5]

1.3 Repair as a Universal Practice

As talk-in-interaction is in principle vulnerable to any of the above-mentioned mishaps, repair is likely to be a practice needed in all languages and cultures (see also Fox et al. 2013:733). The preference orderings with respect to types of repair as described by Schegloff et al. (1977) also seem to hold in everyday talk-in-interaction in most languages.[6] Thus, like turn taking, repair organization appears to have a quasi-universal base.

Yet languages and language types vary in the way this universal base is "inflected" (Sidnell 2007b:241). As recent research has shown, the morpho-syntactic practices of a language can shape the ways in which repair is initiated and carried out in that language. In the following, we will discuss the results of studies on repair in different languages, starting first with self-initiation and then moving to other-initiation. Third- and fourth-position repair will not be dealt with here. We will use the following terminology: the participant initiating repair will be referred to as the *repair initiator*: the participant carrying out the repair will be called the *repairer*. The action of repair initiation will be seen to imply a problem *categorization*, i.e., a "diagnosis" or construal of the problem; the action of carrying out the repair will be referred to as *repair operation* or *repair proper* or simply *repair*. The repair operation entails either that repairers go along with the repair initiator's problem categorization or that they *re-categorize* the trouble source or problem (type).

2. Self-initiation of Repair

There are a number of interactional issues involved in the self-initiation of repair. For instance, how does the speaker make recognizable for the recipient(s) that s/he is initiating repair? How does (do) the recipient(s) know that the next bit of talk is not a coherent continuation of the ongoing TCU, but rather that the speaker is breaking talk in order to repair something just produced or about to be produced? How can the recipient recognize the repairable? How can the recipient know

---

[5] For a discussion of some of these usages see Kitzinger (2013:242–3). On "reference calibration repairs" as a practice for adjusting the precision of formulations for the task at hand see Lerner et al. (2012). On "concessive repair", a constructional schema used for the retraction of overstatements, see Couper-Kuhlen and Thompson (2005).
[6] Moerman (1977) basically corroborates the findings of Schegloff et al. (1977) for English in a study on the preference for self-correction in a Thai conversational corpus. For a replication of the basic context-free structural organization of repair in German see Egbert (1996, 2009).

whether or not the speaker needs help? Finally, how can recipients recognize when the self-repair is over and the speaker is resuming the TCU/turn temporarily suspended? For all of these issues, it is linguistic choices that hold the key.

Self-repair can be initiated with both non-lexical and lexical devices. In the literature, the following non-lexical practices are mentioned: cut-offs, sound stretches or elongations, *uh*s and *uhm*s (i.e., *hesitation markers*), phrasal breaks, restarts, other hitches and peculiarities of articulation, silences/pauses (Schegloff et al. 1977:367; Sidnell 2010:114). Several of these devices can be observed in the following self-initiation of repair ("-" denotes cut-off):

(3.1)   "One course" (Schegloff et al. 1977:367) (adapted)
```
->   A:   W- when's your uh, weh- you have one day y'only have one
          course uh?
```

We can see this speaker cutting off her talk several times. After the first cut-off (notated as *W-*), she recycles the sound /w/ at the beginning of the word *when's*, but shortly thereafter suspends her utterance using *uh* as a delaying device. She then resumes the utterance by producing *weh-*, but again cuts off, abandoning the syntactic structure so far and replacing it with the new structure *you have one day y'only have one course*. (After this she appends a tag question, also transcribed by Schegloff et al. as *uh*.)

All languages appear to make use of such non-lexical devices for the initiation of self-repair. Exact phonetic realizations may differ, however, as reflected in the transcription of delaying devices such as *uh* and *uhm* in American English, *er* and *erm* in British English, *äh*, *ähm*, *öh*, or the like in German, *öö* in Finnish, *ano:* in Japanese, etc.

Lexical devices for the self-initiation of repair include, for instance, particles such as *no* or *I mean* in English (see below). These may be used either alone or in combination with non-lexical devices.

Repair initiations differ with respect to the work they do. Schegloff observes that, generally but not invariably, *uh* or silence/pause is *pre-positioned* in relation to the trouble source, whereas cut-off is *post-positioned* (1979:273). In other words, items such as *uhm* or *uh*, also referred to as "delaying devices" (Hayashi 2003:113), commonly initiate repair on projected talk that has not yet been produced.[7] By contrast, cut-off is positioned after the trouble source. Cut-off stops the turn and prevents a next sound from occurring when due (see also Jasperson 2002:258). It can initiate the repair of some prior item or of the whole turn produced so far. Thus, the way a repair is self-initiated indicates which part of the turn in progress is

---

[7] On uses of *uh(m)*, especially in environments other than self-repair, see Schegloff (2010b). For a recent summary of the relevance of *uh(m)* in conversation see also Lerner (2013:101–2).

being operated on. This is why an account of same-turn repair must deal with the techniques deployed to initiate it (Jasperson 2002:260). In the following sections, we will first concentrate on pre-positioned, and then on post-positioned, initiations of repair.

2.1 Pre-positioned Self-initiation

In pre-positioned initiations of repair, the speaker indicates some trouble in producing the next bit of talk. Let us start with the seemingly simple and omnipresent practice of searching for a word. If you realize that a word is unavailable to you, how do you make it known that you are *searching for a word*? How do you indicate whether you want to solve the problem yourself or whether the recipient should provide some help?

2.1.1 Word Searches

For English and other languages, research has shown that speakers typically initiate word searches with an indication of trouble, for example, through sound stretches, cut-offs, intra-turn pauses, etc. These may co-occur with, or be followed by, *uhm*, *uh*, *m*, or something similar, and/or self-addressed questions such as *What was it again*, and so on.

Here is an example of a word search that is marked in a complex way: first, the item *uh* and a silence of 0.7 seconds are used to initiate repair. (In addition, the sound lengthenings on *wa:s* and *na:med* foreshadow the problem.) The speaker then delivers a self-addressed side remark – *What the hell was her name* – in a low voice, before finding a solution to the problem herself.

```
(3.2)    "Karen" (Schegloff et al. 1977:363) (adapted)
    Clacia:   But, a-another one that went to school with me
->            wa:s a girl na:med uh, (0.7) °What the hell was
->            her name.°Karen. Right. Karen.
```

But the organization of verbal behavior in word searches can be different in different languages and language types. Fox et al. (1996) cite the following case for English:

```
(3.3)    "With a jack" (Fox et al. 1996:204)
->  M:   on the back of this pickup truck [with a,*] (0.4) with a jack.
```

This speaker begins a prepositional phrase postmodifying *truck, with a*, but initiates repair on it by breaking off (represented by *) and leaving a pause. He then recycles the preposition (*with*) and the indefinite article (*a*), and completes the phrase by delivering the noun *jack*. Recycling prepositions and articles is a typical procedure for delaying the production of a noun due next within an English prepositional phrase. This technique can be used, for instance, as part of a word search, as a request for recipient gaze, for the management of overlapping talk, and/ or for the foreshadowing of a dispreferred action (see also Fox et al. 1996:204).[8]

However, in Finnish, which has postpositions instead of prepositions, the recycling of prepositions in order to delay a next content word is not possible. Finnish makes use of pronominal pre-modifiers: demonstrative pronouns like *se* ("it, that, the, this") and pronominal adjectives like *semmonen* ("such"), especially in combination with a lengthening of their final sounds, in order to delay the production of a noun (Kärkkäinen et al. 2007:348). Here is an example from a telephone call in which the first use of the pre-modifier *ton* ("that") ends with a lengthened final sound and thus implies the delay of the noun to follow:

(3.4)   "Telephone call" (Kärkkäinen et al. 2007:348) (adapted)
```
1 Tiina: .hh Ja tota vo-isi-t    sä anta-a    mu-lle
              and well can-CON-2SG you give-INF I-ALL
         .hh And well could you give me
2        to-n:    .mhhth to-n    Eeva-n puhelin-numero-n ku se-
         that-GEN          that-GEN Eeva-GEN phone-number-ACC since it
         ton:.mhhth ton Eve's phone number since she-
```

After the first version of the pre-modifier *ton:* ("that"), which is followed by an inbreath (*.mhhth*), the pre-modifier is recycled before the noun phrase *Eevan puhelinnumeron* "Eve's phone number" is finally produced (line 2). So, pre-positioned grammatical devices, needed for the construction of TCUs anyway, may be deployed as delaying devices in Finnish.

2.1.2 Placeholder Repairs

Some languages use special techniques called "placeholder repairs" (Wouk 2005:241) in order to implement self-repair. In these languages, speakers who are searching for a word use a *dummy* lexical item, mostly translatable as "thing"/ "thingy", at the location of the missing word, while continuing to search for the missing word. Once it is found, speakers then produce the searched-for replacement, although its TCU has already been completed. Languages such as Japanese, Korean, Mandarin Chinese, Indonesian, Russian, Udihe, and Ude reportedly make quite extensive use of this practice (see Fox 2013:3), while English and German use it only occasionally.[9]

---

[8] For practices used in displaying "delicate formulations", among them "hesitating" and "searching for a word", see Lerner (2013).

[9] On the frequent use of placeholder repairs in Indonesian see Wouk (2005). On the use of linguistic constructions to hold a place for a missing word, often accompanied by gestures, by Finnish speakers with aphasia, see Helasvuo et al. (2004).

As Japanese has postpositions rather than prepositions, and no articles, practices like recycling back to a preposition and an article are not possible. Instead, Japanese speakers use demonstrative pronouns like *are* ("that one") or *asoko* ("that place") as placeholders while they are searching for a specific word (Fox et al. 1996; see also Chapter 2 §1). Here is an example:

(3.5)   "No maid" (Fox et al. 1996:205)

```
M: .hh maa   sonna:::  are ga::::  (1.5) u:: meedosan ga   iru         yoona: ie
   well like           that SUBJ          uhm maid   SUBJ  exist such  family
   ya nai kara:,
   be not because
   ... because, like, we are not the sort of family to have that, uhm a maid
```

(*Note*: the abbreviation SUBJ stands for "subject" here.)

Speaker M uses the distal demonstrative *are* ("that one over there") instead of a lexical item in the grammatical slot where the missing item would normally belong. Because it has a forward-looking orientation, *are* functions here as a "prospective indexical" (C. Goodwin 1996:384–5): it requires the recipient to attend to subsequent talk in order to find out the particulars. Following a lengthy pause, speaker M then provides the missing item, thereby retrospectively specifying the referent of the earlier demonstrative (Hayashi 2003:122). So, the same demonstrative *are* that was earlier described as a projecting device in Japanese (see Chapter 2) is also deployed as a device to deal with trouble in finding words.

Distal demonstrative pronouns such as *are/asoko* accomplish two things when used as placeholders. First, they project a later specification and replacement in subsequent talk. Second, there being at least two different resources to choose from – *are* for object/event/etc. and *asoko* for place – the choice of the particular placeholder also specifies the particular domain to which the searched-for item belongs. Placeholders thus project the specific kind of information that will be needed to replace the demonstrative in subsequent talk (Hayashi 2003:126).[10]

A similar practice has been identified in an ethnic style of German called "Turkish German," spoken by adolescents and young adults with Turkish (and other) migration backgrounds in German cities (Kern and Selting 2006b). In this ethnic style, we frequently find the item *dings*, otherwise used by speakers of near-standard colloquial German as a placeholder for, for example, personal names,

---

[10] Judging from the examples presented, the use of *are/asoko* to indicate a word search is often accompanied by other cues for the initiation of word searches, e.g., sound stretches, silences, and/or self-addressed questions (see Hayashi 2003:124). For an analysis of placeholder repairs and other practices used to handle upcoming problems of formulating and establishing referential expressions during turn construction in Japanese, see also Hayashi (2005b). On the usage of postpositions as tying devices across such side sequences in Japanese, see Chapter 6 §1. Hayashi and Yoon (2006) present a cross-linguistic study of similar kinds of demonstratives used as "filler words" in twelve typologically and geographically divergent languages.

taking the place of a common noun. Here are two examples where *dings* is used in the first TCU and then replaced by a common noun in the next TCU:

(3.6)   "Thingy – hand writing" (Kern and Selting 2006b:336) (adapted)
```
1 ->  Eli:  was hatn denn deutsch mit (.) DINGS zu tun;
            what had PART german with      thingy to do
            what does German have to do with (.) thingy
2 ->        HANDschrift;
            hand writing
```

(3.7)   "Thingy – customers" (Kern and Selting 2006b:336) (adapted)
```
4 ->  Esi:  weil    er DINGS    hat bestimmt;
            because he thingy has surely
            surely because he has thingy
5 ->        KUNde;
            customers
```

In the first example, the unit-internal pause is indicative of a word search; in the second example, however, there is no other indication that a word search is in progress.[11] For an item following the completed TCU to be hearable as a replacement of *dings*, it needs to be grammatically fitted to the prior TCU, i.e., have the morpho-syntactic features of case, number, and gender required in this position (Kern and Selting 2006b:340).[12]

So far, we have only shown instances in which speakers initiate a word search and then solve the problem themselves. In many cases, however, word searchers elicit help from the recipient. According to Lerner, word searches are "specifically designed for conditional entry by recipients" (1996a:261). With them recipients are given access to the current turn, should they so wish, and can aid in the search by suggesting candidate solutions. This is what we see happening in the next example:

(3.8)   "Muslims" (Lerner 1996a:261) (adapted)
```
L:  he said, the thing that- that- sad about the uhm black uhm
    (0.3)
P:  muslims,
L:  muslims, he said is that they don't realize...
```

In this case, hitches (the broken off, repeated *that-*), two instances of *uhm*, and a pause display that a word search is underway. Interestingly, the hitches occur

---

[11] For more detail on the prosodic properties and possible origin of this construction see Kern and Selting (2006b:336, 341–2).
[12] In example (3.7), this fitting does not correspond to the rules of Standard German but uses a grammatical form common in Turkish German.

already well before the missing word: their early deployment foreshadows the trouble and thus serves to put the recipient on alert. Lerner points out that P's provision of the item *muslim* also completes the first component of a pseudocleft construction. According to Lerner, in many cases – as in this example – the word being searched for is placed near the end of a unit, so that providing a candidate solution will also serve to terminate the unit (1996a:262).

If the self-initiation of repair for a word search can lead to either self-repair or other-repair, how do searchers make it clear to the recipient whether or not they want help? For this, prosodic and visible resources appear to play an important role.

2.1.3 Prosodic and Visible Resources

Following the display of a word search or other problem in speaking, prosodic and visible cues can be deployed to suggest how participation roles should be distributed in the repair operation. The outcome is either self-repair or other-repair. In this sense, a word search can be thought of as a systematic process of interaction between searcher and recipient organized through verbal, prosodic, and visible resources.

In face-to-face interaction, for instance, verbal resources for indicating word searches can be accompanied by orientational shifts and changes of gaze as well as by manual and facial gestures, including those that might iconically represent some aspect of the searched-for item. Goodwin and Goodwin describe a characteristic "thinking face" enacted during, or at times even before, word searches: speakers withdraw their gaze, look away from their recipients, and produce a facial expression that visually displays continuing involvement in a search, including, for example, lowering the eyelids and pursing or slacking the lips (1986:56ff.). While a thinking face may imply self-repair, speakers can invite their recipients to help by gazing at them. Recipients will then often adapt their prosodic and visible behavior to that of the speaker and join in the search, for instance, by suggesting a candidate solution with a try-marked format (rising intonation).[13]

Hayashi (2003) finds similar practices being used in Japanese conversation. Example (3.5), cited above for the use of placeholder repair in Japanese, shows a case of solitary word search, where the speaker implies that she is aiming to solve the problem herself. However, Hayashi points out that, through the use of gesture and gaze, speakers can invite the recipient to join in the word search and provide a candidate solution. In this way, speaker and recipient(s) collaborate in the resolution of the ongoing word search (2003:127ff.).

---

[13] See C. Goodwin (1980) for the deployment of restarts and pauses at the beginning of turns as a resource for securing recipient gaze and attention.

2. Self-initiation of Repair 123

> Pre-positioned self-initiations of repair, for example, word searches and problems in finding the right formulation, are organized with verbal, prosodic, and visible resources. Typical verbal resources are sound stretches, cut-offs, intra-turn pauses, repetition of function words, etc. However, languages and language types may favor different techniques depending on their grammatical organization: for instance, English speakers appear to prefer the lengthening and/or recycling of elements preceding the searched-for word, while Japanese speakers prefer the use of a placeholder, which they can then replace in a subsequent TCU. Visible cues can suggest whether the repair operation should be carried out as self-repair or as other-repair: the display of a thinking face, with gaze withdrawal, can imply the relevance of self-repair, while gaze directed at the recipient can suggest that other-repair is relevant.

2.2 Post-positioned Self-initiation

With post-positioning, repair is initiated on an item that has already been produced. By indicating that it is in some way insufficient and requires re-doing or fixing, speakers can present themselves as someone who would attend to this type of detail. One nice demonstration of this is cited by Jefferson (1974) from legal proceedings in a traffic court (see also Online-Chapter E §5.2):

(3.9)   "Traffic court" (Jefferson 1974:189)
```
Barrows:   Well? according to thuh- - thee officer...
```

By initially using the form *thuh* of the English article, with a low back vowel, the speaker projects that s/he is going to say a word beginning with a consonant, in this context, for instance, *cop*. But by then replacing *thuh* with *thee*, using a high front vowel, the speaker indicates that a word beginning with a vowel, here *officer*, would be more suitable. In other words, the speaker makes inferrable that s/he is the kind of person who would normally use the item *cop* to refer to members of the police, but that in deference to the court this word is being held back and the word *officer* chosen instead.

Self-repair can thus be closely connected to issues of self-presentation. It can also exhibit sources of trouble with speaker epistemic authority and responsibility. Lerner and Kitzinger (2007) show, for instance, how a speaker's repair of reference to herself from, for example, individual self-reference with "I" to collective self-reference with "we", or vice versa, can be guided by considerations of recipient design and the action to be accomplished. Here is an example in which Dina is telling her friend Bea about a multi-car accident she and her friend saw the day before:

(3.10)   "Awful wreck" (Lerner and Kitzinger 2007:541) (adapted)
```
5      Din:    t hhh En on the way ho:me we sa:w the: (0.5) most gosh
6              u-awful WRE:ck
7      Bea:    Oh↓:::.
8              (0.4)
9 ->   Din:    we have e- (.) I've ever seen. I've never seen a ca:r
10             smashed into
11     Bea:    Mm
12     Din:    such a sma:ll spa:ce.
13     Bea:    °Oh:::.°
```

In line 9 Dina self-repairs her initial formulation *we have e-*, replacing it with *I've e(ver seen)*. As Lerner and Kitzinger explain, *we* is quite appropriate for the description of something that anyone could see and report, but it is not appropriate if Dina is assessing the situation in relation to all other situations she has experienced in her life. This is arguably what motivates her self-repair to *I* (line 9).

As such examples illustrate, repair may be exploited for the purpose of adjusting one's wording to matters of acceptability, or of pursuing agreement and intersubjectivity in interaction. Especially in cases when repair does not address the correction of factual error, self-repairs can reveal how speakers orient to "the normative connections between turn design and sequence/interaction" (Drew et al. 2013:93), how they work to fit their utterance design to the particular sequential and interactional environment it is being used in (see also Raymond and Heritage 2013).

How is post-positioned repair initiation accomplished linguistically? Often, repair is initiated immediately after the first syllable of the repairable, as in the following example:

(3.11)   "Weekend" (Sidnell 2010:114) (adapted)
```
23     Bev:    .hh (.) >Are=you gonna be at my house at what time on
24             uh Fri:- on Sunday?
```

Here Bev cuts off the word *Fri(day)* after the first syllable (line 24), recycles back to the preposition *on*, and substitutes the word *Sunday*.

Since in post-positioned initiations of repair the repairable has already been produced, its location becomes an interactionally relevant concern. Several tasks are thus involved: the speaker must initiate repair in such a way that the onset of repair can be recognized, that the repairable can be located, that the repair operation or its result can be understood, and that the suspended talk can be resumed with as little disturbance as possible. In the following, we address these tasks one by one. Although the basic structure seems to be similar in all languages, some practices differ cross-linguistically.

2.2.1 Initiation Techniques

One technique that is particularly associated with the post-positioned initiation of repair is the *cut-off* (see also Online-Chapter E §4). Jasperson (2002) argues that especially *closure* cut-off is a highly effective means of initiating same-turn self-repair and reports that closure with a glottal stop is very common. He shows that the articulatory details of closure cut-offs are often conditioned by or adapted to the phonetic environment in which the closure occurs; in this way the articulation of the cut-off can foreshadow what the resumption will be. Here is an example, where the **k-* at the end of line 1 indicates a cut-off with velar closure and anticipates resumption with a word beginning with /k/:

(3.12) "Karen" (Jasperson 2002:263) (adapted)
```
1  M:   = 'Cause who *k-
2         <-Ka:ren might have access,
```

Such "opportunistic" closure cut-off deploys articulators that are convenient for both stopping the next sound due as well as starting the resumption. By blocking the air glottally, the speaker can immediately position the oral articulators such that resumption can be started without intervening non-lexical vocalization. This means that the repair can be executed as quickly as possible (2002:279).

Cut-offs appear to be widely used for this purpose across languages. For Finnish, Laakso and Sorjonen (2010) describe cut-off as a general, non-specifying repair initiation device that may be used in any location. It does not project the kind of repair operation that will follow, or even that there will be repair at all. In consequence, it may initiate any kind of repair operation: replacing something, inserting an element into prior talk, or abandoning an utterance in progress and starting a new TCU. Typically, however, repairs started with cut-off lead to the replacement of a word that belongs to the same syntactic and semantic category, as shown in the following example. (Cut-off is represented here by a hyphen, i.e., "-".)

(3.13) "Telephone conversation" (Laakso and Sorjonen 2010:1155) (adapted)
```
6  Veke:  [No<     ]mä me- me< mennään sinne sunnuntaina
          [PRT     ]I  go  we  go-PAS-4 there.to Sunday-ESS
          [Well<   ]I'll g- we're gonna go there on Sunday
7->       kans jo       niinku Tiinan    mutsi- ee faijaha asuu siel.
          too  already like   Tiina-GEN mum      dad-CLI lives there
          already coz Tiina's mum- er dad y'know lives there.
8  Kake:  Aha, Just.=
          I see, right.=
```

(*Note*: the abbreviation PRT stands for "particle" here.)

At line 7, Veke interrupts the category term *mutsi* ("mum") with a cut-off, uses another repair initiation *ee* as a "search sound," and then replaces *mutsi* with a co-hyponym *faija* ("dad").

In Finnish there is one type of self-repair that is exclusively started with cut-offs: this is insertion repair (see below). Here is an example:

(3.14)   "Telephone conversation" (Laakso and Sorjonen 2010:1156) (adapted)
```
Meeri:   Sit  selvästi n-    oma nimi e päällä ja  se: paljonko haluaa.h
         then clearly  n-    own name  on top  and it    much-Q  wants
```
  Then clearly **n- ((your)) own name** e on top of it and how much you want.

Meeri is giving advice on how to tag a bucket that is to be left with the beekeeper when buying honey. After beginning the projected word with the sound *n* (presumably for *nimi* "name"), she cuts this off, and then inserts the specifying modifier *oma* ("own") before producing the noun *nimi* ("name").

Apart from phonetic cut-off, there are lexical devices for initiating post-positioned self-repair. Jasperson reports that *I mean* is typically used when an initial syntactic construction is abandoned and subsequent talk begins with a new syntactic construction (1998:101).[14] This is the case in the following example, where *I mean* is produced with faster tempo (indicated by > <):

(3.15)   "I mean" (Jasperson 1998:101, cited after Kärkkäinen et al. 2007:342) (adapted)
```
L:  ...We could pa:y the: >I mean< the cushion at the institute
    would- (.) would- (0.1) -duh: g:o up significantly if...
```

Lexical items with a similar function have been documented in other languages, for example, German: *ich mein* ("I mean"), *also* ("so"), *ach* ("oh"), *oder* ("or"), *moment* ("(wait) a sec"), *obwohl* ("although"). Furthermore, items like the following are frequently deployed as editing terms after repair initiation: *wie heißen se noch mal/wie heißt das noch mal* ("how do you call them/it again"), *ach nee* ("oh no"), *nee* ("no") (see Egbert 2009:76).[15]

I mean and other lexical devices for initiating repair in English and German are not reserved for the initiation of repair only. But in Finnish the lexical repair initiator *eiku* has been described as deployed exclusively in the initiation of repair (see also §3 below). To our knowledge, the existence of an *exclusive* device for repair initiation has not been reported for other languages.

---

[14] On the use of *I mean*-prefaced utterances as defensive mechanisms in self-repair see Maynard (2013b).
[15] Although the basic organization of self-repair is identical in English and German, the grammatical structure of German is different from English. This leads to linguistically different repair practices (see Egbert 2009:94–5). (For more details see below.)

2.2.2 Locating the Repairable

One way of locating the repairable is through what Schegloff has called "framing" (see also Sidnell 2010:115). This means essentially repeating some of the material surrounding the repaired item, as in the following examples (the repaired segment has gray shading, the repairing segment is in bold, and the framing material is italicized):

(3.16)   "News service" (Sidnell 2010:115) (adapted)
```
4   A:    that has- that works for a larger news service
```

(3.17)   "Press gallery" (Sidnell 2010:115) (adapted)
```
2-4  Q:   so what has the rest of the press gallery:
5          (.)
6 ->       thought about this.uh done about this
```

Example (3.16) illustrates *pre-framing*: one or more items prior to the repairable are repeated. Example (3.17) shows a case of *post-framing*, where one or more items following the repairable are repeated.

2.2.3 Types of Repairables

The target of post-positioned repair initiation can be anything in the prior talk. It can be of very different sizes, ranging from a single sound or prosodic detail to whole turns and indeed entire arguments that the speaker may wish to re-do. In some languages – for instance, Japanese and Finnish – speakers can even replace one bound morpheme with another (Fox et al. 1996; Kärkkäinen et al. 2007; see below). Repairables need not be faulty in any way; as long as speakers choose to repair, i.e., to replace, expand, or modify a first version, that version is retrospectively understood to have been a repairable.

Schegloff (2009a:384, 403) provides an example of a repair of a seemingly minute detail in the speaker's unit-so-far. Shelley is explaining that she is not dropping out of a trip because her boyfriend is not going, but for another reason:

(3.18)   "Funding" (Schegloff 2009a:403) (adapted)
```
1 ->  S:  So: I mean it's not becuz he's- he's- I mean it's
2 ->      not becuz he:'s not going, it's becuz (0.5) his
3         money's not¿ (0.5) funding me.
4         okay¿
```

In line 1 Shelley begins her turn with two unaccented, cut-off references to her boyfriend (*he's- he's-*). She then recycles to the beginning of the TCU.[16] In the

---

[16] Note that the turn-initial *so* is treated as dispensable in the recycling (see also Schegloff 2004).

repaired TCU *I mean it's not becuz he:'s not going*, she now refers to her boyfriend with an accented *he:'s*. This accentuation conveys narrow focus on the element and suggests a contrast with something else. In the event, this turns out to be: *his money's not funding me* (lines 2–3). Thus here, a repair of accentuation is deployed to convey a repaired focus in the TCU.[17]

> The initiation of post-positioned repair can be accomplished through cut-offs, recycling, or pre-framing the troublesome item, through lexical devices such as English *I mean* or Finnish *eiku* (see below), and/or through explicit formulations of the trouble.

2.3 Repair Operations

Speakers can perform different operations on their talk when engaging in self-repair. Schegloff (2013) identifies and illustrates ten types: replacing (i.e., substituting the repairable by another item), inserting, deleting, searching, parenthesizing, aborting, sequence jumping (aborting a sequence in order to pursue an entirely different one), recycling (repeating items, mostly preceding the repairable), re-formatting (changing the grammatical format of a TCU), and re-ordering (of items in a TCU, or of TCUs in a turn). According to Fox (2013:2), recycling and replacing are the most frequently performed types of self-repair, followed by inserting. Deleting is said to be rare; aborting (beginning a TCU, but then abandoning it in order to begin a new one) also seems to occur less frequently than the other types.

In order to understand why speakers self-interrupt and self-repair, we can look at a study by Wilkinson and Weatherall (2011), who investigate this question in a corpus of British, American, and New Zealand English with reference to the practice of *insertion repair*. Insertion repair is a type of same-TCU repair in which "a speaker stops his/her talk at a point where it cannot be possibly complete (in the middle of a word) in order to go back and add something else into the turn-so-far" (p. 66). Here is an extract to illustrate, with the inserted element in bold face:

(3.19)   "Blind date" (Wilkinson and Weatherall 2011:66)
```
Hyla:   this girl's fixed up on a da- a blind da:te.
```

---

[17] See Sidnell (2010:116) for examples of self-repair which involve stressing and "un-contracting" an auxiliary or copula verb. On "modified repeats" concerned with issues of sociorelational positioning see also Stivers (2005).

Here Hyla interrupts her production of the word *date* in order to insert the word *blind* before it.

Insertions are overwhelmingly single words, mostly adjectives – as in this example – or adverbs such as *only, really, completely,* and *extremely* (pp. 69ff.). In their corpus of more than 500 cases of insertion repair, Wilkinson and Weatherall found that over half of all the instances are carried out in the service of *specifying* a referent, often with an adjective, either to differentiate it from a locally possible alternative referent and thus pre-empt possible misunderstandings, or to achieve a better fit between a formulation and an account or assessment (p. 77). In another quarter of their collection, insertion repair is carried out for *intensifying*, i.e., for reinforcing the meaning of the word(s) modified, often with an adverb, in order to achieve a stronger formulation (p. 80). In the rest of the cases, insertion repair is done for *describing, adjusting,* and *adding* (pp. 83ff.). The authors conclude that "inserting is warranted, in the first instance, by the modification it makes to the talk – i.e., the *repairing* action of specifying, intensifying, etc. This modification, in turn, is generated by, and contributes to, the *interactional* action of the turn (e.g., accounting, providing evidence, justifying, etc.)" (Wilkinson and Weatherall 2011:88–9).

> Repair operations have been found to vary across languages. Even though repair may be initiated anywhere in a TCU or turn, in particular the precise points to which the speaker returns in order to start a repair operation have been shown to differ across languages. Research into repair asks the following questions: How do the specific linguistic structures of languages and language types modify the organization of repair? How is the operation of repair constrained by the syntax and morphology of a given language? How do interaction and grammar shape each other in the domain of post-positioned self-repair?

In the following we first report on some of the findings concerning the syntax and morphology of same-turn self-repair in individual languages, and then discuss some larger-scale studies of cross-linguistic variation.

2.3.1 The Syntax of Self-repair in English

Investigating the organization of same-turn self-repair, Fox and Jasperson (1995) and Fox et al. (1996) found that, after breaking off an utterance, speakers do not return to any arbitrary point in the prior utterance when repairing, but instead they orient to syntactic categories. Here are examples to illustrate this (an asterisk indicates the site at which the repair is initiated):

(3.20)   Domain of recycling (Fox et al. 1996:187 or 206) (adapted)
(i)   J: But it- it does i- it does work out if you have just the common
             dena-* denominator here
(ii)   B: in this building- we finally got a-*.hhh a roo:m today in-
             in the leh- a lecture hall,
(iii) K: Plus once he got- (0.8) some* um (1.3)
             he got some battery acid on: (0.2) on his trunk
             or something.
(iv)   M: Okay, well we could- do it from that angle then, because I don't-*
             I don't really.hh encounter that concept problem
(v)   K: Okay, let's see if- before I go and look at the solution if I can-
       C: Mhm
       K: follo-* if I can break it out here

In example (i), the speaker recycles back to the beginning of the noun which was cut off; in (ii) to the beginning of a noun phrase; in (iii) to the beginning of the clause; in (iv) to the subject of the adverbial subordinate clause; and in (v) to the beginning of the adverbial clause, i.e., to the subordinate clause marker *if*. These examples thus suggest that syntactic categories such as nouns (or words more generally), noun phrases, and clauses – excluding as well as including the subordinate clause marker (or connector more generally) – are relevant to speakers: they take them to be holistic entities to whose beginnings they return in the case of repair. Since the recycling goes back to the beginning of syntactic categories, this implies that speakers orient to syntax for the organization of repair (1996:206). The authors conclude that for English the domain of recycling is either the constituent currently being constructed or the clause it is part of (p. 206).[18]

2.3.2 The Syntax of Self-repair in German

Uhmann (2001, 2006) has investigated a particular kind of repair in everyday German conversations: same-sentence self-repair. To qualify as an instance of this, the repair must be done (i) before a sentence in a TCU has reached syntactic completion, and in such a way that (ii) the syntactic integrity of the sentence under construction is not destroyed by the repair (2001:373).

Uhmann finds that repair in German respects constituent boundaries, like in English, but that rather than recycling back to almost anywhere before the repairable (p. 387), speakers observe a strict scope of recycling, as shown in Figure 3.1.

---

[18] The only exception to this generalization is verb phrases (see Fox et al. 1996:n. 16); for more detail see also Fox and Jasperson (1995) and Chapter 6 §5.

2. Self-initiation of Repair

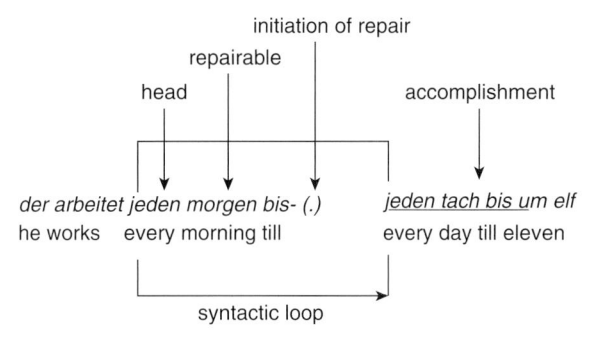

```
                    initiation of repair
           repairable      |
   head       |            |      accomplishment
    |         |            |            |
    ↓         ↓            ↓            ↓
der arbeitet jeden morgen bis- (.)  jeden tach bis um elf
he works    every morning till      every day till eleven
    |_____↑
              syntactic loop
```

Figure 3.1 Uhmann's representation of the scope of recycling (2001:387)

As can be seen here, in order to repair the item *morgen* ("morning"), the speaker does not simply replace the repairable with *tach* ("day"), but instead recycles back to the determiner *jeden* ("every").

Why is this so? Uhmann's claim is that the scope of recycling is constrained by the *functional head* of the phrase with the repairable (2001:373). A functional head is a function word such as an article or preposition that in German precedes the noun in a noun phrase or the prepositional object in a prepositional phrase. According to Uhmann, then, German speakers recycle back to the functional head of the phrase in self-repair: this is the so-called *head rule* (2001:388).[19]

For German, the head rule reportedly works quite well.[20] With relatively free word order, grammatical gender, and a rich case morphology, German requires recycling of larger parts of the utterance than English: i.e., whole phrases (Uhmann 2001:397). For languages such as Japanese with post-positioned heads, on the other hand, the head rule is not expected to work at all; here, repair is likely to be restricted to narrower-scope constituent-internal recycling (2006:196). Uhmann concludes that "same turn self-initiated self-repairs are constrained by language specific syntactic properties (namely functional heads)" (Uhmann 2006:179).[21]

However, Pfeiffer (2010) has examined Uhmann's head rules empirically and found more diversity than these allow. He argues that in addition to syntactic aspects, there is a tendency to recycle back efficiently, i.e., in some cases as little as possible, as in the following example:

---

[19] Special rules apply if the repairable is a functional head itself (see *extended head rule* in Uhmann 2001:392ff.).
[20] In a follow-up study, Uhmann (2006:191) reports that the head rule accounts for 79 percent of her data; the other 21 percent consist of repairs of non-finite verb forms, lexical items, or phonological errors, which are repaired without going back to the functional head of the phrase (pp. 192–3).
[21] See Di Venanzio (2013) for a recent analysis of the role of functional heads in self-repair in German within the theory of the Chomskyan Minimalist Program. She argues that speakers orient to the beginning of the phrase, not the functional head; it is only when the phrase begins with the functional head that the functional head is oriented to.

(3.21)   "Cat toilet" (Pfeiffer 2010:203) (adapted)
```
1   i-mu05:    also [des is einfach zu ZEITaufwendich]
               well that is simply too time-consuming
2   mu05b:          [könn=se höchstens ne ca. (.)   ne] KATze nehmen
                    can you   at most   a               a  cat   take
3                die auf=s KATzenko (.) klo geht
                 who to the cat toiet    toilet goes
                 you can at most take a cat who uses the cat toilet
```

In this example, the speaker intends to produce the prepositional phrase *auf=s KATzenklo* ("to the cat toilet") but omits the sound /l/ from *klo* ("toilet"), mispronouncing the compound noun as *KATzenko*. Yet after a micropause, the speaker does not recycle back to the functional head of the prepositional phrase (the preposition *auf* "to"), but only repairs the second part of the compound noun to *klo*. Pfeiffer surmises that especially in cases of misspeaking, speakers may opt for the fastest and most efficient way to repair the problem and secure comprehensibility. As this kind of repair is not licenced by Uhmann's rules, he concludes that in order to explain recycling, we must take into consideration more factors than just syntax.[22]

Birkner et al. have investigated recycling patterns within prepositional phrases in German and Swedish self-repair (termed "retraction" patterns in their work). They find that there is an even stronger tendency in German than in Swedish to initiate repair early in the prepositional phrase (2012:1431).[23] In both languages, the repair usually involves the production of the noun of the prepositional phrase. In the morphologically more tightly bonded prepositional phrases of German, where prepositions at the beginning of the phrase often project the case marking of the following determiners and nouns, the noun must be anticipated at the latest when choosing the determiner. By contrast, in Swedish, where prepositions and determiners project much less about the noun-to-come, speakers can produce them before deciding which noun to use (p. 1431). Thus, different morpho-syntactic structures within the prepositional phrase lead to different retraction patterns, which in turn suggest different preferences for the initiation of repair as well as for repair operations.

2.3.3 Self-repair in Japanese and Finnish

How is post-positioned self-repair organized in a typologically different language? When comparing the syntax of self-repair in English with that in Japanese, Fox

---

[22] For a more recent analysis of self-repair in German see Pfeiffer (2015).
[23] The locus of break-off tends to correlate with the type of repair: the earlier repair is initiated within the prepositional phrase, the higher the probability for mere repetition of the repairable (e.g., in order to gain time to retrieve the noun due later in the phrase); the later it is initiated, the higher the probability for replacement of the repairable (p. 1431).

et al. (1996) found two significant differences: (i) there is "morphological repair" in Japanese, but not in English, and (ii) the scope of recycling is different in Japanese. Similar findings have been reported for Finnish (Kärkkäinen et al. 2007).

Morphological Repair

In Japanese, certain kinds of morphological repair are possible which are not possible in English. Consider the following example, where the repairable is marked with gray shading:

(3.22) (Fox et al. 1996:202) (adapted)
K: ja   nanji   goro   ni   kuridashi-* soo?
    then   what.time about   OBL   go.out-ADV -COH[24]
    Then about what time (shall we) go out?

Speaker K only replaces the adverbial ending *–shi* by the cohortative ending *-soo*; that means she replaces one bound agglutinating morpheme by another. A process like this is not possible in English, as the following invented example demonstrates: *She looked-* s at the table* (p. 202).

This finding can be accounted for by considering three structural differences between English and Japanese:

i. With respect to the verbal morphology of the two languages, the Japanese verb endings *-shi* and *-soo* are full syllables, each consisting of a consonant and a vowel. English verb endings, by contrast, are typically realized as single consonant sounds (with the exception of *-ing* and *-s* in certain contexts). In other words, they are "unpronounceable" if separated from the word to which they attach (Fox et al. 1996:203). This makes it difficult to use English bound morphemes as independent units in self-repair.

ii. In Japanese, an agglutinating language, each morpheme has a single grammatical meaning (p. 203). By contrast, English inflectional endings often fuse more than one meaning (*-s* in the example above carries the meaning of present tense, third person, and singular).

iii. English verb endings, which mark grammatical agreement, link back to the subject earlier in the clause, whereas in Japanese verbal endings do not function as agreement markers (p. 203).

Fox et al. conclude that in English, verb endings are more tightly "bonded" than in Japanese and thus less able to serve as independent replacements in self-repair (1996:203).

---

[24] Fox et al. describe *-shi* as an "adverbial" inflection, *-soo* as a "cohortative" inflection (1996:202).

A similar kind of morphological repair has been reported for Finnish, another agglutinating language:

(3.23) (Kärkkäinen et al. 2007:345) (adapted)

```
mutta   nyt   selvi-tä-än,              -te-tä-än
but     now   manage-PASS-PERS          CAUSE-PASS-PERS[25]
nämä    marka-t
these   mark-PL
```

but now let us manage, sort out these marks

Here, the speaker initially produces a passive form of the intransitive verb *selvitään* ("to manage"), but then repairs it to the transitive verb form *selvitetään* ("sort out"). The repair is accomplished by inserting the causative morpheme *-te-* after the root of the verb *selvi*, but without recycling the root itself. As in Japanese, Finnish morphemes are often full syllables and have a single grammatical meaning (p. 346).

The Scope of Recycling

In contrast to English, where the domain of recycling can be either the local constituent (word or phrase) or the clause (see above), in Japanese, there is only constituent-internal recycling:

(3.24) (Fox et al. 1996:207) (adapted)

```
M:  tteyuuka koko denwa         kaket-* kakete kite sa,
    I.mean   here telephone ca-  call    come FP
    I mean, (they) ca- called us here,
```

As this example shows, speakers do not recycle back to the beginning of the clause (i.e., they do not say *tteyuuka koko denwa kaket-*, koko denwa kakete kite sa*) but only to the beginning of the noun phrase or verb (here *kaket-* kakete*).

In Finnish too, recycling typically operates within the local constituent: although Finnish is an early projection language, it has very flexible word order and rich agglutinating morphology. Here is an example:

(3.25) (Kärkkäinen et al. 2007:351) (adapted)

```
Doctor:  se syö-mä-ttä oo-t   a-      illa-sta
         it eat-INF-ABE be-SG2 morning? evening-ELA
         it you are without eating ((from)) m- evening onwards
```

Here, in repairing what looks like the word for "morning" to the word for "evening", the speaker backs up to the beginning of the word, not to the beginning

---

[25] In colloquial Finnish, the passive inflection *-taan/-tään* is used for the first-person plural in the present tense. Without an overt subject, this form has an adhortative meaning, i.e., "let us X".

of the clause. However, especially when there is some distance between the repair and the repairable, speakers of Finnish may also recycle to the beginning of the (noun) phrase.

Lexical Initiation Formats and the Type of Repair

Laakso and Sorjonen (2010) show that some lexical repair initiation formats are specialized to project specific kinds of self-repair; in these cases initiation of repair shades into the repair operation itself. One of these is Finnish *eiku*, reserved specifically for the initiation of repair through replacement or abandoning. The first part of this particle is the negation word *ei*, the latter part the connector *ku(n)*, which can have causal, contrastive, or temporal meaning ("as", "when", "while"; 2010:1158). *Eiku* does not occur with insertion repairs; instead, it rejects what precedes and projects an account to be provided by the new word or construction (p. 1158). Here is a case in point:

(3.26)   "Values" (Laakso and Sorjonen 2010:1158) (adapted)

```
1 Doctor:   Alotetaan vaikka nyt näistä     lukemista    mitä tässä nyt sitte
            begin-PAS-4 PRT  now these-ELA value-PL-ELA what here   now then
            Why don't we start off with these values that were

2 ->        on ollu (.) eilen        eikun tossa te- seittemäs päivä.
            is been     yesterday PRT there           seventh  day
            (.) yesterday eikun on the te- seventh.
```

After using the time expression *eilen* "yesterday" (line 2), the speaker produces *eikun* to initiate repair and then replaces the repairable with *tossa te- seittemäs päivä* ("on the te- seventh"). (In this case, the repair itself contains another self-repair, initiated by the cut-off on *te-*.)

There are two further Finnish particles, *tai* and *siis*, that in contrast to *eiku* may initiate repair but are not restricted to repair initiation. *Tai*, which is used to project replacement but at the same time sustains what has been said previously as an alternative, is also used as a connector meaning "or." For initiating repair it needs to be accompanied by another repair marker (pp. 1164–5). *Siis*, which is used to project revision through specification and explanation, is also generally accompanied by another repair initiator.[26]

Laakso and Sorjonen's study thus shows the relevance of different lexical repair initiation formats in Finnish for projecting the kind of repair to follow. To date, a similar division of labor among formats for initiating self-repair has not been attested in other languages.

---

[26] According to the authors, when repair initiations are combined, they follow an order "based on how specifically they project the type of repair operation (replacement, inserting, etc.) that will follow and the way in which they forecast the nature of the forthcoming repair" (Laakso and Sorjonen 2010:1169).

2.3.4 Large-scale Cross-linguistic Studies of Self-repair

Both universal and language-specific principles of self-repair have been explored cross-linguistically by Fox and her colleagues in a large-scale qualitative and quantitative project (see Fox, Maschler, et al. 2009; Fox, Wouk, et al. 2009; Fox and Wouk Forthcoming).

Fox, Maschler, et al. (2009), for instance, report on the morpho-syntactic resources for the organization of same-turn self-repair in English, German, and Hebrew.[27] English and German are closely related Germanic languages, while Hebrew is a genetically quite different Semitic language. Their analysis focuses on three kinds of repair operations: recycle, replacement, and recycle and replacement repairs, as illustrated in the following examples:

(3.27)   Three different repair operations (Fox, Maschler, et al. 2009:248)
(i)   Hey would you like a Trenton::, (.) a Trenton telephone directory
(ii)   and the the moo- thing was the Dark at the Top of the Stairs
(iii)   he's all they were talking about the J- the Niners somehow they started comparing the Niners and the Jets

Example (i) shows a simple recycling; (ii) the simple replacement of a word: what is presumably going to be the word *movie* is replaced with the word *thing*; and (iii) recycling + replacement: the speaker recycles the definite article and replaces the beginning of the name of one team (*Jets*) by the name of the other (*Niners*). The authors find that in all three languages function words are more likely to be recycled, while content words are more likely to be replaced. German, however, has less simple recycling and more replacement than does English or Hebrew (2009:252).

How can self-repair differences between the three languages be explained? Fox, Maschler, et al. relate their findings primarily to word order regularities and morpho-syntactic resources in the respective languages: they claim that word order patterns that have become entrenched through frequent usage – as well as morphological bonding patterns within constituents, for example, agreement in number, gender, and/or case – shape self-repair practices (p. 246 et passim).

To give an example of their reasoning: why are subject pronouns recycled in English more often than in German or Hebrew? Here are two examples:

(3.28)   "It was" (Fox, Maschler, et al. 2009:258) (adapted)
         but it was-* (.) it was bad

(3.29)   "You're like" (Fox, Maschler, et al. 2009:258) (adapted)
         You're li-* you're like o- o- operating in terms of a m- of a slightly more organized life, than you might

---

[27] For details on data collection and coding for the quantitative analysis see pp. 249ff.

2. Self-initiation of Repair

It appears that the following morpho-syntactic regularities of English are responsible (p. 258):

i. English speakers produce an overt subject pronoun in nearly every clause in conversation (in contrast to what happens in other languages).
ii. Subject pronouns always occur at the beginning of utterances (in German they may appear in a range of other locations).
iii. Subject and verb are highly bonded, as the cliticization (attaching) of auxiliaries and copula forms to the subject pronoun reveals (see also Rieger 2003).

Structural regularities such as these make it quite logical for speakers of English to recycle to the subject pronoun more frequently than speakers of other languages.

Fox, Maschler, et al. conclude that it is typological features, rather than genetic closeness, that are responsible for variation in the patterns of self-repair (2009:286). Even closely related languages like English and German may exhibit quite different repair practices. Indeed, although there is no genetic relationship between them, English is found to be much more similar to Hebrew in its self-repair patterns (p. 286).

The findings by Fox, Maschler, et al. (2009) show that the practices of post-positioned repair initiation differ across languages as a result of being shaped by the linguistic structures of the respective language.[28] Their investigations of self-repair allow us insights into grammatical relations as created and maintained by the speakers themselves: self-repair patterns, for instance, reveal the degree of bonding between syntactic categories that speakers consider relevant and attend to.

The morpho-syntactic organization of languages in terms of clausal word order and phrasal structure (pre-positioned versus post-positioned heads, obligatory versus optional realization of constituents, morphological bonding between prepositions and nouns and/or subjects and predicates) shapes, if not determines, the syntax of recycling and replacement in repair operations. Languages appear to differ with respect to whether they reserve lexical items exclusively for the initiation of (particular types of) repair (e.g., Finnish *eiku*) or not.

---

[28] In another study, Fox, Wouk, et al. (2009) present "a cross-linguistic investigation of the site of initiation in same-turn self repair" in seven languages, namely English, Biko (spoken in the Philippines), Sochiapam Chinantec (spoken in Mexico), Finnish, Indonesian, Japanese, and Mandarin Chinese. Sites of repair initiation were found to correlate with repair type (replacement and recycling), word length, and word class. The authors conclude that "there are indeed universal principles at work in shaping site of initiation patterns cross-linguistically" (2009:99).

2.4 Conclusion for Self-initiation of Repair

Self-initiation of repair has been shown to be a highly organized interactional task that features both universal and language-specific practices.

Pre-positioned initiations of repair, for instance in word searches, appear to be similar in many languages and cultures of the world: they reportedly involve sound lengthenings, pauses, as well as delaying devices such as *uh* or *uhm* in English, *äh* or *ähm* in German, and *ano:* ("uhm") or *nanka* ("like") in Japanese, with or without stretching. Apart from this, however, pre-positioned initiations of repair vary according to the linguistic organization of the respective language. In languages with pre-positioned articles/determiners and prepositions, like English and German and to some extent Finnish, these function words can be returned to and recycled in order to postpone production of a next item. In languages with post-positioned, agglutinated morphemes and postpositions like Japanese, this is not possible. Here, a distal demonstrative pronoun like *are* ("that one")/*asoko* ("that place") can be deployed to project that its referent will be provided in a later TCU.

Post-positioned initiations of repair are often implemented by cut-off, but also by trail-off and/or pausing. Patterns of recycling and replacement in same-sentence self-repair have been shown to be related to, and perhaps even determined by, linguistic features such as fixed versus free word order, morpho-syntactic organization (right-headed versus left-headed constituency), and strong versus weak bonding between neighboring words and word classes.

> There is an interdependence between practices of verbal interaction and language structure. On the one hand, the pre- versus post-positioning of the repair initiation results in preferences for the use of delaying devices versus cut-off as initiation techniques. On the other hand, the syntactic structure of languages and language types constrains and shapes the organization of repair, in particular how recycling and replacing are implemented.

3. Other-initiation of Repair

Other-initiation of repair can be followed by either self-repair or other-repair. The latter will be called correction here. We deal with both, starting with other-initiated self-repair.

In other-initiation of repair, the recipient of the turn containing a trouble source locates the trouble, but leaves the repair proper to be carried out by the producer of the trouble source him/herself.[29] Repair initiation in this position is commonly

---

[29] Again, not every repairable is treated as consequential or relevant enough to merit other-initiation of repair. On such "abdicated other-corrections" see Jefferson (2007) and §4.3 below.

referred to as "next-turn repair initiation",[30] but as Schegloff points out, the term "other-initiation" is more appropriate (2000c:211).[31] Benjamin finds that next turn is "the 'first' or 'contiguous' opportunity for other-initiated repair" (2012:104). Thus, recipients wishing to take the *first* opportunity to other-initiate repair do so at the possible completion of the TCU in which the trouble source occurred.

In this section, we report on research dealing with formats for other-initiation of repair, typically in next turn after the trouble source. The basic questions for the recipient here relate to how to design repair initiation so that the speaker of the trouble-source turn will be able to (a) locate the repairable item or issue (What needs to be repaired?), and (b) know or infer what the trouble is (How should it be repaired?). In other words, other-initiators have a twofold task: (a) *locating the trouble source or repairable*, and (b) *categorizing* (Selting 1987a, 1987b, 1988, 1995a, 1996b), *diagnosing* (Svennevig 2008), or *delimiting the trouble* (see also Robinson and Kevoe-Feldman 2010:232ff.). Note that categorizing does not mean that a problem categorization displayed as such by the repair initiator need be accepted by the repairer. The repairer can go along with a repair initiator's categorization or not (see below). The final categorization of the trouble is always worked out by the participants in the context of their interaction.

Other-initiated self-repair is accomplished through what has been called a "retro-sequence" (Schegloff 2007a:217). Its first pair part, the initiation, locates something in prior talk as a trouble source. The initiation places a constraint on the co-participant to provide a response in next turn – the repair proper, constituting the second pair part of a sequence. Other-initiation of repair halts the progressivity of the ongoing activity in order to remedy problems of hearing, understanding, or accepting the trouble source (see also Benjamin and Mazeland 2013:2).[32] In the repair initiation, the repairable can be located through one of several means: repetition, replacement with a question word, rephrasing as a candidate understanding, re-formulation, etc. Normally, the repair sequence is completed when the participants resume suspended topical talk: this implies that the problem has been resolved. Alternatively, the repair sequence may be closed with a receipt of the repair proper through tokens such as *oh* in English, and *ach* ("oh") or *achso* ("oh I see") in German (see Golato and Betz 2008).[33]

---

[30] The precise term in the literature is usually "next-turn repair initiator". But we will refer to "next-turn repair initiation" in order to reserve the term "initiator" for the participant initiating repair.

[31] The reason for this is as follows: "The term 'next-turn repair initiation' incorporates the positioning of these repair initiations – and the trajectory they set off – into their very name, and thereby into a kind of conceptual stipulation to their 'essential' or defining criteria. But occurrence in next turn need not be a defining criterion; it can be treated as an empirical contingency" (Schegloff 2000c:211).

[32] Research has concentrated on verbal and vocal means of repair, but of course repair can also be initiated with visible means, e.g., furrowed eyebrows. See Kaukomaa et al. (2014).

[33] The sequential and epistemic conditions which occasion such explicit closing of the repair sequence need further investigation.

3.1 Conceptualizing Other-initiated Repair

The view in CA is that other-initiation techniques only locate the source of the trouble but do not say anything about its nature (Sidnell 2010:117; see also Schegloff, e.g., 2000c:212, 2007a:101). More recently, however, researchers have argued that the formats of other-initiation imply a construal, diagnosis, or categorization of the trouble source, inviting specific ways of repairing it. In the following we review the different proposals for a typology of repair initiations.

3.1.1 Preference for Stronger over Weaker Other-initiations

Schegloff et al. describe a "natural ordering" of repair initiation formats in terms of their ability to locate the repairable. They identify a preference for stronger over weaker initiations, "stronger" meaning "able to identify the trouble source more precisely" (1977:369). Evidence for this comes from several observations. First, weaker other-initiations, when self-interrupted, are replaced by stronger ones. Second, if more than one other-initiation is needed, they are deployed in order of increasing strength (for examples see 1977:369, n. 15). Svennevig (2008:334ff.) provides an overview of studies whose findings support this view concerning the preference structure of other-initiations.

How do other-initiations rank according to strength? Sidnell presents a scale of forms based on relative power to locate the repairable (2010:117). At one end of the scale, there are what Drew (1997) has called "open-class initiators" such as *what?*, *huh?*, and *hm?*, indicating only that the recipient has detected a trouble source in the previous turn but without locating it more specifically. Category-specific question words such as *who?*, *where?*, and *when?* are classified as more specific, because they indicate the part of speech that is repairable. At the other end of the scale, there are understanding checks with *you mean* plus a re-formulation of the repairable proffered for confirmation or rejection. Of course, these practices may be combined, as in partial repeats with a question word, for example, *you went where?* (Schegloff 1997a:505). Sidnell's representation of the strength scale is shown in Figure 3.2.[34]

Open-class → Wh-word → Repeat + Wh-word → Repeat → Understanding check

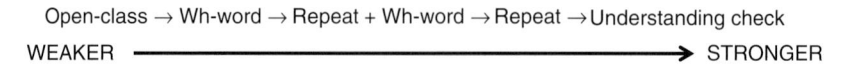

WEAKER ━━━━━━━━━━━━━━━━━━━━━━━━━━━━━━━━━▶ STRONGER

Figure 3.2 Sidnell's typology of other-initiation forms (2010:118)

---

[34] For recent analyses of repair in English conversation that follow this approach see Benjamin (2013) and Kendrick (2015); for Lao see Enfield (2015), and for Siwu, a Kwa language spoken in eastern Ghana, see Dingemanse (2015). The types of other-initiation of repair can, of course, be presented in reverse order, moving from the strongest to the weakest device in locating the trouble, as suggested by Schegloff et al. (1977): (i) understanding check, (ii) partial repeat of the trouble source, (iii) partial repeat with question word, (iv) question word, (v) non-specified trouble/open-class repair initiation.

Robinson and Kevoe-Feldman refine this systematization of repair formats according to the *size of the repairable* (2010:233). Their grouping is as follows:

i. practices for locating *an entire action as the repairable*: open-class repair initiations and full repeats of prior actions, especially questions; versus
ii. practices for locating *some part of an action as the repairable*: other-initiations of repair including question words (*wh*-words or their equivalents in other languages) and partial repeats of the problematic prior turn.

In addition, the authors group repair formats as *practices for delimiting the nature of trouble* (Robinson and Kevoe-Feldman 2010:233–4). Here they distinguish between:

i. open-class repair initiations (prosodically unmarked), by which no type of trouble is ruled out;
ii. *What do you mean?* (prosodically unmarked), by which the problem is delimited as prima facie involving understanding, not hearing or accepting; and
iii. full repeat, which suggests that the trouble is not a hearing problem nor the understanding that a question has been asked, but rather a problem with the entire prior TCU, and thus the entire action.

Yet the aforementioned systematizations of other-initiated repair types according to initiation format (be it through *form* (*wh*-word, repeat) or a *mixture of form and function* (open-class, understanding check)) lead to a problem: despite what may at first appear to be correspondences between form and function, researchers soon come across cases in which a given form is treated as fulfilling another function. Thus, for instance, Drew (1997) found that even though in many cases repair initiations such as *huh?* or *what?* indicate problems of hearing and are responded to with some kind of repetition, they are also responded to with other kinds of repairs, for example clarifications of implicit references. This would seem to compel the conclusion that *huh?* and *what?* are all-purpose initiations that can be responded to with any kind of repair operation. Advocating this view, Schegloff warns that "there do not seem to be systematic relationships between the types of trouble source and the form taken by repairs addressed to them" (1987c:216).

If this warning is meant to caution us that the way repair initiators present or publicly display the problem need not correspond to the "real" problem they have, or in Drew's terms to their "actual cognitive states" (1997:97), we can only agree. With CA methodology it is only possible to reconstruct what is transparent or at least alluded to through observable behavior in the public record of interaction; we cannot handle the question of what participants "really" think or feel. However, if the surface forms of repair initiation are related to how they are overwhelmingly treated through the repair provided, systematic relationships can be identified between type of initiation and type of repair. This is not to say that the problem categorized by the repair initiator always gets dealt with as such by the repairer. The repairer may choose to categorize the problem differently from the initiator, thus **re**-categorizing it. For instance, the repairer can treat the problem as less severe than the initiator suggests, testing whether the repair provided is enough to resolve it; or the repairer can treat the problem as more severe than the initiator suggests and thus pre-empt the need for further repair later. Such exploitation, however, presupposes that (a) there is *prima facie* a systematic relation between repair initiation and repair proper, and (b) there is evidence of a recurrent direction or ordering both in successive initiations of repair and in **re**-categorizations of trouble sources. Such orderings can reveal underlying "preferences" according to which the types of repair and their trouble sources fall on a scale extending from less severe to more severe.[35] The second systematization advocated in the literature is based on this kind of reasoning.

3.1.2 Preference for Less Severe over More Severe Types of Repair

A "preference" among types of repair was first observed by Pomerantz (1984b). She argued that when working on problems of understanding, "a speaker may *try an easy solution first*", or in other words: "try the least complicated and costly remedy first" (p. 156). Such an ordering of repair initiations has been identified and described more systematically in a number of different languages.

Using a corpus of German talk in institutional contexts, Selting (1987a, 1987b) found evidence for a preference hierarchy, according to which it is *preferred* to initiate repair for a less severe or serious problem over a more severe or serious problem. The preference hierarchy specifies that problems of hearing (acoustic problems) are preferred over problems of reference recognition, which are preferred over problems of understanding the meaning of linguistic items, which are preferred over problems of expectation, which are again preferred over more global and severe problems of interaction, including disagreement.

Similarly, on the basis of Norwegian data, Svennevig finds evidence for "a preference for trying the least serious (complicated, sensitive) solution first, that is, addressing problems as hearing problems over addressing them as problems of understanding or acceptability" (2008:333). Svennevig distinguishes between problems of hearing, problems of understanding, and problems of acceptability (as linguistically acceptable and/or acceptable as a social action); his ordering of these problems from treated-as-least-serious to treated-as-most-serious is the same as that found in the German institutional data.

---

[35] The severity of a trouble and its repair can be gauged with respect to, e.g., the progressivity of the interaction or the face-saving needs of the interactants.

Evidence for such a preference hierarchy comes from the following observations:[36]

i. In trying to fix a problem, initiators first initiate repair for a less severe type of trouble, and – if this does not solve the problem – only then initiate repair for a more severe type (Selting 1987a, 1987b; Svennevig 2008:341).

ii. Repairers, if they do not repair the problem as made relevant by the repair initiation, also first treat the trouble as less severe, and only if this does not solve the problem then treat it as more severe. If the repair initiator is not satisfied with the repairer's treatment of the problem as a less severe one, s/he may initiate repair again, thus insisting on her/his original categorization of the trouble. If, on the other hand, the repairer realizes that s/he indeed "really" only had a less severe problem, s/he can indicate this "change of state" in German by explicitly closing the repair sequence with *ach so* ("oh yes") or an equivalent (Selting 1987a:122–3; Golato and Betz 2008).

iii. In comparison to the **re**-categorization of problem types from less severe to more severe, **re**-categorizations in the opposite direction were found to occur only very rarely. The latter cases, when they occur, can be explained by the repairer anticipating that the problem is really more severe and pre-empting the initiation of repair for a more severe problem, thus sparing the initiator the need to do this her/himself later (see Selting 1987a, 1987b; Svennevig 2008). Both repair initiators and repairers can thus be seen to orient to a preference hierarchy according to which less severe types of repair/problems are preferred over more severe types. This preference hierarchy can presumably be accounted for by reference to participants' desire to save face (Goffman 1967).[37]

iv. Hearing repair is initiated frequently, but direct initiations of repair for problems of understanding and acceptability are much less frequent (Svennevig 2008:345).

Svennevig reports that in dealing with problems of hearing and understanding, repairers in his data tend to present repair solutions, but in dealing with problems of acceptability, they are more likely to merely indicate the nature of the problem. By way of explanation, he points to the fact that responsibility is assigned

---

[36] Note that in contrast to the binary distinction between preferred versus dispreferred turn formats and/or actions known from CA research, the notion of preference here is a non-binary one: types of repair are ranked as more or less preferred in relation to other types. The preference hierarchy is evidenced by the participants' treatment of the trouble source (see also Online-Chapter B on preference).

[37] See also Schegloff (2007a:151) and Sidnell (2010:121–2) on the use of repair initiations suggesting hearing trouble before other moves in the context of emerging disalignment and disaffiliation. Kim (1993) makes similar observations for Korean; for related findings in the context of native/non-native speaker interactions see also Mazeland and Zaman-Zadeh (2004). For a discussion of selection principles in the other-initiation of repair see also Egbert (2017).

differently depending on the nature of the trouble source: while initiators of hearing and understanding repair attribute the problem to themselves (they have failed to hear or understand), initiators of acceptability repair attribute the problem to the trouble-source speaker (who has said something wrong or inappropriate) (Svennevig 2008:338–9; see also Robinson 2006).

The systematization of other-initiation in these latter approaches is formulated as starting from the *action* or *function*, i.e., the initiation of repair for a *problem type*, not from the initiation forms. We will follow this approach in §3.2 of this chapter.[38]

3.1.3 A Multidimensional View of Formats for Other-initiation

On the basis of a cross-linguistic, typological study of formats for the other-initiation of conversational repair in eleven languages, Dingemanse et al. (2014) find striking similarities not only in the single forms used but also in the inventories of initiation formats documented.[39] The authors make the distinctions shown in Figure 3.3:

Formats for OIR

Open repair initiation formats

- interjections *huh?* (with Q-int.)
- question words *what?*
- apology-based formats *sorry?* German *bitte?*

Restricted repair initiation formats

formats involving content Q-words
who? (hearing)
German *was?* (hearing)
vs.
German *was.* (reference)
Murrinh-Patha *thanggugu.*
(with spec. reference particle in Australian lg.; see pp. 17ff.)

formats employing repetition

trouble-framing repeats
repeat + *slot*
(= Q-word, candidate understanding, recognizable incompleteness or trouble-presenting repeat) (cf. p. 25)

trouble-presenting repeats
without *slot*
(= presenting the trouble)
(cf. p. 25)

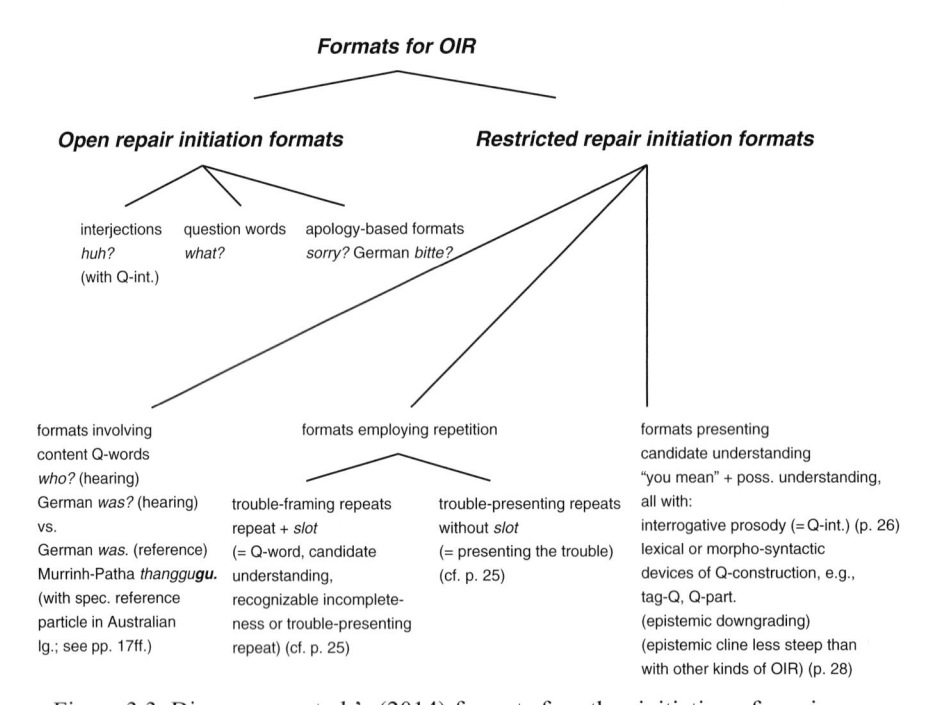

formats presenting candidate understanding
"you mean" + poss. understanding, all with:
interrogative prosody (= Q-int.) (p. 26)
lexical or morpho-syntactic devices of Q-construction, e.g., tag-Q, Q-part.
(epistemic downgrading)
(epistemic cline less steep than with other kinds of OIR) (p. 28)

Figure 3.3 Dingemanse et al.'s (2014) formats for other-initiation of repair

---

[38] Especially for cross-lingustic studies, it has been pointed out that describing and comparing *functions* of utterances, i.e., *actions* across languages, is preferable to comparing and translating utterance forms (see Egbert et al. on repairing reference in English and German (2009:131)).
[39] See also Dingemanse and Enfield (2015) and Dingemanse et al. (2015).

Dingemanse et al. (2014) propose a new multidimensional view of the other-initiation of repair. According to this view there are three main underlying concerns that are relevant for the selection of initiation format and that therefore explain the similarities across languages:

i. capacity to locate and characterize the trouble;
ii. implications for managing responsibility; and
iii. handling of knowledge or epistemic status. (pp. 32–3)

An overview of the initiation formats they distinguish and what these formats imply about trouble, responsibility, and knowledge is presented in Table 3.1.

Dingemanse et al.'s survey shows that the dimensions guiding the selection of repair initiation formats are more complex than hitherto described.[40] Moreover, it

Table 3.1 *Some types of formats and their implications about trouble, responsibility, and knowledge (from Dingemanse et al. 2014:34)*

	Trouble	Responsibility	Knowledge
Huh?	Claims but does not locate or characterize trouble.	No on-record position on responsibility (but A's responsibility is implied).	Claims no knowledge.
Sorry?	Claims but does not locate or characterize trouble.	On-record claim of B's responsibility.	Claims no knowledge.
Trouble-presenting repeat	Claims and locates trouble; characterizes it as higher up Austin/Clark ladder than hearing.	No on-record position on responsibility.	Displays knowledge of what was heard but professes lack of knowledge as to how to interpret it.
Who?	Claims, locates, and characterizes trouble.	No on-record position on responsibility.	Displays that a person reference was heard; claims that it was insufficient to achieve recognition.
Candidate understanding	Claims, locates, and characterizes trouble.	No on-record position on responsibility for trouble, but takes responsibility for solution.	Displays an interpretation of something thereby entailed to have been heard.

---

[40] Their analysis does not take the repair operation following it into account and thus cannot deal with "preferences" like the ones described in the previous section.

sheds light on general principles that single-language studies have not been able to capture. For instance, the authors point out that the prosody of interjections used as initiations of open repair, i.e., items such as *huh?* in English, seems to be connected to the prosody associated with questioning or interrogativity in the respective language. In many languages, these repair initiation formats are delivered with final rising pitch, for instance, *huh?* in English and *Aa?* ("huh") in the Northern Australian language Murrinh-Patha (pp. 9–10).[41] In other types of repair initiation, for example, formats employing repetition, languages may instead make use of utterance-final lengthening (p. 24), question particles (pp. 27–8), or question tags (p. 27). But no matter what device is used, Dingemanse et al. (2014:26–7) claim that the markers of interrogativity associated with other-initiation of repair are designed to index the speaker's position as K-minus [K−], i.e., "not in the know" (see also Heritage and Raymond 2005 and Heritage 2013a on epistemics in interaction, and Chapter 4 §2.5).

3.2 Types of Other-initiated Repair

In the following discussion, we will assume that speakers initiating repair deploy specific practices and formats that display or imply their analysis of the problem, thus making relevant a particular kind of repair operation, or problem treatment, in next turn. Research has focused on repair of the following major trouble sources:[42]

  i. problems of hearing;
 ii. problems of reference;
iii. problems of understanding; and
 iv. problems of expectation or acceptability.

In general, the format of repair initiation chosen by the repair initiator implies that the trouble belongs to one of these categories – at least on the surface. Likewise, the specific repair operation or problem treatment by the repairing party implies that the problem has been categorized in one of these ways – at least on the surface. In most cases, the categorization of the trouble by repair initiator and repairer will match, although contingencies cannot be excluded.

Of course, repair initiations are *displays* only. The problem that is first displayed may not be the "real" problem or even the one that later surfaces in the interaction. Repair initiation techniques are deployed as a resource. Furthermore, the relation between the repair initiation and the repair operation is one of *relevance*; it is not

---

[41] By contrast, in languages where falling intonation is preferred for questions (e.g., Icelandic and Cha'palaa), the interjections for open-class repair also have falling pitch (p. 11).
[42] There is – in principle – an abundance of possible problem types that may need to be worked out in interaction (see, e.g., Selting (1987a) on local problems versus global problems). The ones listed here, however, have figured most prominently in the literature.

a compulsory one-to-one relation. Recipients of the repair initiation may decide that the problem is "in reality" a different one. Thus, the handling of the trouble and its repair is a matter of negotiation between the participants in the interaction.[43]

The specific verbal and prosodic design of the repair initiation is deployed distinctively to locate and categorize the trouble source for the recipient. Our discussion starts with the treated-as-least-severe types of repair and proceeds to the treated-as-more-severe types. In most cases, our examples come from English and German conversation. Where similar practices are found, these languages will be used interchangeably for illustration. Where the languages differ, this will be stated explicitly. Research permitting, we will also include examples from other languages.[44]

3.2.1 Problems of Hearing (and Open-class Repair Initiations)

When displaying a problem as one of hearing, speakers imply that it is only the acoustic decoding that momentarily went wrong, and that nothing more serious is involved – even if it later turns out that this is not the case. Candidate hearings can be used to confirm acoustic decoding or "auditory impressions".

Participants distinguish between where the hearing problem lies in the prior turn (localization) and what its specific nature is (specification).

Implying Non-localized and Unspecified Problems of Hearing

A problem of hearing is *non-localized* if the repair initiation does not indicate where exactly in the prior turn the trouble source occurred, and *unspecified* if it does not indicate what kind of item the problem of hearing pertains to, for instance, whether it is reference to a person, place, or thing. Initiating repair for an unspecified problem of hearing implies that the entire prior turn or TCU was not heard.

Initiation
Three types of "open" formats for the other-initiation of repair have been distinguished in the literature (see, e.g., Robinson (2006) and Dingemanse et al. (2014)):[45]

---

[43] Both the kinds of repair initiation and the relevant repair operations can also be a vehicle for achieving other goals in interaction, from gaining time to exposing the co-participant as ignorant of something. On the specific adaptation and deployment of other-initiated repair in multi-person conversation see Egbert (1997). On practices of other-initiated self-repair that suggest membership categorization as the relevant issue see Egbert (2004).
[44] The differences between languages may be subtle. With respect to English and Korean, Kim shows that even though the repair initiation and operation formats, which, taken together, he calls the *modus operandi* of other-initiated repair, are basically the same, "the two languages may differ in terms of the degrees to which they constrain (or allow) 'opaqueness' of the trouble-source" (1999b:166).
[45] See also Egbert (1996:600) and Egbert et al. (2009:107), who give German examples including the repair initiation formats *häh?* ("huh?"), *hm?*, *wa:s?* ("what?"), *wa?* ("wha?"), and *bitte?* ("pardon?"), all with rising pitch.

i. Interjections like English *huh?*; German *he?*, *häh?* or *hm?*; or Northern Australian Murrinh-Patha *Aa?*.⁴⁶ Such interjections are described as short, all-purpose repair initiation formats. They are remarkably similar across languages: Enfield et al. (2013) found that speakers in all the twenty languages examined made use of a monosyllabic interjection with an open non-back vowel for this purpose. Typically, it is nasalized, has rising intonation, and has an onset with [h].
ii. Question words like English *what?*; German *was?* or non-standard *wa?* or *wat?*; or Korean *mwe?* (see also Kim 1999b), in many languages with rising intonation, but also a morpho-syntactically bare form such as Murrinh-Patha *thanggu* "what", where intonation does not seem to play a role.
iii. Formulaic and apology-based forms such as English *sorry?*, French *pardon?*, or German *bitte?* (lit. "please"), used for the management of responsibility and face-work. In contrast to *what?* and *huh?*, which suggest that the speaker of the trouble source is responsible for the trouble, with *sorry?* or *pardon?* speakers initiating repair imply that they themselves are responsible for the trouble. German *bitte?* is generally linked to the expression of courtesy and politeness in the language (pp. 15–16). These formats are relatively rare in informal interaction, but more common in institutional and other forms of asymmetrical interaction.

The German token, *bitte?* "pardon?", has been thoroughly investigated by Egbert (1996). She claims that, in her materials, *bitte?* is used differently from other repair-initiating tokens: in telephone data, occurrences of *hm?* and *was?* were very rare, while *bitte?* was used frequently (in 40 out of 47 cases); in data with co-present interlocutors, however, *hm?* and *was?* were deployed with about the same frequency, while *bitte?* was used only seldomly (7 out of 50 cases). Egbert's explanation for this is that in co-present interaction *bitte?* is found when there is no mutual gaze between interlocutors: it thus not only initiates repair but also seeks establishment of mutual gaze. However, Dingemanse et al. (2014:16–17) reinterpret Egbert's findings by suggesting that lack of gaze implies a temporary lack of engagement in furthering the progressivity of the conversational project and that the polite form *bitte?* is assuming accountability for the disruption.

Apart from these short forms, there are also more elaborate formats for displaying a problem of hearing. In cases where the problem of hearing results from great distance or bad transmission and the trouble source extends to longer stretches of talk, more explicit repair initations have been observed, such as: *ich hab nich verstanden was sie gesacht habm* "I didn't understand what you were saying"

---

⁴⁶ For Norwegian, Svennevig (2008) mentions the formats *Hæ?* ("Huh?") and *Hva?* ("What?") (pp. 340, 343). For Icelandic see Gisladottir (2015).

3. Other-initiation of Repair 149

(Selting 1987b:132) or °*.hh eh, ich versteh sie kaum*° "uh I (can) hardly hear you" (Egbert 2009:99). These repair initiations take the form of declarative statements with final falling pitch.

Invited Treatment by Repairer

In most cases, formats for initiating repair for a problem of hearing are responded to with a repetition of the trouble-source turn or part of it by the repairer. This is the treatment that such initiating forms invite (see also Dingemanse et al. 2015:4).

According to Drew, the most typical source of trouble leading to "open-class" repair initiation is overlapping talk: this can result in participants not hearing each other (1997:94). Here is the relevant part of the example Drew uses to illustrate:

(3.30)   "Sorry?" (Drew 1997:94) (adapted)
```
1    Mark:     Uh:m Lesley's been teaching the whole of this yea:r?.hhhh
2              Uh::: she went in to do uh:: uh a couple of weeks: for uh:::.hh
3              teacher who had s- back trouble 'n: this teacher had such seve:re
4              trouble that she finished up h.hhhh uh:m she's only- she's (0.4)
5              gonna stop hh (.) eeyuh e-the end of this::: uh m:o:nth.h.hhh
6              [hhhh
7    Lesley:   [Well tell her I may not b[e able to come cz there's so much to do at
8    Dwayne:                             [Oh what from t a k i n g over from her
9    Dwayne:   [(     )o r w h at.
10   Lesley:   [s c h o o :l. To the wedding.=
11   Mark:     =SORRY?
12   Dwayne:   Is is Lesley taking o:ver from her or what.
```

The point to be made here is this: because of overlap, Mark has arguably not heard what Dwayne said at line 8. This is what Mark's other-initiation of repair *SORRY?* at line 11 is designed to display. As is typical in such cases, the speaker of the trouble-source turn, here Dwayne, repeats the relevant part of the trouble-source turn, also making explicit the reference to Lesley, who is present in the room but not speaking on the phone.

But trouble in hearing need not stem from overlap. In the following examples, *huh?* and *what?* are deployed to target a problem with the entire prior turn, although it was delivered in the clear:

(3.31)   "Huh?" (Schegloff et al. 1977:367) (adapted)
```
1      D:   Wul did'e ever get married 'r anything?
2 ->   C:   Hu:h?
3      D:   Did she ever get married?
4      C:   I have no idea.
```

(3.32)   "What?" (Schegloff 1997a:515) (adapted)
```
2        Bonnie:   A:nd (3.0) okay do you think you could come? pretty much
3                  for sure?
4 ->     Marina:   What?
5        Bonnie:   Do you think you could come pretty much for sure?
6        Marina:   Sure.
```

As these examples show, repair initiations like *huh?*, *sorry?*, *what?*, or *eh?* are routinely repaired by the trouble-source speaker delivering a repetition of the entire trouble-source turn, or of those parts that are judged relevant. Both the party initiating repair and the repairer seem to assume that for the solution of the problem a simple repetition of the trouble source is sufficient. In most cases, the repair is initiated in a straightforward manner. This kind of repair is treated as utterly unproblematic.

Often repetitions of the trouble source are not fully identical to it. Schegloff (2004) found that the following elements may be treated as dispensable and therefore left out in the repair (p. 140):

i. discrete turn-initial markers of various sorts, for example, address terms, discourse markers (*well*, *okay*), connectors (*and*, *but*), etc.;
ii. discrete turn-final markers of various sorts, for example, address terms, courtesy terms (*please*), extensions like *or x*, epistemic downgrades (*I guess*), tag questions (*don't you*, *uh?*); and
iii. early positioned constituents of a turn-initial TCU, including subject terms, auxiliary verbs, etc.

In addition, pro-terms and demonstratives may be replaced by full forms and definite descriptions. Schegloff explains that such alterations in the repair turn not only result from their different position in the sequence but also document an orientation to what is being done in the interaction as a whole (see p. 143).[47]

Curl (2005) looks at the phonetic details of the treated-as-repairable turn as well as the repair itself when initiated by a so-called open-class element (*huh?*, *what?*) in American English telephone calls. She finds that repetition repairs vary according to whether the treated-as-trouble-source turn is fitted to the prior sequential context or disjunct from it. *Fitted* turns are those that prolong an ongoing sequence or begin a new one after the prior sequence has been collaboratively closed down

---

[47] For more examples from English see also Benjamin (2013). In Korean, where *ung?* ("huh?") is used for initiating repair of problems of hearing, the repetition of the trouble source by the repairer may feature changed particles due to the structure of Korean and the meaning of agglutinative particles in the two positions. On subtle changes in repetitions after "open other-initiations of repair" in Lao see Enfield (2015).

3. *Other-initiation of Repair* 151

(p. 8). Here is a case in point, where in line 10 speaker B displays his understanding of what speaker A has just told him:

(3.33)   "Working" (Curl 2005:10) (adapted)
         [fitted trouble-source turn]
```
10 ->  B:   o:h °yeah::° (.) she workin' it
11          (0.8)
12     A:   huh
13 ->  B:   she workin' it
14     A:   so (.) anyway she called me a couple of days
15          before she's gonna come home en
```

After A's prior telling (not shown here), B's display of understanding in line 10 is a fitted turn. Yet it is treated as a trouble source by A in line 12 and then repaired by B in line 13. Curl observes that if repair is initiated following a fitted trouble source, as here, repetition repairs like that in line 13 are phonetically and prosodically *upgraded*: they are louder and have longer durations, an expanded pitch range, as well as long-domain changes to the articulator settings, in relation to the treated-as-trouble-source turns (p. 18) (see also Online-Chapter E §9). Some of these features can be seen in the detailed notation shown below.[48]

(3.34)   "Working" (Curl 2005:17)
         [phonetic details with fitted trouble-source turn]

```
1   B:     o:h °yeah::° (.) she  workin' it
           ʃiwə˞kʰinït˥

2          (0.8)
3   A:     huh


4   B:     she  workin' it
           [no differences in tempo]
              {f          }
           ʃywə˞kʰinït˥
```

"Disjunct" treated-as-trouble-source turns are ones that are inappropriately positioned in relation to the prior talk (pp. 10–11). They lack a link to the prior turn and come across as incoherent. Here is an example where repair is initiated on a disjunct trouble source:

---

[48] {f} represents forte loudness.

152   *Repair*

(3.35)   "You inna bathroom?" (Curl 2005:11)
           [disjunct trouble-source turn]

```
1    A:   yer- you know you said a lot of hurtful
2         things too well god damn it
3         (1.8)
4    A:   I'm sick of gettin' trounced on
5         (0.7)
6 -> B:   you inna bathroom?
7         (0.4)
8    A:   huh?
9 -> B:   you inna bathroom?=
10   A:   =no. I'[m just cookin'] (.) din[ner]
11   B:        [inna   kitchen]        [oh ]
12   A:   .hhhhhhhhh s:o- (.) anyway hhhhh that's:
13        what's new here with: that (.) situation
```

According to Curl, in this kind of sequential environment, repetitions of treated-as-trouble-source turns are prosodically and phonetically *non-upgraded*: they are not louder and they have shorter durations, similar or compressed pitch ranges, and no major differences in articulatory settings compared to the treated-as-trouble-source turns (p. 19). Some of these features can be seen in the detailed notation below:[49]

(3.36)   "You inna bathroom?" (Curl 2005:18)
           [phonetic details with disjunct trouble-source turn]

```
1   B:   you inna bathroom
         jɪnəbætʰum

2        (0.4)
3   A:   huh?

4   B:   you inna bathroom
           {allegro    }
           {p          }
         j{ənə}ʷbætũ
```

Curl notes that prosodic upgrading does not seem to be related to the repair of hearing problems (p. 39). As all of her repairs treat, at least on the surface, possible problems of hearing, and as furthermore the majority of the trouble-source turns in her data that occur in overlap (71 percent) are repaired with the **non**-upgraded

---

[49] {p} indicates piano loudness and {allegro} fast tempo. For acoustic phonetic measurements supporting this analysis see Curl (2005:19) as well as Curl (2004: esp. p. 287).

pattern, upgrading does not seem to be related to the repair of problems of hearing. She concludes that it is the lexico-syntactic repetition that is dealing with the hearing problem, while the prosodic-phonetic design of the repeat addresses the sequential fittedness of the original (p. 41).

The prosody of such repair sequences as a whole has been investigated by Couper-Kuhlen (1993:281ff.), again on the basis of English data. She discusses examples of repair of hearing problems and shows that in these sequences timing and rhythm are deployed to set them off from the prior context. See the following example from a radio phone-in in which the moderator Dave is giving the caller Carol a chance to warm up before she takes a try at a riddle:

(3.37)   "Pardon?" (Couper-Kuhlen 1993:281) (adapted)
```
1     D:   what's your
2                    /next door   /
3                    /neighbours /
4                    /like; by the/
5                    /way.
6->   C:                   /pardon?                  /  (slower)
7->   D:                   /what's 'your next door  /
8                          /neighbours like.         /
9     C:                   /^ /
10                         /fine,
```

In contrast to the faster rhythm before (lines 1–5), starting with the repair initiation in line 6, the participants here establish and maintain a slower rhythm and tempo (*rallentando*) while repair is being carried out: see the repetition of the trouble-source turn in lines 7–8. After the repair, Carol leaves a beat of silence but then responds on the next but one beat to Dave's now repaired question. Couper-Kuhlen found that, in contrast to sequences where other types of other-initiated repair are accomplished with faster rhythm and tempo (*accelerando*), trouble displayed as an acoustic problem is recurrently dealt with through repetition using slower rhythm and tempo (*rallentando*) or a marked increase in loudness and pitch height. She explains this finding by reference to the fact that problems of hearing can be attributed to an insufficiency in the channel and are thus less problematic for a participant's face than, for example, problems of understanding, which are attributable to incompetence or insufficiency on the part of one of the interactants (pp. 283–4).

> Repair for a problem of hearing is conventionally initiated with short forms – interjections such as *huh?*; the question word *what?* or equivalents; politeness or apology-based formulae such as *pardon?* – with final rising pitch in English, German, and many other languages. In languages where questioning or interrogativity is associated with final falling pitch or other specific features, it is these that are used on the initiating forms. Initiation formats for a problem of hearing are routinely responded to with repetitions either of the whole turn or of relevant parts of it. The prosody chosen for the repair of hearing problems often shows some kind of general highlighting or upgrading (in English), but this appears to be restricted to the repair of fitted trouble sources only.

Re-categorizations

This is not to deny that repair initiations implying a problem of hearing are on occasion **not** responded to with a repetition of the trouble source. Here is an example from Schegloff et al. (1977), where the repair reveals that the problem has been re-categorized:

(3.38) "What?" (Schegloff et al. 1977:367)[50] (adapted)
```
1      B:   Oh, I was just gonna say come out and come over here and talk this
2           evening, but if you're going out // you can't very well do that
3      C:   "Talk", you mean get drunk don't you.
4 ->   B:   What?
5      C:   It's Saturday.
```

Although what is called open-class repair initiation is conventionally deployed to elicit a repetition of the trouble source, the recipient need not go along with this categorization. S/he can anticipate that the problem may indeed be another one and thus **re**-categorize the problem type when repairing it. This is what we see happening in (3.38) above.

Sometimes a problem initiated with open-class repair initiation is treated as a problem of hearing but then turns out to be something else:

(3.39) "Al Bifferd" (Sidnell 2010:119) (adapted)
```
36   Jon:      Alright, h en ↑Biffer[d's the:re too:.
37   (Guy):                        [(a-)
38   Guy:      e:h?
39   Jon:      ↑Bifferd is the:re too.
40             (0.4)
41   Guy:      Oh is he?
42   Jon:      You know Al Bifferd?
```

---
[50] The symbol "//" indicates the point at which a current speaker's talk is overlapped by the talk of another, here the talk in line 3.

```
43   Guy:     Ye:ah?
44   Jon:     He lives there too he's gotta place down there too:.=
```

Jon's turn in line 36 is partially overlapped by Guy (line 37), who then initiates repair using *eh?*, suggesting an unspecified problem of hearing. Jon now recycles what he has just said (line 39), but when Guy next delays uptake and appears surprised, Jon addresses another possible source of trouble, i.e., that Guy does not know "Bifferd" (line 42) (p. 120).[51]

This usage of the repair initiation *eh?* can be accounted for by referring to the preference for the initiation of less severe problem types before more severe problem types (see above). Instead of revealing the "real" trouble, Guy first tries to solve his problem by initiating repair for the least severe problem possible. Note that he also does not admit his problem after Jon points to it at line 42. Instead of admitting lack of knowledge, Guy waits for Jon to volunteer the necessary information. This example thus speaks to the use of repair initiation for a problem of hearing as a strategic device when the problem is actually more severe. (For other examples see Schegloff 2001.)

Initiations for Problems of Hearing as Vehicles for Other Actions
Open-class repair initiations can also be used as vehicles for other actions: for instance, by parents to prompt a child's use of politeness markers (for an example, see Drew 1997:95); as a response to topical discontinuities (Drew 1997:78); and as a response to sequentially "problematic" prior turns (Drew 1997:84).[52] In these cases such initiations may, but need not, be responded to with repetitions of the prior turn. Nevertheless, their use is not incompatible with the display of a problem of hearing: they can be designed to accomplish a repetition of the trouble source. With topical discontinuities and problematic prior turns, this type of repair initiation allows the initiator to gain time, without indicating that a more serious problem is at stake.

In general, it should be kept in mind that although the "real" problem that a party initiating repair has (which we seldom have a way of knowing) may not be just one of hearing, it can nevertheless be displayed as such. In Svennevig's words, "hearing repair may work as a 'placeholder,' temporarily suspending the progression of the conversation while the repair initiator considers whether repair of understanding or acceptability needs to be initiated" (2008:347). Only if the treatment of the problem as one of hearing does not resolve the matter does the interlocutor who has initiated repair have call to proceed to initiation for a more serious problem.

---

[51] Sidnell concludes that, consequently, "open-class repair initiators invite the speaker of the trouble-source to monitor their prior talk not necessarily for something that was not heard but, more generally, for something potentially problematic from the recipient's point of view" (2010:121).

[52] Schegloff also points out that *what?*, or *what*, can be used as a response to a summons or a pre-announcement in English. This format, although homophonous with repair initiation for a problem of hearing is, however, not related to repair at all; it is instead a go-ahead allowing the interlocutor to proceed to the action that the prior preliminary has projected. A next turn that repeats the summons or pre-announcement would therefore be wholly inappropriate.

Implying Localized or Specified Problems of Hearing

A *localized* or *specified* problem is one in which the repair initiator indicates where exactly in the prior turn the trouble source was located, or what kind of item the problem of hearing pertains to, for instance to a person, place, or other reference made in the prior turn.

Repairs of localized or specified problems of hearing can be initiated by two formats: either a partial repetition or pronominal re-formulation (localization via pre- or post-framing) plus a *class-specific* or *class-unspecific* question word; or a freestanding class-specific question word pointing to the trouble source (specification). Class-specific question words are, for instance, *who?*, *where?*, *when?*, and *how?*. These are called "class-specific" because they single out specific kinds of items as needing repair (Sidnell 2010:124), namely a person reference (*who*), a place reference (*where*), a time reference (*when*), or a description (*how*). The question word *what* can be used both in a class-unspecific and in a class-specific way. A class-unspecific use of the question word *what* merely replaces the trouble source without indicating what it could have been. In its class-specific use, *what* replaces a particular reference to a thing or an event.

Locating + Replacing the Repairable: Partial Repetition/Pronominalization + Question Word

To indicate a localized problem of hearing, the words up to (pre-framing) or following (post-framing) the trouble source are repeated and the trouble source itself is replaced with a question word. The question word can be either class-unspecific, such as *what* in its merely replacing-the-trouble-source usage, or class-specific, such as *who*, *where*, *when*, and *what*. In the languages in focus here, the repair initiation ends with final rising pitch. This can be seen in the next extract for English, where the question mark after *Met whom* indicates final rising pitch.

(3.40)   "Met whom?" (Schegloff et al. 1977:368)
         [Framing + class-specific question word]
```
1      Bea:     Was last night the first time you met Missiz Kelly?
2               (1.0)
3 ->   Marge:   Met whom?
4      Bea:     Missiz Kelly,
5      Marge:   Yes.
```

Marge's repetition of the verb *met* before the question-word *whom?* with rising intonation locates the repairable. In addition, the class-specific question word *whom* conveys that the repair initiator has understood that the trouble source is a name or another person reference form. In the repair, the trouble source is simply repeated.[53]

But the partial repeat of the material before the trouble source can also take a pronominalized form, and the question word can be the class-unspecific *what*:

(3.41)   "Gwaffs" (Sidnell 2010:125–6) (adapted)
         [Framing + class-unspecific question word]
((Mom has just said that she does not think that Virginia should go to the same parties as her older sister Beth because Beth is eighteen and Virginia is only fourteen.))

```
4      Virginia:   [I KNOW::, BUT
5                  A:LL THE REST OF MY: PEOPLE MY AGE ARE GWAFFS. I
6                  promise.they are si:[ck.
7 ->   Mom:                            [They're what?
8                  (.)
9      Virginia:   GWAFFS.
10     ???:        (    )
```

Mom's pre-framing of *what?* with a partial repeat of Virginia's turn (Sidnell 2010:126) – more specifically, a pronominalized repeat – locates the trouble source as the item replaced by the question word. Virginia understands that Mom's repair initiation does not target *si:ck*, which has not been fully produced when Mom starts, but rather the word *gwaff* used earlier. Mom's repair initiation is treated as having made a specific kind of repair relevant: a repetition of the located trouble source only. In this case, the question word *what* replaces the trouble-source item in a class-unspecific way, simply substituting for the trouble-source item without indicating what it could have been.

In sum, with partial repeats or pronominalizations, the party initiating repair claims that s/he has heard the other parts of the TCU, and understood its nature as an action. With the question word selected, the repair initiator, moreover, either conveys what word class or category expression the trouble source is understood to belong to or else simply replaces the trouble source with class-unspecific *what*. Class-specific question words like *who, where, when, what,* and *how* are deployed to indicate the kind of reference or description that the repair initiator failed to hear. Class-unspecific *what*, as Benjamin (2013:141) points out, "can locate any kind of linguistic object for repair" (nominals, noun phrases, verbs, verb phrases/predicates, full clauses, etc.).

Details of the practice "partial repeat/pronominalization + question word" can vary cross-linguistically. Sidnell (2007b) reports on a format for other-initiation of

---

[53] The same technique is used in German. For examples see, e.g., Selting (1987a:85) and Egbert (1996:599, 2009:116).

hearing repair in Bequian Creole that reflects the structure of yes-no interrogatives in that language (p. 240). As there is no subject-auxiliary inversion in Caribbean creoles, prefacing the repair initiation with *if* is used instead:

(3.42)   "Bequia Carnival" (Sidnell 2007b:240) (adapted)
```
1      Benson:   yu biin hii fu kanival (.) Pat?
                 were you here for Carnival Pat?
2 ->   Pat:      if mi bin wa?
                 if  I  was what?
3      Benson:   Bekwe kanival?
                 Bequia Carnival?
4      Pat:      yeah:
                 yeah
```

Line 2 shows an *if*-prefaced partial repeat, isolating *here for Carnival* as the trouble source. As Sidnell points out, *if*-prefacing in this case indicates that the repair initiator has heard the trouble-source turn as a yes-no interrogative (2007b:240). The trouble source itself is replaced by the question word *wa*, arguably in its class-unspecific usage. The repair initiator has thus understood the syntactic structure as well as the kind of action carried out, but requests repair of the trouble source framed by *mi bin*.

Replacing the Repairable: Class-specific Question Word
Freestanding class-specific question words such as *who?*, *where?*, *when?*, and *how?* in English, and *wer?*, *wo?*, *wann?*, *wie?*, etc. in German, initiate repair of specified problems of hearing. They pinpoint particular kinds of items as needing repair. The question words *what?* in English and *was?* in German have not been observed to be used in this way; their freestanding use is normally taken to initiate repair of an unspecified problem of hearing (see above). In the examples in the literature, the question word invariably has rising intonation.[54] Here is a case in point:

(3.43)   "Chicken dinner" (Schegloff 1997a:517) (adapted)
```
6    Nancy:    He's from New York ri:ght?
7              (0.5)
8    Shane:    Long Island
9    Vivian:   Khhh      ·ha [h
10   Michael:              [Whe:re?
11   Vivian:   ·hhh (·) Long Island hh
12   Shane:    Ye:h.
```

---

[54] For more examples in English see Schegloff et al. (1977:367–8), Sidnell (2010:124), and Benjamin (2013: 72–3); for examples in German see Egbert (2004:1486–7, 2009:100).

The repair initiation *Whe:re?* with final rising pitch (line 10) specifies the place name in line 8 as the trouble source. It is responded to with a repetition of the place name in line 11.

Cross-linguistically, Dingemanse et al. (2014:17–18) note that all of the languages they have studied make use of such question words for the initiation of what they call restricted other-initiation of repair. Most languages distinguish between question words for at least the categories "person" (*who*), "thing" (*what*), and "place" (*where*). While in many languages the question word deployed for initiating specified problems of hearing carries final rising pitch, in languages in which final falling pitch is associated with questioning or interrogativity, it can be falling as well.

> Localized or specified problems of hearing are initiated by (a) partial repeats or pronominalizations that localize the trouble source through pre- and/or post-framing and use a class-specific or class-unspecific question word to replace it, or (b) freestanding class-specific question words. In English and German, these have final rising pitch. Such initiation formats invite the producer of the trouble source to repeat the item specified by the question word.

Re-categorizations

Occasionally, however, after the initiation of repair for a specified problem of hearing, the producer of the trouble source responds with something other than a repetition of the trouble-source item, thus **re**-categorizing the problem. In the following case, Mum after a delay initiates repair for a problem of hearing, but Leslie re-categorizes it as a problem of referential recognition.

(3.44)   "Sarah's sister Janet" (Sidnell 2010:125)
```
1  Leslie:  And um .t (0.4) an' Janet's enga:ged?
2           (0.7)
3  Mum:     Who:?
4           (0.3)
5  Leslie:  Sa:rah's sister Janet.
6  Mum:     ^Good gra:cious!
```

As Sidnell explains, it is Mum's 0.7 second delay in initiating repair with rising *who?* that leads Leslie not to treat Mum's repair initiation as a problem of hearing but to surmise a problem of recognition. The repair operation she carries out is typical for problems of referential recognition: the prior referring expression *Janet* from line 1 is replaced by another reference form *Sarah's sister Janet*, in order to improve recognizability (see below).

Similarly, in the following Low German example, a repair initiation using a question word and rising final pitch in line 2 is responded to not as invited, i.e., as a repair of a problem of hearing, but with repair of a prior reference.

(3.45)   "Wer?" (Egbert 1996:599) (adapted)
```
1  Tina:  in't che- ja dat häff so'n schmalt chesicht.
          in the fa-  yes she has such a small face.
2  Rita:  we:r?
          who:?
3  Tina:  usse anna
          our anna
```

Rita initiates repair for a problem of hearing with respect to the person named as the grammatical subject of the prior turn (the question word corresponding to "who" is in the nominative case, line 2). But Tina, who used only a pro-form typical for reference to a child, namely *dat* "she" (lit. "it", line 1), re-categorizes the problem: she repairs not by repeating the pro-form but by providing the name, *usse anna* "our anna". Her repair operation is typical of referential problems: she replaces the pro-form by a full referential form (see below). (For further examples see Egbert 2009:99ff.)

Proffering Candidate Hearings: Partial Repeats
Hearing checks can be implemented in languages such as English and German by repeating either part or all of the prior turn with rising final pitch: this proffers the repeat as a candidate hearing and invites the recipient to confirm or correct it. In the following extracts, partial repeats of the prior turn with rising final pitch are treated as hearing checks by the recipients:

(3.46)   "Columbia?" (Schegloff et al. 1977:369) (adapted)
```
1      A:  I have a: - cousin teaches there.
2      D:  Where.
3      A:  Uh:, Columbia.
4 ->   D:  Columbia?
5      A:  Uh huh.
```

In line 2, D initiates repair on the referring expression *there* in line 1, whereupon A replaces it with the name *Columbia* in line 3. In line 4, D now initiates a hearing check, repeating the name with final rising pitch, thus inviting A to confirm or correct her hearing.[55] A confirms it in line 5.

---

[55] The fact that it later turns out that she cannot interpret the referent of this item and initiates another repair does not mean that at line 4 she is already initiating referential repair, a more severe problem. As the transcript shows, at line 4 she first tries to solve her problem by *prima facie* checking her hearing, even though this may

In the following German example a candidate hearing is corrected:

(3.47)   "Mealworms" (Egbert 2004:1475–6) (adapted)

```
1   Tina:     habt ihr      schon    n paar me:hlwürme
              have you guys already  a few  flou:r  wor
              have you guys already discovered a few
2             entdeckt?   so kleine?
              discovered? so little?
              mea:l worms? such little ones?
3             (0.5)
4   Ronny:    kame:l [wü:rmer?
              ca:mel [wo:rms?
                     [
5   Tina:          [da-
                   [there-
6   Tina:     [meh:lwürmer
              [mea:lworms
              [
7   Stefan:   [he he he he he

              * Ronny, Ina and Tina smile
8             * KAME::Lwürmer HÖ HÖ HÖ HÖ
              * CA::MELworms HE HE HE HE
9   Stefan:   [((laughing))
              [
10  Kerstin:  [(              )
11  Kerstin:  [ey)
              [
12  Ronny:    [nee das  is (mir)   (mal) n
              [no  that is (to me) (PRT) a
              [no (I made) a
13  Ronny:    hör  fehl[er (      )
              hear mist[ake (     )
              hearing  mist[ake (     )
                           [
14  Bärbel:             [HÄ!
```

Ronny initiates a hearing check in line 4 by repeating the version of the trouble source from line 1 as he heard it, with rising final pitch: *kamelwürmer* "camel

_{already foreshadow the referential problem and give D the opportunity to correct or specify the referential expression in line 3. (See below for a longer version of this example.)}

worms". Tina responds by repeating the correct item *mehlwürmer* "meal worms" at line 6. After some laughter and joking (lines 7–11), Ronny explicitly categorizes his hearing as a mishearing (*hörfehler*) (lines 12–13).

> Proffering candidate hearings as hearing checks is accomplished in English and German with partial or full repeats of the trouble-source turn using final rising pitch. This kind of other-initiation invites the trouble-source speaker to either confirm or correct the hearing.

3.2.2 Problems of Reference

Repair for problems of reference can also be initiated in several ways: with an explicit request for specification, with question-word framing, or with a freestanding question word. The latter two have non-rising final pitch in English and German. Speakers who display their problem as referential imply that it is only the recognition or retrieval of a referent that is momentarily not possible, and that nothing more serious is involved – even if retrospectively this turns out not to be the case.

Explicit Request for Specification

The following extract shows a case of repair initiation that categorizes the problem as one of reference, i.e., recognizing what object or person a word is meant to refer to, and explicitly requests specification. It comes from a conversation between an official (S) and a client (K) in a German communal office:

(3.48)   "Which one do you mean" (Selting 1987a:90) (adapted)
```
4      K:    WO kamma erFAHRN was diese    (--)   diese !BAU! da;
             where can one get to know what this         this building there
5            diese !VOR!bau für das verwaltungsgebäude
             this front building for the administration building
             <<dim> für das neue da;>
                for the new one there
6            <<dim>([was das)> beDEUten soll;
                      what that is supposed to mean
7      S:                  [hm,
8            (--)
9      K:    is das HUNde HUNdezwinger?
             is that a dog dog kennel
10           oder [oder FLAschensammelstelle-
             or      or a collecting point for bottles
11     S:         [((laughs))
```

```
12      K:   oder [SONST was;
             or something else
13 ->   S:        [WAS WELches MEInen se denn jetz;
                   what which one do you mean now
14           diesen
             this one
15           [ah ich
              oh I
16      K:   [ja; wemma [da REIN geht hier;
              well if you go in there
17      S:              [WARten se; ich  ich  HOL  ma
                         wait         I       I'll get
18           ich HOL ma son PLAN.
             I'll get such a map
19      K:   das_s [ja FURCHTbar is das ja; ((brief laughter))
             it's terrible it is
20      S:         [moMENT;
                    wait a moment
```

The client K is referring to a new building attached to the administration building that both he and the official know (lines 4–5); he wants to find out what this new building is going to be used for (lines 4, 6–12). But the official S cannot identify the referent and explicitly asks for a more specific description, in line 13: *WAS WELches MEInen se denn jetz;* ("what which one do you mean now").

Locating Plus Replacing the Repairable: Framing + Class-specific Question Word
Occasionally, in initiations of referential repair, the troublesome item is localized through the framing of a question word, which itself replaces the repairable; the whole is then delivered with falling intonation. Here is an example:

(3.49) "Move what" (Sidnell 2010:128)
```
1         Anne:   ((looks at door)) Maybe Cathy, maybe you can move it,
2 ->      Cathy:  °Move what.°
3         Anne:   Move that thing that ('s in the lock)/(yo- in the door).
4         Cathy:  Okay.
```

In this case, Anne is referring to a jacket hanging on the door handle of a door that Cathy has just tried to close. Initiations like this indicate that the repairer cannot find a referent for a word or expression whose meaning is otherwise quite clear (Sidnell 2010:128). They index as problematic the prior speaker's presupposition that the referent is established and presumably identifiable.

Replacing the Repairable: Freestanding Class-specific Question Word
More frequently, however, referential repair is initiated with freestanding class-specific question words, usually delivered with final falling pitch. The question word typically refers back to a pronominal recognitional referring expression in the prior turn that is treated as underspecified. The class-specific question word deployed indicates the trouble source: *what* points to prior reference to (a) thing(s), *who* to prior reference to a person, *where* to prior reference to a place, etc. The following examples show typical formats for the initiation of repair for a problem of reference as well as the typical repair operations invited by these initiation formats.

Here is an example of a repair-initiating *what*, delivered with final falling intonation, that targets an underspecified reference in the prior turn:

```
(3.50)     "Chicken dinner" (Schegloff 1997a:515) (adapted)
1    Shane:    =Lemme have some (0.2) tonight (.) Lemme hav- cz I ran ou:t.
2              (0.4)
3 -> Michael:  What.
4              (.)
5    Shane:    u-Saline solution gonna get some tomorrow.
```

Michael's *What* in line 3, realized with final falling pitch, addresses the reference to "some" in the prior turn (line 1). It invites the trouble-source speaker to clarify the referent of this indexical referring expression, which Shane now does by replacing it with a co-referential full-form *saline solution* in line 5.[56]

On occasion, repair initiators target repairable referents that do not figure explicitly in the prior turn. For this they use the same set of question words (*who*, *what*, *when*, *where*, etc.) with falling intonation. Here are two examples:

```
(3.51)     "Garage sale" (Schegloff et al. 1977:369 n) (adapted)
1    Ben:     They gotta- a garage sale.
2 -> Ellen:   Where.
3    Ben:     On Third Avenue.
```

```
(3.52)     "Parking place" (Schegloff et al. 1977:369 n)
1    Ava:  I wanted to know if you got a uhm whatchamacallit uhm
2          p(hh)ark(hh)ing place this morning.
3    Bee:  A parking place.
```

---

[56] For another example of *what* with falling pitch, see, e.g., Egbert et al. (2009:116); for examples of *where* with falling pitch, see Schegloff et al. (1977:369). For further examples from English see also Benjamin (2013).

```
4     Ava:    Mm hm
5 ->  Bee:    Where.
6     Ava:    Oh hh just anyplace heh heh I was just kidding you.
```

The question-word tokens in these examples could be said to initiate repair for a problem of reference (here to place) that has been left unspecified in the prior turn.[57]

In German, too, referential repair is frequently initiated with single question words with final falling pitch. According to Egbert et al. (2009), for instance, the repair initiation forms *was denn* and *was*, with non-rising intonation – like English *what* – target a pro-term/indexical expression in a prior turn used to refer to a "thing" (not only a real-world object, but also ideas, properties, etc.) and claim that it is underspecified.[58] The repair operation regularly involves specification with a co-referential full-reference form or full noun phrase (e.g., *die Mappe* "the folder", *die Stadette* "the token") (pp. 104–5 et passim). Evidence for this analysis comes from so-called "doubles" (Schegloff et al. 1977), when *was denn* or *was* is followed by a candidate repair of the trouble source. For example: *was denn. dieser wein hier?* ("what. this wine here?"). With these double formats, where the second item is typically stronger (in the sense of locating the trouble source) than the first, the recipient is invited to confirm or reject the candidate referential repair.[59]

As in English, referential repair can also be initiated with other question words in German:

(3.53)   "That chair has suffered" (Egbert 1996:593 and 2009:167)
```
1  Timo:   boh äj der stu:hl hat aber gelitten.
           wow that cha:ir has suffered.
2          (1.0)
3  Rita:   welcher.
           which one.
4  Timo:   dieser hier
           this one here
```

---

[57] As Schegloff points out, there can be a fine line distinguishing a token of *where* that initiates referential repair (and thereby temporarily halts progressivity) and a token of *where* that forwards a telling, thereby serving progressivity (1997a:516ff.). In the cases cited here, the lack of specification of place in the prior turn could be said to impinge upon understanding, so that an analysis as repair seems warranted.

[58] Yet the practice of initiating referential repair with *what/was* is not wholly identical in English and German. While English falling-pitch *what* can be used both as a repair initiator and as a go-ahead in pre-sequences, German *was* is found only in repair initiation (Egbert et al. 2009:125).

[59] For more German examples see Selting (1987a:93ff. and 1995a:291). For English examples see Egbert et al. (2009:122) and Sidnell (2010:132).

In line 3, with the question word *welcher* and final falling pitch, Rita requests repair of the troublesome reference *der stuhl* "that chair" (line 1). Note that in German, in contrast to English, there is morphological agreement between the repairable *der stuhl* and the repair initiation form *welcher*, as well as between the repair initiation form and the repair *dieser* in line 4. All three are marked for masculine gender, singular number, and nominative case.

In initiating repair for person reference, the question word may be combined with other items. Golato (2013) describes how the German repair initiation formats *wer* ("who"), *welcher X* ("which X"), *was für X* ("what X"), *wer is X* ("who is X"), and *wer is nochmal X* ("who is X again") – all with final falling intonation – differ in terms of indicating what specifically the recipient has understood of a reference and thus what needs to be addressed in the repair operation. In contrast to the first three phrasal formats, which presuppose recognizability of the referent and categorize the problem as one of only temporary retrieval, solvable by providing an alternative or additional reference form, initiations of referential problems with full-clause formats such as falling pitch *wer is X* ("who is X") or *wer is nochmal X* ("who is X again") do not presuppose recognizability but ask for an introduction of the referent. This is more akin to the initiation and treatment of repair for problems of understanding (see §3.2.3 below).

Repair initiation for a problem of reference in English and German can be accomplished by (a) explicitly asking for specification, (b) framing a class-specific question word with falling intonation, or (c) using a freestanding class-specific question word with falling intonation (*what*, *who*, *where*, *when*, etc.).[60] In the repair operation following (b) and (c), the problematic indexical referential expression is typically replaced by an alternative, full-form reference. In this type of repair, the assumption that the interlocutor knows and can recognize the referent is maintained; the problem is treated as one of temporary retrieval, not as lack of knowledge.

Preference for Hearing Check over Referential Repair

Evidence for the preference of a hearing check (*prima facie*) over repair for a problem of reference will be seen from examples like the following:

---

[60] Like all other repair initiation formats, the formats for initiating referential repair can be used as vehicles to achieve something other than repair initiation. For examples see Schegloff (1997a:516ff.). Whether or not such a question construction is designed to initiate repair or to implement some other action becomes clear, according to Schegloff (1997a:519), "most notably by whether or not the preceding turn includes some element of that category which could be its targetted trouble-source." For a recent collection of articles on "Reference and repair" see *Research on Language and Social Interaction* volume 45, issue 2 (2012).

(3.54)   "Columbia" (Schegloff et al. 1977:369) (adapted)
```
1  A:  I have a: - cousin teaches there.
2  D:  Where.
3  A:  Uh:, Columbia.
4  D:  Columbia?
5  A:  Uh huh.
6  D:  You mean Manhattan?
7  A:  No. Uh big university. Isn't that in Columbia?
8  D:  Oh, in Columbia.
9  A:  Yeah.
```

The participants seem to be talking about universities here. After the indexical reference *there* in line 1 has been repaired to *Columbia* in line 3, D now checks her hearing or understanding – or at least this is what the format of her initiation of repair in line 4 and especially its treatment by the recipient in line 5 suggests (see also §3.2.3 below). When her hearing is confirmed (line 5), she initiates repair again, this time with *you mean* plus a candidate location of Columbia University (line 6), thus checking her understanding of the referential expression *Columbia*. This understanding is corrected in line 7, however, whereupon the participants then work out that *Columbia* refers to a university in (the city of) Columbia. Even though the problem turns out to be one of the reference of *Columbia*, there does not seem to be anything at line 4 to suggest more than a hearing check.

This example thus supports the claim that next-turn repairers may first check their hearing of a problematic item in the prior turn (a less serious type of trouble) before initiating repair on its reference (a somewhat more serious type).

Different Cultural Practices – Different Linguistic Practices
If cultures have different practices for referring to, for instance, persons, this can result quite naturally in different practices for repairing reference. A case in point is referential repair in Yélî Dnye, as described by Levinson (2005). Yélî Dnye is a Papuan language in which name taboos prohibit their being used for recognitional reference to in-laws (p. 442). In Levinson's example, a succession of other-initiated repair sequences (*Who did?*, *The daughter of Mby:aa did?*, *Kpâputa's wife?*, *Kpâputa's widow, right?*) is used to establish reference to a daughter-in-law when proper names cannot be used for this.

Assumptions concerning the recognizability of person references may vary with the size of a community, and repair practices may be tailored to this, at least in part. On the Caribbean island of Bequia such assumptions are different from those in larger societies or groups. Bequia being a relatively small community, its inhabitants in general assume that they know each other or at least about each other. But identification of person reference may be complicated by the fact that (a) a number of names are used for more than one individual, and (b) individuals may have more than one name in concurrent use. Sidnell (2007c) reports that Bequian Creole has several *who*-based formats for repair initiation of person reference. At least two of them are deployed like similar formats in English or German: *huu?* "who?", which is commonly treated as the initiation of repair for a problem of hearing, and *huu_* ("_" is used to denote "flat" final pitch, i.e., neither falling nor rising). The latter form is used more or less like English *who* or German *wer* (both with falling pitch) to request the replacement of a prior recognitional referring expression with a more specific one (see above). A third repair initiation format, *huu X_* "who X", where X represents a repetition of the referring expression, deals with referential problems resulting from multiple possible referents and appears to be similar to the format *wer is(t) X* with falling pitch described for German (see above). Yet the fourth format, according to Sidnell, shows how repair formats are tailored to specific recurrent interactional problems in the community (2007c:290). *huu neem so_* "who is named so" is specifically tailored to dealing with the problem that, recognizability in this community being more or less presupposed, no person can be attached to the name used in the prior turn. This means that the referent cannot be recognized at all, and thus the assumption of recognizability must be dropped. Consequently, this problem resembles the initiation and treatment of problems of understanding, here with respect to a referential expression (see below).

But also in domains other than person reference, there can be significant differences in practices for referring and for initiating repair on referential expressions. For instance, languages with rich morpho-syntactic resources may allow speakers to indicate the nature of referential problems more precisely than the languages we have considered so far. In Murrinh-Patha, a Northern Australian language which distinguishes between ten noun-classes, the basic form of the initiation of repair, *thanggu* ("what"), can be inflected to indicate referential underspecification of a member of a particular noun-class: for example, *thanggugu* (falling pitch) "what thing of the animate *ku*-class, i.e., animals, meat, spirits, etc." (Dingemanse et al. 2014:19–20).

Furthermore, different cultures can vary with respect to how much their speakers allude to presupposed common knowledge and/or negotiate opaqueness of references in their talk. In Korean conversation, for instance, speakers often use elliptical expressions when formulating topic proffers, making strong presuppositions about shared knowledge (Kim 2001; also 1999a). This can make it necessary for the interlocutor to initiate repair on the indexical reference forms. The repair operation itself may again provide only a phrasal unit or further indexical expression hinting at the referent in question. Here is an example of this practice:

(3.55)   "North Campus Talk – E-mail" (Kim 2001:351–2) (adapted)

```
1    S:   cal toy    -e  -ka-se   -yo?
          well become -CONN -go-HONOR -POL
          Is everything going well?
2         (1.7)
3    H:   ((to his wife R)) cal toy-   cal toy  -e  -ka?
                            well become well become-CONN -go
                            Is everything well- Is everything going well?
4    R:   hhh () hh
5 -> K:   ahcham ku -ke (.) hay-po -si  -ess -eyo?
          DM     that-thing  do -see-HONOR -PST -POL
          Oh, by the way, have you tried that thing?
6         ku -ke?
          that-thing
          That thing?
7 -> H:   mw[e.
          What
          What.
8 -> K:    [e-mail.
9         (0.8)
10   H:   an  hay-po -ass -eyo acik.
          NEG do -see-PST -POL yet
          No, I haven't.
```

At line 5, K asks a topic initial question containing the demonstrative noun phrase *ku-ke* "that thing". Upon completing the TCU, K immediately repeats the demonstrative *ku-ke* (at line 6), as a post-positioned increment to the question (p. 351). At line 7, the recipient H initiates repair with *mwe* "what", with falling intonation, thus displaying that he did not understand K's prior indexical reference term. In response, K repairs the trouble source by providing a phrasal unit, *e-mail* (line 8), which solves the problem. In the example shown here, the demonstrative noun phrase *ku-ke* ("that thing") is first used in the TCU that ultimately becomes the source of trouble, and is then again repeated after completion of this TCU. That is, the speaker here continues to trust that the recipient will be able to identify the referent alluded to until the recipient finally initiates repair. According to Kim, the use of phrasal units after other-initiations of repair is a way for the trouble-source speaker to "help" the recipient resolve the problem. The repair is done not as a response to an initiation of repair by the other but as a (volunteered) continuation of the speaker's own turn (Kim 2001:354).

This practice can be related to the organization of TCUs in Korean as described in Chapter 2 §2.1, namely the strategy of "upshot first and details later", through which the action upshot is presented early in the turn with informationally "light" reference forms, the details being specified later. Repair initiation may easily become relevant as a result. Kim's analysis suggests that in Korean, as in English and German, after initiations of referential repair producers of the trouble source in general maintain the assumption of recognizability. The recipient is provided with another referring expression, not an explanation – at least not immediately. In Kim's words: "One kind of action that is achieved by such a practice is that of achieving a mutually confirmed sense of intersubjectivity and a demonstrably confirmed sense of collusion and mutual intimacy" (2001:364).

> Practices for referring and therefore for initiating repair on referential expressions can vary significantly from culture to culture: taboos concerning names, assumptions concerning the recognizability of persons and things, and presuppositions concerning the amount of knowledge shared by interlocutors influence both the inventory of repair-initiating formats and the ways in which referential repair is initiated and dealt with.

3.2.3 Problems of Understanding

Repair initiation for a problem of understanding may be accomplished by, for example, repeating the trouble source, proffering a candidate understanding, or outright requesting an explanation or other help.

Repeating the Repairable: Partial Repeats
While the repeats with final rising pitch discussed above were heard and treated as hearing checks, other partial repeats with final rising pitch are used less specifically, leaving open whether the problem is one of hearing, remembering, or understanding in the broad sense of knowing what the recipient is talking about. In this case, the pinpointing of a trouble source with a partial repeat invites the prior speaker to confirm or disconfirm one's memory, hearing, and/or understanding in a broad sense, if necessary also to provide an explanation or other help in order to further the initiator's understanding of the problematic item or issue. In contrast to problems of reference, where recognizability remains presupposed, in the initiation and treatment of repair for problems of understanding, recognizability is not presupposed but needs to be achieved, for instance, through the provision of additional information or other help.

In English and German, repair for a problem of understanding can be initiated with partial repeats with final rising pitch. Here is an example of this practice in English:

(3.56)   "Hard-boiled egg" (Sidnell 2010:129) (adapted)
((B has called A in order to find out how to boil an egg.))

```
8      A:    you (.hh) bring it to a boil (.) but then
9            turn it down 'cause you're really not
10           supposed to boil the e::gg
11           (0.4)
12           you let it (.) simmer or you know on me:dium,
13     B:    Ri:ght
14     A:    fo:r [    t w  ]elve minutes.
15     B:         [((sniff))]
16 ->  B:    Twelve minutes?
17     A:    Well I always do it faster than th(h)at (hh)
18     B:    okay=
19     A:    =I just boil the shit out of it [but]
20     A:                                    [How]
21           do you know when it's done?
```

In lines 12–14, Amy tells Betty that in order to cook a hard-boiled egg you let it simmer for twelve minutes. Betty's repeat of *twelve minutes?*, with final rising pitch, pinpoints this as a repairable. Amy does not treat this repair initiation as a hearing check, e.g., by repeating it, but she modifies what she said before by replacing what she knows about how you should do it with how she actually does it (cf. ibid.). Amy thus seems to treat Betty's repeat as indicating that *twelve minutes* is not problematic acoustically or referentially but with respect to its meaning more generally, which she works on by explaining her own simplified procedure for making hard-boiled eggs.

The repetition of an item from the prior turn may be followed by a verbally explicit request for repair of a problem of understanding. Such a case is shown in the following example from a conversation between an official and a client in a German social service office (Off=official; Cli=client):

(3.57)   "Plane table sheets" (Selting 1987a:115) (adapted)

```
1      Cli:  WO bekommt man äh MESStischblätter (.)
             where does one get plane table sheets
             von SENnestadt    und (.) KÖnigbrügge.
             for ((name of town part)) and   ((name of town part))
2            (.)
3      Cli:  genau DIE beiden stAdtteile [bräucht ich.
             exactly those two town parts I would need
4 ->   Off:                              [<<p> MESStischblätter?>
                                               plane table sheets
```

```
5      Cli:    a(l)so?=
               well
6 ->   Off:    =was soll das SEIN;
               what is that supposed to be
7      Cli:    äh: KARten in einem [ziem(l)ich großen Ma?
               uh   maps   on a        rather big sca?
8      Off:                           [a(l)so GRUND GRUNDkarten;
                                       so    ground ground maps
9      Cli:    [ja;
                yeah
10     Off:    [GRUNDkarten;
                ground maps
11             ja d[ie äh:m: die beKOMMT man ((etc.))
               yeah those uhm those you get
12     Cli:        [RICHtig;
                    right
```

In line 4, the official repeats the trouble-source item from the client's prior turn (line 1) with final rising pitch *MESStischblätter?* "plane table sheets" and a bit later adds the question *was soll das SEIN;* "what is that supposed to be", with final falling pitch. In next turn the client addresses the official's problem of understanding by giving an explanation: he first specifies that the item belongs to the category of maps, and then adds that the maps he means are rather large-scale. In overlap the official now proposes the term *GRUNDkarten* "ground maps" as a problem solution (lines 8, 10), which is confirmed by the client (lines 9, 12). (See also the section on requesting explanation below.)

It is not yet entirely clear how recipients who hear the format "partial repeat with final rising pitch" distinguish between its use to initiate repair for a problem of understanding and repair for a problem of hearing. One hypothesis is that prosody and perhaps visible behavior distinguish between the two problem types. In contrast to hearing checks initiated with faster tempo and possibly subdued prosody, the partial repeats shown here are delivered with accentuation and other prosody conveying that their speakers are certain about what they are repeating. The speakers display that they have heard the troublesome item, but cannot ascribe any meaning to it. Another hypothesis is that the boundary between indicating a problem of understanding and indicating a problem of hearing through partial repeats with rising final pitch may be open to situated interpretation and negotiation.

These hypotheses are compatible with Robinson's point concerning the role of epistemic knowledge in interpreting repair initiations with full or partial repeats (2013). His argument is the following. If the recipient figures that the producer of the repeat does *not* have knowledge of the repeated item in context (i.e., is in a [K−] position with respect to the repeated item), the recipient is more likely to interpret the repeat as initiating repair for a problem of understanding. However, if the recipient figures that the producer of the repeat has knowledge of the repeated item in context (i.e., is in a [K+] position with respect to the repeated item), the recipient is more likely to interpret the repeat as foreshadowing some kind of disagreement (2013:265, 283). Robinson finds evidence that in cases where partial questioning repeats are ambiguous with respect to whether their producers are [K+] or [K−], there appears to be a preference for treating partial questioning repeats as implementing [K−] (versus [K+]) actions (p. 285).[61]

Repair for a problem of understanding in English and German can be initiated through partial repeats of the trouble-source turn, typically with final rising pitch.[62] This type of repair initiation for a problem of understanding is routinely dealt with in next turn by the trouble-source speaker confirming/disconfirming the understanding and/or providing more information.[63] The boundary to repair initiation for a problem of hearing is at times fuzzy and may be open to negotiation. Final rising repeats are more likely to be interpretable as initiating repair for a problem of understanding if the initiating speaker is [K−] with respect to the problematic item.

In Mandarin Chinese, it is in particular repeats with the suffixed particle *-a* that serve to check understanding of something troublesome in prior talk (Wu 2006, 2009). Here is an example:

---

[61] Robinson and Kevoe-Feldman (2010) note that full repeats with final rising intonation, mostly of prior questions, can be used as other-initiations of repair designed to locate an entire prior TCU, and thus the entire action, as the repairable. With the full repeat, the repair initiator categorizes the trouble as not involving hearing or understanding, but tacitly claims that the prior questioning action was somehow problematic, either because s/he has trouble understanding the thrust of the question as a whole, i.e., why it was asked or what is meant by asking it or where it is heading (18 out of 20 cases), or because s/he has trouble accepting the action, perhaps even characterizing it as ridiculous (2 out of 20 cases) (pp. 235, 256). However, at least in the latter cases, "neither participant ultimately treats the full repeat as a genuine practice of repair initiation" (2010:253).

[62] Sidnell, however, gives several examples of talk between lawyers and witnesses in legal proceedings showing repair initiation through partial repeats with final falling pitch. These formats allow the repair initiator to challenge something that the other has said in prior talk (2010:130).

[63] This is not to deny that partial or full repeats with final rising (or falling) intonation can be used to implement actions other than repair initiation. Schegloff, for instance, provides examples of next-turn repeats being used to register or acknowledge receipt of prior talk and to target or create a point of reference for a disaffiliative action about to be embarked on next (see 1997a:527ff.). In these cases the repeats are not treated by their recipients as having initiated repair.

(3.58)   "Not many good places in Hebei" (Wu 2009:34) (adapted)
```
1 -> L:  hai,    hebei      jiu mei shenme hao   difang.
         (sigh) (province) just N  what  good   place
         ((sighs)) There are not many good places in Hebei.
2 -> M:  hebei       a?=
         (province) PRT
         Hebei a?=
3 -> L:  =uh.
         PRT
         =Yeah.
4        (0.5)
5 -> M:  langfang  hai    xing.
         (place)   still  okay
         Langfang is okay.
```

By partially repeating a component from the assessment turn in line 1 and suffixing it with -*a*, speaker M in line 2 is heard as seeking confirmation of his understanding of this item. L confirms it in line 3, whereupon M now introduces an exception to the assessment, namely that Langfang, a city in the province of Hebei, is "okay", thus continuing topical talk. According to Wu (2009:35, 40), repeats suffixed with the particle -*a* are deployed and understood as candidate hearings or understandings of the trouble-source turn, that is, they make confirmation or disconfirmation relevant in next position. Note that Wu leaves open whether this repair initiation format is meant to initiate repair for trouble in hearing or in understanding.[64]

Proffering a Candidate Understanding
In order to initiate repair on a problem of understanding, or to check understanding, the repair initiator can also proffer a candidate understanding, i.e., an interpretation, paraphrase, re-formulation, inference, or even a possible specification, for the recipient to confirm or disconfirm.[65] The producer of the trouble source is invited to respond with confirmation or disconfirmation/correction and, if necessary, explanation, further information, and/or other help in understanding the trouble source.

---

[64] In general, prospectively, the *a*-suffixed repeat leaves open whether the problem is one of hearing, understanding, or even accepting/believing the trouble source, but "the specific lexical, prosodic and visual design of the *a*-suffixed repeat may provide important information on the specific type of usage in a specific sequence" (Xiaoting Li, personal communication). In this case, retrospectively, the initiation of repair might indeed be analyzed as dealing with the acceptability of the trouble source and foreshadow M's disagreement, which is made explicit in line 5 (ibid.). As, however, the problem type is not indicated in a formal way, this kind of repair initiation is classified here as one of a problem of understanding (in a broad sense).
[65] On disaffiliative candidate understandings and their claims to epistemic and deontic rights see Antaki (2012).

("You Mean" +) Candidate Understanding

Beginning a turn with the expression "you mean" projects an understanding check from the outset. In general, the proffering of a candidate understanding leads to confirmation or disconfirmation, in the case of disconfirmation followed by correction. A classical example of this practice is the following:

(3.59)   "You mean homosexual?" (Schegloff et al. 1977:368)
```
1     A:   Why did I turn out this way.
2 ->  B:   You mean homosexual?
3     A:   Yes.
```

With this practice, the repair initiator uses *you mean* to preface an alternative formulation of a component in the trouble-source turn as a candidate understanding – here, *homosexual* in line 2 as an alternative to *this way* (line 1). In (3.59), A confirms the candidate understanding in line 3.[66]

Recently it has been argued that *you mean*-prefaced repair initiations are used especially when the trouble source is at a distance from, i.e., is non-contiguous to, its repair (Benjamin 2012). Here is an example of a non-contiguous use (Lottie is asking Emma whether she has put the training wheels on her bicycle):

(3.60)   "Training wheels" (Benjamin 2012:91) (adapted)
```
1   Lot:   um (0.5) (uh) did you put your traini[ng wheels]
2   Emm:                                        [yeah     ]
3          (0.4)
4   Lot:   have you tried th[em
5   Emm:                    [yeah and I still have a little problem
6          I'm scared to death but I'll do it I'll get out there
7          with you
8          (0.2)
9   Lot:   you mean you still topple over with the training wheels
10         (0.2)
11  Emm:   well you got to balance that front wheel too
12         (0.2)
13  Emm:   but I'll do it [I'll do it I'll show you
14  Lot:                  [xx
15  Lot:   okay I'll be down
```

In this case, there is intervening talk (lines 6–7) between the trouble source, Emma's *a little problem* (line 5), and Lottie's formulation *you still topple over with*

---

[66] For similar examples from German see Selting (1995a:273) and, with post-positioned *meinst du* ("do you mean"), Egbert (2009:102).

the training wheels (line 9). The preface *you mean* indexes Lottie's turn as a candidate understanding and invites Emma to confirm, which she does indirectly by asserting that the front wheel requires balancing.

Benjamin hypothesizes that in comparison to minimal formats for understanding checks, i.e., ones that lack the expression *you mean*, the metacommunicatively explicit *you mean* format works through the addition of linguistic material. By using more material, speakers indicate "that the default assumption of a contiguous trouble-source should be overridden" (Benjamin 2012:106). Yet while the use of *you mean* implies non-contiguity, the use of minimal forms does not necessarily imply contiguity. Minimal forms without *you mean* are simply usable in a wider range of situations (p. 106). How this relates to the classic example (3.59) "You mean homosexual?" cited above remains open.

In other languages an equivalent of *you mean* can be used to index understanding checks. Here is an example from Japanese:

(3.61) "You mean you'll move out and come back again?" (Hayashi and Hayano 2013:297)
((Mayumi has told Kyoko that she is going to move to a friend's apartment.))

```
1       Kyo:    Eh jaa! .hh mayumi san soko  DEru        no:?
                RC then      Mayumi TL there move.out    FP
                Well then .hh are you moving out of there, Mayumi?
2   ->  May:    .hhh Un.  >toriaezu<          nikagetsu kan wa.
                     yeah for.the.time.being  2.months  for TP
                .hhh Yeah. For two months, for the time being.
3               (0.7)
4   ->> Kyo:    dete     mata  kaeru    tte koto:?
                move.out again return   QT  thing
                Y'mean you'll move out and come back again?
5       May:    wakannai.=sono  ato   doo  naru   ka.
                not.know  that  after how  become Q
                I don't know.=what will happen after that.
```

In line 4, Kyoko checks her understanding of what Mayumi has implied (line 2) and requests confirmation or disconfirmation. Note that in accordance with the right-headedness of phrases and clauses in Japanese (Chapter 2), the equivalent of the English phrase *you mean*, *tte (yuu) koto*, does not occur at the beginning of the repair initiation turn but at its end.

In yet other languages, the work of *you mean* may be accomplished by particles. For instance, according to Moerman, Thai understanding checks corresponding to those prefaced by *you mean* in English typically employ an interrogative particle or a particle indicating less certainty following the formulation of a possible understanding (1977:876).

3. Other-initiation of Repair

Here is an example in which the particle *nε* (line 5) indicates the uncertainty of MK's interpretation of the meaning of BS's prior turn(s):

(3.62)   "For putting in the seedlings?" (Moerman 1977:881)[67]

```
1  MK: páj wǎ//n ā˙ᵢ páj sǎj (  ) tâŋlûŋ ā⁺
       'Broad //casting ?ᵢ Using (  ) a dibble?'
2  (M): ᶦ( )
3  BS : mm:. sǎj// ¬ tāŋlüŋ =
       'Yeah. Using// ¬ the dibble. ='
4  MK: ᶦsǎj
         ᶦᵈ'Using'
5      = sǎj kâ˙ nε̄
       '= For putting in the seedlings?'
6  BS : mm
       'Yeah'
```

> Other-initiations of repair for a problem of understanding can be implemented through candidate understandings, i.e., alternative formulations of the trouble source proffered to the trouble-source speaker for confirmation. These candidate understandings are often indexed by *you mean* in English, especially if they are at a distance from the trouble source – or by an equivalent expression in other languages, not necessarily positioned turn-initially. In some languages, it is reportedly a particle that marks an alternative formulation as a candidate understanding.

In Korean, where speakers in general assume a high degree of intersubjectivity, and where furthermore the use of unexpressed arguments (so-called "zero anaphora") is a common practice, Kim describes a tendency to use candidate understandings in order to work out allusive and unexpressed references collaboratively (see 1999b:157ff.). Such candidate understandings do not necessarily feature an explicit formal element equivalent to English *you mean*. An example of this is the following:

(3.63)   "(You mean) People (couldn't understand it)?" (Kim 1999b:158–9) (adapted)

```
1   H:   ey. k[u-- kuntey ku--   ku    mal   -ul ku   mal    -ul (.)
         yes that but      that  that phrase-ACC that phrase -ACC
2        taykay--ku— ihay          -lul mos       -ha-te -lakwu -yo
         usually that  understanding-ACC not:able -do-RETRO-QUOT  -POL
         Right. That- but that- I found people could not understand that phrase.
            [
```

---

[67] For details on the notation conventions used in this transcript see Moerman (1977, p. 872, n. 4, and p. 877, n. 10).

```
3     B:         [uhhaha
                 [
4     C:         [huhuhu
5 ->  K:     salam -tul -I    -yo?
             people-PL  -NOM  -POL
             (You mean) people (couldn't understand it)?
6     H:     yey.
             Yes.
```

H's turn in lines 1–2 only alludes to who it is that does not understand the phrase in question. K's understanding check in line 5 now proposes a candidate understanding for confirmation, which H provides in next turn.

However, the status of this practice in Korean is somewhat different from that in other languages. According to Kim, it is extremely common in Korean conversation for recipients to try to guess what their interlocutor is about to say by proffering candidate understandings (1999b:160). At the same time, speakers are concerned to avoid highlighting repair when it becomes necessary (p. 163). Kim thus concludes that not everything that looks like repair in Korean is indeed repair. He argues that we must distinguish between uses of candidate understandings that really do initiate repair on a prior trouble-source from those that are deployed to display co-alignment and interactional collaboration (1999b:165).

Appendor Question, or Increment with Candidate Specification

The term *appendor question* refers to a phrase that is added on as a question to a prior possibly complete turn, syntactically extending its syntax and embodying a candidate understanding of it (see also Chapter 2 §4.1). Like all other-initiations of repair, appendor questions automatically select the prior speaker as next speaker (Sacks 1992a:652, 660–3). Here is an example of an appendor question in English enacted to check understanding:

```
(3.64)     "Across the street?" (Schegloff 1997a:511) (adapted)
1       Roger:    They make miserable coffee.
2       Ken:      hhhh hhh
3  ->   Dan:      Across the street?
4       Roger:    Yeh
5       Ken:      Miserable food hhhh
6                 (0.4)
7       Ken:      hhhh So what'd you do East-er-over Easter vacation
```

With his appendor question in line 3, Dan offers a candidate understanding of who *they* in line 1 refers to; Roger confirms this understanding in line 4.

The following is an example of an appendor question in German. (Ida is talking about her tattoo.)

(3.65)   "At school" (Selting 1995a:275) (adapted)

```
182    Ida:   un weil    ich immer  mutiger bin als andere(h)
              and because I    always more courageous am than others
              and because I am always more courageous than others
183    Nat:   ((laughs ca 1.0)) [((laughs))
184    Ida:                     [oder war besser gesacht
                                 or   was better  said
                                or was, to put it more accurately
185           (ca. 4 secs.)
186    Ida:   hab ich denn `glEich da: (1.0)
              have I then immediately there
              `rIchtig: was `HINge´macht,=
              real         something made
              I put something real there right away
187 -> Ron:   =in der `SCHU´le,
              at  the school
              at school
188           (1.0)
189    Ida:   <<l> ä`NEE:;>
                   no
190           `dAs war irgendwo zu `HAUse mal.
              that was somewhere at home once
              it was somewhere at home one time
```

Ida recounts that she was more courageous than her girlfriends when playing around with applications to the skin and that she applied a real tattoo (lines 182–6). Ron now appends a phrasal continuation to this turn: *in der Schule* "at school" (line 187) with final rising pitch, proposing for confirmation a candidate location where this might have happened. Ida, however, rejects and corrects his candidate understanding (lines 189–90).[68]

"Appendor questions" are also documented in Japanese conversation (Hayashi and Hayano 2013). However, because Japanese is a predicate-final language, the element proffered as a candidate understanding is not grammatically fitted to the end of the prior turn; it is instead an "insertable", normatively belonging earlier in the structure of the trouble-source turn (Chapter 2). Hence, Hayashi and Hayano refer to this practice as "proffering insertable elements" (2013:295). Here is an

---

[68] For more examples see Egbert (2009:101).

example from a conversation between a barber and his customer. ("Backward shampoo" in line 2 refers to the method of shampooing with the customer reclining backward over a sink while facing upwards.) Note that the element in double parentheses at the end of line 1 is not expressed.

(3.66) "Backward shampoo" (Hayashi and Hayano 2013:294)
```
1      Bar:  yappari: (.) nenpaisha no hito    iyagaru (yo)ne,
             after.all   elderly   LK person  dislike  FP
             After all (.) elderly people dislike ((it)).
2  ->  Cst:  bakkushanpuu        o:?,
             backward.shampoo o
             Backward shampoo:?,
3      Bar:  n:.
             Yeah.
4            (0.2)
5      Cst:  soo  ka na:.
             that Q  FP
             I wonder if it's that ((bad)).
```

In line 2 the customer proposes a candidate understanding of an element left unexpressed in the barber's prior turn: a noun (*bakkushanpuu*, "backward shampoo"), followed by the direct object particle *o*. This candidate understanding is formulated as syntactically dependent on the structure of the trouble-source turn, or more precisely, as structurally *insertable* into the barber's turn before the predicate complex *iyagaru yone* "dislike": *yappari nenpaisha no hito **bakkushanpuu o** iyagaru yone* ("After all, elderly people dislike backward shampoo") (2013:469). The barber is invited to confirm this understanding, which he does in line 3.

> Participants use the proffering of a candidate understanding, with or without an expression like *you mean*, in order to check their understanding of the prior turn(s). This practice is designed to invite the recipient to confirm or disconfirm the candidate understanding, and in case of disconfirmation to further explain and/or help the repair initiator in understanding the trouble source.
>
> The practice of proffering an insertable in Japanese is designed to exhibit grammatical dependency on the prior turn, while at the same time initiating repair and aligning with the prior speaker's actions. For the initiator of the repair, the practice serves to display a high degree of attention to and understanding of the trouble-source turn. It is in general deployed to display affiliation with the prior speaker's course of action, keeping the disruption of progressivity to a minimum. However, it can also be used to implement disaffiliation.

In all the examples shown so far, understanding checks proposing candidate understandings were delivered with final rising pitch. However, understanding checks can also have final falling pitch. Here is an example where the participants are talking about their students:

(3.67)   "The students" (Selting 1995a:278–9) (adapted)
```
733    Lea:   <<h> weil ich `IMmer darüber `nAchgedacht hab
                   because I always about     thought    have
                   because I was always wondering
              warUm die   so>=
              why    they so
              why they (are) so
734           =<<h> die `KOMmen mir immer melan`chOlisch vor;=ne,>
                    they seem to me always melancholic          you know
                    they always seem melancholic you know
735 -> Eli:   die stuDENten;
              the students
              the students
736    Lea:   i`jA;
              yeah
737           (1.0)
738           <<h> weil ich `glAube nich>
                   because I believe not
                   because I don't believe
739           <<all> ´wEiß die sagen immer alle die sind> `FAU:L=
                    you know they say always all they are lazy
                    you know everyone always says they are lazy
```

In line 734 Lea says of her students that they seem melancholic. Eli now adds a full-reference form *die studenten* (line 735), which is heard as co-referential with the indexical form *die* in Lea's turn. Although Eli's phrase is produced with falling intonation, Lea nevertheless treats it as a candidate understanding and confirms it in next turn (line 736) before continuing on-topic talk.

Selting observes that candidate understandings with final falling pitch in German invite confirmation more strongly than candidate understandings with final rising pitch (see 1995a:280). This may be related to an observation by Bolden (2010) concerning a similar action in English: an understanding or inferential check about matters in the addressee's domain of knowledge implemented with an *and*-prefaced formulation. Bolden finds that in such formulations "rising intonation [...] suggests a wider epistemic gap between the speaker and the addressee, while falling intonation displays the speaker's stronger epistemic stance" (2010:14).

Couper-Kuhlen (2012a) also finds that final falling pitch on candidate hearings and candidate understandings suggests a heightened degree of epistemic certainty on the part of the repair initiator.

> The final intonation of an understanding check or candidate understanding in English and German may be deployed as an indicator of the speaker's lesser or greater certainty concerning its accuracy. This explains why, in consequence, responses to candidate understandings with final rising pitch (greater uncertainty) exhibit no preference for either confirmation or disconfirmation, whereas responses to candidate understandings with final falling pitch (greater certainty) invite above all confirmation.

Prompting the Prior Speaker to Elaborate

Repair may be initiated because the information a prior speaker has given is not sufficient to understand its meaning or significance. The recipient needs more information, but s/he still presupposes that s/he will then be able to understand. The problem is categorized as one brought about by the speaker having provided insufficient information, not by the recipient lacking the necessary knowledge.

As Lerner (2004) has pointed out, many prepositions, conjunctions, and small function words can work as repair initiations to prompt more information from an interlocutor if they are produced as stand-alones. Turns built, for example, with freestanding *to, for, as, at, with, such as, meaning, and, but, because, except*, etc. prompt the other to extend their prior turn with an increment (see Chapter 2) built around the specific word in the prompt. Lerner calls such words and expressions "increment initiators" when they are used this way. Here are some examples of the practice:

(3.68)   "From" (Lerner 2004:162)
```
1       Jack:    I just returned
2 ->    Kathy:   from
3       Jack:    Finland
```

(3.69)   "And" (Lerner 2004:164–5) (adapted)
```
1       Mary:    I talked to To:ny:.
2                (0.2)
3 ->    Alan:    Ye:h, A:nd¿
4       Mary:    Uh::: he doesn't have too much to say since
5                Bruce moved out, does he
6       Alan:    Mm-mmhh
```

Increment initiators locate something incomplete in a prior turn and begin an elaboration, leaving it to the interlocutor to complete it (Lerner 2004:153). They are typically produced with some lengthening and often with either "continuing" or "flat" intonation (as in (3.69)).

> Incremental initiations of repair are designed to continue and re-open a prior speaker's turn although the latter was presented as complete. They tie to the prior speaker's turn by continuing it in a syntactically fitted way. Because they are recognizably incomplete, they project continuation. The speaker of the increment initiation does not produce the full continuation him/herself but prompts the trouble-source speaker to deliver it (Lerner 2004:174). In this way the repairer can imply that the other should have delivered more but did not.[69]

Requesting Explanation
In addition to checking understanding or prompting the prior speaker to elaborate, repair initiators may request an explanation, specification, or some other help in understanding the trouble-source item or information. When initiating this kind of repair, the repair initiator does not presuppose the recognizability of the problematic item or information. In other words, the problem is not presented as one of momentary retrieval, but as a lack of knowledge that needs remedying. In the repair operation, initiations requesting explanation are commonly dealt with by providing more background, elaborating word meanings, contrasting the item pinpointed with other items, describing the function of the object in more detail, etc. (see Selting 1987a:96ff., 1995a:287ff.).

The following examples show typical practices for initiating this type of repair and typical repair operations for treating the problem.

"What is X", "What do you mean", or the like
In the following example, after Mom has initiated hearing repair with reference to the word *gwaffs* (line 5), and Virginia has repeated the word, Prudence now requests an explanation (line 11):

(3.70) "What's a gwaff" (Sidnell 2010:125–6) (adapted)
((Mom has just said that she does not think Virginia should go to the same parties as her older sister Beth because Beth is eighteen and Virginia is only fourteen.))

```
4     Virginia:   [I KNOW::, BUT
5                 A:LL THE REST OF MY: PEOPLE MY AGE ARE GWAFFS. I
6                 promise. they are si:[ck.
7     Mom:                             [They're what?
```

---
[69] However, it can also be argued that the increment is used to further the progressivity of talk collaboratively, without implying that the other should have delivered more in the first place. This ambiguity shows that prompting the prior speaker to elaborate is a practice revealing the fuzzy boundaries between repair (halting progressivity) and continuation (furthering progressivity).

```
8                        (.)
9     Virginia:     GWAFFS.
10    ???:          (    )
11 -> Prudence:     What's a gwaff.
12                  (3.1)
13    Virginia:     Gwaff is just somebody who's really (1.1) just- ehh!.hh
14                  s- immature.>You don't wanna hang around people like tha:t.<
```

Prudence uses a full-clausal format *What's X* to indicate a problem of understanding (line 11). (*X* stands for a repetition of, or anaphoric reference to, the trouble source.) After a significant delay Virginia responds to Prudence's request for explanation by glossing the meaning of *gwaff* (lines 13–14).

Here is a similar example from German with the format *was ist X* "what is X":

```
(3.71)    "What's that" (Selting 1995a:287) (adapted)
268       Eli:   un das ´ERste mal in einer `SALsadisko.
                 and for the first time in a salsa disco
269 ->    Lea:   <<all> wa[s is> `DAS denn.
                           what's that
270       Cis:           [`´?hm,
271       Eli:   dassis irgnwie ne ne be´stImmte art von `TANZ öh (1.5)
                 it's somehow a a special kind of dance uh (1.5)
                 den die da offensichtlich `tAn´zn,
                 that they apparently dance there
272       ?:     `´hm,
273       Eli:   aber ich hab das also ´nIch unterscheiden kön[nen
                 but I wasn't able to tell it apart
274       ?:                                                  [`´hn,
275       Eli:   von (0.5) ganz normalem `DISko (1.5) `tAnzen.
                 from (0.5) simply normal disco (1.5) dancing.
```

In Lea's repair initiation *was is DAS denn* "what's that" (line 269), the repairable is replaced with the anaphoric pro-form *DAS*. Eli repairs the problem by explaining what the antecedent *SALsadisko* means.[70]

This type of repair initiation may also be combined with a candidate repair solution. In the following example, a client has asked at what time she should come in order to register for a space at the next flea market:

---

[70] Again, it could be argued that this example illustrates the fuzzy boundary between the use of such questions for initiating repair or collaboratively continuing topical talk. For other examples see Selting (1987a:100–1, 1995a: 287–8) and Egbert (2009:100, 105–6).

3. Other-initiation of Repair

(3.72) "What does early mean" (Selting 1987a:98) (adapted)

```
22      S1:    `FRÜH;
               early
23             (0.5)
24      S1:    `GANZ `FRÜH.
               very early
25  ->  K:     was `HEISST ganz früh;
               what does early mean
26  ->         SECHS?
               six
27  ->         SIEBM?
               seven
28  ->         FÜNF?
               five
29             (0.5)
30             <<l> also mir issas e`GAL->
               it doesn't matter to me
31             <<l> ich muss_s nur `WISsen nächstes mal.>
               I just need to know for next time
32      S1:    `JAA;
               yes
33             ich `kAnn ihnen da aber ´KEIne feste `zEitzusage
               `GEben;=´NE,
               but I can't give you a definite time you know
```

Here, the client's initiation of repair for a problem of understanding with *was `HEISST ganz früh;* "what does early mean" (line 25) is immediately followed by three candidate repairs in the form of specifications (lines 26–8). When the official still does not respond, the client adds an appeal that she needs to know (lines 30–1). Now, however, the official shifts the focus from treating K's problem to explaining her own inability to give the client a definite time.

"Who is X"

As discussed above, the most common form of repair initiation for a problem of reference is a question word such as *who* or *wer* with falling pitch, referring back to a purportedly underspecified reference in the prior turn. In the repair operation the problem is typically dealt with by replacing the prior indexical reference form, for example, a pronoun, with an alternative reference form, for example, a full noun phrase. Throughout the sequence, participants uphold the assumption of recognizability, that is, they persist in assuming that the referent is known: the problem is categorized as a provisional one of retrieval only (see §3.2.2).

In German, however, there are repair initiation formats that at first sight look like initiations of repair for a problem of reference, but are nevertheless treated differently by repairers. In particular, repair initiations that target a (person) referent in the prior turn but deploy a full sentential format such as *wer ist X* ("who is X") lead to explanations that resemble the treatment of problems of understanding. The following is a case in point:

(3.73)   "Who is Lobkovitz" (Auer 1984:630) (adapted)

```
1      X:    wie der lobkovitz des erste mal zum präsidenten
             when the PN(PERS)   the first time for president
             when lobkovitz was elected president
             gewählt worden is (.)  [da ham
             elected  was     PERF   then PERF they
             for the first time      they
2  ->  T:                            [wer is lobkovitz
                                     who is PN(PERS)
                                     who is lobkovitz
3      X:    des is der jetzige (der ... drangekommen is)
             that is the present whose-cl turn-(it)-was PERF
             that's the present one (whose ... turn it was)
4      T:    a:so mm,
             I-see
             I see mm,
```

Following the repair initiation *wer is lobkovitz* (line 2), the repairer explains who this person is (rather than offering an alternative recognitional form such as "you know, my next-door neighbor"). Neither the repair initiator nor the repairer in this case assumes that the referent is recognizable; instead, they work toward the provision of additional information that will enable an understanding of who is meant. (For another example see Auer 1984:630–1.)

> Speakers who initiate repair by requesting an explanation target a prior referent with the clausal format *wer ist X* or *was ist X*, often with final falling pitch (rather than the phrasal *wer* or *was* with falling pitch). In doing so, they present the problem not as a temporary one of retrieval only, but as a lack of knowledge that needs supplementing through the provision of relevant information. They thus invite treatment as a problem of understanding rather than as a problem of reference (in the narrower sense dealt with in §3.2.2 above).

Re-categorization of a Problem of Understanding as a Problem of Reference Retrieval

There is evidence that problems of understanding are oriented to as more severe than problems of reference retrieval. One indication of this is the way repair initiation is on occasion re-categorized. For instance, in the following example, from an encounter in a social welfare office, the client (Cli) is trying to tell the official (Off) that he might be able to get a stove for the kitchen in his new flat as a present from Mr N. The official, however, initiates repair for a problem of understanding: he refers to Mr N as someone he does not know and requests the client to explain.

```
(3.74)     "Who is Mr N" (Selting 1987a:122-3) (adapted)
262     Cli:   und `JETZ mit? ähm mit dem mit herr `N;
               and now with uhm with this with Mr N
               (0.5)
263     Cli:   ähn [ich mein ich `WEISS nich ob se mir
               uhm  I mean   I know not     whether they me
               uhm I don't know whether they
264  -> Off:       [`WER is herr `N.
                    who is  Mr    N
        Cli:   den `schEnken oder `nIch.
               that ((=the stove)) give as a present or not
               give that ((=the stove)) to me as a present or not
((5 lines omitted))
270  -> Off:   `WER is der `N.
               who is  that  N
271            (0.5)
272     Cli:   der `HAUSwirt;
               the landlord
273            <<l> von herrn [A  wo  wa  wo  wa  da gewohnt ham.
                    of Mr A       where we where we lived
274     Off:                  [ach `SO; von `A;
                               oh I see  of A
275     Off:   `dEr hat für `sIe so_n (0.5) so_n `HERD.
               he has  for you such a      such a stove
               he has such a stove for you
```

The official's first initiation of repair *wer is Herr N* "who is Mr N" (line 264) is produced in overlap and not taken up by the client. The official subsequently pursues repair by asking again *wer ist der N* "who is that N" (line 270). Both these initiation formats present Mr N as someone who the official does not know, and thus suggest the problem as one of understanding because of lack of knowledge. The client, however, deals with the problem as one of reference retrieval, i.e., as if the official does know who he means but is just momentarily unable to identify him. He provides another recognitional form: *der hauswirt* "the landlord" (line 272), implying that B does not need further explanation. When the official still does not recognize Mr N, the client specifies which landlord (line 273), again presupposing recognizability. In overlap with this, the official now displays recognition and conveys this with a change-of-state token *ach SO;* "oh" (Heritage 1984a), evidencing his understanding that he can now relate Mr N to Mr A (line 275). With this, the official makes clear that the client's (re-)categorization of his problem was justified, because he indeed does know the referent, contrary to his prior repair initiation with its implied lack of knowledge.

> Cases in which repair initiation for a problem of understanding is re-categorized as repair for a problem of reference allow the conclusion that participants treat problems of reference retrieval as preferred over, i.e., less severe than, problems of understanding (see also Selting 1987a:120–4).

3.2.4 Problems of Expectation/Acceptability

The repair initiation formats dealt with so far have suggested the following kinds of trouble:

i. *hearing problem*, implying that it is only the acoustic decoding that momentarily went amiss;
ii. *referential (retrieval) problem*, implying that it is only the retrieval of the referent that is not possible at the moment; and
iii. *problem of understanding*, implying that the repair initiator cannot ascribe a meaning to the trouble-source expressions or turn(s) because of lack of knowledge.

In contrast to these repair initiation formats, when parties initiating repair present a problem as one of expectation (Selting 1987a, 1987b, 1988, 1995a) or acceptability (Svennevig 2008), they convey that what the speaker of the trouble-source turn has said is in contradiction to or in conflict with their own knowledge, expectations, or beliefs about what is true, right, or acceptable. In general, this means that the problem needs to be sorted out before on-topic talk can be continued.[71]

---

[71] On occasion, however, because the sorting out of clashing expectations may take several turns, resolution of the trouble may take the talk in a different topical direction.

3. Other-initiation of Repair

Several different formats for questioning the acceptability of the trouble source and initiating repair for a problem of expectation or acceptability have been described in the literature.

"Why"/"How Come" or their Equivalents + Resumption of the Trouble Source

Repair for a problem of expectation or acceptability can be initiated by questions with *why* in English or *wieso* "why" in German plus repetition or anaphorical resumption of the trouble source, in general with final falling pitch. On occasion, also the question *how come/wie kommt DAS denn* "how come that" can be deployed to the same effect. In most cases, the clash of expectations or norms of acceptability presented in this way needs to be resolved: for example, by an explication of the expectations and/or a clarification of the contradiction.

In the following German example, *wieso* "why" is used in a single-word TCU at the beginning of the repair-initiating turn, followed by a question implying a candidate answer (see Pomerantz 1988).

```
(3.75)     "How so" (Selting 1995a:294–5) (adapted)
101  Eli:  ich `fInde diese `URlaubsregelung an der `Uni
           I find this regulation for vacations at the university
           `VÖLlich `Unsinnig.=´ne,
           totally absurd           you know
102        (0.5)
103  Eli:  ich↑`HAB   nichts von meinem urlaub;=´ne,
           I     have nothing of my vacation     you know
           I can't do anything with my vacation     you know
104        (1.0)
105  Lea:  ´Ich `AU [nich;
           I    also not
           me neither
106  Eli:  man ´Arbeitet ja sowie↑`SO;=´ne,
           one is working anyway          you know
107  Lea:  ja;
           yeah
108  Cis:  `WIEso; `GIBTS da ne offizielle ´URlaubsregel[ung,
           how so    is there an official regulation for vacation
109  Eli:                                              [ja es
                                                       yes there
110  Eli:  `GIBT eine urlaubsregelung.
           is a regulation for vacation
```

```
111         aber es `Ist `Eben `nIcht ´SO,   (0.5)
            but it is just not so
112         wie in jedm: ↑¯SCHULbetrieb—
            like in every school
113         oder an jedm ↑¯ANderem betrieb—(0.5)
            or in any other company
114         wo du ´WIRKlich mal fü:r `fünf wochen im jahr
            where you really once for five weeks a year
            where once a year for five weeks
            alles stehn und `LIEgen lassen ´kAnnst,
            everything stand and leave let can
            you really can drop everything
115         und ´wIrklich ↑`!UR!laub machn kannst.=ne,=
            and really         vacation make can      you know
            and really can go on vacation             you know
116  Cis:   =[`´hm,
117  Lea:   =[`´hm,
```

Eli is complaining about the regulations for taking vacation at the university. She explains that (as a result) she does not really take any vacation but works instead. Cis, in line 108, seems to be surprised at this information and initiates repair by asking *WIEso; GIBTS da ne offizielle URlaubsregelung*, "how so; is there an official regulation for vacation".[72] While Eli has presupposed that there is a regulation for vacation at the university (lines 101ff.), Cis now calls this presupposition into question and initiates repair for a problem of expectation or acceptability.[73] Eli first briefly answers this question in the positive (lines 109–10), before linking the answer back to her complaint and explaining why she disapproves of the university's regulations (lines 111–15): schools and other companies close down for five weeks a year and thus enable their employees to forget work completely during that time. Cis acknowledges this information without coming back to her prior surprise.[74]

---

[72] Egbert and Vöge (2008) argue that, contrary to what dictionaries and our intuitions might tell us, *wieso* and *warum* in German are not synonyms and cannot be directly translated into English as "why". While the question word *wieso* "why" "is doing information seeking only" and in this respect is claimed to be unambiguously affiliative (p. 19), *warum* "how come" "is doing challenging only" and in this respect is unambiguously oriented to as disaffiliative (p. 19 et passim). In contrast to these two question words, English *why* allows for ambiguity between information seeking and challenging (p. 19).

[73] In order to instead initiate repair for a problem of understanding, she could have simply asked for more information, e.g., what the regulation for vacation at the university is, without doubting the presupposition of such a regulation.

[74] In this case, the question word *wieso* is phrased so as to be separate, in its own prosodic unit, prior to the follow-up interrogative sentence; in other cases, it can be integrated into the interrogative sentence, as in *aber wieso `FÄHRS du denn dann wenn*: "but why do you then drive if" (Selting 1995a:296).

Surprised or Astonished Initiations of Repair

Almost all repair initiation formats can be deployed in a prosodically salient, i.e., conspicuous, noticeable, marked way – for instance, with high pitch register, extra loudness, or extra strong accents.[75] This salient prosody overrides all other cues, adds an affective overtone of surprise or astonishment, and is interpreted as the initiation of repair for a problem of expectation or acceptability (Selting 1996b).[76]

Selting (1996b) gives the following examples to illustrate the difference between a prosodically non-salient, and a prosodically marked or salient, format for initiating repair. In the first extract below, Ron uses a prosodically non-salient variant of *bitte* ("pardon"), *bidde*, in order to indicate a problem of hearing:

(3.76)　　Unmarked *"Bidde?"* (Selting 1996b:235) (adapted)

```
1  Ron:  denk ich `schOn daß [das auch (.) <<f> `AUSschlaggebmd ist;>
         I do think that this is also               decisive
2  Nat:                      [ich war <<f>´sIebm `JAHre mit ihm zu`sAmmen.>
                              we were together for seven years
          (.)
3-> Ron: <<all> ´BIDde,>=
         pardon
4  Nat:  =ich war `sIebm `JAHre mit ihm zusammen.=
         we were together for seven years
5  Nat:  =[also da is `schOn (0.6) ne `GRUNDlage oder
          so there was            a    base       or
6  Ron:  =[`AHja;
          oh yeah
   Nat:  ne `BA(h)sis dage`WESen;
         a basis there
```

Here Ron is talking about the duration of relationships and suggesting that Nat's problem with the long-distance relationship she has just described has to do with its short duration (line 1). Nat comes in in overlap with an objection (line 2). In line 3, Ron initiates repair with a prosodically non-salient repair initiation *BIDde*. This is produced with normal accentuation on the first syllable, with rising final pitch and with fast speech rate. In response, Nat repeats her turn from line 2 in line 4, now without "forte" or extra volume (she is speaking in the clear). Her treatment of

---

[75] Benjamin and Walker describe a special case of this in English: a high rise-fall contour used on next-turn repeats that conveys a problem of acceptability (2013).

[76] For Egbert, such prosodically marked versions of other-initiation of repair should not be called repair initiation at all, since they do not display a problem of hearing or understanding (2009:106). However, in this book our understanding of trouble sources that can lead to repair will include problems of unexpected or unacceptable information (see also Svennevig 2008; Benjamin 2013; Benjamin and Walker 2013), on the grounds that they are dealt with in similar ways.

Ron's prosodically non-salient *bitte* thus shows her interpretation of it as indicating a non-localized, unspecified problem of hearing, resolved by repeating the trouble-source turn.

In the next extract, however, Ron uses a prosodically marked version of *bitte*: Ida's information from lines 1–2, namely that her dentist wants to operate on her tattoo, is in conflict with his knowledge and expectations about what dentists do and how tattoos can be removed.

```
(3.77)     Marked "BITte?" (Selting 1996b:235–6) (adapted)
1    Ida:   aber ich `KANN mir das äh:m nochmal ope`rIeren lassen.
            but I can have that   ehm operated on some time
            (1.3)
2    Ida:   ich hab n `ZA[HNarzt=der `mAcht das.
            I know a dentist who's willing to do that
3    Ron:                [wo`ZU:;
                          what for
            (.)
4 -> Ron:   <<h, f> ´BITte?>
            pardon
            (0.8)
5    Ida:   ?`JA(h) ich weiß `Au nich ich hab immer PECH mit [Är(h)ztn.
            well I don't know either        I always have bad luck with doctors
6    Nat:                                                    [((laughs))
            (1.0)
7    Ida:   da bin ich dann mal nach ewigem warten zum zahnarzt gegangn
            once after having waited for ages I went to a dentist
8           (1.0)
9           un sitz im stuhl und hatte: arge zahnschmerzen
            and I was sitting in the chair and had a bad toothache
```

Ron's version of *bitte* in line 4 is produced with normal speech rate, but it features a much higher rise in pitch and extra loudness in comparison to surrounding turns. This repair initiation is not treated as a problem of hearing, but with *JA(h) ich weiß Au nich* ("well I don't know either"). Ida first attends to the surprise Ron conveys about her dentist's unusual offer and then tells the story of how it came about, thus dealing with the basis of his surprise. This demonstrates that Ida treats Ron's prosodically marked initiation of repair as conveying a problem of expectation.[77]

---

[77] For an acoustic analysis of the two versions of *bitte* see Online-Chapter D §3; for other examples of prosodically salient initiations of repair see Selting (1987a:130–47, 1995a:298–304, 1996b).

> Prosodic marking or salience on German repair initiations overrides the verbal format and is regularly heard as initiating repair for a problem of expectation, making a display of surprise or astonishment triggered by the prior speaker's turn.[78] Prosodically marked initiations of repair have different sequential implications from their non-salient counterparts. They are regularly dealt with by the repairer delivering background information that explains the issue or clarifies the contradiction.
> The problem is thus treated as needing resolution before the conversation can progress. The repair initiator can accept the clarification, in which case the participants close the repair sequence by resuming topical talk, or can explicate his/her own knowledge/expectations and thus open negotiation over the matter. In the latter case, problem treatment may change the direction of topical talk, obscuring the boundary between the repair sequence and ongoing topical talk.

Benjamin and Walker (2013) present an analysis of one particular kind of prosodic marking on other-initiation of repair in English: the high rise-fall intonation contour on a repetition of what another participant has just said (see Online-Chapter E §3 for an example and a pitch trace).[79] By using the high rise-fall repetition, the speaker claims that the repeated talk is "wrong", unacceptable, and in need of correction or repair. The contour thus indicates an incongruity between the repeated talk and what the speaker knows, thinks, or believes to be correct, true, appropriate, or acceptable. As Benjamin and Walker explain, this kind of repair initiation implies a "diagnosis" of the nature of the trouble that the prior speaker is called upon to attend to. The further sequential development shows that both participants orient to the trouble as diagnosed by the repair initiator.

Wu (2006, 2009) reports that "question-intoned" repeat formats can be used for other-initiation of repair in Mandarin Chinese conversation.[80] The following example illustrates a question-intoned repeat at line 3:

(3.78)   "Thirty dollars for an hour" (Wu 2009:34)
```
1     C:   ta yi xiaoshi:: fu ni duoshao, xianzai.
           she one hour    pay you how:much now
           How much does she pay you- for an hour:, now?

2  -> W:   pianyi de le. sanshi.
           cheap  NOM CRS thirty
           Cheap. Thirty dollars.
```

---

[78] This, of course, does not mean that any kind of prosodically marked turn initiates repair. In many cases, for instance, prosodically marked news receipts are deployed for the display of surprise but do not disrupt the progressivity of the talk.
[79] Benjamin (2013: Chapter 6) provides further examples.
[80] In a footnote, however, she concedes that "the matter of what constitutes 'question intonation' in a tonal language such as Mandarin is complicated and remains unsettled" (2009:59).

```
3  ->  C:   yi  ge xiaoshi sanshi?
            one c  hour    thirty
            Thirty dollars for an hour?
4  ->  W:   (uh [huh)
            PRT  PRT
            (Uh [huh.)
5  ->  C:       [Bu  pianyi.
                 N   cheap
                Not cheap.
```

C is asking W about the fee that she gets from a graduate student for teaching her Classical Chinese. After W responds *pianyi de le. sanshi.* "Cheap. Thirty dollars." (line 2), C initiates repair at line 3 with *yi ge xiaoshi sanshi?* "Thirty dollars for an hour?", a question-intoned repeat (line 3). This repeat is confirmed by the trouble-source speaker at line 4. However, at line 5, the repeat-speaker launches a disagreeing response: she denies that thirty dollars an hour is cheap. Later in the conversation it emerges that she knows other people who earn only half that fee for a similar job. Wu concludes that question-intoned repeats are used to present what is being repeated as unexpected or having come out of the blue (2009:40, 57).[81]

> There is some indication that prosodically salient repetitions are also deployed in other languages to initiate repair for problems of expectation or acceptability. In English it is a high rise-fall contour on the repetition that diagnoses the problem as one of correctness, appropriateness, or acceptability (Benjamin and Walker 2013).
> In Mandarin Chinese it appears to be "question-intoning" of a repetition that proposes a "momentary breakdown in comprehension of the element being repeated" and implies that it is unexpected (Wu 2009:40).

Re-categorizations of Problems of Expectation or Acceptability
A repair initiation for a problem of expectation can be re-categorized as a less severe problem. We can observe this happening in the following exchange between the official of a communal office (Off) and her client (Cli1):

```
(3.79)    Marked "WAS?" (Selting 1987a:141–2) (adapted)
4    Cli1:   äh: ich wollte gern was beGLAUbigen lassen hier;
             I would like to have something attested
5    Off:    `´jaa,
             yeah
```

---

[81] Question-intoned repeats contrast with *a*-suffixed repeats, which are used as confirmation questions (see §3.2.3 above).

```
6       Cli1:   is mein ZEUCHnis—
                it's my school report
7       Off:    das KOStet allerdings <<all> sag ich ihnen ma gleich
                it costs    however              I'll tell you  straight away
                VORher;> `PRO seite drei `MARK.
                beforehand   per page   three marks
8   ->  Cli1:   <<h,f> ´WAS?>
                       what
9       Off:    ich `MUSS also jetz
                I now have to
10              `JEde beglaubichte `SEIte nehm ich IHnen drei mark;
                each attested page I'll need three marks from you
11              (0.5)
12      Cli2:   wie`sO kostet das denn `GE:L:D;
                why does that cost money
13              der `BRAUCHT das doch für ne (0.5) be`WERbung;
                he needs it for an                      application
```

The client Cli1 needs an official attestation of his school certificate for a job application (lines 4–6, also line 13), but when the official informs him that each page will cost three marks, he responds with a prosodically marked initiation of repair *WAS?* "what?" (line 8). The official starts her repair by alluding to official regulations (*ich muss also jetz*, "I now have to"), but breaks this off and in line 10 merely provides a modified repeat of the information already given at line 7, thus treating Cli1's problem as if it were a problem of hearing. However, Cli2, his partner, now pursues repair by asking why this costs money (line 12) and spelling out her expectation that attestations for job applications should be free of charge (line 13).

> In example (3.79), repair is initiated for a problem of expectation, but re-categorized by the repairer as a less severe problem of hearing. The re-categorization is not accepted, though, and repair for the same problem (of expectation or acceptability) is initiated again, now in another, more explicit format, whereupon the repairer finally explains the regulations in more detail (not shown in the transcript).[82] See Svennevig (2008:340) for a similar example from a Norwegian institutional encounter.

---

[82] For further examples of re-categorizations of problems of expectation as less severe problems see Selting (1987a:141–7).

3.3 Conclusion for Other-initiation of Repair

Even though not all repair initiations are responded to as they are "diagnosed" by the repair initiator, there is a clear relation between the repair initiation format chosen, the problem type it implicitly categorizes, and the repair operation it invites. Table 3.2 presents this relation, with the types of repair ordered from least severe to more severe.

Through the syntax and prosody of the repair initiation in relation to the trouble source, the repair initiator locates, specifies, and categorizes her/his trouble and thus makes relevant a particular repair operation. With respect to syntax, it seems to be relevant whether or not the trouble source is located through pre- or post-framing, and/or is replaced by a question word, or is itself partially/pronominally or fully repeated. The choice of the question word for repair initiation can be used for specifying the trouble source, or not, for example, by using class-unspecific versus class-specific question words: class-unspecific question words leave the trouble source unspecified; class-specific question words specify it as, for example, reference to a person, place, or thing. Verbally explicit initiations of repair, often used in cases of greater distance from the trouble source, are typically formulated as full finite clauses, while many other-initiations of repair are formatted as, for example, noun phrases or prepositional phrases. With respect to prosody, it is relevant whether the final pitch is falling or rising. For instance, in the two languages under primary consideration here (English and German), single question words with rising final pitch are deployed as initiations of hearing repair, whereas with falling final pitch they are understood to be initiating referential repair. The proferring of candidate understandings with final rising pitch suggests that the repair initiator's epistemic status is [K−], whereas with final falling pitch it suggests that the repair initiator is at least partially [K+] (thus inviting confirmation). The use of strong prosodic marking, or salience, in repair initiations suggests that the problem is one of expectation or acceptability, adding an affective overtone of surprise or astonishment, and implying that the problem involves clashing expectations, knowledge, or beliefs.[83]

Repairers may either go along with the suggested categorization of the trouble, or try to repair the trouble with another repair operation, thus implying a **re-categorization** of the trouble. In the latter cases, re-categorizers may follow a "preference" principle according to which repair of less serious problems is initiated first, in order to gain time and/or see if the trouble can be resolved in this way, before initiating repair of a more serious problem. In cases in which

---

[83] In languages other than German or English, the use of final intonation in repair initiation formats is likely to be dependent on the intonation system of the language in question, especially its association with general functions such as declarativity versus interrogativity, and/or its interplay with tone, where relevant (see §3.1.3 above).

Table 3.2 *Types of other-initiated repair, ordered from least to more severe*

Repair initiation examples (from English and German)	Type of trouble implied, repair practice, and initiation format[84] (in English and German)	Implications	Repair operation invited
	Problem of hearing	*Least severe/serious*	
huh? hm? eh? what? was? ('what') sorry? pardon? bitte? ('pardon') ich hab nich verstanden was sie gesacht habm. ("I didn't hear what you said")	*Implying non-localized and unspecified repairable*: "Open" initiation format, with /?/ Explicit initiation format	Acoustic decoding disturbed	Repetition of the trouble source
they're what? met whom? where? who? what? wer? ('who')	*Implying localized or specified repairable*: - *Locating + replacing the repairable*: Q-word framing through partial repeat/ pronominalization (locating repairable) + Q-word (class-unspecific or class-specific), with /?/ - *Replacing the repairable*: Freestanding class-specific Q-word, with /?/	(same as above)	(same as above)
columbia? kame:lwü:rmer? ("camel worms")	*Proffering a candidate hearing*: Partial repeat, with final /?/	Acoustic decoding uncertain	Confirm/correct hearing

[84] In the repair initiation formats, /?/ denotes final rising pitch, /.../ denotes final falling pitch.

Table 3.2 (*cont.*)

Repair initiation examples (from English and German)	Type of trouble implied, repair practice, and initiation format (in English and German)	Implications	Repair operation invited
	Problem of reference	*More severe than* ↑; *less severe than* ↓	
welches meinen se denn jetz; ("which one do you mean")	*Explicit request for specification*	Recognition/retrieval of the referent momentarily not possible	Identification of referent
move what.	*Locating + replacing the repairable*: Q-word framing via partial repeat + class-specific Q-word, with /./	(same as above)	
what. / *where.* / *welcher*. ("which one") / *wer*. ("who")	*Replacing the repairable*: Freestanding class-specific Q-word, with /./		Replacement of prior indexical reference by full reference form (maintaining assumption of recognizability)

	Problem of understanding	*More severe than ↑; less severe than ↓*	
twelve minutes? messtischblätter? ("plane table sheets")	**Repeating the repairable:** Partial repeats with /?/[85]	Check of understanding in an open sense, i.e., of understanding and/or remembering, etc.	Confirm or disconfirm/correct understanding, explication or other help in understanding if necessary
you mean homosexual? across the street? in der SCHUle, ("at school") die stuDENten; ("the students")[86]	**Proffering a candidate understanding:** - (*you mean* +) candidate understanding (e.g., interpretation, paraphrase, reformulation, inference, etc.), with /?/ or /./ - Appendor Q or increment, with /?/ or /./	Understanding of specified item is uncertain and needs to be secured. Implications of final pitch: /?/ or /,/ => [K-] /./ or /;/ => [K+]	Confirmation or disconfirmation/correction
from; and, at	**Prompting prior speaker to elaborate:** Increment initiator, with /,/ or /;/ or /./	Prior information is not sufficient to understand the meaning or significance	Provision of more information by continuing the increment
what's a gwaff. was is DAS denn. ("what's that") was HEISST ganz früh; ("what does early mean") wer is lobkovitz ("who is lobkovitz") wer ist der N. ("who is N")	**Requesting explanation**, with: *what is X. what do you mean (+X). was ist/heißt X.* ("what is X / what does X mean") *wer ist X* ("who is X")	Non-understanding due to lack of knowledge	Explanation or other help in understanding

[85] Also: *a*-suffixed repeats in Chinese. [86] Also: proffering insertable elements in Japanese.

Table 3.2 (*cont.*)

Repair initiation examples (from English and German)	Type of trouble implied, repair practice, and initiation format (in English and German)	Implications	Repair operation invited
	Problem of expectation / acceptability	*More severe than ↑.*	
	Questioning the acceptability of the trouble source with:	Non-acceptance due to unexpected or implausible information	Sorting out, clarification of clashing expectations or beliefs; explanation, perhaps also correction of expectations
WIEso; GIBTS da eine ne offizielle URlaubsregelung? ("how come; is there an official regulation for vacation")	- *why / how come / wieso* ("why") / *wie kommt* ("how come") + resumption of trouble source, with or without implying a candidate answer		
<<f> BIT↑te?> ("pardon") <<h, f> 'WAS?> ("what")	- Surprised/astonished initiation of repair, i.e., with marked/salient prosody	Adding an affective overtone of surprise/astonishment	
james^CAMeron.	- Partial or full repeat with high rise-fall contour[87]		

---

[87] Also: question-intoned repeats in Chinese.

re-categorizers treat the problem as a more severe one, they may wish to spare the co-participant the effort of having to initiate repair on the more serious problem later on her/himself. If re-categorizations do not solve the problem, repair initiators pursue treatment of their problem by initiating repair again.

> Other-initiation of repair and its resolution is not a mechanical operation. In initiating as well as in executing repair, participants take into consideration the situational and sequential circumstances as well as their relationships and assumed or displayed epistemic stances (see also Sidnell 2010:125).

With respect to cross-linguistic aspects we can summarize the results of current research as follows:

i. Language structure shapes other-initiated repair

As Egbert (2009:167ff.) points out, the differences between English and German in the organization of other-initiated self-repair result from the different grammatical structures of these languages, especially the richer morphological marking of nouns and articles/determiners for case, gender, and number in German. Egbert concludes that the basic mechanism of repair is the same for English and German, but that the specific syntactic, morphological, and lexical properties of each language result in different formats for initiating and carrying out repair. The same is true for the other languages included here: Japanese, Chinese, Finnish, etc.

ii. Particular languages (and cultures) have specific techniques for the initiation of repair

Because of cultural restrictions, languages may develop specific techniques for referring to particular classes of people – and thus require special techniques to initiate repair on them. Furthermore, if a language allows constituents to remain unexpressed, interlocutors may well resort, more than in other languages, to "proffering insertables" or other kinds of candidate understandings for confirmation or disconfirmation as formats for the other-initiation of repair. We can thus only agree with Sidnell (2007b:239) when he writes that there is "a good deal of variation across both languages and contexts".

4. Other-correction

According to Schegloff et al. (1977), other-initiated other-repair – or correction – is the most dispreferred kind of repair. The authors report that this kind of repair is least frequently instantiated, and they cite extracts from their data to show that this kind of repair is frequently delayed and/or modulated to mitigate its potential problematic impact for the corrected party. One indication of how dispreferred correction is involves the practice of *embedded correction*, described by Jefferson (1987).

Jefferson shows that other-correction can be carried out in both an *exposed* and an *embedded* way. Constitutive of both kinds of correction is that the participants produce a series of elements in a sequence such that: first, a speaker produces some element (X); second, a subsequent speaker produces an alternative (Y); and finally, the prior speaker accepts the alternative (Y) – or rejects the alternative and retains his/her own original element (X) (1987:88 et passim). In *exposed* correction, the correction is attended to in its own repair sequence. In *embedded* correction, by contrast, the correction is carried out in a by-the-way fashion: it is camouflaged rather than being exposed as a sequence of its own.

Here is one of Jefferson's examples of exposed correction:

(3.80)   "Tomorrow" (Jefferson 1987:87) (adapted)
```
1 -> Larry: They're going to drive ba:ck Wednesday.
2 -> Norm:  Tomorrow.
3 -> Larry: Tomorrow. Righ[t.
4    Norm:                [M-hm,
5    Larry: They're working half day.
```

Larry produces the repairable *Wednesday* (=X) in line 1. Norm provides an alternative next, *Tomorrow.* (=Y) in line 2. Larry now accepts this correction and repeats the alternative, *Tomorrow.* (=Y), in line 3. Together, they produce the series XYY. Jefferson adds that turns carrying out exposed correction (here those in lines 2–4) discontinue the business of prior talk and are occupied with correcting; they are often also accompanied by some accounting for the production of the trouble source and/or the correction.

The same series XYY can be produced in *embedded correction*, in such a way that the correction does not discontinue prior talk nor become the sole business of the turns involved. In consequence, with this kind of repair there is no room for accounting. Here is an example:

(3.81)   "The cops" (Jefferson 1987:93) (adapted)
```
1 -> Ken:   Well- if you're gonna race, the police have said
            this to us.
2    Roger: That makes it even better. The challenge of running
  ->        from the cops!
3 -> Ken:   The cops say if you wanna race, uh go out at four or five in the
            morning on the freeway...
```

Ken refers to *the police* (=X) in line 1, whereupon Roger replaces this referring expression with the alternative referring expression *the cops* (=Y) in line 2. Ultimately Ken adopts Roger's expression *the cops* (=Y) in line 3. Again, the participants collaboratively construct the series XYY, which is constitutive of correction. Nevertheless, in doing so they continue topical talk: correction is carried out by the way, without attracting attention to itself.

Jefferson also identifies cases of what she calls "abdicated other-correction" (2007): in these it can be reconstructed that participants have noticed an error and could have initiated repair on it but instead acknowledge the prior turn as it is and pass up the opportunity to initiate repair, thus minimizing the import of the error. Here is one of her examples:

(3.82) "Gardener" (Jefferson 2007:448) (adapted)
((Helen is complaining to her grown son Edgar about the gardener, who has been hired to do some work for the two of them.))

```
10      Helen: Uh::m it's only that* uh I: faw- I °fah-°.hh I °fah-° found
11             it*,h.h uh very expensive uh ten: pou:nds a(m) a da::y?h.hh
12      Edgar: Yes=
13      Helen: =But* (0.4) uh::m:: (0.9) uh-:: i-i- (.) if::.h.h uhw he
14 ->          won't do what you want* him to do: t-.h twice a week with
15             you 'n twice a wee:k with me.
16 -> Edgar: We:ll we[:  w[e-
17 -> Helen:          °[Uh° [twice a:, a month.
18      Edgar: Well we've got to we've gotta talk to him about it. I haven't
19             mentioned it to him yet.
```

Notice that in lines 14–15 Helen misspeaks when she says *twice a week*: both she and Edgar know that it is twice a month that the gardener comes. Edgar, however, does not initiate repair on this error in next turn; instead, he launches an appropriate response, *well we: we-*, only broken off when Helen herself comes in in overlap with a self-correction (line 17). Thereafter Edgar recycles his response (lines 18–19). Jefferson's point here is that Edgar was in a position to hear that his mother had misspoken in lines 14–15 but "abdicated" correction by letting it pass unaddressed (line 16).

> The practices of embedded correction and abdicated correction indicate that participants in interaction have developed ways of dealing with the dispreference for other-correction that Schegloff et al. (1977) identify. These practices mitigate the impact of correction on the interaction and allow participants to camouflage other-correction when it cannot be avoided.[88]

Both earlier work on other-correction in German (Selting 1987c) and more recent work on other-correction in Finnish (Haakana and Kurhila 2009) distinguish between three rather similar formats, which can be ordered according to the explicitness with which a correction is drawn attention to. Our following summary begins with the most inconspicuous type of other-correction.

4.1 Producing a Correct Version

The most inconspicuous way to carry out other-correction is by simply producing the correct version, i.e., by replacing an item from the prior turn with an alternative, claimed-to-be-correct item in next turn. The correction is often done simply in passing, so that the corrector implies that the trouble is minor – only one of word selection, not a more serious problem of knowledge.

This is the procedure applied in the following example from Finnish, where two boys are talking about a school project they have been doing together.

```
(3.83)    "Amos" (Haakana and Kurhila 2009:161) (adapted)
1  Sami:   heheh s(h)e vid(h)eo oli ihan kau:heen hyvä. .h
           heheh  t(h)he  vid(h)eo was just so: good. .h
2  Pasi:   He
3  Sami:   he he.h (mä ainakin) nauroin..hhh
           he he.h  (at least I) laughed.         .hhh
4          (0.5)
5  Sami:   #@mja:[::.] @#((matkii videon kuuluttajaa))
           #@and: [::. ] @#((imitates the voice in the video))
6  Pasi:         [se ] Jesaja vasta mum  mielest kauhee    oliki.
                  the    nameM  PRT  I-GEN mind-ELA awful-PAR was-CLI
           the Isaiah thing was really awful I think.
7  Sami:   e: Aamos.
           eh Amos.
```

---

[88] This general dispreference, of course, does not preclude the notion that in certain situations or relationships participants may make use of other-correction for achieving goals such as, e.g., exercising power or displaying asymmetry.

```
8   Pasi:    [ai nii Aamos.]
             PRT PRT  name_M
             oh yeah Amos.
```

In line 7, after a hesitation token (*e:*), Sami replaces Pasi's *Jesaja* "Isaiah" from line 6 with the proper name of the prophet, *Aamos* "Amos". Because the boys both have access to the correct name due to their shared project at school, the trouble is treated as a mere slip of the tongue (pp. 162–3).

4.2 Explicitly Correcting an Item

More attention is drawn to other-correction if it is carried out conspicuously, for example, through the replacement of a single item in the prior turn using a prosodically marked or salient form (for instance, high pitch register), or prefacing it with negation, such as *nee* "no" or *X nich* "not X" in German or *eiku* in Finnish.

Haakana and Kurhila (2009) report that other-correcting in Finnish is done with the negative particle *eiku*, a kind of general correction marker (compare its use in self-repairs as described in §2.3.3 above). In their words: "By beginning her correction with *eiku*, the speaker [...] indicates something like 'what you just said is not right; here comes what it should be'" (p. 159). For instance, in the following example Rea replaces the place name Tero has used (*Håkansböle*) with another (*Hiekkis*):

```
(3.84)    "Hiekkis" (Haakana and Kurhila 2009:157–8) (adapted)
1   Tero:   Kati halus    et puol neljä maissa oltas      siella,
            name want-PST PRT half four  around be-PAS-CON there
            Kati wanted to be there at around half past three
2   Rea:    .nss.n [ss
3   Kati:          [Joo::
                    Yes::
4   Tero:   Håkans[bölessä.
            (place name in Swedish)-INE
            in Håkansböle.
5   Kati:          [mut ei se nyt.
                    but NEG it now
                    but it isn't like.
6   Rea:    Ei[ku    Hiekkiksessä.
            NEG + PRT (another place name in Finnish)-INE
            Eiku in Hiekkis.
7   Kati:     [Ei,
               No,
```

```
8    Tero:   Eiku Hiekkiksessä.
             Eiku in Hiekkis.
9    Kati:   Sand↑kulla↑
             (Swedish name of Hiekkis)-NOM
             Sand↑kulla↑
10   Rea:    Sandgullassa.
             (Swedish name of Hiekkis)-INE
             In Sandgulla.
```

By using the repair initiation particle *eiku* in line 6, the speaker Rea draws attention to the fact that she is correcting; she makes the error interactionally salient and projects a response from the recipient (p. 163). If, as in the example given, the trouble source is only a single item, the replacement of one phrase with another can correct the trouble. In line 8, Tero acknowledges the correction by repeating it.

4.3 Explicitly Correcting an Entire Verbal Representation

If an entire verbal representation in a prior TCU or turn needs correcting, explicit other-corrections take the form of *eiku* + alternative clause in Finnish conversation (Haakana and Kurhila 2009). Two instances of this can be seen in the following example. Here is the context: Jaana has been telling a story about the division of an inheritance, where one of the siblings, Veikko, wanted to take more than his share. Jaana's husband, Jaska, played a trick on Veikko: he pretended that a cheap glass plate was a piece of valuable design (lines 2–11, not shown here). At the climax (line 14), Jaska himself enters into storytelling:

(3.85)   "In your hands" (Haakana and Kurhila 2009:166–7) (adapted)

```
13 Jaana:  ja  se kiskasi [sej Jaska,
           and he grab-PST it-ACC nameM
           and he grabbed it from Jaska's,
14 Jaska:              [mää pis- pistin se tohon,   [tolle pualelle,
                       I    pu-  put-PST-1 it-ACC there [that-ALL side-ALL
                       I pu- put it there              on that side,
15 Jaana:                                           [eiku se oli sun
                                                    [PRT it was your
                                                    eiku it was in
```

```
16            käsis[äs,
              hand-PL-INE
              your hands,
17 Jaska:         [>eiku,< mää pisti se >tos<    sivulle  @nii se
                  [PRT      I put-PST it  that-ILL side-ALL PRT  he
                  >eiku,<   I put it there on the side          @so he
18            tuli@ ja (-), [heh heh he,
              came@ and (–), [heh heh he,
19 Mirja:                    [a-haa, [no nii juu.
                             [I see, [well okay yes
```

When Jaska, the protagonist of the story, says that he put the glass plate on the side, storyteller Jaana corrects him by saying *eiku se oli sun käsisäs,* ("*eiku* it was in your hands,"), but this is again counter-corrected by Jaska's *eiku, mää pisti se tos sivulle* ("*eiku*, I put it there on the side") (pp. 166–7).

Interestingly, Haakana and Kurhila's study of repair in everyday Finnish conversation does not confirm the dispreference for other-correction. They find that – especially in multi-party conversations – even though less frequent than self-correction/repair and other-initiated repair in general, other-corrections are not infrequent (2009:154ff., 174). Moreover, other-corrections are usually not modulated. This could be due to the fact that in most of their cases other-correctors were indeed the ones with better access to and knowledge about the corrected matter; they consequently presented themselves with a [K+] epistemic status associated with certainty and confidence.

> Other-correcting in Finnish can be done without explicit marking, or with explicit marking through the negative particle *eiku*. In its least conspicuous form, a trouble-source item in the prior turn is simply replaced in next turn with the correct version: this does not draw attention to the correction. However, with *eiku*, the other-corrector tags part or all of the prior turn as wrong and projects that a corrected version will follow. Typically, other-correctors portray themselves as more knowledgeable; in everyday interaction between friends and family, other-correction is not treated as a problematic or delicate action (Haakana and Kurhila 2009:174).

4.4 Conclusion for Other-correction

Studies on other-repair/correction are scarce and preliminary, but they point to several issues for future research. First, as we have seen, other-correction may be carried out in less conspicuous and more conspicuous ways, thus drawing less or more attention to the co-participant's "fault". There are different turn designs for doing other-correction: with or without explicit negation of the prior correctable, with phrasal or clausal syntax, and with or without prosodic marking or salience. These variants reflect the fact that (a) the correctable can be only a part of the prior turn or the entire presentation of affairs, and (b) the corrector can make the correction less or more salient. The presence of negation-prefacing and/or prosodic salience draws attention to the correction, exposing something said by the other as wrong, while the absence of negation-prefacing and/or prosodic salience does not draw attention to the alternative version. Second, the variant formats for other-correction can imply different problem categorizations or diagnoses: momentary selection of the wrong word, inadvertent production of an error, or a problem of knowledge. Third, although the universal preference for self-correction/repair is not to be disputed, there is reason to believe that the preference structures among other types of repair as suggested by Schegloff et al. (1977) for English conversational interaction may not hold for all situations, participation frameworks, languages, or cultures. Future cross-linguistic research on these issues is needed.

> If other-correction is carried out at all, the format chosen for doing so can involve lesser or greater conspicuousness and imply different problem categorizations or diagnoses of the problem, for example, as a misspeaking (less severe), as a momentary error, or as a lack of knowledge (more severe).

5. Conclusion

Repair is a basic mechanism necessary for the conduct of verbal interaction in all languages. The linguistic details of its organization may vary with constraints set by language types and/or by cultural or institutional conventions. But in all languages and cultures, participants need to have ways of dealing with their own and others' misspeakings, word searches, hearing problems, referential problems, understanding problems, and problems of expectation or acceptability.

Previous research has shown that the types of repair distinguished by Schegloff et al. (1977) are relevant in many, if not all, languages. We have tried to show that there is an internal organization among these types of repair. For all types of trouble source, linguistic structures or formats are deployed systematically both to initiate repair and to repair the trouble; at the same time, they imply type-specific categorizations or diagnoses of the trouble, which can be thought of as ordered relative to one another in terms of seriousness of the problem. Where possible, participants opt for less serious diagnoses and treatments.

The practices of repair and the structure of the language involved are interdependent. In all types of repair the positioning of the repair initiation in relation to the trouble source determines the format of the initiation; the practice of repair thus shapes the linguistic formats used. But the linguistic structures of the respective language constrain, often morpho-syntactically, what its repair formats can do; thus, the morpho-syntax of a language shapes its practices of repair.

Some languages make distinctions and/or afford specialized structures for repair that others lack. Prosody and visible practices have only been investigated for a few languages so far; these, however, show that prosody in particular is systematically deployed in the organization of repair, especially in initiating the type of repair with its implied problem type and in projecting the repair operation due in next turn.

Despite the detailed internal organization of repair practices, repair is, of course, not a mechanical process. The initiation of repair can be contingent on its relevance for the interaction, and the treatment of a trouble source may be subject to negotiation between interlocutors.

Research so far rests on only a few languages. It is an open question whether the attested patterns generalize to other languages and language types around the world.

4

Action Formation and Ascription

In this chapter we broach a further system of organization for the conduct of conversation, this time concerning the formation and ascription of *actions* through turns at talk.[1] As in prior chapters, our focus will be on linguistic resources and their mobilization, primarily in ordinary conversation and across different languages.

As participants take turns at talk, they implement social actions. It has been said that one of the most central concerns of *recipients* in interaction is to figure out "What is the speaker *doing* by that?" (Schegloff 1997a:506), "that" referring to the formal features of a just observed piece of verbal behavior. But it is equally crucial for *speakers* to know how to mobilize linguistic and other semiotic resources in order to be understood as carrying out a particular social action. How forms are assembled by speakers into configurations designed to be recognizable as implementing some particular action is what is known as *action formation*. How such forms are actually understood by recipients to be carrying out a particular action has been referred to as *action ascription* (Levinson 2013b).[2] The following sections will first cover some preliminaries in the study of action formation and ascription, and then examine how language and linguistic structures are mobilized for the implementation of selected initiating actions and their responses, including questions (requests for information and confirmation); offers and requests for action; news deliveries and informings; and finally assessments, compliments, and self-deprecations. In each case our discussion will be motivated by the current state of the art and will incorporate interactional linguistic findings from a variety of languages.

1. Preliminaries

The problem of *action formation* has been characterized by Schegloff in the following way:

---

[1] See Online-Chapter B for a discussion of the asymmetric relationships of *preference* that hold between these actions.

[2] Since actions may not be recognized for what they were designed to be recognizable as, it is preferable to speak of action "ascription" rather than action "recognition" (Levinson 2013b).

... how are the resources of the language, the body, the environment of the interaction, and position *in* the interaction fashioned into conformations designed to be, and to be recognized by recipients as, particular actions – actions like requesting, inviting, granting, complaining, agreeing, telling, noticing, rejecting, and so on – in a class of unknown size?

(2007a:xiv)

Two things are worth noting about this characterization. For one, more is involved in action formation than just language: in addition to the question of which linguistic structures are chosen, it matters how they are embodied (e.g., what tone of voice is used, what gestures accompany them); where they are positioned sequentially (e.g., what turns or turn-constructional units (TCUs) they follow or project); and what kind of environment they are part of (what larger project or activity is underway). Although our focus in the following sections will be primarily on the contribution of *language* to action formation and ascription, it must always be kept in mind that other contextual dimensions and semiotic systems are likely to be involved as well.

Second, as the wording *resources ... designed to be* in Schegloff's characterization makes clear, the linguistic and other formal means involved in action *formation* do not "carry" inherent action-related meaning: there is nothing compulsory about them or their use. Rather, they are *resources*: means afforded by language with which a speaker can make a turn at talk interpretable as such-and-such an action. Just as the root of the word *interpretable* suggests, action *ascription* is inferential. The recipient makes a best guess about what action the interlocutor is implementing. His/her interpretation of this action becomes visible in next turn. If it is congruent with what the interlocutor designed his/her turn to do, talk will proceed apace. If it is not, progressivity may be temporarily halted in order to allow the problem to be remedied and mutual understanding to be re-established (see Chapter 3, especially §3).

1.1 Action and Action Type

What counts as an *action* in interaction? This is surely one of the most intractable issues that interactional linguists are faced with, but it will not do to beg the question entirely. Every bit of conduct that interactants engage in involves a multitude of actions, with varying degrees of granularity: when we speak, for instance, we manipulate our vocal apparatus, raise our larynx, lower our velum, round our lips, etc. (see Online-Chapter E) – all of these are actions in one sense of the word. However, interactional linguists require a level of action description that will allow them to appreciate how the structure and organization of talk-in-interaction impinge upon the choice of linguistic constructions and formats. For this, a less granular view of action is needed.

One way to restrict the notion of action is by focusing on *social* actions in talk. A social action is one that is publicly directed at, targets, or is done in coordination with another, typically co-present human being. This interlocutor will be expected to deal with it next in one way or another. A summons, for instance, targets another, a request enlists the help of another, an informing apprises another of something, etc. Even self-repair is a social action in the sense that it is done for the "benefit" of a recipient. The action of raising the larynx, however, falls outside the purview of social action on this understanding: it is not interpretable as a "doing" in its own right.

Another way to restrict the notion of action in the study of talk-in-interaction is in terms of what the *main job* of a turn is. In Levinson's words, the main job of a turn is "what the response must deal with in order to count as an adequate next turn" (2013b:107). In other words, it is the nature of the responsive action that reflects what the prior turn was taken to be doing. A first turn, for instance, would be described as one type of action, say a "request for action," if it makes *acquiescence* relevant next (the recipient agrees to perform some task in the future), but as another type of action, say a "request for permission", if it makes *granting* relevant next (the recipient agrees to allow the other to perform some act in the future). But a request for action, say, done with a claim to strong authority or in a blunt fashion would not be a different action from a request lacking these features, since the adequate next turn would still be acquiescence by the recipient. As Levinson explains, being blunt or hinting that I am in charge are usually off the record: they may produce "under-currents", but "do not in the normal case change the *nature of the sequential action type now due*" (Levinson 2013b:107).

This means that in order to know what counts as a separate social action in first position, we need to work out whether it makes a different action type relevant in second position. And conversely, to know what counts as a separate social action in second position, we need to work out whether it responds to a different action type in first position. But what is meant by *action type*? To answer this, it is helpful to revisit early conversation analytic work on *adjacency pairs*.

Most turns at talk are organized pairwise, with a first turn, or initiating action, by speaker A projecting a second turn, or responsive action, by speaker B, typically in an immediately adjacent or next position. Speaker B's response must be "typed" to match speaker A's initiating action. That is, if speaker A produces a greeting, speaker B is expected to respond with a *return greeting* and not an appreciation or a thank you. If speaker A produces an offer, speaker B should respond with an *appreciation* and not a return greeting, and so on. The type of first action implemented thus has consequences for the type of response expected next, and conversely the type of response produced makes visible what action type the recipient has ascribed to the prior turn.

1. Preliminaries

Complicating the picture somewhat, however, is the fact that turns at talk can on occasion implement more than one action at a time. Schegloff describes this as one action being used as a "vehicle or instrument" for another (1997a:505). A questioning action, for instance, can be the vehicle for an offer or invitation; an other-initiation of repair can be the vehicle for a challenge. In such cases the responsive turn will also often be "double-barrelled", dealing first with the action of the vehicle itself and then with the action it is serving as a vehicle for. For instance, in the following fragment from a telephone call, Gordon's hairdresser has just informed him that he missed an appointment for that evening. After admitting that he completely forgot the appointment and apologizing, Gordon continues:

(4.1)   "Hair appointment" (Holt Sep-Oct 1988:1:6)
1 Gor: Uh: could I make it next week please.
2 Des: Yes su:re.

Observe that in response to Gordon's turn in line 1, the Desk first says *yes*, a token of affirmation, and then *sure*, a token of acquiescence (line 2). The double-barrelled form that this response takes suggests that Gordon's prior turn is heard as implementing two actions at once: questioning (or requesting information) and requesting an action.

1.2 Social Actions and Speech Acts

Before proceeding any further, it may be relevant at this point to consider whether and how the view of conversational actions presented here relates to the "speech acts" postulated in Speech Act Theory (Austin 1962; Searle 1969, 1976). There may appear to be a number of striking similarities. For instance, many of the social actions talked about in the Conversation Analysis (CA) literature have names identical to those used in Speech Act Theory: question, request, offer, compliment, to name just a few. In addition, the notion of one action serving as a vehicle for another may sound suspiciously like the relation between so-called direct and indirect speech acts. Yet such similarities are only superficial. In reality, there are significant differences between the two approaches to action with far-reaching consequences for what counts as an action and consequently for what the inventory of actions is thought to be.

For one, in contrast to Speech Act Theory, social actions as described by conversation analysts are identified inductively based on empirical observation of sequential contexts in situated talk (Schegloff 1988b). Only those actions for which there is some empirical evidence of participant orientation in naturally occurring conversation are recognized as such. While speech acts are described with respect to their speakers' intentions, which are not directly observable, social actions in interaction are conceived of as produced and responded to in observable interactions (see also Chapter 1, especially §1.1 and §1.2). This means that the set of social actions in interaction is in one sense narrower than the inventory of speech acts, because Speech Act Theory recognizes some speech acts for which there is so far no conversational evidence (e.g., conclude, threaten, fire, etc.).[3] But in another sense the set of documented conversational actions is broader, because counted among the social actions of interaction are various sorts of preliminary actions (pre-announcement, pre-request, pre-invitation), repair and repair initiation actions, and more structurally oriented actions such as conversational openings, pre-closings and closings, etc., for which vernacular terms are lacking altogether, and which Speech Act Theory has not recognized.

Second, conversation analysts consider the set of conversational actions to be *open* in principle. This means that with careful empirical observation new social actions may be discovered, as has happened in the case of Schegloff's "confirming allusions" (1996a). Schegloff argues that speakers can "confirm an allusion" by repeating an explicit formulation their interlocutor has just given of something they themselves had only hinted at. Here is one of Schegloff's examples:

(4.2)   "Verschickert" (Schegloff 1996a:174–5) (adapted)
((Evelyn has been called to the phone.))

```
1          Evelyn:    =Hi:Rita
2          Rita:      Hi: Evelyn:.. How [are you
3          Evelyn:                     [I had to come in another room.
4          Rita:      Oh:.. Uh huh.=
5          Evelyn:    =I fee:l a bi:ssel verschickert.
6                     (0.2)
7          Rita:      W-why's tha:t,
8                     (0.4)
9   ->     Rita:      uh you've had something to dr^ink.=
10  =>     Evelyn:    =I had something to drin:k.
11         Rita:      Uh huh.
```

In response to Rita's question *How are you* (line 2), Evelyn says merely *I feel a bissel verschickert* (line 5), the latter being a Yiddish expression meaning "a little punchy" (Schegloff 1996a:186). When Evelyn is not forthcoming with more detail, Rita now formulates what she surmises Evelyn means: *you've had something to drink* (line 9). What Evelyn does next is what Schegloff calls "confirming an allusion": she repeats her interlocutor's formulation, thereby confirming its interpretation and at the same time confirming that this interpretation was indeed only alluded to in prior talk (1996a:181). "Confirming an allusion" is a type of action

---

[3] For one typology of speech acts see Levinson (1983:240).

1. Preliminaries

that would be inconceivable in Speech Act Theory due to its reliance on a specific kind of composition (repetition) and a specific sequential position (after an explicit formulation of something an interlocutor has only hinted at).[4]

Finally, in contrast to speech acts in Speech Act Theory, social actions in interaction are not restricted to implementation via language. It is true that they are lodged within talk-in-interaction, but many can be carried out non-verbally as well as verbally. Offering and requesting are two cases in point: not only can these actions be implemented admirably by primates (Rossano and Liebal 2014) and pre-linguistic infants (van der Goot et al. 2014), even adult interactants often carry them out with wholly non-verbal means or through a combination of verbal and non-verbal means (Kärkkäinen and Keisanen 2012; Rauniomaa and Keisanen 2012; Rossi 2014).

1.3 Sequence Type and Project

Let us note now that action type is relevant not only for identifying actions but also for understanding a further dimension of structural organization in conversation: sequence and sequence type. *Sequences* are courses of action implemented through turns at talk (Schegloff 2007a:9): they are often composed of one or more adjacency pairs, in the latter case typically organized around a *base pair* (Schegloff 2007a:27). The actions of the base pair determine the *sequence type*. For instance, if I ask you for a favor, for example, to give me a ride to the party, my initiating action or first turn might be *can you give me a ride?*, a "request for action", and your response might be *sure*, an acceptance or "acquiescence". Together these turns build a "request sequence". However, before asking outright for a ride, it might be in my interest to check beforehand whether you are actually going to the party. This could be accomplished by my saying something like *are you going to the party tonight?*, implementing a "pre-request", to which you might reply *yeah*, implementing a "go-ahead" response to the "pre". Together, the two adjacency pairs resulting from the pre-request and the request turns with their responses form a sequence; its type is determined by the action of the initiating turn of the base pair, in this case a "request".

Suppose, however, you respond to my pre-request turn with *no, I'm feeling a bit under the weather.* This would most likely lead to my abandoning the original plan to ask you for a ride, in which case no request sequence would ensue. Nevertheless, my pre-request would be on record as indicative of my plan of action, or project (see also Schegloff 2007a:244). A *project* is thus a "course of action that at least one participant is pursuing" (Levinson 2013b:122). Projects are not equivalent to

---

[4] The fact that the status of "confirming allusions" as a social action has been called into doubt (Levinson 2013b) does not detract from the point being made here: that the set of social actions is, in principle, open.

sequences; in fact, the same project can be pursued through a variety of different sequence types, and the same sequence type can be implicated in different projects. Both sequence types and projects are relevant for action ascription, because recipients rely on the projections created by them to make inferences about what a given speaker is doing in a particular turn or TCU.

1.4 Turn Design and Practices

How does *turn design* make particular actions recognizable? For one, certain *forms*, singly or in combination, are recognizable as performing particular actions in specified sequential positions. For instance, the choice of a syntactic pattern, for example, an imperative construction, can provide the grounds for the inference that the speaker is making a request for action (see below). Or the combination of a particular syntactic pattern with a specific prosodic contour, say, interrogative syntax together with final rising intonation, can suggest that the speaker is asking a question (or requesting information; see below). However, it may also be the *content* of what is said rather than its form that makes a particular action recognizable: for instance, if I tell you how I perceived a situation in which you were involved in order to get you to tell me more about it yourself (*your line's been busy* or *I saw you leaving the house* or *your car wasn't in the garage last night*, etc.), this will be interpretable as "fishing" for information (Pomerantz 1980). That is why analysts prefer to talk about *practices*, a cover term for both form-based and content-based uses of language to implement action (Levinson 2013b:117). Practices are ways of formatting turns and of doing things in turns that make these turns recognizable as performing particular actions and that serve as the basis for ascribing particular actions to them. The relation between practices and actions is many-many: practices can implement different actions, and actions can be accomplished through different practices (Schegloff 1997a:505; see also the preface to Part I and Online-Chapter F). Yet despite this complexity, it is nevertheless possible to identify systematic patterns and routines for language use that guide action formation and ascription.

1.5 "Top-down" versus "Bottom-up" Analysis

Before proceeding to discuss the linguistic design of concrete action types, we should touch briefly on a contentious issue concerning the inferential basis of action ascription. It has been hotly debated whether actions are ascribed in a *top-down* or a *bottom-up* fashion (Drew 2010; Levinson 2013b). The top-down position was first articulated by Schegloff, who wrote that "sequential features of conversation [...] overshadow the contribution made by its linguistic form to what an utterance is doing" (1984:36) and, more pointedly, "it will not do, for a variety of reasons, to use features of linguistic form as sole, or even invariant though not exhaustive, indicators or embodiments of (conversational) objects"[5] (1984:49–50). By contrast, the bottom-up position runs approximately as follows: "We should begin by looking for action in turn design" and "At the core of 'action construction' is the investigation of the (full range of) linguistic resources used to do an action of a certain kind, to be recognized as doing that action, and not to be misunderstood as doing something else" (Drew 2010). Sequential position or turn design? – this in a nutshell articulates the controversy over how action ascription is achieved.

The top-down/bottom-up controversy has a long tradition in discourse functional and interactional linguistic research (Schegloff 1984; Weber 1993; Freed 1994, *inter alia*). But it has recently intensified, with increased attention being paid to action formation and ascription. To shed light on this chicken-and-egg debate, we might note that, to begin with, action ascription is not a question of *either* sequential position *or* turn design but rather of *both-and*. Actions are always recognized in situ on the grounds of both sequential position and turn design. However, two insights from the discussion are worth retaining. The first is that sequences *can* and *do* contribute to action formation and ascription. A turn's location in a sequence creates expectations about what its action will be. This is true not only of turns in second position, but also of first-position turns. If a first turn follows a "pre" that has been given a go-ahead and/or other kinds of prefatory work, its action will be interpretable accordingly. In addition, being part of a larger sequence or project can "change" an action's character (Levinson 2013b). A question that initiates a sequence or project may be a request for information *as well as* a "pre" that broaches or foreshadows some subsequent action (invitation, request, proposal, announcement, etc.). Second, however, and just as important, is the insight that although sequences may inform the understanding of a turn as implementing some action, that turn still needs to be constructed here and now as doing the action – and in talk-in-interaction it is primarily linguistic means that are mobilized to do this (Drew 2010).

We turn now to an examination of how linguistic resources are implicated in the accomplishment of selected initiating action types and their responses.[6]

2. Questions and their Responses

Let us begin by clarifying some important terminological issues. *Question* will be used here as a label for a type of social action by which an interlocutor (questioner)

---

[5] In this context the term "conversational object" refers to a social action.
[6] In the following sections we will use initial capitals for the specific action types as defined.

asks a recipient (questionee) to provide him/her with information concerning something which the questionee is imputed to have more knowledge about.[7] The questioner thereby positions him/herself as an unknowing (or [K−]) party; by the same token the questionee is positioned as a more knowing (or [K+]) party (see also Heritage 2012a, 2012b).[8] Questions, in other words, are actions whose *main job* (see above) is to request information. They make Answers, turns providing the information requested, relevant next. Yet *how* "unknowing" the questioner is can range from having no idea about the matter at all, in which case the speaker is completely [K−], to having more or less clear expectations about what the answer will be, in which case the speaker is partially [K+]. Some analysts refer to the first case as a "request for information" and to the second as a "request for confirmation". Here, both requests for information and requests for confirmation will be called Questions.

Separate in principle from the action type of Question are the various linguistic forms used by languages to mark utterances as *interrogative*, whether polar (in English *yes/no*) or question-word (in English *what*, *when*, *how*, etc.).[9] (In practice, of course, there are systematic mappings between the action type Question and interrogativity: see below.) Most languages use some kind of formal marking for interrogativity, whether morphemic, syntactic, or intonational (Dryer 2008).[10] A morpheme or particle used to formally mark interrogativity will be called an *interrogative morpheme* or *interrogative particle*.[11] A syntactic form used to formally mark interrogativity will be called *interrogative syntax*.[12] And an intonational form used to formally mark interrogativity will be referred to as *interrogative intonation*.[13]

---

[7] Questions that serve as vehicles for other actions, e.g., for requests for action (*can you loan me a pen?*) or for repair initiation (*what did you say?*), will be treated in the sections dealing with those other actions.

[8] Under Question actions we include requests for confirmation, although here the questioner positions him/herself as somewhat more knowing than with requests for information (see below). Requests for repair are treated in Chapter 3.

[9] A third kind of interrogative also recognized by grammarians, so-called "alternative questions" (Quirk et al. 1985:823–4), will not be considered here. See, however, Koshik (2005b) and Koivisto (2017).

[10] However, according to Levinson (2010), Yélî Dnye, a language isolate spoken on Rossel Island off the coast of Papua New Guinea, does not use any linguistic mark for polar interrogatives at all, making them virtually identical to declarative utterances.

[11] Interrogative morphemes or particles are to be distinguished from interrogative tags, such as, e.g., English *isn't it?* or *right?*. Tags are specialized for requesting confirmation; unlike interrogative morphemes or particles, tags do not attach to question-word interrogatives and they can form turns on their own (Hayashi 2010).

[12] Interrogative syntax for polar interrogatives usually involves inversion of the order of subject and verb in a SVO language. Inversion may entail the use of a supporting auxiliary verb, as with English *do*, or not, as, e.g., in Danish or Dutch (Englert 2010; Heinemann 2010). Interrogative syntax for question-word interrogatives typically involves the use of a word questioning who, what, where, when, why, etc. and may also entail subject-verb or subject-auxiliary inversion.

[13] Note that interrogative intonation need not entail rising pitch. As Heinemann (2010) explains for Danish, "question intonation [our *interrogative intonation* in this book] consists of a prosodic curve that is less falling than that applied to bare statements (Grønnum, 2003)." See also Grønnum and Tøndering (2007). In English and German there is no "interrogative intonation": both rising and falling final pitch have been shown to be deployed for different kinds of conversational questions (for German see Selting 1995a; for prosody in wh-questions also Selting 1994c; for English see Couper-Kuhlen 2012a).

2. Questions and their Responses

2.1 Recognizing Questions

Which language practices make turns at talk recognizable as Questions and distinguish them from other action types? How is it that we only rarely find ourselves saying to our interlocutor *Are you asking me or telling me*? Before attempting to answer this question, it is worth observing that on occasion there can be some ambiguity as to whether one is being asked for a piece of information or not. Here is a case in point:

```
(4.3)      "Family dinner" (Schegloff 1988b:57) (adapted)
1    Mother:   Is everybody (0.2) [washed for dinner?
2    Gary:                         [Yah.
3    Mother:   Daddy'n I have t- both go in different directions,
4              en I wanna talk to you about where I'm going
5              (tonight).
6    Russ:     mm hmm
7    Gary:     Is it about us?
8    Mother:   Uh huh
9    Russ:     I know where you're going,
10   Mother:   Where.
11   Russ:     To the uh (eighth grade)=
12   Mother:   =Yeah. Right.
13   Mother:   Do you know who's going to that meeting?
14   Russ:     Who.
15   Mother:   I don't kno:w.
16   Russ:     Oh::. Probably Missiz McOwen ('n detsa) en
17             probably Missiz Cadry and some of the teachers.
18             (0.4) and the coun[sellors.
19   Mother:                      [Missiz Cadry went to the-
20             I'll tell you...
```

When Mother says *Do you know who's going to that meeting?* (line 13) her turn could be taken as a Question asking whether Russ knows something (making *yes* or *no* relevant next) or asking Russ to provide specific information about what he knows (making the names of those attending relevant next). Yet Russ does not respond to Mother's turn in this way. Instead, he treats her turn as a preliminary to a telling, as a Pre-announcement, and furthers this course of action by responding *who* (line 14), thereby soliciting a naming (Terasaki 2004) (see also Online-Chapter F §5). It is only when it later emerges that Mother herself does not know who is attending the meeting (see line 15) that Russ proceeds to inform her (lines 16–18), revealing that he has known all along, but that he had taken her question to be a Pre-announcement rather than a Question.

This fragment is particularly interesting for our discussion, because Mother's turn has all the hallmarks of a genuine Question. For one, its design incorporates two formal features associated with Question actions: *polar interrogativity* (*do you know*) and *question-word interrogativity* (*who is going to that meeting*).[14] In addition, Mother's turn treats the eighth-grade parent-teacher meeting as a *B-event*: something to which the addressee has privileged access (Labov and Fanshel 1977). (This may be due to the fact that Russ has just displayed himself as [K+] about its taking place that evening.) It is such form- and content-based design features of turns that make them recognizable as Questions.

Most of what we know about the relation between Question actions and turn design cross-linguistically is indebted to the large-scale comparative study of question-answer sequences conducted at the Max Planck Institute for Psycholinguistics (Nijmegen) under the supervision of Enfield, Stivers, and Levinson (2010). Their team coded conversational data for both formal questions, i.e., linguistically marked, and functional questions, i.e., ones eliciting information, confirmation, or agreement, in ten geographically and genetically diverse languages.[15] They then quantitatively tracked which formal devices were found with which functions and vice versa. The results are revealing for how Questions, understood as soliciting information or confirmation, are accomplished cross-linguistically.

2.2 Question-word Interrogatives

Question-word interrogatives use so-called "question words" to request specific kinds of information: the who, what, when, where, how and why of a given situation or state of affairs: for example, *Who did you just call?*, *What time did we get back?*, *How far up the canyon do you live?*. In some but not all languages, question words are placed in initial position in the clause, although they may not occupy this position in declarative utterances.[16] English is a language where the question word is typically fronted. However, here are two examples from languages where the question word does not need to be fronted. The first is from Japanese conversation, the second from a conversation in Yélî Dnye, a language spoken on Rossel Island off the coast of Papua New Guinea:

---

[14] In this case the question-word interrogative is embedded as a clausal object complement (X) of the verb "know": *do you know X*.

[15] The languages included were ǂAkhoe Haillom, Danish, Dutch, English, Italian, Japanese, Korean, Lao, Tzeltal, and Yélî Dnye.

[16] Japanese is a language which has been described as leaving the question word *in situ*, i.e., in the position it would occupy in a declarative utterance. However, Hayashi (2010) found that 65 percent of the question-word questions in his conversational data actually had the question word in initial position.

2. Questions and their Responses

(4.4) "Side trip" (Hayashi 2010:2693)
((Looking at a photo from a recent trip.))

H: eh! kore wa **dore:**
    RC *this* TP *which*
    Huh? Which ((side trip)) is this from?

(*Note*: in this example RC stands for "response cry" and TP stands for "topic particle.")

(4.5) "Reason what" (Levinson 2010:2748) (adapted)

Kî   kópu   u   nt:uu   **lukwe**?
DEM.UNMARKED *affair* *3POSS* *reason* *what*
What caused this?

When a question word appears in the initial position of a question-word interrogative, it may or may not be accompanied by syntactic inversion of the subject and verb or auxiliary. In Italian, for instance, syntactic inversion is found following all question words except *perché* ("why") (Rossano 2010:2764). Here is a conversational example showing inversion following the question word *cosa* ("what"):

(4.6) "Underline" (Rossano 2010:2764) (adapted)

B: Cosa sottolinei   tu?
    What underline.2s you
    What do you underline?

In the comparative Nijmegen study of conversational questions and answers, the action of requesting information (speaker wholly [K−]), in contrast to requesting confirmation (speaker partially [K+]), was accomplished on the whole more frequently by question-word interrogatives than by polar interrogatives (Yoon 2010). This initially somewhat surprising finding can be explained by two factors: (i) requests for confirmation were more frequent than requests for information in the data collected, and (ii) requests for confirmation were done exclusively with polar interrogatives (see below). Taken together, these factors account for why question-word interrogatives were more frequent than polar interrogatives in Question actions where the questioner is wholly [K−].

Here is an example of a question-word interrogative in English used to implement a request for information:

(4.7) "Different kinds" (Stivers 2010:2776) (adapted)

```
1    Kim:    These're good so are they all different kinds?,
2            (.)
3    Mark:   Yeah there's uh:: (.) I got the list_
4            (0.6)
```

```
5  ->  Kim:    So why didn't=you buy any of these.
6              (0.2)
7      Mark:   Cuz I haven't even tried them. This is the first time
8              I'm trying them out, tonight.
```

Kim's question-word question in line 5 is interpreted by Mark as implying that she is asking from a wholly [K−] position: consequently he provides an informative answer in next turn (lines 7–8).

By virtue of their question word, question-word interrogatives may appear predestined to implement Question actions. Yet there are occasions when a question-word interrogative does not implement a Question. For instance, it has been observed that some *why*-interrogatives are interpreted not as Questions but rather as Challenges (Koshik 2003); others have been said to implement Complaints (see, e.g., Egbert and Vöge 2008). Here is an example from Günthner's study of reproaches in German (1996b, 2000a). The speaker S has called up the telephone information service to ask for the number of a family Weißer in Konstanz, but the operator A replies that there is no listing under that name:

```
(4.8)     "Telephone information" (Günthner 1996b:284) (adapted)
12    A:  ich habe keine Familie Weißer in Konstanz.
          I don't have a Weißer family in Konstanz
13        nur eine Familie Weiß.
          only a family called Weiß
14    S:  ja die wohnen glaub ich auf der *Reichenau.
          yeah I think they live on the Reichenau
15        und gar nicht direkt *in Konstanz.
          and actually not directly in Konstanz
16 -> A:  WARUM= *SA:↑↓GEN=SIE=DANN=KONSTANZ.
          why do you say Konstanz then
17    S:  tut mir leid. ich dachte die Reichenau fällt unter *Konstanz.
          I am sorry    I thought the Reichenau belonged to Konstanz
18        (2.5)
19    A:  also die *Nummer ist...
          okay the number is
```

As Günthner points out, S's response to the operator's *why*-interrogative reveals that she has not interpreted it purely as a Question (a request for information). Instead S's apology suggests that she took the prior turn to be morally impugning her conduct. This inference is made possible by the fact that in German *why*-turns implementing reproaches typically embody modal particles and extreme case formulations (Pomerantz 1986) as well as prosodic features such as narrow focus on the verb, increased loudness, strong rising-falling pitch contours, and lamento-like syllable stretchings. In (4.8), many of these features are present in the operator's turn. Taken together, they imply moral indignation, a key component of Complaining.

Other *why*-interrogatives are commonly used to implement Invitations rather than Questions or Complaints. Here is a widely cited example from the CA literature:

(4.9)   "Come and see me" (Schegloff 1984:31)
```
1   Ros:    hh ↑Why ↑don't you come'n ↑↑see[me ↓so:me[ti:mes.↓ ]
2   Bea:                                [hh         [I would li]:ke
3           ↓to*:.
4   Ros:    I would like[you to eh <let m[e just]
5   Bea:                [hh             [I: do]n't know just whe:re
6           thi-ih th:is address ↑i[:s:.
7   Ros:                           [Well u-↑whe:re d-uh which part
8           of town do you ↓l*ive
```

Note that Bea's response in line 2 does not treat Rosalyn's *why*-interrogative (line 1) as requesting information: i.e., she does not reply with an Answer such as "because I'm too busy". Rather her response *I would like to* betokens Acceptance, displaying that she has interpreted Rosalyn's *why*-interrogative as an Invitation (see Offers below). It is turns with a particular kind of negative *why*-interrogative, ones formatted as *why don't you X*, that invite an Invitation or Proposal interpretation in English conversation (see also Couper-Kuhlen 2014a).

Finally, we should not leave unmentioned so-called "rhetorical questions", i.e., turns with question-word interrogative form that, however, do not invite Answering (Koshik 2005a; Heinemann 2008). Schegloff (1984) discusses at length a case where a *for whom* turn initially produces some ambiguity as to whether an Answer is required or not. Speaker B is describing a difference of opinion with his high school history teacher concerning the morality of American foreign policy:

(4.10)   "Governments" (Schegloff 1984:28) (adapted)
```
1   B:    An's an (   ) we were discussing, it tur-
2         it comes down, he s- he says, I-I-you've talked
3         with thi- si- i- about this many times. I said,
4         it comes down to this:=
5         =our main difference: I feel that a government,
6         i- the main thing, is- th-the purpose of the
7         government, is, what is best for the country.
8   A:    mmhmm
```

```
9       B:   he says, governments, an' you know he keeps- he
10           talks about governments, they sh- the thing that
11           they should do is what's right or wrong.
12  ->  A:   for whom.
13      B:   well he says- [he-
14  ->  A:                 [by what standard
15      B:   that's what- that's exactly what I mean, he s-
16           but he says...
```

As Schegloff observes, when A produces *for whom* in line 12, B treats it as a Question requesting information and responds with a turn that launches an Answer: i.e., he begins to supply the requested information about what, according to the teacher, is right or wrong policy. However, A's next turn *by what standard* in line 14 overlaps B's reply and displays through its revised, and more pointed, formulation that B has misapprehended A's original turn as a request for information. It was instead an attempt to side with B by providing a bit of his own argument.[17] B adjusts immediately in next turn (line 15), no longer attempting to provide an Answer to an information-seeking Question, but rather expressing Agreement (*that's exactly what I mean*) with A's implication that this is the weak spot in the teacher's argument.

This example, then, shows that question-word interrogatives are not invariably used as turn-constructional devices for Question actions but that they can implement requests for clarification, i.e., Repair initiations, as well. Yet at the same time, it documents the fact that recipients can get action ascription wrong, i.e., as here, they can mistake a Repair initiation for a Question, and this, it can be argued, is due precisely to the systematic relationship between Question actions and question-word interrogatives (see also Chapter 3 §3).

2.3 Polar Interrogatives

Polar interrogatives present whole propositions as hypotheses, requesting that the recipient affirm/deny them (if the questioner is wholly [K−]) or confirm/disconfirm them (if the questioner is partially [K+]).[18] For instance: *Are you married?*, *Aren't you going to stay on?*. Seen cross-linguistically, this can be accomplished with forms marked by interrogative morpho-syntax and/or interrogative intonation, as well as with interrogative tags accompanying declarative

---

[17] In this case, *for whom* is analyzable as a Repair initiation, produced in the name of B and requesting clarification of the teacher's turn.
[18] This is why question-word interrogatives cannot be used to implement requests for confirmation (speaker partially K+): they do not present whole propositions (Hayashi 2010).

clauses;[19] it can also be accomplished under appropriate circumstances with freestanding phrases. Although any of these forms will produce polar interrogativity, some are specialized particularly for requesting confirmation, i.e., for use in situations where the questioner is partially [K+].

We begin, however, with the more general case of requesting information when the questioner is wholly [K−]. Let us examine this in Italian, a language that lacks interrogative morpho-syntax but instead is said to mark polar interrogatives with intonation only.[20] Consider the following Question action in a conversation where speaker A has told speaker B that he is bringing a scooter (the Ciao) to Bologna, and the two have been talking about what kind of gas it uses. After a silence of several seconds the following transpires:

(4.11)   "Scooter" (Rossano 2010: 2767) (adapted)
```
1  ->  B:  F(h)unziona?
           Works.3s
           ((It)) w(h)orks?
2          (0.5)
3      B:  Il Ciao.
           The Ciao
           The Ciao.
4          (1.3)
5      A:  Cosa?
           What?
           What?
6      B:  Il Ciao funziona?
           The Ciao work.3s
           The Ciao works?
7          (0.5)
8      A:  Si' che funziona
           Yes that work.3s
           Yes it works
```

In line 1 speaker B marks his turn as interrogative with final rising pitch. This turn can be heard as implementing a Question action, a request for information (B is wholly [K−]). However, A does not respond immediately with an answer (line 2), even after B has extended his turn in line 3 and made its reference clear. A initiates

---

[19] Tags may involve pro-forms with or without negation and/or syntactic inversion, as is the case for English *aren't you?*, or they may be fixed expressions such as French *n'est-ce pas?* and German *nicht wahr?*, or particles such as German *ne?* or *wa?* and Italian *eh?* or *no?*. Prototypically (but not invariably) tags have rising intonation.
[20] The role of intonation in Italian interrogatives is an issue that requires more research: Rossano reports that in his study of Question actions in conversational Italian, only approximately 60 percent of the polar interrogatives actually had any marked kind of rising pitch (final rise or rise on the last accented syllable) (2010:2759).

repair on the turn in line 5, whereupon B produces a second, more expanded version *il Ciao funzione?* ("the Ciao works?") in line 6. This turn too is marked as a polar interrogative only through its final rising pitch. A subsequently provides the information requested (line 8), thereby displaying that he has recognized the turn as a Question.

Polar interrogatives marked by morpho-syntax or intonation can also be used to implement Question actions when the questioner is partially [K+]. Here is an example of a request for confirmation in Dutch, implemented with a negative polar interrogative. Two brothers are talking about renting DVDs from the library, but Patrick does not have a membership card. He now asks his brother Mike whether he has one:

(4.12) "DVDs" (Englert 2010:2669)
```
1    Pat:  Heb je ook geen bibliotheekpasje (dan).
           have you PAR none library membership card PAR
           Do you not have a library membership card then.
2          (0.4)
3 -> Mik:  Nee.
           no
           No.
```

The negative form of Patrick's turn (line 1) *heb je ook geen bibliotheekspasje (dan)* "do you not have a library membership card then" indicates his suspicion that his brother does not have a membership card either. This positions him as partially [K+]. However, Patrick presents what he thinks is likely to be the case to Mike for confirmation, as reflected in the interrogative form *heb je* with syntactic inversion. Mike confirms this with the particle *nee* ("no").

Yet in Dutch, as in most of the other languages investigated in the Nijmegen study, it is typically polar interrogatives built with *tags* that are used for requesting confirmation. For example, in the following case Matthijs has just told his grandfather about a friend who does Tai Chi:

(4.13) "Tai Chi" (Englert 2010:2670)
```
1    Gfa:  [Een soor-] (0.2) soort yoga is dat niet?
           a                 kind of yoga is that not
           A kin- (0.2) kind of yoga is that, isn't it?
2          (0.2)
3    Mat:  Ja. ((nodding))
           Yes
           Yes.
```

As a candidate understanding of Matthijs' informing, in line 1 Grandfather formulates what he thinks Tai Chi is with *een soor- sort yoga* ("a kind of yoga"). This he presents to Matthijs for confirmation using a tag *is dat niet?* ("isn't it?"). Mattijs confirms with *ja* ("yes") in next turn.

Stivers (2010) observes for her English conversational corpus that nearly all tags were used to implement requests for confirmation, suggesting that there are strong ties between linguistic form and social action type. She concludes: "[…] in considering how question recipients come to understand what sort of action is being put forward and how they should respond, lexico-morpho-syntax is clearly critical" (2010:2778). This is a point that can be expected to hold more generally across most, if not all, languages.

But what about intonation? Can any cross-linguistic generalizations be made about its role in marking polar interrogativity? The short answer here is no. Folk beliefs to the contrary, there is no systematic correspondence between final rising pitch and polar interrogativity, universally speaking. For one, some languages use final *falling* pitch on all types of questions: this is the case, for example, in Finnish, where final rising pitch is encountered, if at all, only on certain declaratives in narrative sequences (Ogden and Routarinne 2005). But second, even for a language such as English, where it has been claimed that, for example, polar questions usually have final rising intonation and that "declarative" questions are obligatorily rising (Quirk et al. 1985:807ff.), interactional linguistic research has shown that this is far from being true. Couper-Kuhlen finds for a corpus of telephone calls on a British radio phone-in program that there are almost as many yes-no questions with final falling as with final rising pitch and that the majority of declarative questions actually have final falling pitch (2012a:131). For English, then, it appears that in order to make reliable generalizations about final pitch in conversational questions it is necessary to take not only the syntactic type of the question but also its action type and the epistemic stance of the questioner into consideration.

2.4 B-event Statements

In addition to lexico-syntax, there is a third way in which turns can be designed to implement something interpretable as a Question action: that is in terms of their content. Many turns that lack interrogative morpho-syntax or intonation are nevertheless interpretable as Question actions, because they make B-event statements[21] that the speaker produces from an unknowing, or [K−], position. This is, of course, particularly relevant for the ascription of Question actions in languages that do not

---

[21] Recall that B-events are ones that are "known to B, but not to A", A being the speaker and B the addressee (Labov and Fanshel 1977:100).

mark interrogativity formally at all, for example, Yélî Dnye (Levinson 2010). However, even in languages that do have the possibility to mark utterances as interrogative, speakers can produce so-called "declarative questions", turns constructed as statements that nevertheless solicit information or confirmation; these are recognizable as Questions because they invariably deal with B-events. Owing to the fact that they establish a binary choice for responding (*yes* or *no*), they function like polar interrogatives. Here is a case in point:

(4.14)   "Staring" (Stivers 2010:2778) (adapted)
((Patrick, Lisa, Jane, and Mary are eating dinner together at a restaurant. Patrick has disclosed that he normally looks not at people's eyes when he talks to them but at their mouth. This is treated as a strange behavior by most of the other interlocutors. In lines 2 and 4 Lisa asks whether this blanket statement of not looking at people's eyes would hold even in the case of a girlfriend.))

```
1     Patrick:   [like () staring.
2  -> Lisa:      [So even like: a girl[frie:nd? Even like a girlfriend,=
3     Mary:                          [huh ((laugh particle))
4  -> Lisa:      =you don't look at her eyes,
5                (1.3)
6     Patrick:   (Well yeah some-
7     Jane:      How could=you- I [could never d^o tha:(h)t.
8     Patrick:                    [Yeah I do- Not all the time but like-
9                (1.1) most of the time. I just look at the mouth. I
10               don't look at [the eye:s_I think it's so bo:ring...
11    Lisa:                    [hhh huh
```

Stivers' point is that Lisa's turn in lines 2 and 4 is treated as a Question addressed to Patrick, not because of interrogative syntax or final high rising pitch or even because of gaze direction,[22] but because it addresses a B-event, which only Patrick can confirm or disconfirm. And Patrick does indeed confirm the proposition, in line 6 with *well yeah some-* and lines 8–9 with *yeah I do- not all the time but like- (1.1) most of the time.*

Pomerantz (1980) has likewise observed that asserting something one knows only partially to someone who knows more will be interpretable as soliciting information from that person.[23] Here is a case in point. Shirley has finally succeeded in reaching her girlfriend Geri on the phone:

---

[22] Lisa is actually not gazing at Patrick at all during lines 2 and 4 and the ensuing silence (2010:2779).
[23] Pomerantz (1980) calls information that one knows directly and has the rights and obligation to know a "type 1 knowable"; information that is known not directly but by report, hearsay, or inference is called a "type 2 knowable" (see also Heritage 2013a:385).

(4.15)   "Busy line" (Pomerantz 1980:186) (adapted)
```
1      Shi:    =.hhh So how're you?
2      Ger:    Oka:y did you just hear me pull up?=
3      Shi:    =.hhhh NO:. I was TRYing you all day.
4  ->          and the LINE was busy for like hours.
5      Ger:    Ohh:::::::, ohh:::::..hhhhhh
6              We::ll, hhh I'm gonna come over in a little while
7              help your brother ou:t,
8      Shi:    Goo[:d.
9      Ger:       [.hh Cuz I know he needs some he::lp,
10     Shi:    .khh Ye:ah. Yeh he'd mentioned that today.=
11     Ger:    =M-hm,=
12 ->  Shi:    =.hhh Uh:m,.tch.hhhh Who were you ta:lking to:
13             (0.6)
14     Ger:    Just no:w?
15     Shi:    .hhhh No I called be-like between ele[ven and
16     Ger:                                         [I: wasn't talking
17             to a:nybody. (b) Bo-oth Marla and I slept until about
18             noo:n,=
19     Shi:    =Oh.
```

Note that in line 4 Shirley volunteers what she knows about Geri's doings earlier that morning by reporting that she has been trying to reach Geri and *the line was busy for like hours*. This is information that Shirley has direct access to herself. By telling this information to Geri, who is clearly the authority on what she was actually doing that morning, Shirley can "invite" Geri to fill her in. In the event, however, Geri resists the "invitation" to come forward with what she was doing. Instead she treats Shirley's informing as a piece of news. Her response is a lengthened change-of-state token *ohh*, suggesting that she now knows something she did not know before (Heritage 1984a; see §4.4.1 below). When she next shifts the topic to talk about coming over and helping out Geri's brother, this is equivalent to withholding an answer to Shirley's implicit Question. Shirley now becomes more explicit and asks pointedly for the information: *who were you talking to* (line 12).

A "my side" telling (see also Online-Chapter F §6) is thus a strategy for "fishing" for information from an interlocutor without mobilizing interrogative morphosyntax, intonation, or tags. As Pomerantz (1980:196) explains it, because a "my side" telling implies that a turn providing the missing information is due next, it is a way of (indirectly) implementing a Question action.

2.5 Questioning and the Epistemic Gradient

Heritage has recently argued that any evocation of a [K−] position in talk addressed to a party who is treated as [K+] on the matter will be interpretable as a Question rather than, say, as an Informing. Through a carefully constructed and systematic comparison, he claims that "relative epistemic status dominates morpho-syntax and intonation in shaping whether utterances are to be understood as requesting or conveying information" (2012a:24). The fact that questioning is always associated with the questioner being more [K−] than the questionee is nicely captured by what he calls the "epistemic gradient" (Heritage 2012a, 2013a), as represented by the following three utterances:

(i) "Are you married?"
(ii) "You're married, aren't you?"
(iii) "You're married."

All three utterances concern information to which the addressee has privileged access, i.e., possesses more knowledge than the speaker. All three would therefore qualify as ways to implement a Question action. Yet they represent different epistemic stances on the part of the questioner, as shown in Figure 4.1.

Heritage's argument is that all three utterances are Question actions because the questioner positions him/herself as more [K−] than the recipient. This stands in stark contrast to Informing actions, where the speaker positions him/herself as more [K+] than the recipient (see §4 below and Online-Chapter C §2).

> There are both form-based and content-based practices for designing turns to be recognizable as Questions: question-word interrogatives and polar interrogatives are two of the most commonly attested means for implementing requests for information and confirmation in a broad range of different languages. Yet interrogativity is not a sure-fire cue for the ascription of a Questioning action, since both question-word and polar interrogatives can be mobilized to implement other actions as well. Interrogativity is, moreover, not the only means for designing Question actions, as many turns are understood to elicit information/confirmation simply by virtue of the fact that they make B-event statements. Thus, the picture that emerges for Question action formation is a complex one, but not one lacking in systematicity.

How are Questions responded to? Not surprisingly, as we shall see, this depends crucially on whether the Question has been implemented by a question-word interrogative or a polar interrogative/B-event statement. But before entering into more detail, let us reflect briefly on what counts as a response.

In the understanding adopted here, a responsive action is not simply an action occurring in second or next position (see also Thompson et al. 2015). There are

2. Questions and their Responses 231

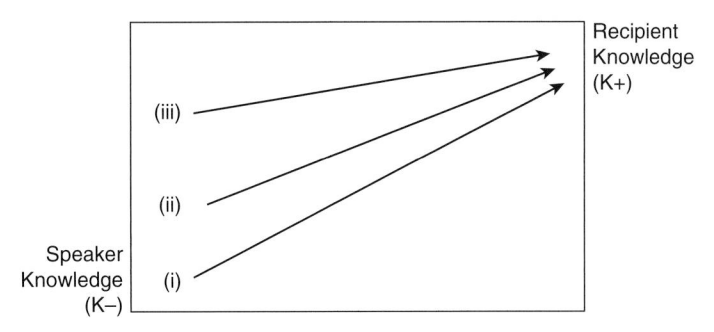

Figure 4.1 Epistemic stance of (i)–(iii) represented in terms of an epistemic gradient (Heritage 2012a:7, adapted)

at least two types of action occurring in next position that do *not* qualify as responsive in the sense used here. For one, the action of passing the floor, for example, remaining silent or producing a continuer, subsequent to an initiating action is *not* a sequence-specific responsive action, but rather one that could be done at any such sequential juncture. Similarly, the action of initiating repair in next position is *not* a response in our understanding. Repair initiation is not specific to a particular type of first pair part but is instead omnirelevant and can be implemented at any point in time (Schegloff 1982, 2007a). Responsive actions, by contrast, have in common that they are "typed": they are specific to a particular type of first pair part or initiating action that they are understood to address.

Responses as we wish to understand them are also distinct from reactions. While the latter can be wholly non-verbal and need not come at transition-relevance places, responsive actions regularly come in slots especially created for them. Although they may be produced in partial overlap with the turn they are directed to, this overlap is typically of the recognitional or terminal sort (Jefferson 1984a; see also Chapter 2 §5.1). In other words, in order to respond, a participant must have ascribed some action to a prior turn, even if that ascription is only a best guess. A turn that comes in non-recognitional, non-terminal overlap with an initiating turn is, generally speaking, not a "response" to it.[24]

An initiating action type can make more than one responsive action type relevant next. The relation between alternative responsive actions for one and the same initiating action is known as *preference* (Pomerantz 1984a; see also Online-Chapter B), more specifically as *action-related* preference. The action that a particular type of first pair part invites is referred to as *preferred*; it is typically

---

[24] The situation looks somewhat different for Assessing first actions. Here agreeing second Assessments are expectable *before* the transition-relevance place and may even come before a recognition point has been reached (Goodwin and Goodwin 1992).

a pro-social one that furthers the course of action or project underway. A responsive action that blocks, obstructs, or deflects the first action and the project it is part of is referred to as *dispreferred*. In the following discussion both preferred and dispreferred responsive actions will be considered.

2.6 Responding to Question-word Interrogatives

Recall that question-word interrogatives single out a specific element in a situation or state of affairs – i.e., who, what, when, where, why, how, etc. – and, when used as Questions, request information concerning it. They project that the formulation provided in the answer will correspond to what the question word has asked, i.e., *who* projects reference to a person, *where* reference to a place, *when* reference to a time, *how* reference to a manner, *why* reference to a reason, and so forth (Schegloff 2007a; Schegloff and Lerner 2009). An answer that provides the information requested by a prior question-word interrogative can be thought of as an *Informing* (see also §4 below). A response that claims inability or unwillingness to provide the information requested by a question-word interrogative is a non-answer and will be said here to do *Disclaiming*.

2.6.1 Informing

Providing information in response to a prior question-word interrogative can be accomplished in different ways. Some of these have been explored in work by Fox and Thompson (2010) and Thompson et al. (2015). Consider, for instance, the grammatical alternatives for responding to a question such as *Who won the feature*: an answerer can say, for instance, "Al won the feature", or "Al won"/"Al did", or simply "Al" (Schegloff 1996b:109). In the first case, the response is a full clause containing the information requested by the question word *who*; in the second, the answer is a reduced clause containing the information requested together with a repetition of the verb or a pro-term standing for it; and in the third, the answer is pared down to the requested information only. Fox and Thompson (2010) argue that these alternatives are not on a par with one another. They point out that question-word interrogatives can be used with two different goals in mind: (a) they can seek specific pieces of information and nothing more (this is called a *Specifying question*), or (b) they can initiate extended talk on a given topic (called a *Telling question*) (2010:135–6). The design of an Informing answer is tailored accordingly: in response to Specifying questions, it is *minimal*, grammatically speaking, while in response to Telling questions, it is *maximal*.

Here is an example of a grammatically minimal response to a Specifying question: the participants in this conversation have been discussing the possibility of

Felicia's elderly mother-in-law coming to live with her; Felicia has just stated that she might then have to move, because her mother-in-law would not be able to handle the drive up the mountain.

(4.16)   "Canyon" (Fox and Thompson 2010:134) (adapted)
```
12      Felicia:                                      [(the the
13              drive) and ↑the dr_iveway hh [(he he).
14      Lisa:                                    [( ) hehehe
15      Molly:   .hhh How ↑ far up the canyon a_re you.=
16 ->   Felicia: =Ten miles.
```

Observe that Felicia does not design her answer to the question *How far up the canyon are you* (line 15) as "We're ten miles up the canyon". Instead she provides only the requested information with a minimal phrase *Ten miles* (line 16).

But now consider how the Telling question *what did you guys do today* is answered in the following fragment:

(4.17)   "Grocery shopping" (Fox and Thompson 2010:136)
```
1       Viv:  So what did you guys do today.
2             (1.8)
3       Nan:  N-mm
4 ->    Nan:  I went grocery sho:pping 'n we went over to the ma:ll
5       Nan:  .pt .hhh
6             (0.5)
7 ->    Mic:  Bought some vitamins=
8       Nan:  =The mall was [pa :   ] :cked.
9       Sha:                [Oh yeh?]
10            (0.5)
11      Nan:  Cause of Valentine's Day?
```

Nancy's response to Vivian's question-word interrogative *So what did you guys do today* (line 1) is not a simple phrase, for example, "grocery shopping": it is clausal, indeed multi-clausal (line 4), and Michael collaboratively expands it with yet another clause in line 7. Nothing in this exchange suggests anything problematic about the question or the sequence. There is thus reason to believe that the kind of question-word interrogative seen here, one that proffers a new topic, is associated with a different set of expectations for an unproblematic answer: arguably here the norm is for an extended response that embraces the topic with multiple clausal forms (see also Chapter 5 §2.2.2 and Chapter 6).

A question-word interrogative invites an Informing action in next turn, i.e., an answer that provides the information requested. But there are different ways of doing this grammatically. If the question-word interrogative implements a Specifying question, that is if it requests a specific piece of information, the Informing is normatively expected to be done in as minimal a fashion as possible, with a phrase (Fox and Thompson 2010). However, if the question-word interrogative implements a Telling question, one that proffers a new topic for subsequent development, then the Informing is expected to be done maximally, with multiple full clauses (Thompson et al. 2015). Both grammatically minimal responses to Specifying questions and grammatically maximal responses to Telling questions are treated by participants as unproblematic ways of answering a question-word interrogative.

2.6.2 Informing but Resisting

Answerers can, however, respond to question-word interrogatives with Informings but at the same time resist the implications and normative expectations of the question. To do this, they can, for instance, respond to a Specifying question with an answer that contains a phrase providing the requested information but embedded in a full-clausal form (Fox and Thompson 2010). Here is a case where this happens: Betty, Teresa, and Jennifer operate a coffee shop and are talking about how late Betty had to work the night before.

```
(4.18)     "One thirty" (Fox and Thompson 2010:134–5) (adapted)
1          Teresa:     You weren't done til two in the morning?
2          Jennifer:   No[:, even later.
3          Betty:           [Oh I was done at three fifteen
4          Jennifer:   She a- had pasta and [then she went back and
5          Teresa:                          [Betty::::
6                      (0.5)
7          Jennifer:   clea[ned more.
8          Betty:          [Well? (°I had to) finish.
9                      (1.2)
10         Teresa:     What time did we get home.
11                     (0.4)
12 ->      Betty:      We got home at one thirty:
13                     (0.9)
```

In response to Teresa's question-word interrogative *What time did we get home* (line 10) – where *we* refers to Teresa and Betty – Betty uses a full-clause format to provide the requested information *we got home at one thirty* (line 12). Such a full-clausal format does more than simply answer a Specifying question: it implies that the question is inapposite and/or that the sequence is in some way problematic (Fox and Thompson 2010:135). In (4.18), the implication appears to be that Teresa's question is asking something Betty should know (after all, she was there). Betty's reading of Teresa's question is thus that Teresa is reproaching her for working so late; her full-clausal response is defensive and implies that she was justified in doing so (2010:139).

Likewise, if the question-word interrogative is a Telling question, an answerer can respond with an Informing but resist the expectation that it should be an extended one by delivering only a phrase as response (Thompson et al. 2015). Here is a case in point:

(4.19) "Pam" (Thompson et al. 2015) (adapted)
((Four women friends have gathered to play a game of Pictionary. Maureen and Abbie have not met before. *NLTS* refers to a local advocacy group.))

```
1      Mau:   how('d) you guys know each other.
2             (0.5)
3 ->   Abb:   Pam.
4             (.)
5      Ter:   hwha:t? y(h)eah ((yawning)) probably [N-L-T-S ]
6      Abb:                                        [N-L-T-S.]
7      Mau:   oh, oh.
8             (0.5)
9      Abb:   yes.
10            (0.5) ((Maureen sniffs))
11     Abb:   recovering N-L-T-S volunteers, did I tell you that I
12            met another: recovering N-L-T-S volunteer this week?
```

Maureen's question *how('d) you guys know each other* (line 1) is directed to Abbie and Terry. Coming as it does virtually out of the blue, it serves to proffer the origin of their relationship as a new topic. Abbie, however, responds only minimally with a simple noun phrase *Pam* (line 3). This response is treated by Maureen as insufficient; in fact, it is not until Terry elaborates somewhat by mentioning their advocacy group, also in minimal form (line 5), that Maureen responds with a freestanding news receipt *oh*, subsequently repeated to form a "double" (Chapter 5 §3.3). This use of a freestanding *oh* to respond to an informing is topic/sequence-curtailing (Heritage 1984a), and Abbie's simple reconfirmation in line 9 collaborates in bringing the sequence to a close. Maureen orients to Abbie's and Terry's minimal responses as declining the topic proffer by doing nothing more herself to keep the topic alive (lines 8, 10). In this case then, a minimal, phrasal response to a question-word interrogative used to implement a Telling question constitutes a departure from the accepted grammatical norm for responding and is treated as problematic by the participants (Thompson et al. 2015).

> Departures from the grammatical norm of minimality for responding to Specifying questions, i.e., the use of non-minimal (full-clause) formats in Informings, is interpretable as doing more than simple answering. Non-minimal forms, because they depart from the grammatical norm, are inferentially rich, one of the inferences being that there is trouble with the question or the sequence. In a similar fashion, when question-word interrogatives implementing Telling questions are responded to with only minimal forms, the grammatical norm for maximality is contravened and it can be inferred that the recipient is declining to embrace the topic.

2.6.3 Disclaiming Ability or Willingness to Inform

Respondents to a question-word interrogative also have the option of *not* providing the requested information at all: this can be accomplished by Disclaiming, refusing to divulge the information requested or denying that they have access to it in the first place. The latter is typically done with an "I don't know" format or the like (see also Heritage 1984b):

(4.20) "Go up Monday" (Fox and Thompson 2010:151)
((Olive has just let her sister Edna know that her (Olive's) husband is out of town visiting his dying mother.))

```
12      Oli:    [So I'm going up uh hhh Monday too:. An' uh,
13      Edn:    W-w uh how [long is he gonna be gone.
14      Oli:               [Y'know.
15 ->   Oli:    hhhh God I don'know, he doesn' know either I mean,
```

When Edna asks *how long is he gonna be gone* (line 13), a Specifying question, Olive does not provide the length of time in a minimal response such as "one week", but instead claims that she does not have access to the information requested (line 15) (Fox and Thompson 2010:151).

Disclaiming responses are often prefaced by *well* in English. Schegloff and Lerner (2009) argue that this is because answers to question-word interrogatives functioning as Questions are normatively expected to be straightforward: the turn preface *well* serves as an alert that the answer will *not* be straightforward. Schegloff and Lerner provide a number of examples in which *well*-prefacing is used in a responsive turn that does not provide the information a question-word interrogative has requested. For instance, in the following dinner-table exchange between Mom and her younger daughter Virginia, Mom has been talking about a local boy

2. Questions and their Responses

who reportedly made off-color comments about her older daughter Beth in a letter to Beth's friend Donna. Mom found out about them from Donna's mother. Virginia now wants to know what was in the letter:

(4.21)   "Letter to Donna" (Schegloff and Lerner 2009:96–7) (adapted)
```
10      Mom:    *Well: I: told Beth>I didn't like that<bo:y,>°I didn't
11              want her having anything to do with him.<
12              (0.2)
13      Vir:    °What did it say.
14              (0.4)
15 ->   Mom:    °(ull) I really [can't tell you.
16      ???:                    [ekhh!
17      Be?:    [([         )] ((loud))
18      Mo?:    [([         ] is mart)
19      ???:     [mghm hgm
20              (0.8)
21      Vir:    °(Y'all) know. .hh
22              (0.5)
23      Vir:    Tell me, plea::se?
24      Pru:    uh[h!
25      Bet:      [You're not old ƒenough. ↑huh hah!
```

When Virginia asks Mom pointedly what the letter to Donna said (line 13), Mom's response is a Disclaiming non-answer: *I really can't tell you* (line 15). This response is prefaced by a reduced version of *well*. Because it does not align with the activity that Virginia has launched by delivering information about the content of the letter, Mom's response could be said to be dispreferred. As Schegloff and Lerner argue, a response that does non-answering is by nature non-straightforward and thus a "natural home" for *well*-prefacing (2009:112).[25]

Disclaiming responses to question-word interrogatives are ones that do not provide the information requested, on the grounds of inability (lack of access) or unwillingness. They are often implemented with "no-access" formats such as "I don't know" (Fox and Thompson 2010). They may also be prefaced by *well*, which serves as an alert to the questioner that the response should be processed as not following straightforwardly from the question (Schegloff and Lerner 2009).

---

[25] Interestingly, Schegloff and Lerner also provide numerous cases of *well*-prefacing with responses that do provide the information requested, if not in a straightforward fashion. They thus conclude that *well*-prefacing is not limited to Disclaiming dispreferred responses (2009:111). See also Chapter 8 §2.2.2.

2.7 Responding to Polar Interrogatives and B-event Statements

In contrast to Question-word interrogatives, which target only one component of a proposition, both Polar interrogatives and B-event statements concern whole propositions. Because of this, the relevancies they establish for a next action are similar. We will treat responses to the two of them together in this section.

2.7.1 Affirming and Confirming

Recall from our discussion above that Polar interrogatives can be asked from a wholly [K−] or from a somewhat knowing, partially [K+] position. B-event statements by definition implement questioning actions from a partially knowing [K+] position. Whether a Question conveys that its speaker is [K−] or partially [K+] is relevant for the type of responsive action made relevant next. Polar interrogatives that are genuine requests for information (questioner fully [K−]) make Affirmation (or Denial) relevant next, whereas polar interrogatives and B-event statements that are requests for confirmation (questioner somewhat knowing, partially [K+]) require Confirmation (or Disconfirmation).[26]

The difference between Affirmation and Confirmation lies in the epistemic stance taken by the responder in relation to that of the questioner. An answerer who *affirms* something said in a prior turn positions him/herself as [K+] and consequently construes the questioner as fully [K−]; the information the answerer provides is thus treated as wholly new and informative for the questioner. An answerer who *confirms* something the other has said, on the other hand, while still positioning him/herself as [K+], construes the questioner as partly in the know. In this case, the information provided in the response is not treated as wholly new or unexpected for the questioner.

In English, the particle *yes* or one of its variants (*yeah, yep, m-hm,* and the like) is used for both Affirmation and Confirmation of positive polar interrogatives and B-event statements; this means that in the case of a minimal response, the distinction between these two action types is not overt. However, in Finnish, different minimal response forms are used for Affirmation and Confirmation. To *affirm* a polar interrogative asked from a wholly [K−] position, the responder *repeats* the finite verb (Sorjonen 2001b).[27] For instance:

---

[26] For this reason, an argument could be made for treating requests for information and requests for confirmation as separate action types. We have opted, however, to treat them as variants of one action type: Question.

[27] As Sorjonen explains, this holds especially for so-called "V-interrogatives", where the interrogative particle is attached to the finite verb and the entire proposition is questioned (2001b:409).

2. Questions and their Responses

(4.22) "Eve's phone number" (Sorjonen 2001b:410) (adapted)

```
1      T:    .hh Ja tota ↑voisit sä antaa mulle ton:
             .hh And well ↑could you give me
2            .mhhthh ton Eevan puhel#innumeron ku – –
             .mhhthh Eve's pho#ne number since
```
((3 lines omitted with T giving the reason for inviting Eeva))
```
6            ni mä (.) ajattelin kutsu [a @sen ja sen]
             so I (.) thought to invite @her and her
7      K:                               [Joo:?        ]
                                         Yea:h?
8      T:    .hh mi[e ↑hen,@           ]
             .hh   hu[sband?@           ]
9      K:          [On-k-s sul ky]↑nä,
                    is-Q-CLI you-ADE  pen
                    Do you have a pen?
10 ->  T:    On?=
11     K:    =.mhh Kaks viis kaks,
             =.mhh Two five two,
```

With her question in line 9, Kaija positions herself as someone who has no preconceptions about whether Tiina has a pen or not. Tiina responds in the affirmative by repeating the finite verb *on* from the question (translatable here as "have") in her answer (line 10). This type of answer provides the questioner with the information requested and therefore does "simple" answering.

By contrast, to *confirm* a polar interrogative asked from a somewhat knowing position, Finnish recipients respond with the particle *joo* (Sorjonen 2001b):[28]

(4.23) "House-warming party" (Sorjonen 2001b:412) (adapted)
((Tiina has called Susanna to invite her and her husband to a house-warming party.))
```
62     S:    ↑Mitä sä sanoit. Kaheskymmenesyhe:ksäs,=
             ↑What did you say. Twenty-ni:nth,=
63     T:    =Nihh,
             =Yes,h
64           (1.0)
65     S:    Ei se oo ens viikonloppu?,
             It isn't the next weekend?,
```

---

[28] Again, this applies to so-called "V-interrogatives", where the interrogative particle is attached to the finite verb and the entire proposition is questioned (2001b:409).

```
66      T:    Ei se ookkaa nyt mut se on sitä seuraava,hh
              It isn't now but it is the one following it.hh
67      S:    Voi-da-an me tul-la.
              Can-PAS-4 we come-INF
              We can come.
68      T:    Voi-tte-ko,
              can-2PL-Q
              Can you,
69  -> S:     Joo::.
70      T:    ↑Ai ku kiva.
              ↑Oh how nice.
```

In line 68, Tiina's question asking Susanna *voitteko* "can you" is positioned immediately after a turn by Susanna telling her *voidaan me tulla* "we can come". Tiina therefore is not wholly [K–] about whether Susanna can come but is only asking for confirmation of what she has just heard. Susanna's response gives this confirmation with the particle *joo*. In Finnish, then, a positive particle (*joo*) *confirms* something the questioner can be expected to know, while a repeat of the verb used in the question *affirms* the state of affairs presented in the question, treating the question as having been asked to elicit genuinely unknown information.[29]

To implement an overt Confirmation in English, speakers must design their response with more than a minimal particle, for instance with a phrase such as "absolutely", "definitely", or "that's right". Here is a case where the latter is used:

(4.24)   "That bit of support" (Stivers 2005:136) (adapted)
((John has been telling his friends about the course he took to stop smoking. Here he is explaining that it was not the scary films they showed that helped him. Don now makes a B-event statement to the effect that it was John's determination that did it.))

```
11      Don:  The point is
12            you wouldn't take that course if you weren't determined in the
13            first[place.
14      Ter:       [(I'm nna [go mo:[my)
15      Joh:                 [Mm hm, [
16      Don:                         [They ju[st- just give you that=
17      Ann:                                  [Well,
18      Don:  =bit of support.
19  ->  Joh:  That's right.
```

[29] An answerer who responds with a *Confirmation* to a polar interrogative which is a wholly [K–] request for information may thus actually be heard to imply that the questioner could have suspected as much in the first place (Sorjonen 2001b; Stivers 2011).

When John responds *That's right* (line 19), he is heard as confirming, from a position of superior epistemic authority, Don's B-event statement *They just give you that bit of support* (lines 16, 18) (Stivers 2005:136).

Alternatively, English speakers can deploy repetition to overtly confirm something that a prior speaker has asked:

(4.25)   "Visitors gone" (Heritage and Raymond 2012:186) (adapted)

```
1    Ver:  Hello:,
2    Jen:  Hello Vera[:?
3    Ver:            [He:llo Jenny have you just got [bahck
4    Jen:                                            [I just got in: en
5          [David] said that you'd called.  ]
6    Ver:  [A h:  ] I thought I'd have caught] you I thought you could
7          have called up for coffee.
8    Jen:  Oh::::. Have they have your visitors g[one then,    ]
9 -> Ver:                                        [They've ↓go]:ne. Yes,
10   Jen:  Oh[:ah.]
11   Ver:    [E::n]:- they've gone to Jea:n's mother's no: [w you kno:w,]
12   Jen:                                                  [Y e: s::    ]:
```

Here Jenny infers from the fact that Vera wanted to invite her over for coffee (lines 6–7) that Vera's visitors have gone. When she now offers this inference to Vera for confirmation (line 8), Vera confirms by repeating it in full: *They've gone* (line 9). Repetitional responses such as this one have been said to assert the respondent's epistemic rights over the matter and thus to confirm rather than affirm the truth of the prior proposition (Heritage and Raymond 2012:186).[30]

Affirming and Confirming are two distinct ways of responding positively to positive polar interrogatives and B-event statements that ask for information and confirmation, respectively. Languages use different resources to make this distinction: in Finnish, for instance, Affirming can be done minimally with a repeat of the verb, while Confirming is done with the particle *joo*. In English, speakers respond with *yes* or a variant thereof to both affirm and confirm; they must resort to more substantial means for overt Confirming: for instance, by choosing phrases such as *that's right* or by repeating the information.

2.7.2 Affirming and Confirming but Resisting

For English, it has been claimed that the grammatical form of a polar interrogative makes relevant a particular type of response, namely one that begins with "yes" or

---

[30] In the environment of prior allusive talk, this is known as "confirming an allusion" (Schegloff 1996a); see §1.2 above. See also Online-Chapter F §3.3.

"no" (Raymond 2000, 2003; see also Online-Chapter B §3).[31] If the polar interrogative is positive, this implies that Affirming and Confirming should be done with the token "yes" or one of its variants. With such a "type-conforming" response, the design of the question as well as the action it is implementing is treated as adequate (Raymond 2000:27). Yet research has shown that respondents have ways of avoiding these entailments and resisting the terms of a question without necessarily denying or disconfirming it.

For one, as Raymond's work has shown, the recipient can design a positive answer to a polar interrogative but avoid using the token "yes". This is what Robyn, Lesley's friend and co-teacher, does in the following exchange:

(4.26)   "Book back" (Raymond 2003:951) (adapted)
((Lesley is asking her colleague Robyn about a book she (Lesley) had requested her to retrieve.))

```
1        Les:   =.hhhh Did um (.).tch (.) Did uh you get that
2               book back
3    ->  Rob:   I've got two books for you:,
4        Les:   Have YOU: [good
5        Rob:             [And
6        Rob:   An' I've got them in my basket 'n they are ho:me. I
7               didn't leave them at school in case you wanted them.
8        Les:   Oh:. right.
```

Had Robyn designed her answer in line 3 with "yes", she would have gone on record as claiming that she has retrieved *one* book and now has it in her possession. But given that she has *more than* one book for Lesley, this is less than the truth. So Robyn departs from the constraints set by Lesley's question and formulates her answer as a full-clausal description of what she does have:[32] *I've got two books for you* (line 3) with a strongly contrastive accent on "two". Answers of this sort retroactively adjust the question that they are answering by qualifying or replacing its problematic terms, and for this reason have been called "transformative" (Stivers and Hayashi 2010): they allow a respondent to resist the constraints of a prior question while still conforming to the expectation of a positive answer.

Bolden's study of responses to questions in Russian reveals another practice for resisting the presuppositions of a question: repeating verbatim the question or part of it as a preface to the answer. In Russian, this practice involves the use of intonation that is non-high rising on the repeat and does not elicit or expect any response from the interlocutor:

---
[31] By the same token, this claim also applies to B-event statements.
[32] The use of maximal (sentential) forms rather than minimal ones for responding to polar interrogatives has also been described by Hakulinen (2001) for Finnish. She points out that when providing a full clausal response, the recipient can distance him/herself from some of the implications of the question (2001:9).

(4.27) "Planted" (Bolden 2009a:133–4) (adapted)
((Tina has just told her friends about a poplar tree near her house that she planted, which has now grown to twice the height of a human.))

```
14      Vic:    Eta ty sp-s-sama sazha?la/
                that you yourself planted
                You planted it yourself?
15              (0.2)
16      Olga:   (O[n prosta tak)
                it just so
                It just
17  -> Tina:    [↓S a z h a l a/
                 planted
18              (.)/(.h)
19      Tina:   ↑On zaletel v garshok v sˇemechkax/
                it flew in pot in seeds
                It flew into the pot as a seed
```

When Victor asks Tina whether the poplar is one that she herself planted (line 14), this presupposes that she intentionally planted it. Tina's repeat of the word *szahala* "planted" targets this word as problematic; she goes on to explain that it planted itself (line 19). Bolden finds that repeating a part of the prior turn as a preface to one's response targets it specifically as making unfounded assumptions; the remainder of the response sets the record straight while still engaging with the prior action (2009a:130).

But in addition to resisting the assumptions of the question, respondents can also contest the advisability of the question being asked in the first place. In English, there are at least two ways of doing this while still providing a positive answer. One has been identified by Heritage (1998): prefacing a positive answer with the particle "oh". Here is one of Heritage's examples:

(4.28) "Learning to speak Chinese" (Heritage 1998:294) (adapted)
((Sir Harold Acton, a well-known British poet and historian, is being interviewed by the broadcaster Russell Harty. In lines 1–2 Acton is referring to his seven-year teaching stint at Beijing University, during which he himself published several well-received translations of Chinese poetry.))

```
1     Act:   .... hhhh and some of the-(0.3) some of my students
2            translated Eliot into Chine::se. I think the very
3            first.
4            (0.2)
5     Har:   Did you learn to speak (.) Chine[:se.
6  -> Act:                                   [.hh Oh yes.
```

```
7                 (0.7)
8      Act:   .hhhh You ca::n't live in the country without speaking
9             the lang[uage it's impossible.hhhhh=
10     Har:           [Not no: cour:se
```

Upon hearing Acton's claim that some of his students translated Eliot into Chinese (lines 1–2), the interviewer somewhat naively asks whether Acton himself learned to speak Chinese (line 5). In response, Acton affirms that he did with *yes*; his affirmation, however, is prefaced with the particle *oh* (line 6). Heritage argues that turn prefacing with *oh* treats the prior question as unexpected and out of place: his reasoning is that *oh* indexes that the question has brought about an attentional change of state. An *oh*-prefaced positive response to a polar question, then, indicates a problem with the appropriateness of the question (1998:294–5).

A related strategy for resisting a polar question's action is to respond with *of course* (Stivers 2011). Stivers argues that *of course* contests the assumption that "yes" and "no" are possible answers at all and thus treats the question as unaskable (2011:87).[33] Here is an example to illustrate:

(4.29)   "Dental work" (Stivers 2011:96) (adapted)
((Dan is complaining to his wife Mona, who is a dental hygienist, that one of his employees has to pay in advance for the dental work he needs.))

```
1      Dan:   He's probably depressed he's gotta
2             pay for all this dental work.
3             (0.5)
4      Dan:   Take all her time to do it.
5      Mon:   ^We can bill your ins^urance,
6             (1.0)
7      Dan:   Can you?
8   -> Mon:   Of course we can.
9             (.)
10     Mon:   Why couldn't we.
```

In response to Dan's complaint, Mona proposes a solution: the insurance company could be billed directly (line 5). After a second's delay, Dan now asks for confirmation: *can you?* (line 7), to which Mona replies *Of course we can* (line 8). This response implies that it is inconceivable that the insurance company could not

---

[33] Although this study is nominally devoted to English *of course*, Stivers (2011) provides examples from Japanese, Italian, and Danish indicating that the equivalent expressions in these other languages work in a similar fashion.

be billed directly (see line 10), thus treating disconfirmation as impossible and Dan's question consequently as unaskable. In other words, *of course* contests the presupposition that both "yes" and "no" are possible answers (2011:97).

> Although respondents may be Affirming or Confirming a prior polar interrogative, they can nevertheless resist some of its constraints, for example, by avoiding using "yes" or its equivalent in their answer, by qualifying or replacing (transforming) its terms, and by repeating the problematic part of the question as a preface before answering. Respondents can also contest the action of questioning in the first place, for example, by prefacing their answer with "oh" or by responding with "of course" or its equivalent. The latter phrase implies that it is impossible for the situation to be otherwise, and that it is meaningless to ask the question.

2.7.3 Denying and Disconfirming

From the distinction between the preferred responses of Affirming and Confirming, it follows that there should also be a distinction between the dispreferred responses of Denying and Disconfirming positive polar interrogatives. Once again, the minimal form *no* and its variants *nope*, *naw*, etc. perform both these actions indiscriminately in English. Finnish, however, again has two options: a negative verb inflected for person and number, and a negative particle *ei* (derived from the negative verb). A negative answer to a genuine [K−] request for information is likely to use a form of the negative verb inflected congruently for person and number. But a negative answer to a partly knowing request for confirmation may use the simple negative particle *ei*. Compare, for instance, the following extracts:

(4.30) "Weekend recommendation" (Kaupunki Euroopassa Sg 377_Part 2)
((A is planning to go away for a weekend with her partner Matti and is asking her girlfriend B for recommendations.))

```
67      A:   mth sano-ppa-s joku semmonen kiva? (0.7)
             mth well (why don't you) tell me some nice? (0.7)
68           kaupun↑ki↑ ?Euroopa-ssa? (0.8)
             city in Europe? (0.8)
69           missä ↑mä↑ e-n oi-s ikinä käy-ny,
             where I would never have been to,
70           (0.3)
71      B:   oo-t  sä  käy-ny  [Amsterdami-ssa?
             be-2SG 2SG visit-PPC Amsterdam-INE
             have you been to Amsterdam?
72      A:                     [( )
```

```
73            (1.0)
74 ->   A:    e-n     oo    >mut< Matti    käy       siel
              NEG-1SG be.STEM but [nameM]  visit.3SG DEM.LOC.at
              I haven't but Matti goes there
              työmatka-lla #koko ajan#.
              work_trip-ADE whole time
              on work trips all the time.
75      B:    ai jaa,
              oh,
76            (0.5)
77      B:    ?se    o-n    kyl i:ha*na*,
              it really is lovely,
78            (0.4)
79      A:    nii,
              yes
```

In this example, B's wholly [K−] Question *oot sä käyny Amsterdamissa* "have you been to Amsterdam" (line 71) is denied by A with a first-person singular inflected form of the negative verb, *en oo* "I haven't (been)" (line 74).

(4.31)   "Godmother" (Kummitäti SKK/SG 435)[34]
((A group of music experts have met to identify and label photographs of well-known musicians and composers for an historical archive. In the following extract, Päivi holds up a photo, showing it to Matti.))

```
101      Päivi:  ↑tää ol-i         sun           kummi#täti#
                 DEM1 be-PST-3SG   you.SG-GEN    godmother
                 this was your godmother
((two lines of concurrent talk omitted))
104      Päivi:  [nii-hän]  se       oli.       ((Matilta))
                 PRT-CLI    DEM3 be-PST-3SG     ((asks Matti))
                 that's how it was
105 ->   Matti:  >ei-ku<    Juka-n.
                 NEG-CLI    [1nameM]-GEN
                 no, Jukka's
106              (0.9)
107      Päivi:  ei mut tämä ↑Aulikki. [eiks tää oo su-n;]
                 no but this Aulikki isn't this your
108      Matti:                       [Aulikki o-j Juka-n] kummitäti.
                                      Aulikki is Jukka's godmother
```

---

[34] This example is also discussed in Koivisto (2015a).

```
109    Päivi:    ↑a:::  [se-hän ol-i-ø niim]
                 oh it was so indeed
110    Liisa:           [<ihan> tot-ta.    ]
                         is that right
111    Matti:    [o-n.]
                 it is
112    Päivi:    [↑mä] luul-i-n     et       tää   o-n       sun           kum°mitäti°
                 I     think-PST-SG1 COMP/PRT DEM1  be-3SG    you.SG-GEN    godmother
                 I thought that this is your godmother
113 -> Matti:    ↑ei::::,
                 NEG
                 no
114    Päivi:    jaa jaa. (.)
                 I see
```

In lines 101 and 112 Päivi directs B-event statements to Matti suggesting that the woman in the photo (named Aulikki) is his godmother. These statements function like polar interrogatives in that they can be answered with "yes" or "no". Because of the epistemic asymmetry involved (Matti is the one to know whether Aulikki is his godmother or not), they request confirmation. Yet at the same time the declarative forms imply that Päivi has a strong suspicion about what the actual state of affairs is. As it turns out, however, she is wrong and Matti disconfirms her suspicion, first by using the negative correction marker *eiku* (Chapter 3 §4.2) and appending a correction (line 105) and then simply by repeating the particle *ei* with a pitch upstep and significant lengthening (line 113).

> As examples (4.30) and (4.31) demonstrate, Denying a prior request for information can be formally distinct from Disconfirming a prior request for confirmation in Finnish. The fact that this distinction can be made lexico-syntactically suggests that it may be a relevant parameter for responding to polar interrogatives and B-event statements cross-linguistically, although in some languages the distinction between Denying and Disconfirming remains covert, i.e., is not expressed through different linguistic forms.

Disconfirming *negative* polar interrogatives and B-event statements is again done differently in some languages.[35] Whereas in English the same word (*no*) is used for minimally denying and disconfirming both positive and negative forms, in

---

[35] Since negatively formatted polar interrogatives in the languages considered here have strong presuppositions associated with them, they are never asked from a wholly [K−] position; they are thus invariably requests for confirmation.

other languages (French and German, for example), there is a separate lexical item dedicated to the disconfirmation of a negative polar interrogative or B-event statement. For instance, in French the word for disconfirming a negative form is "si", while the word for denying or disconfirming a positive form is "non".

In German, Denying or Disconfirming a positive polar interrogative or B-event statement is done by using the response particle *nein* "no" or a variant thereof. For instance, after a B-event statement like *Und du hattest Angst dass sie dein Rauchen feststellen?* "And you were afraid that they would discover your smoking?", which requests Confirmation or Disconfimation, the implied suggestion that the speaker was afraid of being revealed as a smoker can be disconfirmed by responding with *nein* "no". For Disconfirming a *negative* polar interrogative or B-event statement, however, the response particle *doch* is used. For example, in the following exchange Mia and Dor are discussing whether, in an examination for an official health certificate, doctors can discover that an examinee smokes even though the examinee does not want to disclose it:

(4.32)   "Smoker's guilty conscience" (Selting 1992:245) (adapted)
```
1      Dor:   wie HATtese denn nich SCHISS von wegen mit deiner LUNge
              how were  you then not afraid with respect to your lungs
2             röntchen dass se da: (.) dein rAuchen feststellen?
              x-raying that they PART   your smoking find out
              well weren't you afraid that with x-raying your lungs they would determine your
              smoking
3 ->   Mia:   <<tense> DO:CH:-
                         yes ((implying: I was))
4             (.)
5      Mia:   aber das hab ich doch IMmer;
              but that have I  PART always
              but that's what I always feel
```

With her negative polar interrogative in lines 1–2, Dor asks Mia whether she was not afraid that her smoking would be discovered when she went to be examined. In her response, Mia disconfirms that she was not afraid, thus admitting that she was indeed afraid. For this, she deploys the response particle *doch* "yes" (line 3).

> In languages such as Finnish, Denying a positive polar interrogative asked from a wholly [K−] position can be formally distinguished from Disconfirming a positive polar interrogative or B-event statement asked from a partially [K+] position. In some languages, for example, French and German, there are also distinct forms for Disconfirming a negative (as opposed to a positive) polar interrogative or B-event statement.

3. Offers, Requests, and their Responses

Offers and Requests belong to a family of action types that Ervin-Tripp has called "control moves": conversational actions by which a speaker attempts to influence the activities of the interlocutor (1981:196). What distinguishes Offers and Requests from other control moves is that they are concerned with the transfer of an object or a service (Schegloff 2007a:82).[36] Offers and Requests stand in a reciprocal relation to one another: with an Offer, the object or service is to be proffered by the speaker for the benefit of the recipient, while with a Request, the object or service is to be proffered by the recipient for the benefit of the speaker (Couper-Kuhlen 2014a; Clayman and Heritage 2014).[37] Put another way, the transfer of an object or a service can be brought about verbally through either an Offer or a Request.[38]

Because Offers and Requests are actions that, when successful, lead to the same result, they have been said to be alternatives to one another. However, they are not symmetric alternatives. All things being equal, it has been claimed that interactants will "prefer" to accomplish the transfer of an object or service via an offer rather than via a request (see also Online-Chapter B). Evidence for this claim comes from conversational research showing that (a) pre-request sequences are often used to "fish" for offers; (b) offers come early in the sequence, on occasion through anticipatory turn completion, but requests are delayed and done only if no offer is forthcoming; (c) requests are often masked as offers (Lerner 1996b; Schegloff 2007a:83–4).[39]

But how are Offers and Requests designed linguistically? What features make these action types distinguishable and allow one type (Requests) to masquerade as the other (Offers)? These are the questions to be explored in the remainder of this section.

3.1 The Linguistic Design of Offers

Languages provide multiple ways of designing conversational offers. However, research has shown that a language's formats for making offers are not distributed randomly; instead, interactants use different formats selectively according to sequential and interactional considerations (Curl 2006; Drew 2013b; Couper-Kuhlen

---

[36] In our understanding "request for action" is restricted to requests for non-linguistic actions and thus excludes requests for information, which we have called Questions (see §1.2 above).

[37] This understanding of a Request for action thus excludes requests for permission, where there is no transfer of an object or service.

[38] In the discussion to follow, we will use the shorter form "request" to mean "request for action" in the sense specified here.

[39] Curl and Drew call this claim into question on the grounds that in anticipatory completions requesters nevertheless bring their requests to completion (2008:150). For further counter-arguments see also Kendrick and Drew (2014).

2014a). To see this, let us consider first cases where one speaker proposes to assist another in satisfying some need or in resolving some problem: Curl calls these "offers of assistance". In English such offers can be accomplished with turn formats that foreground the recipient's need: *do you want any pots for coffee?*, or with turn formats that foreground the offerer's willingness: *I'll take you up on Wednesday* (2006:1258).

As Curl explains, a format that treats the offer as something the recipient "wants" is never found immediately adjacent to talk about a problem or need: instead, these formats are used only at a sequential remove from any problem-related talk and may even occur without there having been any overt display of a need at all. In telephone talk, offers formatted this way are often placed in the closing section of the conversation. Here is an example:

```
(4.33)     "Chairs" (Curl 2006:1266)
1     Zoe:   we:ll it was [fu:n Clai[re
2     Cla:                [.hhh     [yea::[:h]
3     Zoe:                               [°m]m°[(an')
4     Cla:                                     [I enjoyed every minute o[f it
5     Zoe:                                                              [yah
6            (0.4)
7     Cla:   okay well then u-we'll see: you: Saturda[y
8     Zoe:                                           [Saturday night
9     Cla:   seven thirty
10           (.)
11    Zoe:   ya[h
12 ->Cla:      [.hhhh d'you want me=b:ring the: chai:rs
```

Such offers "educe", i.e., draw forth or bring out, a recipient's need from prior talk and at the same time propose a remedy for it (Curl 2006:1266). They contrast starkly with offers that are made as the reason for the call in telephone talk: these are regularly formatted conditionally with *if X, Y*. In reason-for-the-call offers, the offerer typically spells out how and what they know about the recipient's problem or need and the "if" clause specifies under what circumstances the offer is to be considered relevant: for example, *if there's anything we can do let us know* (2006:1264).

On the other hand, a speaker can make an offer that is directly responsive to a problem or need that a co-interlocutor has just expressed or overtly displayed. In this case, the format chosen is typically one that foregrounds the speaker's willingness to help rather than the recipient's need of help. Here is an example:

(4.34)   "LA depot" (Curl 2006:1271) (adapted)

```
1      Emm:  well anyway tha:t's a dea:l so I don't know what to ↓do about
2            Ba:rbara (0.2) cuz you see she was: depe[nding on:=
3      (L):                                          [(°Y*eh°)
4      Emm:  =him taking her in to the L A⁴⁰ deeple s:- depot Sunday so
5            [he says]
6  -> Lot:   [I:'ll] take her in: Sun[day,]
7      Emm:                          [.h h] ↑OH:: NO LOTTIE.
8            (0.2)
9      Emm:  Oh:[my Go::d.  ] n ]o Lottie,hhh<
10     Lot:     [↑YE:A::↓A:] H.]
11           (0.2)
12     Emm:  No::. That's a hell of a long trip,
13           (0.4)
14     Lot:  WHY::.
15     Emm:  Oh: no. I wouldn't think of it d*ear nhh
16     Lot:  Well it ↑actually only takes a↓bou:t forty ↑minutes,=
17     Emm:  =°Oh: no*:.°
```

Offers formatted this way are produced immediately after an overtly expressed need and are designed to be directly responsive to it, often using the same wording: *she was depending on him taking her in* (lines 2, 4) ... *I'll take her in* (line 6).[41]

In contrast to telephone talk, where it is typically an abstract form of assistance that is being proposed, offers made in co-present interaction often concern a concrete material object, one that may or may not be present in the immediate environment. In such circumstances, offerers are likely to use a two-part format or "action template", according to Kärkkäinen and Keisanen (2012). The first part of the action template establishes the availability of the object, while the second part makes the offer explicit. One or both parts of this action template can be realized non-verbally, i.e., in purely embodied form, circumstances permitting. For instance, if the object in question has been mentioned in prior talk or is otherwise accessible in the environment, full verbalization may not be necessary. But if the referent is not focal, then the target of the offer will first be identified verbally, typically through an existential clause or a clause expressing possession. This is what we observe happening in the following Finnish exchange:[42]

---

[40] Abbreviation for Los Angeles.
[41] Some offers in this position are also made using imperative forms or conditional constructions; however, they never employ the *do you want/need* construction (Curl 2006:1274).
[42] A similar format is documented in English as well (Kärkkäinen and Keisanen 2012). See also Schegloff (2007a:35).

(4.35)   "Lamp" (Kärkkäinen and Keisanen 2012:594–5) (adapted)[43]

```
1    Jukka:      ((WALKS TO THE LIGHT SWITCH, TURNS THE LIGHT OFF))
2                ((WALKS BACK [TO THE CA]MERA))
3    Juha-Pek:              [%(Hx) ]
4    Jukka:      ...(0.8) Joo= (Hx).
                          Okay.
5                ((WALKS [BACK TO THE LIGHT SWITCH, TURNS] THE LIGHT ON))
6                        [^Hirvee erohan täs        [2on2].
                          What a difference this makes.
7    Juha-Pek:                                 [2%@2]@@@[3@@3]
8    Alisa:                                             [3@@3]@@=
9    Juha-Pek:  @@ (H)
10              ...(1.2)
11   Juha-Pek:  [To-ssa    on      To-ssa]  [2työpöydä-llä vielä 2]
                that-INE  be:3SG  that-INE   desk-ADE       also
12              [((POINTS TOWARD LAMP))  ]  [2((SELF-GROOMING))    2]
13   Juha-Pek:  [3tuo lamppu3],
                that lamp
                [3((POINTS)) 3]
                There's also that lamp on that desk,
14              [4jos sää halua-t se-n    laittaa  päälle4]?
                 if  2SG  want-2G 3SG-GEN turn:INF on
                 if you want to turn it on?
15              [4             ((SELF-GROOMING))          4]
16   Jukka:     Ei kyllä täm-tämä varmaan –
                No PRT   thi-this perhaps
                No I think this –
```

Lines 11–13 *Tossa on tossa työpöydällä vielä tuo lamppu* "there's there's also that lamp on that desk", with a simultaneous point toward the lamp, locate the object on offer first, while line 14 *jos sää haluat sen laittaa päälle* "if you want to turn it on" makes the concrete offer.

The two-part format *there's X, if you want Y* is quite different from the *if*-prefaced offers of assistance (*if X, Y*) found by Curl in reason-for-the-call turns in telephone talk. For one, in *if*-prefaced offers of assistance, the "if" clause typically spells out the conditions under which the offer is to be considered relevant: *if there's anything we can do, let us know*. But in a combination like *there's a lamp on the desk, if you*

---

[43] In the following transcript, the symbol ... is used to indicate longish pauses (the exact length follows in parentheses); the numbers inside overlap brackets index which stretches overlap with which.

want to turn it on, the "if" clause does not so much formulate conditions for the offer as implement the offer itself (see also Chapter 7 §2 and Laury 2012a).

> Languages have multiple formats for making offers, including (for English) *do you want X; I'll X; if X, Y; there's Y if you want X*.[44] Yet these formats are not used interchangeably. Instead they are selectively chosen (a) to foreground a recipient's need versus an offerer's willingness to provide assistance, (b) to formulate the conditions under which an offer of assistance is to be understood as relevant, and (c) in the case of a concrete object, to identify and locate what is on offer.[45]

3.2 The Linguistic Design of Requests

As with offers, languages also have diverse formats and practices for making requests. Early work by Wootton (1981a, 1997) on children's requests has been seminal in showing that specific request formats are selectively deployed under different sequential and interactional circumstances. For instance, as early as three years of age, an English-speaking child is sensitive to whether their request will be part of an agreed-upon course of action, in which case s/he is likely to choose an imperative form to implement it, or whether the request comes out of the blue: in the latter case, the *can you X?* format will be preferred (1997:144). It is Wootton's merit to have recognized early on that the way a request is made is not so much a question of social role or politeness, but rather of how the requester construes the situation in which the request is being made.[46] This same principle holds for requesting in adult-adult interaction.

Before examining the design of adult request turns more closely, let us briefly consider how requests as conceptualized here relate to "directives", a term found especially in the literature on parent-child interaction (M. H. Goodwin 2006; Craven and Potter 2010; Goodwin and Cekaite 2012, 2014). In this body of literature, "directives" are turns by parents in which they tell their young children what to do or how to behave, for example, in the context of family mealtime interaction: *Hold it with two hands, don't play, put that down* (Craven and Potter 2010:437), or of getting children ready for bed: *Go, brush teeth, get dressed, come on guys* (M. H. Goodwin 2006:517). Parents' directives are oriented to compliance and, if they meet with non-compliance, are typically re-done in an upgraded form.

---

[44] Couper-Kuhlen (2014a) finds positive imperatives also frequently used to make invitation-like offers (e.g., *Come on down here (I've got beer and stuff)*).
[45] This list is not exhaustive; nor are these parameters necessarily the same cross-linguistically.
[46] See also Wootton (2005). Prior to Wootton's conversation-analytic studies, the social psychologist Ervin-Tripp had also evoked the context dependence of request-form selection (1976, 1981).

It is for this reason that some analysts have argued that directives should be considered different actions from requests: while directives "tell" the recipient what to do and do not treat non-compliance as a viable option, requests merely "ask" the recipient to do something and are oriented toward willingness or ability to comply (Craven and Potter 2010:425). However, given the understanding of action type proposed here (see §1.1 above), directives are similar to requests because they make either compliance or non-compliance the relevant next action. Thus, we will treat both "telling" and "asking" the recipient to do something as possible formats for designing requests, while at the same time acknowledging that particular asymmetric configurations of participant frameworks may favor one set of formats over another.[47]

How are request turns designed linguistically? Curl and Drew (2008) examine requests in a collection of British everyday telephone calls and in after-hours medical calls to the doctor, and identify two frequent linguistic formats: (i) interrogative forms with modal verbs: *could you/would you/will you X?*, and (ii) *I wonder if X*. Intriguingly, both formats occur in everyday as well as in institutional calls.[48] They differ, however, in displaying (i) the requester's *entitlement* (or lack thereof) to make a particular request, and (ii) the requester's awareness (or lack thereof) of *contingencies* that may affect its being complied with. To see this, consider in the next example the way Gordon, who is away at college, asks his mother Lesley to bring him a letter the next time she comes to visit:

```
(4.36)    "Letter" (Curl and Drew 2008:137)
1       Les:   Hello:?
2              (0.3)
3       Gor:   It's Gordon.
4       Les:   .hhhh oh Gordon. Shall I ring you back darling,
5       Gor:   Uh:: no y- I don't think you can.
6              (0.3)
7  ->   Gor:   But uh: just to (0.3) say (.) could you bring up a
8              letter.
9              (.)
10      Gor:   When you come up,
```

Gordon's choice of *could you X* in line 7 does not construe the request as contingent on any prior conditions being fulfilled (the one possible condition, his

---

[47] The scope of what counts as requesting has recently been broadened in studies that expressly incorporate multimodal forms of "recruiting" (soliciting) another's help, often without language (see Drew and Couper-Kuhlen 2014a; Rossi 2014; Kendrick and Drew 2016).
[48] Interrogatives with modal verbs are, however, more frequent in everyday telephone calls, while *I wonder if* formats are more frequent in after-hours medical calls.

mother coming up, is treated as a foregone conclusion in line 10), but rather as wholly unproblematic and non-contingent.

By contrast, this is how Lesley asks her greengrocer to reschedule a home delivery of groceries:

(4.37)   "Deliver another day" (Curl and Drew 2008:142) (adapted)
```
1        Les:   .hh Mister Bathwick (.) uh:m I did ask if you could do
2               me an order on Thu:rsday if I came in and got it
3               ready:,
4        Bat:   (Correct.)
5               (.)
6        Les:   .hh Uh this is Lesley Field h[ere,]
7        Bat:   .hh]=[Yes ]yes]=
8        Les:   =uhm (.) but you know I'm a relief teacher I've been
9               asked to teach on Thursda[y.
10       Bat:                            [Mmhm,=
11       Les:   =.hh And (.) I'm coming in tomorrow: or I could pop in
12  ->          quickly on Wednesday, I wonder.hhh a:re you able
13  ->          to do: (.) deliver another da:y (.) o:r: w-what do you
14  ->          think.
15              (0.4)
16       Bat:   It would be very difficult to deliver another da::y,
17       Les:   Yes.
18       Bat:   Uh:m
19       Les:   .hh Well if I could (0.2) Is it possible for me
20              to leave an order with you.=
21       Bat:   =That's perfectly alright.=Leave the order with us,
22              we'll make it up'n deliver it on Thursday.
```

Lesley's request is preceded by elaborate preliminaries outlining her initial plan (lines 1–3) and explaining why this plan must be modified (lines 8–9). She details various conditions (lines 11–12) and presents her request as an inquiry into the requestee's ability: *I wonder .hhh are you able to do (.) deliver another day* (lines 12–13). She then adds an option for an alternative proposal *or what do you think* (lines 13–14). The *I wonder X* format that Lesley uses for the request itself makes no strong claim of entitlement to make the request and shows an awareness that there may be contingencies affecting whether it can be granted or not. Entitlement and contingency, as Curl and Drew point out, are not objective features of the request situation but rather are construed by the forms that requesters choose (2008:147).[49]

---

[49] See also the discussion of "contingent requests" in Taleghani-Nikazm (2005).

Put another way, speakers display a potential lack of entitlement or sense of contingency by choosing particular forms for requesting.[50]

Entitlement and contingency are especially relevant considerations when the request is not immediately fulfillable and/or is high-cost, as is the case in (4.36) and (4.37). However, what if the request is a simple, low-cost, here-and-now matter?[51] A recent study by Rossi (2012) indicates that what counts in these cases is whether the request is "bilateral", i.e., treated as part of a joint project which requester and requestee have already committed to, or whether it is "unilateral", i.e., initiating a new course of action for one's own benefit. Rossi's data show that in Italian this consideration influences the choice of an imperative form as opposed to a turn-initial benefactive dative + 2nd-person interrogative (*mi X?*). For example, compare the following two requests, both of which target the passing of a plate during the same family meal:

(4.38) "Pass the plate-1" (Rossi 2012:427) (adapted)
```
1 -> Mum:    aldo passami        il piatto.
             Aldo pass-IMP-2s=me the plate
             Aldo pass me the plate.
2    Aldo:   ((passes plate to her))
```

(4.39) "Pass the plate-2"
```
1    Aldo: io sono andato  da loro l'altra sera ((to Friend))
           I  be.1s go-PSTPP by them the other evening
           I visited them last night
2 -> Dad:  mi   p(hh)assi un [pia(hh)ttino, () ((entering the room, to
           Aldo))
           me-DT pass-2s   a plate-DIM
           {will} you p(hh)ass me a pla(hh)te,()
3    Bino:                  [e:h.hhh no:: io::: ((to Aldo))
                             PCL      no   I
                             we:ll.hhh no:: I:::
4    Aldo: ((gets a plate from the cupboard behind him))
```

In (4.38) Aldo has briefly left the table and Mum has begun distributing the food. As he returns, she again announces that she is dishing out portions for everyone. In this context, her request that Aldo pass his plate is clearly part of the joint and mutually agreed-upon project underway. The imperative form selected does not index any uncertainty on the part of the requester but instead "expects" compliance.

---

[50] A further practice for displaying lack of entitlement in requesting is the production of an account, either before or immediately after the request: see Taleghani-Nikazm (2006: Chapter 4).
[51] Keisanen and Rauniomaa (2012) call these "situated" requests; their study focuses on the organization of participation and attention during the pre-beginning phase of request sequences in face-to-face co-present interaction.

In (4.39), by contrast, Dad's request that Aldo pass him a plate is not an integral part of a shared activity but is interjected into a conversation between Aldo and his friend Bino. The request has nothing to do with their talk but is instead self-serving, as Dad has just entered the dining room and realized that he does not have a saucer for the fruit allotted to him. For this context the choice of a *mi X?* format is better suited: it presents the request as self-directed (dative of benefaction[52]) and the requester as not knowing whether the requestee will comply or not.

In this section we have reviewed contrasting forms for conversational requesting in English (*could/would you X?* versus *I wonder if X*)[53] and in Italian (imperative versus *mi X?*).[54] Further formats for conversational requesting have been documented in other languages, including a contingent *wenn* ("if")-format for German (Taleghani-Nikazm 2005), a freestanding *jos* ("if") construction for Finnish (Laury 2012a), and a *trzeba x* ("one needs to X") construction for Polish (Zinken and Ogiermann 2011).

> To date, studies of everyday requesting among adults are in agreement that the relevant criterion for selecting among alternative request formats in a given language is not politeness but rather considerations such as entitlement, contingency, and bilaterality. Moreover, these studies underline that the selection of one request form over another has consequences for the subsequent unfolding of the sequence. Studies of requesting in institutional contexts such as at the copy shop (Vinkhuyzen and Szymanski 2005), in home-help situations (Lindström 2005; Heinemann 2006), or at the kiosk (Sorjonen and Raevaara 2014) suggest that similar considerations are relevant in these settings as well, although they play out in institutionally specific ways.

3.3 Requests Masquerading As Offers

Let us take stock of what we have seen so far, using the case of English as an example. Offerers choose from among the formats *do you want X*; *I'll X*; *if X, Y*; *there's X if you want Y*, while Requesters choose from among the formats *could/would you X?*; *I wonder if X*; *we need X/I want X*. The fact that non-overlapping sets of conventionalized forms are used for implementing Offers and Requests suggests that these action types can be recognized and distinguished from one

---

[52] In the example given here, the dative is grammatically required by the valence of the verb *passare*. However, Rossi notes that even when the dative of benefaction is *not* grammatically required, it is often selected in such turns.
[53] Desiderative statements such as *we need water* or *I want my book back* are further formats used frequently for everyday requesting in English (Couper-Kuhlen 2014a).
[54] Rossi (2012) also notes the use of *Hai X?* "Do you have X?" as a format in Italian for requesting an item in the recipient's possession.

258 Action Formation and Ascription

another on formal grounds. This is what lays the groundwork for their exploitation, as, for example, when one action masquerades as another. Here is a case in point:

(4.40)   "Beauty parlor" (Schegloff 2007a:85–6) (adapted)[55]
((Emma, who has recently separated from her husband, has spent the weekend alone. Her sister Lottie has just returned from an out-of-town trip and is now calling to find out how Emma got along in her absence. Prior to this extract Lottie has offered twice to come down and take Emma out somewhere but each time Emma has rejected the offer.))

```
19      Emm:  I: MISSED YOU BUT I: [I MEAN EV↑ERY DAY'S BEEN A NI:CE DA:Y.
20      (L):                        [()
21            (0.3)
22      Emm:  [There's a:l]ways]
23 ->   Lot:  [↑Don't you ]want]me to come dow:n 'n get you tomorrow and take
24 ->         you dow:n to the beauty parlor?
25            (0.3)
26 =>   Emm:  What fo:r I ↑just did my hair it looks like pruh- a
27            profess↓ional.
28            (0.3)
29 ->   Lot:  ↑I mean uh: you wanna go to the store or anything over at
30 ->         the Market [Ba:sket] or an ]ything?]
31      Emm:             [.hmhhh  ].thhh].hhh.h ]h Well ↑HO[NEY] I]
32 ->   Lot:                                              [or ]Ri]chard's?
33            (0.2)
34 =>   Emm:  I've bou↑:ght EVerythi:ng?
35            (0.9)
36 =>   Emm:  If [you wa ]nt ↑ME TO go to the beauty parlor I wi:ll,
37      Lot:    [°Oh:..°]
38            (.)
39      Lot:  ↑Well I just thought maybe we could go over to Richard's for
40            lunch then after I get my hair ↓fixed.
41      Emm:  Alri:ght.
42      Lot:  Oka:y,
```

The formats that Lottie chooses to implement her actions in lines 23–4 and 29–30 are those associated with Offers (*do you want X?*, *don't you want X?*), and in each case Emma responds in a way that documents her understanding that Lottie is proposing to do something *for* Emma that will primarily benefit

---

[55] This excerpt is also discussed in Clayman and Heritage (2014) and Couper-Kuhlen (2014a).

her (Emma): she professes not to need what Lottie is ostensibly offering (*I just did my hair, I've bought everything*). Yet Lottie's sheer insistence hints that more may be at stake, and Emma's turn *if you want me to go to the beauty parlor I will* (line 36) unmasks the offer for what it really is, namely a Request, proposing that Emma do something that will primarily benefit Lottie. Lottie essentially acknowledges as much when she admits that she was hoping they could go to Richard's for lunch together (lines 39–40), whereupon the two agree on this joint course of action.

> Requests, designed to benefit the requester, can be masked as offers, designed to benefit the requestee. This may be thought to render them more acceptable. Yet participants will often reject something that is presented as an offer because it implies a lack or need on their part, while they will readily accept it if presented as a request: it allows them to do the other a favor. Both requests and offers turn on the question of benefaction: who is the beneficiary? who is the benefactor? Yet these roles, as Clayman and Heritage (2014) have recently pointed out, are to a certain extent malleable, and consequently the boundary between requests and offers is on occasion fuzzy.

3.4 Responding to Offers and Requests

The initiating actions of Offer and Request have in common that they make similar aligning [+] and disaligning [−] action types relevant next (see Online-Chapter B §2). Vernacularly, however, we might wish to say that an Offer is *accepted* (or *rejected*), while a Request is *complied with* (or *refused*). In the following we will adopt these terms as labels for the [+] and [−] variants of responses to Offers and Requests, respectively.

3.4.1 Acceptance and Compliance

It appears to be symptomatic for Offers in English conversation, especially if they are made with a *do you want* format that foregrounds a need on the part of the addressee, that they are more likely to be rejected than accepted.[56] If such everyday Offers are accepted at all, the acceptance is made reluctantly and/or kept to a bare minimum.[57] Here is a case in point:

---

[56] Davidson, for instance, cites numerous examples of Offers that are declined (1984, 1990). For more evidence see also Couper-Kuhlen (2014a).
[57] This does not, however, apply to Invitations, which for reasons of space are not dealt with here. See, however, Drew (1984), who discusses Invitations and how they are dealt with at some length.

(4.41)   "Coffee maker" (SBL 2:1:6) (adapted)

```
1       Tes:   = hh But uh (0.2) then: uh what time shell: we be o- shall
2              I- is there- (.) *e-nothing hh Do you want any pots for
3              coffee or a[(nything?)]
4   -> Bea:               [W E :LL? I ]: have[-v]
5       Tes:                               [h ] You know I have that great
6              big glass: °coffee m:° hhh maker it makes ni:ne cu*:p[s.
7   -> Bea:                                                        [Well
8   ->         ^sa:y now ^that's an idea YE:s I would like to use[˘tha:t.]
9       Tes:                                                     [N o : w ]
10             I: can I:'ll bring the: insi:de to it y'see I: jus:t use
11             powdered (.) (s-) coffe[e<b u t]
12  -> Bea:                           [Uh we:l]l i-you [do:n't ^NEED] the-]=
13      Tes:                                           [I  h a v e  ] the ]=
14      Tes:  =[i : n s ˘i : de.]
15  -> Bea:  =[i-you DO:n't need] to:. I hhave: I have my electric
16  ->         percolater for the co°˘ff*ee.° hhhhh=
17      Tes:  =˘Oh[:.
18  -> Bea:      [But I: would like to have a: larger conta[iner,hhh
```

Bea's initial response to Tess' offer of pots for coffee is formatted as the beginning of a rejection *well I have* (line 4). However, when Tess now specifically mentions a *great big glass coffee maker* (lines 5–6), Bea reconsiders the offer, evaluating it positively, *that's an idea*, and provisionally accepting it: *yes I would like to use that* (line 8). Overall, however, Bea's acceptance of this offer is more reluctant than enthusiastic, as can be seen from her concern to keep it to an absolute minimum (not the "inside", just the "container", lines 12–18). Note also that her accepting turns are not straightforward but prefaced instead with *well* (lines 7–8) and *but* (line 18).

In contrast to Offers, Requests are more likely to receive straightforward, positive responses – at least in everyday English adult conversation (Rauniomaa and Keisanen 2012; Thompson et al. 2015).[58] Moreover, there are dedicated linguistic formats for doing Compliance. As with Offers, responses to Requests are sensitive to the way the initiating action is done. However, the mapping is not simple or one-to-one (Thompson et al. 2015).

Recall that Requests in non-institutional contexts in English are frequently implemented with, for example, modal interrogatives (*could/would/can you X?*)

---

[58] Wootton argues that even parental nongrantings of children's requests are oriented towards a preference for granting, in that they are formulated positively as deferment or reduction, e.g., *will you read me this story – well after I've washed the dishes I'll read you that story (.) yes*, not *no, I won't read you the story now* (1981b:63).

3. *Offers, Requests, and their Responses* 261

and imperatives (*do X!*). The following excerpts show such Requests being accepted:

(4.42) "Ham" (Thompson et al. 2015:301)
```
1        Les:   well can you get the ham at lunch time?
2   ->   Ski:   okay then,
3        Les:   few piece:s,
((4 lines omitted))
8        Ski:   yes.
9               (.)
10  ->   Ski:   I ↑wi:ll;
((a split second later))
13       Les:   ↑am I:- invited tonIght.
14              (1.2)
15       Ski:   ↓I don't think so:,
16              (0.6)
((15 lines omitted))
32       Les:   ↑let me know if [I a:m,
33  ->   Ski:                   [I'll let you kno:w,
34              ye:s. yes.
```

What is significant about these responses is that the forms used to signal compliance, *okay*, *I will*, *I'll X*, and *yes*, are not distributed, as one might expect, according to the syntactic form of the request. That is, it is *not* the case that *yes* only complies with an *interrogative* request while *I will* only complies with an *imperative* one. Instead, there appears to be a paradigm of forms (including *yes* and *I will*) for complying with requests across syntactic format type, each of which, however, has different affordances and accomplishes different work.[59] The most commonly used forms for Compliance in English are: *okay*, *alright*, *sure*; *I will*; and *I'll do X/Y* (Thompson et al. 2015). However, it should be noted that it is primarily in telephone conversation that verbal tokens of compliance are common, especially if the request cannot be fulfilled immediately (Houtkoop-Steenstra 1987). In co-present interaction, the most common way to respond favorably to an immediate Request is with embodied fulfillment (Rauniomaa and Keisanen 2012; Rossi 2014).

Example (4.42) above shows the token *okay* being used in response to a unilateral request targeting a deferred action: responses of this type (including *alright* and *sure*) mark simple, unproblematic Compliance. Significantly, however,

---

[59] Although the argument is illustrated here with English examples, the same appears to hold for Finnish as well (Sorjonen 2001a).

yes or *yeah* in response to this kind of request is routinely considered insufficient.[60] We can see evidence of this in the following excerpt, where Emma is asking her grown daughter Barbara to call her father, with whom Emma has been having marital problems, and persuade him to come to their Thanksgiving dinner (Hugh is Barbara's husband):[61]

(4.43)   "Barbara" (Schegloff 2007a:95) (adapted)
```
5         Emm:   AND BARBARA would you CA:LL im toni:ght for me,h
6                (.)
7   ->    Bar:   Ye:ah,
8         Emm:   .h HU:H?h
9         Bar:   Well if ↑he doesn't co:me I won't uh:: (0.2) t-dra:g (.)
10               Hugh and ↓everybody do:wn↓
11        Emm:   CUZ I:'D L::OVE to (.) cook for you,
12  ->    Bar:   We:ll I don't- you know I don't wanna get in↓vo:lved down- I
13               don't wanna haf: you know I'll come dow:n over the weekend'n
14               stay with you but I don't want you know Hugh to come: (.) down
15               if it's a ↓mess,
((6 lines deleted))
22        Emm:   =[Uh will YOU CALL HIM TONI:GHT [for me,=
23  ->    Bar:                                  [°Yeah°
24  ->    Bar:   =Ye:ah,
25        Emm:   ↑PLEA-:SE,=
26  ->    Bar:   =Ye:a[h.
27        Emm:        [An' reverse the↓cha::rge, °.hhh°
28        Bar:   ↑↑Oh: don't be sill↓y.
29        Emm:   .t.h[hhh.h]hh
30        Bar:       [No:.  ]
```

Barbara's *yeah*s in lines 7, 23, 24, and 26 are not treated as marks of compliance with Emma's request but rather as preliminaries to possible rejection.[62] Following each *yeah*, Emma either re-issues her request (line 25) or offers incentives to make it easier for Barbara to comply: *I'd love to cook for you* (line 11) and *reverse the charge* (line 27). Emma does not stop pursuing a more committed response to her request until the following transpires:

---

[60] By contrast, in response to low-cost, immediate-action, bilateral requests formatted with polar interrogatives, *yes* or a variant thereof is an unproblematic way to respond favorably: e.g., *do you wanna hold on a minute?* – *yeah* (Thompson et al. 2015).
[61] This excerpt is also discussed in Thompson et al. (2015).
[62] In this respect, *yeah* is like a *nii* response to a Finnish request, which as Sorjonen shows, merely acknowledges the proposed plan as a possible course of action but does not commit to complying with it and may foreshadow refusal (2001a:127).

(4.44)   "Call him tonight" (Thompson et al. 2015:266–7) (adapted)
```
1        Emm:  [nyeah,.t.h w[ill you HELP M]E OU:T OF [THI:S:,]
2    -> Bar:              [O k a y.]                  [Yeah ↑I]'ll call
3    ->          him to↓ni:ght, hh
4                (0.2)
5    -> Bar:  [and you can call] [me]
6        Emm:  [A:LRIGHT   DEA:]R [.h][h.hh]
7    -> Bar:                       [↑you] call me at n:ine tomorrow
8    ->       ↓mo[rning.
9        Emm:     [.t alright darling I APPRECIATE *I[T.
10       Bar:                                        [oka:y,
```

Only when Barbara commits explicitly to performing the task Emma is requesting (lines 2–3, 5, and 7–8) is the sequence brought to a close (lines 9–10).

Explicit commitment to comply with a request is done in English with either *I will* or *I'll do X/Y*, where X is a formulation of what is being requested that uses the same words as the requester and Y is a formulation that uses different words. In (4.44) Barbara chooses the same wording as Emma's request in (4.43), *will you call him tonight for me* (line 22), to mark her commitment: *I'll call him tonight* (lines 2–3).

Initial observations suggest that Offers in everyday English conversation, especially when made with a *do you want (me) to X* format (Curl 2006), are only reluctantly accepted, if at all. The formats deployed for doing so include *well I have X ... but ... I would like Y*. By contrast, Requests are more likely to receive positive (complying) responses. English requestees signal verbally that they will comply with a low-cost request by saying *okay/ alright/sure*, or they commit explicitly to performing a high-cost, deferred action by saying *I will* or *I'll do X/Y*, where X and Y represent either a re-use or a paraphrase of the wording of the request.[63] Reports from other languages suggest that this is a more widespread pattern: Lindström, for instance, finds that in Swedish the repetition of the action verb used in the request together with an indexical expression referring to the action requested displays a stronger commitment to comply than a simple *ja* "yes" (1999:125–34); see also Steensig and Heinemann (2014) for responses to requests in Danish.

3.4.2 Rejection and Refusal

Although definitive studies remain to be done, initial observations suggest that Offers in English conversation are rejected by recipients implying that they have no need of what is on offer. Consider, for instance, the following examples (those cited from §3.1 above are renumbered here):

---

[63] The *I'll do Y* format can also be used in "bargaining", when requestees partially accept what is requested but formulate their own terms of acceptance (M. H. Goodwin 2006; Thompson et al. 2015).

(4.45)   "Cards" (SBL 2:1:6) (adapted)
```
27      Tes:    Do you need any ca:rds
28              I have (0.2) I have a couple of de:cks that've never
1               been o:pened.
2   ->  Bea:    So have I:, I gotta[couple of [new] ones, ]
3       Tes:                        [hhh       [ˆAw] ˇright] ho [ˇney.
4       Bea:                                                    [Ah ha:h,
5   ->  Bea:    But thanks a lo:t,hhh
6               (.)
7       Tes:    [eh heh huh]
8   ->  Bea:    [A n : d  u]h, I don't think I need anˆythi:ng,
```

(4.46)   "Beauty parlor" (= (4.40) above) (adapted)
```
23      Lot:    ↑Don't you want me to come dow:n 'n get you tomorrow and take
24              you dow:n to the beauty parlor?
25              (0.3)
26  ->  Emm:    What fo:r I ↑just did my hair it looks like pruh- a
27  ->          profess↓ional.
28              (0.3)
29      Lot:    ↑I mean uh: you wanna go to the store or anything over at
30              the Market [Ba:sket]or an ]ything?]
31  ->  Emm:               [.hmhhh ].thhh].hhh.h ]h Well ↑HO[NEY] I]
32      Lot:                                                [or ]Ri]chard's?
33              (0.2)
34  ->  Emm:    I've bou↑:ght EVerythi:ng?
```

What we find in each case is that the recipient responds with a report of something they have or have just done: (4.45) *I've got a couple of new ones* (line 2); (4.46) *I just did my hair* (line 26), *I've bought everything* (line 34). In other words, objective facts or circumstances are reported as a way to implicitly claim that there is no need for what the Offerer is proposing.[64] In (4.45) Tess interprets Bea's *So have I* (line 2) immediately as a rejection of her offer, which she now "finalizes" by indicating acceptance: *alright honey* (line 3).[65] In (4.46), Lottie also interprets Emma's report *I just did my hair it looks like a professional* (lines 26–7) as an actual rejection, because in lines 29–30 she proceeds to modify the offer in order to deal with its inadequacy and make it more acceptable: *I mean you wanna go to the store or anything over at the Market Basket or anything?* (Davidson 1984:107). Even

---

[64] Negative responses to Offers are thus very similar to those declining Invitations (Drew 1984).
[65] With a "rejection finalizer" such as *oh, okay, alright* produced post-rejection, the offerer indicates that they are going along with or accepting the rejection rather than contesting it (Davidson 1990:163).

Emma's *well honey I* (line 31) is enough to display upcoming Rejection, which is arguably why in line 32 Lottie now expands her offer to include going over to Richard's (Davidson 1984:110).

In sum, when Offers are made with a format that foregrounds the recipient's need, Rejection will often be accomplished by evincing no need. On the other hand, if an Offer is made with a format that foregrounds the speaker's willingness, then it is more likely to be rejected by reference to the imposition it would create. We can observe this happening in example (4.34) from §3.1 above (renumbered here):

(4.47)   "LA depot" (= (4.34) above) (adapted)
```
1      Emm:   Well anyway tha:t's a dea:l so I don't know what to ↓do about
2             Ba:rbara.hhhhh (0.2) cuz you see she was: depe[nding on:=
3      (L):                                                [(°Y*eh°)
4      Emm:   =hhim taking her in to the L.A. deeple s:- depot Sunday so
5             [he says]
6      Lot:   [I:'ll  ] take her in: Sun[day,]
7  -> Emm:                               [.h h ] ↑OH:: NO LOTTIE.
8             (0.2)
9  -> Emm:   Oh: [my Go::d.  ] n]o Lottie,hhh<
10     Lot:       [↑YE:A::↓A:] H.]
11            (0.2)
12 -> Emm:   No::. That's a hhell of a long trip,
```

When an Offer is made in response to an overtly expressed need, the recipient can hardly reject it on the grounds of not needing assistance. In these cases rejections are typically made directly and firmly, as here with *oh no Lottie* (lines 7 and 9), and justified on the grounds that the imposition would be too great: *no that's a hell of a long trip* (line 12).

How are Requests refused? As with Offers, there does not appear to be a specific linguistic format dedicated to implementing a negative response type in English, aside from the negative particle *no*. Rather than outright Refusal with *no*, however, conversationalists are more likely to turn down requests using practices similar to those for rejecting Offers: they report circumstances that are to be understood as rendering the request unnecessary or as impeding compliance with it:

(4.48)   "Scoot in" (Thompson et al. 2015:255) (adapted)
((Michelle is asking Mom to move closer so they will all be visible to the camera.))
```
1      Michelle:   Well scoot in though so they can see you.
2                  (0.6)
3  -> Mom:         I think they can see us fine. hehehehehehe
```

(4.49)   "Ten dollars" (Couper-Kuhlen 2012d:290) (adapted)
((Virginia is asking her mother to give her an increase in allowance.))

```
4      Vir:    'hh But >I don't have a car< and >I don't drive< so plea
5              uhh! 'hh Mom, just- >I'm not talkin' about that< ^please,
6              just let me have ten dollars¿ plea::se.<I MEAN THAT'S NOT
7              ASKING too much I mean rea:lly.
8              (2.8)
9  ->  Mom:    Well Virginia, (0.5) I: just don't know.
10             (.)
11     Vir:    uhhh!
12             (2.0)
13     P/V:    (Wha['d you)
14 ->  Mom:        [We're NOT made out of money.
```

Although the requests in (4.48) and (4.49) both receive Rejection as a response, this is not done directly: instead, indirect practices are deployed either claiming that the purpose of the action requested has already been achieved (*I think they can see us fine*), or reporting circumstances that can be interpreted as precluding compliance (*we're not made out of money*). The request is thereby rendered either superfluous or non-grantable.

> To date no specific linguistic formats for Rejecting (offers) have been identified, but recurrent *practices* are observed: for example, immediately rejecting an offer on the grounds of there being no need for it or it being too great an imposition. When Refusing (requests), speakers are also likely to deploy indirect strategies such as claiming that the request is not necessary or presenting grounds on which lack of compliance can be inferred.

4. News Deliveries, Informings, and their Responses

Although most utterances have been said to contain at least some "new" information that is not available situationally or from prior discourse, not every utterance is implementing the action of delivering news or informing. The latter category of action is reserved for those utterances that are specifically designed to report something newsworthy or informative to the recipient. In transmitting this information, the news deliverer or informer conveys the belief that the other party is non-knowing but should be knowing (Heritage 1984a). S/he thus assumes a [K+] position vis à vis a [K−] recipient (Heritage 2012a). News deliveries and Informings make a receipt of the news or informing relevant next. By receipting the news or informing, the recipient confirms the newsworthiness or informativeness of the information and shows that s/he is now in the know (Heritage 1984a).

A successful News delivery or Informing sequence thus results in the recipient becoming [K+].[66]

Pieces of information and other "announceables" are not intrinsically newsworthy or informative; rather they are constructed as such through the way they emerge and are treated in talk.[67] In the following excerpt, for instance, Emma refers in line 6 to a recent death that is "new" for her recipient,[68] but she does not present it as "news". Instead, it is the information about Bud's golf game that she treats as newsworthy:[69]

(4.50)   "Riverside golf" (Maynard 2003)
```
1 ->  Emm:  =Bud's gone to play go:lf now up Riverside he's just leaving
2            (0.2)
3 =>  Lot:  Oh:.
4            (0.5)
5     Emm:  So: Kathryn and Harry were supposed to come down last night
6           but there was a death in the family so they couldn't come
7 ->        so Bud's asked Bill to play with the company deal so I
8 ->        guess he can play with him so
9 =>  Lot:  Oh:: goo::d.
```

The information about Bud's golf game is constructed as newsworthy in part by its position: it is reported as the first topic in the telephone call: *Bud's gone to play golf now up (to) Riverside he's just leaving* (line 1).[70] Lottie treats this report as news-for-her by producing *oh* in next turn, i.e., she conveys that it has brought about a change of state in her knowledge (Heritage 1984a). Emma now continues with more details, namely that Bud's original golf partner had to cancel at the last minute due to a death in the family and that Bud has asked Bill to be a substitute and he has agreed. It is this last piece of information that Lottie treats as newsworthy by responding with *oh* plus an assessment. The information about the death in the family is disregarded: Lottie lets it pass without commentary.

How does Lottie know to treat Emma's turns as News rather than, say, as B-event Questions or Complaints? This is the question we will address here. Put more

---

[66] Informings are thus epistemically the mirror image of Questions, where it is the speaker who is positioned as [K−] and the recipient as [K+], and where the outcome of a successful sequence is the speaker becoming [K+] (see §2.5 above).
[67] Of course it is also possible for recipients to treat something as news-to-them, although it was not presented as an announcement or piece of news (see Thompson et al. 2015:55).
[68] Evidence for this can be seen in the fact that she uses the indefinite article *a* rather than the definite article *the* in referring to it.
[69] This data extract is also discussed by Terasaki (2004:174) and Thompson et al. (2015:66).
[70] As Terasaki points out, "an apparent constraint on the delivery of announceable news is that it be told on the first opportunity to tell" (2004:182). If a first opportunity to tell is missed, then the news rapidly becomes "old" and may not be told at all.

generally: how are News and Informing turns built linguistically? What provides for their recognizability and distinguishability? Before tackling these questions, we explore the distinction between a News delivery and an Informing.

4.1 News Deliveries Distinguished from Informings

Proffering information in conversation can be done in various ways. For one, a piece of information can have a precursor turn in the form of a "pre-announcement" (Terasaki 2004). Subsequent to a pre-announcement, a "go-ahead" response by the recipient functions to solicit the projected news:

(4.51)   "Professor Deelies" (Terasaki 2004:195) (adapted)
```
1  ->  D:  .hh Oh guess what.
2  =>  R:  What.
3      D:  Professor Deelies came in, 'n he- put another
4          book on his order.
```

Pre-announcements have been said to provide for the tellability of information that is not already known to the recipient. A response such as "I already know" in line 2 would have blocked the proposed delivery of D's news on the grounds that it is known. Pre-announcements are recognizable because they typically contain a question word standing for (and consequently projecting) the new information – in line 2 this is the word *what* – along with main verbs such as *hear, tell, know,* or *guess* (Terasaki 2004:197). They are routinely delivered in turn formats that elicit a response. On these grounds, it is easy to see why in the following exchange Kid could mistake Mom's turn in line 5 for a pre-announcement:[71]

(4.52)   "Meeting" (Terasaki 2004:202) (adapted)
```
1         Kid:   I know where you're going.
2         Mom:   Where.
3         Kid:   To that (meeting).
4         Mom:   Right. Yah!
5  ->            Do you know who's going to that meeting?
6  =>     Kid:   Who.
7         Mom:   I don't know!
8         Kid:   Oh:: probably: Mr. Murphy and Dad said probably
9                Mrs. Timpte and some of the teachers.
```

---

[71] This example was seen in a slightly different form as (4.3) in §2.1 above.

4. News Deliveries, Informings, and their Responses

But aside from sequences in which information is pre-announced by a would-be teller and then solicited by a recipient, information can also be elicited from a teller by a would-be recipient,[72] as in the following exchange:

(4.53) "Own apartment" (Heritage 1984a:310) (adapted)
((Nancy and her friend Hyla are talking about Hyla's would-be boyfriend Richard. Hyla has just announced that she called him long-distance on the spur of the moment.))

```
1   -> Nan:  =.hhh Does he have his own apa:rt[ment?]
2   => Hyl:                                  [.hhhh] Yea:h,=
3      Nan:  =Oh:,
4            (1.0)
5   -> Nan:  How did you get his number,
6            (.)
7   => Hyl:  I(h) (.) c(h)alled information in San Francisc(h) [o!
8      Nan:                                                    [Oh::::.
9            (.)
10     Nan:  Very cleve:r,hh=
11     Hyl:  =Thank you[:   I-   .hh-.hhhhhhhh] hh=
12  -> Nan:            [What's his last name,]
13  => Hyl:  =Uh:: Freedla:nd..hh[hh
14     Nan:                      [Oh:,
```

Each of the single arrowed turns in this exchange elicits information, which the double-arrowed turns provide in response. These double-arrowed turns instantiate Informings, described by Heritage as acts with which "tellers propose to be knowledgeable about some matter concerning which, they also propose, recipients are ignorant" (1984a:304). Subsequent to the double-arrowed turns, the recipient indicates that the information just provided has brought about a change of state in her knowledge, i.e., that she is now [K+].

Informings – as they will be understood here – differ from News deliveries in that they typically occur in second position, subsequent to a turn that elicits information (see §2.6.1 above). Their informativeness does not need to be established, for example, via a pre-sequence, but is brought about *ipso facto* by the eliciting question. By contrast, News is delivered in first position; its newsworthiness is staged by the teller or news deliverer, who may need to ascertain beforehand whether it is already known or not. Yet both News deliveries and Informings make the same type of responsive action relevant next, namely a News receipt or Newsmark indicating that the recipient, although previously uninformed, is now

---

[72] Maynard refers to such cases as *news inquiries* (2003:90).

informed (see §4.4 below). For this reason we shall treat these two action types here together.

How are News and Informing turns built linguistically? Their differing sequential positions result in their being designed in rather different ways.

4.2 The Linguistic Design of News Deliveries

The job of News turns is to construct a piece of information as newsworthy. If there is a pre-announcement projecting them, the pre-announcement will prepare the ground by proposing that there is some piece of news that is tellable; typically it will do so without specifying what the news is.[73] The pre-announcement may or may not foreshadow the valence of the upcoming News. The News turn itself asserts the information, in declarative form, as (a) recent and (b) non-ordinary, both features serving to upgrade the teller's [K+] claim (Heritage 2012b). In line 1 of (4.50) above, for instance, Emma presents Bud's going to play golf as a recent happening (using the perfect tense form, *Bud has gone*, rather than the simple past, *Bud went*), a happening that has consequences for the present (subsequently described with the continuous form of the present tense + *just*: *he's just leaving*). She goes on to detail how Bud's golf game came about in a way that was not foreseen and is thus a "non-ordinary" event (lines 5–8).

News deliverers typically also give some hint as to how they evaluate the news, i.e., whether it is good or bad. We can observe this happening in the following excerpt, where the news is occasioned by a so-called "topic initial elicitor" in line 1 (Button and Casey 1984):

```
(4.54)      "New gold bridge" (Freese and Maynard 1998:204) (adapted)
1       Lot:    What's new with you:.
2   ->  Emm:    .hhhh Oh::I went to the dentist 'n [uh::G ]od he wanted to pull=
3       Lot:                                      [Ye:ah?]
4   ->  Emm:    =a tooth 'n [make me a  ] new go:ld uh:.hhhh (.) bridge for
5       (L):                [(t'hhhhh)]
6                   (.)
7   ->  Emm:    EI:GHT HUNDRED DOLLARS.
8   =>  Lot:    °Oh:: sh::i[:t.°]
9       Emm:               [ Shi ]:t.
10                  (0.2)
11      Emm:    Is ri:ght.
```

---

[73] In Terasaki's words: "Pre-Announcement Firsts are designed to withhold their news while precursing it" (2004:190).

In this fragment Emma's News is that her dentist wanted to make her a gold bridge for a large amount of money. Her stance toward the sum of eight hundred dollars is configured by the way she produces her turn. In addition to delaying the announcement of the dentist's fee until late in the sequence, when she does name it, it is with loud volume, slow tempo, and a marked rhythm on the accented syllables: /bridge for (.) /eight hundred /dollars. As Freese and Maynard point out, this delivery cues a stance of indignation and extreme displeasure over the exorbitance of the fee (1998:204).

Importantly, as we have noted, valence is not intrinsically given in a piece of news but must be construed as good or bad by the participants. This happens primarily through language. Both lexical and prosodic devices are mobilized for ascribing valence, often already in the pre-sequence: *hey we got good news!* as opposed to *did you hear the terrible news?*. Freese and Maynard (1998) find that *good* news is routinely delivered with one or more of the following prosodic features: high pitch level, wide pitch range, sharp pitch step-ups, loud volume on key words, and fast or accelerating tempo. *Bad* news by contrast tends to be announced with low pitch level, narrow pitch range, stretched vowels with falling pitch, breathy or creaky voice quality, key words that are quieter, and slow or rallentando tempo (gradually slowing down). The authors add, however, that these prosodic cues only *propose* a valence for the news; the recipient can align with this proposed valence or not. Interestingly, they find that when the news being delivered concerns the speaker's own self, the use of prosodic valence cues is restrained on the delivery but pronounced, if not exaggerated, in the reception. Their explanation for this is that the deliverer may be warding off accusations of "bragging" (in the case of good news) or "whining" (in the case of bad news) by downplaying its emotive content (1998:215).

News delivery turns can be designed to elicit surprise (see also Online-Chapter C §4). Surprising news turns are ones that present the news as possibly counter to what the recipient might expect (Wilkinson and Kitzinger 2006). Here is a case in point (the symbol $ refers to smile voice):

(4.55)   "Reversal" (Wilkinson and Kitzinger 2006:155–6)[74] (adapted)
```
1    Andi:    .hhh well: (.) speaking of bottoms are you sitting
2             dow:n.
3    Betty:   Ye:ah.
4    Andi:    Well (.) we have some news for you:.
5    Betty:   What.
6    Andi:    .hhh that (.) may come as $a bit of a surpri:se. ehhh!
7    Betty:   I see- $what are you telling me.$=
```

[74] This example was first discussed by Maynard (1997, 2003).

```
8      Andi:    =hhhh! Bob and I are gonna have a baby.
9  ->  Betty:   <°O:h my: go:od↑ness°> hho- (0.5) did you have a
10              reverse- he have a reversal?
11     Andi:    Yeah.
```

As Wilkinson and Kitzinger point out, the news that Andi and Bob are going to have a baby is presented as a source of surprise to their recipient Betty, who knows that Bob has had a vasectomy (lines 9–10). This is accomplished by cueing the information as something that will take Betty's breath away (*are you sitting down*, lines 1–2) and by pre-announcing it with the understatement that it will come as *a bit of a surprise* (line 6). All this creates a backdrop for the dramatic and unexpected announcement in line 8 that Andi and her partner Bob are expecting a baby. Such a sequence sets the news up to be a source of surprise, and the recipient aligns by responding in next turn with the surprise token *oh my goodness* (line 9).

By contrast, in the following sequence the news of a friend's pregnancy is presented not as a source of surprise but rather as something that was quite expectable:

```
(4.56)    "Big gap" (Wilkinson and Kitzinger 2006:155)
1   ->  Pau:  So::.hh But- oh Alison's pregnant. Again.
2   =>  Chl:  Oh ri:ght. Yeah.
3       Pau:  Which I heard today as well when I popped into ()
4             an' she's like (going) [  ()   ]
5       Chl:                         [.hh So] there'll be quite a big gap
6             betwee:n (.) them.
7       Pau:  Four. (.) Four yeah four.
8       Chl:  yeah
9       Pau:  So: uh four year[s.]
10      Chl:                  [Oh] right. Not as big as I thought. Yeah.
```

Paul presents the news of Alison's pregnancy, which he claims to have heard that same day (line 3), as something to be expected. This is evidenced by the fact that the news lacks dramatic staging and by the addition of the increment *again* (line 1), implying that a pregnancy has occurred at least once before. Chloe's response is a simple news receipt *oh right*, also lacking any display of surprise. The two participants are thus aligned in treating this piece of news as fully within the bounds of the expectable in the world as they know it.[75]

Turns serving as surprise sources have predictable characteristics that contribute to the configuration of the news as counter to expectation (Wilkinson and Kitzinger 2006). For instance, they may involve negative observations (*I got to six*

---

[75] As Wilkinson and Kitzinger point out, this kind of alignment between speaker and recipient in news deliveries "invoke(s) and reproduce(s) mundane understandings of what is normative for their culture" (2006:158).

centimeters and I hadn't had no pain at all) and extreme case formulations (*all, only, even*) (Pomerantz 1986; Edwards 2000). As in example (4.54), surprise source turns may contain numerical values (cost, age, size, etc.), implying a contrast between expectation and reality (Wilkinson and Kitzinger 2006:157). Such practices are among those that allow news deliverers essentially to solicit a display of surprise in next turn.[76]

4.3 The Linguistic Design of Informings

How are question-elicited Informing turns designed? Unlike first-position News delivery turns, which are likely to be full clauses with fully explicit syntactic constituents (*Bud's gone to play golf now up (to) Riverside, Professor Deelies came in and he put another book on his order, Bob and I are going to have a baby*), second-position question-elicited Informing turns are typically minimal, providing only the information lacking in the prior question (Thompson et al. 2015). If an information-eliciting question is a polar interrogative, then the Informing can be accomplished with a simple particle *yes* or *no* (Raymond 2003; see also Online-Chapter B §3.1).[77] We can observe this happening, for instance, in line 2 of example (4.53) above:

```
(4.53´)   "Own apartment" (excerpt)
1   ->  Nan:   =.hhh Does he have his own apa:rt[ment?]
2   =>  Hyl:                                   [.hhhh] Yea:h,=
3       Nan:   =Oh:,
```

Turns like *yeah* may seem minimal indeed, yet they are fully informative in the context of an immediately prior polar question that has elicited them.

If the information-eliciting question is a Specifying question-word interrogative, i.e., one that asks for a specific piece of information (Fox and Thompson 2010; Thompson et al. 2015; §2.2 above), then, as we have seen, the Informing can be accomplished with a simple phrase providing the missing information (see §2.6.1 above). An example of this is seen in line 13 of (4.53) above:

```
(4.53´´)  "Own apartment" (excerpt)
12  ->  Nan:   What's his last name,
13  =>  Hyl:   =Uh:: Freedla:nd..hh[hh
14      Nan:                       [Oh:,
```

---

[76] Of course, recipients can express surprise in the absence of a news delivery turn constructed to elicit it. And they can withhold an expression of surprise, although the prior turn has been built to elicit one (Wilkinson and Kitzinger 2006:158).
[77] In some languages, e.g., Finnish, the default form for simple answering is not a particle but a verb repeat: see, e.g., Hakulinen (2001) and Sorjonen (2001b).

Here too the minimally designed turn *Freedland* is fully informative in the context of the question that has elicited it.

On the other hand, if the information-eliciting question is a Telling question-word interrogative, i.e., one that asks for an explanation, a story, or an account (see §2.2 above), then the informing is more likely to be accomplished via a full clause or series of clauses (Thompson et al. 2015 and §2.6.1 above). An example of this can be seen in line 7 of (4.53):

(4.53‴) "Own apartment" (excerpt)
```
5   ->  Nan:    How did you get his number,
6               (.)
7   =>  Hyl:    I(h) (.) c(h)alled information in San Francisc(h) [o!
8       Nan:                                                       [Oh::::.
9               (.)
10      Nan:    Very cleve:r,hh=
```

Here the eliciting question, *How did you get his number* (line 5), invites a more substantial Informing and the Informing is accomplished with a full clause *I called Information in San Francisco*. In fact, had Hyla attempted to do her Informing with only a minimal form such as *Information*, for example, it would have come off as marked in this context, i.e., as designedly insufficient and therefore doing more than simple informing.[78]

Informing turns, then, are parasitic on the questions that elicit them. In the default case, they are as minimal or as maximal in form as the elicitation calls for.

News deliveries and Informings both position the speaker as [K+] and the recipient by consequence as [K−]. Yet while News deliveries occur in first position sequentially, possibly subsequent to a pre-announcement, Informings as understood here are elicited by prior turns and thus appear in second position. This difference in sequential location has an effect on their linguistic form: News deliveries are substantial, consisting of one or more full clauses, while Informings are often minimal, consisting of a particle (when elicited by a polar interrogative) or a phrase only (when elicited by a Specifying question-word interrogative), unless a Telling question-word interrogative has been deployed to elicit an explanation, story, or account. News deliveries can be constructed to elicit surprise by being presented as extreme cases and/or counter to expectation.

---

[78] The same holds analogously for Informings that are maximal in form when elicited by polar interrogatives or Specifying question-word interrogatives: the fact that they are designedly overdone conveys that something more is at stake (Thompson et al. 2015).

4.4 Responding to News and Informings

Recipients who align with News and Informings, i.e., provide "preferred-action" responses, treat the prior turn as having imparted news or been otherwise informative. A non-aligning, dispreferred response, on the other hand, rejects the newsworthiness of the prior turn. The latter is what we find happening in the following exchange:

```
(4.57)      "Terminal" (Maynard 1997:105) (adapted)
1      Sally:   In any eve::nt?hhhhh That's not all that's ne:w.
2      Judy:    What e:lse.
3      Sally:   .t.hhhhh Well Vickie'n I have been really having
4               problems.
5      Judy:    M-hm,
6      Sally:   .hh An' yesterday< I talked to her..hhhh A:n' (0.3)
7 ->            apparently her mother is terminal.
8               (0.5)
9 =>   Judy:    .tch Yeh but we knew that befo[:re.
10     Sally:                                 [.hhh Ri:ght. Well,
11              (.) now I guess it's official.
12     Judy:    Mm-hm.
```

In this excerpt Sally prefaces her news with two preliminary turns, one projecting that something newsworthy will follow (*that's not all that's new*, line 1) and another projecting its moral dimensions (*Vickie and I have been really having problems*, lines 3–4). After a go-ahead from Judy (line 2) and a continuer (line 5), Sally delivers her news as something recently learned (*and yesterday I talked to her*, line 6) that is at once dramatic and tragic (*apparently her mother is terminal*, line 7). Yet Judy rejects this information as newsworthy: *yeh but we knew that before* (line 9). Sally must now justify why she has told her interlocutor something she already knew; she extracts herself from the situation by claiming that the news is now *official* (line 11).

Example (4.57) allows us to register the fact that responses to News and Informings are on occasion *non-aligning*. We focus now, however, on the much more frequent case of *aligning* responses. There are two major types of aligning response to News and Informings in conversation: (i) News receipts and (ii) Newsmarks (Heritage 1984a; Maynard 2003). *News receipts* are primarily backward-looking responses: they convey that the speaker has been informed of something that s/he previously did not know. They also propose that the informing is complete and that the recipient does not need to know more; in other words, that the sequence can now be closed. If we return to the example seen in §4.2 above, we can observe a prototypical News receipt being used:

(4.58)   "Riverside golf" (= (4.50) above)
```
1 -> Emm:   =Bud's gone to play go:lf now up Riverside he's just leaving
2               (0.2)
3 => Lot:   Oh:.
4               (0.5)
```

Newsmarks, on the other hand, are not only backward-looking but also forward-looking. They highlight some aspect of the prior News or Informing turn as newsworthy and invite or encourage more talk on it. Rather than curtailing the sequence, Newsmarks work to prolong it:

(4.59)   "Lobster" (Chicken dinner)
```
28 -> VIV:  u-Shane ate lobster (0.5) this afternoon
29              (0.2)
30 => NAN:  [R e a l l[y?
31 => MIC:  [(He)     di[d?
32    SHA:               [Yeah:,=
33    NAN:  =Where[a:t.
34    VIV:        [A half Maine lobster in u-that ma::ll? They have
35              this (.) place it was Cafe: Mandarin?
```

In the following we examine the linguistic devices that serve as News receipts and Newsmarks in English and other languages.

4.4.1 News Receipts and Newsmarks in English

Let us begin with what is perhaps the most widely studied News receipt token of all: English *oh*. It was Heritage's (1984a) groundbreaking study of *oh* in everyday conversation that first drew linguists' attention to the importance of this unassuming and inobtrusive bit of language. Heritage calls *oh* a "change-of-state" token. The state in question can be one's orientation, awareness, or attention; a change can be brought about by a noticing (*oh that teeshirt reminded me [STORY]*) or, for example, by an inappropriate question that causes a marked shift of attention (*did you learn to speak Chinese – oh yes*) (Heritage 1998; see also §2.7.2 above). But the state can also be that of one's information and knowledge; such a change is often brought about by a News delivery or Informing. It is the latter type of change of state we will be concerned with here.

As Heritage explains, *oh* works in a way quite distinct from *mm-hm* or *yes* in response to a News delivery or Informing. Whereas tokens such as *mm-hm* or *yes* avoid treating a prior turn as informative, *oh* confirms that a prior turn has "involved the transmission of information from an informed to an uninformed party" (1984a:304).[79] In response to News or an Informing, *oh* can be freestanding or have further turn components accompanying it. Typically, a freestanding *oh* will work to curtail the sequence, while *oh* + assessment will treat the informing as complete and *oh* + request for further information will treat it as incomplete (1984a:305). We can observe an *oh* + assessment news receipt at work in the continuation of (4.50) from above:

(4.60)   "Riverside golf" (= (4.50) above)
```
5        Emm:  So: Kathryn and Harry were supposed to come down last night
6              but there was a death in the family so they couldn't come
7   ->         so Bud's asked Bill to play with the company deal so I
8   ->         guess he can play with him so
9   =>  Lot:  Oh:: goo::d.
```

Importantly, the freestanding news receipt *oh* in English has final <u>falling</u> pitch. When freestanding *oh* is produced with <u>rising</u> pitch following a piece of News or an Informing, it works to encourage more talk:

(4.61)   "Company deal" (Thompson et al. 2015:66) (adapted)
((In this phone call Emma is telling her friend Nancy about Bud's game of golf in Riverside.))
```
1   ->  Emm:  .hhhhh [Bud just left] to play go:1f he's gotta go to Riverside=
2       Nan:         [ °ye h ah° ]
3   =>  Nan:  =[↓oh:.    ]
4   ->  Emm:  =[on a compan]y dea:l so,.t.h[hhhhh
5   =>  Nan:                               [oh::?
6       Emm:  ↑GOD [it's be-]
7       Nan:       [to River]side toda:y?
8       Emm:  .hhh yeah they: they're gonna tee off at twelve it's a company
9             dea:l so (.)
```

Nancy's first *oh* (line 3) is produced with falling pitch and timed to be responsive to the information that Bud just left to play golf: it functions as a standard News receipt. However, her next *oh* in line 5 is done with rising pitch and timed to be responsive to the information that the game will be in Riverside as part of a company deal. The prosodic format prevents *oh* from working to receipt this piece of news: rather than proposing that the informing is complete and the sequence can be closed, rising pitch *oh* solicits more information and works to keep the sequence open. Evidence for this will be seen here in the fact that although

---

[79] The uninformedness may be due to a lack of information, to misinformation, or to a temporary inability to recollect (Heritage 1984a:338).

Emma has already begun to launch her next topic (*God it's be-*) in line 6, she breaks off after the production of Nancy's rising pitch *oh* and begins to explain why Bud's game is in Riverside (lines 8–9). In the meantime Nancy has added an appendor question, *to Riverside today?*, initiating repair on Emma's news and possibly foreshadowing disagreement (line 7) (see also Chapter 3 §3.2.3).

English *oh* is thus a many-faceted object: its prosody is crucial in cueing its interpretation as a response to News and Informings (Local 1996; Reber 2012; Thompson et al. 2015). As has been stressed in the literature, *oh* does not invariably display surprise (Heritage 1984a; Local 1996). But a recent study by Reber (2012) shows that with one specific prosodic formatting, namely with lengthening, extra high pitch, and a sharp rise-fall contour (optionally with extra loudness and rhythmic timing), an "extra high and pointed" *oh* systematically displays not only that the prior news was informative but also that it was unexpected for the recipient:

```
(4.62)      "Keith to stay" (Reber 2012:108) (adapted)
1         Mum:    have you been busy this WEEK?
2         Les:    .hh yes I HAVE been busy;
3   ->            =katherine's had uh h kEIth to STAY?
4                 (-)
5         Mum:    so oh is it KEITH uh-
6   ->    Les:    REDgrave,
7   =>    Mum:    <<h>> [ðU] >; ((extra high and pointed))
8                 DID she?
9                 (-)
10        Les:    Y[ES,
11        Mum:    [<<smile> i thought that was over ↑LONG since;>
12                hi [hi
13        Les:       [<<hh> well yes but he's still a FRIEN[D?>
14        Mum:                                              [yes GOOD;
15        Les:    he's got a girlfrien:d in uhm (.)
16                Edinburgh,
```

Mum's News receipt *oh* in line 7 is done with extra high and pointed prosody cueing surprise. Evidence for this will be seen in the fact that she adds the Newsmark *did she?* next (line 8), encouraging more talk on the subject of Katherine's overnight guest. When Lesley confirms the news, Mum acknowledges that she did not expect this to happen: *I thought that was over long since* (line 11). Lesley next orients to Mum's display of surprise by explaining why the visit was nothing out of the ordinary: *well yes but he's still a friend* (line 13).

English Newsmarks include pro-repeats like that in line 31 of (4.59), *he did?*, and line 8 of (4.62), *did she?*, but also *oh*-prefaced pro-repeats (*oh he did?*, *oh did she?*) as well as "assertions of ritualized disbelief" (Heritage 1984a:339) such as *really?* and *you're kidding* (Maynard 1997:107). With the exception of *you're kidding*, Newsmarks can have either rising or falling pitch but in American English appear to encourage more talk only with rising pitch (Thompson et al. 2015).[80]

Like *oh* and other News receipts, Newsmarks are prosodically and phonetically malleable; they can be finely adjusted in terms of duration, pitch, loudness, and vowel quality to cue various types of affective display in response to News and Informings. As Freese and Maynard (1998) explain, Newsmarks often display sensitivity to the valence of news as good or bad well before any lexical evaluations are made. Consider, for instance, the following exchange:

```
(4.63)     "Old Time Music Hall" (Freese and Maynard 1998:209)
1 -> Leslie:  We had a ↑very nice evening at the(k) (0.3) Ditchit- (0.2)
2             Old Time Musi[c Ha:ll.]
3 => Mum:                  [↑Oh : :] ↓did ↑you ↓that's goo↑[:d
4    Leslie:                                               ['hhh An'
5             Gordon went to watch Big Country las' week at um the Sharring
6             Pavillion (Chetsham Mallet)?
```

In line 3 it is clear from the way Mum says *oh did you* that she is treating Leslie's news as good although she does not say so until afterwards.[81]

4.4.2 News Receipts and Newsmarks in Other Languages

News receipts and Newsmarks are just beginning to come under scrutiny in languages other than English.[82] Golato's work (2010, 2012b) on German has been pioneering here, and the results are revealing. In German, Golato argues, there is not just one particle but at least *two* that do the work of receipting News and Informings, *achso* and *ach*, with a very clear division of labor between them. Whereas the particle *achso* frequently forms a TCU of its own and displays that the new information has been both heard and understood, the particle *ach* is typically followed by more material in the same TCU and displays only that the news has been registered but that its implications are not necessarily understood. The material that follows *ach* may request confirmation, as in the following example:[83]

---

[80] Kaimaki (2012), however, examines the non-valenced newsmark *oh really* in British and American English data and finds no systematic differences between rising or falling pitch in terms of how the news telling sequence develops sequentially thereafter.
[81] Note that Leslie has introduced a positive valence by saying ↑*very nice evening* in line 1.
[82] See Mori (2006) for a study of the Japanese token *hee*, which in one of its functions can serve as a change-of-state marker. Kaimaki (2012) discusses the Greek non-valenced news receipt *a ne* (literal translation = "PARTICLE yes"), Heinemann (2009) touches on the Danish change-of-state particle *nå*, and more recently, Koivisto (2013, 2015a, 2015c) examines the change-of-state particles *ai niin*, *aa*, and *aijaa* in Finnish.
[83] Alternatively *ach* can be followed by an assessment of the information (Golato 2010:167), a use not shown here.

(4.64)   "To Spain" (Golato 2010:165) (adapted)[84]
((Ingo has called to speak to his friend Mark but has been informed by Mark's roommate Thomas that he is at his girlfriend's place. Thomas now begins to volunteer more information about Mark's plans.))

```
1      T:   der hat ja jetzt auch frei,
            he now also has time off, you know
2      I:   >ja,<
            >yes,<
3      T:   und hatte glaub mittwoch seinen letzten tag
            and i believe wednesday was his last day
4   ->      gehabt bei der ↑sparkasse und jetzt am mittwoch
            at the credit union and this coming wednesday
5   ->      oder d- (.) dienstag- oder mittwoch fahrn die ja
            or t- (.) tuesday- or wednesday drive they PRT
            or t- (.) tuesday- or wednesday they are going
6   ->      nach spanien.
            to spain.
            to spain.
7      I:   ja,
            yes,
8           (.)
9   =>  I:  ach dienstag oder mittwoch schfahrn die schon nach spanien?
            oh tuesday or wednesday spgo they already to spain?
            oh they are already leaving tuesday or wednesday for spain?
10     T:   dienstag abend oder mittwoch früh
            tuesday evening or wednesday morning
11  =>  I:  achso:.
            oh i see.
12          (.)
13     I:   ja. nun das is ja ...
            yes. well that is ...
```

In line 7 Ingo initially produces a continuer, treating Thomas' informing as incomplete. However, when Thomas does not continue (line 8), Ingo registers the news so far with *ach* and appends a candidate understanding requesting confirmation in line 9: *ach dienstag oder mittwoch schfahrn die schon nach spanien?* ("oh they are already leaving Tuesday or Wednesday for Spain?"). It is only when Thomas confirms this that Ingo responds with *achso* (line 11), conveying that he now fully understands and accepts the information.

[84] This excerpt is also discussed in Golato (2012b:246).

As Golato points out, similar interactional tasks may be handled differently in different languages (2010:170). Whereas English appears to have only one word *oh* with a rich array of prosodic variants for indicating a shift from uninformed to informed and from not understanding to understanding, German has two different words for these two processes.[85]

In addition to separate particles for marking informedness and understanding, languages may also have distinct particles or particle combinations for indicating a cognitive shift from not-remembered to now-remembered or recollected information.[86] Here is an example from German, which uses the particle combination *achJA* or *ahJA* with prosodic prominence on the second syllable for this purpose (Betz and Golato 2008):

(4.65)   "Rigoletto" (Betz and Golato 2008:63) (adapted)

```
1      M:   und dann abends äh gehmer in die oper. .hhh
            and then at night uh we'll go to the opera. .hhh
2           und [ da gibts ]
            and there is (playing)
3      I:       [was läuft?]
                what's playing?
4      M:   isch glaub riguletto.
            I think riguletto.
5           (0.5) ((no other background sound hearable))
6      M:   .h muß jetzt- ja doch riguletto .hhhh
            now I have to- yeah that's it riguletto .hhh
7      M:   naja [un-]
            well  an-
8      I:        [von] wem isn des nochma?
                 who wrote that again?
9  ->  M:   .hh ve- äh verdi
            .hh ve- uh Verdi
10          (.)
11 =>  I:   achJA. dann kenn isch des auch
            oh that's RIght. then I know it too
12     M:   ja:
            yea:h
```

---

[85] In English this distinction can be made explicit by contrasting *oh* (simple registering of the news) with *oh I see* (claiming understanding).

[86] In Danish speakers use *najà* to claim that they are just realizing matters not previously considered (Emmertsen and Heinemann 2010). See also Koivisto (2013) on *ai niin* in Finnish. The English equivalent would appear to be *oh that's right* (Heritage 1984a:338, note 12).

In using the particle *achJA* here (line 11) Ines signals that she has just now recollected the information Markus has provided her with in line 9. The implication is that she previously knew who composed the opera but had temporarily forgotten. This is also inferrable from the way she elicits the information: both the modal particle *denn* (cliticized onto the verb form *ist*) and the adverb *nochmal* in her question (line 8) work to suggest that she is, or at least has been, [K+] with respect to the composer of *Rigoletto*. Following *achJA*, Ines indeed now goes on to claim that she knows the opera (line 11).

As Betz and Golato explain, use of the particle combination *achJA* for indexing just-now-remembered information is not coincidental: *ach* in German marks the news and claims a change of state, while stressed *JA* confirms or acknowledges the information, thereby claiming that the speaker has independent access to it (2008:91). The particle combination is typically followed by a display of this independent knowledge, after which the sequence is brought to a close.

In addition to cognitive changes of state, languages may also employ the same or different news receipt tokens for indicating various sorts of affective changes of state associated with an informing. Mori reports, for instance, that the particle *hee*, often considered a standard news receipt token in Japanese, can be manipulated prosodically to reflect differing degrees of interest and/or surprise: "The more surprising or significant a piece of news is, the more likely it seems for the recipients to extend and raise the pitch of *hee*" (2006:1191). She notes cases of freestanding *hee* lasting up to two seconds in duration.

German, on the other hand, appears to have a separate particle reserved for marking *affective* changes of state subsequent to informings (Golato 2012b). This is the particle *oh* (not to be confused with English *oh*), which is usually produced with a back mid-high monophthong and often lengthened. It is used instead of more "cognitive" change-of-state tokens such as *ach*, *achso*, or *achja* as a way to receipt news and at the same time display what is purported to be a concurrently experienced emotive or affective stance. Here is a case where the affective stance is one of surprise and empathy:

(4.66)   "Four women" (Golato 2012b:259) (adapted)
((Xavier is telling his friend Ingo about having problems getting a date for a picnic.))

```
1    X:   klaus nino und ich, wir wollten halt frauen einladen.
          klaus nino and I, we simply wanted to invite women,
2    I:   >ja,<
          >yeah,<
              *smile voice*
3    X:   und ich *hab hier <voll> den träller gekriecht,* ich
          and I *was totally hosed,* I
```

```
4       X:   hab (.) vier frauen angespochen,
             asked (.) four women,
5       I:   und? ((smile voice))
             and?
6   ->  X:   bin alleine hingedüst.
             went alone.
7   =>  I:   o:::h.
             o:::h.
8       X:   da hab' ich mir gestern erstmal richtig die kante
             because of that I really got hammered
9       X:   [gegeben.
             yesterday.
10      I:   [ha ha ha
```

Note that Ingo's *o:::h* (line 7) is accomplishing more than merely receipting the news that Xavier went to the picnic alone. Xavier has constructed his mini-narrative around the expectation that he would find a date: when he now – after a suspenseful delay (line 5) – announces that he was unsuccessful, this is not only unexpected but implies a disappointment. Empathic moments of this sort call for empathic responses (Heritage 2011), which is what Ingo's *oh* can be heard as doing.

> What English does with the simple word *oh* together with myriad forms of phonetic-prosodic variation is often accomplished with different particles in other languages.[87] The tasks which News receipts and Newsmarks must address include displaying cognitive shifts from uninformed to informed, from non-understanding to understanding, and from not remembering to just-now-recalling, as well as indexing shifts in attentional state (anticipated news versus counter-to-expectation news) and in affective state (good versus bad news) associated with News and Informings.

5. Assessments, Compliments, Self-deprecations, and their Responses

Assessing actions involve evaluating persons, objects, states of affairs, and situations positively or negatively: for example, *Adeline's such a swell gal*, or *I never was a great bridge player*. As Pomerantz, whose work has been seminal in this area, points out, assessing something requires that the person doing the assessing

---

[87] It is worth noting, however, that English does have other "sound objects" which can be found in response to informings, among them *ah* and *oo* (Reber 2012).

has access to or experience/knowledge of what is being assessed (1984a:57–8). Limited access makes it necessary to indicate the evidential basis for one's assessing: *you sound happy, she seems like a nice little lady*. Lack of sufficient access to what is being assessed can be grounds for refusing to engage in an assessing activity at all: *I don't know, I didn't really get to talk to him that much, I can't say*.[88] But provided two participants both have access to a given referent, a first Assessment by one makes a second Assessment of the same referent by the other relevant next (Pomerantz 1984a:59).

In this section we follow Goodwin and Goodwin (1987, 1992) in making a number of terminological distinctions for the description of Assessments. First, we will say that a turn or TCU that carries out an evaluation in the sense described above implements an *assessment action*. A series of turns engaging in assessment actions together create an *assessment activity*. The object of an assessing action or activity will be referred to as an *assessable*. Finally, within an assessing action or turn we will distinguish between an *assessment segment* and an *assessment signal*. While an assessment segment, as its name suggests, refers to a specific and delimitable part of the turn at talk, an assessment signal can be non-segmental, displaying a speaker's involvement in a more diffuse way. An assessment segment is thus a special kind of assessment signal. To illustrate using one of the Goodwins' examples, where the assessable is asparagus pie:

(4.67)   "Asparagus pie" (Goodwin and Goodwin 1992:161)

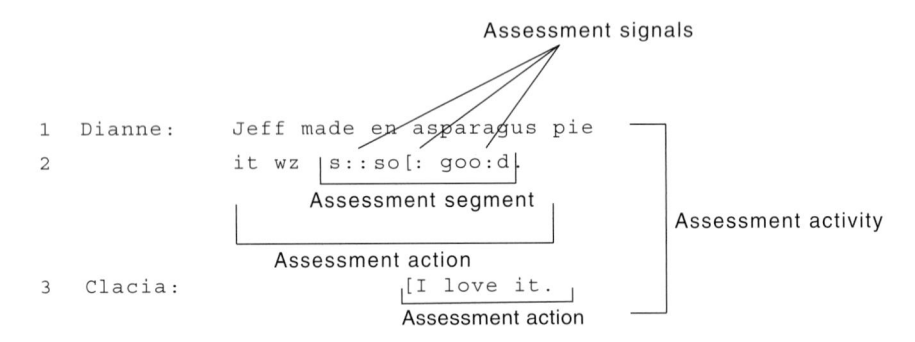

```
                             Assessment signals
                                    ↗ ↑ ↖
1  Dianne:   Jeff made en asparagus pie
2            it wz |s::so[: goo:d|
                   Assessment segment
             |_____|
                  Assessment action                Assessment activity
3  Clacia:                    |[I love it.|
                              Assessment action
```

In this example Dianne's and Clacia's turns together constitute an assessment activity, while *it wz s::so: goo:d* and *I love it* implement assessment actions. Within the TCU *it wz s::so: goo:d* the adjective phrase *s::o: goo:d* is an assessment segment, while the sound and syllable lengthenings on *s::o:* and *goo:d* work as assessment signals.

---

[88] These three (attested) TCUs were produced in response to a co-interlocutor's invitation to assess a non-present flatmate: *So what did you think?*

5. Assessments, Compliments, Self-deprecations, and their Responses

What kinds of things do speakers assess? Importantly, assessables are not only persons or concrete objects, like the asparagus pie in (4.67). They can also be abstract political or social matters, bodily movements as in sports or dance, musical performances, manipulations of physical objects – virtually any and all imaginable beings, objects, states of affairs, and situations, immutable as well as mutable (Fasulo and Monzoni 2009). Some assessables are present in the here and now of talk-in-interaction; others are part of a past experience that is being reported on in current talk.

Assessments can occur in various sequential environments in talk-in-interaction: (a) as initiating moves for the evaluation of a person, object, state of affairs, or situation being experienced in the very moment or having been experienced on an earlier occasion (= first Assessments), (b) as responsive moves in a turn after a first assessment (= second Assessments), (c) as recipient moves during and after stories and extended tellings (= "extended-telling" Assessments), and (d) in "third" position to propose closing a prior sequence (= sequence-closing Assessments). Lines 2 and 3 of example (4.67) illustrate (a) and (b) respectively. Examples (4.68) and (4.69) below show cases of extended-telling Assessments and sequence-closing Assessments, respectively:

(4.68)   "Nurses" (NB IV:1)
((Lottie is talking to her sister Emma on the phone. In lines 2–3 she is referring to the property she rents out at the beach.))

```
1        Lot:     [°O  h  : ] (well)°]         [Maybe I'll see you
2                 Sa: tur (.) Oh I (.)   .hh.hh I rented the↓ uh(p) (.)
3                 apartment fou:r ↓to: uh↓: (0.3) two uh nurses from uh::
4                 (0.3) I think it's the Presbyterian hospital in
5                 Whitti↓er.
6        Emm:     You ↑DI::D?
7                 (.)
8        Lot:     Ya:h. Gee they were rea:l real ni:ce k-uh[ :↓:↓: ]
9   ->   Emm:                                              [Well how]
10  ->            wonder↓ f*u:l.=
11       Lot:     =They work in surgery one is an older woman e- a-an:: it
12                seemed li:ke (.) she had raised ↓this: (.) gi↓rl.
13       Emm:     YE:ah:?
14                (0.2)
15       Lot:     tShe's rea:l (b) (0.2) uh fa*:t this girl but ↑th*ey just
16                wanted someplace to co:me you kno:w, to kinda get awa:y
17                from everything up there
18       Emm:     .khh Oh they gonna stake it take it all winter?
```

```
19      Lot:    .hh (.) Yeah but they're jus:t coming li:ke one has to work
20              one weekend an' one [ has ] to work the ↓other weekend ↓an'=
21      Emm:                        [Oh:.]
22      Lot:    =they g-eh you kno:w the [y ↑won't be there all the time so(d)
23      Emm:                             [(     )
24              (.)
25      Lot:    'n Jeesu-us thha-at's th:at's goo:d. [you  know]=
26      Emm:                                         [M   m   :]=
27 ->   Emm:    =↓THA:T'S good ↓Lottie <Then you've got eyuh u-w'did the
28              uh: the (b) ↑Hilt boy lea:ve?h
29      Lot:    .t No he's not leav'ing until the seventh.
```

(4.69)   "How have you been" (TG)

```
1       Ava:    °(Any way). 'hh How've you bee:n.
2       Bee:    'hh Oh:: survi:ving I guess, hh[h!
3 ->    Ava:                                   [That's good,
4               how's (Bob),
5       Bee:    He's fine,
6 ->    Ava:    Tha::t's goo:d,
```

In (4.68) Emma's phrasal extended-telling Assessment *well how wonderful* (lines 9–10) is produced after Lottie has added an evaluation of her new tenants: *gee they were real real nice* (line 8). Lottie now continues with a more extended telling about the tenants, brought to a point of possible completion with *jeesus, that's good you know* (line 25). Emma's next turn *That's good Lottie* (line 27) is a clausal extended-telling Assessment, hearable as evaluating the whole of Lottie's story and thereby proposing to close it down. Immediately after this Emma moves the talk to a new topic (Thompson et al. 2015:211).

In (4.69) Ava uses *that's good* twice to implement a sequence-closing Assessment, once in line 3 after Bee has responded to her inquiry *how have you been* (line 1) with *oh surviving I guess* (line 2), and again in line 6 after Bee responds to her second inquiry *how's Bob* (line 4) with *he's fine* (line 5). These turns are hearable as evaluating the immediately prior second-position turn and proposing to close down the sequence.[89]

The discussion in the following sections focuses on type (a), first Assessments, and type (b), second Assessments. Type (c), extended-telling Assessments, and Type (d), sequence-closing Assessments, are dealt with in Chapter 5 §3.3.1. See

---

[89] The difference between a telling Assessment and a sequence-closing third Assessment is, then, primarily one of scope: telling Assessments have larger units within their scope than do sequence-closing third Assessments (Thompson et al. 2015).

also Online-Chapter C §1 for a discussion of epistemic priority and subordination in Assessment sequences.

5.1 Assessing Actions in First Position

Assessing actions in an initiating position can be broken down into subcategories depending on how the assessable relates to the participants and what its valence is, i.e., whether it is positive or negative. For instance, if the assessable is an external object, situation, or third party that belongs to the *recipient's* domain or territory, then a *positive* assessing action by the speaker will be hearable as a Compliment (Golato 2005).[90,91] Since non-compliment Assessments and Compliments call for different types of response in next turn, it is customary to think of them as distinct action types. On the other hand, if the assessable is something that belongs to the *speaker's* domain or territory, a *negative* assessing action by that speaker will be hearable as a Self-deprecation (Pomerantz 1984a).[92] This action, too, calls for a different sort of response compared to an Assessment or Compliment, and is typically considered a separate action type.[93]

In sum, assessing actions form a *family* of related action types, of which Assessment, as illustrated in (4.67)–(4.69), is only one kind. The following examples illustrate the action types of Compliment and Self-deprecation respectively in English:

(4.70)   "Lovely luncheon" (NB VII)
((Edna has called her friend Margy to thank her for the recent luncheon at which Edna was a guest.))

```
1 ->   Edn:   =Oh honey that was a lovely luncheon I should have ca:lled you
2 ->          s:soo[:ner but I:]l:[lo:ved it. It was just deli:ghtfu[:l. ]=
3      Mar:        [((f)) Oh:::]  [°(        )                      [Well]=
4      Mar:   =I was gla[d     y o u] (came).]
5 ->   Edn:              [and your f:] friends] are so da:rli:ng,=
6      Mar:   =Oh:::: it wz:
```

---

[90] *Negative* assessing actions of something within the recipient's domain or territory could be thought of as Criticisms or Reproaches, an action type not discussed here for reasons of space. See, however, Günthner (2000a).
[91] As Golato points out, however, positive evaluations of recipients can also accomplish other actions, such as reproaching or rebuking a co-present party: e.g., *Mary's sitting up nicely* said in the presence of children who are not (2005:86).
[92] Pomerantz (1978a) also discusses the action type Self-praise, which is found when a speaker makes a *positive* evaluation of him/herself or of something within his/her domain or territory. Given the social constraint of Self-praise avoidance, however, these cases are rare and consequently will not be discussed here. See Wu (2011) for a study of self-praising in Mandarin conversation.
[93] Schegloff treats both self-deprecations and compliments as accomplished through the vehicle of an Assessment (2007a:73).

(4.71)   "Great bridge player" (SBL 2:2:3)
((Claire and her friend Chloe are revisiting the game of bridge they played together the day before this telephone call.))

```
1      Cla:   °^uhhh hu hu°˜WE::ll, [ah-
2  ->  Chl:                         [AND I n:ever ˜was a
3  ->         gr(h)ea(h)t br(h)idge [play(h)er]Cl(h)a[(h)ire?]
4      Cla:                         [°˜Y*e::h°] hhh   [Well I ]think you've
5             always been real good and I'm sure gla::d that uh hhhh when
6             I look ba:ck o:ver it (0.2) *eh an' I told Frank e-I (.)
7             ca:n't understand how you'n Jo: hhh u-my: ^GO::d *eh:(.)t-
8             ^talk about Gl:^a:˜dys hhhh I just sa:t there throwing
9             things i:n not counting a:nything at lea:st I count little
10            b*it ˜n*o: [w, [Tha]t's little bit better?
11     Chl:                [Ya[:h?]
12     Cla:   =°hhh-hhhh°
```

We will examine such Compliment and Self-deprecation turns more closely in §5.4 below.

5.2 The Linguistic Design of Assessments

How do speakers build assessing turns? What makes an Assessment action recognizable as such? As with Questions, languages appear to have dedicated ways of implementing Assessments. In English, for instance, one of the most frequent formats appears to be the following:

(4.72)   Assessment format in English ("objective assessment") (adapted from Goodwin and Goodwin 1987:22)
[it/that/(s)he] + [copula] + ([adverbial intensifier]) + [assessment term]
Example: it was so good

Linguistically, this format could be described as a copular construction in which an evaluative adjective or noun phrase (assessment term), with or without an adverbial intensifier, predicates a quality or characteristic of a third-person assessable, typically in subject position.[94] As Goodwin and Goodwin (1987:22) point out, such a format begins by referencing the assessable and then builds up to the assessing component. The adverbial intensifier, if present and placed before the assessing component, allows the recipient to begin aligning with the projected term even before it is produced, as happens in example (4.67).

---

[94] This format is an example of what Fox (2007) has called a "social action format".

An Assessment format like the one shown in (4.72) has been called "objective", in the sense that it formulates a quality of the assessable that is presented as inherent and enduring (Wiggins and Potter 2003:516). It can be contrasted with another type of format used in assessing that has been called "subjective":

(4.73)   Assessment format in English ("subjective assessment")
[I] like/love/detest/hate [assessable]
```
Example: (Pomerantz 1978a:100) (adapted)
1      K:   Those tacos were good!
2      B:   You liked them...
3  ->  K:   I loved them, yes.
```

An Assessment format like that in (4.73) does not present the evaluation as an inherent, enduring characteristic of the assessable, but rather suggests that it is a personal stance, the subject's internal reaction to the referent, and is therefore "subjective".

If we now compare (4.73) *I loved them* and (4.67) *I love it* in their respective sequential contexts, it will become clear that Assessments differ in terms of whether a specific item or a class of items is being evaluated (Wiggins and Potter 2003). Whereas *I loved them* in (4.73) refers to the specific tacos referenced in K's prior turn, *I love it* in (4.67) evaluates asparagus pie in general. In other words, in (4.67) Clacia is not claiming to have experienced the same asparagus pie as Dianne, but only typical members of the class of asparagus pie. The distinction between evaluating a specific item and a class of items can be relevant for how participants position themselves with respect to their rights to assess (see also Online-Chapter C §1).

5.3 Epistemic Primacy in First Assessments

By producing a first Assessment with a simple, unmarked form (as in line 2 of (4.67) and line 1 of (4.73)), it has been argued that speakers make an implicit claim to have privileged access to the assessable and therefore primary rights to evaluate it (Heritage and Raymond 2005). The inherent claim of epistemic primacy brought about by "going first" in an assessing activity can, however, be modified – downplayed or enhanced – by specific linguistic devices. Heritage and Raymond distinguish *downgraded* first Assessments from *upgraded* ones. A first Assessment can be downgraded by *evidentially marking* that one's access is only secondary.[95] For instance:

---

[95] In home-birth helplines such as the one described by Shaw and Kitzinger, evidential markers in the call-taker's positive assessments of the mother (e.g., *that sounds very sensible*) have been said to *strengthen* the Assessment, owing to the fact that they formulate the basis on which the Assessment is being made and, in doing so, increase its plausibility (2012:225).

(4.74) "Nice little lady" (Thompson et al. 2015:152) (adapted)
```
1     Bea:   hh hhh we:ll,h I was gla:d she could come too last ni:ght=
2 ->  Nor:   =sh[e seems such a n]ice little [l a d y]
3     Bea:      [(since you keh)]             [dAwful]ly nice little
4                person. t hhhh hhh
```

An evidential such as *seem* indicates that the evaluation about to be made is not based on immediate first-order access to the referent but on derivative knowledge.

A first Assessment can also be downgraded in English by appending a *tag question*:

(4.75) "Second earring" (Heritage and Raymond 2005:24) (adapted)
```
7       Mum:   she's been in hot water with her mum today,
8       Les:   why?
9       Mum:   .hh we:ll. (0.2)
10             uh you know (.)
11             there's a craze with the girls now to have (.) a
12             secon:d. (1.1) ring ih- a secon:d uh earring in on[e ear.
13 ->   Les:                                                    [oh:
14 ->          it's very chea:p isn't it.
15      Mum:   it's very cheap yes
```

Mum's description of the earring craze among young girls (lines 11–12) is done from a [K+] position, as reflected, among other things, in the *you know* preface to her turn (line 10). Lesley claims access to the assessable when she evaluates it as *very cheap*, but at the same time she pays tribute to Mum's more privileged epistemic position by appending a tag *isn't it*. As Heritage and Raymond (2005:20) explain, first Assessments with appended tag questions are not assertions demanding agreement (as would be the case with the simple *it's very cheap*), but rather questions demanding answers.[96] By virtue of their doing questioning from a partially [K−] position, English tag questions in first-position Assessments thus index a subordinate epistemic stance.

By contrast, a first Assessment can be *upgraded* epistemically if it is formatted as a negative interrogative:

(4.76) "Pat" (Heritage and Raymond 2005:33) (adapted)
```
1 ->   Edn:   e-that Pa:t isn't she a do:[:ll?]
2      Mar:                              [iYe]h isn't she pretty,
```

In this case Edna chooses a negative interrogative form *isn't she* to evaluate Margy's friend Pat as *a doll*. While it is Margy who has privileged rights to assess

---
[96] Or in this case, statements + tags requesting confirmation.

Pat (Edna did not know her prior to Margy's luncheon), Edna compensates her subordinate epistemic position by presenting her evaluation in a format that strongly invites agreement: she uses a negative interrogative form that is tilted toward a positive answer. This formatting choice suggests that Edna has a settled opinion on the matter and is in no way subordinating herself to Margy's superior knowledge.

In some languages the kind of access the speaker claims to have to the assessable is marked systematically via particles. For instance, in Japanese the particle *yo* in turn-final position on a first Assessment indexes that the speaker has privileged access to the assessable, i.e., knows it better than the recipient (Hayano 2013). (This is presumably the equivalent of an upgraded first Assessment in English.) The following example shows *yo* at work:

(4.77)   "Salmon" (Hayano 2013:50)
((Eiko, Nami, and Kayo are having a lunch break. Eiko has pieces of salmon in her lunch box and offers them to Nami to try. As part of the offer she makes an assessment of the salmon.))

```
                    [[((Eiko puts her lunch box in front of Nami))
1 ->   Eiko:   [[kono shake oishii yo. chotto tabete goran.
                 this salmon good  FP  a_little eat   try
               This salmon is good yo. Try (it).
2 ->           kosuko no shake.
               Costco L  salmon
               (It's) salmon from Costco.
3                   [[((Nami reaches toward the lunch box))
                    [[(0.2)
4      Nami:   hmm:::.
               ITJ
               I see.
5                   [((Nami eats the salmon))
                    [(3.3)
6      Eiko:   nanka shio:mi mo    choodoii tte iu ka,
               like  saltiness also temperate QT  say or
               (It's) like, the saltiness is right (or something),
7      Nami:   aa:: honto da,
               ITJ   true  CP
               Oh::: (you are) right,
8              (0.2)
9 ->   Nami:   oihii    oihii.
               delicious delicious
               (It's) good (it's) good.
```

By using the particle *yo* at the end of her first TCU (line 1), Eiko signals that she is assessing something she has directly experienced but that she assumes the recipient has not. Once Nami has tried the salmon, she agrees with Eiko's positive evaluation (lines 7, 9) but, in doing so, confirms her own epistemic subordination by not using *yo* (line 9) (Hayano 2013:51).

First Assessments can be designed in English with formats that present them as "objective" (*X* + *copula verb* + *assessment term*) or as "subjective" (*I love/hate X*). The epistemic primacy claimed through being the first to assess some assessable can be downgraded linguistically with evidential markers and/or tag questions and upgraded with negative interrogatives. In languages such as Japanese, the type of speaker access to an assessable (privileged or not) is marked with epistemic particles.

5.4 The Linguistic Design of Compliments and Self-deprecations

How are Compliments and Self-deprecations designed? How can they be identified as such? The issue here turns on whether the valence of an evaluation is positive or negative and on whether the assessable belongs to the domain of the speaker or the recipient. Both dimensions can be marked linguistically (Golato 2005).[97] Thus, in (4.70) the semantically positive characteristic of being *darling* is attributed to an assessable belonging to Margy (*your friends*), while in (4.71) the negative characteristic of not being *a great bridge player* is attributed to the speaker herself (*I never was*). These linguistic cues leave little doubt that Edna's turn in (4.70) is a Compliment, while Chloe's in (4.71) is a Self-deprecation.

Yet in the absence of clear linguistic marking, it will be up to the recipient to decide whether the referent of a positive assessing action lies within their domain or not. Recipients may thus have a certain amount of latitude in deciding whether to treat a positive evaluation as a Compliment. Likewise, it may be up to the recipient to decide whether the referent of a negative assessing action lies within the domain of the speaker and should therefore be treated as self-deprecative. These distinctions, as we show below, are not without consequence: the interpretation of an interlocutor's assessing action as a (third-person) Assessment, a (second-person) Compliment, or a (first-person) Self-deprecation is crucial for deciding on an appropriate next action.

Like Assessments, Compliments have been shown to be accomplished with recurrent linguistic forms (Golato 2005; Shaw and Kitzinger 2012; Keisanen and Kärkkäinen 2014).[98] While Keisanen and Kärkkäinen find *you*-subjects,

---

[97] See also Keisanen and Kärkkäinen (2014) for a multimodal approach to compliments.
[98] Whether the same holds for Self-deprecations is an open question at this time. To our knowledge, there has been no empirical study of the self-deprecative formats used in talk-in-interaction.

present-tense copula *be*-verbs, and positively valenced adjectives and noun phrases to be the most common forms in the everyday compliments they examine (2014:652–3), Shaw and Kitzinger, whose study is based on calls to a helpline for mothers planning a home birth, stress that Compliment turns are more diverse in their materials. In particular, they find a recurrent use of evidentials: *It sounds as if your body worked very well*, *You obviously handled the contractions well*, as well as a frequent use of "reaction tokens" such as *oh* and *ooh* to enhance the sincerity of the call-taker's positive Assessments (2012:225).

Golato (2005) reports that many Compliment turns in German have "verb-first constructions", thus violating the prescriptive norm for German that declarative sentences should have the topic position before the verb filled with a subject, complement, or adjunct constituent: in other words, they have an empty topic slot and begin immediately with the verb (see also Auer 1993). In some cases, the subject appears after the verb as in *kannste gu:ut* [lit. can you good] "you do that well" (p. 73) or *habt ihr schöne ro:sen hier* [lit. have you nice roses here] "you've got nice roses here" (p. 74). In other cases, the subject is not mentioned at all: *schmeckt gut, inge* [lit. tastes good first-name] "this tastes good, Inge" (p. 73). Golato argues that the empty topic position allows German speakers to index a strong cohesive relation between the compliment and the surrounding talk or action.[99]

Self-deprecation turns appear to have a less predictable linguistic make-up. Pomerantz (1984a) mentions self-deprecative turns such as: *I'm trying to get slim, … In my old age I'm slowing down, I have no dates, I was wondering if I ruined your weekend, I'm so dumb I don't even know it, It's not bad for an old lady, I never was a great bridge player, She talks better than I do, I'm no bottle of milk, She was almost as bad as I was, I'm talking nonsense, I'm being irritable right now by telling you, I have my desk full of trash*, etc. (pp. 83–95) – most of which make reference to the speaker having some negative quality. However, the forms that are used to do this are quite varied.

Compliment turns in talk-in-interaction are typically designed with a small number of recurrent formats. For English, these include *[you] + [are] + [positive ADJ/NP]*, *how/what [positive ADJ/NP] you are*, and *you [positive NP]*. For German, "empty topic" or verb-first constructions have been noted as especially frequent. Further patterns await discovery. Self-deprecations typically attribute some negative quality to the speaker but the linguistic forms deployed in doing so appear to be more diverse than for Compliment turns.

(Note: *ADJ* = adjective; *NP* = noun phrase.)

---

[99] "Topic" here refers to the grammatical position before the left sentence brace in German, the front field (see also Chapter 6 §2.1) as a "topic slot" in a topic-comment strecture.

5.5 Responding to Assessments

Responses to assessing first actions are themselves generally assessing actions. Yet these second Assessments can implement different actions: they can *agree* with the evaluation of the first Assessment or they can *disagree* with it. Agreement and Disagreement are not on a par with one another as second actions, however. Depending on the sequential environment, one is preferred, in the sense that it furthers the project underway and is therefore considered pro-social, while the other is by contrast dispreferred. Preferred second actions tend to be implemented in a simple, straightforward fashion without delay, whereas dispreferred actions are often delayed and accompanied by accounts, excuses, or justifications (see also Online-Chapter B).

Recall that assessing actions establish different preferences for the next action depending on whether they are interpreted as Assessments, Compliments, or Self-deprecations. This is because normative expectations concerning what counts as a pro-social response vary according to whether the evaluation is of a "neutral" assessable (belonging to neither speaker nor recipient) or is instead praising the recipient or denigrating the speaker. As Pomerantz (1984a) shows, based on a dataset of assessing actions in English conversation, the preferred response to an Assessment in English is *Agreement*. We can observe this preference at work by returning to the example seen above for Assessment (renumbered here):

```
(4.78)    "Asparagus pie" (Goodwin and Goodwin 1992:161) (= (4.67) above)
1         Dianne:   Jeff made an asparagus pie
2                   it was s::so[: goo:d.
3   =>    Clacia:              [I love it.
```

The responsive turn *I love it* (line 3) is a positive Assessment, *agreeing* with its prior, the Assessment *it was so good*. The simple, straightforward, and immediate way in which the responsive action is carried out here points to the fact that it is both unproblematic and preferred in this context of occurrence.

As Pomerantz observes, responses to Compliment actions are more complicated. This is due to the fact that they involve two conflicting preference systems, one dictating that Assessments should be agreed with, and the other stipulating that self-praise should be avoided (Pomerantz 1978b). Consequently, responses to Compliments in Pomerantz's English data lie somewhere between Acceptance/Agreement and Rejection/Disagreement. This can be observed in the example for Complimenting from above:

5. Assessments, Compliments, Self-deprecations, and their Responses

(4.79)   "Lovely luncheon" (NB VII) (= (4.70) above)
((Edna has called her friend Margy to thank her for the recent luncheon at which Edna was a guest.))

```
1 ->  Edn:  =Oh honey that was a lovely luncheon I should have ca:lled you
2 ->        s:soo[:ner but I:]l:[lo:ved it. It was just deli:ghtfu[:l. ]=
3     Mar:       [((f)) Oh:::]   [°(           )              [Well]=
4 =>  Mar:  =I was gla[d     y o u] (came).]
5 ->  Edn:            [and your f:] friends] are so da:rli:ng,=
6 =>  Mar:  =Oh:::: it wz: ((two discontinued))
```

Margy does not outright agree with Edna's compliments *that was a lovely luncheon*, *I loved it*, and *it was just delightful* (lines 1–2) by saying something like "yes, I thought so too" in next turn. Instead, she deflects the compliments by shifting the assessable away from the quality of her luncheon to the fact that Edna came to it. With *I was glad you came* (line 4), Margy presents Edna's coming as something that pleased her, i.e., she transforms her response into a subjective, positive evaluation of what Edna did. We will return to other practices for responding to Compliments shortly. But meanwhile, how is Agreement done in response to an Assessment?

5.5.1 Agreement in Response to an Assessment

It turns out that the practices used to accomplish Agreement as a responsive action can vary significantly in different languages. In English, according to Pomerantz (1984a), the primary way to agree with a prior Assessment is to *upgrade* it by using a stronger evaluative term or an intensifier. For example:

(4.80)   "Fair old upset" (Holt July 86:1:4)
```
1 ->  Gwe:  Mind you this is a fair old upset for him as well at the
2 ->        wrong time is[n'it
3 =>  Les:               [Oh I think it's terrible.
```

(4.81)   "Nice little lady" (Thompson et al. 2015:152) (adapted) (= (4.74) above)
```
1     Bea:  hh hhh we:ll,h I was gla:d she could come too last ni:ght=
2 ->  Nor:  =sh[e seems such a n]ice little [lady  ]
3 =>  Bea:     [(since you keh)]           [dAwful]ly nice little
4 =>        person. t hhhh hhh
```

In (4.80) Gwen's evaluation *this is a fair old upset* (line 1) is upgraded in Lesley's response with a stronger evaluative term *it's terrible* (line 3). And in (4.81) Norma's evaluation *she seems such a nice little lady* (line 2) is upgraded with the intensified *awfully nice little person* (lines 3–4) in Bea's response. Such upgraded second evaluations are treated by participants as unproblematic and unconditional Agreeing actions in English.

By contrast, *same*-evaluations in next turn are said to provide only *weak* agreement in English. Evidence for this comes from the fact that they are often followed by Disagreement, as in the following cases:

(4.82)   "Big obligation" (Three gals)
((The participants are talking about having one's elderly parents live nearby.))
```
11 ->  Linda:    =(But) it's a ↑big obligation also=
12 =>  Felicia:  =It is. It is. {nodding}
13 =>  Felicia:  .hhh (.) But ↑he's happy to be able to do it I [think.
14     Linda:                                                   [Uh huh
```

(4.83)   "Nice guy" (Chicken dinner)
```
37 ->  Sha:  He's [a nice [guy
38     Vi?:       [(.t)   [
39 =>  Viv:               [Oh he's a nice gu:y.
40           (0.3)
1      Sha:  I rib um a lot.
2            (2.7)
3  =>  Viv:  But- when- That's the: problem when you try to carry
4            on a conversation with him
```

Although both Felicia in (4.82) and Vivian in (4.83) are agreeing with a prior Assessment, the fact that they take over the same-evaluation term in doing so renders their agreement weak.[100] In fact, both speakers continue with *but*-prefaced TCUs elaborating ways in which the prior evaluation does not hold.

A third practice for doing agreement with a prior Assessment is to *downgrade* the lexical evaluation made in the prior turn. Like a same-evaluation in English, this response provides only weak agreement:

(4.84)   "Pat" (Heritage and Raymond 2005:33) (= (4.76) above)
```
1 ->  Edn:  e-that Pa:t isn't she a do:[:ll?]
2 =>  Mar:                             [iYe]h isn't she pretty,
3           (.)
4 ->  Edn:  Oh: she's a beautiful girl.=
5 =>  Mar:  =Yeh I think she's a pretty gir[l.
```

Although Margy is nominally agreeing with Edna's evaluation of Pat, her adjective *pretty* in line 2 is semantically weaker than Edna's *a doll* in line 1 and

---

[100] Note that same-evaluation responses can be done either without re-using the assessment term as in example (4.82) *it is*, or with a repeat of the assessment term as in (4.83) *oh he's a nice guy*. For cases with accented copulas, Thompson et al. argue that the latter exhibit somewhat more agency than the former (2015:199).

is thus heard as downgrading the evaluation. Similarly, when Edna now upgrades her subsequent evaluation of Pat to *beautiful*, Margy once again downgrades it by using the comparatively weaker adjective *pretty* (line 5).

In the cases shown above, the strength of the Agreeing response appears to turn on lexical choice. However, a study by Ogden (2006) shows that the way a second evaluation is formatted *prosodically* and *phonetically* in relation to a first Assessment can influence the strength of an agreeing response in English. Ogden claims that lexical upgrades in second Assessments are only heard as strongly agreeing if they are also prosodically-phonetically upgraded, i.e., have expanded pitch spans, more dynamic pitch contours, higher pitch, slower tempo, and/or closer articulations (Ogden 2006:1762). For an example illustrating an agreeing second Assessment that is both lexically and prosodically upgraded by comparison with the prior turn, see example (E.3) in Online-Chapter E.

A lexically upgraded second Assessment that is prosodically-phonetically downgraded, by contrast, does not come off as strongly agreeing but instead as projecting Disagreement. Here is a case in point (see also Figure 4.2):

(4.85) "Cash in today" (Ogden 2006:1770) (adapted)
((Skip and Fred are colleagues and in this phone call are talking about the fact that there has been an inflow of cash that day.))

```
5       Fre    =thanks 'n I, I've also heard about the- of course
6              about the cash in toda:[y.
7   ->  Ski                          [gYes::. yes isn't that
8   ->         good at l:ong la:[st.  [((sniff))
9   =>  Fre                           [that [s- that's (.) very good
10  =>         news. but of cour[se it (0.3)
11      Ski                     [khhhhhhhh
12      Fre    we'll have to pay out a lot of that I [guess
```

Despite the fact that Fred's response in example (4.85) has a lexical upgrade *very good* (line 9), it is produced with a narrower pitch span and less dynamic pitch contours than those used in Skip's prior Assessment (see Figure 4.2 below). This prosodic downgrade contributes to the fact that Fred's response comes off as projecting Disagreement. And in fact, the disagreement comes to the fore when he says next: *but of course we'll have to pay out a lot of that* (lines 10, 12).

Why should lexical and prosodic upgrading be a default way to do Agreement in English? One explanation can be found in Heritage and Raymond's (2005) observation that "going first" with an Assessment places that speaker in an epistemically superior position. By the same token it sets the agenda for the response, obliging the recipient to respond taking account of the terms that the first speaker has established. A second assessor who agrees runs the risk of being seen as merely

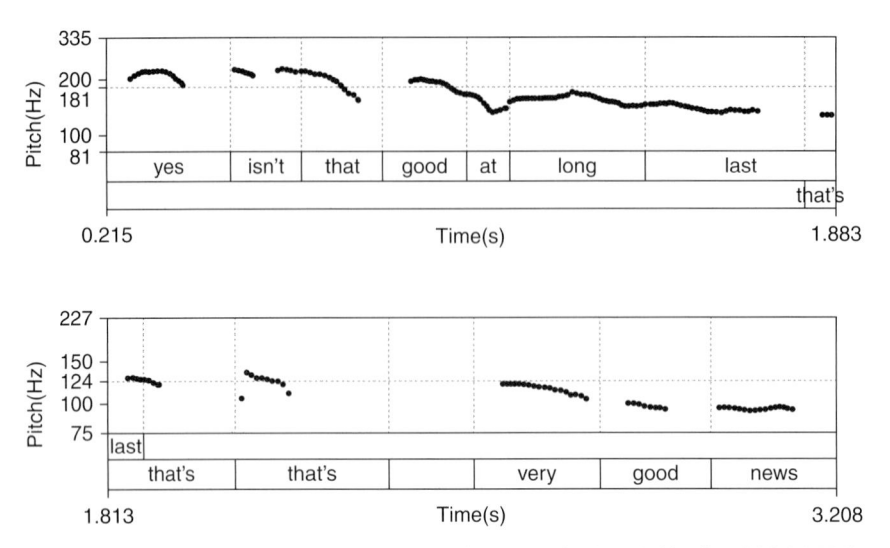

Figure 4.2 Pitch trace of the Assessments in example (4.85) (Ogden 2006:1771)

going along with the first assessor, rather than as being an epistemically independent agent. By lexically and prosodically *upgrading* a second Assessment, however, the second speaker can offset this risk and create the impression of agreeing on his/her own terms.[101]

> Agreement in response to a first Assessment in English can be accomplished through a lexical upgrade, a lexical same-evaluation, or a lexical downgrade. Lexical upgrades are generally said to indicate strong agreement if they are also prosodically upgraded: by choosing their own assessing term, respondents display epistemic independence. (This independence can, however, risk challenging the first assessor's evaluation.) Lexical same-evaluations, when minimal and prosodically downgraded, and lexical downgrades are generally said to indicate only weak agreement: they are often followed by Disagreement. Responding to a first Assessment is thus a balancing act: merely going along with what the other has said can imply a lack of commitment, while choosing an assessment term of one's own displays more commitment and independence of judgment. Yet in some cases, this can be perceived as challenging the interlocutor's evaluation.

How is Agreeing with a first Assessment done in other languages? From recent research it is emerging that particles can be used to reinforce same-evaluation second Assessments in some languages. When this happens, same-evaluation responses are

---

[101] In their study of the grammar of responsive actions, however, Thompson et al. (2015) point out that upgraded second Assessments can display such a degree of epistemic independence that they actually become challenges to the first Assessment because they "re-author" it (p. 180). They can thus be a site for disaffiliation (p. 191).

not weak at all but the default way to do unproblematic Agreement. In German, for instance, same-evaluation second Assessments are clearly agreeing if they are preceded by the particle *ja* "yeah" (Uhmann 1996:305):[102]

(4.86)   "Nice age" (Uhmann 1996:305)
```
1      H:    wie alt,
             how old
2      X:    ja:: so:: sechsenzwanzig glaub=ich
             oh about twenty-six I think
3   -> H:    "schö::nes Alter
             nice age
4   => X:    ja ne heheh (0.8) 'best(h)en 'Jah(h)re
             yeah huh hehe (0.8) prime years
```

Auer and Uhmann (1982) argue that paraphrases such as *schönes Alter* "nice age" and *beste Jahre* "prime years" should be considered semantic equivalents; as such, when accompanied by an agreeing particle, they function as same-evaluations indicating unproblematic Agreement.

In Finnish, unproblematic Agreeing responses to first Assessments are done by repeating the verb. When the particle *niin* ("in that way") prefaces the verb repeat, it takes up the evaluation of the prior turn anaphorically and the response expresses strong Agreement with it (Sorjonen and Hakulinen 2009). For instance:

(4.87)   "Nice fields" (Sorjonen and Hakulinen 2009) (adapted)
```
8   -> V:    =Kyl siin    pelaa joo ei se tos    >et ne    oli
             sure it.ESS Ø plays yeah NEG it there PRT    they was
             =Sure one can play on it yeah it won't there >so those were
9   ->       kyl kivat kentät oikeestaan tuolla (1.2) .mt Olarissa.
             sure nice fields   actually there            Olari.INE
             real nice fields there in fact (1.2) .tch in Olari.
10  => S:    Niin on. Nehän    on tosi hyvät.
             so   is  they.CLI is true good.PL
             They were. Indeed they were so nice.
```

Finally, in Japanese, with the particle *ne* in final position, same-evaluation Assessments are the default way to show full affiliation, i.e., agreement (Hayano 2013:69).[103] Turn-final *ne* in Japanese assessing is a means to mark shared access to a referent (see also Online-Chapter C §2.2.1):

---

[102] Disagreement-implicative same-evaluation second Assessments, by contrast, are prefaced by *haja* or *aja*, while downgraded second Assessments have *naja* (Uhmann 1996:315).

[103] In Hayano's conversational data, 64 percent of second Assessments that were treated as unproblematically affiliative were done with same evaluations (and overwhelmingly marked with *ne* or *yone*), while only 36 percent were lexically upgraded (and marked with *yo*) (2013:69).

(4.88) "Thick" (Hayano 2013:54)
((Kayo is a pottery instructor and is making a critical observation here about her student Eiko's pot.))

```
1  ->  Kayo:   de- (0.2) a^tsui ne.
                And       thick  FP
                And- (0.2) (it's) ^thick ne.

2  =>  Eiko:   atsui desu [ne:.
                thick CP    FP
               (It's) thick ne:.

3      Kayo:              [un:.
                           ITJ
                           Yeah:.
```

According to Hayano, because first assessors in Japanese can signal shared access through the use of *ne*, second assessors are not vulnerable to being seen as epistemically dependent merely by virtue of "going second". They can use same-evaluations without the risk of appearing epistemically subordinate (2013:70).[104]

> There is a growing body of evidence from languages such as German, Finnish, and Japanese that same-evaluations in these languages are not weak agreements at all, but instead – especially when reinforced by particles – actually the default way to achieve congruence and shared commitment in the evaluation of an assessable.

5.5.2 Agreeing but Asserting Epistemic Independence

Recent work on epistemics in conversation has shown that who is agreeing with whom in Assessment sequences is a very real concern for participants (Heritage and Raymond 2005, Raymond and Heritage 2006). Placed in a sequential position that automatically subordinates them epistemically, second assessors may well wish to push back and assert their epistemic independence. How to effect this "resistance" while still agreeing is a delicate matter. In the following we consider three linguistic devices in English and other languages that have been shown to index epistemic authority and/or independence in Agreeing responses.[105]

i. *Oh*-prefacing

As Heritage (2002a) explains, the particle *oh* in English responses conveys that a prior turn has occasioned a marked shift of attention. When the prior turn is an

---

[104] Lindström and Heinemann (2009) and Mondada (2009) discuss cases from institutional interactions in Swedish/Danish and French, respectively, where *upgraded* second Assessments are actually avoided due to their unwanted implications.

[105] One of these, *oh*-prefacing, can also be used with Disagreeing second assessments as well (Heritage 2002a).

5. Assessments, Compliments, Self-deprecations, and their Responses

Assessment, *oh*-prefacing indicates that it has brought about "a review, recollection, and renewal of the speaker's previous experience and judgment" (2002a:201). This implies that the evaluation the speaker is giving now, rather than being occasioned by the first Assessment, was actually formed earlier on independent grounds. The practice of *oh*-prefacing can be used both in cases (a) where the second assessor has equivalent access and equal rights to assess the referent, and (b) where the second assessor has privileged access and rights to evaluate the referent. Here is a case where the participants have equivalent rights:

(4.89) "Too depressing" (Heritage 2002a:203) (adapted)
((Emma and Lottie are referring to the television coverage of Robert Kennedy's assassination.))

```
8      Lot:   Uh I wouldn't even turn it o:n I [mean I]: just .t.hhh
9      Emm:                                    [Uh-uh]
10 ->  Lot:   It's too depres[sing.]
11 =>  Emm:                  [Oh:::]::↓it is terr:ible↓=What's ne:w.
12     Lot:   Gee nothing Emma ((turn continues))
```

Both Lottie and Emma share equal rights to evaluate the television reports of Kennedy's assassination. When Lottie "goes first" and declares that she does not want to watch them because they are *too depressing*, this puts Emma, who agrees, in the position of appearing to be just going along with Lottie's Assessment. By prefacing her agreeing turn with *oh*, however, Emma can convey that she had reached this conclusion independently of Lottie's having introduced it.

For a contrasting case in which the second assessors have privileged access and rights, see example (C.6′) in Online-Chapter C. Here too, second assessors index that they are agreeing with the first assessor's evaluation from a prior established and independent position by prefacing their Agreeing assessment with *oh*.

ii. Modified repeats

English speakers can also push back from second position by formatting their Agreement as a "modified" repeat of the first Assessment (Stivers 2005). The term *modified repeat* refers to a repetition of the prior assessing turn with the main accent falling on the copular verb. Example (4.82) from above (renumbered here) shows a case where the modified repetition is *partial*:

(4.90) "Big obligation" (Three gals) (= (4.82) above)

```
11  ->  Linda:    =(But) it's a ↑big obligation also=
12  =>  Felicia:  =It is. It is. {nodding}
```

Here only the subject and copular verb of the first Assessment are repeated in the Agreeing response.

But the repetition can also be *full*, in that the assessing term itself is also repeated:

(4.91)   "Great coat" (Thompson et al. 2015:167) (adapted)
```
1       Abbie:   that's a great coat.
2                (.)
3   ->  Abbie:   that looks very warm.
4   =>  Stacy:   it is very warm.
```

In both (4.90) and (4.91), speakers are agreeing with prior Assessments from second position. Yet they could have shown their alignment by simply saying *yeah* or *mhm*. Instead, by re-doing the original evaluation with an accented copular, they mark that they are doing more than simply Agreeing: they are asserting their own superior rights to make the judgment and are thus confirming the Assessment from a position of authority (Stivers 2005).

One explanation for how this works may be that placing a main accent on an auxiliary or copular verb in English gives rise to the implication that a claim with the opposite polarity has been asserted or presupposed ("it's not warm") and is now being countered ("it is warm").[106] Abbie's first Assessment *that looks very warm* can be heard as allowing for the possibility that the coat is not warm. Therefore, in responding *it is warm*, Stacy is essentially counter-asserting, denying that her coat might not be warm, something that can only be done from a position of authority. In a sense then, a modified repeat format embodies epistemic authority in Agreeing.

In Thompson et al.'s (2015) study of Agreeing second assessments with accented copula verbs, the authors find that "partial modified repeats" (minimal clausal forms in their terminology) – as in (4.90) with *it is* – usually have downgraded prosody and occur in environments of trouble. They thus instantiate a weaker form of agreement (or symmetry of commitment) than "full modified repeats" (expanded clausal forms) as in (4.91) with *it is X*. The latter typically have upgraded prosody and occur in situations when participants are assessing something in the immediate environment. In these cases, recipients display greater agency by producing a same-evaluation in expanded form: they re-use the same term "for themselves" (p. 173).

Do other languages have the equivalent of modified repeats? A recent study by Sidnell and Enfield (2012) suggests they do. The authors describe practices in three different languages for demonstrating epistemic authority while Agreeing from second position, all of which involve repetition of the prior Assessment. In each case the repeated second Assessment is "modified" slightly differently, in

---

[106] This type of accent placement has been called "polarity" focus (Gussenhoven 1984:45).

5. *Assessments, Compliments, Self-deprecations, and their Responses* 303

a way motivated by the specific resources of the language in question. In Caribbean Creole English, an authoritative second Assessment involves a repetition of the prior assessment preceded by the word *if*. For instance: *hii ruud yuno* ("he's rude you know"), – *if hi ruud?* ("if he's rude"). Here the *if*-prefaced turn does not initiate repair but instead functions as a second Agreeing assessment implicating sequence closure (p. 314). In Finnish an authoritative second evaluation is done with an explicit subject and repeated verb in either Subject-Verb or Verb-Subject word order. And in Lao a factive perfective particle, *lèq1*,[107] is appended to the repeated evaluation. In all three cases the effect is to mark the second speaker as having stronger epistemic authority to assess, although all responders are nominally "agreeing" with the prior evaluation (Sidnell and Enfield 2012).[108]

iii. Particles and other practices

Finally, it should be pointed out that some of the same practices used to epistemically upgrade first Assessments can also be deployed to index epistemic priority in second-position Agreements. This includes, for example, for Japanese the use of the epistemic particle *yo* in second Assessments:

(4.92)   "Ayumi" (Hayano 2013:49)
```
5 ->  B:  demo a^yumi chan yoku shaberu ne:, igaini       ne:,
          but  ayumi  END  much talk    FP   unexpectedly P
          But A^yumi talks a lot ne, unexpectedly ne,

6 =>  G:  ayumi chan wa yoku  shaberu yo an[o ko    wa.
          ayumi  END  TP  often talk    FP that girl  TP
          Ayumi talks a lot yo, that girl (does).

7     B:                              [nn.
                                       ITJ
                                       Yeah.

8     G:  nn-
          ITJ
          Yeah-
```

As Hayano explains it, G here agrees with B in line 6 but at the same time expresses epistemic primacy: she knows better than B that Ayumi talks a lot. This is reflected not only in the fact that she does not repeat the word *igaini* "unexpectedly", indicating that unexpectedness is an element of the Assessment she does not agree with, but can also be seen in the fact that she adds on an expression of the

---
[107] The numeral at the end of this word represents its lexical tone.
[108] There are also "collateral effects", or side effects, attendant on each of these practices due to the specific lexico-grammatical forms used and their affordances in the respective language. We reserve a discussion of these for Chapter 9.

subject *ano ko wa* "that girl (does)", implying her own judgment that Ayumi is generally a talkative person. She also uses the particle *yo*, claiming exclusive or primary rights to the knowledge (2013:52).

As for English, although tag questions have a downgrading effect with first Assessments, they have an epistemic strengthening effect when appended to Agreeing second assessments. This is because they constrain the interlocutor to respond on the terms set by the second evaluation. The second assessor is thereby able to claim greater epistemic authority:

(4.93)　"No expertise" (Holt May 1988 1:5)
((Robbie and Lesley are talking about one of the teachers at the school where Robbie now teaches. Lesley has formerly worked as a replacement teacher at the same school.))

```
35      Rob:  but I ↑look at what she does with he[r (?class )=
36      Les:                                     [I k n o: w,=
37 ->   Rob:  [and it's n:↑o↓thin[g. (really)
38      Les:  [I kno:w.          [no:.
39 =>         no it's no- there's no uh:m expertise ↓there is there.
40      Rob:  not really [but I suppose we do learn and she hasn't been
41      Les:             [no.
42      Rob:  =to other schools ((turn continues))
```

In this exchange, Lesley agrees with Robbie's evaluation that the teacher in question accomplishes nothing with her class. However, by formatting her turn as an independent evaluation, *there's no expertise there*, and appending the tag question *is there*, Lesley presents herself as having greater epistemic authority and puts Robbie in the position of having to go along with her evaluation.

Finally, a negative interrogative also makes a claim of epistemic priority when deployed in second-position Agreements:

(4.94)　"Pat" (Heritage and Raymond 2005:33) (= (4.84) above)

```
1 ->    Edn:  e-that Pa:t isn't she a do:[:ll?]
2 =>    Mar:                             [iYe]h isn't she pretty,
3             (.)
4       Edn:  Oh: she's a beautiful girl.=
5       Mar:  =Yeh I think she's a pretty gir[l.
```

In line 2 Margy uses a lexical downgrade in her response to Edna's first Assessment of Pat, but she also frames it as a negative question, constraining the interlocutor to answer with a confirmation. Edna cleverly avoids this constraint, however, by upgrading her subsequent evaluation and prefacing it with *oh*, indexing her own epistemic independence.

> This section has reviewed a number of ways in which speakers who are responding with an Agreeing evaluation in second position can push back against the inherent claim to epistemic priority associated with first Assessments. The practices reviewed include (a) *oh*-prefacing in English, (b) modified repeats in English and related devices in other languages, as well as (c) the use of particles in Japanese, and tag questions and negative interrogatives in English. This list is by no means exhaustive; other ways of claiming epistemic authority from second position await discovery.

5.5.3 Disagreement in Response to an Assessment

How do speakers *disagree* with a prior Assessment? As Pomerantz (1984a) points out, Disagreements are typically dispreferred responses and as a rule delayed through silence, repair initiations, requests for clarification, and the like. If and when finally done, Disagreements are typically mitigated and indirect in form. In this connection then, it comes as no surprise that *prosodic* downgrading on a verbally *agreeing* response should foreshadow Disagreement (Ogden 2006), and not vice versa, prosody being far less accountable than words.

Among the verbal devices deployed for Disagreement is the so-called *yes ... but* construction, attested *inter alia* in English, German, Danish, and Finnish (Barth-Weingarten 2003; Steensig and Asmuss 2005; Niemi 2014). When a turn is formatted with this construction, it begins with what looks like Agreement but then moves, more or less quickly, into Disagreement. Pomerantz refers to this pattern as the "agreement plus disagreement" turn shape (1984a:72). Here is an example:

(4.95)   "Accidents" (Pomerantz 1984a:73) (adapted)
```
1  A:   ... cause those things take working at,
2       (2.0)
3  B:   (hhhhh) well, they [do, but-
4  A:                      [They aren't accidents,
5  B:   No, they take working at but on the other
6       hand, some people ...
```

The design of B's turn in line 3, with its delay, audible pre-beginning, and *well*-preface, already adumbrates a problem in seconding A's Assessment from line 1. Yet she first expresses agreement with A's position *they do*. When A reiterates her position, in partial overlap, with a negative assertion *they aren't accidents* (line 4), B again first agrees *no, they take working at*, before launching a counter to A's assertion *but on the other hand* (lines 5–6). The *yes ... but* construction allows recipients to initially present ways in which they agree with another's first Assessment before moving to state some disagreement. Although it is the disagreement component that is sequentially implicative for next turn, with this practice recipients can avoid blatantly contradicting their co-interlocutor.

In some contexts, however, more directly antagonistic practices for disagreeing are customary. M. H. Goodwin describes the device of "format tying" in argumentative sequences, which is common, for instance, among young black children in the United States (Goodwin and Goodwin 1987). In her words: "participants frequently tie not only to the type of action produced by the last speaker but also to the particulars of its wording" (M. H. Goodwin 1990:177). Here is an example from her data, where the first action is a negative Assessment (an insult) and the next action disputes that evaluation by re-directing it to the instigators of the insult:

(4.96)   "Dance steps" (M. H. Goodwin 1990:183)
((A group of girls are practicing steps for a future dance contest against the boys. The girls sing as they practice original dance steps.))

```
1 ->  Tony:    You sound terrible.
2 =>  Martha:  We sound just like you look.
```

But format tying is also used by adults, as in the following argumentative sequence:

(4.97)   "Weird" (Before bed)
```
1         Oli:  speakers have like CODES?
2               (11.9)
3         Oli:  <GOD!.hhh> <stage whisper>
4               (0.3)
5         Ste:  <<f> (wha-/wel-) it's im[PORtant.>
6         Oli:                          [<<pp> DO::cuments (   )>
7               <<p> huh!>
8         STe:  you don't think ANything's im[portant
9    ->   Oli:                               [it's W:EI:RD!
10              (1.0)
11   =>   Ste:  it's not WEI:RD;
12   =>         it's what- <<declination unit> it's NECessary.
13   =>         it's SCIence.>
14              (2.4)
15        Ste:  i mean it's a SO:FT science but it's SCIence
```

Here Stephie re-uses Oliver's format *it's X* in Disagreeing with the import of his Assessment: she first denies it with *it's not X* (line 11) and then positively assesses what *is* the case with the format *it's Y* (lines 12–13).

> Disagreeing with a prior Assessment can be done in a mitigated fashion with a *yes ... but* strategy, conveying first weak Agreement followed by Disagreement. Constructions dedicated to accomplishing this have been attested in a variety of languages, including English, German, Danish, and Finnish.[109] But Disagreement can also be direct and explicit, for instance, through the practice of format tying, using elements from a prior turn for its reversal in the response.

5.6 Responding to Compliments and Self-deprecations

Disagreement is also one of the practices that has been identified as a way to respond to Compliments. But let us first consider Compliments in a somewhat broader perspective. As Pomerantz (1978b) explains, Compliments can be treated as (i) *supportive* actions (similar to Offers and Invitations), making Acceptance or Rejection relevant next; in this case, Acceptance would be the preferred response. Or Compliments can be treated as (ii) *assessing* actions, making Agreement or Disagreement relevant next; in this case Agreement would be the preferred option. In (4.98), we find recipients *accepting* the Compliment, typically via an expression of appreciation:

(4.98)　"Loveliest record" (Pomerantz 1978b:84)
```
1   ->  A:  Why it's the loveliest record I ever heard.
2           And the organ-
3   =>  B:  Well thank you.
```

On the other hand, in (4.99) we find recipients *agreeing* with a prior Assessment:[110]

(4.99)　"Organ music" (Pomerantz 1978b:85) (adapted)
```
4   ->  A:  The organ music came out so
5           beautiful[ly in it.
6   =>  B:          [I thought it did too,
```

When Compliments are treated as Assessments, two different sets of preferences are in play: (a) as Assessments, Compliments make *agreement* relevant next; (b) as positive evaluations of the recipient, Compliments make *avoidance of self-praise* relevant next. These preferences are in conflict with one another, i.e., they cannot both be satisfied at once: to agree with a compliment is to engage in self-praise; to avoid self-praise is to disagree with the Assessment.

Therefore, as Pomerantz and others have pointed out, recipients have a variety of solutions for the conflict of preferences: they can (a) agree but scale down the

---

[109] The strategy is, however, subject to language-specific constraints. For instance, since Finnish has two "yes" particles (*nii* and *joo*), it also has two "yes but" constructions that are functionally distinct (Niemi 2014).
[110] Agreements can, of course, occur together with Acceptances/appreciations; however, the latter tend to come first: *Well thank you* + *uh I thought it was quite nice* (Pomerantz 1978b:85).

praise, (b) disagree with diminutions and qualifications of the praise, (c) reassign the praise by shifting the referent, and (d) return the praise (Pomerantz 1978b). Strategy (a) we have already observed above in example (4.84), where in response to Edna's praise of Margy's friend Pat: *that Pat isn't she a doll?* (line 1), Margy downgrades her agreement by saying *yeah isn't she pretty* (line 2). Strategy (b) can be observed in the following example:

(4.100) "Christmas card" (Pomerantz 1978b:98) (adapted)
```
1 ->   B:   By the way I loved your Christmas card,
((3 lines omitted))
5 =>   A:   I had a hard time, but I didn't think they were
6 =>        too good, ...
```

Strategies (c) and (d) can be seen in the following excerpt, where Edna is praising Margy for how she handles her family responsibilities while at the same time hosting luncheon parties:[111]

(4.101) "Just delightful" (NB VII)
((Margy has just announced that her mother will be coming to stay with her for an indefinite amount of time. The table in line 8 is a reference to the luncheon that she recently hosted where Edna was a guest. Bud is Edna's husband.))
```
1  ->   Edn:   =Ma:rgy I- I: mar[vel]at you really.eh you fascinate me,=
2       Mar:                       [hhh]
3       Mar:   =hh=
4  ->   Edn:   =I[ve never] seen a ga:l li[:ke you. ]
5       Mar:      [hOh(h)o ]              [°E(h)edn]a, #:::[ah]
6       Edn:                                             [I ] mean it.
7  =>   Mar:   ((f)) °nNo[: no: ((n))no. ]
8  ->   Edn:             [.hhYou do every]thing so beautifully and your table
9  ->          was so beau- I told Bud I said honestly. .hhhhh ih was jus:t
10 ->          deli:ghtful to come down there that day and mee[t these]
11      Mar:                                                  [We :ll ]
12             (.)
13 ->   Edn:   [ga:ls] 'n: ]
14 =>   Mar:   [ I:. ] just] was so:- tickled that you di:d, Bu[t uh].hh=
15      Edn:                                                   [°Mmm]
16 =>   Mar:   =I like to do that stu:ff an' u-[I he-]=
17      Edn:                                   [°Ya h]=
```

[111] This excerpt also includes a case of rejection of a Compliment: In line 7 Margy flatly rejects Edna's praise *I marvel at you, you fascinate me* (line 1) and *I've never seen a gal like you* (line 4).

In line 14 Margy reverses the praise implicit in Edna's *it was just delightful to come down there that day and meet these gals* (lines 9–13) by positively assessing the fact that Edna made the effort to come in the first place (Strategy d). And in line 16, Margy shifts the referent of *your table was so beau-* away from herself to the activity of *doing that stuff*, which she treats as simply something she likes (Strategy c).

Interestingly, although complimenting is presumably a universal action and Compliment responses are therefore likely to be found in all languages, the practices used by speakers to deal with their conflicting preferences can differ significantly. In German, for instance, Compliments are not accepted with appreciation markers as in English with *thank you* (Golato 2002a:557). Instead they are more frequently accepted using one of three practices unattested in English: (i) confirming the compliment assertion, (ii) positively assessing the fact that a compliment was made, or (iii) agreeing with the compliment and pursuing further agreement. Here are examples of each of these:

(4.102) "Onion pattern" (Golato 2002a:557) (adapted)
((A is complimenting B on her china.))

```
1 -> A:  ihr habt ja           so en schönes zwiebelmuster  hier,
         you have MODAL PARTICLE so a  nice       onion pattern here,
         you have such a nice onion pattern here,
2 => B:  joa:
         ye:s
         ye:s
```

(4.103) "Nice at your place" (Golato 2002a:557)

```
1    A:  Aber heute abend hier  war's  schön bei euch
         but today evening here was it nice  at yours
         but it was nice this evening here at your place
2    B:  schön
         nice.
         that's nice.
```

(4.104) "Excellent meat" (Golato 2002a:558)
((A is the guest. In line 1, he is gazing at B, who barbecued the meat.))

```
1 -> A:  übrigens    (.) das fleisch exzel[lent
         by the way (.) the meat     excel[lent
         by the way (.) the meat excel[lent
                                         [
2 => B:                                  [super ne?
                                         [super right?
                                         [super right?
```

```
3      A:     exzellent
              excellent
              excellent
4      B:     joa.
              yeah.
              yeah.
```

In (4.102) recipient B confirms A's assessment of her onion-pattern china as *schön* "nice" with the affirmative particle *joa* "yes"; in (4.103) B assesses as *schön* "nice" the fact that A has complimented her on the pleasant evening; and in (4.104) B implicitly agrees with A's evaluation of the meat as *exzellent* "excellent" by pursuing further agreement that it was *super* (line 2).

As for responding to Self-deprecations, it is the kind of overt, unmitigated Disagreement seen, for example, in (4.97) that is considered the normatively appropriate response in English. In other words, in such contexts Disagreement is delivered as a preferred action. This is because, as Pomerantz has put it: "When conversants disagree with prior self-deprecations, they show support of their co-conversants" (1984a:81).[112] Here is a case where we can see this preference at work:

(4.105)   "Great bridge player" (SBL 2:2:3) (= (4.71) above)
((Claire and her friend Chloe are revisiting the game of bridge they played together the day before this telephone call.))

```
1         Cla:   °^uhhh hu hu°˜WE::ll, [ah-
2  ->     Chl:                         [AND I n:ever ˜was a
3  ->            gr(h)ea(h)t br(h)idge[play(h)er]Cl(h)a[(h)ire?]
4  =>     Cla:                        [°˜Y*e::h°] hhh    [Well I ]think
5  =>            you've always been real good
```

Claire counters Chloe's self-criticism here by building evaluative terms into her response that stand in direct contrast to Chloe's: *never great* (lines 2–3) → *always real good* (line 5). In other words, although her responsive turn *I think you've always been real good* is a positive assessment,[113] it disagrees with its prior, a Self-deprecation: *I never was a great bridge player*. The simple and immediate way in which this responsive action is carried out points to the fact that it is both unproblematic and preferred in its sequential context.[114]

---

[112] Consequently, silence and other forms of withholding subsequent to a Self-deprecation are interpretable as *Agreeing* with the criticism, i.e., as performing the dispreferred alternative action (Pomerantz 1984a:95).
[113] Because of its positive evaluation of the other, this kind of response could be said to be complimenting the other. In fact, Self-deprecations can reportedly be used to do "fishing for compliments" (Golato 2005).
[114] For further examples of this practice see Pomerantz (1984a:83–90).

> Strategies for responding to Compliments can differ from language to language and culture to culture. In English, for instance, recipients will be observed to downgrade the compliment, to mildly disagree with it, to deflect it onto another referent, and/or to return the praise. In German, by contrast, recipients observably confirm the complimentary assessment, positively assess the fact that it was made, and/or pursue agreement that the positive evaluation is shared. In English, the normatively preferred way to respond to Self-deprecations is with unmitigated Disagreement. Whether the same practice is found in other languages and cultures is an open question at this time.

6. Conclusion

Our discussion of action formation and ascription has been organized around four different families of initiating actions: Questions, Offers/Requests, News/Informings, and Assessments/Compliments/Self-deprecations. In Questions and News/Informings the engine driving the sequence is *epistemic*, with the initiating speaker assuming either a [K−] (Question) or a [K+] (News/Informing) stance (Heritage 2012b). In Offer and Request sequences, on the other hand, the driving engine is *deontic-benefactive*, with the initiating speaker instigating something of benefit to self (Request) or of benefit to the other (Offer) (Stevanovic and Peräkylä 2012; Clayman and Heritage 2014). Finally, in Assessment/Compliment/Self-deprecation sequences, the driving engine is *evaluative*, with the initiating speaker inviting agreement (Assessment/Compliment) or disagreement (Self-deprecation) (Thompson et al. 2015:290).

With the state-of-the-art review in this chapter we hope to have revealed how deeply implicated language and linguistic resources are in the formation and ascription of actions in talk-in-interaction. Much work remains to be done in exploring the linguistic design of action types, both in single languages and cross-linguistically.

5

Topic and Sequence

The subject matter of this chapter concerns another "generic organization for conversation" summed up by Schegloff in these words: "How are actions implemented through successive turns formed up to be 'coherent' with the actions of the prior turn (or *some* prior turn), and what is the nature of that coherence?" (2010b:133). As Schegloff explains, talk-in-interaction comes not just in single, unrelated turns but rather in "clumps" of turns that appear to cohere with one another (1990). There are at least two possible ways of accounting for such coherence. One is in terms of *topicality*: the clumps can be thought of as created by the orderliness of topical talk (a content-related notion). The other is in terms of *sequentiality*: in this case the clumps might be said to come about through the organization of sequences of turns or courses of action (a structure-related notion). In this chapter we consider both types of orderliness and the linguistic resources used to achieve them.

1. Distinguishing Topicality from Sequentiality

On many conversational occasions, topicality and sequentiality go hand in hand: a sequence of turns at talk will also be on topic; and vice versa, on-topic talk will form a single course of action. Yet the two notions are analytically distinct, and situations can be found in which topical coherence and sequential coherence are at odds with one another. A prime example of this will be found in the "BB gun" conversation analyzed by Schegloff (1990, 2007a). Fourteen-year-old Bonnie has called her erstwhile boyfriend Jim to request the loan of his BB gun. The conversation begins with an opening and a brief discussion of an upcoming youth meeting they are to attend. It then continues as follows:

(5.1)   "BB gun – Pre-sequence and request" (Schegloff 1990:56) (adapted)
```
1    B:   But- (1.0) Would you do me a favor? heheh
2    J:   e(hh) depends on the favor::, go ahead,
3    B:   Did your mom tell you I called the other day?
4    J:   No she didn't.
```

```
5          (0.5)
6    B:   Well I called. (·) [hhh]
7    J:                       [Uhuh]
8          (0.5)
9    B:   ·hhh 'n I was wondering if you'd let me borrow your
10         gun.
11         (1.2)
12   J:   My gun?
13   B:   Yeah.
```

Schegloff notes that this spate of talk does not appear to be topically coherent, dealing as it does with a favor, Bonnie's previous call, and Jim's mother – yet it is sequentially cohesive because it forms a pre-sequence, beginning with a preliminary to a preliminary, or pre-pre, in line 1 (see Online-Chapter F §5) and culminating in Bonnie's request to borrow Jim's gun (lines 9–10) (see Chapter 4 §3.2).

The turns that follow this pre-sequence (not shown here) are also topically diverse: the topics have to do, among other things, with what kind of a gun Jim has, the drama class in which Bonnie will be performing "Annie Get Your Gun," what a pantomine is, and finally whether Bonnie is a good actress.[1] Yet the turns in which these topics are talked about are sequentially fitted to one another: they are either clarifying the first pair part – Bonnie's request – in one way or another, or preparing the ground for the second pair part – the request response – that it has projected (see §3.1 below). Approximately eighty lines later, Jim delivers his response to Bonnie's request:

(5.2)   "BB gun – Response" (Schegloff 1990:58) (adapted)
```
79   J:   You a good- (·) uh::: (1.8) actress?
80         (1.0)
81   B:   No: heheheh?
82         (0.5)
83   J:   Then how d'you come out to be A:nnie.
84         (1.0)
85   B:   No- I'n- it's just that- everybody in the class has
86         to do a different- (·) pantomime, you know?
87   J:   Uhuh,
88         (0.4)
89   B:   An :
90   J:        [Y]eah:, you can use it,
```

---

[1] For the transcript of this part of the conversation see Schegloff (1990:56ff.).

Topically speaking, Jim's complying response *yeah, you can use it* (line 90) comes out of the blue and appears to have little or nothing to do with what the participants have just been talking about – whether Bonnie is a good actress. Yet it is sequentially coherent because it is the second pair part that Bonnie's request in lines 9–10 has projected and because it is produced when all intervening insert sequences have been brought to a close. Schegloff's argument is that this spate of talk (lines 1–90) is topically disjunct but is held together through its sequential organization. Needless to say, other examples could be found demonstrating the reverse situation, where successive discrete sequences are held together cohesively by having a single topical focus.

> Topicality and sequentiality are two types of orderliness providing for the coherence of clumps of turns in conversation. Although new topics often correspond to new sequences and vice versa, the two orders of cohesiveness are analytically independent, and situations can be found in which diverse topics are talked about in one sequence and/or in which the treatment of one topic extends over several sequences.

2. Topic Management

What is a topic and how is topical talk organized? Conversation analysts have shied away from trying to find a warrantable and defendable definition of *topic* in the sense of content, i.e., "what talk is about". Instead, they have focused on *topicality* as something procedural that speakers achieve via orderly practices.

2.1 Topicality

As Sacks so astutely observes, participants do not just say everything they want to say the first chance they get; instead, they place their *mentionables* methodically such that they will appear to naturally "come up in the course of conversation" (Sacks 1992a:535). It is incumbent on conversation analysts to work out what methods participants use to achieve the "natural" flow of topics in conversation.

One of these methods, Sacks points out, is to fit mentionables to what has just occurred in prior talk. New topics that are introduced are tied to what has been talked about before. Speakers who do not manage to do this but produce "a large number of specific new topic starts" (Sacks 1992b:566) run the risk of being called "lousy" conversationalists.

A large part of doing topical talk, then, is fitting what one wants to say to what has just been said without bringing the prior topic to an analyzable end: this is referred to as "topic shading" (Schegloff and Sacks 1973:305). Topical shifts that are accomplished this way are said to be *stepwise* moves or transitions (Maynard 1980; Jefferson 1984c; Sacks 1992b): for an example see (5.8) below. In such cases the boundary between one topic and a next is virtually imperceptible: topics appear to flow continuously one from another (Button and Casey 1985).

New topics that are not fitted to prior talk are said to be brought about by *disjunctive* topic changes (Maynard 1980; Jefferson 1984c): for an example see (5.9) below. In these cases, participants work expressly to mark their turn as *not* fitted to what has gone before. By disengaging the upcoming turn from prior talk, they in essence instruct their co-interlocutor not to look for any connection between what they have been talking about before and what will now be said. The new turn is done as a break with prior talk, typically when it has been closed down with an "analyzable end" (Schegloff and Sacks 1973). See also §3.3 below.

In telephone conversations, as Button and Casey (1985) have pointed out, there are three locations in the overall structure of a conversation where it is routine for topical talk to be generated disjunctively:

  i. subsequent to conversational openings, after an exchange of greetings/speaker identifications and *how-are-you*s – this is the so-called "anchor position", where a *first topic* can be expected, one that as a rule will be understood to be the reason for the call (Schegloff and Sacks 1973; Schegloff 2010);
 ii. in the body of a conversation, when a prior topic has reached a point of possible closure – this can happen if topical talk atrophies, i.e., if participants do not keep the topic alive by feeding it with new topical materials (Maynard 1980), or if a topic is expressly wrapped up, for example, with an aphoristic summary (Schegloff and Sacks 1973) or a formulation of its gist (Heritage and Watson 1979; see also Online-Chapter F §7); and
iii. in conversational closings, where one party opts to move out of closing and to re-establish topical talk (Schegloff and Sacks 1973; Button 1987).

Regardless of whether speakers are producing on-topic talk, shifting topic stepwise, or beginning a new topic disjunctively, managing topicality in conversation is always a collaborative, interactive phenomenon. It cannot be done alone. On-topic talk and stepwise transitions must generate further topical material from the recipient if topical talk is not to break down (Maynard 1980). Even disjunctive topic beginnings must be embraced by the recipient if they are to succeed (Button and Casey 1985; Schegloff 2007a:170). It is for this reason that we speak here of topic *management*, meaning that not just speakers but also their recipients are heavily implicated in the pursuit and accomplishment of topical talk.

> Rather than investigate topic as a content notion, conversation analysts focus on topicality, studying how interlocutors accomplish topical talk methodically through a range of techniques and procedures for beginning a new topic, shifting topic stepwise, changing topic disjunctively, and closing down a topic. Managing topicality in conversation invariably involves the co-interlocutor; in this sense it is a collaborative achievement.

2.2 Some Linguistic Resources for Managing Topic

In this section we describe a selection of practices for achieving topical talk in conversation that depend on the use of concrete linguistic resources. We begin by looking at devices used in the initiation of topics, then at ones found in moving from topic to topic, and finally at ones used to close down topical talk.

2.2.1 "Uh(m)" and High Onsets in First Topics/Reasons for the Call

Although *uh(m)* is frequently thought to convey hesitation and/or trouble in talk, when used turn-initially at anchor position this particle is one hallmark of a reason-for-the-call turn in English telephone conversations (Schegloff 2010). We find it, for instance, in the following extract, where Marcia has called her acquaintance Sue, and after exchanging routine identifications/greetings and *how-are-you*s, proceeds to the announcement of a piece of news (line 8):

```
(5.3)      "Tickets" (Schegloff 2010:147-8)
0                ring
1      Sue:     H'llo:
2      Mar:     Hi: 's Sue there?
3      Sue:     Yeah, this is she¿
4      Mar:     Hi this's Ma:rcia.
5      Sue:     ↑Hi Marcia, how're you:.=
6      Mar:     =Fine how're you¿=
7      Sue:     =Fi:ne¿
8 ->   Mar:     Uh::m: We got the tickets, [and'a (    ]) put them in=
9      Sue:                                [Oh goo:d. ]
```

Marcia's news, that she *got the tickets* (line 8), is hearable as the reason for her call by virtue of its placement in first-topic position. It is marked as such not through explicit naming, for example, "the reason I'm calling is to tell you that . . .", but indexically through, among other things, the lengthened *uh::m:* at its outset. *Uh(m)* frames this anchor-position turn as disjunct from what has gone before.

2. Topic Management

By minimally delaying the production of a next utterance (see Online-Chapter E §4), it displays this utterance as having a different status from prior talk and therefore as being worthy of special attention.

Interestingly, if either the caller or the called party pre-empts anchor position to launch something other than the reason for the call as first topic, *uh(m)* is not used. In other words, it does not mark the beginning of *any* first topic, but is instead reserved specifically for the beginning of the reason for the call, even when the latter is deferred. For instance, in the following extract, Alan, who is making a number of calls to invite people to a surprise birthday party for one of his friends, is prevented from introducing his reason for calling in anchor position when Mary pre-empts the first-topic slot with a news delivery concerning something that just happened the day before (data not shown here). Only once this first topic has been jointly closed down (lines 10–12) does Alan move to announce his reason for the call (lines 13–14), the invitation to his party. *Uh* appears at the beginning of this turn (line 17):

```
(5.4)        "Surprise party" (Schegloff 2010:153-4) (adapted)
1        Ala:    So. I don't know if Bruce is all- Bruce, (·)'s gonna
2                talk to Marcie anymore he doesn't wanna even see her
3                anymore.
4                (0.6)
5        Mry:    Well that's good, [at least it's (o:[:fen.)
6        Ala:                      [So he         [
7        Ala:                                     [eeYeah. Finally.=
8        Ala:    =That[s what   I- ]
9        Mry:         [(Close) the] su:bject,
10       Ala:    This what hhIhh told him I go "It's ab(h)out t(h)i:me."
11               You kno[w.
12       Mry:           [Go:::::[::::[:d]
13  ->   Ala:                   ['hhh [Ok]ay Well the reason I'm calling=
14       Ala:    =There[is a reason behind my madness.
15       Mry:          [°( ).
16       Mry:    Uh-huh,
17  ->   Ala:    Uh next Saturday night's a surprise party here for p-
18               Kevin.
19               (0.2)
20       Ala:    ·p! And if you can make it.
21       Mry:    OH REALLY::::=
22       Ala:    =Yeah.
23       Mry:    Is it his birthda:y?
```

```
24      Ala:    e-hyihh-hih- No::  we're j(h)us(h)g(h)iving him-
25              ˙hhhhh surprise birthday p(h)arty for the
26              h(h)el[l of it.]=
27      Mry:           [O H :,].=
```

This fragment shows that *uh(m)* is not used to mark any first topic but is dedicated specifically to framing the reason-for-the-call turn or a pre-sequence thereto (Schegloff 2010).

Reasons for the call and pre-sequences projecting them have also been shown to be marked by extra high pitch onsets (see Online-Chapter E §3) in telephone calls to radio phone-in programs (Couper-Kuhlen 2001). For instance, in the following excerpt taken from a program broadcast in Berkeley, California, shortly after the beginning of the first Gulf War, the caller moves immediately after an exchange of greetings to announce the reason for his call (line 6):

(5.5)   "Freedom" (Couper-Kuhlen 2001:37) (adapted)
```
1    Leo:   BOB,
2           you're on the GIant sixty eight;
3           thanks for CALLing.
4    Bob:   HI leo.
5    Leo:   HI bob.
6    Bob:   uhm i ↑WANTed to say something about uh-
7           a COUple of things about uhm-
8           the WAR;
9           our attack on uh iRAQ;
10          uhm a LOT of people are saying it's about OIL;
11          i think it's about uhm FREEdom.
            ((turn continues))
```

Bob's turn beginning in line 6 is not only prefaced by *uhm* but also has an extra high pitch peak on its first accent, in the word *wanted*. This pitch peak is significantly higher than the one in Bob's prior greeting turn (line 4) and projects that Bob is about to produce a lengthy turn: its high beginning leaves plenty of room for further turn-constructional units (TCUs) to follow at lower levels. Accordingly, the moderator withholds intervening talk and gives Bob an opportunity to present his concerns in full.

However, just as in mundane telephone talk, the reason for a caller's call is on occasion not presented as a first topic. This can happen when first topics are appropriated for other business, which is what we find happening in the following fragment:

(5.6)   "First-time caller" (Couper-Kuhlen 2001:46) (adapted)

```
1    Leo:      theREsa's been hanging on from el graNAda;
2              theREsa THANKS:,
3              you're on the GIant sixty eight KAY en bee ar.
4    Theresa:  HI leo.
5    Leo:      HI theresa.
6    Theresa:  ↓I'M a first-time CALLer-
7    Leo:      GLAD you called.
8    Theresa:  uhm:-
9              ↑I'M kind of unHA:Ppy;
10             because I DON'T feel (.) the media-
11             is ACcurately reFLECTing;
12             the feelings of MOST people;
13             reGARDing this persian GULF conflict.
14             (1.0)
               ((turn continues))
```

Observe that Theresa's turn in line 6 is positioned at what might be called anchor position. Yet it is not prefaced by *uh(m)*; nor does it begin with a high onset. In fact, its first accented syllable *I'm* is pitched significantly lower than in Theresa's greeting turn in line 4. This design displays that Theresa's turn is doing something other than presenting the reason for her call; consequently, the moderator does not withhold talk at the first transition-relevance place as he did in (5.5). However, in lines 8 and 9, when Theresa finally does launch a turn with lengthened *uhm:* and a high pitch onset, he treats this as the reason for her call and allows her space to present her concerns (see the one-second pause in line 14, which follows a syntactically and prosodically complete unit that might otherwise lead to turn transition).

> *Uh(m)* and high pitch onset are particularly appropriate devices for marking a turn as launching the reason for a call. Both herald in a break with what has gone before: *uh(m)* because it delays the production of the next word due; high onset because it marks a departure from the overall descending line of pitch declination in prior talk. These cues – in two different perceptual modalities, verbal (lexical) and vocal (prosodic) – create strong grounds for the projection that the upcoming turn will be doing something different, something particularly relevant and meaningful for the activity underway. At anchor position this is likely to be the caller's reason for calling.

2.2.2 Polar Interrogative Structures for Proffering a Topic

When a prior topic has been brought to possible closure, an environment for the start of a new topic is created. Next speakers who now wish to generate topical talk have a number of options: they can invite the recipient to propose a newsworthy topic of their own with, for example, a *topic initial elicitor* such as "What's new with you?" (Button and Casey 1984); they can solicit talk on a specific topic related to the recipient with an *itemized news inquiry* such as "How's your foot?" (Button and Casey 1985); or they can provide for topical talk by making their own *news announcement* such as "Bud just left to play golf" (Button and Casey 1985; see also Chapter 4 §4.2). Distinct from these options for generating a new topic is that of a *topic proffer* (Schegloff 2007a). Speakers who put forward a topic with a topic proffer make that topic available for talk but do not actively pursue or further develop it themselves. Instead they leave it up to the recipient to embrace or reject it in next turn.[2] Proffered topics are typically recipient-oriented, that is, ones for which the recipient is an authority. This makes them particularly appropriate (a) for the recipient to decide whether topical development comes about, and (b) for the topic to be developed by the recipient, if at all.

Topic proffers rely heavily on a specific set of linguistic resources with the appropriate affordances: among these are polar interrogatives and B-event statements, or so-called "declarative" questions (see Chapter 4 §2.4).[3] Schegloff cites the following examples:

(5.7)   Polar interrogative structures as topic proffers (Schegloff 2007a:170–1) (adapted)

(a) TG, 14:1–3

```
1        Ava:    °That's goo[d,
2   ->   Bee:               [Do you have any-cl- You have a class with
3   ->           Billy this te:rm?
```

(b) TG, 10:2–3

```
1   ->   Bee:    °(I 'unno)/°So anyway) °hh Hey do you see v- (0.3)
2   ->           fat old Vivian anymore?
```

(c) TG, 4:35–6

```
1   ->   Bee:    Eh-you have anybody: that uh:? (1.2) I would know from
2   ->           the English department there?
```

---

[2] This distinguishes them from "itemized news inquiries," in which the speaker "makes a sequential commitment to the object of the news inquiry" (Button and Casey 1985:15) and pursues topical talk on it even in the face of curtailing moves by the co-interlocutor (pp. 27ff.).
[3] Question-word questions, with many of the same affordances as polar interrogative structures, can also serve as topic proffers (Couper-Kuhlen 2012a:129): see Chapter 4 §2.2 and §2.6.

(d) SN-4, 16:02
```
1   -> Mar:   So (are) you da:ting Keith?
```

(e) Stolen, 2:22
```
1   -> Mar:   'hhh So: you're ba:ck.
```

Each of these turns addresses something in the recipient's experience or expertise. But more importantly, through their interrogativity, each creates an opportunity for the recipient to provide more talk on the subject, and at the same time places the responsibility for talk on the recipient. Next turns will often include a positive or negative response token (*yes* or *no*), aligned or not with the polarity of the question, and either an expanded or a minimal response. Grammatically aligned and expanded responses, such as "yes" + expansion following the proffers above, embrace the topic proffered and engender more talk on it; grammatically non-aligned and minimal turns, such as "no" without expansion, decline to develop what has been proposed as a topic (Schegloff 2007a:171; see also Online-Chapter B §3.1).

Polar interrogative structures are particularly well suited as topic proffers because they afford multiple ways in which a response can be topic-embracing (or topic-rejecting). For one, by virtue of their interrogativity, they allocate next turn to the recipient. Second, by virtue of their polarity, they embody grammatical relevancies for a grammatically preferred (=topic-embracing) as opposed to a dispreferred (=topic-rejecting) response (see also Online-Chapter B §3.1). And third, because they are generally clausal, they provide lexico-syntactic substance for the recipient to work with in generating more topical talk.

2.2.3 *"Actually" in Topic Shift versus Topic Change*

As noted above, when speakers do move to new topics in a next turn, they can do so in a way that links to prior talk (topic *shift*) or is instead disjunctive with it (topic *change*). Using the English particle "actually" in turn- or TCU-*initial* position, for instance, announces a topic shift: it suggests that what is about to be said has just been thought of and was triggered by something in prior talk. Clift calls "actually" in such cases a "touch-off marker" (2001:285). Here is an example:

(5.8)   "Complicated lunch" (Clift 2001:284) (adapted)
((J = Julia, M = Mary. J has brought some books to M; she is now sorting through them. M's daughter Vanessa has been ill, which is why M has refused Vanessa's offer to cook lunch.))

```
1     J    =(h)£I haven't bought any for a long ti- I've had a clear
2          ou:t,£ you (see) Jane Grigson English Food. (0.2) ↑That
3          Margaret Costa's is a classic, they've reprinted [it now.
4     M                                                     [Oh well
5          Vanessa'd probably lo:ve that.
6          (0.4)
7     M    [I must tell her that. She probably kno:ws [anyway. She's
8     J    [So::.                                     [Yes, now.
9     M    =always reading books [on cookery.
10    J                          [D'you want (.) uh- (.) does she just
11         read cookbooks,
12         (0.3)
13    M    She coo:ks.
14         (0.2)
15    J    Yea:s. (0.2) Yes,=
16 -> M    =Actually toda:y, she was (0.1) had a (0.8) complicated
17         lunch packed, a- [uh- planned.
18    J                     [Mm.
19         (0.4)
20    M    And I said firmly (0.2) n:o::.
21         (0.1)
22    J    Uh huh.
```

Through its preface with "actually", M's anecdote concerning Vanessa's complicated lunch packet (lines 16–17) is presented as touched off by prior talk – presumably the information that Vanessa not only reads cookbooks but also cooks herself (line 13).

By contrast, when "actually" is placed in TCU- or turn-*final* position, it marks a disjunctive topic change: the material preceding it is presented as contrasting with prior talk and having more relevance than what preceded:

(5.9)   "Phoning Scott" (Clift 2001:279) (adapted)
((G = Gordon, D = Dana. G has been telling a story about getting home in time for his music lesson at 5.30, having been driven back by a friend. When approached for a ride, the friend was obviously reluctant to leave just then.))

```
1     G    And I said I've gotta be home by
2          five thirty (.) hh.hhh And and his face just dropped.
3          (0.5)
4     D    ↑Uh[h
```

```
5      G     [.tch.hhh And I said ↑No.hh N(h)o (h) I'm
6            se(h)r(h)i(h)ous. (.) You drive me home no:w.
7            (.)
8      G     .hhhh
9            (0.2)
10     G     And he did.
11           (0.5)
12     G     .hh Uh hh(h) and then: uh.hh And I didn't feel guilty
13           about it at a[ll.
14     D                 [°hn]=
15     G     =.tch hhhhh ↓Which is probably very bad of me.hhh I
16 ->        ↑thought I might (.) phone Scott tonight actually .t1
17           Cz uh[m
18     D          [Ye::h.
19     G     he c' probably do with a bit of cheering up
20     D     [Ye:[h
21     G     [.hh[So I thought I'll (.) give him a bell,.t.hhh See
22           ho[w he's g]ett[in on,
23     D       [(Do a) ]    [synchronized phoning
24     D     .hhhhh
```

Gordon's story about his insistence on his friend's driving him home in time for his guitar lesson and not feeling guilty about it gets little uptake from Dana (lines 7–9, 11, and 14). It is at this point that he changes to a new topic: *I thought I might (.) phone Scott tonight*,[4] marked with turn-final "actually" (lines 15–16). When "actually" is placed after new topical material, its contrastive quality comes to the fore: the new topic is implied to be more relevant than what came before (Clift 2001:280). Clift argues that this is related to the fact that *actually* in other contexts is found in turns that correct by means of counter-informing (p. 253).

> The particle "actually" indicates that the turn or TCU it accompanies is moving topic. However, the position of "actually" within the turn unit is crucial for the distinction between topic shift (with a link to prior talk) and topic change (with disjunction): in turn- or TCU-initial position, "actually" conveys that the new material being presented is related to prior talk, having just been occasioned by it, while in turn- or TCU-final position "actually" brackets its material and presents it contrastively as more relevant than the prior topic.

---

[4] Note that the use of a full form "Scott" cues this turn as beginning a new sequence (see §3.2.2 below).

2.2.4 Figurative Expressions in Topic Transition and Closing

Figurative expressions have been described in the literature as fully clausal, relatively "fixed" expressions whose semantic content is to be understood metaphorically rather than literally (Drew and Holt 1995, 1998). Examples include *have a good innings* (meaning "have a long and successful life" in British English) or *make a hole in one's pocket* (meaning "cost a lot of money"): these expressions do not refer to a unit of play in cricket or to an opening in the pouch of a jacket or pair of pants. Instead, when used figuratively, they can summarize metaphorically what speakers have been talking about so far and serve to initiate topic closing. Here is an example where this happens (Lesley is telling her mother about an acquaintance, the church warden, who recently died at an advanced age):

```
(5.10)      "Good innings" (Drew and Holt 1998:499) (adapted)
17    Lesley:   .hhh He was a p- uh: Ye:s. Indee:d.hh He was a
18              (0.2) .p a buyer for the hoh- i- the
19              only horse hair factory left in England.
20    Mum:      Good gracious,
21              (0.3)
22    Lesley:   And he was their buyer,
23              (.)
24    Mum:      Hm:::
25    Lesley:   .t
26    Mum:      Hm:.
27->  Lesley:   So he had a good inni:ngs did[n't he.
28    Mum:                                   [I should say so:
29              Ye:s.
30              (0.2)
31    Mum:      Marvellous,
32    Lesley:   .tk.hhhh Anyway we had a very good evening o:n
33              Saturda:y.
34              (.)
35    Mum:      Ye:s?
36    Lesley:   We went to North Cadbury: and Gordon came too...
```

Lesley's turn in line 27 brings to conclusion the report of the deceased man's life by metaphorically summarizing it as "an innings". Through its design with a figurative expression, this turn begins to detach talk from the progressive development that would be achieved with more topical detail. Moreover, by casting the man's life in a positive light ("a *good* innings"), it displays how Lesley assesses the matter. Together, the summary and the assessment propose a possible closing of the topic. In next turn (lines 28–9) Mum agrees with Lesley's assessment and declines to develop the topic any further (lines 30–1). This now provides Lesley with a warrant to move to a new and unrelated topic, which she does after audible inbreaths and the discontinuity marker *anyway* in line 32.

Example (5.10) illustrates a typical topic transition sequence, which Drew and Holt schematize as shown in Figure 5.1.

> 1 —> Speaker A: Figurative summary
> 2 —> Speaker B: Agreement (or other expression of contiguity)
> 3 —> Speaker A: Agreement/confirmation
> 4 —> Speaker A/B: Introduces next topic

Figure 5.1 Standard topic transition sequence (Drew and Holt 1998:506)

In the case shown in example (5.10), step 3 is skipped and step 4 is implemented disjunctively by A, with multiple indications of separateness from prior talk, including raised pitch and amplitude, inbreaths, and prefatory discontinuity markers (see also §3.2 below).

Yet in a follow-up to their work, Holt and Drew (2005) point out that step 4 need not be a disjunctive topic change. Instead, the figurative expression itself can provide material for, or even touch off, further topical talk. In this case, what follows the figurative expression is something different from what preceded it, but the transition has been a stepwise one. Here is a case in point (Deena has been telling her cousin Mark about preparations for her daughter's upcoming wedding):

```
(5.11)     "Hole in your pocket" (Holt and Drew 2005:50) (adapted)
7      Deena:   'n no:w (.) believe it or not it's
8               u-only nine weeks a[way it's beginning to
9      Mark:                       [()
10     Deena:   build up agai[n we're
11     Mark:                 [ehhh hhehh hheh hhuh.
12     Deena:   checking[up on eve[rything to make su:re
13     Mark:            [.hhhhhh  [.hhhh
14              [it's.hhhh everything's still going ]=
15     Deena:   =[everything's    (.)    you kno:w  ]=
16     Mark:    =I KNO:W YE[S:::
17     Deena:              [Bu:t uh:m[: I tell you ]=
18     Mark:                         [.hhhhhh     ]=
19 ->  Deena:   = Mark it does make a hole in your=
20 ->  Deena:   = pocket [though (I [warn you [)
21     Mark:            [.hhh      [Well I [k- I can
22              well imagine we.hhhhh we had a s:mall
```

```
23              do: just a local thing here in Cary
24              this (.) the last year about this time
25              last year. Which was just a little (0.2)
26              .hhhh private thing which we organi:zed, h
27              .hhh uh:m:: (0.4) a:n:d uh: it was
28              surprising how much: actual effort went
29              into that we just hired the village ha↓ll...
```

With the figurative expression *it does make a hole in your pocket though* (lines 19 and 20), Deena can be heard to propose closing down the topic of her daughter's wedding and its expense. But Mark uses Deena's figurative expression as a link to a mentionable of his own, namely the private party he himself organized a year before (lines 22–5), which – so it is implied – also created a hole in his pocket. The figurative expression here, then, serves as a pivot, affording a bridge from Deena's topical talk on the wedding to a new but related topic of Mark's, his own private party (Holt and Drew 2005:46).

> Figurative expressions are one method among others (including, e.g., repetition and non-metaphorical assessment: see §3.3 below) routinely used to propose topic closure. Their generic nature makes them well suited for summarizing, and their positive or negative coloring brings off an assessment, with which the co-participant can agree or disagree. Once such a topic-bounding move is in place, co-participants can refrain from further topical talk, thereby providing a warrant for the introduction of a new, disjunct topic. Or they can use the figurative expression as a pivot for stepwise transition to a new but related topic.

2.2.5 "Okay" and "Alright" in Topic Closure and Transition

Unlike figurative expressions, which are substantively fitted to the specific topic to be closed down, the freestanding particles *okay* and *alright* can function as generic devices for proposing to "bound" off a topic.[5] Because *okay* and *alright* make no substantive contribution to topical talk, they are heard as embodying a "pass", tentatively initiating pre-closing. The next speaker can use the opportunity to introduce a new topic, or – in the absence of further mentionables – can acknowledge the move by responding with a second "pass", whereupon conversational closing can be collaboratively pursued (Schegloff and Sacks 1973). Here is an

---

[5] In addition to *okay* or *alright*, other minimal acknowledgement tokens such as, e.g., *yes* or *yeah* can be used in next position prior to a topic shift (Jefferson 1993a). As Jefferson points out, this practice allows recipients to display (minimal) attention to an interlocutor's topic while transitioning to one of their own.

example where B's first *alrighty* (line 7) proposes to close down the prior topic and the second *alrighty* (line 10) effectively closes it down:

(5.12)   "Alrighty" (Schegloff and Sacks 1973:318) (adapted)
```
1         B:    Well that's why I said "I'm not gonna say anything, I'm not
2               making any comments [about anybody"
3         C:                       [Hmh
4         C:    Eh yeah
5         B:    Yeah
6         C:    Yeah
7         B:    Alrighty. Well I'll give you a call before we decide to come
8               down. O.K.?
9         C:    O.K.
10        B:    Alrighty
11        C:    O.K.
12        B:    We'll see you then
13        C:    O.K.
14        B:    Bye bye
15        C:    Bye
```

But *okay* and *alright* are not only backward oriented and closure-relevant. They can also project additional turn components that transition to new topics and activities (Beach 1993):

(5.13)   "Study" (Beach 1993:343–4) (adapted)
```
1              A:    =I couldn't get over after that anyway
2                    I've got so many errands and stuff to run=
3     1->     B:    =Okay=
4              A:    =that's perfect=
5     *->     B:    =Okay well just ha:ve uh:m
6              A:    Are you gonna have her pick you ↑up
7                    or what [(   )]
8              B:            [We:ll] see: I: don't know I think
9                    I'll probably just go home by myself because
10                   I have this appointment. but why don't you have
11                   her call me tonight. Is she gonna be home tonight?
12             A:    I would hope so=
13    2->     B:    =Okay=
14             A:    =I guess I'm gonna be leaving here at six to go
15                   back to school >I've got a class tonight.<=
16    3->     B:    =Okay=
```

```
17      A:    a::nd so all I can do is- you know if I- if I
18            don't talk to her before I leave I'll just leave
19            her a note- message to call you tonight.=
20  *-> B:    Okay and do you remember how to get here? or do
21            you want me to give you direc[(tions)]
22      A:                                 [She:   ]gave me
23            some instruction.
              ((call moves to closing))
```

The freestanding *okay*s here (at 1→, 2→, and 3→) are, on the one hand, acknowledging the prior informings but, on the other hand, hearably on their way to something more (*→). This is evident from the way B continues at the next opportunity: *Okay well just ha:ve uh:m*[6] (line 5) and *Okay and do you remember how to get here?* (line 20). Beach's point here is that in each case with *okay* B is working up to a new matter (1993:344).

> *Okay* and *alright* are generic devices for putting a topic in a "state of attrition" and thereby bringing about topic closure.[7] At the same time they can serve as transitional pivots and project further turn components dealing with new matters.

In this section we have reviewed a selection of linguistic devices that serve to manage topic (others remain to be discovered): speakers use them selectively to begin new topics, to bring ongoing topics to a close, and to move from one topic to another in a stepwise or disjunctive fashion. Related to but analytically distinct from topic management is sequence organization, to which we turn now.

3. Sequence Organization

Recall that sequentiality involves the organization of turns at talk into sequences. In this section we first review the structure of sequences and then examine how linguistic resources are used to organize them.

3.1 Sequence and Sequential Structure

Sequences can be thought of as coherent, orderly, and meaningful successions of turns, brought about when participants collaboratively pursue courses of action

---

[6] Presumably B is on the way to saying "have her call me tonight" (see lines 10–11 below).
[7] Hayashi and Yoon (2009) show that Japanese and Korean have similar solutions (the particles *un* and *um* respectively) for this general organizational task in interaction.

through turns at talk (Schegloff 2007a:2). They are typically organized around a *base* adjacency pair, the one whose actions underlie the sequence as a whole (2007a:27) (see also Chapter 4 §1.1).[8] In the "BB gun" conversation excerpted in examples (5.1) and (5.2) above, the base adjacency pair is constituted by Bonnie's request in lines 9–10, *I was wondering if you'd let me borrow your gun*, and Jim's response, *Yeah:, you can use it*, in line 90 (see also Schegloff 1990).

Base adjacency pairs can be expanded by further adjacency pairs or sequences. These expansions are positioned at one of the following locations: (i) prior to the first part of a base pair (pre-expansion), (ii) in between the first and second parts of a base pair (insert expansion), and (iii) subsequent to the second part of a base pair (post-expansion). The structure of an expanded sequence of turns at talk can thus be schematized as shown in Figure 5.2, where A and B are separate speakers and the first and second pair parts in question belong to a base pair.

```
                              ←Pre-expansion
       A    First pair part
                              ←Insert expansion
       B    Second pair part
                              ←Post-expansion
```

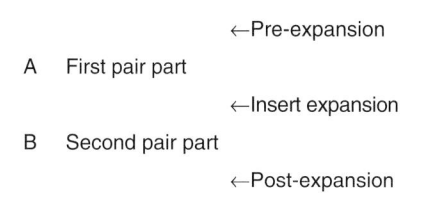

Figure 5.2 Schema of expanded sequence structure (Schegloff 2007a:26)

Pre-expansions are adjacency pairs that are preliminary to the first pair part of the base sequence and may project what kind of specific action the first pair part will implement (see also Online-Chapter F §5). A case in point was seen in lines 1–8 of example (5.1): here the pre-sequence is launched by Bonnie's *would you do me a favor?*, which on production appears to project an upcoming request (Schegloff 2007a:47).

Insert expansions delay the production of the second pair part: they can be oriented either backward to problems of hearing or understanding of the first pair part ("post-first": Schegloff 2007a:100), or forward to acquiring the information needed to implement the second pair part ("pre-second": Schegloff 2007a:106). An insert expansion was seen in lines 12–13 of (5.1) above, with Jim's repair initiation *My gun?*. This is a post-first insert expansion because it seeks to clarify an item in Bonnie's request.[9] Lines 79–88 of (5.2) show another insert expansion, one launched by Jim's *You a good- (') uh::: (1.8) actress?* (line 79). This is a case of

---

[8] As Schegloff points out, there are also types of sequence organization not based on adjacency pairs, for instance, some forms of extended tellings and/or storytelling episodes (2007a:9).
[9] This post-first insert expansion sequence is itself internally expanded and that internal expansion again internally expanded, etc., in subsequent talk (data not shown here). In fact, as Levinson (2013a:157) points out, there are up to six degrees of internal expansion, or recursion, in this part of the conversation.

a pre-second insert expansion: Jim is trying to establish whether the granting of Bonnie's request is justified.

Post-expansions can be minimal, consisting of, for example, sequence-closing thirds and the like, or non-minimal, including other-initiated repair, disagreements, rejections, challenges, and reworkings of the first pair part (Schegloff 2007a:117–68). Here is an instance of a non-minimal post-expansion sequence from the "BB gun" conversation, brought about by Bonnie's initiation of repair:

(5.14) "BB gun – Minimal post-expansion" (Schegloff 1990:58) (adapted)
```
90        J:   Yeah:, you can use it,
91             (0.4)
92   ->   B:   ˙hh Ca:n?
93        J:   >Yeh-<
```

Although sequence organization has been described most thoroughly based on English materials (Schegloff 2007a; Stivers 2013), a recent study by Kendrick et al. (2014) found cross-linguistic evidence of its relevance in a broad sampling of genetically and areally diverse languages. This suggests that sequence structure is not a unique characteristic of English or of any specific language per se, but rather part of a universal infrastructure for social interaction that all human languages and societies have in common (see also Levinson 2006 and Chapter 9).

> Sequence structure is one of the generic "orders of organization" in conversation; it regulates how successive turns at talk are "formed up" to be coherent with one another (Schegloff 2007a:xiv). As the phrase "form up" implies, sequence structure is not simply given; nor does it come about automatically. Instead it must be achieved. That is, pre-expansion sequences, insert expansion sequences, and post-expansion sequences must be constructed and made recognizable as such through the collaborative work of the participants in a conversation.

In the following we survey what is known so far about how linguistic resources are implicated in making turns recognizable as beginning a sequence and/or closing a sequence, as well as how they can be used to frame a sequence as misplaced or to return to a prior non-adjacent sequence.

3.2 Some Linguistic Resources for Marking Sequence Beginnings

As a rule, new sequences begin when prior sequences have been closed down. Yet as Schegloff has pointed out, "sequences – however apparently 'over' – can turn out not to have been over if the next thing that happens adds to them" (cited in Couper-Kuhlen 2004:336). That is, sequences are only closed for sure if what happens next is sequentially unrelated. But since the default understanding of a next turn is that it relates to the immediately preceding turn (Sacks 1992b:559), participants must do extra work to construct a next turn as doing something sequentially new: they must work to counter the assumption that what they are about to say is related to prior talk (Heritage 1984b:261).

3.2.1 Inbreaths, High Onsets, and Clicks

One set of resources that next speakers can exploit to mark an upcoming turn as beginning a new sequence involves prosody and phonetics (see also Online-Chapter E). For instance, next speakers can use *extra high pitch* from the very start of their turn (Online-Chapter E §3).[10] This is what we find happening in (5.15) below. Guy has called his friend Jon to explore the possibility of a golf game that day or the next. The conversation opens with mutual recognition and identification, followed by greetings and a jocular exchange concerning how each of the men "looks". Then in line 17 Guy moves to initiate something sequentially unrelated:

(5.15)   "Play a little golf" (Couper-Kuhlen 2004:337–8) (adapted)
```
1              (0.9)
2     Jon:   Hello:?
3     Guy:   Johnny?
4     Jon:   Ye:h.
5     Guy:   Guy Detweiler.
6     Jon:   Hi Guy how you doing.=
7     Guy:   =Fine.
8              (.)
9     Jon:   You're looking [goo:d,
10    (G):                  [(.hhh)
11    Guy:   ↑Grea:t.hhh
12             So are you:.hh-hh
13             °Grea:t.
14             Gotta° nice smile on your face ['n every] thing.
15    Jon:                                    [°(    )°]
16             ↓Ye↓ah.hh
17->  Guy:   .hh.hh.hhh <<f>↑Hey> uh hhwhhkhh
```

---

[10] Note that this resource is roughly the same as that used in reason-for-the-call turns (see §2.2.1 above). However, the *practices* involved are different in that in one case (reason-for-the-call turns) a new topic is being indexed, while in the other it is a new sequence beginning. As we show in §2.2.1 and below, the two (new topic and new sequence) are not necessarily the same.

```
18->         <<f>↑My ↑son-in-law's down an:d uh:↓::,>
19           hh thought we might play a little golf::
20           ↓either this afternoon or tomorrow
21           would you like to (0.3) .hhh (0.3) get out? uhh
22           (.)
23   Jon:    Well this afternoon'd be alright
24           but I don't think I'd  better tomorrow,
```

What we observe Guy doing in line 17 is setting off the turn he is about to launch from prior talk by audible inbreaths and extra pitch height on the prefatory attention-getter *hey* and the first content words, *my son-in-law's*. The pitch peaks on the syllables *my son* are not only higher than those at the beginning of Guy's prior TCUs, for example, line 14; they are also high in Guy's habitual pitch range (Couper-Kuhlen 2004:340). In addition, lines 17 and 18 are noticeably louder than line 14 (Goldberg 1978). Guy is thus exploiting a cluster of prosodic resources to mark what he is doing in lines 17 and 18 as beginning a new sequence.

It is true that the turn Guy launches in lines 17–18 is also a new topic. However, new topics – especially when they are broached in a stepwise fashion – routinely lack the prosodic cues that new sequence beginnings display. An example of a stepwise topic shift that is not beginning a new sequence will be seen, for instance, in example (E.13) in Online-Chapter E. Moreover, the same prosodic cues (high pitch onsets and sudden increases in loudness) as seen in lines 17–18 of (5.15) above are also found on turns in which speakers are moving off topical talk and into closings: these are also new sequence beginnings but not new topics. Consider, by way of illustration, the following fragment from a conversation between Lesley and her friend Lucy. The topic of talk here has been an upcoming women's group meeting at which Lesley is scheduled to give a presentation on acupuncture:

```
(5.16)     "Acupuncture needle" (Wright 2011a:1084)
7    Les:   .hhhh and I [was going to try and get ho]ld of a needle=
8    Luc:               [  w e l l   I     d o n ' t  ]
9    Les:   =but then I thought .hhh we:ll I don't know  perhaps I won't
10          .hh the- (0.2) e-hh who do I know it's been  stu(h)uck in uh
11          heh he:h hih
12   Luc:   huh huh ho ho[ho ho [ho
13   Les:                [.hhh [so I haven't got hold of a needle
14   Les:   uh huhh huh huh.[.hhhh
15   Luc:                   [perhaps it's just as well=
16   Les:   =[eh
```

```
17      Luc:    =[could have a few people faintin[g    [at the si-:ght of=
18      Les:                                           [ehh[heh huh
19      Luc:    =i-:t[eh ah [ah
20->    Les:         [.hhh [yep (0.2) [⊕]¹¹ (.) o:[k a[y then]
21      Luc:                                          [.hh[Okay  ] Les see you
22              tomorrow[()
23      Les:            [bye:
24      Luc:    bye::
```

Lesley's turn in line 20 has multiple indications of disjunction: it begins with an audible inbreath and, following a first unit (*yep*) that closes down the prior sequence and a brief pause, it proceeds to initiate the action of closing the call with *okay then*. *Okay then* does not introduce a new topic, yet it is designed with the prosodic markings of a new sequence beginning: it has a pitch upstep and is produced high in the speaker's pitch range in addition to having wider pitch span and greater loudness than the prior *yep* (Wright 2011a).

Note that Lesley's new sequence beginning in line 20 is also prefaced with a *click*, represented by [⊕], which Wright's work (2005, 2011a) has shown to be a routine feature of multi-unit turns that transition from on-topic talk into the closing section of a telephone call. In fact, in a more recent study Wright (2011b) makes the argument that clicks are *generally* produced at the boundary between any two disjunctive sequences of talk (see also Online-Chapter E §7).

> Prosodic and phonetic features such as audible inbreaths, high pitch onsets, increased loudness, and clicks all serve as resources for marking a next turn as beginning a new sequence rather than continuing a possibly complete sequence in prior talk. They do so by breaking with the prosodic-phonetic trajectory of what has come before and iconically displaying – with a new intake of breath, a new pitch and loudness declination, and a new adjustment of the articulatory organs – that the speaker is about to launch talk that is also sequentially new.

3.2.2 Full Noun Phrases

In contrast to turns in second position, whose form and interpretation can in many ways rely on the turn preceding it, first-position turns that initiate new sequences must be interpretable without appeal to the prior sequential context. One way to achieve this in English is through the use of *full noun phrases* rather

---

[11] The symbol "⊕" represents a bilabial click (see Online-Chapter E §7), the symbol "-" in lines 17 and 19 a glottal stop (Wright 2011a).

than anaphoric pronouns for the mentioning of (human) referents (Fox 1987). Consider, for instance, the following fragment from a four-party face-to-face conversation:

(5.17)   "Honeymoon" (Fox 1987:70–1) (adapted)

```
1      M:   A:nd ( ) as far as that goes my father's on his honeymoon.=
2           =yah ha:h hah
3      K:   Oh::. Very [nice
4      M:             [(Ye:ah)
5->    K:   Where'd he go,
6      M:   Well I had thought he was going to Acapulco because it was
7           such a hush hush secret where he'd be go:ing.
8           (0.8)
9      M:   'n I thought he didn't want anybody to know or something
```
((11 lines omitted in which Mark explains that his father went north instead))
```
21     K:   You like the lady?
22          (0.4)
23=>   M:   She's ni:ce. She's a nice lady. I like her.
24          (0.3)
25     K:   Ah[hh
26     M:     [Friendly.
27          (1.0)
28     M:   But-the ba:d thing was that um::,
29          (0.3)
30=>   M:   I had to mo:ve my dad's furniture
31          (0.7)
32     M:   from his place in Santa Monica= I had to have
33          let the movers in (-) so.
34          (0.7)
35     M:   Being to:tally drunk from that orgy on Saturday night
36          I (had) to get up (0.2) and go do:wn. (0.2)
37          Santa Monica with Hillary.
```

Observe that when Mark begins a new sequence with the announcement that his father is on a honeymoon (line 1), he refers to him with a full noun phrase, *my father*. Karen evaluates Mark's news positively in next turn and pursues the topic with a question, now using a pronominal form to refer to Mark's father, *Where'd he go* (line 5). The use of the pronoun *he* (as opposed to *your father*) displays that Karen is expanding the prior sequence rather than treating it as closed and launching a new one (Fox 1987:22). Something similar happens in the adjacency pair of lines 21–3: Mark's father's wife is referred to as *the lady* in Karen's sequence-initiating turn, but as *she* in Mark's response.

This is a robust pattern: full noun phrases are used when human referents are mentioned for the first time in sequence-initiating turns but pronominal forms are used to refer to the same referent in subsequent turns within the sequence. In fact, as Fox (1987) argues, if a full noun phrase is used for a referent who has already been mentioned in prior discourse, this is generally taken by participants as beginning a new sequential unit.[12] A case in point was seen in lines 28–30 of (5.17) above, where Mark now refers to his father as *my dad*. Since no other same-gender referents have been mentioned in the meantime, Mark would actually have had the option here of saying *I had to move his furniture*. His choice of a full noun phrase, however, construes his turn as beginning a new sequential unit, which, as it emerges, becomes a complaint story (Fox 1987:71).

Full forms, and specifically full noun phrases, are a lexico-syntactic resource for designing a turn to be understood as beginning a sequence rather than as continuing it. In English conversation, a human referent is routinely referred to with a full noun phrase on first mention, and thereafter with a pronominal form within the sequence. The use of a full form for a referent who has already been mentioned can construe the turn as beginning something new.

3.3 Some Linguistic Resources for Initiating Sequence Closings

How are sequences brought to a close? Here too participants have dedicated practices, for which lexico-syntax and prosody serve as useful resources. One such practice involves the initiation of a "sequence-closing sequence" (Schegloff 2007a:186). The first turn of a sequence-closing sequence may be, for example, a summary assessment (see §2.2.4 above) or a formulation of the gist or upshot of the prior talk (Heritage and Watson 1979, 1980; see also Online-Chapter E §7). These turn types propose sequence closure. If the recipient agrees or aligns with the assessment or formulation in next turn, s/he will be understood to be collaborating in the sequence closure. The third position of a sequence-closing sequence serves to ratify the other's alignment and/or to launch a new sequence (Schegloff 2007a:187).

---

[12] The practice does not work mechanistically, however. Fox's study of conversational anaphora also unearthed cases of full noun phrases being used *within* sequences in conjunction with disagreement or to convey overt recognition (1987:62–4). See also Ford and Fox (1996) and Online-Chapter F §1.

Alternatively, a sequence-closing sequence can be initiated with an appraisal expression that projects no more talk, for example, *never mind*. If the recipient now passes up the opportunity to take an extended turn at talk, or withholds talk altogether, the first speaker can propose and embody sequence termination by repeating the appraisal object, for example, *never mind (.) never mind*. Following this "double saying," the way is clear to start a new sequence (Curl et al. 2006). In the following we examine these practices more closely.

3.3.1 Sequence-closing Assessments

As pointed out in the discussion of figurative expressions and topic closure above (§2.2.4), summaries are useful devices for proposing closure because they do not tie back to the preceding turn only but instead encompass the whole of a prior stretch of talk. Not all summary assessments employ figurative expressions, however.[13] Here is an example of a non-figurative summary assessment used to propose sequence closure:

(5.18)   "Doing alright" (Jefferson 1984c:212)
((At Shirley's instigation, Geri is bringing her up to date on a mutual friend Dana who is "in competition" to study law.))

```
1         G:   Bu:t, he does feel tha:t (1.0) you know, (.) he's
2              proud of the fact that he got into the finals. ·hhh
3              and he doesn't ca:re if he doesn't make the finals
4              and go o:n ·hh[   [t o - ] Berkeley or wherever,=
5    ->   S:                 [Ri[:ght.]
6         G:   =·h[h and then-
7    ->   S:      [Ri:ght.
8              (.)
9         G:   become a Harvard attorney I mean he doesn't care
10             about ↓that. at [all.↓
11   ->   S:                   [Right.
12   ->   S:   Ri[ght.
13        G:     [So.
14        S:   ·hh So he's doing alright.
15        G:   Ye:ah
16   ->   S:   Two twenty Joey,
17             (0.4)
18        S:   ·hhhh Twenty after two.
19             (.)
```

---

[13] Drew and Holt claim that figurative summaries, however, are "stronger" than non-figurative ones in bringing about topic and sequence closure (1998:504).

```
20  -> S:     'hh Well I'm glad to hear he's doing reasonably
21             well.
22     G:     Ye:ah,
23  -> S:     'hh Uh:m what was I gonna tell you.
```

In addition to a number of minimal acknowledgments with *right* (lines 5, 7, 11, and 12), Shirley also uses a *non-figurative summary assessment* – *so he's doing alright* (line 14) – to bring the topic of Dana's competition to a close. Following a brief off-phone interaction with Joey (lines 16–18), who is in the same room with her, she resumes talk by re-doing this summary assessment in a more elaborate form: *well I'm glad to hear he's doing reasonably well* (lines 20–21). Geri's subsequent minimal response now gives Shirley a warrant to launch a new sequence, which she does in line 23.

Another practice for proposing sequence closure, particularly in extended tellings, involves the use of an *assessment in a "that's X" format*, where X is an assessing term such as *great, good, wonderful* (Thompson et al. 2015). As Thompson and her co-authors emphasize, the expanded clausal assessing form, for example, *that's good*, must be distinguished from its corresponding phrasal variant, for example, *good*: phrasal forms are used by recipients to treat an extended telling as not yet complete, while expanded clausal forms display an understanding that the telling is now possibly complete (p. 201).[14] Here is a case where the recipient in a lengthy storytelling episode is clearly working to bring the telling to a close with *that's X* assessments:

(5.19)   "Fruit" (Thompson et al. 2015:209)
((Lottie is telling Emma about a recent out-of-town visit to her friend Adeline and what she bought on her way home.))

```
1   Lot:    so:: (.) and then: u-Adeline ↓bou:ght some too::=
2   Emm:    =°m[m hm,°
3   Lot:       [and that's:: about the uh oh:.hh and then coming home I
4           bought:: (.) they had tangeri:nes ten pounds for a do:llar
5           so I got te[n pounds [and I g]ot some casa:ba and then I bought
6   Emm:               [mm::     [↓m:m.]
7           (.)
8   Lot:    ↓uh:: (0.3) uh Edna back a box of da:tes [↓'cause]
9   Emm:                                              [°↓oh:]*::=
10  (Lot):  =[(°.hh°)
```

---

[14] Presumably the use of this pattern is related to the presence of the discourse deictic *that*, which has wide scope over the whole of a prior telling.

```
11  -> Emm:       =[that's ni[:ce,°  ]
12     Lot:                  [you kno]:w,
13                (.)
14     Lot:       [she:<]
15  -> Emm:       [°tha:]t's [↓nice  ] Lottie°]
16     Lot:                  [she fed] the ca: ]:[ts and ]
17  -> Emm:                                      [that's] °beau:tiful.°
18                (0.3)
19     Emm:       .tk..hhhhhh well [you had a] ↑beau:tiful <now you feel=
20     Lot:                        [°(o:↓kay.)°]
21     Emm:       =like a new ↓ga:l..hh [your ↑NER::VES have
22     Lot:                              [mm
23                (0.4)
24     Emm:       y'know there's so many other wonderful people arou:nd you.hh
25                .hhh uh it's good to get awa:y from:: your family sometimes
26                you-ih can be yours:↑E:lf. You [know what I me] EA:N?
27     Lot:                                      [ye::ah.        ]
28                ye:a[h.
29     Emm:           [.huhh uh getting ba:ck to this Vi:afo:r:m foam, Lottie
30                is your NAIL A:LRIGHT no:w?
```

Emma's first clausal assessment comes in lines 9 and 11, *oh that's nice*, at the hearable conclusion of Lottie's three-part list of what she bought on her way home. But the assessment emerges in overlap with Lottie's turn extension *cause.hh you know* (lines 8, 10, 12), whereupon Emma re-does it in line 15 with a terminal address term *that's nice Lottie*. Again Lottie's turn extension *she fed the cats* (line 16) prevents Emma's assessment from being in the clear and Emma re-does it yet again with *that's beautiful* (line 17). These repeated attempts to positively assess Lottie's story suggest that Emma has a stake in bringing the telling to a close, and indeed she can be observed next to launch into an elaborate summary assessment (lines 19–26). Lottie's minimal acknowledgments now provide Emma with a warrant to begin a new sequence, directed to a topic that ultimately concerns herself (she is currently suffering from a toenail infection).

> Two formats for assessing can be deployed to propose sequence closure: one is the summary assessment, a valenced resumé of what the sequence has dealt with so far. The other is a *that's X* assessment, where *X* is an evaluative term such as *good* or *too bad*. Both formats have the whole of a prior telling in their scope, which makes them particularly apt devices for this task.

3.3.2 Formulations

Like sequence-closing assessments, *formulations* also encompass the whole of a prior stretch of talk. They have been described as "a means for constructing an explicit sense [...] of the talk thus far" (Drew 2003:296). With formulations speakers either summarize the gist of prior talk or draw out its upshot or implications (Heritage and Watson 1979; Persson 2013). (See also Online-Chapter E §7.) Formulations are well suited for sequence closing because they "fix" the sense of what has been going on in a collaborative and reflexive way (Heritage and Watson 1980:255).

Persson's recent study of formulations in French talk-in-interaction (2013, 2014) argues that not all formulations are necessarily closure-implicative.[15] Although they make confirmation from the recipient relevant next, only some formulations project the relevance of imminent sequence closing; others invite the recipient to expand the sequence. In French these two types of formulation are distinguished by intonation: expansion-relevant formulations have final rising pitch on the last accented syllable of the TCU, while closure-relevant formulations have final (rising-)falling pitch. Here is an example illustrating the closure-relevant type of formulation:

(5.20) "Apply next year" (Persson 2013:30) (adapted)
((C is calling a university to ask whether it is still possible to apply for a particular study program. H is the receptionist who answers.))

```
1    H:   ah ben non c'est terminé là::depuis [le quinze mai hain]
          oh no the deadline has passed now since May fifteenth you know
2    C:                                       [(c'est terminé)]
                                               (it has passed)
3         (0.2)
4    C:   [m d'a]ccord o[key]
          m okay I see
5    H:   [.oui]         [oui] hh
          yes             yes hh
6         (.)
                                        (r----)(f------) (app---)
7 -> C:   il faudra que je:: j'postule l'ann{ée pr }{ochaine} {q[uoi]}
          it be.necessary.FUT that I I.apply the year next       like
          I'll have to apply next year huh
8    H:                                                         [ma]is voilà
                                                                 that's right
```

---

[15] In contrast to Drew (2003) and others, for Persson formulations do not require prefacing with a metacommunicative expression such as "you mean" or "what you're saying is" (2013:21).

```
9              (.)
10      H:     oui hh
               yes hh
11             (.)
12      C:     m d'accord (m[ais) c'est] pas grave merci au revoir
               m okay      (well)  no big deal  thank you goodbye
13      H:                [.ouais    ]
                           yeah
14      H:     au revoir
               goodbye
```

Observe that when the caller formulates in so many words the upshot of what the receptionist has just told her, *il faudra que je:: j'postule l'année prochaine quoi* "I'll have to apply next year huh" (line 7), the receptionist produces only two minimal confirmations next, *mais voilà* "that's right" and *oui* "yes", treating the prior as needing no further elaboration. This simple confirmation in essence collaborates in closing the sequence, whereupon the caller initiates closing of the conversation as a whole (line 12).

Persson argues that it is the distinctive intonational configuration of the caller's formulation in line 7 that renders it closure-relevant: there is a pitch step-up at the beginning of the last content word *prochaine* "next" and a significant pitch fall extending over the rest of the TCU (see Figure 5.3).

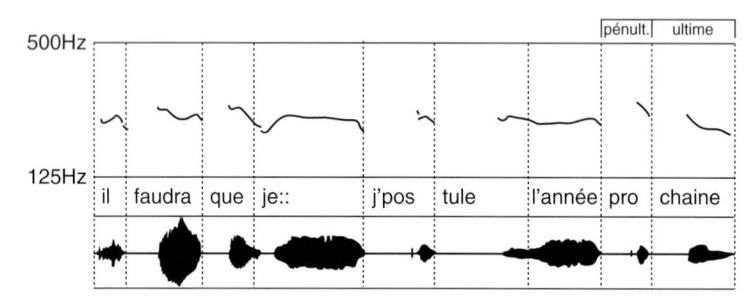

Figure 5.3 Pitch trace of line 7 in example (5.20) *(Persson 2014:85)*

By contrast, other cases in Persson's data suggest that a final *rising* pitch movement on the last content word of a formulation calls for sequence expansion in the form of explanations, justifications, and excuses. (See Online-Chapter E §7.)

> Among the numerous practices that can be used to propose sequence closure are formulations, versions of prior talk based on candidate understandings that can either summarize its gist or draw out its implications. Formulations in general make confirmation or disconfirmation relevant in next turn. In French such formulations are closure-relevant only if they have a distinctive intonational configuration: a rising-falling contour on the last syllables of a TCU. With a final rising contour they are sequence-expanding. Whether other languages make a similar distinction between sequence-expanding and sequence-closing formulations is still an open question.

3.3.3 Double Sayings

Like formulations, double sayings require collaborative work to bring about sequence closure. At a point that is ripe for sequence and topic closure, a speaker can propose closure by producing an *appraisal* – a clause-size object that displays an understanding of prior talk but does not project more talk, for example, *never mind, it might do, c'est la vie* (see also Schegloff 2007a:193). If the recipient indicates that they too have nothing more to say on the matter by, for example, withholding talk, then the first speaker can bring about sequence closure by re-doing the appraisal, thereby producing what Curl et al. (2006) call a "double saying". (See also Online-Chapter E §3.)

As Curl and her co-authors stress, double sayings have a characteristic prosodic-phonetic shape: the second part is typically lower in pitch and has a more compressed pitch range than the first part; its primary stress is shorter. However, the loudness level remains constant across the two parts, and there are no major articulatory shifts involved. Here is a case in point:

(5.21) "Never mind" (Curl et al. 2006:1726–7)
((Lesley and her co-teacher Robbie are talking about a colleague of theirs at school.))

```
1     Rob:  you know she's very.hh sometimes she's quite helpful
2           and other times I feel you know I don't know where I
3           stand with her
4     Les:  no
5           (0.2)
6     Les:  no no
7 ->  Rob:  never mind
8           (.)
9 ->  Rob:  never m[ind
10    Les:         [no
11          (0.3)
12    Rob:  anyway (.) I will let you (0.2) [go
13    Les:                                  [oh yes
```

Following a summary assessment of what she thinks about their colleague (lines 1–3) and minimal acknowledgment/agreement from Lesley (lines 4–6), Robbie's first *never mind* in line 7 indicates that she has nothing more to say on the subject. Nor does Lesley come in next with any further talk of her own at this point. There thus appears to be mutual consent between the two participants that the sequence can be closed down. This is what Robbie now achieves by producing a second *never mind* (line 9) that is equally as loud as the first but lower and more compressed in terms of pitch. Together her two turns constitute a double saying, one that with the collaboration of the interlocutor brings about sequence closure. The way is now free for a new sequence, or in this case pre-closing of the conversation, which is what Robbie initiates in line 12.

> Double sayings are particularly well suited for closing down sequences (a) because through their repetition they iconically embody "nothing new to say", and (b) because built into their structure, they provide interlocutors with an opportunity to prolong the sequence should they wish to do so. The achievement of sequence closure thus comes about through collaborative work.

3.4 Some Linguistic Resources for Marking Misplaced Sequences

Although sequence closure is a place where new sequences can begin, on occasion it happens that a new sequence is begun out of place. Misplaced turns, when they occur, are typically marked as such: the marking displays that although speakers are positioning their turn at a place where it does not belong, they at least recognize and acknowledge its ill-fittedness (Schegloff and Sacks 1973:319–20). Misplaced turns routinely lead to side sequences (Jefferson 1972).

3.4.1 Lexical Markers of Misplacement

Lexical devices for marking a misplaced turn in English include dedicated phrases such as *by the way* or *incidentally*. In the following example a *by the way* misplacement marker is used to introduce a content-related turn that moves out of conversational closings:[16]

(5.22)   "Good luck" (Jefferson 1972:315) (adapted)
```
1      A:  Forgive me sir, I'm gonna have to go.
2      B:  O:kay.
```

---

[16] Note that *by the way* is preceded here by *uh*, which serves to interrupt the projected trajectory of closings (see also Schegloff 2010 on some other uses of *uh(m)*).

```
3       A:   Nice [talking to you.
4       B:        [I enjoyed talking.
5       A:   [Thank you very much.
6       B:   [Thank y'very much. Okay,
7       A:   Bye bye.
8  ->   B:   Uh-by the way:::, Have a-a-Good luck in the hospital.
9       A:   Thank you.
10      B:   [Okay bye bye.
11      A:   [Mm bye bye.
```

Although in line 7 A produces the first pair part of a closing sequence (*bye bye → bye bye*), B does not respond with the relevant second pair part next, but instead moves out of closings in order to wish his interlocutor well in the hospital (line 8). In addition to *by the way*, misplaced turns can also be marked by, for example, *oh*-prefacing, where the particle indexes an extra-conversational noticing or something just remembered (Heritage 1984a). Here is a case in point:

(5.23)   "Twenty-three bonito" (Couper-Kuhlen 2004:342–3) (adapted)
((Lottie is telling Emma about her recent fishing expedition.))
```
1       Lot:   =Was KIND of FO:GGY, (.)
2              We GO:T TWENTY THREE BONITO but
3              (.)
4       Emm:   [eh hoh] HOh] ho hoh< ]
5       Lot:   [GOD we] had] mo:re da]:mn fu:n.
6       Emm:   Oh: Lo:ttie no: [ kidding ]
7       Lot:                   [N-hn-No k]idding=
8              =we got

((five lines omitted in which Emma relays the news to her husband off-phone))

14      Emm:   ↑TWENTY three-.hh.hh.hhu
15  ->         Oh did uh::
16             NOT TO CHANGE the subject but did you kno::w
17  ->         BILL WENT OUT ON THA:T (.) DEA:L with the gu-
18             a:ngling club 'n he won a pri::ze
19             did he tell yo[u? He]
20      Lot:                 [No: he] didn't ↑tell me he won a prize
21             he told me he went ou:t
22             but he didn't tell me he won a pri(:ze)
```

Emma is in the process of exclaiming over the size of Lottie's fishing catch (line 14) when she unexpectedly breaks off and, after a brief inbreath, launches into something projectably unrelated: *Oh did uh::* (line 15). This new unit has the prosodic markings of a new beginning, with sudden high pitch on *oh* and an even higher pitch peak on *did*. The *oh*-preface indexes the matter as having suddenly popped up, perhaps touched off by something in Lottie's story. Yet the misplacement is abrupt enough to warrant an account, which is what Emma does next by interjecting *not to change the subject but did you know* (line 16). Through this unit she orients to the prematurity of her new sequence and topic beginning – the prior unit had not been properly closed down – but implies with her dangling *but* that there is an unspoken motivation for doing so.

> Sequentially misplaced turns can be marked lexically by dedicated phrases such as *by the way* or *incidentally*, or by *oh*-prefacing, where *oh* indexes something just thought of or just noticed in the ambient surroundings. Such misplacements typically initiate side sequences, leading to the need to return to the prior sequence at their completion (see below).

3.4.2 Repetition Repairs without Prosodic-phonetic Upgrading

Sequentially misplaced turns that are not marked as such may produce puzzlement on the part of next speakers. Drew (1997) has described a number of such situations and noted that if repair is then initiated on the troublesome turn, it will be done with an open-class repair initiator of the sort *huh?*, *what?*, *sorry?* (see also Chapter 3 §3.2.1). Here is an example where this happens:

(5.24)   "Big repairs" (Drew 1997:87) (adapted)
```
1    Mum:      I'm not planning any big (0.2) any big things this
2              (0.2) repai:rs this yea:r,
3    Lesley:   No:. Well-
4    Mum:      I've just had my kitchen painted bu[t
5    Lesley:                                      [.h Well there's
6              no point in it if you don't need it. is there.
7              (0.3)
8    Mum:      What's that love,
9              (0.3)
10   Lesley:   There's no point in spending money if you don't need IT.
```

As Drew explains it, Lesley begins a response to Mum's announcement in lines 1–2 already in line 3: *No:. Well-*. But she now discontinues this turn, whereupon Mum adds a qualification to what she has just said: *I've just had my kitchen painted but* (line 4). Consequently, when Lesley now resumes her discontinued turn with *Well there's no point in it if you don't need it. is there* (lines 5–6), it no longer fits the sequential context. It is arguably this sequential misfit that prompts Mum's open-class repair initiation *what's that love* (line 8).

In (5.24) Lesley repairs the trouble source by repeating in so many words what she originally said (line 10). This affords her an opportunity to display some orientation to the misplacement of her turn retrospectively. Her solution is an elegant one: she replaces the *it* of the original turn, designed in line 10 to be understandable by reference to "big repairs" (line 1), with a full noun phrase *spending money*. The latter phrase contributes to transforming her turn into a generic statement of universal validity, which is easy for others to agree with. Thus, although superficially Lesley is merely "repeating" the trouble-source turn, the anaphoric resolution allows her to reshape it into something sequentially more appropriate.

Alternatively, speakers can use the prosodic-phonetic configuration of their "repetition" repair to retrospectively index the sequential misplacement of the trouble-source turn. As Curl's studies (2004, 2005) have shown, repetitions of trouble-source turns following open-class repair initiations can be done either with upgraded prosody and phonetics – i.e., expanded pitch range, longer word durations, louder volume, and more distinct articulations than the original – or with non-upgraded prosody and phonetics. In her data, it is sequentially *disjunct*, i.e., misplaced trouble-source turns that are routinely repeated with no upgrading: the repetitions have a more compressed pitch range, with similar or shorter word durations, similar articulations, and quieter volume than the original (Curl 2004:291). For an example see (3.35) in Chapter 3. This finding suggests that speakers of sequentially misplaced turns whose interlocutors have initiated repair with an open-class format may retrospectively mark the misplacement by prosodically-phonetically "downgrading" their repetition repair.

Should a sequentially misplaced turn be unmarked lexically and subject to open-class repair initiation, it can be retrospectively displayed as misplaced when repaired with repetition. To accomplish this, the repetition must be done *without* upgraded prosody and phonetics, i.e., by using a more compressed pitch range and lower volume as well as roughly the same durations and articulations compared to the original.

3.5 Some Linguistic Resources for Returning to a Prior Non-adjacent Sequence

Because misplaced turns as a rule lead to side sequences, they can occasion a further organizational problem for interactants: how to return to an ongoing sequence after completion of the side sequence. But also in other circumstances speakers need to be able to mark that what is being said next should be understood *not* by reference to the last turn, but by reference to something said earlier than last turn. Sacks describes one way to handle this problem: "a speaker produces an utterance that is indeed related to some prior utterance, but it's not related to the directly prior utterance, but some utterance prior to the directly prior utterance" (1992b:349). Sacks uses the term "skip-connecting" for this, but only if the speaker skip-connects to their own last-but-one utterance. As will be seen shortly, however, what we will call *back-connecting* can also be accomplished over longer distances and to other speakers' turns.

A number of linguistic resources can be mobilized to back-connect: for instance, discontinuity markers such as *anyway* will indicate that what follows does not tie to immediately preceding talk (Schegloff 1984:38). Alternatively, speakers can tie back to earlier talk with meta-phrases such as *getting back to* ... (line 29 of (5.19) above is an example of this). In the following sections we review further linguistic practices for returning to prior talk.

3.5.1 Recycling and Prosodic Continuation versus Restarting

Perhaps the most straightforward way to back-connect is to recycle all or part of the turn unit that occurred just before a prior sequence was discontinued. Local (1992) observes that such recycled talk can be designed prosodically either as a *continuation* of prior talk, or as a *restart*.[17] The distinction depends on how pitch and loudness levels at the beginning of the recycled talk are manipulated (see Online-Chapter D §3.1). If they match the pitch and loudness levels in the original, then the return is construed as a *continuation* of prior talk. If they are hearably different, then the recycled talk is construed as a *restart*: it is presented as if for the first time. Here are two examples that illustrate this difference:

```
(5.25)     "Canyon" (Local 2004:381)
1      Lot:   Uh::::. (.) Let's see hit the Riverside Freeway and then
2             when you see the River:side (.) Freeway when it says
3             Indio and San Diego [turn] off] the:re=
4      Emm:                       [Mm: ] h m]
5      Emm:   You're all freeway all the wa::y
6             (.)
7      Lot:   .t And then you go through the ca:nyon you kno[:w.]
8      Emm:                                                  [Yea]h:
```

[17] Local's "restarts" correspond roughly to what Sacks calls "re-beginnings": "it's perfectly plain that speakers do things like reasserting a line that they earlier started to take, that got nowhere. But if they do that over any distance, then they tend to do it by reference to a re-beginning" (1992b:349). Local claims, however, that returns to prior talk – even over some distance – can also be done as continuations.

```
9                  (.)
10   ->   Lot:     And the:n: uh[:
11        Emm:              [I hate that °canyon°
12                 (0.9)
13        Lot:     No I'm ta:lking about the other canyon after you pass:
14                 uh:.hhh Rive[r s  i[: d e ]
15        Emm:                 [.t.hh[Oh: y]a:h
16                 (0.7)
17   ->   Lot:     uAnd then it says turn to: Indio and [San]Die:]go=
18        Emm:                                          [M m]hm: ]
19        Lot:     =and then you go on there about five mi:les and then
20                 you're in:
```

Lottie is describing to Emma the route she took on a recent trip: *And then you go through the ca:nyon you kno:w* (line 7). However, she breaks off her next unit *And the:n: uh:* when Emma interjects an assessment of the canyon (line 11). Emma's comment leads to a side sequence clarifying which canyon Lottie meant. It is at the close of this sequence that Lottie finds herself needing to return to where she left off in her route description. In line 17 she recycles the suspended material, and in doing so, matches its original pitch and loudness levels. That is, she makes the recycled unit sound like a continuation of the discontinued one.

Now compare the following return:

```
(5.26)    "Bullock's" (Local 2004:382)
1         Emm:     Isn't this funny you and I: would have it h
2                  (0.4)
3         Emm:     This is ri[: dicul]ous.]
4    ->   Lot:              [e:very ]body]'s got .hh Isn't tha:t funny we
5    ->            were in a p-uh:[:
6         Emm:                    [Oh: God it's terrible Lottie m:y toenails
7                  .hehh they just look so sick those big t:oenails it just
8                  u- makes me: sick You know they're diss (.) u-dea:d (.)
9                  Everything's dead I d- I sat ou:t (.) today and I said my
10                 Go:d am I just (.) dy:ing it's: (.) like I'm ossified
11   ->   Lot:     no I- we were in: some [pla:ce uh don't know if it was
12        Emm:                            [((sniff))
13        Lot:     Bullock's==or some pla:ce (0.4) I guess it was Bullock's
14                 A:nd somebody was ta:lking about it a:nd I: bet there
15                 were .hhh te:n people arou:nd the:re and they a:ll
16                 started to say well they had the sa:me thing
```

In lines 4–5 Lottie cuts off her summary assessment *everybody's got* (the reference is to a toe fungus) to launch a story touched off by it: *we were in a p-uh:*. But Emma interjects an emotive complaint about her current state of health, forcing Lottie to temporarily abort her story. At the close of Emma's complaint turn, after summarily dismissing Emma's fears (*no* in line 11), Lottie now returns to her story, recycling the beginning *we were in: some pla:ce* . . . The recycled material, however, is noticeably louder and higher in pitch than the original. That is, it is presented as a restart, as a new contribution to the conversation.

> When talk is suspended for a side sequence and then picked up again afterwards, the return can be accomplished through recycling *with* prosodic matching of pitch and loudness or *without* prosodic matching. The former presents the return as a continuation of prior talk, while the latter, with a marked increase in pitch and loudness, configures the recycled material as a restart, as being done for another first time.

3.5.2 Turn-initial Connectives in Continuing versus Resuming

Local's dichotomy between prosodically contextualized "continuing" versus "restarting" suspended talk is a relevant distinction when the return is accomplished through recycling. However, there are other techniques for implementing a return to a prior, non-adjacent sequence that do not depend on recycled material: one of these is the use of a connective as a turn preface (see also Chapter 8 §2).

To appreciate the work that connectives can do in turn-initial position, it is necessary to introduce a distinction made by Jefferson (1972), using terminology that is only partially equivalent to Local's "continuing" versus "restarting". Jefferson claims that if a next speaker returns to material further back than the just prior turn, the return can be accomplished either as a *continuation* of earlier talk or as a *resumption*: resumption marks that there is a problem in accomplishing the return, while continuing covers it up (1972:319).[18] This distinction can be effected *inter alia* through the choice of turn-initial connective.

For instance, in Dutch talk-in-interaction following an inserted repair sequence within an extended telling, the suspended telling can be picked up again with a turn that begins with the connective *en* "and" or with the connective *maar* "but". *En* links the next unit to the prior talk by simply adding more material to it: the intervening repair sequence is treated as something incidental that can be "deleted" by simply going on. But *maar* frames the return as a contrast with what has come in

---

[18] While Local's "continuing" and Jefferson's "continuation" appear to be roughly equivalent, Local's "restart" highlights the newness of the return action, while Jefferson's "resumption" highlights its problematicity.

between; it treats the intervening repair sequence as a digression (Mazeland and Huiskes 2001). Here is a case where the work that the two connectives do can be compared:

(5.27)   "Hiking story" (Mazeland and Huiskes 2001:145–6) (adapted)

```
22      Bob:    nou↓eh:: (.) we zijn daar aa::ngekomen (0.7)
                well uh:: (.) we got there (0.7)
23              en eh: (.) we zijn naar 't (.) Lac du la:Gileppe gerejen
                and uh: (.) we then drove to the (.) Lac du la Gileppe
24              (.)
25 ->   Eric:   't wa:t=                              repair initiation
                the what=
26      Bob:    =Lac du la Gileppe (.)
                =Lac du la Gileppe (.)
27              dat is een heel groot stu:wmeer
                that's a very big artificial lake
28              (1.5)
29 ->   Bob:    ·hh en eh::: (.) nou: da (.) daar was 't o-   continuation
                ·hh and uh::: (.) well there (.) there was too-
30              eh:: (.) hEE:l erg regenweer (.) daar was
                uh:: (.) very rainy weather (.) there was
31              ammel snee::uw en eh ha::gel en zo (.)
                all snow and uh hail and so (.)
32              toen hebben we op een of a:ndere:: (.) mt (.)
                then we sat at some (.) mt (.)
33              afdakje hebben we (.) onder gezeten (.)
                canopy we sat (.) under it (.)
34              hebben we erwtensoe:p gemaakt ·hhh
                made pea soup ·hhh
35              en hebwe:: (.) 'n heleboel gegeten
                and ate (.) lots of it
36              we hadden voor twee: dagen eten bij (.) ·hh en eh::
                we had two days of food with us (.) ·hh and uh::
37              (2.0)
38      Bob:    nou: (.) toen- toen werd 't droo:g (.) wonder
                well: (.) then- then the rain stopped (.) wonder
39              boven wonder (.) hh toen zijn we aa::ngelopen (.)
                of all wonders (.) hh then we started to walk (.)
40              toen was 't al na:cht (.) of toen was 't al avond
                it was already night by then (.) or already evening time
```

41		toen was 't al d<u>o</u>nker (.) toen zijn we <u>aa</u>ngelopen (.)	
		it was already dark then (.) then we started to walk (.)	
42		en eh:: (.) he'we ongeveer v<u>ie</u>:r	
		and uh:: (.) we did about four	
43		of v<u>ij</u>:f kilometer gelopen of zo:=	
		or five kilometers or something:=	
44 ->	Eric:	=in 't d<u>o</u>nker?=	***repair initiation***
		=in the dark?=	
45	Bob:	=ja	
		=yes	
46		(.)	
47	Eric:	oh (.) wij veronderstelden (.) dat (.) dat jullie	
		oh (.) we supposed (.) that (.) that you guys	
48		<u>ui</u>tgewerkt waren (.) zo gauw 't donker waren (.) w<u>a</u>s=	
		were finished (.) as soon as it were dark (.) was=	
49	Bob:	=nou (.) we zijn t<u>oe</u>:n gewoon d<u>oo</u>rgelopen	
		=well (.) we just walked on then	
50		want we hadden nog geen sl<u>aa</u>pplek	
		because we didn't have a place to sleep yet	
51		(.)	
52	Eric:	>jaja=	
		>yes yes=	
53 ->	Bob:	=·hh **maar** toen eh (.) nou toen zijn we gewoon	***resumption***
		=·hh but then uh (.) well then we just	
54		de b↑o:ssen <u>i</u>ngelopen (.) we hadden geen lamp bij	
		walked into the woods (.) we didn't have a light with us	
55		en da was wel heel lastig	
		and it was really very difficult	
56	Eric:	jaha	
		yhes	

Notice that when Bob continues his story after the repair sequence Eric has initiated (lines 25–7), he does so by back-connecting with *en* "and" (line 29). What follows is a next component (the weather) in the story he is telling: this weather report is added on, not to the immediately preceding repair sequence, but to the hiking story being recounted (2001:146). By contrast, when Eric again initiates repair with a candidate understanding in line 44, Bob first deals with the trouble it is indicative of, and then resumes his story with *maar* "but" in line 53. In this case what follows is *not* a next story component, but one that was already introduced in line 41 with *toen zijn we aangelopen* "then we started to walk". That is, an earlier component is first recycled before the story is resumed. Mazeland and Huiskes argue that this is an indication that the intervening talk is being treated as a digression, something from which it is necessary to return before moving on. The return is done as non-incidental and not unproblematic (2001:147).

> Jefferson's distinction between unproblematic continuing and more problematic resumption of talk after a side sequence can be seen at work in Dutch storytelling, where speakers whose story has been suspended due to other-initiation of repair *continue* by adding a next story component with *en* "and", but *resume* by recycling the story component prior to suspension with *maar* "but" before moving on.

A study by Local (2004) uncovered a similar use of English *and uh(m)* in turn-initial position for continuing talk after a side sequence. Interestingly, this *and uh(m)* is quite distinct from turn-initial *and*, in that the former (but not the latter) has a stable cluster of prosodic-phonetic features associated with it: it is typically preceded and/or followed by breathiness or pause, it is not louder than surrounding talk but is noticeably slower, it has relatively level pitch located roughly in the middle of the speaker's pitch range, and each syllable carries a beat, lending it an equal-equal (or DA-DA) rhythm. The vowel of its first syllable is full (non-reduced); this syllable may begin with creaky voice or glottal closure; there is no break between the syllables (2004:392). Local observes that it is this realization of *and uh(m)* that characterizes returns to a prior activity after intervening side sequences.

Preliminary observations by Walker suggest that something similar may hold for turn-initial *but uh(m)* when accompanied by such prosodic-phonetic features (2013:467). *But uh(m)* in other environments, for example, in sequence exiting (Schegloff 2009b), is realized differently. However, it is as yet unclear whether back-connecting *but uh(m)* contrasts functionally with *and uh(m)* following side sequences.

> In English, back-connecting to prior talk after a side sequence can be done with turn-initial *and uh(m)*. *And uh(m)* is distinct from turn-initial *and*: it has a stable cluster of prosodic-phonetic features including slow delivery, mid-range level pitch, and full vowel quality. In contrast to turn-initial *and*, which can link to immediately preceding talk, this variant of *and uh(m)* is reserved for connecting back over intervening talk.

3.5.3 Turn-final Particles and Delayed Actions

So far the linguistic devices we have described for back-connecting have all been located at the beginning of turns or TCUs. Bolden (2009c), however, describes a linguistic resource for back-connecting in Russian that invariably appears in turn-medial or turn-final position: the post-positioned discourse particle -*to* (derived etymologically from the indexical pronoun *tot* meaning "that"). This particle is used, *inter alia*, in sequence-initiating turns to mark that the action being implemented does not tie back to immediately preceding talk but to something earlier. It is typically attached to a word that repeats a bit of the prior talk, thus enabling an appropriate connection to be made. Here is an example where we can see the particle at work:

(5.28) "New van" (Bolden 2009c:338–9) (adapted)[19]

((Dina is on her way out of the house when Zhenya calls. In line 2 she is apologizing for having been out of touch.))

```
1     ZH:   [Nu |ladna/
            Okay then
2     DI:        [.h |Zhen'ka/ [izvini/
                    Zhenja I am sorry
3     ZH:                      [Ty savsem ischezla/
                                You've totally disappeared
4     DI:   .h da ty znaesh chëta vchera, mashinu kupili/=
            You know yesterday we bought a car
5     ZH:   =D[a/ ja   zna]ju
             yes  I    know
6     DI:   [Celyj den'-] (.) doma ne byla/=A sevodnja my idëm
            We weren't home the entire day/ and today we are going
7           .hh eh- abmyvat' Mishkinu kupch(h)uju(h)/
            to celebrate Misha's deed of purchase
8     ZH:   Da,/ da/ [da/[(   )
            yes yes yes
9     DI:            [.h [Vot/ubegaem/ ja praspala/ ja usnula/
                         We are running out/ I overslept/ I fell asleep
10          (.)
11    ZH:   [(Kakuju-)
             what
12    DI:   [Ja utram chëta ochen' rana-
             For some reason in the morning very early I-
13    ZH:   Kakuju mashinu vy kupili/ Kamu/
            What car did you buy/ for whom
14    DI:   Mne:/ Ve:n/
            For me/ A van
```

---

[19] In this transcript, a slash [/] indicates a unit boundary with a somewhat falling pitch contour.

```
15   ->   ZH:    A/=U tebja zh byla [novaja/ vrode by/
                oh with you PRT was   new     seems PRT
                Oh you had a new car I believe
((several lines omitted))
44        DI:       [I on ↑xarasho ochen' vygadna pradal/
                    And he sold it very profitably
45                  my dazhe ne azhidali/
                    we didn't even expect it
46   ->   ZH:       A zachem tebe ven ta/
                    PRT why   you  van PRT
                    What do you need a van for
47                  (0.2)
48        DI:   Nu nam n^u:zhen/ On-mne takoj ven ↓zdaravenyj
                We need one/ It's not so huge
```

When Dina explains that the reason for her absence is that she bought a new car the day before, and when it emerges that the car is a van for herself, Zhenya challenges this, first by implying that Dina already had a new car and did not need another one (line 15). What follows is a longish interlude in which Dina explains that she gave her car to Misha, who then sold his old one (data not shown here). Now Zhenya returns to her prior (critical) course of action with another challenge – *A zachem tebe ven ta* "what do you need a van for" (line 46) – attaching the *-to* particle (pronounced /ta/) to the word *ven* "van". The presence of this particle marks Zhenya's turn as connecting back to her prior activity.

In sum, without the particle *-to*, a sequence-initiating turn such as the one in line 13 is displayed as launching a new course of action, while with the particle *-to*, a sequence-initiating turn such as the one in line 46 is marked as continuing a prior activity, here that of critically challenging Dina's car purchase. As Bolden points out, this use of *-to* has more to do with actions and their sequentially delayed position than with invoking an "old" topic. In fact, both lines 13 and 46 repeat words from prior discourse and could be said to hark back to prior topics (2009c:387). But only line 46 connects back to a prior activity and it is marked with *-to*.

> The post-positioned particle *-to* in Russian can be used turn-medially or turn-finally to index a return to a possibly completed course of action in prior talk. Although it typically attaches to a word that is a repetition from earlier talk, it is not used so much in the service of re-invoking a prior topic as of reinstating and continuing a prior action or activity.

4. Conclusion

With example (5.28) we have come full circle, having once again seen evidence that topicality can be meaningfully distinguished from sequentiality in conversational interaction (see §1 above). Both notions refer to underlying systems of organization that promote the coherence of turns at talk, and these systems often work hand in hand. However, as our discussion has shown, some linguistic devices are sensitive to one order of organization to the exclusion of the other. In the case of the high onset in English (§3.2.1) and the discourse particle *-to* in Russian (§3.5.3), the conversational evidence points to their work being primarily sequential rather than topical. In the case of, for example, figurative expressions and/or *okay*, on the other hand, their work appears to be at once topical <u>and</u> sequential. On occasion researchers cast their analysis in one framework rather than the other; Clift's analysis of *actually* (2001), for instance, is framed entirely in terms of topicality, while Mazeland and Huiskes' (2001) analysis of *maar* is framed in terms of sequentiality. More research will be needed to tease out whether this choice is an analytic necessity.

Part II

How are Linguistic Resources Deployed in Interaction?

Preface

Before the reader embarks on the second part of this book, a word of caution is in order. As pointed out earlier, Interactional Linguistics advocates a cross-linguistic approach to the study of language in social interaction. Yet when examining linguistic resources and their use in interaction, how can we be sure we are talking about the *same* resource across languages? To take an example, the term *clause* in English has no satisfactory equivalent in German. If we try to compare an English clause to a German *Satz* ("sentence"), we will find ourselves comparing two very unlike entities.[1] Moreover, the characteristics of clauses vary significantly across languages: whereas in English, clauses can be either finite or non-finite (Quirk et al. 1985:1120), the Finnish *lause* ("clause") is by definition finite (Hakulinen et al. 2004:827). Branching out even further to include other non-Indo-European languages, what we know as, for example, a "relative clause" in English – i.e., a clause that modifies a noun or noun phrase and is introduced by a relative pronoun linking it to its antecedent – does not exist in Japanese, since Japanese places modifying clauses directly before the word they modify as adjective-like attributive verbs without a relative pronoun: *tempura-o tsukutta hito* "tempura-OBJ made person"[2] (Kuno 1973). The crux of the matter then is that categories developed for the description of one language do not necessarily transfer to other languages, much less to *all* other languages.

Language typologists have thought long and hard about this dilemma.[3] Far from claiming that linguistic categories are universal, they would instead advocate comparing, for example, grammatical relations across languages in terms of *comparative concepts*: concepts that rely on very basic, general, even primitive notions that can be

---

[1] German *Teilsatz* ("sub-sentence" or "sentence part") is also not particularly helpful, as the term implies that this unit cannot stand alone, making it quite different from the English clause, which can. See also Chapter 6.
[2] The abbreviation OBJ stands for "object".
[3] For enlightening discussions see Dryer (1997), Croft (2001), and Haspelmath (2010).

established independently of specific languages. The comparative concept of *relative clause*, for instance, might be described as "a clause that is used to narrow the reference of a referential phrase and in which the referent of the phrase plays a semantic role" (Haspelmath 2010:672). This understanding would make it possible to treat both (English) *the man who came to dinner* and (Japanese) *tempura-o tsukutta hito* "tempura-OBJ made person"[4] as conceptually comparable. The label used to refer to them can be considered of secondary importance.

In the following chapters, we will attempt to compare linguistic categories to the extent possible in terms of basic conceptual-semantic notions. At the same time, we will follow Dryer (1997) and restrict our discussion to languages where there is enough isomorphism between them to justify using one and the same label for the phenomena in question. Because a thorough understanding of language-specific grammar will be needed for proper comparison, heavier focus will be placed on English and German in this part of our book than elsewhere. The labels used to refer to cross-linguistic "categories" will be English ones for the sake of convenience only.

A final word relating to our use of the term *linguistic resource*. What counts as a linguistic resource? Recall from the preface to Part I the way we are conceptualizing the term here: a *resource* for talk-in-interaction is a form-based entity, including *verbal* forms such as phones and other sound objects, morphs, words, phrases, clauses, sentences, and recurrent larger discourse units; combinations of forms in (construction) formats; and *non-verbal* forms or devices such as prosodies, facial/bodily gestures, and bodily position and movement, to the extent that they accompany language and interface with it systematically in the communicative process. Distinct from, but related to, resources in this understanding are *practices*, the recurrent ways in which concrete linguistic and other forms and formats are deployed for specific purposes in social interaction. Although practices are carried out with resources, they cannot always be described in terms of specific forms but sometimes only in terms of principles for the use of such forms. A good example might be *repetition*. Repetition is a recurrent practice, for example, for confirming an allusion (Schegloff 1996a) or for other-initiating repair (Robinson and Kevoe-Feldman 2010). With respect to form, it can be described as the "resaying" of an interlocutor's prior utterance. When this is done in a specifiable sequential location, other-repetition can be analyzed as accomplishing the action of, for example, confirming an allusion or other-initiating repair.

---

[4] Regardless of whether this construction is interpreted as "the person who made tempura" or "the person (someone) made tempura for", it would satisfy the definition cited above of "relative clause", since the referent (*person*) plays a semantic role in the clause that narrows it down (*someone made tempura (for someone)*).

Part II: How are Linguistic Resources Deployed in Interaction?

We return to such linguistic practices in Online-Chapter F – see also §3 there on repeating and repetitions. But before doing so, we examine various types of linguistic resources and their deployment in talk-in-interaction, ordered from larger (sentences, clauses, phrases: Chapter 6) and largest (clause combinations: Chapter 7) to smaller (particles as one-word constructions: Chapter 8). The smallest resources (prosody and phonetics) are dealt with in Online-Chapter E.

6

Sentences, Clauses, and Phrases

As Sacks, Schegloff, and Jefferson note, turn-constructional units (TCUs) are formed, *inter alia*, by syntactic units such as sentences, clauses, and phrases (1974:720). In this chapter we will systematically explore these structures as resources for building turns and implementing actions in talk-in-interaction.

1. Analyzing Sentences, Clauses, and Phrases in Talk-in-interaction

In linguistics, the sentence has traditionally been viewed as the basic unit of description, as the largest syntactic entity that can be captured with traditional linguistic tools, and as the unit with respect to which smaller component units such as embedded clauses and phrases function (morpho)syntactically. Linguistics, however, has often had a fundamental bias toward written language (see, e.g., Linell 2005). It has dealt primarily with written texts, which are fully present in a visual medium and are prototypically produced well before they are read, in the absence of direct interaction between writer and reader. Spoken language, however, is by nature fleeting and ephemeral; in talk-in-interaction it arises from a continual moment-by-moment exchange between participants, who have little time to think or plan between contributions. Thus, the syntactic units deployed in conversational turns – sentences, clauses, and phrases – need to be fundamentally flexible, adaptable to the local exigencies of interaction. If we deal with these units here, it is not because linguists have traditionally thought them relevant, but because they have been shown to be oriented to as relevant by participants in social interaction.

When referring to *sentence* and/or *clause*, researchers in general mean to denote a grammatical unit formed with a predicate, most often a verb or a verb complex, and the grammatical constituents or phrases that need to accompany it in order for it to be interpreted as complete. Yet the terms *sentence* and *clause* do not have the same status in the grammars of all languages.[1] Different linguistic traditions may have reason to

---

[1] For divergent understandings of the clause see, for instance, Laury and Ono (2014) and Laury et al. (Forthcoming).

make different distinctions. To take English and German as examples, English grammarians generally conceive of *sentence* as a superordinate category only, and refer to the simple sentence with a special term, namely *clause* (see Figure 6.1). For analyses of syntactic units in English, thus, *clause* is the basic term.

```
                    Sentence (in English grammar)
                   ┌──────────────┼──────────────┐
        clause            compound sentence       complex sentence
        (=simple sentence) (=coordinated clauses) (=main clause + subordinate clause(s))
        (SVO word order)   (SVO word order)       (SVO word order)
```

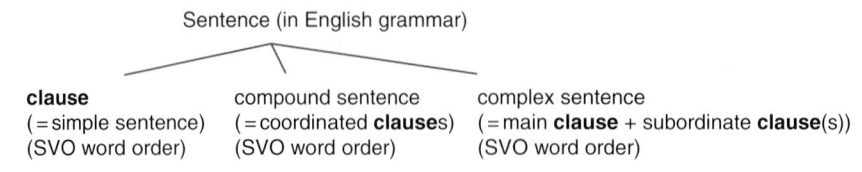

Figure 6.1 Hierarchy of terms for sentence and clause in English grammar

German grammarians, however, take *Satz* "sentence" to be the basic term, both in superordinate and in subordinate categories, with the hierarchy of terms shown in Figure 6.2 indicating the most important subcategories for canonical exemplars with Subject-Verb-Object (SVO) and Subject-Object-Verb (SOV) word order.

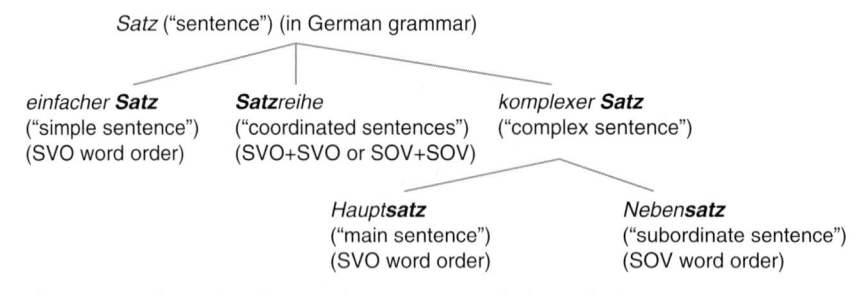

```
                    Satz ("sentence") (in German grammar)
                   ┌──────────────┼──────────────┐
        einfacher Satz      Satzreihe         komplexer Satz
        ("simple sentence") ("coordinated sentences") ("complex sentence")
        (SVO word order)    (SVO+SVO or SOV+SOV)
                                         ┌──────────────┴──────────────┐
                                      Hauptsatz                   Nebensatz
                                   ("main sentence")         ("subordinate sentence")
                                   (SVO word order)           (SOV word order)
```

Figure 6.2 Hierarchy of terms for sentence and clause in German grammar

The terminological differences between English and German are related to the different word orderings in the two languages. In English, where main and subordinate clauses share the same word order (SVO), syntactic descriptions can start from the clause as their lowest common denominator. In German, main and subordinate clauses have different word order, however: normatively speaking, main clauses have the verb in second position (i.e., SVO or, when another constituent is topicalized, XVO[2]), while subordinate clauses have the verb in final position (i.e., SOV). Therefore, German grammar must start from a larger and more complex unit in order to be able to encompass both main and subordinate clauses; in other words, here the lowest common denominator is *Satz* "sentence".

In German talk-in-interaction, however, both main and subordinate clauses can be thought of as the smallest syntactic units organized with reference to

---

[2] In this abbreviation X stands for some element other than the subject.

predicates. Regardless of whether they are formed as main or subordinate, clauses share many properties, especially their projectability and their flexibility. In German talk-in-interaction, subordinate clauses can even be used on their own as TCUs separate from a (host) main clause (see Günthner 1993, 1996a; Auer 1998). Moreover, at least some syntactically subordinate structures are evolving toward syntactically coordinated structures (see Auer 1998; Günthner 2000b).[3] With this in mind, in spoken German the clause can also be looked upon as the basic unit, and sentences as a more complex combination of clauses. Thus, despite the different terminology, common ground can be found in research on German *Sätze* ("sentences") and English *clauses* in talk-in-interaction. For present purposes, we shall adopt the following definitions:

> *Clauses* are grammatical units that consist of "predicates (in English these are verb complexes) and the phrases that 'go with'" them (Thompson and Couper-Kuhlen 2005:484). *Phrases* are grammatical units expressing the core and non-core arguments that accompany predicates (Thompson Forthcoming), while *sentences* are understood to be grammatical units consisting of either a single clause or a combination of clauses.[4]

This section will show that what we as researchers conceive of as sentences, clauses, and phrases are syntactic schemata or construction types which participants mobilize in the production and recognition of TCUs in talk-in-interaction. As, however, the production of TCUs is an interactional process in time that is subject to local contingencies, sentences, clauses, and phrases must be conceived of as fundamentally dynamic units with flexible beginnings, middles, and ends.

1.1 An Eye-opener

Schegloff (1979) opened the eyes of many linguists by showing that even when speakers misspeak, both the repair processes dealing with these mishaps and the syntactic structures they are embedded in are highly systematic (see also Chapter 3). For this reason, he speaks of a "syntax-for-conversation". Taking "sentence" as the basic unit, Schegloff looks at within-sentence repair, describing – *inter alia* – the effects of repair on the syntactic form of a "sentence" (in our terminology, a clause). He notes various ways in which the practices of repair can

---

[3] See also Thompson (2002) and Lindström (2006) on epistemic phrases like *I think* and *I guess*, which erode the distinction between "main" and "complement" clauses in English and Swedish, with the omission of complementizers like *that* being a contributing factor. See also Chapter 7 §4.1.1.
[4] In some places in this section, we adopt the coordinated expression "sentences and clauses" in order to point to similarities between the two unit types. In other places "clause" will be used as the more general term, including both main and subordinate clauses.

change the syntax of clauses, for instance, when speakers expand phrases, modify clausal structure, subsume a clause under a "frame" (e.g., *I think*) or by contrast "deframe" it by converting an independent clause into a subordinate one, transform a question into an assertion, etc. (pp. 263–6). Thus, even though repair may become necessary and may change the structure of clauses, it is always performed in orientation to clauses as units.

As we have seen in Chapter 2, speakers attend to the boundaries of units in turn taking. In order to ensure that a self-repair is initiated before the recipient takes over, speakers must get it initiated before the next possible completion of the TCU. If they are producing a clause, the self-repair will thus have to be initiated within the boundaries of that unit. Schegloff concludes (referring to the clause as "sentence"): "What is thought of in terms of current syntax as the 'integrity' of the sentence is, therefore, systematically subordinated to other sequential requirements" (Schegloff 1979:269, emphasis from the original omitted; see also Hayashi 2004a). In other words, the structure of "sentences" needs to be adapted to the local tasks of turn taking, repair, and sequence organization. This fits well with early research by C. Goodwin (1979, 1981), who showed that speakers orient to ongoing recipient behavior as they produce "sentences," adapting them to the local contingencies of the interaction (Chapter 2 §1.1).

> From an interactional linguistic perspective, sentences, clauses, and phrases are interesting because they are syntactic structure types that regularly occur in turns. This means that they must be described with regard to the properties they exhibit and the work they do when used as turns at talk.

1.2 Conceptualizing Sentences, Clauses, and Phrases Interactionally

What kind of grammatical description do we need to capture the properties relevant for analyzing sentences, clauses, and phrases in social interaction? For interactional linguistic descriptions, the following models have become important.

i. Typological word order models

The position of the verb (V) or predicate in relation to the subject (S) and object(s) (O) in simple sentences or clauses distinguishes languages as *verb-second* (e.g., English (SVO); German main clauses (SVO/XVO), in which the pre-verb position can be filled with either the subject (S) or any other topicalized constituent (referred to as X here; see below)), or *verb-final* (e.g., Japanese,

Korean, Turkish, German subordinate clauses (SOV)).[5] The basic position of the verb is often related to other morpho-syntactic properties of the language, such as whether it has predominantly prepositions or postpositions, inflecting or agglutinating morphology, case marking, etc. In interactional linguistic research, the basic position of the verb is assumed to result in different kinds of projection: SVO languages enable early projection of possible utterance trajectories, SOV languages, late projection (Chapter 2 §1.1).[6]

ii. Topological field models

For the representation of German and Swedish syntax, different fields or positions in the linear progression of sentences and clauses have been shown to be relevant for different tasks in the organization of sequential interaction. See, for instance, Auer (1991, 1992a, 1996a, 1996b) for German, and Lindström (2006) for Swedish. More detail on topological field models is provided below.

iii. Online syntax

For Auer, "syntax is a formal(ized) way of human language to make projection in time possible" (2005a:14). He develops the notion of *online* syntax for the description of the real-time emergence of syntactic structures in spoken interaction, with particular regard to processes of projection, retraction, and expansion (2000a, 2007a, etc.). In this model, syntactic descriptions are devised so as to capture the three most fundamental characteristics of spoken language in interaction (Auer 2007a:96):

– its incremental production: syntactic structures are projected and delivered bit by bit, in real time, such that recipients can follow and understand them without delay;
– its dialogical character: syntactic structures are used in turns at talk that are jointly achieved; they are monitored from the outset by co-interlocutors and they are open to co-construction; and
– its use of constructions: these partly fixed and partly open structures (in the sense of recent models of usage-based *construction grammar*; see below) allow recipients to respond without delay after a prior speaker's turn completion.

All the above models will prove relevant in the following review of interactional linguistic research on sentences, clauses, and phrases in diverse languages.

---

[5] To our knowledge, verb-first languages (VSO) have not been analyzed in an interactional linguistic framework.
[6] See also Tanaka (e.g., 2000a), Kim (e.g., 2001), Steensig (2001), Hayashi (e.g., 2004a), and Couper-Kuhlen and Ono (2007b).

1.3 Sentences, Clauses, and Phrases As Emergent Constructions

It was C. Goodwin who first advocated a view of the "sentence" as emerging in the real time of conversation (1979:97–8). But in a somewhat different sense, sentences – as well as clauses and phrases – are also viewed as emergent in Hopper's understanding of "emergent" grammar. In contrast to traditional *a priori* grammar, which postulates a pre-existing system of grammatical categories along with rules for combining their members into well-formed sentences, Hopper thinks of grammar as "emergent," i.e., "epiphenomenal to the ongoing creation of new combinations of forms in interactive encounters" (2011:26). By this he means that language does not have fixed structures, but speakers engage in "structuration" (see also Linell 1998:59–60): they build on structures previously heard and used, modify them, reconfigure them, and re-use them, always in slightly different ways and in adaptation to the situation at hand. In this way, speakers create and re-create structures, constructions, and grammar. Emergent grammar on this understanding is an online phenomenon (Auer and Pfänder 2011:14).

To see how constructions are structured and re-structured on concrete occasions of use, consider the following example. Doris and Angela are talking about a woman named Sam (".." and "..." denote pauses):

(6.1)   "Sam" (Hopper 2011:31) (adapted)
```
1   Doris:    ... Sam has been,
2             .. has taken such an interest in this retirement bit.
3             .. (H) ... That it-
4             .. it really surprises me.
5   Angela:   .. Well she's begun to listen.
6   Doris:    .. Yes she has.
```

In lines 1 and 2, Doris produces a possibly complete TCU that ends with final falling pitch (the self-repair is not relevant for the argument here). In this construction, *such a/n* is deployed as an intensifier in the single-clause evaluative utterance *Sam has taken such an interest in this retirement bit*. However, when Angela does not respond (line 3), Doris continues her turn and retrospectively integrates the continuation into a biclausal utterance *Sam has taken such an interest in this retirement bit that it really surprises me*. In other words, as a reaction to Angela's lack of response, Doris transforms her first construction into a second, more complex one. This second construction was not planned from the outset but is a result of her online analysis of what is going on: the construction of her sentence is adapted to this local contingency. Put differently, it is interactionally accomplished.[7]

---

[7] See Helasvuo (2001a, 2001b) for an analysis of clauses and noun phrases in Finnish as emergent constructions.

1. Analyzing Sentences, Clauses, and Phrases in Talk-in-interaction 365

Adopting a usage-based notion of grammar[8] (Bybee 2006, 2010) as advocated by, for instance, Hopper (1987, 1988, 1998, 2011), Auer (2005a, 2006b), and Fox and Thompson (2007), we can conceive of sentences, clauses, and phrases in spoken interaction as emergent in another sense: they are the products of sedimented routines; in the case of example (6.1), Doris' clause combination can be seen as the online product of two sedimented routines.[9]

> Temporality and projection are essential components of emergent grammar. In this view, sentences, clauses, and phrases are emergent products of sedimented and shared routines for organizing projection in interaction. They have open as well as fixed components, and are produced incrementally, in real time. They are constantly being re-analyzed and adapted to the contingencies and exigencies of the ongoing interaction.

1.4 Cross-linguistic Evidence for the Interactional Relevance of the Clause

It is participants' grammatical and pragmatic competence that allows them to use sentences, clauses, and phrases as formats or gestalts in the accomplishment and recognition of turns at talk. However, these units are constructed differently in different languages. In this section we examine research that has explored the interactional relevance of the clause (or simple sentence) cross-linguistically. Similar arguments could be made for certain types of complex sentences and for phrases, although to our knowledge this has not yet been done cross-linguistically.[10]

Comparing data from English and Japanese, Thompson and Couper-Kuhlen argue that the clause is mobilized by participants both for recognizing the possible completion of a turn and for projecting what social action is being accomplished with it. Extending a claim made for Japanese (Tanaka 1999) to all languages, they write: "The clause, then, with its crucial predicate, appears to be a unit which facilitates the monitoring of talk for social actions" (2005:812).[11]

In order to warrant the claim that (simple) sentences and clauses are oriented to by participants in interaction, researchers have pointed to the placement of

---

[8] A "usage-based" model views grammar as "the cognitive organization of one's experience with language" (Bybee 2010:8–9).
[9] A question in debate is how prior instances of constructions are represented in the mind: "as concrete utterances remembered in their individual shape, or as more or less abstract patterns filtered out of this prior experience?" (Auer and Pfänder 2011:9).
[10] See, however, Laury and Ono (2014), who compare clause combining in Finnish and Japanese conversation.
[11] Other units that do not consist of clauses themselves are often "constructed *with reference to* a nearby verb or predicate" (p. 812, n. 6, emphasis in the original).

responses, to co-constructions or collaborative turn completions, and to turn expansions (Selting 1995b; Thompson and Couper-Kuhlen 2005; Lindström 2006). As we shall see, all these interactional phenomena are organized around the clause, although the ways that clauses are built and the types of grammatical projection they enable vary significantly from language to language.[12]

1.4.1 Next-turn Onset

Cross-linguistically, as we have seen, predicates come at different positions in the clause: this means that projections of upcoming transition-relevance places (TRPs) are possible quite early in some languages but are delayed in others (Chapter 2). Nevertheless it is the (possible) final boundary of clause-like units in all these languages that typically signals the moment in time when a next speaker can legitimately come in.

In German, for instance, next-turn onsets are overwhelmingly begun just at or very shortly after the first possible completion of a prior speaker's clause (see also Sacks et al. 1974:721 for examples from English). In the following case, the first possible completion point of Ron's clause is denoted with "#":

(6.2)   "Changing universities" (Selting 1995b:303) (adapted)

```
1 Ron: du könntes auch: öh (--)   nach der zwIschenprüfung
       you could  also  uh         after the intermediate-exam
       you could also uh           after the intermediate exam

       n die ↑UNI       noch mal wEchseln # fü[r die (prüfung);
       the university   again    change      for the ((final)) exam
       change the university again           for the final exam
2 Ida:                                       [<<f>JAa, aber>
                                              yes   but
3 Ida: das: MÖCHT <<all> ich nich=das> LOHNT sich nich (1.0) für mich;
       I don't want that                it isn't worthwhile    for me
```

Ron's turn begins with a pronominal subject followed by a finite modal auxiliary *könntes* "could", projecting that the clause will not be complete until an accompanying main verb is produced. Ida's response begins shortly after Ron has delivered this component: *wechseln* "change", i.e., at the first possible completion point of his clause. Note that Ida's turn inadvertently ends up in overlap with Ron's *für die Prüfung* "for the final exam", a de-bracketed element he has added on as an increment (Chapter 2 §4).

---

[12] The centrality of the clause as the basic unit of interaction universally is currently being debated. Evidence is accumulating that in some languages, e.g., Mandarin, the phrase may be more important (Tao 1996), while in others, e.g., Nuuchahnulth, it may be larger units composed of multiple predications (Nakayama 2002): see also Laury et al. (Forthcoming) and Thompson (Forthcoming).

1. Analyzing Sentences, Clauses, and Phrases in Talk-in-interaction 367

In an early projection language like German, insertions into clauses and internal repairs do not erase participants' orientation toward possible completion, but only suspend the expectation of continuation and completion. For instance:

(6.3) "Party" (Selting 1995b:304) (adapted)

```
1  Ron: EInen: auftritt hatten wir auch zum beispiel auf: ähm
         one show had we ((=R and his band)) also for example at uhm
         one show we ((=R and his band)) had for example at uhm
         auf der fete vom:    (--)    kulTUR (0.9)
         at the party of-the (MASC) ((first part of the name of the
                                          cultural summer festival))
         at the party of the         ((first part of the name of the cultural summer
                                          festival))
2  Nat: SOMmer;
         summer (MASC)
         ((second part of the name of the cultural summer festival))
3  Ron: <<l, all> kulTURsommer ja.
                  cultural-summer yes
                  ((suggested name)) yes
4         <<l, all> nEe=nIch>=
                  no    not
5         =SOMmer heiß_das NICH;
           it is not called summer
6         kul <<all>vonner (FEM)> kultureTAge;=
           cul         of-the (FEM) cultural-floor
           cul         of the ((name of the cultural summer festival))
7         =die h[am
           they have
8  Nat:        [ach; hm,
                oh   hm
9         (--)
10 Nat: kul[tur()
         culture()
11 Ron:    [fete hIer gemacht ((räuspert sich)) im: im zenTRALbereich.
            party here made ((clears throat)) in-the in-the central-area
            had a party here      ((clears throat))   in   in the central area
12 Nat: hm,
```

Despite all the trouble he encounters in delivering this turn, Ron pursues the construction and completion of two clauses here: *einen auftritt hatten wir auch zum beispiel auf der fete von der kulturetage* "one show we also had for example at the party of the cultural summer festival" and *die haben fete hier gemacht im zentralbereich* "they had a party here in the central area". Apart from Nat's collaborative prompt in line 2, her next-turn responses in lines 8 and 12 do not come until Ron has completed these two clauses in lines 6 and 11.

In an early projection language like German, moreover, speakers claim a legitimate right to complete projected clauses. In the case of a competitive incoming, they can be observed to compete for the floor in order to end the projected clause. For example:

(6.4)   "It will be over one day" (Selting 1995b:305) (adapted)
```
1   Ron:   un ich dEnke das wird (-) [<<cresc>irgdnwann>
           and I think  it  will                one-day
           and I think it will                  one day
2   Ida:                              [         ja; sOlange
                                                yeah that long

    Ron:   [<<f> vorBEI sein;> ne,]
           over      be       you know
           be over            you know
    Ida:   [    BRAUCHS du ja] auch gar nich mehr.
           need      you PART PART  not any more
           you don't need any more

3   Ron:   hm,
```

When Ida comes in in the middle of Ron's clause, he increases his volume (notated as *crescendo* and *forte*) and continues his turn until the end of the clause. He thus fights for the legitimate right to complete the unit and turn (French and Local 1983; see also Chapter 2 §5.1).[13]

In a delayed projection language like Japanese, however, this type of behavior has not been reported. Nevertheless, participants appear to orient to predicates (and thus to clauses) as projecting possible TRPs, especially when they are marked as "final" predicates by the presence of utterance-final elements such as particles, nominalizers, and copulas (Tanaka 2000a:21ff.). Together, the predicate and the utterance-final elements signal turn completion. (See also Fox et al. 1996; Tanaka 1999, 2000a; Hayashi 2003, 2004a; and Chapter 2.) Here is an example where we can observe this happening:[14]

---

[13] Note that projection is not the same as determination: projected constructions can, of course, be broken off, resulting in fragments, or changed, yielding, e.g., *apokoinu* or pivot constructions (see also Auer 2000a, 2005a; and below).

[14] For a further example see line 3 in example (B.8) (Online-Chapter B).

(6.5)   "Yōko" (Tanaka 1999:116) (adapted)
((B is reporting to F about his wife Yōko, who went to a beach the previous day.))

```
1   -> B:  Mata jyūni ji   goro kara itta ttsu no ne:=
           again 12 o'clock about from went say  FP FP
           ((She)) says ((she)) went out again from about 12 o'clock

2             [Yōko     ga (.) 'N
              [((name)) NOM   yeah
              [Yōko did, yeah
              ((post-predicate addition))

           =[
3      F:   ['N ( )
            [Yeah ...
```

In line 1 B produces a syntactically complete utterance with a predicate component *itta ttsu* marked as final by the particles *no ne* (in boldface); the subject is left unexpressed, because Yōko is already being talked about. It is at this point that speaker F comes in with a receipt of the news (line 3), inadvertently overlapping an appended specification of the subject *Yōko ga*, which B produces in post-completion (Tanaka 1999:116). Crucially, however, the next speaker has timed her incoming in relation to the final predicate component of the prior turn.

1.4.2 Co-construction or Joint Utterance Completion

Participants also orient to the clause as a unit in co-constructing utterances: they add either the second clausal component of a multi-clausal unit or the last word or two of a monoclausal unit (Thompson and Couper-Kuhlen 2005:822). For this, they rely on their knowledge of clausal formats.

While in English early projection allows, for instance, a first speaker's "if" clause to be completed by a second speaker's "then" clause (Lerner 1996a) and/or a second speaker to provide the last words or phrases of a projected simple clause, in Japanese, due to its late projectability, co-construction is typically delayed. Most frequently, Japanese co-constructing second speakers supply only the terminal element of an emerging monoclausal unit, as in this example:

(6.6)   "Phones" (Hayashi 1999:479) (adapted)
```
1   H:  asoko o:: (0.2) teteteto orite[itta]ra shoomen ni:,=
        there o               go.down:if       front   in
        If you go down there, in front of you,

2   K:                                 [u:n]
                                       Uh huh.

3   K:  =u:n.
        Uh huh.
```

```
4    H:   denwa ga- ano mi [dori] no denwa ga:[:]
          phone SB  uhm  green    LK  phone SB
          Phones, uhm, green phones
5->  K:                   [aru.]               [a]ru aru.
                          exist                exist exist
                          are there.           are there, are there.
```

In line 5, K produces the late, yet predictable, predicate that completes the emergent clause.

1.4.3 Extensions of Sentences and Clauses

When speakers extend their turn after the possible completion of a TCU, they again orient to the clause but differently in different languages. Schegloff (2001:9) found that 85 percent of the increments he analyzed were added to host turns that were clauses. Thompson and Couper-Kuhlen note that increments in English are regularly phrases that appear elsewhere in the final position of a clausal TCU (2005:495). Here is an example:

(6.7)   "By any chance-1" (Thompson and Couper-Kuhlen 2005:495) (adapted)
```
2       Guy:    Have you got (.) uh: Seacliffs phone number?h
3               (1.1)
4  ->   Guy:    by any chance?
```

The phrase *by any chance*, produced here as an increment to a turn initially treated as complete, can occur elsewhere as part of a single clausal TCU:

(6.8)   "By any chance-2" (Thompson and Couper-Kuhlen 2005:496) (adapted)
```
1 ->   Guy:    Is Cliff dow:n by any chance?
2              =do you know?
```

In Japanese, there are very few, if any, grammatical formats in which such phrases occur at the end of clauses; adverbials and noun phrases (NPs) accompanying predicates occur instead early in the clause (Thompson and Couper-Kuhlen 2005:496). If Japanese speakers need to extend their clause for turn expansion, they are more likely to make an NP explicit that could have appeared early in the clause but did not. This can be seen in the next example:

(6.9)   "Australia" (Thompson and Couper-Kuhlen 2005:496) (adapted)
((Aki is the name of a female friend, "-chan" a diminutive suffix.))
```
1      R:    soshitara @ oo- asoko_i ikanakatta - n   da   tte.
             then        Au- there   go:not:PAST  NZR COP  I.hear
             I hear ((she)) didn't go ((to)) Au- there then
```

1. Analyzing Sentences, Clauses, and Phrases in Talk-in-interaction   371

```
2   ->  R:   [oosutora]ria; akichan
             Australia
             Australia           Aki
3       H:   [doko e?   ]
             where to
             to where?
```

After line 1, which is grammatically, prosodically, and interactionally possibly complete, speaker R continues her turn by making the unspecified/unexpressed referents from line 1 explicit (line 2). *Oosutoraria* "Australia" specifies *asoko*; *Akichan* supplies the missing subject in line 1.[15] However, neither *Oosutoraria* nor *Akichan* are phrases that would be found in the final position of a clause in Japanese; instead, they would normally precede the verb *ikanakattan* "didn't go" and other utterance-final elements.

> Interlocutors provide evidence for the reality and relevance of the patterns that linguists call *clauses* (simple sentences) by using them to gauge when a next turn is due, to jointly construct an ongoing turn with their co-participant, and to extend a turn at talk beyond its possible completion. Although clausal structure varies from language to language, the interactional practices used are precisely the ones allowed by the clausal grammatical formats of a given language (Thompson and Couper-Kuhlen 2005:828).

1.5 Packaging of Sentences, Clauses, and Phrases

How are sentences, clauses, and phrases packaged prosodically as interactionally relevant entities? Research on English and Finnish conversation has found that as a rule the clause *core*, consisting of the predicate and its "obligatory" accompaniments, is produced within a single intonation unit (Helasvuo 2001b:145–6), while peripheral elements, or adjuncts, may occur in separate intonation units. This suggests that the syntactic bonding among clausal constituents is closest in the clause core. If, exceptionally, an argument is packaged in a separate intonation unit, it is likely to be an object, which indicates that the bond between the subject and the predicate is stronger than that between the predicate and the object (Helasvuo 2001a:33).

The prosodic packaging of syntactic units is closely related to action formation: in many cases, a prosodically packaged syntactic unit conveys a single action or identifiable component of an action. In German, for instance, the separate

---

[15] Recall that core arguments do not need to be expressed in Japanese if it is clear from the context what they are (see also Chapter 2 §1.1).

packaging of syntactic units such as phrases or single words in their own separate intonation phrases, with their own accented syllable and thus focused information, is often used to render these units separate actions or action components. As a case in point, consider the German adverbial *genau* "precisely": this word may be formatted at the beginning of a TCU either as a prosodically separate unit for explicit confirmation (example (6.10)) or as prosodically integrated into a neighboring clause or phrase (example (6.11)):

(6.10)   Prosodically separate adverbial (Selting 1995b:307–8) (adapted)

```
Ida:  geNAU;      da musst ich ARbeiten;
      precisely   then must I  work
      precisely   then I had to work
```

(6.11)   Prosodically integrated adverbial (Selting 1995b:307–8) (adapted)

```
Ida:  genau       da    musst ich ARbeiten und dann: war ich noch auf
      precisely   then  must I  work       and then  was I  PART to
      ner Anderen fete eingeladen.
      another party invited
      precisely then I had to work and for later I was invited to another party
```

In example (6.10), the prosodic packaging in a separate intonation phrase makes *genau* "precisely" interpretable as a separate confirmation token, whereas in example (6.11) the packaging of the same item as part of the following intonation phrase makes it interpretable as an initial modifier of the temporal adverbial *da* ("then") at the beginning of the following sentence. While example (6.10) is formatted to convey two actions, example (6.11) suggests the interpretation of a single action.[16]

Likewise, at the end of simple sentences, phrases may be formatted as continued and thus prosodically integrated parts of prior possible sentences or clauses (example (6.12)), or as prosodically separate extensions, so-called "afterthoughts" (example (6.13)). Compare the following examples:

(6.12)   Prosodically integrated extension (Selting 1995b:308) (adapted)

```
1 Lea:  also aKUT war das dadurch        dass ich so ne komische LEHrerin
        well acute was it through-this that I    such a funny   teacher
        well it was acute because I had such a funny teacher
->      hinten drin sitzen hatte beim schülerinformationstach; ne,
        at the back sitting had at Pupils'-Information-Day    you know
        sitting at the back of my class at Pupils' Information Day you know
2 Eli:  hmhm,
```

---

[16] Similarly, left dislocations and other constructions serving as resources at the beginning of turns and TCUs may also be packaged prosodically as either integrated into or separate from the clause that follows them (see §4 below and Pekarek Doehler et al. 2015).

Here, we see a complex sentence combining a main clause ending in the cataphoric pro-form *dadurch* (*also aKUT war das dadurch*, literally "well acute was it through this"), plus a following subordinate clause ending with a finite verb form (*dass ich so ne komische LEHrerin hinten drin sitzen hatte*, literally "that I such a funny teacher at the back of my class sitting had"), plus a following extension (*beim schülerinformationstach* "at Pupils' Information Day"), followed by a final discourse particle (*ne*, "you know"). The entire complex sentence up to the final discourse particle is packaged as a single prosodic unit. Each clause has its own primary accent and the entire prosodic unit ends with mid-falling final pitch.

But syntactic phrases and clauses can also be added on to the end of prior sentences and clauses, and packaged in their own intonation phrases. In the following extract, Eli is explaining why her students are different from Lea's:

(6.13) Prosodically separate extension (Selting 1995b:308–9) (adapted)

```
1      Eli:   ich hAb mir      keine geDANken darüber gemacht;
              I   have myself no    thoughts       about-it made
              I didn't think about it
2      Lea:   hm,
3      Eli:   zumAl        ich auch ÜBERwiegend studenten hab die: (2.5)
              the-more-so-as I also mostly      students have who
              especially since I mostly have students who
              die also schon !ÄL!ter sind;
              who PART already older   are
              who are already older
4      Eli:   d[ie:: [schn ein studium  !A:B!geschlossen ha[m;
              who    already one degree finished          have
              who have already finished one degree
5      Lea:   [hm,                                           [hm,
6      Cis:          [hm,
7   -> Eli:   **oder: faMI:lie habm;**
              or     family    have
              or have family
8      Eli:   im beRU:F     stehn;
              in employment are
              are working
9      Lea:   hm,
```

In example (6.13), lines 1–7 altogether contain five clauses that constitute a complex sentence. Line 1 is a main clause packaged in its own intonation phrase; line 3 is a subordinate clause ending with the finite verb form (*zumAl ich auch ÜBERwiegend studenten hab* "the more so as I mostly students have"), which is immediately extended by a relative clause specifying the NP, *studenten* "students".[17] In line 4, Eli adds another relative clause packaged in its own intonation phrase: *die:: schn ein studium !AB!geschlossen ham* "who already one degree finished have". This relative clause is extended in line 7 through an additional verb phrase: *oder: faMIlie habm* "or family have", again packaged in its own separate intonation phrase. In principle, the clauses in lines 4 and 7 could have been phrased as a single, prosodically integrated unit: *die:: schn ein studium !AB! geschlossen ham oder: faMIlie habm* "who already one degree finished have or family have". Yet, in the extract given, the two clauses are delivered "incrementally". This way, each clause can be given its own accented syllable and focused information: each is then hearable as a separate action component.

> At the beginning as well as at the end of sentences and clauses, prosodic packaging determines whether items are produced and made hearable as parts of the clause or as separate clauses or phrases of their own. Separate intonational packaging contributes to the accomplishment and interpretation of separate actions or action components.[18] Yet we do not only rely on prosody for the interpretation of syntactic units as TCUs and therefore actions: it is the interplay of prosody and syntax, the fulfilling of context-sensitive projections within the sequential context, that is relevant (Selting 2001a:252).

2. Internal Organization of Clauses

The internal organization of clauses, i.e., their morpho-syntax, has often been described in terms of "word" order or constituent order. For interactional linguists, the questions are: What determines the order of constituents in a given TCU? How is the syntax of clauses related to the tasks that need addressing within TCUs? The following section will show how the topological fields of sentences and clauses in talk-in-interaction (see §1.2 above) are used for accomplishing routine tasks within the TCU. The internal flexibility of clauses in talk manifests itself through practices, for example, for the construction of pivots, also called *apokoinou* constructions, and for the insertion of parentheticals and other embedded clauses. We will concentrate here on pivots; for parentheticals, see Chapter 2 §1.4. In concluding this section, we deal with the expression of tense in finite clauses

---

[17] Eli leaves a pause of 2.5 seconds after the relative pronoun, but then resumes and completes it by adding *die also schon !ÄL!ter sind* "who PART already older are" without a prosodic break.
[18] This is not to deny that the production of talk in general – and of sentences, clauses, and phrases in particular – is embedded in multimodal interaction and that, consequently, the analysis of these units in face-to-face interaction needs to incorporate the description of the visible aspects of the interaction as well. This is where we expect future work to make new contributions.

as an interactional resource for English speakers and consider how *not* expressing tense in independent infinitive constructions can also be a resource for constructing TCUs and implementing actions.

2.1 Word Order

As we have seen, the order of constituents in clauses has repercussions for the projectability of possible clause completion. However, even when a language shows relatively fixed basic word order patterns in written language, in spoken interaction the order of constituents is always adapted to the exigencies of verbal interaction (Ford and Mori 1994).

It is most plausible to assume that the order of words and constituents in clauses has developed to what it is now because – given other typological features of the language or language type – this order has proved to be useful in carrying out recurrent tasks in social interaction. Indeed, there seems to be a clear relationship between the tasks to be dealt with in TCUs and the linguistic elements that occupy structural positions in the clauses that constitute them. This has been shown in detail for languages such as German and Swedish, where the structural organization of TCUs is nicely mirrored by the structural organization of clauses (see below).

According to Schegloff (1996b), the tasks to be dealt with in TCUs include the following:

i. *pre-beginning* – projecting the onset of talk (p. 92);
ii. *beginning* – starting a TCU with a recognizable beginning (p. 77);
iii. *TCU ending* – finishing a TCU with a recognizable syntactic, prosodic, and action/pragmatic completion (p. 83), including:

   a. *pre(possible) completion* – making the beginning of the transition (relevance) space recognizable before possible completion (p. 84); and
   b. *post(possible) completion* – providing for re-completion of the TCU via increments and "post-completion stance markers" (p. 92).

Lindström (2006) presents a schematic diagram of the structural organization of the TCU as shown in Figure 6.3.

Possible turn			
Pre-segment, link to prior	TCU core		Post-segment, link to next
^	Beginning	(Pre) Completion	^
Yeah, so	I say that would bum you out then,		hunh

Figure 6.3 Structural organization of a TCU (Lindström 2006:83)

This diagram shows a possible turn as being organized around a TCU core, which is optionally preceded and followed by pre-segments and post-segments, respectively. The TCU core itself consists of a beginning segment and a completion segment, the latter including a pre-completion. How is such structure realized in different languages?

2.1.1 English and Swedish with Relatively Fixed SVO

English is a language with relatively fixed SVO order in clauses: the verb (complex) comes after the subject of the clause in most cases. This can be seen in the following example, arranged to show clause structure more clearly:

(6.14) "A Tree's Life" (Thompson and Couper-Kuhlen 2005:813) (adapted)

			Subj. NP	Verb (complex)	Prep. Phrase
12	Alice:	when	Ron	gets home	from wor=k,
13			...I	wanna spend time	with Ro=n,
14		because	Ron...	usually doesn't get home	till (@)nine or ten.
15	Mary:	...yeah.			
16	Alice:	unlike Tim	he	has to w=ork	for every little dime
					that he makes.

These clauses begin with a subject NP followed by a verb (complex) and other phrases, in this case prepositional phrases, or objects, often made relevant by the verb. The clauses may be preceded by coordinating conjunctions such as *and* or *or*, or by subordinating conjunctions such as *when* or *because*, as well as by other elements such as *unlike Tim*, or adverbials such as *however* or *frankly*. In each case the clause could be extended by another phrase. For instance, *in the evening* could easily be added to the end of lines 12, 13, or 14. Line 16 shows an extension of the NP *every little dime* by the relative clause *that he makes*. As this example shows, with certain prosodic changes, speakers of English can lengthen their clauses with more words, without making such prolongations recognizable as extensions for the recipients.

Swedish is another language with relatively fixed constituent order, referred to as "verb-second" or XVO order: this means that virtually any constituent can come first but the finite verb must follow next. Lindström argues that the structure of a TCU as shown in Figure 6.3 above is matched by the topological word order fields of expanded clauses in Swedish. He represents the latter as shown in Figure 6.4 (see next page).

According to this representation, the inner clausal frame consists of a front field, a middle field, and an end field. The inner clause can be extended by a pre-front field and/or a post-end field. When the topological fields are filled, they are often recognizable as distinct linguistic segments designed for each particular field. For

2. Internal Organization of Clauses

Pre-front field	Expanded clause					Post-end field
	Inner clausal frame					
	Front field	Middle field			End field	
	Clausal base	Finite	Subject	Adverb	Infinite Nominal Adverb	
Ja,	i morgon	kan	hon	inte	träffa Mats där,	eller hur?
Yes,	tomorrow	can	she	not	meet Matt there,	right?
Idiomatic English: *'Yes, she cannot meet Matt there tomorrow, right?'*						

Figure 6.4 Topological word order fields of expanded clauses in Swedish (Lindström 2006:85)

instance, the following types of pre-segments are identified as occurring in the syntactically isolated pre-front field of the clause (2006:86ff.):

i. *pre-starts* such as conjunctions, discourse particles, terms of address – these are not integrated as constituents into the clause (e.g., *hördu* in Swedish, "listen, you know");
ii. optional *appositionals* such as conjunctional or stance-indexing adverbs, which may be used as either pre-segments or as syntactically integrated constituents of the clause (e.g., *i varje fall* "in any case, anyway"); and
iii. other TCU-framing devices such as question frames, left dislocations, and certain responsive formats that are syntactically separate but closely bound to the inner clause that is projected to follow (e.g., *jag undrar* "I wonder").

These elements accomplish pre-beginning tasks in the TCU.

In contrast to the pre-beginning, the beginning of a TCU contribution normally coincides with the start of the front field of a clause; in Swedish this is most frequently the subject of the clause or a question word. The distinction between pre-segments in the pre-front field and integral beginnings of the syntactic core of the TCU in the front field is warranted by two observations: first, pre-segments are not syntactically integrated into the core TCU clause, and second, in recycling the beginning of TCUs, pre-segments are not recycled, but the beginnings of core TCU clauses are (2006:93).

As in English, in Swedish a sentence or clause is possibly syntactically complete when its structural projections are fulfilled, i.e., when grammatically obligatory and pragmatically necessary complements of the finite verb have been produced in the end field. The pre-completion of the end field is a point to which recipients orient in placing continuers, launching collaborative completions, and prematurely starting next turns (2006:98).

The post-end field is constituted by post-possible completion segments, added on with or without a prosodic break and/or delay. These can be, for instance, syntactically optional phrases fitted to the end field, or delayed extensions or insertables, stance markers, or tag questions (2006:104ff.). This field can be relevant for negotiations over turn transition.

For Swedish, then, the clause can be described as composed of a succession of structural fields that are relevant for the accomplishment of recurrent tasks in TCU organization. As fixed SVO or XVO languages, English and Swedish share the feature that the end of clauses is not clearly demarcated.[19]

2.1.2 German with Mixed SVO/XVO and SOV

Other languages have more clearly defined clause endings, for instance, German, Japanese, Korean, etc. (see also Chapter 2). Let us take a closer look at German, which has been investigated in detail by Auer (1991, 1992a, 1996a, 1996b). In contrast to English and Swedish, German is a mixed verb-second (SVO or XVO) and verb-final (SOV) language: in main clauses, the finite verb comes in second position following another constituent, but non-finite parts of the verb phrase such as participles, separable verb prefixes, and infinitives often occupy clause-final position; in subordinate clauses, even the finite verb is placed in the final position of what Lindström calls the "inner clausal frame" (see Figure 6.4 above). As a result, clauses are more clearly delimited in German than in English or Swedish: there are non-finite components of the verb phrase or finite verbs themselves in the final position of the inner clausal frame whose occurrence marks clause completion. Elements following this are clearly recognizable as postpositioned. German is thus a language displaying possible completion of clauses more clearly than many other languages.

German sentences and clauses are structured by reference to what is called the sentence brace (*Satzklammer*), which is formed by the initial and final parts of the verb phrase or predicate. Its topological fields in speech are represented by Auer (1996b) as shown in Figure 6.5 (see next page).

Sentences and clauses in spoken Standard German can be said to feature a front field, a middle field, and an end field. These positions are defined in relation to the two components of the verb or predicate, the left (initial) and the right (final) sentence brace, which demarcate the fields, but do not themselves belong to any of the fields. The front field is defined as the field before the initial part of the verb. It can only be occupied by a single constituent: either the subject or a topicalized constituent from the middle field that changes

---

[19] Another language with less clearly marked syntactic completion is Finnish, which has been described as a language with free or discourse functional word order (Helasvuo 2001a:31). In Finnish, the subject need not be overtly expressed and the order of subject and verb may be deployed for interactional meaning. Finnish can use word order as a resource to cue discourse categories such as perspective or point of view, e.g., in agreeing second assessments. This contrasts with other languages, for instance English, where verb-initial word order is used for constructing grammatical distinctions such as declaratives versus interrogatives and imperatives (Hakulinen and Sorjonen 2009).

2. Internal Organization of Clauses 379

natürlich *of course*	allein *alone*	kann *can*	man's nicht *one it not*	schaffen *make*	
mich hat besonders angesprochen *me has particularly pleased*	es *it*	geht *is*	auch um die Zusammenarbeit *also a question of collaboration*		in den Gruppen *in the teams*
wenn ich Dich da gehabt hätte *if I had had you there*	ich *I*	hätt *had*		getobt *been furious*	
pre-front field	**front field**	*left brace*	**middle field**	*right brace*	**end field**

Figure 6.5 Diagrammatic representation of the sentence brace in spoken German (adapted from Auer 1996b:296)

places with the front field constituent.[20] The middle field is the field between the initial and the final parts of the verb. The end field is the field after the final part of the verb. It can be filled by a variety of elements: for example, subordinate clauses, right dislocations, appositionals (e.g., *übrigens* "by the way"), extrapositions, incremented insertables, and afterthoughts (Auer 1996a; see also 1991, 1992a).[21] In addition, speakers make use of a pre-front field before the front field. Typical constructions in the pre-front field are, for example, adverbials (*nämlich* "namely", *natürlich* "obviously", *nur* "only", etc.),[22] subordinate clauses, left dislocations and hanging topics (see below), conjunctions, address terms, and attention-getters (Auer 1996b). While pre-front field elements are concerned with orienting to and responding to the prior turn, end field elements and post-end field elements, such as tag questions like *ne*, or *nicht wahr?* (not shown in Figure 6.5), are concerned with organizing the transition to the next turn.

---

[20] Topicalization is the fronting of constituents from their canonical middle field position to the front field for reasons of focusing. Since there can only be one constituent in the front field, the original front field constituent, normally the subject of the clause, can be said metaphorically to "swap places" with the topicalized constituent and is realized in the middle field.

[21] These elements basically correspond to the increment types presented in Chapter 2 §4.

[22] See Deppermann and Helmer (2013) on the use of *also* "so" in pre-front field position at turn beginnings as a practice for explicating presumably shared inferences from the partner's prior turn, and on the use of turn-initial *dann* "then" in front field position as a practice either for formulating a unilateral inference from the partner's prior turn or for presenting a next action as a consequence from the partner's preceding action.

> Just as there are tasks to be accomplished prior to the beginning of a TCU core and after it, so there are specific syntactic positions – topological fields – designed for particular linguistic elements and practices that accomplish these tasks.[23] In Swedish and German, the structural positions for the organization of a TCU are mirrored by matching topological fields in the linear organization of spoken clauses and sentences.

The structuring of the clause in terms of topological fields progressing from the front field constituent through the middle field toward the end field implies that, upon beginning a clause, both speaker and recipients know roughly what it will take for the clause to come to possible completion. The number of middle field and/or end field constituents is determined by the lexically conditioned kind and number of obligatory objects or verb complements. The syntactic structure of sentences and clauses thus functions as a guide along the path of sentence or clause progression in TCUs. The presence of final parts of the predicate in clause-final position in German enhances the recognizability of possible sentence and clause completion points (for the relevance of syntactic structure for projection see Chapter 2 §2).

Interestingly, as Lindström (2006) observes, an investigation of grammatical constructions from this perspective suggests a re-analysis of some of the structures of traditional grammar. Constructions such as *I mean* or *ich finde/ich denke* "I find/I think" in German, etc., which have traditionally been analyzed as the main clause of a complex sentence, often occur in the pre-beginning of TCUs, with clauses following in the core TCU (see also Thompson and Mulac (1991a) and Kärkkäinen (2003) for English constructions with *I think*). Interactionally, the clause in the core TCU is more important than what has conventionally been called the main clause (see also Chapter 7 §4.1.1). Thus, when traditional grammar classifies the pre-beginning segments as main clauses and the core TCU clauses as subordinate clauses, this analysis seems odd from an interactional linguistic point of view. Interactionally more adequate is the analysis of pre-beginning segments as constituents or constructions suitable for the pre-front field. Likewise, if the same constructions are used following the TCU core, now in their inverted syntactic form (*finde ich/denke ich* "find I/think I" in German or *tycker ja* "think I" in Swedish), they are deployed in post-end position, just like the tags *weißt du?*, *nicht wahr?*, or *ne?* (variants of "you know") in German. Rather than classifying them as post-positioned main clauses, their re-analysis as post-end field segments or constructions suitable

---

[23] The topological field model has been shown to be especially relevant for northern Germanic languages; however, there is no evidence to date that it is similarly relevant for, say, Mandarin, Japanese, or many native American languages (Sandra A. Thompson, personal communication).

2. *Internal Organization of Clauses*

for the accomplishment of post-completion is interactionally more appropriate (Lindström 2006:107ff.).

2.2 *Pivots*

The adaptation of word order to the tasks to be solved in interaction gives rise to constructions specific to spoken language, ones that are looked upon as "non-standard" in traditional grammar books. One such construction is the pivot or *apokoinou* construction. Without naming it as such, Sacks (1992b) gives an example of what is today called a pivot construction in one of his 1969 lectures:

(6.15) "Mariposa" (Sacks 1992b:145–6) (adapted)
```
1   B:   We were in northern California, up- (0.2) weh(hhh)- (0.4) way up
2        in the mountains too.
3        (0.4)
4   A:   Oh well we went up there oh:: about thr- 'hh I'd say about three
5        weeks ago we was up at Maripo:sa,
```

Sacks analyzes A's turn (lines 4–5) as doing correction but at the same time as producing a single sentence that does the business of two sentences.[24] Speaker A first produces the clause *we went up there about three weeks ago*, but then uses the segment *about three weeks ago* to begin another clause: *about three weeks ago we was up at Mariposa*.

Schegloff (1979:275–6) describes pivot elements as a special case of repair initiation. Here is one of his examples:

(6.16) "Middle one" (Schegloff 1979:276) (adapted)
((M is looking at a picture of V and his family.))
```
1   M:   I saw it but I never looked you know at did-eh-deh-deh-middle one
2        looks just like,
```

In this case, the phrase *the middle one* is part of the first clause: *I never looked at the middle one*, but then is used as the beginning of a new clause: *the middle one looks just like* ... Schegloff conceives of *the middle one* as a "shifter," belonging both to the prior and to the next syntactic clause. In retrospect, the unit comes off as re-structured, because the shifter or pivot is heard as the initiation of repair.

Elsewhere, pivots have been defined differently, largely due to a consideration of their prosodic properties. In the following, given space considerations, we restrict

---

[24] This is what Sacks (1992b) says: "if, within the first sentence of your utterance you start to do a correction, whatever sort of correction, you're still within that sentence. If you can produce such a correction as indicates that, from the correction on, now the hearer needs to remonitor for sentence completion, then what you can do is produce almost a complete sentence and start a correction that allows you to do another complete sentence. ... You end up having in effect done two sentences" (p. 146).

our discussion to pivots that are produced in one intonation phrase, excluding cases with prosodic breaks between any of the three parts.

2.2.1 Pivots in German, English, and Swedish

The first papers to look systematically at pivots – or at *apokoinou* constructions, as they have been called in linguistic and rhetorical research – were on so-called "double-bind sentence structures", with most examples coming from Dutch (Franck 1985) and German (Scheutz 1992, 2005). Scheutz refers to the pivot elements as A, B, and C: both A plus B and B plus C construct syntactically possible clauses, but all three together, delivered in a single intonation phrase, yield a syntactic structure that does not conform to the rules of standard written German. Yet these pivots are not uncommon in spoken German. They are built highly systematically and they are deployed for specific functions in talk-in-interaction. Despite some formal flexibility, Scheutz identifies three basic types of pivot construction in spoken (Austrian) German.

i. Type 1: true mirror-image construction

(6.17)   "Something awful" (extract from Scheutz 2005:105)
```
des is     was FURCHTbares    is des.
that is    something AWful    is that.
That's     terrible           is that.
A          B                  C
```

B is the pivot element, A and C are called the initial and final periphery. The peripheral items occur with reversed word order: while part A has X + verb (*des is*), part C has verb + X (*is des*).

ii. Type 2: syntactically less integrated mirror-image construction

(6.18)   "Technically" (extract from Scheutz 2005:108) (adapted)
```
der is halt (-) sagn=wir (-)    handwerklich    is=er net ein=so
he is well (-) say-PL1=we (-)   technically     is=he not a=such
He is, well, let's say,         technically     he's not so [good].
A                               B               C
```

Here, there is an additional particle *halt* in part A, and a parenthetical *sagn=wir* ("let's say") between part A and part B of the construction, separated from the surrounding parts of the construction by pauses. Nevertheless, there is no break in the intonation contour. Rather, the integration of the entire construction in one intonation phrase suggests that it is a single unit. In contrast to the mirror image constructions here, parts A and B together do

2. Internal Organization of Clauses

not form a complete clause; completion is only reached after the entire construction.

iii. Type 3: modified mirror-image construction

(6.19)   "Six years" (extract from Scheutz 2005:109) (adapted)
```
dann bin=i      no     sechs    jahr als verheiratete frau
then am-PP=I    still  six years as a married           woman
Then I spent another   six years as a married woman
A                      B
war=I no      bei   meine eltern.
was=I still   with  my    parents.
I was in my parents' home.
C
```

In this type, the initial and the final parts of the construction are not identical. Nevertheless, the pivot part fulfills the same syntactic function in both syntactic strings and the entire construction is produced in a single intonation phrase. In this example, the initial part A and the final part C are different with respect to their time reference. (For further detail see Scheutz 2005:107ff.)

Some pivots or *apokoinou* are more sedimented than others: mirror-image constructions are the most sedimented and occur most frequently; others are more likely to be heard as self-repairs (Auer and Pfänder 2011:11–12).[25] According to Scheutz, the three types of pivot construction fulfill different functions in talk-in-interaction: while the first two types are used to organize topic, the third type is used for repair.

Norén (2007), in a detailed study of *apokoinou* in Swedish talk-in-interaction, describes pivots as instances of a family of emerging grammatical constructions. He argues that they are a participant's method to address local tasks that arise in the course of utterance production (p. 1). The use and functioning of an *apokoinou* construction in Swedish can be grasped from this extract:

(6.20)   "In the end" (extract from Norén 2007:5–6) (adapted)
((From talk between a pregnant woman (=K) and her gynecologist (=L) at a Swedish maternity health care center during an ultrasound examination. K has remarked before that the child in her uterus moves around less than she expected. Then L continues.))

```
11   L:   >men man ska ju känna< att de
          but you should feel that it
12        rör sej ((beep sound)) (0.4) n↑ån gå:ng
          moves                  (0.4)  once in a
```

---

[25] For more recent analyses of pivot constructions in one variety of spoken German see Betz (2008, 2013); also Clayman and Raymond (2015) for English.

```
13      emellanå[t.]
        while
14  K:          [ja] å d↑e va're men inte
                yes and that's how it was but not
15      >såd↑är<of::ta som ja trodde att >ja
        so          often as I thought that I
16      [skulle< kä]nna¿
        would feel
17  L:  [    ja::  ]
             yes
18  L:  >å sen så blir de< också lugnare på
        and then PRT gets it also calmer at
        and then it also gets calmer in
19      slutet blir de tr↑ängre i magen,=
        end-the gets it narrower in belly-the
        the end it gets narrower in the belly (uterus)
20  K:  =a:¿
        yes
```

The *apokoinou* construction in lines 18–19 is analyzed as responding to the woman's concern that her baby does not kick as much as she had expected. In the first part of the construction, the doctor tries to *reassure* the woman with medical information, stating that usually the baby calms down toward the end of the pregnancy. Having reached the adverbial *på slutet* "at the end", however, the doctor shifts perspective and produces an *explanation* for why the baby calms down near the end of pregnancy (it gets narrower in the uterus) (2007:7). With this *apokoinou* construction then, two actions are accomplished within the same TCU: first the doctor reassures his patient, and then he shifts to an explanation. In general, according to Norén, *apokoinou* constructions in Swedish conversation are used for three main functions: (i) shifting between projects, for example, shifting perspective on some topical aspect (as above); (ii) parenthetic handling of expressions or actions, i.e., to insist, confirm, or focus on expressions or actions; (iii) organizing local communicative projects, i.e., closing, demarcating, and leaving local projects, resuming turn progression, and/or skip-connecting to pending communicative projects (2007:357).[26]

Such pivot constructions have been found to be structured and deployed systematically in a number of languages as resources for dealing with particular tasks in

---

[26] On language-dependent syntactic differences of pivot constructions in Swedish and Finnish see Lindström (2013).

talk-in-interaction. They appear to be an efficient device for accomplishing two actions in one syntactic construction.

Walker (2004a; also 2007) devotes a chapter to the phonetic analysis of TCUs with pivots such as that shown in the following example:

(6.21) "Beautiful bone" (Walker 2004a:172) (also Walker 2007:2219) (adapted)
((Talk has been about colors of dresses that Lottie and Emma have seen on a recent shopping trip.))

```
2   Emm:    but I('d) love the bone[27] was so beautiful the
            pink was exquisite
```

In the TCU in line 2, the pivot *the bone* is both the ending of the preceding and the beginning of a following grammatical construction:

(a) but I('d) love the bone
(b) the bone was so beautiful

Walker interprets pivot constructions in terms of turn formation: the end of one grammatical structure is also used as the beginning of another one. The speaker must thus deploy phonetic resources in order to prevent the recipient from inferring that a point of possible grammatical completion conveying the TRP of a TCU has been reached after (a). This entails avoiding phonetic features that could signal unit or turn completion (e.g., a final pitch configuration and/or slowing down) and moving directly into the second part of the construction, without pause or delay. Phonetically, then, pivots are presented as cohesively fitted both to the prior and to the upcoming part of the construction (Walker 2004a:197; also 2007:2236).[28]

Pivots in German, English, and Swedish are an interesting variation on clause and TCU construction – one that results from the merging of two clauses into a single construction. Although they are often considered to be non-standard constructions, they exhibit systematic syntactic patterns. Prosodic and phonetic features are deployed to distinguish pivots from repairs: in the case of pivots, speakers package the parts phonetically and prosodically as a single unit. This normally prevents their being heard as repair. However, when the final part is modified in comparison to the initial part of a pivot construction, such as in Scheutz' "modified mirror-image construction", pivot constructions may nevertheless be exploited for doing (inconspicuous) repair. Pivots are deployed as a resource in talk-in-interaction; they are an efficient device for accomplishing more than one action in a TCU. Pivot constructions thus provide powerful evidence for the fundamental flexibility and adaptability of syntax to the exigencies of interaction.

---

[27] "Bone" in this context refers to an off-white color with gray tones.
[28] In this sense the continuation of talk at the end of the pivot is just a special case of continuing talk within a TCU (see Chapter 2 §4.1).

2.2.2 Pivots in French

In French, pivot constructions are reportedly used more frequently than in German or English (Horlacher and Pekarek Doehler 2014:598), and they are also structured differently from those in the languages dealt with so far (Pekarek Doehler 2011a:77–9; Pekarek Doehler and Horlacher 2013; Horlacher and Pekarek Doehler 2014; see also Horlacher 2012; Pekarek Doehler et al. 2015). Horlacher and Pekarek Doehler distinguish the following types of pivots in French:

i. [NP – clause – NP or infinitival VP]
   A   B   C

This type is called a "double dislocation pivot": it represents a highly sedimented or routinized pattern that amalgamates left and right dislocation (Pekarek Doehler and Horlacher 2013:96ff.). One variant can be seen in the following example, where the pivot is shaded in gray:

(6.22)   "Not possible" (Pekarek Doehler 2011a:77)
```
Lae:   ça    c' est pas possible ça.
       DEMᵢ CLIᵢ is  not possible DEMᵢ
       that's not possible
```

In this construction the pivot part (*c'est pas possible*) is a complete clause, featuring a clitic pronoun *ce* (assimilated to *c'*) combined with a copula verb (*est* "is"). The clitic pronoun (*c'*) can be read as having a co-referential argument of the verb in the pre-pivot as well as in the post-pivot parts of the construction. The demonstrative pronoun *ça* ("that") realizes this co-referential argument: it is deployed both prior to the clause, suggesting a left dislocation construction (*ça c'est pas possible*), as well as following the clause, suggesting a right dislocation construction (*c'est pas possible ça*) (see §3 below). The entire construction is produced without a prosodic break, in a single intonation phrase. According to Pekarek Doehler, this construction is a sedimented format for evaluative statements, often strong assessments, occasionally with an undertone of indignation or enthusiasm (2011a:77).

In a variant of this construction type, the post-pivot does not feature an NP but an infinitival verb phrase, as in the following example:

(6.23)   "Critical" (Pekarek Doehler and Horlacher 2013:98) (adapted)
```
8 Cat:   ça    c'    est: difficile d'avoir l'esp- >l'esprit< critique.
         DEMᵢ CLI.Nᵢ is   difficult [to have      DET spirit critical]ᵢ
         it's difficult to be critical
```

While these patterns are recurrently used at the beginning of turns to proffer assessments following some elaboration in the prior turn, another variant of the construction type is deployed for managing reference formulation, in particular for referential adjustment. Here is an example:

(6.24)   "Papers" (Pekarek Doehler 2011a:77–8)
((*Les feuilles* refers to sheets of paper spread out on the table between the participants.))

```
2  Mar:   .hh d'accord (.) eh ben merci? (.)
             o.k.              well thanks
3          euh ça   je veux les prendre les feuilles?
                this_i I  want them_i take  the papers_i
           I want to take the papers
4          (..)
5  Mar:   Voilà.
           there you go
```

Again, the pivot part (*je veux les prendre*) is a complete clause, containing the indexical pronoun *les* "them". And again, together with the co-referential demonstrative pronoun *ça* in the pre-pivot part, the syntax at first suggests a left dislocation construction (*ça je veux les prendre* "this I want to take them"). But then the indexical pronoun *les* ("them") is retrospectively expanded into a co-referential full NP *les feuilles*. Now the clause can also be heard as a right dislocation construction (*je veux les prendre les feuilles* "I want to take them the papers"). In this case then, the pre-pivot and the post-pivot parts of the construction are not identical, although both still extend the indexical pronoun in the clausal part of the construction (see pp. 77–8). Typically, the post-pivot contains a fuller referential expression than the pre-pivot. This kind of pivot construction is designed to execute referential repair in a way that is minimally disruptive to the turn in progress (Pekarek Doehler and Horlacher 2013:100ff.).[29]

ii.   [clause – NP – clause]
       A   B   C

In this pattern, a clause followed by a right dislocation is followed by another clause that retrospectively treats the pivot NP as a left dislocation. Again, the pivot construction amalgamates a right and left dislocation structure, but now the pivot is an NP and the pre-pivot as well as the post-pivot parts of the pattern are full clauses. Here is an example (PRO.REFL = reflexive pronoun):

---

[29] In another type of pattern, which Horlacher and Pekarek Doehler (2014) describe as *pivotage* or "pivoting", the post-pivot part of the construction is added only after a prosodic break. As this is more like a final turn extension (see §3 below) than what we are calling a pivot construction, we will not discuss it here.

(6.25) "Image" (Horlacher and Pekarek Doehler 2014:597) (adapted)

```
1 Mac: elle    va          s'effacer        l'ima(ge)   elle va
       it_i is.going.to  PRO.REFL fade away  the image_i  it_i is.going.to
       it's going to fade away the image it's going to
2      s'effacer         au fil du temps.
       PRO.REFL fade.away after a while
       fade away after a while
```

Here we first see the clause *elle va s'effacer* "it is going to fade away" followed by the right dislocated element *l'image* "the image", which is co-referential with the pronoun *elle* "it" in the prior clause. The NP *l'image* is then followed by another clause *elle va s'effacer au fil du temps* "it is going to fade away after a while", in which the pronoun *elle* is co-referential with the prior NP. The latter can now be retrospectively re-interpreted as an element that is left dislocated from the final clause. The prosodic configuration of this entire pattern is in a single intonation phrase, preventing any part of it from being heard as a restart or as an independent clause (p. 597).

Both these construction types (i and ii) are used to extend the turn beyond a point of possible completion. They manage self-repair, upgrade the speaker's stance, manage the progressivity of talk, and/or deal with lack of recipiency (2014:597 and elsewhere). Pivot patterns in French thus provide particularly telling evidence for an emergent grammar that results from local needs in the conduct of interaction.

Pivotal constructions are deployed in talk-in-interaction in numerous languages, but the details of their structure can differ. In all cases, pivots are formed of three parts, A, B, and C, with both A plus B and B plus C constituting grammatically possible constructions according to the normative "rules" of grammar in the language concerned. Yet the entire construction A plus B plus C does not conform to what may be considered "standard" in the language. Pivot constructions merge or amalgamate two different syntactically possible clauses into one construction, designed to achieve two actions in a single TCU.

Pivot constructions can have different degrees of sedimentation, from more fixed to more ad hoc patterns. In all cases, part A of the construction type projects continuation, which is then realized by adding part B. The B part ends in a point of possible syntactic completion, yet the lack of a prosodic break prevents this point of possible syntactic completion from being heard as such and foreshadows the addition of part C. At the end of part C, the TCU is normally complete both syntactically and prosodically.

Pivot constructions have been shown to be deployed for diverse interactional purposes including, for example, topic management, unobtrusive repair, and handling problematic recipiency.

2. Internal Organization of Clauses

2.3 Finiteness versus Non-finiteness

In this section we consider how the distinctions of tense in finite clauses can serve as resources in social interaction. Then we show how *not* making such distinctions in independent non-finite clauses can also be a useful interactional resource.

2.3.1 Finiteness: Tense and Temporal Reference

Tense is a grammatical category that allows speakers to locate events and situations temporally. Typically, this is done by relating them to the moment of speaking, but other temporally situated events and situations can also be used as reference points. An event or situation can be located anterior to, simultaneous with, or posterior to a speaker's "now" or to some other point in time (past – present – future).[30] The relative position of an event can be further specified temporally with reference to a particular point or interval on the time line: for example, *September 23rd, the following Tuesday*, or to another temporally situated event, such as *when I got home*.[31]

When are tense distinctions and other references to time relevant in interaction? To date, there has not been much interactional research on this dimension of language. What little there is has been concerned primarily with the use of temporal and aspectual categories in conversational storytelling: we deal with this research in Online-Chapter D. However, there are isolated references to tense contrasts in other sequential contexts of interaction. One of these is with respect to assessments.

Goodwin and Goodwin (1987), for instance, observe that the contrast of tenses between two speakers may be deployed to convey different access to and experience of an event or item being assessed. Here is their example:

(6.26)   "Asparagus pie" (Goodwin and Goodwin 1987:24) (adapted)
```
Dianne:   Jeff made en asparagus pie
          it wz s::so[: goo:d.
Clacia:              [I love it.
```

Dianne assesses Jeff's asparagus pie in the past tense, presenting her assessment as based on the experience of a particular pie on a specific occasion prior to

---

[30] The location of an event as past, present, or future (tense) is distinct from, but related to, its presentation as completed or ongoing (aspect). Aspect has not yet been explored from an interactional linguistic perspective and will not be dealt with further here.
[31] A preliminary study by White and Raymond (2014) suggests that the type of temporal reference made to particular moments in time, e.g., whether speaker-centered, recipient-centered, or shared, can do additional interactional and interpersonal work.

the moment of speaking. But Clacia, who agrees in a partially overlapping next turn, presents her assessment in the present tense: she does not address the specifics of a particular pie but generalizes over multiple instantiations of (Jeff's) asparagus pie (1987:27). Thus, participants deploy tense in this sequence as a resource to index different types of epistemic access to the assessable.[32]

Another context in which tense contrasts have been shown to be relevant is problem presentation in medical interaction, specifically when patients with acute problems visit primary-care physicians. In this context, both doctors and patients normatively orient to a problem-presentation phase of the consultation, under the control of the patient, and an information-gathering phase, under the control of the doctor (Robinson and Heritage 2005:481). When patients present the history of their medical problems with narratives in the *simple past tense*, these are treated as incomplete problem presentations; by contrast, with *present-tense* forms patients lead up to a description of their current concrete symptoms. It is the latter that serve as a transition to the next phase of the consultation – information gathering by the physician. This can be seen in the following excerpt:

```
(6.27)    "Sore throat" (Robinson and Heritage 2005:485) (adapted)
1    Doc:   An' what can we do for you today.
2    Pat:   .hh well I was here on september=h < twenty third >
3           because I had < bronchial > (.) > an' I < was put on
4           z:ithroma[x.
5    Doc:             [Mm hm,
6    Pat:   .hh the following: tuesday wednesday I had such a
7           sore throat I could hardly swallo[w.
8    Doc:                                    [Mm [hm,]
9    Pat:                                        [.h ]h I came
10          i:n fo:r a culture an' it was negative.
```

This patient mentions a diagnosis (*bronchial*), a treatment (*z:ithromax*), and a concrete symptom (*sore throat*) in the simple past tense (with the verb forms *was*, *had*, *could*, *came in*). But the physician treats these tellings as an incomplete problem presentation: he only provides continuers (*Mm hm*, in lines 5 and 8), whereupon the patient pursues the presentation of her problem.[33]

By contrast, when patients mention concrete symptoms being experienced in the here and now, and use present-tense forms to do so, physicians treat this as

---

[32] See Heritage (2002a:212) and Hayano (2011:61) for similar cases in English and Japanese, respectively.
[33] See also Heritage and Clayman (2010:113–14), who discuss this exchange in its full trajectory.

2. Internal Organization of Clauses

a possibly complete problem presentation and move to the information-gathering phase of the consultation:

(6.28)   "Chest pains" (Robinson and Heritage 2005:486)
```
1  Doc:  Wha̱t, can=I do:, for yo̱u tonight.=hh
2  Pat:  We:ll=h I have=h (.) chest pains.
3  Doc:  Hha:=hh=oka:y,
4        (0.2)
5  Doc:  How long have they been going on.
```

After the doctor's opening of the problem-presentation phase (line 1), this patient briefly states his current, concrete symptoms with the present-tense verb form *have* (line 2). The doctor now registers and accepts the patient's presentation (line 3) and leaves a bit of time for the patient to possibly produce more talk (line 4). When this is not forthcoming, the doctor moves into information gathering (line 5), treating the problem presentation as complete (2005:486).

> Tense contrasts have been shown to be relevant in assessment sequences, where they index different types of access to the assessable. A past-tense assessment such as *it was so good* is based on the experience of the assessable on one particular occasion, while a present-tense assessment such as *I love it* generalizes over a class of instances on which the assessable has been experienced. In primary-care doctor–patient consultations the patient's presentation of symptoms in the past tense is oriented to as leading up to and projecting the presentation of current symptoms in the present tense. Only the latter is treated as completing the problem-presentation phase of the consultation: it leads to the next phase – information gathering by the physician.

2.3.2 Non-finiteness: Infinitive Constructions

While finite clauses are characterized by tense distinctions, non-finite clauses lack tense. Yet it is not uncommon – at least in German and Finnish – to build turns at talk with non-finite, infinitive constructions.[34] Let us look at some examples:

(6.29)   "Family" (Deppermann 2006:246) (adapted)
((Father to child))
```
1  Va:   GUten MO:Rgen, (.)
         good morning
2        !AUF!stehen-
         to get up ((=get up!))
```

---

[34] See also §4.2 below for the use of non-finite clauses in German "dense constructions."

Here a freestanding infinitive form is used as a directive to bring about the desired action. It is understood from the context that the recipient is the person who is to carry out the action. (Note that a colloquial English translation requires the imperative form.) Deppermann refers to this construction as a "deontic infinitive": it is used to impose, impede, or permit an action by the recipient on normative grounds (2006:243).

Yet there are also situations in which infinitive constructions of this type can be used to issue a complaint:

(6.30)   "Always clean up" (Deppermann 2006:247) (adapted)
((Interaction between father and child))

```
1  Va:  jetz machste- (-) hh erst mA:l dein z↑Immer,
         now you clean up (-) your room first
2  Ki:  =Immer Auf[räumen-
         always to clean up ((=always clean up))
3  Va:            [un dann schAUn wer mal.
                   and then we'll see
```

In contrast to *jetz machste erst mal dein zimmer* "now you clean up your room first" (line 1), which conveys that the recipient is to carry out the action immediately, the infinitive in line 2 is not used to bring about an action that the speaker is treating as a norm, but rather to implement a complaint about the constraining character of a norm that is treated as having been established externally (Deppermann 2006:243). The infinitive construction does not locate the action temporally; moreover, lacking both grammatical subject and object, it leaves unexpressed what is to be cleaned up and who is to do it (Deppermann 2007: 247–50). This makes it an apt means for generalizing the situation (cleaning up has now become something that is "always" (*immer*) insisted upon) and evaluating it negatively as coercion.

In Finnish a freestanding infinitive construction can also be deployed in the service of evaluating (Etelämäki and Visäpää 2014). Here is an instance where this happens:

(6.31)   "Pinging cash register" (Etelämäki and Visäpää 2014:487–8) (adapted)
((Pirjo has been telling her friends about a group of Finns she watched buying large amounts of cheap food in Sweden.))

```
7  Pirjo: [kyl se   semmost se[ittemääsataa oli melkei jokaisel
           PRT DEM3 DEM3.ADJ-PAR seven-PAR.hundred-PAR be-PST almost each-ADE
           it sure was something like seven hundred for each of them
8  Jonna:                     [MÄ EN TAJUU       MÄ EN   JA:KSAIS
                               1SG NEG-1SG understand 1SG NEG-1SG be.able.to-COND
                               I don't understand I wouldn't have the energy
```

```
9           HEI IKI:NÄ?[:
            PRT ever
            like ever

10 Anu:                [ja raahata jostai,=
                       PRT drag-A-INF some-ELA
                       and to drag from somewhere (like)

11 Jonna: [nii:i
          PRT
          yeah

12 Ulla:  [nii:i
```

In line 7 Pirjo is describing the overindulgence of the Finnish shoppers she has observed when Jonna comes in with a first negative evaluation of their behavior. She claims that she would not have the energy to go to so much trouble (to "save" money) – ever (*ikinä*). Anu now chimes in with another negative evaluation, expressed with a freestanding infinitive: *ja raahata jostai* "and to drag (everything) from somewhere (to somewhere else)". Here too, the infinitive construction leaves time, person/number, and modality unexpressed: that is, it is not stated who is dragging what where, or when this happens. This allows Anu as story recipient to generalize from a singular event (which she did not experience personally) to the more general situation of consumers going to great length to economize and having to lug all the cheap goods home. Located sequentially as an addition to Jonna's negative evaluation (see the *ja* "and" preface), this infinitive turn is likewise hearable as an affect-laden condemnation of the Finnish shoppers.

> Freestanding infinitives can be used in both German and Finnish to construct turns at talk. In German they have been documented as a means for implementing requests, suggestions, and permission-givings – as well as complaints, where they negatively evaluate what is implied to be an externally established normative constraint.
> In Finnish, freestanding infinitives are also found in evaluative contexts, for example, when interlocutors are co-evaluating an assessable. In both languages, freestanding infinitive constructions – because they do not express time, person/number, or modality – allow speakers to generalize over specific and singular events and to reference more abstract, potentially universal situations.

3. Extensions of Clauses

Clauses can serve as host constructions and be extended ad hoc with diverse pre-positioned and/or post-positioned elements. When they are recurrent, these pre-positionings and post-positionings sediment into grammatical constructions. In this section we describe some common constructions involving initial and final clausal extension in selected languages (see also Chapter 2 §4 for a discussion of incrementing).[35]

3.1 Initial Extensions: Left Dislocation and Other Pre-positionings

Traditionally, in research on the grammar of spoken language in discourse, initial extensions have been dealt with under labels such as *left dislocations* and *hanging topics*. The description of these structures has mirrored the development of research on language in interaction (see Ochs and Schieffelin (1976, 1983) for early work on English, and Duranti and Ochs (1979) for Italian).[36]

In left dislocations, referents are first introduced with a full NP and then referred to again with a pro-form in the clause that follows. Thus, from the perspective of normative grammar, there is a superfluous constituent in the clause. Here is an example from English (the initial reference form and the subsequent co-referential pro-form are in bold):

(6.32)   "My father" (Ochs and Schieffelin 1983:158) (adapted)
((K has been talking about the fact that his car radio was taken from his car.))
K: They cleaned me out. And **my father** oh **he**'s// **he**'s fit to be tied.
R: Tell Daddy to buy you some more.

In this example, the referent is first introduced with *my father* and then taken up again with the co-referential pro-form *he* in the following full clause.

For English it has been argued that there are at least two kinds of left dislocation (Geluykens 1992). One type – by far the more frequent – is deployed for the interactional and collaborative introduction of referents into the discourse (p. 49). In these cases, the referent is mentioned in its own prosodic or intonation phrase, typically with final falling pitch (p. 114), and is often followed by a pause. This creates a structural opportunity for recipients to acknowledge recognition of the referent, before the speaker launches a subsequent clause with that referent as an argument. Here are two of Geluykens' examples:

---

[35] Note that we distinguish terminologically between "extensions" of clauses and other grammatical units and "expansions" of TCUs, turns, and other units in the organization of interaction.
[36] In contrast to Schegloff's (1980) "preliminaries to preliminaries", which constitute sequential devices for action projection, the constructions dealt with here are turn-constructional devices for action projection. Located at the beginning of TCUs and turns, left dislocated elements project more to come by virtue of their grammatical incompleteness.

(6.33)   "Last paragraph" (1992:35) (adapted)
```
1  A:   now ?u:hm (.) the ↑last ˋ´paragraph- (- - -)
2  B:   [yes]
3  A:   [u:hm] I seem to reˋmember it (.) being different
        from what's printed
```

(6.34)   "Bernadette Devlin" (1992:35–6) (adapted)
```
1  A:   n u:hm (- - -) uh ↑Bernadette ˋDevlin.
2       [ˋnow]
3  B:   [ah] yes
4  A:   she (was) ´born in a place called ↑ˋCooks´Town,
5       County Tyrone
```

In the first example, the referent is mentioned first with a full referring expression *the last paragraph* (line 1) and then mentioned again with a minimal referring expression, the pronoun *it*, in the clause that follows (line 3). In the second example, the referent is referred to first as *Bernadette Devlin* (line 1) and then again with the pronoun *she* at the beginning of the clause in line 4. (The minimal referring expression can thus occupy different argument roles within the following clause.) In both these examples, the recipient in fact explicitly acknowledges the referent: see line 2 in (6.33) and line 3 in (6.34). This does not need to be the case, however: in some instances, acknowledgment is only tacit.

In the examples above, the referent is presented as irrecoverable (not derivable from prior discourse, p. 53) and topical (talked about in subsequent discourse, p. 69); for this reason it could be said to be "introduced" through the left dislocation. But Geluykens also identifies a second type of left dislocation that is non-referent introducing. This type is used, for example, for contrasting and listing. The following example shows a contrasting usage:

(6.35)   "North of Crawley" (Geluykens 1992:87) (adapted)
```
1 A: and we had to go down [s] . [m] round [k] Crawley to find it --
2 C: yeah - -
3 A: no (.) no ˋ´North of Crawley, that's it, (.)
4    there's an interchange there but that in fact doesn't really
     help
```

In line 3, *North of Crawley* is the left dislocated constituent and *that's it* the full clause. According to Geluykens, this left dislocation construction is used to highlight the contrast between the prior focus on *Crawley* and the new one on *North of Crawley*. Since *Crawley* has just been mentioned, the left dislocated element does not introduce a new referent into the talk. In contrast to referent-introducing dislocated elements, which mostly end with falling pitch and are often followed by a pause, non-referent-introducing ones often carry an accent with rising final pitch and are not followed by a pause (pp. 113–14). In other words, they are not "exposed" prosodically the way referent-introducing left dislocations are: this can be seen by comparing (6.33) and (6.34) with (6.35) above.

For German, researchers also distinguish between two types of dislocated elements at the beginning of TCUs: *left dislocations* and *hanging topics*. Both are positioned in the pre-front field of the clause (see Figure 6.5 in §2.1 above). Often, they can only be distinguished on prosodic grounds.[37] Consider, for instance, the following examples (co-referential NPs and proforms are printed in bold face and indexed with $_i$):

(6.36)   Left dislocation (Selting 1993:295) (adapted)

```
1 L: un (.) die lEhrer_i die_i SAßen da alle auch (.) um so größere TIsche herum,
     and      the teachers they sat there all also     around such big tables
     and      the teachers were also sitting around at such big tables
```

(6.37)   Hanging topic (Selting 1993:297) (adapted)

```
1 L: diese ganzen FRAUenthemen_i von wegen emanzipatiOn un so, (-)
     these all    women topics    regarding emancipation and so
     all these feminist topics    concerning emancipation and such stuff
2    die_i wern von den mEisten frauen DIE sich damit beschäftigen und
     they are by most of the women who concern themselves with that and
     they are    by most of the women who are concerned about them and
3    die da so: HINterstehen (---) irgnwie so hOchgejubelt und (.)
     who support that              somehow played so much up and
     who support that              played up so much somehow and
     mh auch so exTREM ausgebreitet; ne,
     also so extremely expanded      you know
     are so extremely expanded       you know
```

Both constructions deploy co-referential expressions at the beginning of the turn, thus creating more linguistic weight in this position than referentially necessary. In some cases, as in (6.36), the first and the second mention of the referent are packaged in the same intonation phrase; these are treated as left dislocations. In other cases, as in (6.37), the first mention of the referent is packaged in an independent intonation phrase; these have been described as hanging topics. With hanging topics, the pre-positioned phrase may be expanded and followed by a pause before the clause with a co-referential expression follows in a new

---

[37] It is sometimes claimed that congruent case marking between the pre-positioned constituent and its co-referential pronoun characterizes left dislocation but not hanging topic. However, Selting (1993) argues that this distinction is not watertight. In examples (6.36) and (6.37) there is congruent case marking for both the left dislocation and the hanging topic.

intonation phrase (as in (6.37)). In German, both constructions are deployed as marked forms of topicalization.[38] But while left dislocations continue a prior topic locally, hanging topics return to a prior topic at a distance, i.e., they backskip to a topic which has been either provisionally completed or for some reason discontinued in prior talk. Both constructions project more talk on the referent and topic thus introduced or reintroduced (Selting 1993).

Left dislocation has been documented in a number of other languages, among these Italian, where it is reported to be particularly frequent (Monzoni 2005). In Monzoni's examples the left dislocated element is always prosodically integrated with the following clause. Here is a case in point:

(6.38) "Melon" (Monzoni 2005:145) (adapted)
((During a schism phase in a multi-party conversation, Lina comes in from the kitchen and brings some melon; the others are already eating ham.))

```
4   Li:    [allora ↑IL MELONE_I LO_I MANGIATE= COL        PROSCIUTTO::↑?
            so      the melon_i it_i eat-2^nd_PL with-the ham
            ↑THE MELON_I DO YOU EAT IT_I = WITH THE HAM::↑ then?
```

According to Monzoni, Lina is interjecting a new topic into the current talk of the others here. To attract their attention, she introduces the new referent *il melone* first and then produces a clause about it: *lo mangiate=col prosciutto* "do you eat it with the ham" (line 4). In Italian, such left dislocations are used for accomplishing abrupt topic changes, introducing new referents that are disconnected from the prior topical talk. With this device, speakers can mark the abrupt topic change, as if to instruct the recipient(s) not to rely on the previous talk for an understanding of the new and upcoming turn (Monzoni 2005:146).

Left dislocation constructions are also reported to occur frequently in French, another Romance language (Pekarek Doehler et al. 2015). Pekarek Doehler (2011a) conceives of French left dislocations as "emergent products of partially routinized interactional projection practices" (p. 47). She shows that although they are considered to be highly grammaticized, they are molded in real time and adapted to accommodate to locally emergent interactional contingencies. While retaining the terms "left [and right] dislocation" for clarity, she makes it clear that these terms are misleading:[39] the constructions are actually resources oriented to

---

[38] Scheutz (1997) has suggested using a combination of topological, morpho-syntactic, and prosodic criteria to position such initial extensions of TCUs and turns on a continuum ranging from maximal integration to maximal disintegration.
[39] The terms "left dislocation" and "right dislocation" stem from early generative approaches to syntax, which conceive of dislocated constituents as resulting from "movement" transformations operating on a basic sentence structure in which all constituents have their canonical topological place.

the temporal unfolding of talk at the beginning (and end) of TCUs (p. 50).[40] Here is one of her examples of left dislocation (PREP = preposition):

(6.39)   "My mother" (Pekarek Doehler 2011a:51) (adapted)
```
1  Jul:  ma mère    elle arrive pas à     me    parler en allemand.
         my mother_i she_i succeeds not PREP to me speak in German
         my mother (she) can't manage to speak in German to me
2  Mar:  mhm
         mhm
```

Jul's contribution at line 1 begins with the referent *ma mère*, a full NP, which is then referred to again with the pronoun *elle* in the following clause.

Pekarek Doehler describes left dislocations as constructions that are used as "shared adaptive resources for action" (2011a:54). She makes three observations that support this claim. First, she observes that they can be co-constructed, as in the following case:

(6.40)   "Devil" (Pekarek Doehler 2011a:55) (adapted)
```
1  A:  (alors que) le (.) diable (.) eh: c' [est:
       Whereas     the  devil_i         it_i's
2  B:                                   [c'est
                                        it_i's
3      tout ce qui est mauvais.
       all that   is  bad
4  A:  oui
       yes
```

In its local sequential context, an NP such as *le diable* "the devil" at the beginning of an emerging TCU recognizably projects continuation: here this continuation is furnished by the recipient. When speaker A hesitates after producing *le diable*, speaker B comes in with *c'est* (almost simultaneously with the start of A's continuation, which also deploys *c'est*) and then completes the utterance in the clear. A and B thus co-construct this TCU.

Pekarek Doehler also observes that, secondly, a left dislocated element can be formatted with a "try marker" (Sacks and Schegloff 1979) in order to invite a recipient response:

(6.41)   "Water" (Pekarek Doehler 2011a:59) (adapted)
```
1  Xav:  mais (..) on connaît jamais un mot (..) qu'est-ce qu'
         but       we never know      a  word        what
```

---

[40] What Pekarek Doehler describes as left dislocations in French can be produced as prosodically integrated into the following clause or not; she does not make a distinction between what has been called left dislocation and hanging topic in German (see above).

3. Extensions of Clauses 399

```
2            il veut dire vraiment.
             it means      really
3            (0.6)
4            du genre^euh: (.) l'acqua?
             like              l'acqua
5    Mar:    ouais
             yeah
6    Xav:    euh: enfin, (.) >on sait que c'est de l'eau<.
             well            one knows that it's  PART water
7    Mar:    ouais
             yeah
```

While discussing problems of translating words from one language into another, Xavier introduces the word *l'acqua* as an example (line 4). He produces it with rising pitch here: that is, it is proffered to the recipient for confirmation. After Marina has provided confirmation (line 5), Xavier continues with an utterance referring to *l'acqua* with *ce* "that/it", cliticized to *c'*. Seen retrospectively, Xavier has thus produced a left dislocation construction: *l'acqua ... on sait que c'est de l'eau* "l'acqua$_i$ ... one knows that it$_i$'s water". Note, however, that this production does not result from a predefined syntactic project: non-confirmation of the referent by the recipient would undoubtedly have led to a different sequential trajectory. Rather the phrase *l'acqua* is retrospectively formed into a left dislocation structure, in response to the co-participant's display of recognition. The left dislocation construction is thus a contingent product of the temporal process of securing understanding between the participants (2011a:64).

Finally, Pekarek Doehler observes that, in complex turns, first parts of left dislocation constructions can be followed by syntactically independent inserts (parentheticals) or syntactically linked expansions (e.g., appositive relative clauses) before the second part is produced. Here is an example:

(6.42)   "Swiss Germans" (Pekarek Doehler 2011a:64) (adapted)
```
1    Noa:    parce que les suisses alémaniques=et j'ai pu
             because   the Swiss Germans        and I was able to
2            le constater ..h euh eux       veulent surtout
             witness it         they (stressed PRO) want above all
3            pas être confondus non [plus avec des allemands.
             not to be confused either    with the Germans
4    Cec:                           [mh
```

The parenthetical phrase *et j'ai pu le constater* "and I was able to witness it" (lines 1–2) is inserted after the first mention of the referent *les suisses alémaniques* "the Swiss Germans", before the construction is continued with a co-referential pro-form *eux*. Here, the uptake of the suspended construction with a stressed pro-form helps the recipient keep track of the complex syntax of the TCU. In other words, the construction of a left dislocation in such cases provides a resource that can help make a complex clause recognizable and understandable for the co-participant (2011a:67).

As Pekarek Doehler rightly observes, the phenomena illustrated in examples (6.40)–(6.42) provide evidence that grammar is emergent and distributed among speakers. Even though there are regular patterns called left dislocations, these are not pre-fabricated and then inserted into talk but are rather constructed locally through participants' orienting to syntax in progress. They emerge step by step as practical solutions to current tasks that need to be dealt with by the participants of the interaction.[41]

In addition to left dislocated constituents, there are also other kinds of syntactic constituents that can be positioned before the clause at the beginning of TCUs, for instance adverbials (such as German *nämlich* "namely", *nur* "only") and subordinate clauses.[42] For spoken German, Auer (1996b, 1997) describes these grammatically as occupying the topological pre-front field, i.e., the position before the first constituent of an unexpanded clause. Here are some of his examples in tabular form:

Table 6.1 *Adverbials and subordinate clauses as pre-front field elements in German (adapted from Auer 1997:55)*

	PRE-FRONT FIELD	FRONT FIELD	REST OF CLAUSE
(i)	núr;	das	ist mit nem finanziellen áufwand verbunden;
	only	that	is connected to financial expenditures
(ii)	wobei (.)	ich	hab féstgestellt daß es nicht zwíngend die pollen sind: die mich dahinraffen-
	whereby (=which reminds me)	I	have discovered that it isn't necessarily the pollen that make me feel so bad
(iii)	wenn ich da mal kurz réingehn darf;	das	is=das is ein teil des problems;
	if I can come in for a second	that	is that is a part of the problem

---

[41] In this way of thinking, the prosody of a left dislocation construction, i.e., whether it is produced as integrated into the following clause or not, is not a question of choosing between pre-defined construction types such as left dislocation or hanging topic, but a result of local contingencies in the interaction.

[42] Lexical items such as response particles (e.g., *yeah/yes*), discourse markers (e.g., *so*), address terms/vocatives, and other attention getters (e.g., *hey*) can, of course, also appear in this position (see Chapter 8).

Table 6.1 (cont.)

	PRE-FRONT FIELD	FRONT FIELD	REST OF CLAUSE
(iv)	mích: hat besónders ange-sprochen – ah	Sie: – Sie	légen wert auf- f´ührungsqualitäten,
	to me it was most appealing	you you	attach importance to managerial abilities

The constituents shown here in the pre-front field are syntactically and prosodically heterogeneous. In examples (i) and (ii) the pre-positioned elements are adverbial; in examples (iii) and (iv) they are clausal (see also Chapter 7). What they all have in common is that, although they can be packaged in their own intonation phrases, they are recognizably incomplete in their sequential contexts and cannot constitute TCUs on their own. They are deployed to take over speakership, to frame and/or foreshadow an upcoming TCU or turn, i.e., to project more to come. What precisely this "more" will be cannot be predicted in advance. As Auer (1996b:320) points out, such underspecified syntactic openings can be of interactional advantage when used at the beginning of a turn.

> In this section we have examined a number of linguistic elements, with varying syntactic and prosodic relations to the following talk, that are used at the beginning of TCUs to extend host clauses: left dislocations in English, German, Italian, and French, as well as hanging topics and other pre-front field elements in German. All pre-positioned elements have in common that they are incomplete syntactically and cannot constitute TCUs in and of themselves. Consequently, they project more to come.
>
> The fact that many languages have been shown to have constructions providing for pre-positioned clausal extensions suggests that there are recurrent interactional tasks at exactly this position in the TCU: among these are the need to start a turn but delay its official beginning so that, for example, referents can be confirmed, "old" or non-active topics can be revived, and/or in general early understanding can be secured. All this is accomplished with partly sedimented constructions that are nevertheless locally emergent and adapted to the temporally unfolding contingencies of interaction.

3.2 Final Extensions: Right Dislocation and Other Post-positionings

Just as clauses can be extended through pre-positionings, so they can undergo extension through the post-positioning of syntactic constituents after their possible completion.[43] This happens, for instance, in the case of right dislocation, where a syntactic constituent of a clausal utterance is taken up again with a co-referential element afterwards. But more generally, we speak of final clausal extension when any kind of syntactic constituent "belonging" to a clause is added on to it after possible completion, as in the case of "incrementing" (see also Chapter 2 §4). This section deals with some of the grammatical constructions that involve final extension in selected languages. The focus is primarily on non-clausal elements that are added on, i.e., in topological terms ones that occupy the post-end field of clauses (see §2.1 and §2.1.2 above); post-end field stance markers like *really*, tag questions like *right?* or *you know?*, etc. are not dealt with here; clausal extensions are dealt with in Chapter 7.

One of the more well-known constructions for final extension of a clause is what is known in English and German as "right dislocation" or *Rechtsversetzung* (Auer 1991, 1992a; Geluykens 1994; Selting 1994a). A right dislocated structure is commonly understood to be one in which a referent contained in an initial clausal utterance is taken up again with a co-referential element positioned after completion of the clause. As in the case of left dislocation, the result is a clause with an extra component, one of its constituents having been doubled. Geluykens (1994) observes that the co-referential term added on, frequently an NP, is often semantically more informational than the original element, a pronominal with potentially problematic recoverability (p. 51). Since in his English data there is typically a pause between the original clause and the post-positioned re-mentioning of one of its constituents, Geluykens argues that the process of right dislocation is akin to self-repair. Here is one of his examples (the initial reference and the right dislocated element are in bold):

(6.43)   "Tree in the middle" (Geluykens 1994:52) (adapted)
((A and C are looking through a collection of paintings.))
```
1    A:   well I don't think I want to ((2 syllables))
2         you know they're a bit too sort of strong (.)
3    C:   [mhm]
4    A:   [for] my room – so I thought I'd wait till he he had
5         another lot
```

---

[43] For the placement of syntactically non-integrated items such as vocatives and tags after possible clause (or TCU and turn) completion see Chapter 8.

```
6    C:    [mhm]
7    A:    [I] like `´THAT One best (-)
8          the (tree) in the `MIDdle (-)
9          but I think it's too er
10         it would dominate the room a bit too much
```

In line 7 speaker A singles out the painting he likes best with *that one*, but the ensuing pause – when C could be expected to respond with an assessment of his/her own – indicates a possible referential problem. A addresses this by substituting a more informative NP, now describing the picture as *the tree in the middle* (line 8).

Geluykens notes, however, that not all right dislocations in conversation are instances of self-repair. For instance, the following examples show two cases where the referent of the NP in the initial clause is quite clear, although it is nevertheless taken up again in post-position:

(6.44)   "Difficult question" (1994:114) (adapted)
```
1    A:   (-) erm (.) well I mean it's a (.) terribly difficult
2         question to answer that because (.)
3         it entirely depends on the person (.)
```

(6.45)   "Absolutely pathetic" (1994:115) (adapted)
```
1    B:   (-) (I mean it's) absolutely pathetic that sort of thing
2         darling even I don't do that
```

The right dislocated elements here, *that* (line 2) in (6.44) and *that sort of thing* (line 1) in (6.45), are not delivered after an intervening pause (as is the case in (6.43)). Instead, the two parts of the construction (clause + dislocated element) form one prosodic unit together. Moreover, the dislocated elements are not handling referential problems: their referents are known to both speaker and recipient. Geluykens calls such right dislocations "emotive": they are typically used when the speaker is expressing a positive or negative evaluation of a referent (1994:114).

This analysis suggests that there are at least two functionally distinct types of right dislocation in English: one used in self-repair and another for "emotive" purposes (p. 123). It also implies that a purely syntactic analysis of right dislocation is insufficient: to capture the full range of its usages, prosody must be taken into account as well.

Prosodic packaging has been shown to be an important resource for the interpretation of right dislocated extensions in German as well. Compare the following examples:

404 *Sentences, Clauses, and Phrases*

(6.46)   "Foundation launching" (Selting 1994a:312) (adapted)

```
703 Eli:   ´wAs is eigentlich so
           what is PART so
           what is actually
704        `SCHWIErig daran an dieser `stIftungsgründung;
           difficult with-it with this foundation-launching
           so difficult about it, this foundation launching
705 Lea:   ((clears [her thr[oat))
706 Cis:          [((laughs[for about 2 se[conds))
707 Eli:                   [[((laughs for a[bout 2 seconds))
708 Lea:                                   [(da sind)
                                            (there are)
                                            (there are)
709 Lea:   [<<f> proble´MAtisch warn die `fOrderungen;>
             problematic    were the   demands
             it's the demands that were problematic
710 Eli:   [<<all> d is do schon> seit ↑!JA:HR:N! im gespRäch.
             t has          for years         been talked about
             it's been talked about for years
```

(6.47)   "Women" (Selting 1994a:314) (adapted)

```
138 Nat:   `nIch nur ´DAS,
           not only that
           sondern da `fInde die sin (---) inzwischen sehr `UNkritisch
           but       there find they have meanwhile    very uncritical
           geworden.
           become
           but I think they have become very uncritical in the meantime
139        (--)
140 Nat:   <<l> `FRAUN.>
                women
141 Ida:   `´JA[a,
             yeah
142 Nat:      [aso sich SELber geg[enüber;=[das is
               like toward themselves       that is
143 Ron:                          [.hh     [<<f> ach SO; ja;>
                                            oh       I see
```

In both cases, after possible clause completion, an indexical pronoun in the clause (*daran* "with it" and *die* "they") is followed by a co-referential full NP. In the first example, the dislocated element (*an dieser stIftungsgründung* "with this foundation launching", line 704) is prosodically integrated with the prior clausal unit, without any break. As a result, the extension is unobtrusive: it ensures understanding *en passant* (p. 312). In the second example, the dislocated element *FRAUN* "women" in line 140 is added only after a silence in which the recipients refrain from responding, and it is presented in low pitch register. This presentation makes it sound *exposed*: the extension comes across as Nat's doing a re-completion of her turn in order to elicit a response from her recipients. In fact, when Ron does respond, it is with *ach SO; ja;* "oh, I see" (line 143), implying that there was indeed a problem of understanding.

In general, Selting argues, right dislocations in German in which a full referential item is added quickly and without a prosodic break can be said to secure understanding in a by-the-way, unobtrusive fashion, while right dislocations in which a full referential item is added with a prosodic break, often after a lack of recipient uptake, pursue a response in an exposed, on-record fashion. Thus, different prosodic formattings of right dislocation in German, as in English, accomplish different kinds of interactional work.

In French – much as in English and German – Pekarek Doehler (2011a) and Pekarek Doehler et al. (2015) also observe that right dislocations are often emergent constructions: a TCU initially constituted by a clause containing a clitic pronoun and ending with falling pitch is subsequently followed by a pause and then expanded with a lexical NP that is co-referential with the clitic in the prior TCU. For example:

(6.48) "Your parent" (Pekarek Doehler 2011a:70) (adapted)

```
1   Cat:  franchement (..) je pense que: c'est: (1.0) si: t'as vraiment
           frankly            I think that it's          if you really have
2         un parent qui a: (1.4) dévié,
           a parent    who has        gotten on the wrong track
3   Els:  ((laughter 6.4 s))
4   Cat:  qui a vraiment pris un très mauvais chemin,
           who has really taken a very bad path
5         (1.0) euh: (1.5) soit (...) tu prends le même chemin que
                            either       you take the same path as
6         lui? (1.1) soit tu vas á l'opposé
           him/her    or   you go in the opposite direction
7         et tu le détestes.
           and you hate him
```

```
8          (1.0)
9          euh: ton: parent qui a- (1.2) dé[vié.
                your parent who has        gotten on the wrong track
10  Els:                               [(dévié)
                                        gotten on the wrong track
```

This excerpt comes from a classroom discussion on the relationship between children and their parents. Catherine ends her argument with *et tu le détestes* "and you hate him", where the clitic pronoun *le* refers to a parent who has gotten on the wrong track (first introduced in lines 2–4). After this, a response is relevant. But when her recipient Elsa does not provide this response for one reason or another,[44] Catherine resumes the turn and adds a full NP referential form (line 9), thus taking her turn to another point of possible completion. This time, in overlap with Catherine's completion, Elsa chimes in with a completion of Catherine's turn.

Pekarek Doehler stresses the emergent character of such constructions. The syntactic project is not simply extended, but revised: "What so far has appeared to be an SVO structure, ending on a TRP, is repackaged as an RD" (2011a:73). This makes it look very similar to the process of "incrementing", another type of post-positioning – albeit non-co-referential – leading to a final extension of the clause.

In English, "incrementing" extensions can take the form of various syntactic constituents, including NPs, adverbs, adverbial phrases, prepositional phrases, relative clauses, and adverbial clauses (Ford et al. 2002:18). Here are some examples, with the extensions marked in bold:

(6.49)   Incrementing extensions of clauses in English (Ford et al. 2002:18ff.) (adapted)

(i)   Have you been to New Orleans? **ever?**
(ii)   We could've used a little marijuana. **to get through the weekend.**
(iii) ((...)) it drips on the front of the cars? (.) **If you park in a certain place?**
(iv)   An' how are you feeling? (0.4) **these days,**

These extensions are all formatted as constituents of the prior clause, regardless of whether there is a pause before the post-positioned extension or not. Ford et al. find that such extensions are used for continuing the action of the prior clause: they re-complete the turn when uptake is lacking at a TRP (2002:25; see also Chapter 2 §4).

Yet as clauses in English seldom show clear syntactic completion points, this kind of clausal expansion is often not easily recognizable. Had it been appropriate

---

[44] Video data would presumably clarify this question.

in context, for instance, examples (ii)–(iv) above could have been realized in one prosodic unit, without any noticeable extension. This is shown in (ii')–(iv'):

(ii')   We could've used a little marijuana to get through the weekend.
(iii') ((...)) it drips on the front of the cars if you park in a certain
        place?
(iv')   An' how are you feeling these days,

Thus, the recognizability of the extensions in (ii)–(iv) rests on their being produced in their own prosodic unit, separated from the clause in the first prosodic unit.[45]

The picture is different in German, however. Here, possible sentence completion points are for the most part clearly recognizable syntactically. As explained in §2 above, German clauses are structured around the sentence brace (*Satzklammer*), typically with a final right-hand brace demarcating clause and sentence completion clearly. When this brace is present, post-positioned extensions can be recognized independently of their prosodic configuration. Auer (1991, 1992a, 1996a, 2006a, 2007b) was the first researcher to systematically investigate sentence extensions beyond such completion points and take prosody into account (see especially 1996a). He determined that the most important post-positioned extensions of a clause in German are the following (marked in bold face):[46]

i. Retrospective syntagmatic extensions, i.e., continuations of a clause beyond its right-hand sentence brace (first possible completion point) with an item that normatively belongs within the prior clause, at the position indicated by the symbol @:

(6.50)   "Probably" (Auer 1996a:64) (adapted)
1   B: die ham gestern@ zuviel geSCHNAPselt. (-)
          they have yesterday too much schnapps drunk
          they drank too much schnapps yesterday

2   ->   [**wahrscheinlich.**
          probably

3   A: [ja:,
          yes

---

[45] Example (i) constitutes an exception in this respect: here, normatively speaking, the adverbial *ever* must be positioned *between* the auxiliary and the main verb: *have you ever been to New Orleans*. Consequently, if example (i) were to be produced in one prosodic unit, it would not correspond to normative word order.

[46] Auer refers to these extensions as "expansions"; we have adjusted his terminology to conform with usage elsewhere in this book. The following list is restricted to *syntactic* extensions only. Purely semantically linked extensions are discussed in §5 below.

The adverbial *wahrscheinlich* "probably" is added after the final sentence brace, the second part of the verb *geschnapselt* "drunk schnapps". Because it actually belongs before the object complement *zuviel* "too much", this could be thought of as an "insertable" increment (see Chapter 2 §4). The extension is formatted as prosodically separate.[47]

ii. Prospective syntagmatic extensions, i.e., continuations of a clause that lacks a right-hand brace:

(6.51)   "Kuantan" (Auer 1996a:67) (adapted)
```
1     S:    ehm (.) un was halt TOLL       is is die OSTküste: (.)
                  and what PART fantastic is is the east-coast
                  and what is fantastic is the east coast
2     ->          so (.) d von kuAntan an        HO:CH;
                  like from ((name)) starting up
                  like starting from Kuantan upwards
```

In this case, the clause in line 1 does not have a right-hand brace and therefore has no syntactic demarcation of possible completion; the local adverbial *so von kuantan an hoch* "like starting from Kuantan upwards" is simply fitted grammatically to its provisional end and could be thought of as a "glue-on" increment (Chapter 2 §4). Like "incrementing" extensions in English, this extension is only recognizable as an extension because it is prosodically separate from the clause that precedes it.

iii. Retrospective paradigmatic extensions, i.e., continuations that "replace" an element in the prior clause (SBJV = subjunctive):

(6.52) "Cheating" (Auer 1996a:66) (adapted)
```
1    K:    du: DES däd=      i=It MOgeln;
           you that do.SBJV I not cheat
           hey that I wouldn't do cheat
```

The infinitive *mogeln* "cheat" could be said to "replace" *des* "that" in the possibly complete prior clause. Since *des* and *mogeln* are co-referential, this is an instantiation of "right dislocation" (see above). Here, as is often the case, the "replacement" extension is not prosodically separate but integrated into the intonation phrase that packages the prior clause.

---

[47] Auer (2007b:652–3) points out, however, that in cases of brief, prosodically integrated adverbial extensions after the final sentence brace, as in *hier wird @ ORdentlich gegessen **heute*** "here is being @ orderly eaten **today**" (= "we're eating in an orderly fashion here today"), it is difficult to argue that these are extensions, because they are not doing an action of their own and have become "normal" constructions in spoken German.

3. Extensions of Clauses

> In this section we have reviewed two types of syntactic post-extension of the clause: a co-referential type known as "right dislocation" and a more general (not necessarily co-referential) type known as "incrementing". Viewed cross-linguistically, post-positioned syntactic extensions of the clause are omnipresent in talk-in-interaction (see, e.g., the contributions to Couper-Kuhlen and Ono 2007a). They can be produced by the same speaker or by the interlocutor (see also Sidnell 2012); they can add something to the prior clause or they can "replace" something in it; they can be prosodically integrated with the prior clause and therefore camouflaged, or prosodically separated and therefore exposed. And they can serve many different sequential and interactional functions (see also Chapter 2 §4).

The languages exemplified above are SVO (English, French) or mixed SVO/XVO and SOV (German) languages with inflecting morphology. But similar constructions are also documented in Korean, a strict SOV language with agglutinating morphology. Kim (2007) explains how light, allusive reference forms in a first Korean clause are often retroactively elaborated after its completion (see also Kim 2001). Since clausal completions are clearly demarcated through sentence-final suffixes, modal markers, aspect markers, and honorific markers attached to the verb (p. 575, n. 4), this cannot be done with glue-ons as in English (Couper-Kuhlen and Ono 2007b). Instead, in Korean it is done with insertables, i.e., with constituents that could have been placed in a normative pre-verbal position. The following examples from Korean conversational data illustrate a subject, an object, a locative phrase, and an adverbial clause respectively as post-predicate elements in clausal extension. (The post-verbal extensions are in bold face; implicit items in the clause are put in parentheses in the translation.)

(6.53) Post-predicate elements in clausal extension in Korean (Kim 2007:575) (adapted)

(i) mikwuk -iya::, **suthail-i.**
America-COP:IE style-NOM
It is (just like department stores in) America, **The style (is).**

(ii) keki -se haycwu -ci -anh -na? **kulen -ke?**
there-LOC do:for:you -COMM -NEG -NONCOMM like:that -thing
Don't (they) do (that) for you there? **Things like that?**

(iii) il -ha-kosip-eyo.(.) **kakey-eyse.**
work -do-want -POL store -LOC
I want to work. (.) **In the store.**

(iv) mal -un chama mos ha- keyss-e. (2.5)
Telling -TOP not:have:the:heart not:able do- MOD-IE

khun ay -tul -i -ntey.
`big kid-PL -COP -CIRCUM`
I didn't have the heart to tell them. (2.5) **Given that they are big (grown-up) kids.**

In Korean such post-predicate elements serve to re-complete the turn and prompt uptake by the recipient. But Kim argues that in addition to addressing various states of recipiency, the post-verbal elaboration of a prior implicit item is constitutive of a turn-tying practice in which a recipient first repeats a (predicative) element from the prior turn and thus occasions the need for post-predicate elaboration (2007:595). (For more on the prosodic fitting of such extensions with the prior host TCU in different kinds of turn expansion, see Chapter 2 §4.) Often these constructions are designed to display an affect-laden stance in the host construction first, and only then, when necessary, to mitigate the speaker's stance with a post-predicate elaboration (2007:599).[48]

Speakers of very different languages treat the ends of sentences and clauses flexibly. When necessary, they produce clause and sentence extensions (and thus create emergent constructions) to deal with local interactional contingencies. In doing so, they make use of grammatical constructions suitable for post-positioning in their respective languages. For a systematic analysis of these post-positionings, not only syntax and prosody but also semantics and pragmatics in the local sequential context need to be taken into account (see also Auer 2007b:657).

---

4. Other Clausal Variants

The normative description of unexpressed constituents in clauses differs from language type to language type. For languages like English and German, grammarians and linguists have traditionally argued that clauses lacking obligatory constituents result from "ellipsis" – the deletion or omission of communicatively redundant constituents to form abbreviated versions of full clauses. However, since in a given context full and abbreviated versions of clauses have different interactional implications, it is more appropriate from an interactional linguistic point of view to investigate such "curtailed" clauses as TCUs in their own right and to describe their "locally specific grammar(s)" (Schegloff 1996b) (see also Selting 1997a; Thompson et al. 2015; and Schwitalla 2012 on short forms).

---

[48] On different kinds of clause extensions or turn continuations in Japanese see Couper-Kuhlen and Ono (2007b: 535–45). On right dislocation constructions in Mandarin Chinese see Luke and Zhang (2007). On varying preferences for different types of turn continuation in different languages and possible language-typological explanations for them see Chapter 2 §4.

In the following sections, we will take a closer look at two different kinds of non-normative clauses deployed systematically in talk-in-interaction, one in English and one in German.

4.1 "Argument Omission" Constructions in English

Languages such as Chinese, Japanese, Korean, and Thai are usually described as leaving constituents unexpressed if they are "given" or known in context. This has been referred to as *pro-drop* or *zero anaphora*. Since both terms are problematic from an interactional linguistic perspective, we will speak here of *argument omission*. The choice of argument omission over overt reference forms has been discussed with reference to notions such as topic continuity, cohesion, and return-pop.[49] More recently, however, a form of argument omission has also been noted in English conversation and described as an orderly resource for the conduct of interaction. Oh (2005, 2006) identifies several sequential environments in which the routine dropping of a personal reference term is deployed as a practice (2005:269). In one of these, speakers format a current TCU as a second saying through the use of subject omission. Here is a case in point (the omission is denoted by ⌀):

(6.54) "Wouldn't know" (Oh 2005:271) (adapted)
((Mike and Curt are talking about a car spring that Mike is interested in acquiring.))

```
4      Mike:  =I think theh-the:re used to be a place up in Toledo that'd
5             make them for you if you give them the dimensions you want,
6             (0.3)
7      Curt:  Well? see I don't know any, I wouldn' know what- (0.4)
8             what dimensions to even start to give them.
9             (0.4)
10 ->  Curt:  ⌀ Wouldn' know what the hell he'd want.
11     Gary:  Go down there 'n measure hi:s.  .hh
```

By formulating the TCU in line 10 without a subject, Curt obliges his recipients to search prior talk in order to locate the missing referent. The repetition of *wouldn't know what* leads them to the TCU in lines 7–8. The subject omission in line 10 thus conveys that its TCU is a resaying, or second saying, in relation to the prior TCU (p. 272). When self-referential omission is used to index a second saying in this way, it often implies a request for recipient uptake and alignment.

---

[49] For more detail and references see Oh (2005:268–9); for a critical discussion of the notion of "zero anaphora" in Japanese see Ono and Thompson (1997).

In another sequential environment, the use of subject omission displays that the TCU so cued is performing a subsidiary, secondary action in relation to a prior major action. An example of this usage can be seen in the following:

(6.55)   "Used to work" (Oh 2005:288) (adapted)
```
1     Curt: Did you know that guy up there at-oh. What the hell is his name
2  ->       ⌀ used to work up at (Steeldinner) garage
3  ->       ⌀ did their body work. for them.
4     Curt: Uh:::ah,
```

By designing his utterances in lines 2 and 3 with subject omission instead of the pronoun *he*, Curt cues the descriptions he is offering in the service of referent recognition as implementing a secondary, subsidiary action to the primary action of telling a story about *that guy*. Subject omission in this case indicates that the clause incorporating it is not to be understood as an independent TCU performing a main action itself, but only as acting in the service of identifying the referent (2005:291).

In both these environments, the lack of a subject reference term displays the secondary nature of the TCU relative to a preceding TCU, one that includes an overt referential form (p. 287). If full-reference forms are used in these or similar environments, the speaker implies the separateness or independence of the second TCU with respect to the first: the implication is, for instance, that the second TCU is replacing the first or reasserting the position it conveyed (pp. 292ff.).[50]

Subject omission in English is far from being an ungrammatical mishap, or a strategy of linguistic economy, or a result of the speaker's laziness in talking. Instead, it is systematically deployed as a resource for accomplishing interactional tasks, including displaying a subsequent action as secondary to a prior, major one.

4.2 *"Dense" Constructions in German*

Non-normative clause types have also been documented in German talk-in-interaction. One type is called *dichte Konstruktionen* "dense constructions" (Günthner 2006a, 2007). These have been described as recurrent, conventionalized, even grammaticalized, partly fixed structural schemata, designed and

---

[50] In a follow-up study, Oh (2006) shows that subject omission in English may also be used for resuming the prior TCU after a parenthetical insert, for displaying maximal continuity, and for avoiding a choice among alternative reference forms.

deployed to manage specific interactional tasks, especially in the course of telling stories about past events. Günthner identifies four major types and gives structural descriptions with reference to the topological field model of the German clause:

i. *Verb-first constructions with narrative present-tense forms*

(6.56) "Car accident" (Günthner 2006a:99) (adapted)

```
10      Lisa:    =ich versuch EINzuparken bei de klara,
                 I try to park at Klara's
11 ->            KOMM an das AUto daNEben ran, [hh]
                 graze the car next to mine
12      Petra:                                    [hm]
13 ->   Lisa:    hh' STEIG aus,
                    get out
14 ->            SEH nix,
                 don't see a thing
15               gegenüber   von mir PARKT en ↑TYP.
                 across from me there's a guy parked
```

The common structure of the constructions in lines 11, 13, and 14 is as follows, with shading indicating the core fields that have been left empty, in this case the front field (Günthner 2006a:101):

front field	+ **initial sentence brace**	+ **middle field**	+ **final sentence brace**	**post field**
	finite verb		infinite verbal parts	
(empty)	(obligatory)	(optional)	(optional)	(empty)

These are equivalent to the "argument omission" constructions of English analyzed by Oh (2005).

ii. *Non-finite constructions*

(6.57)   "Easter visit" (Günthner 2006a:105) (adapted)

```
35      Klara:   ich hab (.) ge geklingelt,
                 I rang (the bell)
36               seh d die MAra kommen,
                 see ((name)) come
37               hi <<hi> verSTECK mich.>
                         hide myself
38      Pia:     hihi (<<hi> du FEIGling.>)
                             you coward
39 ->   Klara:   hihihi ICH (.) [NIX wie] WEG.
                        I   (.)  just away
```

Constructions such as the one in line 39 have the following structure, this time with the initial sentence brace left empty (Günthner 2006a:107):

front field	+ **initial sentence brace**	+ **middle field**	+ **final sentence brace**	**post field**
	finite verb		non-finite verbal parts (optional)	
(obligatory)	(empty)	(optional)		(optional)

iii. *Non-finite-constructions without subjects*[51]

(6.58) "Panic attacks: Tina" (Günthner 2006a:110) (adapted)

```
207      Tina:     und hab im AUto mich abjelenkt,
                   and have in the car myself distracted
                   distracted myself in the car
208 ->             .h <<all> mein KOPFtuch abjemacht,>
                              my head scarf taken off
                   took off my head scarf
209 ->             <<all> det ZWANzig mal zuSAMmengelescht,>
                          it twenty times folded
                   folded it twenty times
210 ->             <<all> it wieder UFFjerollt,>
                          it again unfolded
                   unfolded it again
211 ->             <<all> ne ROlle drausjemacht,>
                          a roll out-of-it made
                   made a roll out of it
212 ->             <<all> nen KNOten drinjemacht,>
                          a   knot  into-it made
                   made a knot in it
213                um diesen WEG     von heinersdorf nach HAUse; (-)
                   in order this way from heinersdorf to home
214                zu überBRÜcken.
                   to bridge
                   to bridge the way home from Heinersdorf
```

Here, the structure is even more reduced: two fields are empty (Günthner 2006a:109):

---

[51] See also §2.3 above for other uses of non-finite constructions without subjects.

front field	+	initial sentence brace finite verb	+	middle field	+	final sentence brace non-finite verbal parts	post field
(empty)		(empty)		(obligatory)		(obligatory)	(optional)

iv. *Minimal phrases*

(6.59) "Panic attacks: Gabi" (Günthner 2006a:114) (adapted)

```
174    Gabi:   es ging auf EINmal,
               it started all of a sudden
175            aus HEIterem himmel LOS.
               out of the blue
176            KEIne LUFT mehr gekriegt,
               got no more air
177 ->         SUper herzrasen,
               super heart racing
178 ->         und und KOPFschmerzen,
               and and headache
179            die OHren gingen zu-
               ears stopped up
180 ->         SCHWINdelig-
               dizzy
181            und alles und
               and all and
182            .h da BIN ich
                  then I
183            ich HAB dann das FENster erst RUNtergemacht,
               I first closed the window then
```

In this case, three fields are empty; the structure is as follows (Günthner 2006a:115):

front field	+	initial sentence brace finite verb	+	middle field	+	final sentence brace non-finite verbal parts	post field
(empty)		(empty)		(obligatory)		(empty)	(optional)

As the examples illustrate, the linguistic material in these clauses is reduced: constituents are often left unexpressed that would be obligatory in normative clauses. This reduction not only eliminates contextually redundant elements but simultaneously serves to focus on the few constituents that remain. The constructions are often combined list-like, in one TCU after another, iconically depicting fast and dramatic developments in the story.

> The non-normative clause types dealt with here – subject omission in English and "dense constructions" in German – are recurrent patterns with their own structure; they are not interchangeable with other kinds of sentences and clauses. These constructions have developed and are designed to do important work in the conduct of spoken interaction. Although the normative grammars of languages such as Chinese, Japanese, and Korean on the one hand, and English, French, and German on the other hand, are quite different, the grammatical practices of talk-in-interaction in these languages may not be as different as they seem, due to the universal nature of the tasks to be managed in social interaction.

5. Phrases

Phrases are syntactic units, consisting generally of more than one word, whose head is a noun, adjective, adverb, or pre/postposition. While clauses and sentences can stand alone as independent units, their parts, phrases, cannot. Yet in talk-in-interaction, phrases are commonly deployed as formats for building complete TCUs (and actions). Like sentences and clauses, phrases are also dynamic, flexible units, adaptable to the contingencies of interaction.

In this section we examine phrases cross-linguistically as a means for accomplishing actions in talk-in-interaction, with special attention to NPs and prepositional/postpositional phrases.[52] But first we explain in what sense phrases can be said to have flexibility and projectability.

5.1 The Flexibility and Projectability of Phrases

Phrases can have further phrases and clauses embedded as optional elements within them. Thus, they are in theory indefinitely "extendable" (Quirk et al. 1985:43).

The extendability of phrases makes them eminently suitable for use in turn continuation. For instance, here is a case from English conversation where the speaker Vanessa extends a final NP from her own (provisionally complete) turn:

---

[52] Languages with SOV structure are more likely to have *postpositions* following a noun phrase than *prepositions* preceding it. For this reason, many typologists speak of "adpositions" (Dryer 2013). In the following, however, we shall retain the more unwieldy "pre-" and "post-" nomenclature, as it captures more transparently the directional way these structures work in interaction.

5. *Phrases* 417

(6.60) "Purple dress" (Clift 2007a:61) (adapted)
((Vanessa is Mary's twenty-something-year-old daughter; she is wearing a summer dress.))

```
1         Mary:   Listen, I don't know how dressy this is going to be
2                 tomorrow. (0.4) I don't think you want to wear that dress
3                 do you?
4                 (1.1)
5         Van:    This dress¿
6         Mary:   Mm.
7                 (1.2)
8         Van:    I could, I mean if its bla:zingly hot, I might wear this
9                 dress.
10                (0.2)
11  ->    Van:    Or my purple dress.
12                (0.8)
13  ->    Van:    Which is pre[tty.
14        Mary:               [Mmm.
```

When there is no uptake to Vanessa's turn in lines 8–9, she expands its final NP *this dress* first by appending a coordinate NP, *or my purple dress* (line 11). The latter extension again receiving no uptake (line 12), she then extends its final NP with a relative clause, *which is pretty* (line 13) (see also Chapter 7 §4.2). Over time then, Vanessa's original NP *this dress* becomes *this dress or my purple dress, which is pretty.*

But an interlocutor can also extend a co-interlocutor's turn by adding to their (turn-final) phrase:

(6.61) "Volvo 345" (Clift 2007a:70)
((Edgerton has asked after Donald's health; Donald has had problems in his leg and foot.))

```
1         Don:    I've bought myself a Volvo three four fi::ve.
2   ->    Edg:    Which is autom[atic.
3         Don:                  [automatic.
4         Edg:    Yes.
5   (->)  Don:    Which is magnificent.
```

Here Edgerton expands the final NP in his co-interlocutor's turn *a Volvo three four fi::ve* (line 1) by adding on the relative clause *which is automatic* (line 2). Don confirms this co-completion in line 3 and then expands the NP again himself in line 5.

Phrases also permit projection. However, the grounds on which the projections are made can be quite different. Take, for instance, the Finnish NP:

here, determiners and modifiers precede the head and agree with it in case and number. This means that on production of the determiner and/or modifier, it is already clear what the case and number of the whole phrase will be (Helasvuo 2001a:36). In the English NP, on the other hand, it is the order of elements that has projective force: the quantifier *some*, for example, when unstressed, projects a following head, for example, *some virus* (2001a:37).

Within prepositional phrases it is the projective force of the preposition that permits it to be used as a so-called *increment elicitor* in English talk-in-interaction (Lerner 2004). Lerner describes prepositions as having "maximum grammatical projection" (2004:158), meaning that on production they strongly call for completion of the phrase. Thus, when speakers use a preposition as a stand-alone, it can "prompt" the other to say more in order to finish the phrase. This suggests that phrases have strong internal cohesion. Here is a case where the recipient uses this device to elicit the completion of an increment to the prior turn (see also Chapter 3 §3.2.3):

(6.62)   "Finland" (Lerner 2004:162)
```
1        Jack:     I just returned
2   ->   Kathy:    from
3        Jack:     Finland
```

And here is a case where an original questioner deploys an increment elicitor to prompt the respondent to provide a more substantial answer to their question (the underscore in line 3 represents a "flat" intonation contour):

(6.63)   "Food service" (Lerner 2004:163)
```
1        Therapist:   What kind of work do you do?
2        Mother:      on food service
3   ->   Therapist:   At_
4        Mother:      uh post office cafeteria downtown
5                     main point office on Redwood
6        Therapist:   °Okay°
```

In Japanese talk-in-interaction, postpositions lack projective force by definition. However, as work by Tanaka (1999) and Hayashi (2001, 2004b) has shown, they can be used in utterance- and turn-initial position to establish a backward link to a prior NP. This practice thus also builds on the internal cohesion of a phrase. Here is a case where a recipient deploys such a practice to answer a prior question pre-emptively:

5. Phrases

(6.64) "Ten days" (Hayashi 2001:319)

```
1 Aiko:  de! nan'nicikan     gurai °sore     tte.°
         and for-how-many-days about that-one QT
         And, for about how many days, that one?

2 Mami:  ga tookakan.
         SP for-ten-days
         is for ten days
```

The post-positioned *ga*, a subject particle, is used at the beginning of Mami's turn to link back to the NP *sore* "that one" at the end of Aiko's prior turn. That is, *sore* "that one" is incorporated into Mami's answer as the subject of the predicate *tookakan* "for ten days": *sore ga* "that one" (Hayashi 2001:319). According to Hayashi, the practice of beginning a turn with a postposition allows recipients *inter alia* to pre-emptively answer a prior question and close off an emerging adjacency pair that risks taking the conversation in a potentially problematic direction (2001:327).

> Like clauses, phrases have internal cohesion and allow varying degrees of projectability. In SVO languages such as English or Finnish, pre-head elements in an NP strongly project an upcoming head and prepositions project the NPs that follow them. The latter is what makes freestanding prepositions deployable as *increment elicitors*: they prompt completion of an initiated but as yet incomplete phrase (Lerner 2004). In SOV languages such as Japanese, projection is weaker in NPs and postpositional phrases. However, speakers can exploit the cohesiveness of postpositional phrases by beginning a turn with a postposition that links back to an NP in a prior turn at talk. This practice allows them to steer or re-direct the trajectory of a developing course of action (Hayashi 2001:338).

5.2 Building Actions with Phrases

Like clauses, phrases can be used to build turns and implement actions in talk-in-interaction. A well-known example is the use of phrasal formats for the other-initiation of repair: *Columbia?* (NP), *Met whom?* (verb phrase), *Across the street?* (prepositional phrase) (see also Chapter 3 §3). Somewhat less well known, however, is the use of unattached or "free" NPs as found, for example, in turn continuation (Ono and Thompson 1994; Helasvuo 2001a, 2001b; Ford et al. 2002).[53]

---

[53] Even less well known is the use of phrasal forms to initiate subsidiary sequences (Mazeland 2013:488), a practice that will not be dealt with here.

A "free" NP is an NP that is not part of any neighboring clausal construction in its context of occurrence (Helasvuo 2001b:105). The NPs that constitute left and right dislocations (see above) can be analyzed as constituents of the clause they precede or follow; moreover, they are primarily concerned with reference. Free NPs, by contrast, function predicatively (Ono and Thompson 1994). This can be seen from the following example:

(6.65) "Sibbie's sister" (Ford et al. 2002:27) (adapted)
```
1       Bee:    Oh Sibbie's sister had a ba:by bo::y.
2       Ava:    Who?
3       Bee:    Sibbie's sister.
4       Ava:    Oh really?
5       Bee:    Myeah,
6       Ava:    [°(That's nice)°
7       Bee:    [She had it yesterday.
8  ->           Ten:: pou:nds.
9       Ava:    °Jesus Christ.°
10      Bee:    She had a ho:(hh)rse hh .hh
```

The NP *ten pounds* (line 8) is not a syntactic constituent of the clause *she had it yesterday* (line 7) nor does it function to clarify a referent; instead, it is an independent construction predicating the weight of the baby. Like a syntactically dependent "increment" (Chapter 2 §4), this free NP occurs when uptake is lacking or insufficient (see Ava's barely audible turn in line 6), and it provides an additional TRP for a response. However, unlike "increments", free NPs display a stance toward what has just been said: in addition to its extreme nasal delivery, Bee's *ten pounds* in line 8 has significant lengthening on both words. This affective coloring models the kind of alignment that is being sought from the recipient (Ford et al. 2002:26).

Free NPs have also been documented in Finnish, where their default case marking is nominative (Helasvuo 2001b:114). In German, not only NPs but also adjective phrases can be used as "free" constituents, the latter lacking inflection altogether. Auer refers to such free constituents as *appositional* in his taxonomy of sentence extensions (see §3.2 above): although they are semantically tied to a prior clause, they are not grammatically fitted to it (1991:151–2). Here is one of his examples:

(6.66) "Mercedes" (Auer 1996a:77) (adapted)
```
1    M:   dann=zahl=I nomal zehndausend Mark drauf,=
          in that case I pay another ten thousand marks in addition,=
```

```
2          (na)=hab=i=n fanTAstischn (.)  h gä tä I (.)  gEll,
           =and I get a fantastic         (.) h GTI   (.) you know,
3    F:    m:,=
4 -> M:    =absolut NEU,
           absolutely new,
```

Although the adjectival phrase *absolut neu* "absolutely new" (line 4) is semantically linked to the NP complement *n fantastischn gä tä I* "a fantastic GTI" of the prior clause (line 2), it is not morpho-syntactically inflected to be part of it. If it were, it would be marked for the accusative case, like the other elements of that NP: *einen absolut neuen* "an absolutely new one". Instead, this freestanding adjective phrase is added, without inflectional marking, to the possibly complete TCU in line 2, arguably to do the work of a "post-completion stance marker" (Schegloff 1996b:92): like the free NP in (6.65), it conveys a stance toward what the speaker has just said.

> NPs (and other phrasal types) can be used as "free" constituents to build TCUs in turn continuation. In these cases, they follow a possibly complete TCU ending in a TRP, but they are not morpho-syntactically part of it. Instead, they merely "lean" on it for semantic interpretation. The deployment of free phrasal constituents is a practice for dealing with lack of (sufficient) uptake: the phrasal constituents themselves provide another point of possible completion, and thus another TRP at which recipients can respond. But they are not merely extensions of the prior turn, they also convey retrospective alignment toward what has just been said, modeling a stance for the uptake being sought.

Freestanding phrasal units – whether NPs, pre- (or post)positional phrases, adjective phrases, or adverb phrases – can also be used to build wholly independent turns at talk. This commonly happens in responsive position (Mazeland 2013:487). For instance, as we have already noted, phrases are the default format for providing simple answers to specifying question-word questions (see Chapter 4 §2.6). But phrasal units are also used in second assessments that agree with first assessments:[54]

(6.67)   "Nice little lady" (Thompson et al. 2015:152) (adapted)
((With reference to an old acquaintance of Bea's who Norma has just met.))
```
1    Bea:    hh hhh we:ll, h I was gla:d she could come too last ni:ght=
```

---

[54] However, Thompson et al. (2015:150) find that in American English such phrasal assessments are rare compared to the much more frequent clausal ones.

```
2     Nor:    =sh[e seems such a n]ice little [lady    ]
3 ->  Bea:       [(since you keh) ]           [dAwful]ly nice little
4 ->           person. t hhhh hhh we:ll, I: just
```

Here Bea agrees with Norma's assessment of her friend *she seems such a nice little lady* (line 2) by using a simple NP *awfully nice little person* (lines 3–4).[55]

And phrasal units are used to respond to news reports and informings:

(6.68)   "Next Thursday" (Thompson et al. 2015:87)
```
1     Cla:    mMm hm hhh hhh well we're gonna have a meeting uh::m hh uh
2             Jo at ah:: (.) THUR:SDAY:: e-October the seventh that's
3             next Thu:rsda:[y.
4 ->  Jo:                   [next Thurs[day.
5     Cla:                              [hhh hhh
6             at eleven thirty at the Gir:l's Clu:b here in: uh:m (0.2)
7             hhh in Santa Ba:rbara at fi:ve thirty one East Or:tega.hh
```

Phrasal repetition of information delivered in a prior turn – as here, with falling intonation (line 4) – has been described in English and German as a practice for receipting instructions (Goldberg 1975) and/or for confirming central information (Auer 2014a:551).

In all these cases, phrasal forms build a full-fledged turn at talk, one that is implementing an independent action. Yet the interpretation of these phrasal turns is crucially dependent on their position as responses to prior, typically clausal turns. Auer describes the relation between such initiating and responsive turns as symbiotic, with the first structure serving as a "host" for the second. The host provides structural positions that remain latent for use in subsequent talk (Auer 2014a:549). Accordingly, a phrasal answer to a question-word question (here in German) might be represented as follows:

(6.69)   "At Göttingen" (Auer 2014a:555) (adapted)
```
1   A:    WO     warn wir stEhngeblieben-
          where  had  we   stopped
          where were we?
2         ach so [bei GÖTtingen;
          oh yes  at Göttingen
3   B:           [bei GÖTtingen;
                  at  Göttingen
```

---

[55] It is worth noting that this singular noun phrase lacks a determiner, as do the other instantiations of phrasal agreeing second assessments reported in Pomerantz (1984a). This practice awaits further investigation.

1 A:		WO	warn	wir	stEhngeblieben-
		where	had	we	stopped
2	ach so	bei GÖTtingen;			
	oh yes	at Göttingen			
3 B:		bei GÖTtingen;			
		at Göttingen			
		Advb	**V$_{fin}$**	**Subj**	**V$_{inf}$**

In line 2 A provides a candidate answer to his/her own question from line 1 in full overlap (and full agreement) with the answer that B gives in line 3. Both candidate answer and answer are formatted as prepositional phrases: *bei Göttingen* "at Göttingen". Interpretively, they fit in the slot established by *wo* "where" in the prior question (line 1). The structure provided by *warn wir stehengeblieben* "had we stopped" in line 1 remains latently available for the interpretation of the phrases in lines 2 and 3 (Auer 2014a:555).

> Freestanding phrases can be used in English to build turns that respond *inter alia* to specifying question-word questions, to first assessments, and to news deliveries and informings. In these sequence types, phrasal responses are full-fledged actions: they provide simple answers, agreeing assessments, and (with falling intonation) confirmations/registerings of prior information. Moreover, they are the *default* way to accomplish such actions. Yet their interpretation is dependent on a prior (clausal) turn, whose structural "slots" remain latently available for them.

6. Conclusion

Sentences, clauses, and phrases are syntactic construction types that are mobilized by participants for the design of TCUs and the implementation of social actions. Although they vary in size – phrases are typically smaller than clauses (having fewer words) and sentences often larger (when they encompass multiple clauses) – all may have internal structure with syntactic heads and optionally other accompanying elements. Participants tacitly know and recognize these construction types, including their beginnings and their completions, from past interactional history and linguistic socialization.

Internally, sentences, clauses, and phrases are cohesive. In languages that are predominantly left-headed, "early" heads project what is likely to come next and bring the unit to completion; in languages that are predominantly right-headed, "late" heads complete the unit, retrospectively establishing cohesive relations with elements that have come before. In order to be used for the implementation of social actions, sentences, clauses, and phrases are prosodically packaged as interactionally relevant units. In some languages (e.g., Swedish and German), the interactional tasks that need to be dealt with in TCUs are mirrored by the topological fields of the clause and the morpho-syntactic elements that routinely fill them.

Externally, sentences, clauses, and phrases exhibit fundamental flexibility and adaptability to the contingencies and exigencies of the interaction at hand. In the case of clauses, this is attested to by their initial and final extendability through various types of grammatical constructions suitable for pre- and post-positionings. Initial extensions (e.g., left dislocations) allow participants to respond to and/or deal with issues relating to prior talk; final extensions (e.g., "increments") allow participants to deal with organizing the transition to the next unit or turn. There is thus a systematic relationship between the interactional tasks to be accomplished and the grammatical structures used for these purposes.

Because of their fully articulated structure, sentences and clauses are particularly well suited for carrying out independent actions, for example, launching new topics or initiating new sequences, independent of the prior speaker's contribution (Mazeland 2013:487; also Thompson Forthcoming). By contrast, the use of other syntactic unit types is more restricted. Constructions with subject omission (English) and phrases more generally are dependent formats that rely on their relation to a syntactic host construction, or host action, for interpretation. Their form contextualizes the action being carried out through it as a dependent or secondary one. "Dense" constructions (German) are used in special contexts for the depiction of fast and dramatic developments in the complication part of a story.

The usage of sentences, clauses, and phrases is sensitive to position in the turn. In multi-unit German turns, for instance, Deppermann (2012) finds that sentences typically do not occur at the beginning of turns but only later (see also 2013). The reason for this is that speakers must first address the tasks of (i) taking over the turn and establishing a common focus of interaction, (ii) conveying understanding, alignment, and/or affiliation with respect to the prior turn, and (iii) dealing with the projections built up in the prior turn. Only then do they (iv) deliver their own projects. Tasks (i)–(iii) rely heavily on prior utterances and can in most cases be achieved through non-sentential/non-clausal forms. However, task (iv) often involves something "new", i.e., not projected by the prior speaker: this may be a new topic, a new action, an action that breaks with current projections, or a complex presentation. This is where sentences and clauses become relevant: they are deployed as resources for presenting and making interpretable the action being carried out as something independent from a prior speaker's TCU, turn, or action (Deppermann 2012:10–11).

6. Conclusion

Finally, the usage of sentences, clauses, and phrases is sensitive to position in the sequence. Recall that in response to specifying question-word questions in English, clausal and phrasal formats are not interchangeable. In this sequential position it is phrasal forms that are treated as unproblematic, while clausal forms signal some kind of problem (Fox and Thompson 2010; also Chapter 4 §2.6). More generally, recent research indicates that phrasal forms in responsive position engage with the prior turn, while non-repetitional full-clausal responses are maximally independent of the turn they are responsive to (Thompson et al. 2015:277–81). This corroborates Mazeland's description of phrasal TCUs as "practices for using sequential position as a resource, relating the action in current TCU to the action in prior turn and exploiting this relationship for shaping next turns as recognizable types of next actions" (2013:489).

7
Clause Combinations

1. Introduction

In this chapter we consider clausal complexes as resources for talk-in-interaction. Clausal complexes can be thought of as formed by two processes that traditional descriptive grammarians have called *coordination*[1] and *subordination*[2]: clausal coordination is the linkage of two or more independent clauses to form what is called a compound sentence; clausal subordination is the "embedding" of one or more dependent clauses within a "main" or matrix clause to form a so-called complex sentence (Quirk et al. 1985:987).[3] Why do we use the term *clause combination* here? There are at least two very good reasons. For one, descriptive grammars base their understanding of clausal coordination and subordination on the "sentence", which – in its traditional understanding – is a problematic notion for the analysis of conversation (see Chapter 6). Second, the reality of clausal linkage in unscripted talk is far more complex than is suggested by the concepts of coordination of one clause with another, or subordination of one to another.[4] For instance, in the following English fragment,[5] the clause *it's so funny* in line 32 is linked to a whole chunk of subsequent discourse (lines 33–40):

---

[1] *Coordination* has been described as referring to "syntactic constructions in which two or more units of the same type are combined into a larger unit and still have the same semantic relations with other surrounding elements" (Haspelmath 2007:1). Some grammarians have described the two units which are coordinated as being at the same "rank" or "level."

[2] *Subordination* has been described as involving "clauses which are grammatically dependent on another clause or on some element in another clause" (Thompson et al. 2007:237–8). The authors distinguish three types: complement clauses, relative clauses, and adverbial clauses. We deal with the first two types in §4 and with the last type in §3 below.

[3] *Embedding* is typically understood to mean that the dependent clause functions as an element, or constituent, in the superordinate clause.

[4] See Matthiessen and Thompson (1988) for further arguments in support of the notion of clause combining as opposed to coordination/subordination. Our use of the term *clause combining* in this book is somewhat broader than theirs, which is restricted to hypotaxis and specifically to circumstantial relations.

[5] See also Laury and Ono (2014), who present case analyses of clause combining in Finnish and Japanese conversation, highlighting the complexity of the process.

1. Introduction

(7.1) "Contradiction" (Santa Barbara Corpus of Spoken American English 028)
((Jeff is talking to his girlfriend Jill long-distance. In this fragment he is telling her about an Asian guy he met earlier that day while playing basketball at the beach.))

```
1    Jeff:    A=nd,
2             .. we just,
3             .. <@ we just got in one of those  .. conversations where
4             @>,
5             .. (H) you just talk about everything.
6             @@@ (H)
7    Jill:    Un[hunh=].
8    Jeff:        [Like,
9             like] r=eal politica=l,
10            and,
11            (H) and,
12            .. everything from Norm- --
13            um,
```
((9 lines omitted involving a self-repair operation))
```
23   Jeff:    [(H)] from Nixon,
24            to like Rush Limbaugh,
25            to abortion,
26            to capital punishment,
27            @@
28   Jill:    Whoa[=].
29   Jeff:        [Like],
30            .. yeah,
31            you know what,
32            and <X it's X> so funny,
33            cause he's,
34            .. he's a Catholic,
35            ... (TSK) a=nd,
36            (H) you know,
37            like I nailed him on the contradiction <X you know X>,
38            he's like pro-capital punishment,
39            ... but --
40            and.. pro-life?
41            @=
42   Jill:    Unhunh[=].
```

Disregarding the tokens *you know* (lines 36 and 37) and *like* (lines 37 and 38) in the latter part (lines 32–41) of Jeff's extended turn, we might wish to say that the connector *cause* in line 33 links what follows it to the prior clause *it's so funny* (line 32) in a cause or reason relation. But the linked material that is serving as a reason for the funniness of Jeff's experience is more than a subordinate clause (*he's a Catholic*) or even a conjunction of two subordinate clauses (*he's a Catholic and . . . I nailed him on the contradiction*). It also includes the clause *he's pro-capital punishment but – and pro-life* (lines 38–40), which has no explicit marker of coordination or subordination but is semantically and pragmatically dependent on *contradiction* (line 37), being a description of its content.[6] Actually, it might be useful to say that lines 38–40 stand in a dependent relation to *I nailed him on the contradiction*, although the link between them is not explicit; rather this is a case of *asyndetic* linkage: there is no overt verbal indication of the syndetic relation holding between the two parts. Yet observe that there is a prosodic indication of the relation: the two lines 37 and 38 are "run on" with no temporal break or pitch step-up between them (see also Online-Chapter E).[7] That is, the two units in lines 37 and 38–40 are combined with one another prosodically. Altogether then, Jeff's turn, specifically lines 32–41, could be considered one large clause complex, although in terms of coordination and subordination it does not appear to be cohesive at all.[8]

It is in order to be able to handle complex structures of this type that we have chosen to speak of clause combinations in this chapter. In the sections that follow, we will consider both syndetic and asyndetic combinations to the extent that the latter are prosodically linked.

It has been pointed out in the literature that there is a cline, or continuum, in clause-combining constructions extending from *parataxis*, in which two or more relatively independent clauses (or clause complexes)[9] are combined with one another, through *hypotaxis*, where an independent clause is combined with one or more dependent clauses, to *subordination*, where a dependent clause is wholly embedded within an independent clause – its matrix – forming one of its constituents (Hopper and Traugott 1993:169–70).[10] We adopt this classification with slight

---

[6] In other words, lines 37–40 are paraphrasable as "I nailed him on the contradiction **that** he's pro-capital punishment but ... pro-life". This analysis is supported by the fact that the definite noun phrase *the contradiction* in line 37 is built to project an upcoming dependent clause, either a content clause or a restrictive relative one.

[7] In terms of pitch, for example, line 38 begins where line 37 left off. For other types of prosodic linkage in English asyndetic clause combinations see Thumm (2000); Couper-Kuhlen (2009c); and especially Barth-Weingarten (2009).

[8] We note, moreover, that this whole complex structure (lines 32–40) is itself linked via the coordinator *and* to something preceding, not simply to line 26 but rather, arguably, to the whole chunk of talk in lines 2–26.

[9] With the distinction *independent* versus *dependent* clause we mean "able to stand by itself" or "not able to stand by itself."

[10] This classification differs from that of many grammarians, who see hypotaxis and embedding as two different kinds of subordination.

adjustments here[11] and begin with a discussion of paratactically linked clause combinations.

2. Paratactic Clause Combinations

Prototypically speaking, paratactic combinations express additive, contrastive, or alternative relations between clauses and/or clause complexes with the help of dedicated connectors such as (in English) *and*, *but*, and *or*.[12] For instance, here is an example of a turn, taken from the same conversation as (7.1) above, that is constructed with additive clause combinations linked by the connector *and*:[13]

(7.2) "Ecstasy" (Santa Barbara Corpus of Spoken American English 028)
((Jill is telling her boyfriend Jeff about her recent pregnancy test.))

```
1        Jill:   Yeah,
2                there was such drama.
3   ->           There was drama,
4   =>           and there was suspense.
5   =>           (H) And then there was relief,
6   =>           (H) and [then there was] ecstasy.
```

Observe that the three *and*s here are alike in that they all link clausal units and stand in initial position with respect to the second unit or conjunct. But they function differently according to whether they are connecting material to a prior finished or unfinished unit. (This is reflected in the capitalization of *and*, or lack of it, in the transcript.) The unit beginning with *and* in line 4 is projected by line 3 *there was drama*, which ends in rising pitch, suggesting that at the end of line 3, Jill is indicating that another item will follow. The unit beginning with *and* in line 5, on the other hand, has not been projected by line 4 *and there was suspense*: this is because line 4 ends in low falling pitch, suggesting that on its completion Jill may have reached the end of her turn. Thus, when she begins again in line 5, after a brief inbreath, Jill is heard as continuing a turn that had already reached a point of possible completion. The difference between what happens prosodically at the end of line 3 and the end of line 4 has been referred to as "forward linking" and "backward linking" in clause combinations (Chafe 1988:19). Observations of this sort have important implications for clause combining.

---

[11] Hopper and Traugott (1993:172) use the term "parataxis" to refer only to asyndetic clausal combinations; we broaden it here to include combinations with an overt coordinator, as long as the units being combined are at the same level of structure, i.e., are both relatively independent.

[12] As our later discussion will show, circumstantial relations such as cause, condition, and concession can also be expressed paratactically. See also Haspelmath (2007:2), who identifies causal linkage as in *She died, for the apple was poisoned* as one major type of *coordination*.

[13] In this and the following examples, we use single arrows to mark the first part of a paratactic or hypotactic clause combination and double arrows to mark the second part.

> Paratactically combined clauses are linearly ordered, meaning that one of the units comes first and the other is placed second in relation to it. Since in conversation paratactic clause combinations are produced in real time, this means that the second clause or clause complex can be projected lexically,[14] syntactically,[15] and/or prosodically by the first clause or clause combination, or can be added on retrospectively after the first unit has come to possible completion.

The generalization above holds not only for additive clause linkages (see also Barth-Weingarten and Couper-Kuhlen 2011 for English), but also for contrastive ones (e.g., Barth-Weingarten 2009 for English) and for alternative ones (see, e.g., Koivisto 2017 for Finnish).

There is another observation to be made concerning the real-time production of clause combinations and the role of prosody in forming them: this can be seen from the following fragment, here a case of contrastive linkage with *but*:

(7.3) "Bear Lake" (Santa Barbara Corpus of Spoken American English 028) ((Jeff is telling Jill about a mutual friend Rob, who has gone off to spend several days alone in a cabin overlooking Bear Lake.))

```
1   -> Jeff:   ..(H)(TSK) Yeah I think he was trying to get a girl to go with him but,
2                @[@@@@@@@@]
3      Jill:   [Oh,
4                @@@@@@@@]
5   =>          (H) [2but that2] fell through.
6      Jeff:   [2(H)=2]
7                So he went from like the romantic .. sexual getaway,
8                to,
9      Jill:   @
10     Jeff:   you know,
11               a soul searching .. (SNIFF) bond with nature .. type of (Hx) deal.
```

Observe that the connector word *but* appears in line 1 at the end of the first conjoined unit rather than at the beginning of the second conjunct, as was the case with *and* in extract (7.2). *But* is heard here as attached to the first conjunct because it is run on prosodically from *Yeah I think he was trying to get a girl to go with him*: in other words, there is no break in timing, pitch, or loudness between *him* and *but*.

---

[14] Lexical projection can involve, for instance, the use of "correlate" words that point to an upcoming clausal continuation: for instance, in German *dadurch weil* ... "for the following reason because ..." (Gohl 2006:231).

[15] Syntactic projection can involve constructions with specific constituent ordering that project more to come, as, for instance, with verb-first constructions in German: *hätt ich zu dem Zeitpunkt gewusst* ... "had I known at that time ..." (Auer and Lindström 2011:247); and Swedish: *har de gått mer än sex timmar å ingenting har hänt*, "if six hours have passed and nothing has happened" (Auer and Lindström 2011:239).

Rhythmically speaking, *but* is cliticized onto the prior accented syllable *with*, yielding a trisyllabic foot *WITH him but*: /DA da da/ (see also Online-Chapter E). Jeff now pauses, ending the prosodic unit with slightly rising pitch and thus projecting that he will continue. However, his *but* is so strongly projective that, after a spate of joint laughter, Jill is able to propose a candidate completion herself: *but that fell through* (line 5). In a case like this, we might then say that the connector *but* has "detached" itself from its default position at the beginning of the second conjunct and cliticized onto the end of the first conjunct.[16]

> What we see here is a very general phenomenon, one that can be observed with all connector words, whether additive, contrastive, or alternative: the connecting word can be produced prosodically as attached to the end of the first unit, thereby projecting not only that the turn will continue but also how it will continue.

Because of the strong projection that a "detachment" process like the one seen above creates, there are important implications for language change. As Mulder and Thompson (2008) point out, in some varieties of English, such as Australian English, *but* has developed from a connector – which, as shown in (7.3) above, can sometimes be left dangling – into a turn-final particle, one that is treated not as leaving the turn so far incomplete, but as actually completing it (see also Chapter 8 §2.3.1). Here is an Australian English fragment that demonstrates such a turn-final *but*:

(7.4)　　"New people" (Mulder and Thompson 2008:192)

```
1     Cathy:   We've had new people join our [group].
2     Megan:                                 [yeah].
3     Sally:   Kylie,
4  -> 		   She was a bit of a bitch but. (Hx=)
5     Cathy:   um.
6     Sally:   She [was].
7     Cathy:       [Al]icia.
8     Sally:   Alicia.
```

Sally's final fall-to-low intonation after *but* as well as her exhalation at the end of line 4 imply that her turn has reached a point of possible completion.[17] And indeed

---

[16] Obviously, such a "detachment" analysis is only meaningful for languages in which a coordinating conjunction can be said to be positioned by default before the second conjunct. It would not apply, for instance, in Finnish, where coordinating conjunctions are treated as having their default position at the end of the first conjunct (Hakulinen et al. 2004; Koivisto 2012). See also Haspelmath (2007:2).

[17] The effect of this turn-final *but* is thus similar to turn-final *though* in other English dialects (see also Barth-Weingarten and Couper-Kuhlen 2002).

this is how Cathy treats it, because in next turn she produces not a continuer, which would suggest that Sally's turn is incomplete, but rather a turn that treats the prior assessment as complete by acknowledging it, if only minimally (line 5). It is presumably the minimal nature of Cathy's acknowledgment that prompts Sally to reaffirm her assessment in line 6. Mulder and Thompson (2008) conclude that *but* is following a path of grammaticization from "conjunction" to "final particle", a path that is common to all English varieties, although others may not have progressed along it as far. In fact, the same grammaticization path for contrastive markers is documented in other, unrelated languages, for example, Japanese (Mori 1999a, 1999b; Ono et al. 2012) and Finnish (Koivisto 2012). Moreover, analogous paths of development are observed for additive and alternative markers: Koivisto (2012) describes a comparable development for Finnish *ja* "and"; the German tag *oder* "or" (see example (7.13) below) has presumably developed similarly.

Above we observed that conjunctive markers such as *and*, *but*, and *or* can attach themselves to the end of a first conjunct prosodically in a process that is relevant for turn construction. But paratactic clause combinations can undergo further processes of condensation and fusion: when this happens with *and*, so-called *hendiadic* constructions can emerge (Hopper 2001a). *Hendiadys* is a Greek term ("one by means of two") for a figure of speech that represents one conceptual entity through the conjunction of two distinct constituents, often in a single intonation phrase. Conventionalized examples of clausal hendiadics in English are, for instance, *go ahead and sit down*, *go and complain*, *try and come* (Hopper 2001b).

Note that not all clauses conjoined with *and* – even if they share a subject – constitute hendiadic constructions. Here is a case of **non**-hendiadic clausal conjunction: in lines 12 and 14 of (7.5) below, the two clauses have the same understood subject and are linked with *and*; yet because of their prosodic delivery, they map onto separate turn-constructional units (TCUs) and are interpretable as describing two distinct events:

(7.5)   "Gladys" (Barth-Weingarten and Couper-Kuhlen 2011:269)
((Claire and her friend Chloe are talking about a recent bridge game and how poorly Gladys, one of the other women there, played.))

```
1    Cla:    ↑I can just get e-uh ((smiling))
2    Chl:    hhehhh hh[ehh
3    Cla:             [she say[↓:s uh↓]
4    Chl:                     [d i d y ][ou notice] ()
5    Cla:                                [is that al]right with you dear?
6    Cla:    hhh she ta:lks [so En]glish you know] hhh
7    Chl:                   [yah.] she's ↑su    ]ch a do:ll
8                                                a[nd you know=
9    Cla:                                         [uh-h
```

```
10    Chl:    =she almost makes me pull my hair ou [t when] I w a ] tch her pla:y
11    Cla:                                         [ehhhh]↑heh heh↑]
12 -> Chl:    hhhh I shoul [d ↑get u:p,
13    Cla:                 [hhhh
14 => Chl:    and go (to) the bathroom or put some ma(h)ake [(h)up (h)on=
15    Cla:                                                  [u
16    Cla:    =h [n hn
17    Chl:       [bec(h)uz she ↑just about ↑hhehhh=
18    Cla:    = hhhh
19    Chl:    dri(h)ves me [in↑sane she won't get those ↑trumps out hhe:hh
20    Cla:                 [°he°
21    Cla:    I know
```

To underline how excruciating she finds it to watch Gladys play bridge, Chloe suggests in line 12 that she should leave the table (*I should get up*). Chloe produces this unit with slightly rising pitch, intimating that she will continue talking. In the event, she does deliver another clause, linked to the first one with *and*, describing possible activities once she has left the bridge table: *go (to) the bathroom or put some make-up on* (line 14). The prosodic design here results in Chloe's turn being multi-unit, the first clause having projected more talk, with the successive predicates *get up* and *go to the bathroom* encoding what are conceptually two separate actions that take place at different moments in time.[18]

However, additive clause combinations such as the one in (7.5) can also be compacted and condensed, for instance, by avoiding prosodic boundaries before or after *and* and/or by reducing the phonetic substance of the conjunction. When such fusion and reduction take place, the two clauses are likely to be heard as part of the same TCU. If they share a subject and the first verb is "light", with little semantic content of its own, then the clause combination – instead of expressing two predicates and separate actions – becomes interpretable semantically as a hendiadys, i.e., as a single predicate expressing one action. In line 12 of (7.6) below, the speaker uses a hendiadic clause combination:

(7.6)   "Money borrower" (Barth-Weingarten and Couper-Kuhlen 2011:271)
((Bea and her friend Dinah are talking about a mutual friend Marty who is a compulsive money borrower.))
```
1       Bea:    =Well that's what I mea:n.
```

---

[18] On other occasions, and produced under a single intonation contour, *get up and go to the bathroom* could, of course, encode what is conceptually one action: see below.

```
2            It isn't the: money as [much as]
3    Din:                        [No money] doe:s:
4            didn't mean anything or I'd do it for ↑M-ARty
5            only ee-it's: it's just this: uh:: (0.7)
6            hh ↑you kno:w now for instance wu-
7            she: used to borrow from me
8            she borrowed twice:: from me once.
9    Bea:    Uh huh
10   Din:    hhh A:n:: (0.5)
11           I wu-I was sitting in her hou:se
12 ->        and: Re:j Oakley came'n de↑livered something.
13           and she: w- h said she didn't have the cha:nge
14           would I loan her the money to pay him
15           and she'd pay me later:.
16           and I: said well you already borrowed from me twice:
17           and never offered to pa:y
18   Bea:    Oh huh[:
19   Din:          [hhh And ↑she produ:ced money enou:gh
20           to pa:y Rej Oakley and me bo:th.
```

Dinah is telling a story about her friend Marty's odd behavior with respect to borrowing money. In line 12 she relates that on one occasion *Rej Oakley came 'n delivered something*. With a different prosodic design, this could refer to two actions: Rej Oakley first coming by, and Rej Oakley then delivering something. But with no prosodic breaks on either side of *and* as well as with the connector being heavily reduced phonetically, the prosodic-phonetic design here suggests that *came and delivered* is conceptually one action, taking place at a single point in time.

But if Dinah wanted to refer to a single action, why did she not just simply say "Rej Oakley delivered something" rather than using a hendiadic construction consisting of two (conjoined) predicates? A study by Drew (1998) on conversational complaining suggests one possible motivation. Drew is concerned to account for why a speaker would say "I took the drink and I drank out of it" rather than simply "I had a drink", or "he came up to me and he said" rather than simply "he said …".[19] Drew's argument is that using two predicates instead of one *overdetermines* the description and attributes a moral dimension to the behavior being described: it construes the behavior as deliberate, intentional, and purposeful,

---

[19] Note that in Drew's examples the (co-referential) subject is repeated in the second predicate (*he came up to me and **he** said*), whereas in conventionalized cases it is typically omitted (*he came and ∅ delivered*).

rather than accidental, inadvertent, or unconscious. Such a depiction can be crucial in portraying a third party's behavior as egregious or reprehensible (1998:318ff.). In the case of (7.6) above, it is not Rej Oakley whose conduct is being presented as complainable, but rather that of Marty, Dinah's friend. In this instance then, Dinah, in using two predicates instead of one, conveys the deliberateness of Rej's behavior, and can imply that her friend should have anticipated that he was coming and had her money ready. However, instead of this, Marty is depicted as feigning surprise at Rej's arrival and being caught empty-handed, making it necessary to ask Dinah for a loan.

> Speakers deploy clause combinations as resources: linked clauses can be separated into two prosodic units for the purpose of turn and sequence organization, or they can be condensed into one unit for specific types of turn design. This flexibility is made possible through various forms of lexico-syntactic expansion ("he came up to me and he said") versus deletion ("came and delivered"), as well as through various phonetic-prosodic means such as stretching versus reduction/elision of sound segments, and exposing versus suppression of prosodic boundaries.

In the following we review further uses to which paratactic clause combinations can be put in talk-in-interaction. This overview includes studies of paratactic and asyndetic constructions encoding not only additive, contrastive, and alternative relations but also circumstantial relations such as cause, condition, and concession. To capture the fact that the same or similar work can be accomplished by paratactic, or paratactically used, connectors in a wide variety of languages, these connectors will be referred to in quotation marks; language-particular connectors will appear in italics.

2.1 Agenda-invoking with "And"

Heritage and Sorjonen (1994) examine *and* when it is used to preface questions in informal medical encounters. They distinguish a use such as the one in (7.7) from one such as in (7.8) (HV stands for health visitor, M for a new mother):

(7.7)   "Georgina" (Heritage and Sorjonen 1994:5)
```
1        HV: What are you going to (.) call her?
2    ->  M:  Georgi:na.
3            (1.0)
4    =>  HV: An:d you're spelling that,
```

436   *Clause Combinations*

(7.8)   "Husband" (Heritage and Sorjonen 1994:5)
```
1        HV:    Okay so that's your clinic fo:rm.
2        M:     (                    )
3        HV:    An' all I put on here is you:r (0.7) there's a
4               bit about you:::, (0.9) it sa:ys here that you're
5               twenty o:ne is that ri:ght?
6        M:     That's right.=
7   ->   HV:    =How old's your husba:nd.
8        M:     Twenty s- uh twenty six in April.
9               (0.5)
10  =>   HV:    **And** does he wo:rk?
11       M:     He wo:rks at the factory yes.
```

Heritage and Sorjonen observe that in (7.7) *and* is linking the question it prefaces to the interlocutor's immediately prior answer *Georgi:na* (line 2), while in (7.8) *and* links the following question to the speaker's own prior question, *How old's your husba:nd* (line 7) (1994:5). The authors argue that *and*-prefacing as in (7.8) invokes and sustains an orientation to a larger routine or agenda-based activity, here, in the case of health visits, the bureaucratic form-filling task that health visitors must execute as part of their daily routine. The more general point with respect to clause combining is that turn-initial *and*-prefacing is a resource for "skip-connecting", which Sacks describes as follows: "a speaker produces an utterance that is indeed related to some prior utterance, but it's not related to the directly prior utterance, but some utterance prior to the directly prior utterance" (1992b:349). See also Chapter 5 §3.5. Skip-connecting is found not only in medical interviews but is in general needed whenever a speaker wishes to tie what they are about to say back to one of their own turns rather than to the immediately preceding turn.[20]

2.2 Resuming a Topic with "But"

Related to *and*-prefacing for the linkage of non-adjacent turns is the use of "but" to resume a spate of talk that has been temporarily abandoned. Mazeland and Huiskes (2001) describe this phenomenon in Dutch, where the connective used is *maar* "but". Resuming talk with *maar*, they argue, is different from seamlessly continuing earlier talk with *en* "and" (for more on this distinction see Chapter 5 §3.5.2). *Maar* indicates a contrast at the level of discourse organization. Here is an example where it is used to resume a storytelling that is suspended when the story recipient initiates repair:

---

[20] See also Maynard (2013b), who discusses English *I mean* as a device for skip-connecting in complaint sequences.

2. Paratactic Clause Combinations

(7.9) "Alexander" (Mazeland and Huiskes 2001:143–4) (adapted)
((Jan and Ans are high school students who are sitting at a table doing homework together.))

313	Jan:	weet jeh, (.) >op me ouwe school ↑hè (0.4)
		listen, (.) at my former school, you know (0.4)
314		daar zat zo'n go:zer en die(jie-) die mocht ik
		there was this guy and he (uh-) I didn't like
315		niet zo↓:h (0.3) en da was heel grappig:
		him very much. (0.3) and this was really hilarious
316		[(want e:h)
		(because uh)
317	Ans:	[(°hoe heet(t)↓ieh°)
		(°what was his name.°)
318		(0.5)
319	Jan:	↑wat=
		what?=
320	Ans:	=en hoe heette die
		=°and what was his name
321		(.)
322	Jan:	alexander,
		Alexander,
323		(1.3)
324	Ans:	>op welke school heb je geze:t:n dan.=
		which school was it.
325	Jan:	=op sint maart↓`ns:.
		=Saint Martin's. ((name of the school))
326		(.)
327	Ans:	o↓:h.
		o:h.
328		(0.3)
329	Ans:	(lage ge↑:)
		(Lower Quay,) ((name of the school's area))
330		(0.2)
331	Ans:	goe[d. [(°>ga verder)]
		right. (go ahead)
332 ->	Jan:	[**maar** di [e e : : : :]:h (.) die e:h (0.6)
		but this u : : : : :h (.) this u:h (0.6)
333		die (°jongeh°) (0.3) die mocht ik niet zo.=
		this (°boy°) (0.3) I didn't like him very much.

```
334            =>da was ook 'n heel vreemde vogel:,< ·h
               it was really a very strange guy, ·h
335            en laa↓:tst >toen: zag ik zij↓n:- (.) zijn adres
               and not so long ago I saw his-        (.)   his address
336            en z'n naam bij CHIN↓a express ↑hè (0.4) omdat
               and his name at China Express you know,    (0.4)   because
337            ie zich had opge- opgegeveh. (.) bij mijn wer:k,
               he had si- signed himself up      (.)   at my work,
338            ·hh (°om)dat ie d'r o↑ok wou werke
               ·hh (because) he wanted to work there too,
               ((story continues))
```

What Jan projects to be a *hilarious* story is temporarily halted when Ans asks for the name of the boy in question (line 317). Yet the ensuing repair *Alexander* (line 322) does not lead immediately to a continuation of the story, since Ans again expands the sequence by asking which school the boy went to, initiating a post-expansion that risks shifting the focus of talk and derailing Jan's story (lines 324–31). It is this type of side sequence, one with a potentially competing line of talk, that promotes story resumption with *maar* (line 332). By using *maar* as a preface to his turn, Jan treats the intervening sequence as a digression, indexing the return to the story line as "non-incidental, non-unproblematic" (Mazeland and Huiskes 2001:147). Thus, "but" – like "and" – can also be used as a resource for construing the relationship of one's current turn to one's own prior talk.

2.3 Building Subsequent Versions with "Or"

Related to the backward tying that can be accomplished with "and" and "but"[21] is the use of "or" in building subsequent versions of invitations, offers, requests, and proposals. "Subsequent version" refers here to a second or later attempt by a speaker to deal with the possible or actual rejection of an invitation, offer, or the like if acceptance or commitment to comply is not immediately forthcoming on a first attempt (Davidson 1984:103). For instance, in the following fragment, Claire suggests to her friend Chloe that they play partners at their next bridge club meeting:

```
(7.10)    "Play partners" (SBL 025-28) (see also Davidson 1984:103)
1    Cla:    ^You know (what) would be kinda ni::ce: (.) too: hh *uhh (.)
```

---

[21] Mazeland and Huiskes argue that the resumptive use of *maar*, strictly speaking, does not skip-connect like *and*, because it does "long distance tying" rather than "turn-over-turn", or last-but-one, linkage (2001:159).

```
2                     t hh I was  [thinkin a] bout going u-when we go over to church
3        (Chl):                   [(°Okay°)]
4        Cla:         °*u::w::°^why wouldn't it be nice to play ^pa:rt˘n*ers.
5   ->                (0.7)
6   =>   Cla:         Or wouldn't you ˘li*:ke th*a:t.˘
7                     (2.8)
8        Chl:         tch WE:ll, (0.2) I don't know how would we get ˘p*artners.
9                     you mean just (.) keep your partner?
```

Claire's proposal, couched as an assessment that playing partners would be "nice", is met with silence by Chloe in line 5. What Claire now does in line 6 is issue a subsequent version of her proposal, displaying that it was somehow unacceptable and attempting to deal with the possibility of its being rejected. Claire's subsequent version is prefaced by *or*: it provides an alternative that makes it easier for Chloe to give an *agreeing* response ("wouldn't you like that" – "no I wouldn't").[22]

Something similar happens in the following fragment, where a "detached" *or* can be observed:

```
(7.11)     "Visit" (Davidson 1984:116)
1   ->   A:    Uh: would it be: alright if we came in a little early
2              or
3              (0.2)
4   =>   A:    would that upset you[r
5        B:                        [I: don't think so.
```

In line 4 a subsequent version of A's request (from line 1) also presents an alternative that, in the face of possible rejection, will make it easier for B to respond with an agreement ("would that upset your (schedule)" – "yes it would"). Interestingly, however, the *or*-preface comes as a post-extension to the original request (line 2). Davidson concludes that requesters, inviters, and offerers monitor for *immediate* acceptance of what they are promoting, i.e., at the first possible completion point – here at *a little early* (line 1). Absence of a sign of acceptance at this moment is taken as rejection-implicative (1984:116). This accounts for why the alternative connective *or* is already delivered in line 2.

---

[22] See Heritage (1988:137) for a further instance of this phenomenon, where a subsequent version after an invitation is formatted with *or*.

> All paratactic connective words indicating an addition, contrast, or alternative can be used in turn or TCU-initial position as resources for skip-connecting or backward tying to prior talk. Their precise work – whether it is invoking an agenda, resuming a suspended topic, or offering an alternative in the face of possible rejection – is related to their lexico-semantic potential, with words such as "and" displaying additivity, words such as "but" displaying contrastivity, and words such as "or" displaying alternativeness in their sequential environment.

Yet connectors expressing circumstantial relations such as cause, condition, or concession (see §3 below), for example, can also be used paratactically, as the following sections will show.

2.4 Accounting for "How I Know This" or "Why I Say This" with Reason Combinations

The distinction between parataxis and hypotaxis in the expression of cause/reason is particularly clear in German, where it is reflected in the position of the finite verb: with a paratactic cause or reason clause the verb appears in second position; with a hypotactic cause or reason clause it is placed in final position.[23] In the following fragment, the speaker uses the connector *weil* "because" hypotactically with verb-final word order:

(7.12)   "Seeing a doctor" (Günthner 1996a:325) (adapted)

```
138   ->   Sonja:    hh auf der andern Seite wär der Kielmann vielleicht besser
                     hh on the other hand Kielmann might be better
139   =>             weil der gleich en Röntgengerät da hat.
                     because he has an X-ray right there.
140        Kaja:     ja genau.
                     yes that's right.
```

Here Sonja treats the fact that Dr Kielmann has an X-ray machine in his office as the reason for his being the better choice of a doctor to see.

But in the following fragment the speaker uses *weil* "because" paratactically with verb-second word order:[24]

(7.13)   "Flying" (Günthner 1996a:327)
((Udo has been invited to Maria's house for dinner. *Blasrohr* is a local political magazine.))

---

[23] In English this distinction appears to be carried by prosody: a pitch reset on a conjoined *because* clause signals a paratactic relation to the preceding clause or clause complex (see Couper-Kuhlen 1996b).
[24] This use of *weil* comes close in meaning to that of *denn* "for", whose use in colloquial German is, however, subject to regional and genre-specific constraints (Gohl 2006:151).

```
22  ->  Udo:     ihr habt nich s- (.) zufällig s'Blasrohr. (-) oder?
                 you don't happen to have the Blasrohr here      (-) do you
23      Maria:   °he. eh.°
                 °no°
24  =>  Udo:     weil da is ja em Peter sein Flugartikel drin, (-) über? (-)
                 because Peter's article on flying is in it       (-) about  (-)
```

In line 24 Udo is not treating the fact of Peter's article being in the *Blasrohr* as the reason for Maria's having the magazine or not; instead, Udo is providing a reason, or account, for *asking* whether Maria has the *Blasrohr*. In other words, the reason clause here is one step removed from what it is providing a reason for: it is paraphrasable as "I ask you because ...".

German speakers also use *weil* "because" paratactically when the clause it introduces is providing a reason for how the speaker knows something. This is illustrated in the following fragment:

(7.14)   "Pork meat" (Günthner 1996a:328) (adapted)
((Fritz and Gabi are talking about symbols and "indicators" of cultural assimilation among Muslims.))

```
48      Fritz:   aber de- [des war (        )              ]
                 but th-   that was (        )
49  ->  Gabi:            [aber s'isch (-) scheine-] SCHWEInefleisch IST
                          but it's     (-) pork-         pork is
50  ->           glaub=auch=so en indiKAtor
                 such an indicator I believe
51  =>           weil (-) ich hatte auch en persischen freund
                 because (-) I also had a Persian friend
52  =>           (        ) früher und da war ↑IMmer der indi↑kator
                 (        ) before and there was always the indicator
53               die fragen sich gegenseitig (-)
                 they ask each other
54               ißt du flei- SCHWEInefleisch
                 "do you eat mea- pork"
```

Here Gabi is not presenting the experience with her Persian friend as a reason for the consumption of pork being a mark of cultural assimilation among Muslims, but rather as a reason for, or account of, how she *knows* that this is the case.[25]

---

[25] For a summary of research on German hypotactic and paratactic *weil* clauses see also Selting (1999b) and Schwitalla (2012:142–3) and the references given there.

Accounts for why the speaker has just said something or how the speaker knows what they have just claimed can also be provided asyndetically, with no verbal indicator of linkage between the clauses involved. For instance, Gohl (2000, 2006) cites the following example:

(7.15)   "Church" (Gohl 2000:86) (adapted)
((The participants have just had their Christmas dinner and are now talking about going to church later in the evening.))

```
1        Erik:     gott sei dank muß ↑i (.) <<all> ↓heut nimme in(d) kirch.>
                   thank god I don't have to go to church today anymore.
2                  i dät schnarche.
                   I would snore.
3                  (1.0)
4        Uwe:      des isch ebe des was [((5 Silben))
                   that's what              ((5 syllables))
5   ->   Kai:                           [da: kommsch eh net
                                         you won't get round to snoring
6   ->             zum schnarche-
                   there anyway
7   =>             mir werdet eh schtande.
                   we'll have to stand anyway.
8        Maria:    (nei) nei mir ganget so früh daß me net schtandet.
                   (no)  no  we'll go so early that we won't have to stand.
```

Kai gives an account here in line 7 for why he is claiming that his brother Uwe will not be able to sleep during the Christmas evening church service: it will be so crowded that they will have to stand. This account is not linked in any verbally explicit way to what it is accounting for, namely Kai's assertion that his brother will not be able to fall asleep at church (lines 5–6); yet its status as a reason for this assertion is indisputable. As a TCU, line 7 is prosodically projected by the level intonation contour at the end of line 6, a sign of turn continuation in German (see Chapter 2 §2.3). Thus, because the two units in lines 5–7 have both a semantic and a prosodic link, they are interpreted as forming a clause combination with one another, the fact in line 7 providing the reason for the claim in lines 5–6.

What do speakers gain from presenting accounts paratactically and/or asyndetically? Both Günthner and Gohl stress that paratactically formatted accounts are produced in specific sequential circumstances, namely when participants are carrying out sensitive actions such as making a request (7.13), producing a strong assertion (7.14), or responding in a dispreferred fashion (7.15). A paratactically formatted reason clause, as Günthner (1996a) points out, is an action of its own. This stands in contrast to hypotactic reason clauses, as in example (7.12), where the reason merely supports the turn's main action, an assessment.[26] Thus, paratactic *weil* "because", and its asyndetic variants, serve as resources for presenting a reason as an *account*, i.e., for implementing a social action that explains some ongoing action in the conversation. These resources are used for reasoning at "the level of overt explanation in which social actors give accounts of what they are doing" (Heritage 1988:128).

2.5 Taking Exception to Something Just Said with Adversative Combinations

Similar to the paratactic use of the causal connector *weil* "because", German speakers also have an option to use the concessive connector *obwohl* "although" paratactically. As with *weil*, the distinction between a paratactic and a hypotactic use of *obwohl* is reflected in word order. In the following fragment, *obwohl* is used hypotactically, with the verb in final position (see line 19):

(7.16)   "Coffeeklatsch" (Günthner 1996a:337)
```
16      Hanna:    eh:m da kamen wir (.)
                  ehm we got to talking
17                da erzählte sie- die erzählte daß
                  she told me that she- she
18  ->            SIE=jetzt=anfängt=sich=zu=bewerben,
                  she's started to apply for jobs
19  =>            ob[wohl] ihre Habil noch nich fertig is.
                  although she hasn't finished her post-doc thesis yet
20      Sara:     [ mhm ]
                   mhm
21      Hanna:    ehm (-) und dann kamen wir da irgendwie drauf
                  ehm and then somehow we got on to the topic
```

Here the speaker is expressing a relationship of contradiction or dissonance between two states of affairs: her friend applying for jobs already and her not having finished her post-doctoral thesis. Despite this dissonance, the claim in the first clause is still understood to hold its validity. But in the next fragment *obwohl* is used paratactically, with the verb in second position:

(7.17)   "Skiing" (Günthner 1996a:339) (adapted)
((Gero has to make a phone call but does not know the number. He decides to call Information.))
```
32 -> Gero:   DU=ich brauch en kleinen STIFT.
              hey I need a small pencil
```

---

[26] The supportive role of the reason clause in (7.12) is reflected in the fact that the recipient's next turn addresses the assessment, not its reason.

```
33                  (0.5)
34      Tom:        moment mal (...)
                    just a second (...)
35 => Gero:         ob↑wohl NEE eigntlich weiß ichs auch AUSwendig. glaub=ich.
                    although no actually I know it by heart I think
36                  (0.5) WEI:L ich nämlich die Vorwahl is: (0.5)
                    (0.5)   because I namely the area code is        (0.5)
37                  NU:LL FÜ:NF eh: (1.0) drei drei acht.
                    zero five eh:       (1.0)   three three eight
```

With this paratactic use of *obwohl*, the speaker is not expressing a concessive relationship of contradiction or dissonance between needing a pencil and knowing the number by heart. Were this the case, he would be saying that he still needs a pencil: *ich brauch en kleinen Stift, obwohl ichs eigentlich auch auswendig weiß* "I need a small pencil, although I actually know it by heart". Instead, this speaker is retracting his earlier request and saying that he does not need a pencil anymore at all. A paratactic *obwohl* clause thus expresses an adversative, rather than a concessive, relationship between two adjacent turn units, and the action it implements is accordingly different from that of a hypotactic *obwohl* clause.

Paratactic *obwohl* "although" combinations can also be produced collaboratively by two different speakers:

```
(7.18)       "Summer heat" (Günthner 1996a:345) (adapted)
1   ->  Klaus:   das is echt s'BESte BIER. (-)
                 this is really the best beer (-)
2   ->           ich mein von den alkoHOLfreien.
                 I mean among the alcohol-free ones
3                (-)
4   => Hans:     hhm. obwohl es gibt schon BESsere
                 hhm. although there are better ones
5                zum beispiel BECKS is bei weitem TRINKbarer
                 for example Becks is much more drinkable
```

In line 4 Hans adds an *obwohl* "although" clause to Klaus' assertion in line 1 that the beer he is drinking is by far the best of the alcohol-free brands. Yet Hans' *obwohl* clause does not express something dissonant or unexpected in the light of Klaus' assertion: it refutes it altogether.

Why use an *obwohl* "although" clause if one is taking back something one has just said or refuting something another speaker has just said? The answer may lie in considerations of "face", the image one wishes to convey of oneself and/or attribute to others in the public sphere (Goffman 1967). Using a linguistic format that, at least on the surface, implies mere dissonance between a claim and one's expectations, without affecting the validity of that claim, is by far less face-threatening than an outright denial of the claim. That the claim itself is being refuted with paratactic *obwohl* is not part of the semantics of the connector but merely a pragmatic implicature stemming from its use in specific contexts; for this reason, it is arguably less of a face threat than an on-record assertion to the effect "what I've/you've just said is wrong".

2.6 *Conceding and "Show Concessions" with Concessive Combinations*

As we have just seen, a "concessive" connector such as *obwohl*, when used hypotactically, expresses a concessive semantic relation between clauses and clause complexes, but when used paratactically, expresses an adversative relation to a prior clause or clause complex. But concession is not tied to hypotaxis. If we adopt an action-based understanding of concession, then we find that concessive relations between clauses and clause complexes are often expressed paratactically.[27] In action-based terms *concession* can be thought of as a two-part conversational routine that involves (i) acknowledging the validity of an interlocutor's assertion but (ii) claiming that a potentially contrasting assertion also holds (Couper-Kuhlen and Thompson 2000; Barth-Weingarten 2003).[28] Here is an example:

(7.19)   "Steep" (Barth-Weingarten 2003:1) (adapted)
((Betsy is planning a trip to Australia with her husband Dave and wondering how much money she should save in order to pay the airport taxes when leaving. Mora has just explained that it is twenty dollars per person.))

```
1          Mora:    [so keep that [in the back of your purse.
2          Betsy:   [hm-          [forty dollars.
3                   yes.
4          Dave:    <<p> i think it's a chEat,>
5          Betsy:   [<<subdued laughter>hhh>
6    ->    Mora:    [<<singing> ha ha we:ll> (-) yes (-) I think it's a
                    bit steep mysElf,
7    =>             but (0.7)
8          Dave:    yeah.
```

---

[27] Similarly, conditional relations between clauses can be expressed paratactically: see Thumm (2000) for more on paratactic/asyndetic conditionals in English conversation.
[28] Studies by Lindström and Londen (2013) and Niemi (2014) suggest that this routine is not particular to English but is instead a wider practice also found, e.g., in Swedish and Finnish respectively. See Steensig and Asmuss (2005) for a related study of *yes but* constructions in German and Danish and Chapter 4 §5.5.3.

```
9   =>  Mora:   .hh but then they do it to cover their grOund costs;
10  =>          [and (0.7) and (0.7)
11      Betsy:  [hmm;
12      Wally:  pay for the airport [presumably.
13  =>  Mora:                       [pAy for the Airport;
```

The paratactic clause combination of interest here is in lines 6–13: *I think it's a bit steep myself, but then they do it to cover their ground costs; and pay for the airport.* The contrast that is being set up is one between the airport tax being steep (and therefore unjustified) and it being used to cover ground costs and pay for the airport (thus justified). Mora uses this contrast first to acknowledge that Dave is right in assessing the airport tax as *a cheat* (line 4), but then to claim that there is nevertheless a redeeming value to its being reinvested for upkeep and maintenance.[29]

What do such paratactic concessive clause combinations afford their speakers? One answer lies in the domain of preference organization (Online-Chapter B §2). As Pomerantz (1984a) has argued, producers of first assessments who claim knowledge of, or access to, a referent, and presume that the recipient also has access to this referent, invite that recipient to proffer a second assessment of it in next turn. In most cases, this second assessment will be normatively expected to *agree* with the first.[30] A recipient who *disagrees* with a first assessment is thus placed in the awkward position of having to contravene a normative preference. One way to deal with this dilemma is to postpone the disagreeing component in next turn, for example, by prefacing it with initial agreement components (Pomerantz 1984a:72); see Chapter 4 §5.5.3. This is precisely what a concessive clause combination does: it allows the recipient to agree or align, if only partially, with a co-participant's assessment and in doing so to avoid categorical disagreement. Concessive clause combinations can be used to suggest aspects of the matter on which participants *can* agree, thus creating an environment for "agreement" through the acknowledgment that two potentially incompatible perspectives can nevertheless be reconciled with one another (Couper-Kuhlen and Thompson 2000).

Conversational concessive routines have a number of features in common with what has been called "show concession" in the literature (Antaki and Wetherell 1999; Lindström and Londen 2013). Here is an example of a show concession pattern:

---

[29] Chapter 2 §2.2 discusses such a pattern as the action-specific projection of a multi-unit turn.
[30] Exceptions to this rule of thumb are first assessing turns that involve self-deprecation, where the normatively preferred response in next turn is a *disagreeing* one (Pomerantz 1984a:74); see also Chapter 4 §5.6.

(7.20)   "Sedge" (Antaki and Wetherell 1999:8)
```
1    Resp:   there's no way I can influence
2            the Federation of Labour
3            I might [hate them you know
4    Int:            [yeah
5    Resp:   [willing to go out and shoot the
6    Int:    [yeah
7    Resp:   whole lot of them. [But
8    Int:                       [((explosive
9            laughter))
10   Resp:   I can't influence them.
```

In contrast to the conversational concessive routine illustrated in example (7.19), which involves two speakers (one making an assertion and the other conceding its partial validity but insisting on a potentially contrasting claim), "show concessions" are single-speaker patterns. They are often found when a speaker has made a challengeable or, as in (7.20), an extreme assertion: *there's no way I can influence the Federation of Labour* (lines 1–2).[31] There follows a potential counter-argument against this claim: *I might hate them you know, willing to go out and shoot the whole lot of them* (lines 3, 5, and 7),[32] but then comes a contrasting reassertion of the original claim: *But I can't influence them* (lines 7 and 10). As Antaki and Wetherell observe, show concession "calls attention, in a rhetorical fanfare, to the fact that (the speaker) is all too aware of the simple challenge to his statement, and easily rebuts it" (1999:9). This makes the original claim sound even stronger and more defensible.

2.7 Projecting Failure with First Verb Combinations

The last type of paratactic clause combination to be discussed here has been referred to as a *first verb* pattern. The term "first verb" comes from Sacks, who introduces it to describe the following use of *want* in storytelling: "... a lady wanted to go in the main entrance ... and they wouldn't let her go in" (1992b:181). Sacks remarks that *wanted* here projects, on its occurrence, that another clause will follow having to do with the *failure* of the event talked about in the first clause. Schulze-Wenck's extended study of this use of first verbs in English conversation

---

[31] Of course, logically speaking, there are ways: bribes, infiltration, blackmail, etc. Thus, this assertion is an overstatement. With the concession that follows, the speaker shows that s/he has thought through other alternatives. The reprised assertion is then all the more insulated against criticism (Antaki and Wetherell 1999: 23–24).
[32] As Antaki and Wetherell point out, the counter-argument in this case is itself so extreme that it can hardly be taken seriously (1999:20).

(2005) reveals that in its fullest form the first verb pattern is tripartite, consisting of (i) a first verb clause[33] referring to past time and evoking a counterfactual alternative world, for example, with *wanted to, tried to, thought that, was going to, should have, was supposed to*, etc. (FV); (ii) a clause asserting the failure or non-occurrence of the intended or planned event (NEG); and (iii) a clause accounting for the failure or non-occurrence of the event (ACC). We find all three of these components realized in the following fragment:

(7.21)   "New factory radio" (Schulze-Wenck 2005:323) (adapted)
((Alina is telling her interlocutor about how her boyfriend's radio was stolen from his car.))

```
1        Ali:   Hector's radio=,
2               with -
3               i- it was bro=ken,
4   ->          we WERE GONNA s- --                              FV
5   ->          take it out and send it back to the factory,
6   ->          to get a new factory,
7   ->          .. (H) radio,
8   =>          we never got a chance,                           NEG
9               because,
10  =>          the back window was broken                       ACC
11  =>          and they stole <X it X>.
12  =>          ... The radio.
```

In this instantiation of the pattern, the link between FV (*we were gonna s- take it out and send it back to the factory*, lines 4–6) and NEG (*we never got a chance*, line 8) is asyndetic, while that between NEG and ACC (*the back window was broken and they stole it ... the radio*, lines 10–12) is conveyed explicitly with *because*. On other occasions, "but" can be used to introduce NEG, and ACC can be asyndetic. But despite such variation, the pattern itself is robust and predictable – in fact, so predictable that both NEG and ACC can be absent but will still be implicitly understood. As Schulze-Wenck points out, this can be of strategic value: for instance, by not spelling out the reason why an anticipated event did not take place, a speaker can imply that it is inexplicable (2005:342).

What does a first verb construction achieve for interactants? It is, first of all, as Sacks explains, a means for building a multi-unit turn: this is because FV projects both NEG and ACC; consequently, the speaker's turn may not be hearably complete until these projected parts have been produced. This may account for why first verbs

---

[33] As Schulze-Wenck points out, first verbs are complement-taking predicates (see also §4.1 below): they are followed by a finite or non-finite clausal complement describing the event or action that was originally planned/attempted/desired (2005:326).

are regularly found in storytelling. But a first verb clause combination can also be a useful resource in other sequential environments: for instance, in justifying or explaining some course of action, where the evocation of an alternative (if counterfactual) world implies that one has considered other options. Or in complaining, where a first verb clause combination can be used to present a state of affairs as not what one had expected or anticipated and indeed as inexplicable. For more on these and related uses, see Schulze-Wenck (2005:340ff.) and Jefferson (2004c).

> Among the paratactically linked clause combinations examined here, some rely heavily on the presence of a particular connective word, while others may lack a verbally explicit connector altogether. However, what they all have in common is that they are not simply coincidental or haphazard juxtapositions of unrelated clauses, but are instead closely connected and motivated clause combinations whose first parts prospectively foreshadow later parts and/or whose later parts create retrospective ties to earlier parts.

The clauses in the combinations discussed above are all at the same level of structure with one another, that is, no one part is subordinate to another. It is this feature that differentiates paratactic clause combinations from hypotactically related ones, to which we turn now.

3. Hypotactic Clause Combinations

In this section we consider clause complexes in which the clauses and/or clause complexes hold an independent-dependent relation to one another. We begin by discussing those in which one clause or clause complex stands in an "adverbial" relation to another clause or clause complex.

Adverbial clauses and clause complexes are ones that express notions such as time, place, manner, means, reason, condition, concession, purpose, result, etc. (see Quirk et al. 1985:1078–112 and Matthiessen and Thompson 1988). The term *adverbial* for this category is, however, misleading: actually, such clauses do not "belong to" or "modify" a verb only, but rather a whole predicate, if not a whole clause or clause complex. Moreover, they are not "subordinate" to a superordinate verb, predicate, or clause in the sense of being embedded in it, but rather they stand in a dependent, or hypotactic, relation to a larger unit of discourse (Matthiessen and Thompson 1988).

Since adverbial clauses indicate when, where, how, why, in what manner, by what means, under what conditions, despite what, for what purpose, with what result, etc. a larger chunk of discourse holds, they might be said to express *circumstantial* relations with respect to this discourse unit (Thompson et al. 2007). Their dependence on a larger unit of structure is often indicated explicitly: in many languages with a morpheme, word, or lexical unit that has traditionally been called a "subordinator" or "subordinating conjunction" (including *when, because, if, although*, etc. in English; *wenn, wo, weil, obwohl* in German; *lorsque, parce que, si, malgré que* in French, etc.) and in some languages also with word order (e.g., verb-final position in German and Swedish dependent clauses versus verb-second position in independent clauses). (On paratactic clause combinations with German *weil* and *obwohl* see §2 above.)

Hypotactic clauses are characterized by the fact that they can appear either before or after the clause or clause complex they relate to. In English, pre-posing or post-posing a circumstantial clause does not involve any structural changes in the main or the dependent clause. But in German, for instance, this is not the case: pre-posed circumstantial clauses are closely integrated into the structure of the main clause. Because they appear in the front field, the verb must follow immediately in second position; the subject is then realized in the middle field (Auer 2000b; see also Chapter 6 §2.1.2).[34] Here is an example of a pre-posed conditional *wenn* "if" clause from German conversation:

(7.22)   "Down to the point" (Auer 2000b:174)
wenn sie=n JOB haben wollen, (.) **müssen sie**=n bisschen da aufn PUNKT kommen
if you want to have a job,   you need to get down to the point

Yet, had this conditional clause been post-posed, it would have appeared in the post field and no subject-verb inversion in the main clause would have been necessary:

(7.22')   "Down to the point" *(constructed)* (Auer 2000b:174)
sie müssen n bisschen auf=n PUNKT kommen wenn sie=n jOb haben wollen
you need to get down to the point   if you want to have a job

Thus, pre-posing versus post-posing of "adverbial" clauses is not without structural consequences in German; nor is it a free choice in languages in general. Ford (1993) finds that in English conversation speakers have preferences for "adverbial"-clause positioning that are reflected in relative frequency: causal clauses (with *because*) are virtually always post-posed in her conversational material, while conditional clauses (with *if*) are pre-posed at least half the time (1993:24).[35] The prevalence of pre-posing with conditional clauses has also been attested in

---

[34] Under certain circumstances, "main clause" word order can also be used following a pre-posed *wenn* "if" clause: see Auer (1996b, 2000b) for more on this.
[35] Concessive clauses (with *although*) show a tendency for post-position, but there were very few exemplars in Ford's collection (1993:24).

German conversation (Auer 2000b). In fact, pre-position for a conditional clause has been said to be "natural", in the sense that semantically a conditional clause establishes the grounding for a more focal main clause (Ford 1993) and pragmatically it functions as a topic-introducing device (Haiman 1978).

It has been suggested in the literature that conditional clauses can be seen as related to polar interrogatives in discourse: compare *If he comes, I will stay* with *Will he come? I will stay*. In fact, as Haiman (1978) has observed, conditional sentences might be thought of as condensed versions of conversational routines involving polar questions:

(7.23)   "Establishing preconditions" (Haiman 1978:571) (adapted)
```
1  A:   Will he come?
2  B:   Yes.
3  A:   Well then, I'll stay.
```

The same line of thinking can be expanded to include other types of "adverbial" clause, for example, reason:

(7.24)   "Asking for reasons" (constructed example)[36]
```
1  A:   We have to go now.
2  B:   Why?
3  A:   The shops are about to close.
```

> Many bipartite grammatical constructions have grown out of, or emerged from, the sequential routines of mundane conversation (Hopper 1987, 1998; Bybee 2006).[37]
> In a conversation analytic perspective, this process corresponds to a trade-off between sequence organization and turn construction (Schegloff 2007a): what on one occasion is accomplished via a succession of (cross-speaker) actions can, on other occasions, be "collapsed" into a single speaker's (expanded) turn.[38]

When hypotactic clause combinations are used in conversation, they are produced with prosody and in real time (see also Chafe 1984, 1988). Two implications follow from this observation.

i. Post-posed hypotactic clauses may or may not be projected prosodically by prior talk.

---

[36] See also Gohl (2006:74ff.) for examples in German. Bolden and Robinson (2011) discuss *why* interrogatives in English as a means of directly soliciting accounts.
[37] Linguists first attested this process in early language acquisition and described it as movement from vertical to horizontal construction (Scollon 1976; Ochs and Schieffelin 1983).
[38] For further examples of this process see Couper-Kuhlen (2011).

In her corpus of conversational English, Ford (1993) found that while a majority of post-posed *temporal* clauses were produced after *continuing* intonation at the end of the first unit, the majority of *causal* clauses were produced after *final* intonation at the end of the first unit (pp. 132–5).[39] Post-posed *conditional* clauses were not frequent, but more were produced after continuing than after final intonation. These are intriguing findings, because they suggest that whereas post-posed temporal and often conditional clauses are for the most part projected by prior talk, post-posed causal clauses are not always "planned". Instead, they are what Ford calls "post-completion extensions", added on after a turn has come to a point of possible completion. Here is an example of a causal clause used in post-completion extension from Ford's collection:

(7.25) "Modern art" (Ford 1993:121) (adapted)
((B is talking about the trouble she has been having in finding the textbooks for one of her classes.))

```
1      B:    The mo:dern art. The twentieth century a:rt there's about
2            eight books,
3      A:    Mm [hm,
4      B:       [An' I went to buy a book the other day. I [went]
5      A:                                                  [(mm)]
6  ->  B:    'hh went down to N.Y.U. to get it.
7  =>        Because it's the only place that car[ries the book.
8      A:                                        [Mmm
```

As Ford explains, B is telling a story here about how expensive the textbook is for her modern art course. In lines 4 and 6, she reports *going down to N.Y.U to get it*. But why she would go to NYU, which is in Greenwich Village, to get it, when it is mutually known to both her and her interlocutor that she lives on Long Island, is not recoverable from the context. B's post-completion turn extension with a causal clause, *Because it's the only place that carries the book* (line 7), is thus motivated by self-editing and problem-anticipation: during the course of her turn B arguably realizes that her interlocutor will not fully understand if she does not add an explanation. This she does with a "because" clause added after possible turn completion.

> Not only causal but all circumstantial clauses lend themselves to being added on after a turn or TCU has been brought to potential completion if it later emerges that more circumstantial information is needed to further the interlocutor's understanding and/or help avoid misunderstanding.

[39] Ford's intonational categories are based on Chafe (1984, 1988), for whom *final*, or "period", intonation refers to pitch at the end of an intonation unit that falls to low, and *continuing*, or "comma", intonation to pitch at the end of an intonation unit that does not fall to low, i.e., is slightly rising, slightly falling, or level.

3. Hypotactic Clause Combinations

ii. Pre-posed hypotactic clauses invite collaboration and co-production.

Although many hypotactic clause combinations are produced in the order [independent clause, dependent clause], this is not to say that the opposite order [dependent clause, independent clause] is not attested. On the contrary: it is especially with the expression of temporal and conditional relations that the order [dependent clause, independent clause] is found in English conversation (Ford 1993).

Clause combinations with pre-posed temporal and conditional clauses create what Lerner has called "compound turn-constructional units" (1991, 1996a, 1996b) (see also Chapter 2 §1.5). Compound TCUs have a multicomponent structure that consists of a preliminary component and a final component, the first of these projecting the second. Here is one of Lerner's examples, where the preliminary component of a compound TCU comes in line 5 and the final component in lines 7–8:

```
(7.26)     "Noon Saturday" (Lerner 1996b:307) (adapted)
1      Mark:   ·hhhhh Oka::y now
2              here's the plan.
3      Joan:   Okay.
4      Mark:   ·pk ·hhhhhh uh:m
5  ->          if I don't see you?
6              (0.7)
7  =>          ·hhh why don't you call me sometime before
8              noon Saturday.
9      Joan:   Okay.
```

As Lerner explains, the real-time production of a clause combination such as that in lines 5–8 allows for early recognizability of the structure once the preliminary component has been delivered: *if I don't see you?* (line 5). This preliminary component is prosodically complete, and with the ensuing pause in line 6, speaker Mark creates an "interactive turn space" (Iwasaki 2007, 2009), within which the recipient could produce a continuer or other mark of alignment.[40] But just as importantly, such a preliminary component projects the kind of unit that will be needed to complete the turn, making it possible for recipients to anticipate this unit and provide the final component themselves. This is what we see happening in the following fragment:

---

[40] In fact, in (7.26) Mark could be said to be monitoring for such a signal (see his audible inbreath at line 7), although in the event none is forthcoming.

(7.27)   "Ten o'clock" (Lerner 1996b:315)
```
1  ->  A:   If for any reason you
2  ->       uh can't be there at ten
3           o'clock [let me know.
4  =>  B:          [I will call you
5      A:   All right
```

Here the recipient can no doubt project that after the pre-posed "if" clause speaker A will continue with a *request* for speaker B to call. It is this structural recognizability and the projectability of the final component that allow B to pre-empt A's upcoming request and – in the guise of a collaborative turn completion – produce a final component that *offers* to call instead. In Lerner's words, "by merely voicing what can be treated as a continuation of another's utterance, B associates himself with the TCU as a whole and with the collaboratively produced proposition it carries" (1996b:310).

> Pre-posed hypotactic clause combinations create compound TCUs. The preliminary component of such compound TCUs provides an opportunity for possible co-completion by allowing the co-participant to anticipate when the final component is due and what form it should take. Co-participants can use this opportunity to convert foreshadowed dispreferred actions into preferred ones.

In the following, we review some uses to which specific types of pre-posed and post-posed hypotactic clauses can be put.

3.1 Designing versus Adding on Accounts with "Because"

Earlier we pointed to the fact that post-posed hypotactic clauses can be projected by a stretch of prior talk or, on the other hand, can be added post hoc after a prior turn unit has come to a point of possible completion. This distinction is especially relevant in the case of cause or reason clauses, which in everyday conversation can be used by speakers to deliver *accounts* for something they have just said or done, referred to here as *accountables*.[41]

Here is an English example of an account that is projected prosodically by the prior accountable:

---

[41] Accounts can, of course, also be delivered *before* an accountable action has been produced; for more on anticipatory accounts see Schegloff (2007a:68).

(7.28)   "Granny coming" (Couper-Kuhlen 2012d:282)
((Leslie's daughter Katherine, who is at college in the north, is making plans to return home for a Christmas visit. When she comes home, she will need to be picked up at the station.))

```
1      Les:   ↑↑anyway=
2             ↑=whEn do you think you'd like to come HOME love.
3             (.)
4      Kat:   uh:m- (.)
5             we:ll brAd's going down on MONday.
6             (0.7)
7      Les:   MONday.
8             WE:LL ah-:hh .hh w:
9   ->        ↑mOnday WE can't mAnage,
10  =>        becuz (.) ↑GRANny's coming mOnday.
11            (0.4)
12     Kat:   OH:.
13            (0.5)
14     Kat:   c'd- (0.3) dAd couldn't pick me UP fr'm: (.)
15            ee- even from GLAStonbury could he,
```

In line 9 Leslie rejects her daughter's implicit request to come home on Monday. But the slightly rising pitch at the end of this unit projects that more talk, most probably an explanation or account, will follow. In line 10 she delivers this account. In (7.28) then, Leslie's turn includes an account by design: the accountable is construed, on record, as something requiring explanation. This may well have to do with the dispreferred nature of the action being accomplished: denying a grown daughter's wish is, in the "web of moral accountability" (Heritage 1988:138) that social interaction entails, an accountable action. Accounts in such rejection contexts are expectable and, if not provided, are noticeably absent (Ford 2001a, 2001b).

Yet the need for an account cannot always be anticipated. Here is a case where a speaker initially delivers an action without an account, i.e., construes it as conforming to normative expectations, yet this action is subsequently treated by co-participants as accountable:

(7.29)   "Going to church" (Couper-Kuhlen 2012d:286–7) (adapted)
```
34    Mic: Boy I feel guilty about not going to ch[urch,
35    Sha:                                        [Mn
36    Viv: nuhh [h_huh]
37    Sha:      [I ha] [ve to (take) off]
38    Mic:            [it's:: second w]e[ek
39    Nan:                              [Well it's NOT [L I K E]=
40    Mic:                                             [It's the]=
```

```
41   Mic: =[second week I haven't ] go:n  e   a   n   d   ]
42   Nan: =[the Catholic °church°] you don't have to fee]l guil[ty
43   Mic:                                                      [An' uh:.
44        (0.7)
45   Mic: You get into that habit of not going then you don't go:.
46        [you know?
47   Sha: [(Look.)
48 -> Sha: **I have to start going.**
49        (0.4)
50 => Sha: **Cuz I'm getting really tense:.**
51        (0.7)
52   Mic: Ye[:ah.
53 => Sha:    [**And that really ca:lms you.**
54        (.)
55   Nan: Yeah it doe:s it's (.) It's like medication.
```

Shane's turn in line 48 *I have to start going* builds off of Michael's prior self-deprecation *boy I feel guilty about not going to church* (line 34) and the accompanying account *you get into that habit of not going then you don't go* (line 45). Yet rather than responding with reassurance, as does Nancy in lines 39 and 42, Shane's response is a self-attentive statement concerning his own intention to go to church: *I have to start going* (line 48). When this action receives no uptake (line 49), Shane continues his turn by adding on an account, *cuz I'm getting really tense* (line 50), and a split second later, *and that really calms you* (line 53). This account is not designed as part of an action complex, as in (7.28), but is instead prompted by the lack of uptake: it is produced "on demand".

The production of an account by design versus on demand has sequential implications for what happens next. Accounts designed as part of action complexes are not topically implicative: that is, as a rule they do not get talked about in what happens next. In (7.28), for instance, Katherine does not proceed to inquire about the details of Granny's visit but instead addresses the upshot of Leslie's denial and how to deal with it (lines 14–15). By contrast, when an account is produced on demand, it is done as an action on its own and is therefore topically implicative for subsequent talk. In (7.29), the co-participants do not follow up on Shane's declared intention to go to church but rather on his assessment-like account that going to church is calming (lines 52 and 55).[42]

---

[42] See Couper-Kuhlen (2012d) for further discussion of this distinction.

> Hypotactic causal clause combinations are used in conversational accounting. When the account is projected, i.e., designed as part of an action complex, the accountable action is construed normatively as in need of an account. When actions are delivered without accounts, they are construed as conforming to normative expectations and therefore as not requiring an account. If an account is given later, it comes off as having been produced on demand, reflexively rendering the prior action accountable after all.

3.2 Verb-first Forms in Conditional Clauses

Recall that conditional clauses can be seen as related to polar interrogatives. This is actually one explanation for the fact that, in colloquial German and especially colloquial Swedish, conditional clauses can be marked by verb-first word order rather than by a connective word such as *wenn* "if" (German) or *om* "if" (Swedish): *Haben Sie Fragen, können Sie mit mir Kontakt aufnehmen* or *Har ni frågor, kan ni kontakta mig* "Have you (= if you have) questions, you can contact me" (Auer and Lindström 2011:219).[43] In Swedish conversation, both verb-first and *om* conditionals have roughly the same frequency, but they are not distributed similarly. Instead, speakers use the two conditional forms in different contexts and sequential environments. As Auer and Lindström explain, verb-first conditional clauses in Swedish cluster in various types of expert discourse: they are used by representatives of institutions to describe standard procedures resulting in law-like consequences. Here is an example of a verb-first conditional used by a Swedish pharmacist giving advice on an emergency call line:

(7.30) "Lamp oil" (Auer and Lindström 2011:239) (adapted)
((Call to a poison control center. The caller's child has licked some lamp oil.))

```
1  ->  P:  e:h har de gått mer än   sex timmar å  ingenting har hänt,
           erm has it been more than six hours   and nothing's happened,
           ehm if six hours have passed and nothing has happened
2  =>      då kan man i princip avskriva de hela,
           then one can in principle write off the whole thing,
```

In Swedish, the verb-first conditional construction is found not only with auxiliary-like verbs, as here, but also with full content verbs. In everyday contexts, it is used when speakers are presenting a definitive stance on some subject matter. In doing so, they construe themselves as "experts" and the situation as having indisputable consequences, thus lending their turn a certainty that facilitates sequence closure. Here is a fragment where this can be observed:

---

[43] In English this possibility is restricted to hypothetical conditionals with *were*, *had*, or *should* (Quirk et al. 1985:1094).

(7.31)   "Music styles" (Auer and Lindström 2011:245) (adapted)
((High school students are being interviewed about musical styles.))

```
1   I:   ä de nåt som ni skulle kunna lyssna på hemma?
         is it PART something you could listen to at home?
2   A:   mm
3   B:   mm
4   C:   aa
         yes
5   A:   a om de kommer på radio      så stänger ja ju inte av den typ
         yes if it comes on the radio  I won't of course turn it off like
6-> D:   a kommer den på radion       så skulle ja ju inte stänga av den nä
         yes comes it on the-radio
         yes if it comes on the radio  I wouldn't of course turn it off no
```

What is noticeable here is that first the *om*-conditional in line 5 is used by speaker A to explore the option of listening to the music at home. But this turn is re-worded in line 6 by the next speaker, D, with a verb-first conditional that presents the same situation as having definitive consequences: not turning off the radio is now construed as a consequence with law-like certainty. With this construction the second speaker achieves "doing being an expert" and manages to have the last word.

> In Swedish both the connective *om* "if" and verb-first syntax can be used to indicate hypotactic conditional clauses. *Om* focuses more on the condition; its consequences are treated as hypothetical. Verb-first syntax in a conditional clause, on the other hand, presents the consequences as indisputable, given the condition. Verb-first conditionals serve as a device for invoking expert status during talk.

3.3 Freestanding "If" Clauses

Earlier we pointed out that what characterizes a hypotactic clause of circumstance is that it stands in a dependency relation to an independent clause. Yet there is at least one well-known use of a *stand-alone* hypotactic circumstantial clause without any accompanying or projected independent clause: this is the case of freestanding conditional "if" clauses.[44] Laury (2012a) has recently described these structures in everyday Finnish conversation. She finds that independent *jos* "if" clauses occur in contexts where participants are planning or negotiating some activity and that they

---

[44] Strictly speaking, freestanding "if" clauses are, of course, not hypotactic clause combinations at all. We nevertheless discuss them here because they arguably emerge from hypotactic combinations.

3. Hypotactic Clause Combinations

are used to convey the speaker's deontic stance (see Online-Chapter C §3) toward a possible action or state of affairs associated with it. In other words, with an independent *jos* "if" clause, the speaker is understood to be advocating what is in the clause as desirable or undesirable. Consequently, such turns are treated as directives, i.e., as requests, proposals, or suggestions. Here is an example:

(7.32) "Pitcher" (Laury 2012a:225–6) (adapted)
((Missu is organizing a house-warming gift for a mutual friend and has called Anna to include her in the project.))

```
1     Anna:   joo:, (.) siis mentäskö me yhe:ssä sitä ostaav
              OK,       so should we go together to buy it
2             vai [°mitä me tehtäs°.]
              or what should we do.
3     Missu:      [  .hhhh       ] ei ku mää aattelin n- tai siis
                                   no because I am thinking    or actually
4             > me aateltii Viken kans mennä tänä iltana se<,hh
                Vikke and I thought we'd go    this evening to
5             (.)
6     Anna:   jo[o:?
              yeah?
7     Missu:    [hakeen siält se kannukin?
                get that pitcher from there too.
8     Anna:   °joo?,°
              yeah?,
9 ->  Missu:  niij jos tota, te maksasitte sittem meille takas.
              PTC   if  PTC  2PL pay-COND-2PL then  1PL-ALL back
              so if um, you would pay us back then.
10    Anna:   joo-o? totta kai.
              yeah,  of course.
11    Missu:  niin nii mitenhän k- miltä kuulostaa oisko ne
              so so how what does (that) sound like would they be
12            kiva:t vai o[isko sulla jotaim >muita ideoita<.h
              nice or would you have some other ideas.
13    Anna:               [joo (kyllä).
                           Yes.
14    Anna:   ↑kyllä mum mielestä ne ois tosi hyvä.
              I think they would be really good.
```

In this fragment Anna first offers to help Missu buy the house-warming gift (lines 1–2), but Missu replies that she and another friend have already planned to get the pitcher that evening (lines 3–7).[45] This Anna acknowledges in line 8. Missu now follows up with a turn prefaced by *niij* "so" and the conditional marker *jos* "if": *niij jos tota te maksasitte sittem meille takas* "so if um you would pay us back then". However, she delivers this unit as a stand-alone (with final pitch falling to low): it does not project more to come; nor does she go on to produce any independent clause to accompany it. Anna's response is an immediate *joo-o* "yeah", reinforced with *totta kai* "of course" (line 10). That is, Anna treats Missu's turn as transition-ready on completion of the "if" clause, and she responds with a token of commitment to comply (Sorjonen 2001a), suggesting that she has interpreted it not in terms of epistemic conditionality but rather deontically, as a request.

Finnish *jos* "if" clauses, especially those with second- or first-person subjects and conditional marking on the verb (as in (7.32)), have grammaticized for the promotion of desirable/undesirable future actions and consequently are understood in everyday conversation, under the appropriate circumstances, as directive actions – requests, proposals, and suggestions – (Laury 2012a).[46]

The same general phenomenon has been attested with freestanding "if" clauses in English conversation, where they are found in conjunction with offers and proposals (Ford and Thompson 1986; Ford 1997:401–5). It is likely to be widespread cross-linguistically (see also Evans 2007).

3.4 "Although" as a Concessive Marker

Recall that we also discussed the concessive relation between clauses under the category of "Paratactic clause combinations" (§2.6 above). This is because concession is commonly expressed through parataxis (and/or asyndesis, i.e., the juxtaposition of clauses without any linking element between them) in talk-in-interaction, despite the fact that many languages have dedicated concessive subordinators: English *although*, German *obwohl*, French *quoique/bien que*, Italian *anche se*, Finnish *vaikka*, etc. Speakers could thus theoretically make use of these subordinators for hypotactic clause combinations. Yet Ford's study of adverbial clauses in English conversation (1993) turned up only three tokens of *although* in close to two hours of talk. Why should "although" clauses be so rare in English conversation? And more generally, if circumstantial relations can

---

[45] The pitcher is presented as a known entity ("that pitcher") through the use of the determiner *se*.
[46] Laury observes that independent *jos* clauses with second-person subjects are typically understood as requests, while those with first-person plural marking tend to convey proposals for joint action (2012a:233).

be expressed with both subordinators and coordinators (as is the case for reason, condition, and concession), under what circumstances do speakers opt for hypotaxis, and under what circumstances for parataxis? In this section we consider these questions with respect to the English concessive connector *although* and its synonymous variant *though*.

Ford's initial findings on "although" clauses have been corroborated in larger corpus-based studies of spoken English (Biber et al. 1999:842; Barth 2000). In fact, when "although" clauses are considered in their conversational contexts, it turns out that they are not simply lexically explicit versions of paratactic concessive combinations. Instead, "although" clauses have their own home environment in multi-unit turns, where they are used to restrict the validity of one's own prior claim (Barth 2000). Here is an example:

(7.33)   "Gastric ulcer" (Barth 2000:421)[47]
((Antony Clair interviewing a well-known neurologist, Colin Blakemore, on the BBC.))

```
1         Clair:    .hh so there's a sense of lIving what on
2                   borrowed tIme even;
3                   that this is tIme you hadn't expEcted;
4                   you pAck it full;
5    ->             you nEver know when the/-
6    =>             =although in fact that partIcular problem was EAsed as uh
7                   the Ulcer,
8                   and the blEEding,
9                   [and/
10        Blake:    [i hAd an operAtion when I ws I think twEnty;
11                  uh gastrActomy,
```

The interviewer here orients to his own somewhat overdramatized presentation of Blakemore's health challenges (lines 1–5) by breaking off what was projectably something like *you never know when the (death bell will toll)*, and restricting the validity of what he has just said by conceding *in fact that particular problem was eased* (line 6). With this retroactive restriction, the interviewer is able to forestall any objection by Blakemore that he has overstated the facts. Although his "although" clause is not a straightforward correction of what he has just said, it nevertheless comes close to the "corrective" use of German *obwohl* "although" discussed above (§2.5).

---

[47] The symbol "/" is used here to indicate break-off, and "-" to represent final level intonation.

> Lexical subordinators conveying concession have specialized and acquired their own contexts of use in conversation, English *although* being a case in point. It is reserved for situations in which speakers restrict the validity of something they have just said. What is striking is that the conversational uses of concessive subordinators are not unrelated cross-linguistically, as testified by a comparison of English *although* and German *obwohl*.

4. Subordinate Clause Combinations

Recall that subordinate clause combinations are ones in which a clause can be considered wholly contained within a larger constituent (§1 above). Two kinds of subordinate clause combinations have been studied in particular by interactional linguists: (i) *complement* clauses, which function as the subject or object of a matrix clause,[48] and (ii) *relative* clauses, which function either to modify or to stand in apposition to a noun/noun phrase or a larger clause/clause complex.[49] Our discussion will focus on the conversational uses of these two structures.

4.1 Complement Clauses

Typologically speaking, languages can have different *complement types*: English, for instance, has "that" clauses (*that Sue visited Rome*), infinitive clauses (*for Sue to visit Rome*), gerundial/verbal noun clauses (*Sue's visiting of Rome*), and participial clauses (*Sue, visiting Rome, …*) (Noonan 2007:54). Associated with such complement types are often *complementizers* – a word, particle, clitic, or affix that serves to identify the clause as a *complement clause*. Finite indicative complement clauses in English, for instance, can have *that* (*I know **that** Zeke knows Harry*) or *if* (*I don't know **if** Zeke knows Harry*) (Noonan 2007:55).[50] Predicates that have complement clauses as their subjects or objects are termed "complement-taking predicates" (Noonan 2007:53).

How are complement clauses used in conversation? One of the more surprising findings to emerge from interactional linguistic research into this question is that what may look like object complementation in conversation is actually not a clause combination at all. This is because the putative matrix subject + verb, or "complement-taking phrase" (Thompson 2002:132), has grammaticized into an epistemic, evidential, or evaluative marker for the content of the complement clause. Here is an example from English conversation to illustrate:

---

[48] An example of a subject complement clause in English might be *[That Eliot entered the room] annoyed Floyd*; an example of an object complement clause, *Zeke remembered [that Nell left]* (Noonan 2007:52).
[49] In the case of *This man [**who I have for linguistics**] is really too much*, the relative clause modifies a noun or noun phrase (Fox and Thompson 1990a:298), while in the case of *We just noticed you were open [**which is nice**]* (Tao and McCarthy 2001:654), it stands in apposition to a clause complex.
[50] English object complement clauses can also be introduced by a question word, as in *I don't give a shit [**what she thinks**]* (Thompson 2002:127), although not all grammarians would consider this *what* a complementizer.

(7.34)   "Lettuce on tooth" (Thompson 2002:132)
((At a birthday party; after Kevin was discovered to have lettuce on his tooth, everyone has jokingly commented on it, and Kendra has asked for a toothpick.))
```
1        Wendy:   ... everybody's getting uh,
2                 tooth obsessed.
3  ->    Ken:     I guess we a=re.
```

Traditional grammar would analyze Ken's turn in line 3 as a combination of two clauses, [*I guess X*] and [*we are*], with [*we are*] standing for *X* and functioning as the object of the matrix verb *guess*, the complementizer *that* having been deleted. Yet Thompson has argued that *I guess* and other complement-taking predicates like it function in such cases as *phrases* (Chapter 6 §5) indicating the speaker's epistemic or evidential stance toward what is expressed in the clause that follows. On this understanding, *we are* is not a complement clause that is subordinate to a matrix clause; nor is *I guess we are* a biclausal combination: instead, this utterance is *monoclausal*, with *I guess* serving as an epistemic adverbial phrase. Evidence for this will be seen, among other things, in the fact that *I guess* can "float away" from the complement-taking position and occur in other positions: for example, *because **I guess** she uh= has had enough → because she uh= has had enough **I guess*** (Thompson 2002:134). For this reason *I guess* as well as *I think* have been referred to as "epistemic parentheticals" (Thompson and Mulac 1991a, 1991b; see also Kärkkäinen 2003).

The findings concerning *I think* and *I guess* have since been extended to other finite indicative complement-taking predicates in English conversation (Thompson 2002).[51] Based on a collection of over 400 cases of apparent object complementation, Thompson found overwhelming evidence that (i) complement-taking phrases have epistemic, evidential, and/or evaluative meaning, with the epistemic category being by far the largest, and (ii) the most frequent epistemic phrases – i.e., those with the verbs *think/thought*, *know/knew*, *guess*, and *remember* – are formulaic: they appear with first-person subjects and lack complementizers. Typically, it is the complement clause, not the complement-taking phrase, that carries the main action of a turn or "constitute(s) the speakers' interactional agenda" (2002:134). This can be seen, for instance, in the following fragment:

(7.35)   "Lunch" (Thompson 2002:152–3) (adapted)
```
1        Laura:   well,
2                 Isn't she healthy?
3                 .. I mean,
```

---

[51] Thompson's (2002) study, however, excludes the verb *say* on the grounds that reported speech raises its own separate issues.

```
4                        she -
5      ->                I know she has [X]
6         Ruth:                          [more] or less.
7         Laura:      .. she has [something wrong with her gallbladder,
8         Mom:                   [gallbladder and,
9         Mom:        .. heart trouble,
10                    ... and [back problems].
11        Laura:         [she has heart trouble],
12        Ruth:       .. she has an enlarged heart.
((lines omitted))
13        Laura:      maybe she's .. a semi hypochondriac
((lines omitted))
14     ->  Mom:       I think .. that that's ... closer to the <@truth@>.
```

In this fragment the speakers are discussing the health of one of their family members. The claims about what this family member's health problems reportedly are come either in simple clauses – *she has heart trouble* (line 11), *she has an enlarged heart* (line 12), *(she has) gallbladder and heart trouble and back problems* (lines 8–10) – or importantly, in a complement clause prefaced by an epistemic phrase: **I know** *she has something wrong with her gallbladder* (lines 5 and 7). Just as Laura's final analysis **maybe** *she's a semi hypochondriac* (line 13) is a simple clause prefaced by an epistemic adverbial, so Mom's verdict on the situation (line 14) is a complement clause prefaced by the epistemic marker *I think*.[52] In other words, the main actions in (7.35) are all assertions, and these actions are implemented either by simple clauses or by complement clauses that behave similarly.

Thompson's findings have been corroborated in a number of studies on other languages. We single out three of these here to illustrate the seminal character of her findings and how they play out in different languages.

4.1.1 German Complementation with glauben *"believe"*

Imo (2011) has studied the use of clause combinations with *glauben* "believe/think" in German conversation. He finds that the epistemic phrase *ich glaub* "I believe/think" is routinely followed by a main clause with verb-second word order: for example, *ich glaub ich guck mal aufm STADTplan* "I think I'll look it up on the map" (Imo 2011:171).[53] Compared to the fabricated – and indeed implausible – clause

---

[52] The presence of the complementizer *that* in line 14 does not change the functional analysis of *I think* as an epistemic stance marker; its stance-marker interpretation is facilitated by the pause that follows it. See Kärkkäinen (2003) for more on *I think*; its use with versus without a complementizer is discussed on p. 156.
[53] Strictly speaking, this is a "hybrid" form in German resulting from the fusion of two constructions: *ich guck mal aufm STADTplan nach* (literally "I look PRT up on the map"), and *ich guck mal aufn STADTplan* (literally "I look PRT at the map").

combination *ich glaube, dass ich mal auf dem Stadtplan (nach)gucke* "I think that I'll look it up on the map", where the matrix clause becomes very prominent (p. 172), an initial *ich glaub* phrase serves as an epistemic frame for the clause that follows it: it is this latter clause that implements the main action of the turn.

Interestingly, like English *I think*, the German phrase *ich glaub* can also appear in non-initial position in the clause it accompanies, but when it does, it is likely to have the inverted order of subject and predicate *glaub ich* "believe/think I". With this order the phrase can be seamlessly embedded, both syntactically and prosodically, within another utterance and serve as a modal particle:

(7.36) "Interruption" (Imo 2011:179) (adapted)
((From a radio phone-in in which a priest is offering to help callers with psychological problems.))

```
1    H:   ja entSCHULdigen sie wenn ich jetzt unter[BRECh]e;
          yes excuse me if I interrupt you now;
2    C:                                             [ja. ]
                                                    yes.
3 -> H:   ihr problem ist glaub ich ganz GUT bei unsern hörern und
          your problem has I think (lit.: think I) reached our audience
4         bei unserer expertin angekommen,
          and our expert very well,
```

The *glaub ich* phrase in line 3 here has no pauses before or after it; nor does it carry an accent: it is instead a fixed idiomatic phrase, incorporated like a particle within the utterance rather than on its edges. *Glaub ich* has thus moved further away from a matrix clause + subordinate clause combination than a pre-positioned *ich glaub*, the latter still being analyzable as a concatenation of subject and predicate (Imo 2011:182). (See also Auer and Lindström 2015 for a similar phenomenon in Swedish.)

Imo further observes that when such phrases in German are negated, the complement clause that follows is regularly marked as subordinate through the use of the complementizer *dass* "that" and verb-final position. Here is an example:

(7.37) "Church" (Imo 2011:166) (adapted)

```
1    W:   deine ELtern gehen nich in die kIrche?
          your parents don't go to church?
2    H:   NEE:.
          no:.
3         (0.5)
4    W:   .hh des WUNdert mich irgendwie.
          I'm surprised to hear that.
```

```
5              (1.0)
6       H:     NEE:.
               no:.
7              machen se NET,
               they don't do it,
8    ->        wobei ich nich glaub (.) dass ses       aus überZEUgung nicht machen
               although I not believe    that they-it out of conviction not do
               although I don't think (.) that they don't do it because of their conviction
9              sondern weils halt dann halt (noch) zu wenig lUscht oder (.)
               but because in the end they're not interested or
10             zu fAUl oder sOnschtwas sin;
               they're too lazy or whatever;
11             also sie sin schon potentielle .hh WEIHnachtskirchen kandidaten.
               actually they are potential        .hh Christmas-church candidates.
```

As Imo points out, when a matrix clause containing *glauben* is negated, as in line 8 here, it is made more prominent than the following clause: it is this that accounts for the canonical subordination pattern found in the *dass* clause here (Imo 2011:167; see also Auer 1998).

4.1.2 Interrogative Complementation in Estonian

While Thompson's original study intentionally excluded the complement-taking predicate *say* on the grounds that this verb raises issues related to reported speech, Keevallik (2011) has shown that a similar analysis can be made for verbs of speaking in Estonian, which are frequently combined with interrogative complement clauses, as in *Ütle mis ma tegema pean* "**Say** what I have to do" or *Räägi kuidas sul läks täna* "**Tell** how it went today" (2011:39). Although normative Estonian grammar would treat the verbs "say" and "tell" as transitive and therefore as requiring object complementation, Keevallik argues that when they are used in the imperative form with a following (indirect) interrogative clause, the imperative "main clause" is more particle-like, functioning as a preface that projects a following question and urges a response. Evidence for this can be found in the fact that it is the interrogative complement clause to which the recipient responds in next turn. Here is an example where this can be seen:

```
(7.38)    "Granny home" (Keevallik 2011:51) (adapted)
1       H:     kesse kuuleb seal.
               who is speaking
2       V:     Üllar?
               Üllar ((name))
```

```
3  -> H:   Ullar oled  jah? (.) kule räägi
           NAME  be-2SG yeah     PART tell-IMP-2SG
           you're Üllar. Listen, räägi
4          kas sul     vanaema ka  kodus
           QUES you-ADS granny  too home-INS
           your granny is at home/is your granny at home
5          [on vä.]
           is QUES
           too
6     V:   [jaa,   ] ma kutsun kohe.
           yeah, I'll call her right away
```

Note that Estonian does not distinguish dependent versus independent clause status through word order or auxiliaries (Keevallik 2011:42), so that lines 3–4 could be translated either as an indirect interrogative, "Tell whether your granny is at home too," or as an independent clause: "Tell: is your granny at home too". With the latter translation, the particle-like status of *räägi* "tell" is in full evidence. Keevallik notes that all such prefaces with verbs of speaking in the imperative are typically incorporated as enclitics into the following intonation unit (pp. 48 and 52): thus, it is not that their prosody differentiates between a dependent and an independent reading, but rather that their prosodic subordination leads to a profiling and foregrounding of the following clause.

As Keevallik points out, the interrogative alone, *kas sul vanaema ka kodus on vä* "is your granny also at home" (lines 4–5), would have been enough to elicit the required information in (7.38). So the issue becomes, why is the *räägi*-preface used at all? The answer appears to be that it is a preface for question turns that initiate a new topic or sequence: it indicates a boundary between one course of action and another, forewarning the addressee that a question (and change of topic) is about to transpire (Keevallik 2011:53–4).

4.1.3 The Complementizer Että in Finnish

Characteristic of the English, German, and Estonian clause combinations discussed above was the absence of a complementizer or other indication of syntactic dependency in the complement clause: it is as if this absence "liberates" the clause, allowing it to act more independently. In Finnish, however, the complementizer *että* "that" is *not* optional: instead, it is obligatory with all complement-taking predicates. Yet interactional linguistic research has shown that in Finnish too complement clauses with *että* can occur independently, without an accompanying complement-taking predicate.[54] When this happens, *että* functions like a particle indicating that what follows will be a paraphrase, summary, or upshot of something that has preceded:

(7.39) "Christmas coffee" (Koivisto et al. 2011:83–4) (adapted)
((Liisa is recounting an incident at their summer cottage when during a nap after lunch her husband Keijo started snoring loudly, startling one of their friends, Pena.))

```
10      Liisa:   >ja tota< Pena meni siihe l:a:ttialle
                 and uhm     Pena stretched himself on the
11               pitkälleej ja (0.3) ja tää kuulek
                 floor and        (0.3)  and he ((=Keijo)) imagine
12               ku se yks kaks (.) krh ku sä
                 when he suddenly (.)  krh when you ((=Keijo))
13               aloit. (.) siis Pena kuules se varmast
                 began.   (.)  I mean Pena you see he surely
14               kaks metrii hyppäs
                 jumped two meters high
15               [nyt se kuolee?, hehehe hehe
                  he's dying now?, hehehe hehe
16      Keijo:   [no::e:i nyt sentääm mutta tota pikkusen
                  well:: not quite like that but a little
17      Raija:   nii:n
                 ye:ah
18      Liisa:   >kuulese< s:e on< se
                 >you see it< i:t is< it
19               [on hirveetä.
                  is terrible.
20 ->   Tyyne:   [että pelästy           tosissaan niin,
                   PTC  be frightened-PST really     so
                 that he really was so frightened,
21      Liisa:   nii. se todella pelästy että: et miten<
                 yeah. he really was frightened that what<
22               miten tolle nyt on käyny.
                 what has happened now to that guy ((=Keijo))
```

In line 20, when Tyyne says *että pelästy tosissaan niin* "that he really was so frightened", she is formulating a candidate understanding of the main point of Liisa's story, which Liisa confirms in next turn. But notice that there is no

---
[54] See Evans (2007) for a typological study of clausal "insubordination".

complement-taking predicate in Tyyne's prior talk, or in any of the prior turns to which Tyyne's *että* clause could be said to be a complement.[55] Instead, *että* appears to be functioning here as a particle that prefaces a re-working of something someone else has said (Koivisto et al. 2011:85). For further examples of this phenomenon see Seppänen and Laury (2007) and Laury and Seppänen (2008).

> The complement clause combinations discussed here all manifest a tendency toward monoclausality: rather than functioning as a matrix clause + subordinate clause combination, we find the matrix clause "reducing" to a phrase that accompanies the erstwhile subordinate clause, which is now free to form the main thrust of the turn. Or, as in Finnish, we find the erstwhile subordinate clause acting freely on its own, without an accompanying matrix clause. In both scenarios, we are left with only one clause implementing the action and the TCU in question.

Let us now look at relative clauses, where monoclausality is also a relevant notion, at least for some types.

4.2 Relative Clauses

In traditional grammar, relative clauses are understood to be clauses that either modify or stand in apposition to another constituent in a larger sentence-level construction: this constituent is referred to as their antecedent. Prototypically speaking, relative clauses are said to contain a *relativizer*, which relates them to their antecedent. Scholars who have studied relative clauses empirically in conversational data argue that there is not just one relative clause construction but rather a set of relative constructions related to one another through family resemblances (see, e.g., Fox and Thompson 2007; Birkner 2008).

One frequent type of relative clause in English – where the noun phrase that is co-referential with the antecedent is an object, adverbial, or oblique constituent in the relative clause – routinely *lacks* a relativizer: for example, *that's [something] I'm not used to* (p. 299).[56] In this type of relative construction the main clause is usually semantically "empty", the antecedent is not lexically specific, and the relative clause itself contains only short verbal expressions. In Fox and Thompson's words, such a construction is for all practical purposes *monoclausal* (2007:308). Here are further examples:

---

[55] It cannot be heard as a complement to *se on hirveetä* "it is terrible" (lines 18–19), because it is produced in full overlap with line 19.
[56] In this and the following examples, the antecedent will be placed in square brackets and the material in the relative clause will be underlined.

(7.40)   Quasi-monoclausal relative constructions (Fox and Thompson 2007: 310–12)

```
is that [the one] I bought?
there was [something] we needed
that's [the way] it is
is there [any way] he could meet us?
```

The argument is that in such cases the "main clause" is hardly clausal at all: due to this, and to the fact that the relativizer is lacking, the boundary between main clause and relative clause has virtually disappeared (p. 312).

Yet not all relative clause constructions are monoclausal in this way. Grammarians of English traditionally recognize two subtypes of biclausal relative constructions: those with so-called *restrictive* and those with so-called *non-restrictive* relative clauses. In the former, the relative clause is conventionally understood to "define", or restrict, the extension of a nominal antecedent, while in the latter it merely presents supplementary information concerning the antecedent. For instance, compare the following two relative clauses in English with the relativizer *which*:

(7.41)   "Pubs" (Tao and McCarthy 2001:652)

```
I do need a car, there's not much happening around here ... and we go to a few
of the pubs which are quite far away
```

(7.42)   "Viennese coffee" (Tao and McCarthy 2001:652) (adapted)

((The speaker is bemoaning how expensive a cup of coffee is in Vienna for a British tourist))
```
And these two cups of coffee cost 50 shillings which is equivalent to two
pounds fifty
```

Whereas in (7.41) the relative clause *which are quite far away* identifies which pubs the speaker goes to, in (7.42) the relative clause *which is equivalent to two pounds fifty* does not identify its antecedent *50 shillings*, but rather provides additional information concerning it. Non-restrictive relative clauses are said to be omissible: they can be left out without changing the meaning of the utterance.

The latter case, in (7.42), instantiates a type of non-restrictive relative clause known as *adnominal*: its antecedent is nominal, i.e., a noun. By contrast, a non-restrictive relative clause whose antecedent is another clause is known as a *sentential* relative clause (Quirk et al. 1985:1245). Here is an example:

(7.43)   "Open shop" (Tao and McCarthy 2001:654)

((Customer to shopkeeper))
```
Hi we were just passing and we just noticed you were open which is nice
```

In (7.43) the relative clause *which is nice* does not modify any one noun in prior talk but instead the whole clause *you were open*. Sentential relative clauses are said to correspond to coordinated clauses introduced by *and*: "we just noticed you were open and that is nice" (Tao and McCarthy 2001:654).

But are these subtypes of relative clause distinct and meaningful categories for participants in interaction? Tao and McCarthy (2001) find that it is often hard to distinguish restrictive from non-restrictive relative clauses in spoken discourse. Although in English they are punctuated differently in writing,[57] and it has been claimed that there is a corresponding intonational difference in speech, in actual fact the matter is much more complex. This also emerges from Birkner's (2007, 2008) large-scale study of the relative clause in German talk-in-interaction. Birkner finds that, intonationally, non-restrictive (or "appositional") relative clauses in her data are more likely than restrictive relative clauses to have "disintegrated" prosody – that is, to be delivered in an intonation phrase separate from the matrix clause, each with its own main accent. However, a good one third of her clearly restrictive relative clauses also have "disintegrated" prosody, while only one third has "integrated" prosody, i.e., is delivered in the same intonation phrase as the matrix clause with one main accent. A final one third of her restrictive relatives are delivered in the same intonation phrase as the matrix clause but with two main accents. Birkner concludes that, for participants in interaction, delivery of a relative clause with separate intonation is hardly sufficient to determine whether that clause is restrictive or non-restrictive.

Yet a number of interactional linguistic studies have shown that certain types of restrictive and non-restrictive relative clause constructions can serve as resources for participants in the conduct of conversation. In the following sections we examine two of these.

4.2.1 Restrictive Relative Clauses for Formulating Reference

As Schegloff (1972) and Sacks and Schegloff (1979) have observed, there are many different ways in which reference to a discourse entity can be formulated for the achievement of recognition. For instance, if I wish to refer to my uncle, I can say *Tom, Tom Smith, a relative of mine, Sally's father, Bob's brother, this guy I know in New York, a doctor, he*, and so on. The point is that speakers choose a specific reference form, among the many possible ones, that is designed for the particular occasion and for the particular recipient in question (see also Online-Chapter F §1). In formulating recipient-designed reference, a noun phrase with a restrictive relative clause can on occasion be more appropriate than a simple noun phrase.

To see this, consider the following example from Fox and Thompson (1990b):

---

[57] Non-restrictive relatives are set off by commas from the rest of the sentence in English, while restrictive relatives are not.

(7.44)   "This fellow" (Fox and Thompson 1990b:185) (adapted)
((Bee and Ava are students who used to attend the same college but are now at different institutions. They are talking on the telephone here.))

```
1        Bee:    nYeeah, 'hh This fellow I have-(nn)/(iv-)"fellow"; this
2                ma:n. (0.2) t! 'hhh He ha::(s)-uff-eh-who-who I have for
3                Linguistics [is real]ly too much, 'hh[h=       ]
4        Ava:                [Mm hm? ]               [Mm [hm,]
5        Bee:                                            [=I didn't notice it
6   ->           but there's a woman in my class who's a nurse 'n. 'hh she
7                said to me she said did you notice he has a ha:ndicap and I
8                said wha:t. You know I said I don't see anything wrong
9                with him, she says his ha:nds.=
```

In this excerpt Bee is launching a story about her linguistics professor. Central to the story is a noticing by one of the other students in her class. Significantly, Bee refers to this person as *a woman in my class who's a nurse* (line 6). Why does she not just say "a nurse?" Fox and Thompson (1990b) observe that it is not only the identity of the person as a *nurse* that is relevant for Bee's story (this identity provides the professional expertise needed to make the noticing credible). But the woman's identity as a *member of the class* is also needed to provide an occasion for the noticing. A simple noun phrase such as "a nurse" or "a woman in my class" would invoke only one of this person's relevant identities. But by building a complex noun phrase with a restrictive relative clause attached to the noun, the speaker can capture both identities with one reference form (Fox and Thompson 1990b:187).

> Restrictive relative clauses are useful in formulating reference to a discourse entity when there is more than one aspect of that entity that is relevant on the particular occasion of use.

4.2.2 Non-restrictive Relative Clauses as Increments

Clift (2007a) observes that non-restrictive relative clauses introduced by *which* in English talk-in-interaction can be used to implement one of two social actions: *elaborations* or *assessments* (p. 56). In the case of elaboration, the non-restrictive relative pursues common understanding of a problematic reference, as in:

(7.45)   "Esserleen" (Clift 2007a:53) (adapted)
((Emma is asking Nancy about a course she has just taken; Mr. Bradley is Nancy's class teacher.))

4. Subordinate Clause Combinations 473

```
1      Emma:  Did you learn a lo:t in cla[:ss¿
2      Nan:                       [There were:
3             (.)
4      Nan:   Well I'll tell you one thing that I do feel I'd learned'n I
5             told Mister Bradley (0.2) too: h-uh: (.) afterwards becuz
6             he: is tryin:g to: .hhhhh- .hh He has another year to go
7             at Orange Coa:st, h en then he wants to esta:blish: uh:n (.)
8  ->         something that would be co:mparable: to Ess:erleen:.
9             (.)
10 =>         Which is the: (.) uhm (.) .hhhhh thing that they have
11            in the Big Su:r¿h
12            (.)
13     Nan:   You know for all of this: uh [inten]sive thou:ght busin[ess¿]
14     Emma:                               [mm:. ]                   [mm  ]
15            hm
```

When Emma shows no sign of recognizing what Nancy is referring to with *Esserleen* (line 8), Nancy adds an increment providing supplementary information, that it is a "thing" in Big Sur (lines 10–11). This still does not trigger recognition, however (see line 12), so she further specifies that it deals with "intensive thought" (line 13). Both pieces of supplementary information are delivered in a non-restrictive relative clause introduced by *which*, whose antecedent is *Esserleen* (lines 10–13).

But non-restrictive relative clauses introduced by *which* can also be used to pursue a common assessment or stance toward something the speaker has just said, as in:

(7.46)   "Always eating" (Clift 2007a:53–4) (adapted)
((Mary is preparing dinner while talking to her daughter Vanessa and son-in-law Adam, who have come to stay. David is a neighbor.))

```
1       Mary:   David (.) came in last night and I was: (0.4) ↑is this
2               mine?
3               (.)
4       Van:    Yes.
5       Mary:   >Okay.< .h I was: uhm: (0.2) it was >quarter past >>twenty<<
6  ->           past< eight. (0.2) He said EVERY TIME I COME HERE YOU'RE
7  ->           EA(H)TING.
8               (0.4)
9  =>   Mary:   [£Which is true.£ Whatever time he picks, we're=
10      Van:    [(audible expiration) hh
```

```
11              =always eating.
12              (0.3)
13    Adam:     Heh heh.
14              (0.2)
15    Mary:     [And I was [late last
16    Van:      [Well-   [(they- they- they pick-)
17    Adam:              [(Maybe) you sit at table longer than [most people.
18    Mary:                                                    [Mm?
19    Adam:     [Maybe you sit at the table- a lot of people (---- you do.)
20    Mary:     [Probably. But I was late last night anyway.
```

When the punchline in Mary's story *every time I come here you're eating* (lines 6–7) receives no immediate uptake (line 8), she adds the evaluation, with a non-restrictive relative and in smile voice, that David's assertion is true (line 9) and then launches what is projectably an account in line 15. This leads to her recipients now taking up the punchline and themselves providing explanations for David's remark (lines 16–19).

Note that the non-restrictive relative in (7.45) is adnominal – it modifies *Esserleen* – while the one in (7.46) is sentential: the antecedent is not a noun but a whole clause complex *every time I come here you're eating*. This suggests that adnominal non-restrictive relatives are particularly well suited for pursuing resolution of a referential problem, while sentential relatives are more appropriate for evaluating or assessing a larger segment of prior talk.

Both of these relative clauses are produced as increments, after a prior turn has been brought to possible completion (see also Chapter 2 §4). As Clift points out, when such increments are produced by the speaker on the next beat or after a brief gap in talk, they are motivated by a pursuit of alignment. However, non-restrictive relatives can also be produced as increments *after* the recipient has delivered a response, in which case – because they re-complete the speaker's turn despite the recipient's intervention – they can imply through their disattention to the prior response that that response was inapposite, inappropriate, or undesired. Here is a case where this happens:

(7.47)   "Two scones" (Clift 2007a:67) (adapted)
((Nan is Lesley's elderly mother-in-law. This fragment takes place on the phone after an exchange of greetings.))

```
1  ->   Nan:   .kh We:ll, (0.8) You said phone Mon:day e:veni:ng?=
2        Les:   Yes if you want anyth[ing.
3  =>   Nan:                         [Which I'm doing?
4        Les:   Ye:s,=
5        Nan:   =No:w I want tomorro:w (0.3) two sco:nes
```

Lesley's response to Nan's pre-request in line 1 makes it clear that she is offering to do a favor for Nan. But Nan's increment *which I'm doing* (line 3) presents her call as dutifully meeting an obligation, thereby disattending to – and sequentially deleting – the altruistic intentions Lesley makes visible in line 2 (Clift 2007a:69).

Non-restrictive relative clauses are useful resources for re-completing a speaker's turn if it has not received proper uptake, or if it runs the risk of doing so. Adnominal non-restrictives are particularly well suited as increments when the understanding of a referent must be secured, while sentential non-restrictives are tailored for displaying a stance toward a larger segment of talk. Through their placement, these increments can either further alignment between the participants, or – as in the case of post-other-talk – lead to disalignment if they disattend to the intervening talk.

---

5. Other Clausal Combinations

There are other types of clause combinations traditionally thought of as biclausal that are used as resources in conversation: among these are diverse *cleft* construction types as well as what is known as *extraposition*.

Cleft constructions are said to involve a "division of the sentence into two clauses" in order to give prominence to one of its items (Quirk et al. 1985:1383). At least two different types are recognized in English:

(7.48)   *It*-cleft (Hopper and Thompson 2008:100) (adapted)

((Talking about a tape recorder that does not have a certain capability))

    ... it's the dual one that doesn't,

(7.49)   Pseudo- or *wh*-cleft (Hopper and Thompson 2008:100)

    ... (H) Well what we're trying to get at,
    ... is potential ... versus ... actual.

In (7.48) Quirk et al.'s (1985) "sentence" would presumably be *the dual one doesn't*: it is divided into a clause with an "empty" subject pronoun *it* together with a form of the copula verb *be*, followed by a constituent that is singled out for special focus, with the rest of the "sentence" following after the linking word *that*. In (7.49) Quirk et al.'s "sentence" would presumably be *we're trying to get at potential versus actual*: it is divided into a clause with a *wh*-word standing for the constituent singled out for focus and another clause with the constituent itself following the copula verb.

Extraposition is described by grammarians as involving the "postponement" of a subject nominal clause, which in English can be finite or non-finite, to the end position in the "sentence", with an anticipatory *it* replacing it at the beginning of the sentence (Quirk et al. 1985:1391):

(7.50)   Extraposition (Hopper and Thompson 2008:100) (adapted)
```
it's possible ((...)) that I would change
```

As we shall see from a consideration of these constructions in talk-in-interaction, cleft and extraposed configurations often do not consist of two clauses syntactically combined into a single complex construction and thus do not always deserve the label "biclausal" (Hopper and Thompson 2008). Yet they clearly do serve – in one form or another – as resources for participants, in particular when the latter are faced with the task of constructing a multi-unit turn. In the following we report on interactional studies of clefting, specifically pseudoclefting, and extraposition in English, German, and French conversation.

5.1 Pseudoclefts

English grammarians describe the structure of a canonical pseudocleft construction schematically as in Figure 7.1, where the identically subscripted constituents are understood to be co-referential.

[*wh*-constituent$_i$ + remaining clause] *is/was* [focused constituent$_i$]

Figure 7.1 Schematic representation of canonical pseudocleft in English (adapted from Collins 1991:27)

The focused constituent[58] in pseudoclefts is typically a noun phrase, a non-finite clause, or a finite nominal clause introduced by *that*. Departures from this pattern are considered "deviant" or "incomplete" (Collins 1991:44).

Yet Hopper (2001a) observes that in naturally occurring English conversation there are very few of these canonical pseudoclefts to be found. Instead, what we observe are cases in which, for instance, the focused constituent is a finite clause without *that*, as in the following excerpt:

(7.51)   "Third-graders" (Hopper and Thompson 2008:108) (adapted)
```
1     Sharon:      ... (TSK) (H) <Q Oh,
2                  well,
3->                .. what you do with those third-graders,
4                  you know,
5=>                is you just like,
```

---

[58] The focusing of constituents aims at foregrounding them against the background of other information in the clause. In English and German, focusing can be done *inter alia* through grammatical devices such as those discussed here, and/or prosodic devices such as accentuation (see also Online-Chapter E).

```
6=>                  (H) take them,
7=>                  and put them,
8                    you know,
9=>                  with one of the smarter fourth-graders,
10                   who's very [ver]bal,
11     Carolyn:            [uh ].
12     Sharon:       and .. and well-beha=ved.
13                   (H) And you have them work as a team,
14                   you know,
15                   so that the (H) fourth-grader can help the third-
16                   grader Q>.
```

Here the pseudocleft "piece" is *what you do with those third-graders* (line 3), but the constituent that follows the copula verb *is* (line 5) is an independent clause *you just like take them and put them ... with one of the smarter fourth-graders* (lines 5–9).

Similarly, Hopper finds that the copula verb *is* is frequently missing in conversational pseudoclefts:

(7.52) "Cook all the fish" (Hopper and Thompson 2008:107–8) (adapted) ((Marilyn, Roy, and their friend Pete are fixing dinner together. Marilyn is trying to figure out how to make two pieces of fish serve three people.))

```
1      Roy:          ... I could eat ... o = one of those.
2      Marilyn:      ... you could?
3      Roy:          well,
4                    ... [but I] won't.
5      Pete:              [@ @ ]
6                    then [I guess] –
7      Roy:              [I mean],
8      Marilyn:          [okay.]
9      Pete:         [divide] [it in half.
10     Roy:          [well don't] –
11     Marilyn:      [then I'll] –
12     Roy:          y-
13->                 what you oughta do though Mar,
14=>                 ... cook all the fish.
15                   ... cause –
16                   we won't use it,
17                   ... if you don't cook it.
```

Hopper concludes that it would be better to describe the pseudocleft "sentence" as consisting of a pseudocleft fragment or "piece", which only possibly terminates with *is* and is only possibly followed by a continuation (2001a:112). The pseudocleft piece projects this continuation, without revealing very much about its form or content. That is, it serves as a turn-holding device to delay, and arguably call attention to, the production of an upcoming, more significant segment of talk. In this sense it is a resource for dealing with the temporality of talk-in-interaction.

Hopper goes on to observe that the verbs in the pseudocleft pieces in spontaneous English conversation come from a very restricted lexical set: "*do, happen, need, make, use, say* (usually in some form such as *what I'm saying*), *tell*" (2001a:117). This suggests that only certain things are projected: *what x does* frames the continuation as an action, *what happens* frames it as an event, and *what x is saying* frames it as a (re)formulation or paraphrase (Hopper and Thompson 2008:105).

In what interactional situations do speakers resort to pseudocleft constructions? Kim (1990) finds them being used in two specific sets of circumstances:

i. when a speaker wishes to indicate an episode boundary or topic shift, as in:

(7.53)   "Fruitcake" (Kim 1990:726–7) (adapted)
((Clare and her friend Marylou are trying to sell fruitcake to raise money for their club. Clare has just said she does not like to approach people she knows, and Marylou has added that this is because they feel obligated.))

```
1      Cla:   =khhhh Ye::ah? I: uh (.) asked my neighbor a:n' uh (.)
2             sh*e *uh f-first she said she would cuz we had them marked
              do:wn
3             so hhhh (.) m t she bought one la^:st year 'n so when I
4             went 'n took it out she didn't want it becuz it was sli:ced.
5             Well it was sli:ced la^:st y*ea˘:r.
6      Mar:   M[m: hm?]
7      Cla:    [hhhhh] hhh But I mean it's just something that you
8             [f e e l ]like]they-]*e : : : : ]
9      Mar:   [But see] I d ]idn't]even know it was] sli:ced.
((11 lines omitted dealing with Marylou's surprise at finding the fruitcake already sliced))
21 ->  Cla:   Any˘wa::y I'm: u haa- uh what I'm ha:ving to do to people
22 =>         ^I ˘know: i:s cut them up en sell them hhhh uh: a pound and a
23 =>         half for a dollar sixty fi˘*:ve.[59]
24     Mar:   Oh you're doing tha:t,
25     Cla:   hhhhhh We:ll I'm doing it to the few people ^I know bec'z
```

[59] Note that Clare presumably means here "cut the fruitcakes up", not the people she knows.

```
26              every time I say three twenty five they look at me like hh
27              (.) ^you must be ^nuts woman,
```

When the side sequence initiated by Marylou in line 9 has come to a point of possible completion, Clare now resumes her telling with *anyway* (line 21) and a pseudocleft construction (lines 21–22) projecting how she deals with the people she knows: she offers them smaller packages of fruitcake for less money. Together these two devices (*anyway* and the *wh*-cleft) indicate a shift in topic, from the fruitcake being already sliced to a strategy for making the price more reasonable. Kim's observation is that the pseudocleft construction is crucial in establishing a link between what has gone before and what is projected to come next in conversation.

ii. when a speaker deals with a problem in prior talk, as in third-position repair.

Third-position repair occurs when a speaker initiates repair in response to an interlocutor's displayed misunderstanding. This is what happens in the following case:

(7.54) "BB gun" (Kim 1990:736) (adapted)
((Bonnie has called her erstwhile boyfriend Jim to find out if she can borrow a gun from him for a theater performance she is taking part in at school.))[60]

```
9       B:      ·hhh 'n I was wondering if you'd let me borrow your
10              gun.
11              (1.2)
12      J:      My gun?
13      B:      Yeah.
14              (1.0)
15      J:      What gun.
16              (0.7)
17      B:      Don't you have a beebee gun?
18      J:      Yeah,
19              (0.8)
20      B:      (I'm a-) It' [s-]
21      J:                   [Oh] : I have a lotta guns.hehh
22      B:      Yuh do:?
23 ->   J:      Yeah. aWhat- I meant was which gun.
```

---

[60] See Chapter 5 §1, where this conversation is also discussed with respect to the notions of topic and sequence.

Jim's question *what gun* in line 15 has as a possible inference that he does not own a gun at all, which is why Bonnie checks her assumption that he does in line 17. The following sequence reveals that Jim actually has a number of guns, leading him to repair his earlier turn using a pseudocleft piece as a frame: *what I meant was* (line 23). As Kim points out, both the pseudocleft piece here as well as the one in example (7.53) frame the upcoming talk as "the heart of the matter", contrasting it with what has been said before (1990:740).

Pseudocleft constructions are not only an English phenomenon. Günthner (2006b, 2011a) finds equivalent structures in German conversational interaction with many of the same properties. German pseudocleft pieces are often evaluative or affective frames for what follows. They may not have a following copula verb, and if a clause or clause complex follows, it can have varying degrees of syntactic integration: a complementizer can be present or absent, the verb can be either in second or final position. Here is an example where there is maximal independence between the two parts of the construction: there is no copula verb linking the pseudocleft piece with what follows, and the next clause has main clause word order:

(7.55) "Restaurants in Münster" (Günthner 2011a:168) (adapted)

```
17      Bert:   also ich denke=ja,
                well I think,
18      Udo:    hm?
                hm?
19  ->  Bert:   was immer äh- e- entSETZlich is,
                what is always eh- h- horrible,
20  =>          du KOMMST inne restaurAnt rein,
                you enter a restaurant,
21  =>          und dat riescht schon so Ü:BEL.
                and it smells so terrible.
22      Udo:    hm.
                hm.
23      Bert:   da biste doch ech=schon beDIENT. ne?
                then you've had enough already. right?
```

The pseudocleft piece *was immer entsetzlich is* "what is always horrible" (line 19) is not followed by a copula verb. Moreover, what it projects turns out to be an independent clause complex: *du kommst inne restaurant rein, und dat riescht schon so übel* "you enter a restaurant, and it smells so terrible" (lines 20–21). As Günthner points out, such a pseudocleft piece functions like a topicalizing discourse marker of the type *was XY angeht* "as far as XY is concerned" (2006b:76). This observation leads her, along with Hopper (2004) and Hopper and Thompson (2008), to refer to pseudocleft pieces as *projector* constructions (2008a, 2008b): they project more talk by the same speaker, which can be a syntactically dependent or independent clause, or even a stretch of talk extending over several TCUs (2011a:166).

Pekarek Doehler (2011b), who has studied pseudoclefts in French conversation, also finds that they are best described as "projector constructions". She notes that rather than the canonical pseudocleft constructions described by traditional grammar, it is configurations like the following that are found in her data:

(7.56) "Fear of the unknown" (Pekarek Doehler 2011b:134) (adapted)
```
1     P:   donc on va devoir retravailler la di-
           so   we will have to rework        the di-
2          la motivation différemment
           DET motivation   differently
3->   F:   ce qui est intéressant par rapport à
           what is  interesting with regard   to
4->        ce que:: vous disiez,
           what     you  said
5=>        eh:hm vous parliez là de:de littérature et tout,
                 you   talked there about literature  and all
6=>        .h moi je vois avec mes élèves qui pourtant sont au
              I     see  with my  pupils  who still    are  in
7          collège le fait de travailer par immersion,
           high school the fact of working by immersion
8          (.) où    ils sont vraiment confrontés à
               where they are   truely   confronted with
9          des texts authentiques en allemand,
           DET authentic texts      in German
10         sur les zed des statistiques et caetera,
           on  the "zeds" of statistics   et cetera
11         .h il y a cette: crain:te de l'inconnu::
              there is this      fear    of the unknown
12         qui se qui c- qui disparaît petit à petit?
           that   that    that disappears step by step
13         ((turn continued))
```

For Pekarek Doehler, the configuration that Fabio produces here (lines 3–12) is only remotely related to a standard pseudocleft construction in French, which is said to consist of a free relative clause initiated by *ce qui* (subject) or *ce que* (object), followed by a dummy pronoun + copula *c'est* "it is", and finally by a noun phrase, an infinitive clause, or a finite nominal clause (introduced by *que*) (p. 123). Here the pseudocleft piece *ce qui est intéressant* (line 3) is not followed by *c'est* nor by a finite nominal clause introduced by *que*. Instead, what follows is a succession of independent clauses: *vous parliez là de littérature et tout* "you talked about literature and everything" (line 5), *je vois avec mes élèves . . .* "I see with my pupils" (line 6), *il y a cette crainte de l'inconnu* "there is this fear of the unknown" (line 11). Arguably it is the latter clause, with its following relative *qui disparaît petit à petit* "that disappears step by step" (line 12), that is what is "interesting" and is thus the point Fabio is making with his turn. As Pekarek Doehler notes, the pseudocleft piece *ce qui est intéressant* is simply a projective device that allows the speaker to construct a multi-unit turn at talk with a delayed main point.

> Pseudocleft constructions in English, German, and French conversation are only rarely like the canonical structures described in traditional grammars. Instead, they consist of pseudocleft "pieces" – question-word clauses – that may or may not be followed by a copula verb and a syntactically dependent complement clause. Often it is one or more independent clauses that follow. For this reason pseudocleft pieces have been called "projector" constructions: they allow speakers to project that more talk will be forthcoming but they only loosely foreshadow what it will be or how far it will extend.

5.2 Extraposition

Extraposition has traditionally been thought of as a process whereby a nominal clause, typically a subject nominal clause, is positioned "outside" the sentence, i.e., at its end, with an anticipatory pronoun (in English *it*, in German *es*) replacing it earlier in the sentence: for example, *To hear him say that surprised me* → *It surprised me to hear him say that* (Quirk et al. 1985:1392). The assumption has been that these two forms are variants of one and the same "sentence", and that the non-extraposed variant is the more basic one.

Yet interactional linguistic studies of extraposition in talk-in-interaction have found no evidence to support either of these assumptions (Couper-Kuhlen and Thompson 2006, 2008; Günthner 2009, 2011a). In both English and German conversation, non-extraposed utterances are rare, while extraposed utterances abound. Moreover, although extraposed utterances in the two languages are bipartite, the parts are not on a par with one another. Instead, the first part is typically an epistemic, evidential, or evaluative frame for the second, more substantial part: for example, *it's possible*, *it turns out*, *it's nice* in English or *es kann sein* "it can be", *es kommt vor* "it happens", *es ist schade* "it's a shame" in German. These frames project clausal continuations that can be either finite (introduced by *that* or *dass*) or non-finite (introduced by *to* or *zu*). In both languages, the complementizer *that* or

5. Other Clausal Combinations

dass can be missing in what follows the frame. In German, when the complementizer *dass* is left out, the verb in the clausal continuation comes in second position (as in main clauses) and not in final position (as in subordinate clauses).

In the following German example, the two parts of the extraposition structure are syntactically integrated through the presence of *dass* and verb-final position in the clausal continuation:

(7.57) "Decisions" (Günthner 2009:29) (adapted)
((In this "Big Brother" excerpt, Jörg, Alida, and Hanka are discussing how to organize their household budget. At issue here is whether each person should buy their own yogurt, or two of the group should buy enough for everyone.))

```
862    Jörg:    GANZ schnEll [geht das.]
                very quickly    it can happen
863    Alida:                [nEe aber_s] kann nicht s'
                             no but it won't w'
864             =denn horten sIe ihr_n kiste joghurt,
                then everybody will hoard their box of yogurt
865             und a' zwanzig [Andere] sitz_n da- (.)
                and   twenty    others will sit there (.)
866    Jörg:              <<p> [genau.]>
                                 exactly
867    Alida:   .h EEn joghurt wär OH_nich schlecht.
                .h one yogurt wouldn't be a bad idea
                [weißt]_te
                you know
868    Hanka:   [ja ]
                yeah
869    Alida:   dat is Och blöd
                that's stupid too
870             (--)
871             nA: ich weiß AUch nich wie_s am GÜNstigsten ist,
                well: I don't know either how it'd be most economical
872 ->          aber es kAnn nich sein,
                but it can't be
873 =>          =dass zwEI leute über Alle entscheiden.
                that two people decide for everyone else.
874             =das GEHT nich.
                that won't work.
```

Here the material framed by *es kann nicht sein* "it can't be" is a subordinate clause introduced by a complementizer: *dass zwei leute über alle entscheiden* "that two people decide for everyone else", with the verb *entscheiden* in final position. This creates a relation of syntactic dependency between the two parts of the extraposition structure.

The following German example, however, illustrates an extraposition with a syntactically independent clausal continuation:

(7.58)   "Left alone" (Günthner 2011a:177) (adapted)
((From a telephone conversation between two girlfriends.))

```
46     Sina:   [ja- glaub ich gern.]
               yea-  I can believe that.
47     Nine:   [kannst du   (echt) ]
               you can      (really)
48->           es is halt schOn (.) sch' be (.) SCHISSen,
               actually it's pretty  (.)  aw  (.) awful,
49=>           weißt (.) ER meldet sich NIE;
               you know (.) he never calls me;
50=>           ECHT NIE.
               really never.
51     Sina:   hm.
               hm.
52=>   Nine:   (ähm) un wenn ich ihn dann mal SEH;
               (ähm) and when I run into him;
53=>           zUfällig,
               by accident,
54     Sina:   [hm]
               hm
55=>   Nine:   [is'] isses auch hh' zIemlisch <<p> depriMIErend.>
               it'   it's also       quite depressing.
```

The extrapositional structure here is located in lines 48–55, with the phrase *es ist halt schon beschissen* "actually it's pretty awful" serving as a frame for what follows. Yet the telling that ensues is not syntactically dependent on this frame: it is not introduced by *dass*, and the verb *meldet* in *er meldet sich nie* "he never calls me" is located in second rather than final position in the clause. The framed material is not only separated from the frame by the discourse marker *weißt* "you know", it is also syntactically independent and its length is expandable, as witnessed by the incremental extension in lines 52–55.

In English, the same options – syntactic integration versus non-integration – are available in extrapositional structures. Here is a case, for instance, of syntactic non-integration between the two parts:[61]

(7.59)   "How cute" (Couper-Kuhlen and Thompson 2008:452)
((Middle-aged Nancy is telling her friend Emma about the other students in the night-school psychology class she has been taking.))

```
1          Nan:    they are so cute ↓yeah they really.
2                  they were just (.) ve:ry.hhhhh very very sweet with me:
3     ->           a:nd it was so funny
4     =>           in fact one of the kids came up to me:
5                  (.) one of the young.hhhh fellas that (.)
6                  Ra:lph's about twenty two:,
7          Emm:    mm h[m:¿]
8          Nan:        [a: ]nd he had been,h in, (.)
9                  one of my mi:cro groups right at the very beginning,
((24 lines omitted))
34    =>   Nan:    .hhhhh en then afterwards Ra:lph
35    =>           came up and he said (.)
36    =>           I:'d like (.) Nancy? (0.2)
37    =>           he said I'd like to (0.2)
38    =>           take you over to Shakey's and buy you a ↓bee:r. (.)
39         Nan:    uhhhh ↓huh[↓huh.h]hhh
40         Emm:               [h o : w] ↓cu::te.
```

The extrapositional structure begins in line 3 with the fragment *and it was so funny*, which projects that Nancy will go on to say next what was funny. However, there follows a rather circuitous story, which does not end until a recognizable "funny" climax is reached in lines 37–38. In this case then, the framed material of the extrapositional structure extends over several seconds and many lines of transcript.

When and why do speakers use extrapositional structures in conversation? Couper-Kuhlen and Thompson (2008) investigate this question in English conversation with respect to evaluative frames that assess something in upcoming talk. They point out that in cases of *non-integration* in particular – when the framed material is prosodically separate and syntactically independent of the frame – the

---

[61] Example (7.1) at the beginning of this chapter illustrates a case in which the material following the extrapositional frame *it's so funny* is syntactically integrated, but through the subordinator *because* rather than the complementizer *that*.

frame serves as a story preface (see Online-Chapter D §1). In example (7.59), for instance, *it was so funny* projects that a story will follow which will deal with something that will be found to be assessable in this way. Such a preface is an assessing action of its own that frames the whole subsequent telling, which consists of several events presented in a succession of TCUs.

Yet on other occasions, the extrapositional frame and the material it frames are *integrated* into one prosodic unit and one single TCU. An example of this will be seen in the following:

(7.60) "Get in for free" (Couper-Kuhlen and Thompson 2008:457–8) ((Teresa has been telling her friends about recently going to a cheap-rate movie theater and not having to show her ticket.))

```
1        T:   I hate myself mentally for go(h)ing there=
2        J:   =I know.
3             (2.0)
4   ->   T:   .hhh it is great that we got in for free though.=
5        J:   =mhmm.
```

Observe that in this case the material framed by the extraposition fragment *it is great* is formulated as syntactically dependent on the frame and is integrated prosodically with it. Together the two parts build a single TCU. Couper-Kuhlen and Thompson observe that this kind of extraposition structure is frequently mobilized to propose sequence and topic closure (2008:457). In example (7.60), for instance, Teresa, after having made a deprecatory remark about her moral "weakness" in going to a cheap movie theater (line 1), uses an extrapositional structure to highlight the more positive aspect of her experience (line 4). This "summary assessment" (Chapter 5 §3.3) allows her to wrap up the prior topic and prepare the ground for a shift to something new.

> Extrapositional structures consist of two unequal parts: (i) an initial epistemic, evidential, or evaluative clause with a dummy pronoun that serves to anticipate and frame (ii) a subsequent, more important clause or succession of clauses. In both English and German the two parts of an extrapositional structure can be syntactically and prosodically integrated – or syntactically independent and/or prosodically separate. Syntactically and prosodically integrated structures build single TCUs and can be used as a resource for proposing topic and/or sequence closure, as, for example, in summary assessments. Non-integrated structures are used to construct multi-unit turns; the framing part can serve, for instance, to project and preface an upcoming story or extended telling.

5.3 Other Projector Constructions

Both extraposition frames and pseudocleft pieces are projective devices that can be mobilized for the construction of multi-unit turns. But there are other types of "projector constructions" as well. All have in common that a first clausal piece prefigures a next clausal or multi-clausal spate of talk by the same speaker. What follows need not be syntactically or prosodically integrated with its frame, and can be of indeterminate length. The two parts are nevertheless treated as belonging together and forming a larger whole. In a broad sense they thus instantiate a form of clause combining. In this section, we discuss two well-known projector constructions in German: *die Sache/das Ding ist ...* "the thing/point is ... " and *es ist so ...* "it's like this ... "; for a discussion of selected projector constructions in French see Pekarek Doehler (2011b).[62]

Die Sache/das Ding ist ... "the thing/point is ... " is known as a nominal construction with a matrix clause formed by an abstract noun such as "thing, point, problem" as subject and a copula verb as predicate, followed by a complement clause as predicate nominal. Yet in conversational German, what follows the matrix clause is typically more important than the matrix clause itself; moreover, it is often not grammatically subordinate and can consist of more than one clause or clause complex (Günthner 2008b, 2011a, 2011b). Here is an example:

(7.61)   "Panic attack" (Günthner 2011a:173) (adapted)
((Olga is describing to her friend Eva the difficulties she has had driving her car after suffering a panic attack.))

```
21        Olga:   es hat mich SEHR v viel überWINdung ge[kOstet;]
                  I really had to force myself;
22        Eva:                                           [un      ]
                                                          and
23        Eva:    hm?
24   ->   Olga:  d das ding is hAlt; (-)
                  th- the thing is PRT;
25                <<all> is nunma so;>
                   it's the way it is
26        Eva:    hm
27   =>   Olga:   wenn_du das EINma hAst,
                  once you have it,
28   =>           dat LÄSST dich NICH (mehr) los.
                  you can't escape it.
29                ECHT. NICH.
                  you really can't.
```

---
[62] Aijmer (2007) discusses a related construction in English: *the fact is that ...*

As Günthner points out, what the speaker is doing here in line 24 is delaying the main point of her turn. The metapragmatic construction *das ding ist halt* "the thing is PRT" projects that the crux of her argument is coming next: this allows her to hold the floor while she thinks through how to formulate what she wants to claim (2011b:25).

Related to *die Sache/das Ding ist* is another projector construction in German: *es ist so ...* "it's like this ..." (Auer 2006b). This construction has many of the same characteristics as *die Sache ist*: it projects at least one further clause, which may but need not be grammatically dependent. Yet in contrast to *die Sache ist*, the *es ist so* frame is completely empty semantically: *es* "it" is a dummy element linked via the copula verb *ist* "is" to a deictic *so* "like this", pointing forward to an upcoming stretch of talk (Auer 2006b:298). This stretch often involves several syntactic/ prosodic units of talk dealing with a complex or intricate state of affairs. Here is an example:

(7.62)   "Boat neighbor" (Auer 2006b:299) (adapted)
((B is calling A to back out of a get-together they had planned for that evening.))

```
1        A:   <<nach hinten zu Theo> theo geht der thomas zum WEINfest?>
              ((to Theo in the background)) Theo is Thomas going to the wine festival?
2             (2.5)
3        B:   weißers NEDde?=
              doesn't he know?=
4        A:   =der theo meint er glaubt es NICHT bei dem wetter.
              Thomas says he doesn't think so with this weather
5        B:   bei dem WETter
              with this weather
6   ->        weil bei UNS isches SO:
              because it's like this with us
7   =>        (-) wir ham doch n SCHIFFSnachbar. (-)
              we have a boat neighbor
8   =>        und der hat uns jetzt beSTIMMT schon das ZEHNtemal
              and he has invited us now for at least the tenth time
    =>        zum ESsen eingeladen;
              to have a meal with him
9   =>        [und IMmer hatten wir was Andres vor;
              and we've always had something else planned
10       A:   [mHM
11  =>   B:   jetz ham mir gsa (gd) mir gehn heut Abend mit DEM
              now we've said we're going with him this evening
              ä: (-)   nach BEburg.
              uhm (-) to B'burg.
```

Why does speaker B preface the talk in lines 7–11 with the semantically empty *bei uns isches so* "it's like this with us" in line 6? Auer observes that when this construction is used, it prefaces a complex turn consisting of several TCUs: it is thus serving to secure the floor for more than one TCU. At the same time it disrupts the contiguity of talk: what is projected to follow is not immediately related to what came before. This break and the ensuing delay appear to be in the service of buffering a delicate and/or face-threatening action, as can be observed in example (7.62) (2006b:302–3). Here the upshot of B's report about having accepted one of their boat neighbor's multiple invitations for a meal that evening is that B will not be able to join A as planned.

> Projector constructions such as German *die Sache/das Ding ist* ... "the thing/point is" and *es ist so* ... "it's like this" are relatively fixed schemata for prefacing a complex, multi-unit turn at talk. They project more same-speaker talk, while giving the speaker time to plan what to say next and how to say it. Both can be followed by subordinated complement clauses with *dass* "that", but are more often followed by one or more syntactically independent clauses. While *die Sache ist* ... projects metapragmatically that the upcoming stretch of talk will contain the crux of the matter, *es ist so* ... is semantically empty: it simply delays the gist of the turn, thereby breaking contiguity with prior talk. This makes it suited for introducing delicate and/or face-threatening matters.

6. Practices of Clause Combining: Co-construction, Incrementation, Projector Frames

In this chapter we have reviewed a range of clause combinations, all of which can be conceptualized, roughly speaking, as bipartite. That is, they consist of two parts, each of which is itself minimally a clause (or clause-like). Often there is a word – a conjunction, complementizer, or relativizer – linking the two parts; in the absence of such a word, the link is asyndetic.[63]

Yet one of the more striking facts about these clause combinations is that although they may be conceptualized as bipartite constructions, implying symmetry between the two parts, in naturally occurring interaction the parts are produced one by one, in real time. In other words, what is called Part 1 comes *first* in time, and what is called Part 2 comes *next*.[64] This fact has important implications for the way these clause combinations figure in practices for the conduct of conversation.

---

[63] In the case of asyndesis, the only overt indication of linkage is prosodic (see §1 above).
[64] This applies first and foremost to languages with Subject-Verb-Object (SVO) or if there is another constituent X before the verb, XVO main-clause word order. In languages with Subject-Object-Verb (SOV) word order, the situation is more complex and still needs full investigation. For a first foray see, e.g., Ford and Mori (1994).

The temporal unfolding of bipartite structures can lead to asymmetry between the parts.

Consider first that a second part in a bipartite structure – unlike a first – builds on the first part by virtue of coming second. This is why one practice of clause combining in talk-in-interaction involves a co-interlocutor *completing* a bipartite structure begun by their interlocutor. Examples of this practice were seen above in (7.3) and (7.18). But the practice is a more widespread one: in general, if any first Part 1 is produced by one participant, the next Part 2 can be provided by another participant. The process is, of course, facilitated if Part 1 projects what it will take for the combined structure [Part 1 + Part 2] to be complete (Lerner 1991, 1996a). This happens, for instance, with pre-posed "if" clauses, which project a following "then" clause: for examples where this leads to joint turn construction, see §3 above.

But even if Part 1 does not project a Part 2, clause combinations can be jointly produced:

(7.63)   "Flat water" (Ford 1993:127) (adapted)
((D is talking about how Nepalis and foreigners react differently to health conditions in Kathmandu. W is the recipient. C and H have both lived in Nepal.))

```
1        D:    They don't like the taste of boiled water, y'know,
2              they ya offer 'em boiled water, (Ah.)
3        W:    [The ta- what ta-?
4   ->   D:    [There's no ta- there's no ta:ste to it.=
5   =>   H:    =Because it gets flat.=
6        D:    =Yeah.=
7        C:    =It doesn't (have all that junk in) it, y'know?
```

Here D's claim in line 4 is designed as an independent clause: with its final fall-to-low pitch, the structure is possibly complete at the end of this line. It makes no further projection of another clause to follow. Yet H appends a dependent reason clause to it in line 5. Together, lines 4 and 5 retrospectively form a hypotactic clause combination.

Thus, one practice of clause combining in talk-in-interaction can involve joint production or co-construction. A second practice involves same-speaker incrementation (Chapter 2 §4). Examples of this practice were seen in (7.25), (7.29), (7.45), and (7.46). But more generally speaking, all the structures with an independent clause in first position can be designed such that on its production Part 1 is a possibly complete TCU. Part 2 is then only added if and when it is needed. Here is a case, for instance, of an assessing turn that is initially built to stand alone (line 10):

(7.64) "Second pregnancy" (Couper-Kuhlen and Thompson 2008:449–50) ((Beth has been talking about the differences between her first and her anticipated second pregnancy, saying that having been through one pregnancy, she can enjoy anticipating the phases of the second one more than she could the first time.))

```
1          Beth:    I just pretend like I'm really going to,
2                   really- looking forward to every little aspect of the thing.
3          Ann:     are you pregnant now?
4          Beth:    nno:, no, but we c- probably will be before, long,
5          Ann:     yeah?!=
6          Don:     =hhm.=
7          Beth:    =mmhm?
8          Ann:     wo:w.
9          Beth:    so it's really,
10  ->              It's nice though.
11                  Y'know, (0.5)
12  =>              to be able to say like
13  =>              no:w you start into the new phase and,
14         Ann:     mmhm::.
15                  that's [nice.
16         Beth:           [yea:h.
```

When Beth produces *it's nice though* in line 10, her TCU is possibly complete: with it she is not only assessing her situation but also proposing topic and sequence closure. Were Ann to follow up with a minimally agreeing turn, the ground would be ripe for a topic shift. But Ann does not come in at this point, even when Beth pursues uptake with *you know* (line 11). So Beth now adds a non-finite clause to her prior turn, specifying what it is that she finds nice (lines 12–13); this ultimately resolves the problem of recipiency. Retrospectively, lines 12–13 together with line 10 instantiate an extraposition construction. But it is one that has developed incrementally over time.

The practice illustrated in example (7.64) can be found with all clause combination types in which Part 1 can build a TCU and implement a social action on its own. If bipartite structures result, these are not pre-planned, but rather come about in real time through clausal incrementation. In §2.1–§2.3 we saw examples of this process with paratactic clausal increments introduced by "and", "but", and "or" (see also Barth-Weingarten 2009; Barth-Weingarten and Couper-Kuhlen 2011; Koivisto 2017); in §3.1, with hypotactic clausal increments (see also Ford 1993 and Günthner 1993, 1996a); and in §4.2, with subordinate, relative clause increments (Clift 2007a). In all of these cases, clause combining proves to be a practice that can be mobilized in the service of anticipating problems of understanding and handling recipiency after a first clausally formatted action.

A third practice of clause combining in interaction involves those structures in which Part 1 is a syntactically dependent or incomplete clause, unable to build a TCU or implement a social action on its own. This is the case with many preposed "if" clauses, with matrix clauses containing complement-taking predicates, and with projector constructions. When such a Part 1 occurs, it projects that a Part 2 will be needed to complete the structure. These types of clause combinations are particularly useful in the construction of multi-unit turns. When particular kinds of projective first parts are recurrent, they can become sedimented (semi-fixed) and function as frames for a more substantial second part. This happens, for example, with *I think/ich glaub* (§4.1.1), with pseudocleft "pieces" (§5.1), and with projector constructions in general (§5.3). In these cases the framed material, especially when finite, no longer needs to bear marks of its syntactic "dependence". And it is "free" to extend as far as needed, over as many TCUs as necessary for the purpose at hand.

Practices with clause combining in talk-in-interaction can be observed in the joint construction of a cohesive series of turns at talk and in the same-speaker construction of multi-unit turns through projector frames and clausal incrementation. Multi-unit turns can be planned in advance with projector frames, or they can evolve over time with incrementation. Clause combining in interaction thus contributes not only to the articulation of complex material but also interactionally to the mutual alignment of participants and the negotiation of intersubjective understanding.

---

7. Conclusion

Clause combinations are a grammatical phenomenon, but because grammar serves to deliver action in talk, they are also a resource for accomplishing action and interaction. As bipartite structures, clause combinations are particularly well suited for implementing action complexes (see also Chapter 2 §2.2). But because interaction takes place in time, clause combining can also be used as a practice for incrementally building multi-unit turns, or for jointly constructing a cohesive series of turns at talk with one's interlocutor. Action and temporality are thus key notions in an interactional linguistic approach to clause combining.

8

One-word Constructions: Particles

1. Introduction

In addition to sentences, clauses, and phrases (Chapter 6) and clause combinations (Chapter 7), speakers also mobilize single words for constructing turns at talk (Sacks et al. 1974:702). Here is one of Sacks et al.'s examples to illustrate:

(8.1)   "Mittie's husband" (Sacks et al. 1974:702)
```
1    Jeanette:   Oh you know, Mittie- Gordon, eh- Gordon, Mittie's
                 husband died.
2                (0.3)
3    Estelle:    Oh whe::n.
4    Jeanette:   Well it was in the paper this morning.
5    Estelle:    It wa::s,
6 -> Jeanette:   Yeah.
```

In line 6, Jeanette confirms her informing from line 4, namely that Mittie's husband's death was in the paper that morning, with a single word, *Yeah*. This word builds a turn and implements a social action in its own right. Yet it is not inflected morpho-syntactically to indicate a grammatical relationship to other words in a larger syntagma; nor is it syntactically dependent on a prior turn. English *yeah* and its variants, *yes* and *yep*, are what are known as *particles*. A large part of this chapter is devoted to reviewing the work that such particles do (including, e.g., *uh-huh* and *hm*) as resources for turn construction and action implementation in talk-in-interaction. Excluded from the discussion here are modal particles (German *Abtönungspartikeln*) on the grounds that they are syntactically integrated in the utterances they accompany, and one-word repair initiators, which are treated in Chapter 3. Other one-word constructions such as terms of address are dealt with in Online-Chapter F §2.

Because particles are not morpho-syntactically inflected for a role within a larger syntagma nor syntactically dependent on neighboring constructions, they are in a sense independent one-word constructions.[1] Yet although they can build turns at talk alone (as seen in (8.1)), particles can also appear turn-initially and/or turn-finally as prefaces, codas, and/or post-completion components of turn-constructional units (TCUs) that serve as hosts for them. For instance, in the first of the following two extracts the particle *yeah* appears as a turn-initial preface, and in the second its variant *yes* appears as a turn-final particle:

```
(8.2)     "Smith" (Sacks et al. 1974:702)
1     Guy:     Is uh Smith down?
2 ->  Eddy:    Yeah he's down,


(8.3)     "Jillian" (Heritage and Raymond 2005:25) (adapted)
1     Ver:     =Jillian, she can be a litte nasty litte bi[tch.
2     Jen:                                                 [Well you were
3              say:↑ing there's something in that_=It's a sha:me
4              i[sn't i:t.]
5     Ver:      [Yeh  a::n]d-
6              even Jean said she couldn't do eh uh she said she's always
7              glad when they go:.
8     Jen:     Yeh.h well of course you see Bill is so good with them as
9              well is[n't h[e:.
10 -> Ver:            [.kl  [That's ri:ght yes.
```

In (8.2)–(8.3), the pre-positioned and post-positioned particles are not delivered as separate prosodic units; had this been the case, they would have built TCUs of their own within multi-unit turns. Instead, they are initial and/or final components of single-unit turns – although, despite their prosodic integration, they are not syntactically integrated with the clausal structure they preface or follow.

What is the linguistic status of particles? As we have stressed, these one-word constructions do not enter into syntactic relations with other units. Moreover, they lack semantic content: many particles – although they may derive from lexical items[2] – have bleached to a point beyond recognition. But one-word constructions are not only devoid of syntax and semantics: many are not even lexemes in the strictest sense of the word, English *uh(m)*, *mm*, *uh-huh*, and the like being cases in point. Yet all have phonetic substance and serve systematically as resources for the implementation of social action in conversation. As freestanding objects they can work, *inter alia*, to summon a next speaker, to pursue a response, to implement

---

[1] Where single words have the potential to be syntactically integral parts of larger syntagmas, as in the case of, e.g., English *what*, the recognition of a one-word construction depends on its intonation (Sacks et al. 1974: 721–22).
[2] The most frequent lexical sources of particles are conjunctions and adverbs: see Koivisto (2012, 2015b) and Heritage (2015) for examples.

a responsive action, to acknowledge a prior turn affiliatively or disaffiliatively, and to claim attention and understanding. As turn-initial or turn-final objects, they can, for example, project imminent topic shift, convey epistemic independence, foreshadow non-responsiveness or non-straightforwardness, and organize pivotal boundaries in turn construction. In this sense, particles are not the "detritus" of conversation[3] (Schegloff 1982:74) but rather part of its very fabric – its warp and weft. This confirms their status as objects worthy of interactional linguistic interest.[4]

2. Particles

In the understanding adopted here, particles are small, uninflected words that can either stand alone as TCUs or occupy various positions in the TCU, foremost among these being at its beginning and at its end. In these sequence and turn positions, particles can appear as single objects or in combination with one another. When they co-occur, it is often in a prescribed order: for instance, in English we find, for example, *oh no* (but not "no oh"), *oh well* (not "well oh"); in German, for example, *ja doch* "yes indeed", *ach nein* "oh no", *na ja* "well"; in Finnish, for example, *no siis* "well I mean", *no nii* "right", *ai niin* "oh that's right". Particles can also co-occur with address terms; typically the order is [particle + address term]: English *oh Ron* or *well Michael* (Clayman 2012:1855).

Prosodic configuration can be decisive for the work that freestanding single particles do. Gardner (1997), for instance, shows that in Australian English conversation, if the particle *mm* is produced as an independent TCU with a falling contour, it will be taken as a problem-free receipt of the prior utterance, functioning as a weak acknowledger. If *mm* has a falling-rising contour it will be treated as a continuer, implying that the talk it is oriented to is incomplete, while if *mm* has a rising-falling contour, it does the work of a weak assessment token equivalent to *good* (1997:133). For a full appreciation of particles as resources for turn construction and action implementation, prosodic shape thus must not be neglected.

Single particles can be reiterated, as in English *no no* (Stivers 2004) or German *ja ja* (Golato and Fagyal 2008; Barth-Weingarten 2011a). Stivers investigates this phenomenon in a number of languages, arguing that the reiteration of a unit of talk is more than simply an intensification of the single unit. For instance, by saying *yes yes yes yes* (under one intonation contour), the speaker is not just acknowledging

---

[3] Schegloff describes conversational "detritus" as bits of talk "apparently lacking semantic content, and seemingly not contributing to the substance of what the discourse ends up having said" (1982:74).
[4] As Sorjonen writes with respect to the Finnish response particles *niin* and *joo*, they are part of an *activity grammar*, i.e., "they belong to semiotic tools through which members of a speech community collaboratively and in a systematic fashion go about constituting activities in and through which they manage their relationships and practical tasks in the everyday life" (1996:321).

a prior turn several times, but is instead addressing the whole course of action that the turn is part of and is suggesting that the prior speaker should now halt that course of action. Here is an instance where we can observe this happening:

(8.4)   "Robert Sawyer" (Stivers 2004:268) (adapted)
((The doctor in this medical encounter is trying to elicit the name of his young patient.))

```
1      Doc:   Now you're::
2             (0.2)
3      Mom:   Sawy:er.
4             (0.3)
5      Doc:   Ye:[s.]
6      Mom:      [Ro]ber[t (Sawyer).]
7  ->  Doc:             [Yes yes   ye]s yes:: yes::.
8             (0.4)
9      Mom:   A very bad cough.=I had to call the doctor...
```

Although the doctor's query is ostensibly addressed to his patient, the boy's mother pre-emptively provides their family name in next turn (line 3) and then, following the doctor's acknowledgment, the boy's full name (line 6). It is in overlap with this latter turn that the doctor now produces a TCU consisting of five tokens of *yes* under one intonation contour (line 7). Stivers observes that the doctor's reiteration of *yes* here is not simply acknowledging the information provided in line 6, but is instead suggesting that the whole course of action underway should now be halted, perhaps also conveying some annoyance at the mother's persistent intervention (2004:269). As this example shows, the reiteration of a particle can be a practice of its own, independent of that accomplished by a single token (see also Golato and Fagyal 2008; Heinemann 2016).

Note that particle reiteration depends crucially on prosody for its status as a separate practice. Had the *yes* tokens in (8.4) been produced in separate intonation contours, each would have been a discrete lexical TCU, implementing, for example, acknowledgment or confirmation.

The work of freestanding and non-freestanding particles is also dependent on their position in the sequence and/or turn. A freestanding particle such as *okay* can occur in second or third position, where it will either respond to the initiating action or close off the prior sequence respectively (Heritage 2013b). A non-freestanding particle may do one job turn-initially but another job turn-finally. For instance, the word *but* at the beginning of a TCU projects upcoming talk that will be contrastively related to what preceded (Chapter 7 §2), but the same particle at the end of a TCU can indicate that the turn is possibly complete and ready for transition to next speaker (Mulder and Thompson 2008; Chapter 7 §2). Finally, the sequential position of a turn will affect how its turn-initial particle is heard: an *oh* that prefaces an *initiating* action will indicate that something has just been noticed, realized, or remembered (Bolden 2006), while an *oh* that prefaces a *responsive* turn such as a second assessment, for example, will convey that the speaker has reached this judgment on epistemically independent grounds (Heritage 2002a and Chapter 4 §5.5.2). An *oh* that prefaces a third-position, *sequence-closing* turn – for example, *oh good* or *oh thanks* – will be heard as registering receipt of the information just provided, with the rest of the turn conveying acceptance of the prior action (Schegloff 2007a:136).

Particles are small, uninflected one-word constructions that serve as resources for building TCUs (freestanding particles) or for prefacing/completing TCUs (turn-initial/turn-final particles). A consideration of prosody is crucial for appreciating the work that freestanding and non-freestanding particles accomplish. Particles can occur singly or in combination, and can be reiterated multiple times. When a particle is reiterated within the bounds of a single intonation unit, this can constitute a separate practice, independent of what a single instance of that particle might do. In addition to the composition of units constructed with particles, their position within the turn and/or sequence is also decisive.

2.1 Freestanding Particles

When particles are mobilized to build TCUs of their own, these TCUs as a rule do not initiate sequences (for this, more substance is needed: see Chapter 6 §6), but they are instead *responsive* actions or *continuer* actions within already initiated sequences. In the terminology to be used here, *responsive* actions are particular actions (e.g., acknowledgments, confirmations, news receipts, agreements, etc.) that the type of initiating action (e.g., assertion, question, informing, assessment, etc.) has made relevant next (see also Chapter 4 §2.5). A *continuer* action, by contrast, is an action that is made relevant by a bit of talk but that passes up the opportunity to initiate repair or do a responsive action in a full turn (Schegloff 1982:87). The producer of a continuer action displays through that action that the prior speaker should go on talking, i.e., continue the unit underway. Verbal formats for continuer actions are called *continuers* (1982:81).

In the following sections, we survey a selection of freestanding particles[5] as used in a variety of different languages to implement responsive and continuer actions.

---

[5] In the usage to be adopted here, a *freestanding* particle will be understood to mean one that builds a TCU on its own. This TCU may be the only unit in the turn or may be followed by further units in a multi-unit turn.

Included are discussions of positive and negative response tokens, change-of-state tokens, tokens for acknowledgment and agreement/affiliation, and continuer tokens. This survey is by no means exhaustive; rather, it is intended to illustrate the ubiquity of particle usage across languages. The aim is ultimately to come to an appreciation of the sequential and interactional work that can be done with particles cross-linguistically.

2.1.1 Positive and Negative Tokens in Response to Polar Questions

Positive and negative tokens include, for instance, *yes* and *no* in English or *ja* and *nein* in German. In these two languages, the positive and negative particles are used to minimally affirm/confirm or deny/disconfirm the propositional content of a polar question. Yet this is only one type of "answering system" documented in the languages of the world. Typologically speaking, in addition to (a) the yes-no type of answering system, there is also (b) an agree-disagree type, where positive and negative particles (e.g., *right* or *wrong*) are used to agree or disagree with the propositional content of the question, and (c) an echo-answer type, where typically the verb of the question is "echoed", or repeated, in affirming/confirming the content of the question (Sadock and Zwicky 1985).

As mentioned above, English belongs to category (a): *positive* polar questions make relevant a response with the particle *yes* for affirming or confirming and the particle *no* for denying or disconfirming (Raymond 2000, 2003; see also Chapter 4 §2.7.1 and §2.7.3). For *negative* polar questions, affirming/confirming is accomplished with *no* (A: *You don't like tomatoes?* B: *No*), while denying and disconfirming is done with *yes*, typically together with a positive pro-repeat (A: *You don't like tomatoes?* B: *Yes, I do*). In Russian, another language with a yes-no answering system, the particle *da* is used for simple affirmation of a positively formulated question, and *net* for affirmation of a negatively formulated one (Bolden 2016).[6]

Japanese, by contrast, is considered to be an agree-disagree language, where minimal responses to polar questions instantiate category (b). It uses positive particles such as *un*, *hai*, and *ee* to agree with the content of a prior question, and negative particles such as *ie*, *iie*, *iya*, and *uun* to disagree with it (Hayashi 2010). One typical characteristic of the Japanese answering system can be observed in the following extract, where the initiating action is a negatively formulated B-event, a request for confirmation, functioning like a polar question:

---

[6] Russian, however, can also use echo repeats (category (c)) to confirm the content of a prior question, although these appear to be reserved for cases in which the recipient is conveying an epistemic stance that is incongruent with that of the questioner (Bolden 2016; see also Online-Chapter B §2).

(8.5)   "Never heard of it" (Hayashi 2010:2699)
```
1    C:   >kiita koto< nai?        soo yuu no?
          heard  N    not.exist such     N
          ((You)) have never heard of such a thing?
2 -> A:   u::n kiita koto nakatta
          yes  heard  N   not.exist
          u::n (=Yes) ((I)) had never heard of ((it)).
```

Whereas with a yes-no answering system, a *negative* particle would be used to *confirm* the content of a prior negative question (A: *You have never heard of such a thing?* B: *No*), in an agree-disagree system, as illustrated here, a *positive* particle is used to *agree* with the content of a prior negative question (A: *You have never heard of such a thing?* B: *Yes* (= "that is right")).

Category (c), the echo-answer type, is said to be instantiated by languages such as Welsh and Finnish (Sorjonen 2001a, 2001b).[7] In Finnish, simple, unproblematic answering of a polar V-interrogative (one in which the interrogative morpheme is suffixed to the finite verb, implementing a request for information) is accomplished with a verb repeat (A: *Ajoiks Anna Helsinkiin eilen?* "Did Anna drive to Helsinki yesterday?" B: *Ajoi* "Drove") (Sorjonen 2001a:35). A positive response with the positive particle *joo* would convey the implication that the questioner already has access to the information asked for, thus confirming it (2001a:414; see also Chapter 4 §2.7.1).[8]

> Simple, unproblematic answering of polar questions is accomplished minimally with positive/negative particles in some languages, but with verb repeats in others. In the former case, the particles (a) either affirm/deny or confirm/disconfirm the content of the question (English, German, French, Italian, Russian, etc.), or they (b) agree/disagree with it (Japanese, Korean). In the last case (c), verb-repeat languages, affirmation is accomplished by repeating the verb of the question, and particle responses are reserved for special circumstances and do more than simple answering (Finnish, Welsh).

When positive and negative particles are used to answer polar questions, their delivery can be modulated prosodically and/or phonetically in ways that carry implications for the trajectory of the sequence and/or for the alignment between participants (Raymond 2000, 2010; Bolden 2016). In English, for instance, rather

---

[7] Welsh and Finnish, however, also have particles that can be used to answer polar questions under special circumstances, and might thus be considered to have "mixed" answering systems (Sorjonen 2001a:406).
[8] By contrast, in Estonian – a "mixed"-system language – the positive particle *jah* or *jaa* and negative particle *ei* are the formats used for simple, unproblematic answers to polar questions, with verb repeats being reserved for special circumstances (Keevallik 2010).

than using a flat or slightly falling pitch contour on *yes* or *no*, a respondent can produce the particle with slightly rising pitch, which will project more same-speaker talk and thus postpone the transition relevance point (Raymond 2010:117).[9] Alternatively, a respondent can project turn completion by saying *yep* or *nope* instead of *yes/yeah* or *no*, with the lip closure of the final voiceless plosive /p/ iconically indicating "no elaboration" (Raymond 2000:43). In Russian, as Bolden's (2016) study shows, the positive particle *da* "yes" following a polar question requesting confirmation of a piece of news or an informing can be modulated prosodically to indicate the presence or absence of evaluative congruence, i.e., agreement concerning the evaluative or affective stance taken toward the information. Here is a case where the prosodic delivery of *da* "yes" suggests that the participants do not share an evaluative stance:

(8.6)   "Plus two" (Bolden 2016:46–7) (adapted)
((Oleg, who lives in Russia, is talking to Vova, who is currently in Minnesota. The conversation takes place in March.))

```
1      Oleg:   (A)u vas schas (t') e¿at' pjatnacat'/
                Is it fifteen degrees now where you are
2      Vova:   .hh n- U nas net/<Schas u nas znaesh gdeta
                No ((it's)) not/ Now we ((have)) you know about
3              no:,l'/ pljus dva:/
                zero, plus two
4              (.)
5      Vova:   vot tak/=
                like that
6      Oleg:   =↑Pljus dva?↓ u vas/
                You have plus two
7 ->   Vova:   Da::/
                yes
8      Oleg:   A xatja chevo ya/ vy zhe na severe.
                But why am I/ You are in the north
```

Oleg's request for confirmation, *Pljus dva? u vas* "you have plus two" (line 6), is delivered with a strong rising-falling contour suggestive of astonishment, given his assumption that it would be much warmer in Minnesota (line 1). But Vova's confirmation with *da* "yes" in line 7 is prosodically subdued: it does not match the pitch extremes of Oleg's prior turn and does not align with the astonished stance

---

[9] See also Lindström (2009), who describes a "curled *ja*" in Swedish that projects a non-aligning stance when used to respond to an inquiry (p. 138).

it conveys. Instead, the implication is that the information Vova has delivered is not surprising at all (Bolden 2016:47). More generally, a minimal particle that confirms a piece of news or an informing in response to a polar question that has requested confirmation conveys evaluative congruence in Russian if it is matched prosodically, but non-congruence if it is not matched (Bolden 2016:49).

Positive and negative particles can be upgraded – and the work they do can be reinforced – through the addition of a further particle. This is what happens in Dutch with *ja* "yes" and *nee* "no" when the particle *hoor* (literally "hear") is appended to them (Mazeland and Plug 2010). *Ja hoor* and *nee hoor* not only confirm prior polar questions, they implement an upgrade that has been called "full" confirmation – a type of confirmation that proposes local sequence closure in the interest of advancing a larger, more encompassing course of action (p. 166). Here is a case in point:

(8.7)   "Very nice" (Mazeland and Plug 2010:165) (adapted)
((Mrs L has called the travel agency desk to change her holiday booking. She is concerned to know whether one of the places she is now considering is "pleasantly crowded".))

```
1        MsL:   (en) dat >zegge ze< dat 't ook heel e:h
                (and) this one they say that it must be very u:h
2               leuk moet we:zeh
                nice as well
3               (.)
4   ->   Dkl:   ja hoor. da's     op zich     ook best
                yes hoor that-is in itself also rather
                yes hoor. that's in principle also
5               wel leuk. e:h (is) ook wel 'n vrij e:h
                PRT nice         is also PRT a rather
                quite nice indeed, u:h is also a pretty u:h
6               (1.1) vrij   groot plaatsje
                      rather big   place
                (1.1) pretty big village.
7        MsL:   ook druk?
                also crowded?
8               (0.2)
9   ->   Dkl:   'n beetje- ja hoor:.
                a  bit     yes hoor
                a bit- yes hoor.
10              (1.6)
11              °hm.°
```

The travel agent provides a preferred response to both of Mrs L's requests for confirmation (lines 2 and 7): the place she is considering is *heel leuk* "very nice" and *druk* "crowded," and she does so by confirming with *ja hoor* on both occasions (lines 4 and 9). Even though these confirmations are accompanied by downgrades *op zich ook best wel leuk* "in principle rather nice indeed" (lines 4–5) and *'n beetje* "a bit" (line 9), they come off as full, unconditioned confirmations, in the sense that they promote local sequence closure and thereby advance the larger course of action that the customer's questions are implementing (2010:166).

Positive and negative particles that are used in affirmation or confirmation of polar questions can be modulated prosodically and/or phonetically in ways that have implications for the trajectory of the sequence and/or the alignment of the participants. While slightly rising intonation on English *yes/yeah* or *no* projects more talk to come, the addition of a final voiceless bilabial plosive, producing *yep* or *nope*, projects "no elaboration". A matching pitch contour on Russian *da* "yes" or *net* "no", when used to confirm a prior piece of news or an informing, implies evaluative congruence between the participants, while a non-matching contour implies non-congruence. The positive and negative particles *ja* "yes" and *nee* "no" in Dutch can be upgraded by the addition of a further particle *hoor* "hear", in which case they implement full confirmation, promoting local sequence closure in the interest of progressing a larger course of action.

2.1.2 Change-of-state Tokens in Response to News and Informings

The delivery of a piece of news or an informing in informal conversation calls minimally for a news receipt – some indication that, as a result of the prior action, the recipient's store of knowledge has undergone a change of state from uninformed to informed. As Heritage's (1984a) study has shown, it is the particle *oh* that is the primary means for accomplishing this in English (see also Chapter 4 §4.4.1). *Oh* is often accompanied by further turn components, either promoting an elaboration of the news or informing (*oh has she?*), or assessing it as good or bad news (*oh good, oh how awful*) (1984a:302–303). By contrast, when *oh* is produced as a stand-alone response with falling pitch, it is sequence-curtailing: it proposes that the recipient is prepared to treat the prior news or informing as complete for all practical purposes and that the sequence can now be brought to a close (1984a:312).

By contrast with English, which is said to have only one change-of-state particle,[10] namely *oh* (with numerous prosodic-phonetic variants (Local 1996)), other languages have been shown to have significantly more. German, for instance, reportedly has at least four different particles for conveying a change of state: *ach*,

---

[10] See, however, Reber (2012), who identifies *ah* and *ooh* as two further (affect-laden) particles for responding to informings in English.

achso, *achja*, and *oh*, each of which does distinct interactional work. Only one, *achso*, is a standard news receipt in the sense that its speaker claims to now be informed of something not known before and to fully understand its implications (see also Chapter 4 §4.4.2). Japanese has at least six response particles whose use overlaps with English *oh* in one way or another: *aa*, ↑*ee*, *haa*, *hoo*, *hee*, and *huun*. A division of labor holds between these particles, with *aa* reportedly being the closest to the English change-of-state token *oh* (Tanaka 2010:305). Finnish also has a set of particles that convey that the prior turn has delivered new information: *ai*, *aijaa*, *aha(a)*, *jaa*, *ja(a)ha*, *m-hy*, *vai niin*. Of these, the particle *aijaa* is said to be the "neutral" one, in the sense that it does not display any affect per se nor function as a topicalizer (Koivisto 2015c).[11] In addition to this "neutral" news receipt token, Finnish – like German and Japanese – has other particles dedicated to conveying more subtle dimensions of the change of state brought about by news and informings.

In fact, as more work is done cross-linguistically on news receipts, it is becoming evident that changes of state with respect to knowledge are multi-faceted and that these facets can be interactionally relevant (Heinemann and Koivisto 2016): their interactional relevance becomes evident when participants use different response particles to orient to them. Some languages, for instance, have distinct change-of-state particles for discriminating between simply receipting a piece of new information and more fully understanding its implications: this is the case with German, where *ach* is used for the former and *achso* for the latter (Golato and Betz 2008; Golato 2010). Other languages have distinct particles for discriminating between claiming that one is now informed where one was previously uninformed and claiming that one has just now realized something relevant for the prior talk: this is the case in Danish, which uses *nå* for the former and *nåja* for the latter (Emmertsen and Heinemann 2010).[12] German, too, has a separate particle (*achja*) for cases in which the informing is treated not as new information but as information previously known and just now remembered (Betz and Golato 2008).[13] But some languages go a step further and distinguish between claiming that one already had independent access to the information but is just now recollecting it and claiming that one now understands something that was unclear before or that conflicted with one's previous assumptions. This is the case in Finnish, where the particle *ai nii(n)* is used for the former but the particle *aa* for the latter (Koivisto 2015a, 2015c).

---

[11] Unlike English *oh*, however, Finnish *aijaa* is not a sequence-closing token (Koivisto 2015c).
[12] Emmertsen and Heinemann note that the realization can be "caused by the speaker's recollection, recognition, or understanding of relevant matters" and that the realization token *nåja* can be used to remedy prior potentially disaffiliative turns by indicating a change in the speaker's epistemic access (2010:109).
[13] Both Danish *nåja* and German *achja* consist of a change-of-state token (*nå*, *ach*) and an acknowledgment token (*ja*, *ja*), which may account for why they do similar work (Emmertsen and Heinemann 2010:114).

To appreciate this distinction, consider the following extracts:

(8.8) "German" (Koivisto 2013:284–5) (adapted)
((Oona has just told her friends that she will be coming to school late the next day: her classes do not start until 10 a.m.))

```
1     Milja:   ↑miten siul voi alkaa kymmeneltä
               how is it possible that your classes start at ten.
2              (0.3)
3     Oona:    helposti. ((looking at her calendar))
               easily.
4              (0.7)
5     Oona:    [miul   ei   oo   ilmasua.]
               I don't have drama.
6     Milja:   [mikä siul o, >mikä siulla o,<]
               what do you have what do you have
7     Lotta:   mikä siu-l on sit eka tunti.
               what's your first lesson then.
8              (1.0)
9     Oona:    [saksa. ((looking at her calendar))
               German.
10    Milja:   [(äyy::)
11 -> Lotta:   >#ai nii#<  siul    o    <sak°sa°>.
               PRT PRT            2SG-ADE  be-3 german
               ai nii you have German.
12             (0.2)
13    Milja:   mut meil onki ilmasua ja sit meil on hyppy°tunti°.=
               but we have drama and then we have a free period.
```

In line 11, Lotta acknowledges that she knew about Oona's German class but simply forgot about it: she does this by saying *ai nii* "oh that's right". She then goes on to repeat the information that she should have remembered: *siul o saksa* "you have German".

Now consider, by comparison, this exchange:

(8.9) "Baking" (Koivisto 2015a:114–5)
((B has just reported that she and her parents have bought a food processor.))

```
1     A:   oottekste jo kokeillu leipoo sillä hh. hh
           Have you already tried to bake with it.
2     B:   no ku se on niinku: tilattu ni sit se [tulee vasta
           well it's been like ordered so it will arrive only
3 ->  A:                                         [a↑a:
```

```
4    B:   [(-)
5    A:   [ai se tulee sit joskus     vast.
          PRT DEM come  then sometimes not.until
          oh it will arrive only later.
6    B:   joo;
          yes.
7    A:   okei.
          okay.
```

In this instance A's inquiry (line 1) is based on a faulty assumption, namely that B has already received her new food processor. When B corrects this understanding, A now says *aa* "oh" (line 3) and then provides a candidate formulation of the actual state of affairs (line 5). By comparison with (8.8), it would not be possible for B to respond with *ai nii* "oh right" here, because the information she has received is not something that she actually knew and is only now recollecting. By the same token, if Lotta were to have responded *aa* in (8.8), she would have been heard as claiming not simply to have forgotten that Oona has a German class at 10 a.m., but to be under the mistaken assumption that she did not.

As the non-interchangeability of Finnish *ai nii* "oh that's right (I forgot)" and *aa* "oh (*I thought* ...)" in these sequences suggests, recollecting information and revising one's understanding of a situation because of it are two different "cognitive" dimensions of responding to informings, which are made overt through the use of distinct particles (see Weidner 2016). While this distinction can be circumscribed in English and other languages, it is not always encoded overtly through distinct particles.

In addition to cognitive aspects, languages can also mobilize distinct particles for the display of different affective dimensions in responding to news and informings. In English, for instance, *ah*, typically with low or low falling pitch, has been identified as a way of responding to negatively valenced informings, for example, bad news or troubles telling (Reber 2012).[14] In German responses to informings, *oh*, typically with level or low falling pitch, does the work of conveying an emotional change-of-state that can be interpreted either as disappointment/despair or empathy/sympathy depending on context (Golato 2012b). In Japanese, both *hee* and *eh*, when lengthened and produced with a high flat or rising pitch contour, in addition to conveying a change-of-state, can index concomitant surprise and/or disbelief (Mori 2006; Hayashi 2009).

---

[14] The English particle *wow*, by contrast, when delivered with narrow pitch span just below the middle of the speaker's pitch range, does not distinguish between positive and negative valence and can be used to respond to both good and bad news (Local and Walker 2008).

> Languages differ in the use they make of freestanding particles for responding to news and informings. While English has primarily one change-of-state particle, *oh*, whose production can be modified prosodically and phonetically to convey different cognitive and affective nuances, other languages have multiple change-of-state particles with partly distinct interactional functions. This suggests that responding to a piece of news or an informing in interaction is a complex affair: some languages use distinct particles to discriminate cognitive dimensions such as registering an informing as new information, displaying an understanding of its implications, conveying that the informing has led to a recollection or a sudden realization, and/or indicating that it has brought about a revised understanding of the situation. Some languages use distinct particles to discriminate affective dimensions of a response to news and/or an informing such as empathy or surprise, or whether it is being taken as good news or bad news.

2.1.3 Tokens for Acknowledgment and Agreement/Affiliation in Response to Assertions

"Assertion" will be used here as a label for a composite action category that includes both descriptions of states of affairs and assessments (Stivers 2005). Assertions make acknowledgment (e.g., *yeah*), agreement/affiliation (e.g., *yea:h!*), and/or confirmation (e.g., *that's right*) relevant next (see also Chapter 4 §5.5).[15] As Jefferson (2002) has shown, in response to assertions, recipients can use minimal response tokens either for simple *acknowledgment* of what an interlocutor has said,[16] or to display *affiliation* with what has been said. While tokens used for acknowledgment merely indicate "I (hear and) understand what you have said", tokens used for affiliation convey "I feel the same way", "I'd do the same thing", "I'm with you" (Jefferson 2002:1345).[17] In English, minimal acknowledgment and minimal affiliation are accomplished with the particles *yes/yeah* and *no*. Yet speakers of British English and American English diverge in their practices for distinguishing minimal acknowledgment from minimal affiliation (Jefferson 2002).

As Jefferson observes, this divergence is particularly noticeable in responses to negatively framed utterances. For instance, in American English mundane conversation, a negatively framed assertion is routinely acknowledged with *yeah*. Here

---

[15] To date, it appears that confirming an assertion is accomplished primarily with clausal formats: English *that's right* or German *das stimmt* (Gardner 2007; Barnes 2012; Betz 2015a). For that reason confirmation will not be discussed further here.

[16] What Stivers describes as "bland agreement" to an assertion, in English accomplished with *yeah* (2005:134), would also belong in this category.

[17] See also Müller (1996), who discusses the use of Italian *si* "yes"/*non* "no" and other tokens such as *certo* "certainly" and *bene* "fine" for affiliating with assertions as opposed to merely acknowledging them, i.e., displaying non-affiliation. He shows that the distinction is dependent on the timing and intonation of the token with respect to the talk it is dealing with.

is a case in point (the symbol (–) refers to negative framing, the symbol (+) to a positive token):

(8.10)   "Another one" (Jefferson 2002:1348)
```
1      Joan:   (-)    because I said, now I don't even have time to order
2                     another one from these other catalogue=
3 ->   Linda:  (+)    =e[Y e :]ah.
4      Joan:          [thing]
5      Joan:   (-)    .hhh 'Cause it wouldn't get here in time for
6                     Christma[s.=So,]
7 ->   Linda:  (+)            [Yeah, ]
8      Joan:          .mp.hh-.hhhh She said well...
```

Joan's negatively framed assertions *now I don't even have time to order another one from these other catalogue* (lines 1–2) and *it wouldn't get here in time for Christmas* (lines 5–6) are acknowledged by Linda with *yeah* on both occasions (lines 3 and 7). With this token, Linda simply conveys that she has heard and understood what Joan has just said.

But now compare how the recipient in the following American English exchange responds to a strong, morally charged assertion that is negatively framed:

(8.11)   "Mother's Day" (Jefferson 2002:1355)
((Nancy, talking to a friend of hers, is rehashing a conversation she just had with her former mother-in-law, who hadn't heard from her son (Nancy's ex-husband André) on Mother's Day. He later told his mother that he'd spent all of Mother's Day trying to call her.))
```
1      Nancy:  (-)    a:nd she: (.) knows better than tha:t because André
2                     never stayed home all day to call ↓anybod[y,h.hhh] hh
3 ->   Emma:   (-)                                            [n::No:,]
```

As Jefferson points out, Nancy's *André never stayed home all day to call anybody* (lines 1–2) is a morally charged assertion invoking how things are but ought not to be; in other words, it is affiliation-implicative, making relevant a sign of support, agreement, sympathy, or the like from the recipient (2002:1349). Emma responds with a lengthened *no* that is hearably affiliative (line 3). Thus, for American English, following negatively framed assertions, it is a (+) token, *yes*, that does simple acknowledgment, but a (–) token, *no*, that does affiliation.

In British English mundane conversation, by contrast, the practices for acknowledgment and affiliation differ. Here it is a *no* (–) token that is used to implement simple acknowledgment following a negatively framed assertion:

(8.12) "Deena's wedding" (Jefferson 2002:1360)
((Deena's daughter is getting married.))

```
1     Deena:      And eh the other thing Mark if they hadn't got a hou:se?
2                 (-) then there's no way we would be lavishing out on a
3                 ↑wedding °for them we'd° (.) you kno [w we would...
4 ->  Mark:  (-)                                      [No:.
```

Deena's statement that she and her husband would not be willing to fund a lavish wedding for her daughter if the latter did not have a house (line 2) is acknowledged by Mark in his next turn with *no* (line 4).[18] Deena's assertion is made in a matter-of-fact way and is not strongly affiliation-implicative; Mark's response treats it simply as heard and understood.

But in the following case, Mum's statement that despite British Telecom's £17 service charge for her telephone she has never had any service from them is morally charged:

(8.13) "British Telecom" (Jefferson 2002:1356)
((Leslie and her mother are complaining together about British Telecom: on top of high prices, there's a £17 service charge.))

```
1     Mum:     (-) I've never ↓had any service from them. ↑Ne↓ver.
2 ->  Leslie:  (-) No:. No:.
3                  (.)
4     Leslie:      Oh I haa (.) we ha:ve,
5     Mum:         °Ha [ve yo [u°
6     Leslie:         [.hhh [Because they're a:lways going wrong here
7                 [at Bridgewater,
8     Mum:         [(Tha:t's it. ↑yes.)
```

Notice that Leslie's response to Mum's strong assertion in line 1 – somewhat of an overstatement since Mum is presumably using British Telecom's services at the very moment – is also done with a slightly lengthened *no*, but one that is repeated with separate prosodic packaging (line 2). According to Jefferson, there is evidence that the use of multiple (separate) *no*s is a recurrent practice in British English mundane conversation for conveying affiliation and agreement with a negatively framed, affiliation-implicative assertion (2002:1357).

---

[18] This pattern holds not only for negatively framed statements followed by "you know" (as here) but also for statements with "I don't know", and for negatively framed statements delivering background information (Jefferson 2002:1366).

> Acknowledgment and affiliation are two ways of responding to assertions, and both American and British English use the particles *yes* and *no* to implement these responsive actions. Yet their practices for deploying the two particles differ. American English speakers use a (+) token, *yes* or *yeah*, for acknowledging a prior negatively framed assertion, while British English speakers use a (–) token, *no*, in the same environment. American English speakers deploy a (–) token when a negatively framed assertion is affiliation-implicative and they wish to make a display of support, understanding, sympathy, or the like, while British English speakers use multiple instances of the (–) token to convey such affiliation. The two varieties thus distinguish acknowledgment from affiliation consistently but use different practices with *yes* and *no* tokens to do so.[19]

In some languages there are distinct particles for distinguishing the responsive actions of acknowledgment and affiliation subsequent to assertions. Finnish, for instance, has two "yes" particles, *joo* and *niin*, which are dedicated to neutral registering and to conveying affiliation, respectively (Sorjonen 2001a:280). The distinction between them is particularly noticeable following A-event statements[20] that are affiliation-relevant. The particle *nii(n)* makes a claim of affiliation, as in the following extract:[21]

(8.14)   "Problems with money" (Sorjonen 2001a:135) (adapted)
((P suffers from high blood pressure and is explaining to the doctor why he thinks the new medication he has been taking may not be effective.))

```
8       P:   Kyllä nyt-ki iha
             I had for example now
9            rauhalline viiko-n-loppu ett-e(-n tehny) °mitää°,
             quite a peaceful weekend so that (I didn't do) °anything°,
10           (0.5)
11      P:   Mut ei se vaikuta silti.
             But still it doesn't have an effect.
12           (0.8)
13 ->   P:   Mut se on ainoa että ne (.) raha-huole-t    paina-vat
             but it is only that the    money-worry-PL press-PL3
             But the only thing is that the (.) problems with money
```

---

[19] The situation appears to be different in Danish, where Heinemann (2005) finds that both acknowledgment and affiliation with a prior negatively framed assertion are done with the negative particle *nej* "no".
[20] In contrast to B-event statements (see Chapter 4 §2.4), A-event statements concern states of affairs or situations about which the speaker (A) has knowledge but to which the recipient (B) lacks direct access.
[21] In this and the following transcript, 0 stands for "zero person", often roughly equivalent to generic "one" or "you" in English; ## stands for creaky voice.

```
14 ->         0 (vähän).
              0 little
              do burden 0 (a little).
15            (.)
16 =>   D:    Nii::,h
17            (.)
18      D:    Joo: ne on sielä kuitenki koko aja-n miele-ssä °ja°,
              Joo: they are there anyway in mind all the time °and°,
19      P:    #O[n:#    °ne siel (joo)°,         ]
              #They# a:re there a yeah)°,
20      D:         [viiko-n-loppu on lyhyt aika.]
                    a weekend is a short time.
21            (0.5)
22      P:    °(.Joo ja)°,
              °(.Joo and)°,
```

P's turn in lines 13–14 contains a so-called "zero-person" construction, which makes the reference open or generic and allows the speaker to avoid a direct reference to himself. At the same time, this construction invites the recipient to fill in the relevant reference and identify with the experience. In line 16 the doctor responds with a lengthened *nii::*, displaying that he recognizes the state of affairs as a possible one that legitimizes P's account. In doing so, he affiliates with P (Sorjonen 2001a:136). Lines 18 and 20 can be seen as a demonstration of this affiliation.

Now consider, by contrast, the following exchange:

(8.15)   "Party fuss" (Sorjonen 2001a:155) (adapted)
((Two sisters, Mervi and Jaana, are discussing plans for a celebration of their father's birthday, which will take place at their parents' place. Here they are deliberating over when they will leave again.))

```
6       M:    Oo-t-ko-s sinä sitten millonka jo lähö-ssä
              When is it that you are going
7             poe(k[kee).       ]
              away.             ]
                   [
8       J:         [No ku mu-l] o-is perjantai-na tö-i:-tä?,
                   Well 'cause I'd have to wo:rk on Friday?,
9             (0.4)
10      M:    °Ai jaa:.°
              °Oh I see:.°
11            (3.1)
```

```
12     M:    .hh Elikkä sinu-n pit:tää sillo jo torst°tai- na
             .hh In other words you mu:st then leave already on
13           lähtte-e°.=
             Thursday.=
14 ->  J:    =Nii:.mhh .hhh Ja varmmaa niin se< (.) juhla-häly-n
              PRT            and probably PRT     the.GEN party-fuss-GEN
             =Nii:.mhh.hhh And probably after the party fuss
15 ->        jäläkkeen 0 n'nku lähtee-k(h)i jo     iha mielellää. .hhh=
             after     0 like leaves-CLI   already just PRT
             0 is als(h)o like quite happy to leave..hhh=
16 =>  M:    =Joo[:.
                 [
17     J:    [°Tai no e-n >tiiä<°.hhh Mut ↑toisaalta
             °Or well I don't know.°   .hhh But ↑on the other hand
18           ol-is ihan kiva ol-la vähän pite-mppä-än mut<
             it would be just nice to stay a bit longer but<
```

In lines 14–15, Jaana also uses a zero-person construction "after the party fuss one is quite happy to leave", perhaps in part to justify her plan to leave the festivities early. This turn format invites Mervi to identify with Jaana's point and support her plan. But Mervi responds only with *joo* (line 16), registering the prior assertion but withholding any affiliation with it. Jaana orients to the lack of affiliation, and possible display of disaffiliation, by now backing down from her prior stance (lines 17–18) (2001a:156–7).

In Finnish, acknowledgment and affiliation following assertions are distinguished from one another through the use of different particles. Following an affiliation-relevant utterance, *nii* makes a display of affiliation, claiming "I see your point, I agree with you", while *joo* responds to the factuality of the utterance, registering it as understood but not addressing any possible affiliation-relevance.

2.1.4 Continuers

Rather than implementing a type-specific response at a point of possible completion in ongoing talk, for example, confirming/disconfirming information, receipting a piece of news, or acknowledging/affiliating with an assertion, recipients can pass up the opportunity to take a full turn at talk and simply invite their interlocutor to continue talking. Objects that are used to this effect are called *continuers* (Schegloff 1982).[22]

---

[22] Continuers may be wholly non-verbal, as in the case of head nods. However, given the linguistic focus of this volume, these will not be discussed here.

In English, the category of continuer includes particles such as *uh-huh*, *mm-hm*, and *mm*. Continuers are distinct from acknowledgment tokens in that, rather than being concerned with receipting the prior turn adequately, their primary job is to ensure that the prior speaker retains the floor (Gardner 2001:34).

Note that conversation analysts are careful to avoid the term "backchannel" (Duncan and Fiske 1977) for this type of object: they maintain that "signaling attention and understanding" is a gross under-specification, if not misrepresentation, of the work that continuers do. As Schegloff observes, a description in terms of "backchanneling" does not distinguish continuers from other practices for displaying understanding; nor does it do justice to the fact that, in producing a continuer, the recipient is specifically *not* undertaking whatever type-specific action might otherwise be appropriate and is also *not* initiating repair on the other's talk, which could be taken to foreshadow disagreement (1982:85–88). Continuers, then, betoken that an extended unit of talk by the co-interlocutor is underway, i.e., is not yet complete, and that the co-interlocutor should now continue talking and complete the unit (1982:81). The use of continuers is a practice for collaboratively achieving an extended turn at talk (C. Goodwin 1986a:207).

Continuers such as *mm-hm* have been contrasted with minimal acknowledgment tokens such as *yeah* (Jefferson 1984d): an *mm-hm* does "passive recipiency",[23] while a *yeah* can imply incipient speakership, i.e., that the recipient-so-far is about to take over the floor (Jefferson 1993b). Here is an example where we can see the two particles, *mm-hm* and *yeah*, at work:

(8.16) "Cleaning up" (Jefferson 1984d:203)
```
1         L:   I didn't have five minutes yesterday.
2         E:   I don't know how you do i:t.
3              (0.3)
4         L:   I don't kno:w. nh hnh
5         E:   You wuh: work all day toda:y.
6              (0.3)
7         L:   Ye:ah.
8              (0.2)
9         L:   Just get Well I'm (.) by myself I'm kind of cleaning up
10             from yesterday.
11   ->   E:   Mm: hm,
12             (0.2)
13        E:   ·t·hhh [hhh
14        L:          [°A-and° (.) °I was just g-washing the dishes,°
15   ->   E:   Yeah we're just (.) cleaning up here too:.
```

[23] Jefferson (1993a) argues that *mm-hm* is more passive than *uh-huh*.

With her *mm-hm* in line 11, Emma invites Lottie to continue talking about being by herself and cleaning up from the day before. Moreover, she leaves space for this to happen (lines 12 and 13), and when Lottie does continue (line 14), Emma assumes a recipient role. However, Emma then produces a *yeah* and shifts into talk about her own activities (line 15). Jefferson finds that this is a systematic pattern for many American English speakers: *mm-hm* is used to invite the other to continue, while *yes* or *yeah* is a precursor of upcoming speakership (1984d:206).[24]

Continuers such as *uh-huh* have also been contrasted with minimal assessments such as *oh wow* (C. Goodwin 1986a). The former are often placed *within* turns: that is, although they may come close to the possible end of a TCU, the current speaker continues the turn even before the interlocutor's continuer has come to an end. By contrast, minimal assessments come *between* units: even if a current speaker's turn is still ongoing, that speaker will delay production of the next unit until the interlocutor's minimal assessment has been completed. Consider, for instance, the following conversation between two friends, who are complaining about the advice given in the "Dear Abbey" newspaper column:

```
(8.17)      "Dear Abbey" (C. Goodwin 1986a:206) (adapted)
1      Hyla:      One time I remember, ·hh this girl wrote
2                 and her, ·hh she was like (.) fifteen or
3                 six[teen and] her mother doesn't let her wear
4  ->  Nancy:        [Uh hu:h,]
5      Hyla:      ·hh nail polish or sh(h)ort ski:::rts
6                 or:[:: ·hhhhhh]
7  ->  Nancy:        [Oh: wo:(h)w]=
8      Hyla:      =Oo::h no I remember what yesterday was
```

As Hyla is approaching the end of her parenthetical *she was like fifteen or sixteen* (lines 2–3), Nancy produces an *uh huh* (line 4). Hyla, however, moves immediately into the next unit *and her mother doesn't let her wear nail polish* (lines 3 and 5) without waiting for Nancy's *uh huh* to be completed. In lines 5–6, Hyla now begins a three-part list, *nail polish or short skirts or*. But when Nancy launches an appreciation of this information with *oh wow* (line 7), Hyla audibly delays, with a long inbreath, until it is completed (see the overlapped .hhhhhhh in line 6). Only then does she continue her turn, which coincidentally moves to something she has just remembered (line 8). Goodwin's argument here is that *uh huh* and *oh wow* are doing different work and that this is reflected in the way Hyla times her turn continuations. *Uh huh* does the work of a continuer: it treats the

---

[24] Jefferson's examples indicate that such a pre-shift *yeah* can be produced either as a turn preface (see (8.16)) or as a freestanding particle. Note that the *yeah* in line 7 of (8.16) is not an acknowledgment token and therefore not discussed further here.

unit Hyla is just completing as a preliminary to something else, simply inviting Hyla to go on. *Oh wow*, on the other hand, works as an assessment: it treats the specifics of what Hyla has just said. Were Hyla to continue before this assessment is fully articulated, the latter might no longer be appropriately placed (C. Goodwin 1986a:210).

> The use of continuers such as English *uh-huh* and *mm-hm* at points of possible completion in ongoing talk is a recipient's practice. This practice is characterized as much by what it does *not* do as by what it does: it does not treat the talk so far as ready for a type-specific response; nor does it convey a problem with the talk so far by initiating repair on it. Instead, the action carried out is simply to display an understanding that the current turn is not yet complete and to invite the speaker to continue.[25] In contrast to *uh-huh* or *mm-hm*, the particle *yeah* is used systematically by many American English speakers as a precursor to taking over speakership themselves. Continuers are often overlapped by the current speaker's continuation of the turn, whereas minimal assessments such as *oh wow* are not: instead, the turn continuation is delayed until the assessment has been produced in full. This suggests that continuers deal with the talk so far as preliminary to more talk, whereas minimal assessments deal with the particulars of what has just been said.

2.2 Turn-initial Particles

In most cases, whether a particle positioned at the beginning of a turn is free-standing, i.e., builds a TCU of its own, or is a turn-initial preface, i.e., constitutes part of the TCU that follows, depends to a large extent on its prosodic delivery. If a first particle is intoned in one go with what follows, without prosodic breaks such as pauses or lengthenings or pitch breaks/resets – i.e., if it is "through-produced", as many conversation analysts would say – it does not deliver an action on its own but works as a pre-beginning of the TCU that ensues. For instance, in the second turn (line 2) of example (8.2) above, *yeah he's down*, the particle *yeah* is a pre-beginning or preface[26] for the following turn components *he's down*.

Turn-initial position encompasses not only actual turn beginnings but also "effective" turn beginnings (Heritage 1998). In other words, although a particle may not be the first element uttered in a turn, it can still function as if it were *virtually* turn-initial. Consider, for instance, the following case:

---

[25] On the relevance of prosody, in particular final pitch, of continuer tokens in Australian English see §2 above. Systematic analyses for other varieties of English and for other languages are still needed.

[26] The terms *pre-beginning* and *preface* will be used interchangeably here.

(8.18)   "How've you been" (Heritage 1998:328)
1   E: How've you been.
2 -> L: Well- (0.2) **oh** fi:ne. Ye:ah. Goo:d.

Although *oh* is not the first word uttered in the turn at line 2, it is nevertheless in virtual turn-initial position: it serves as a pre-beginning or preface in the TCU whose other component is *fine*. This TCU moves away from the action that is foreshadowed by *well* and subsequently abandoned. In general then, the initial particle of a second, third, or later TCU in a multi-unit turn can be said to be in "effective" turn-initial position if that TCU involves a shift away from the action/ activity of the prior TCU(s) (Heritage 1998:328).

When turns beginning with a particle are later recycled for repair, the turn-initial particle is typically left out or dispensed with (Schegloff 2004). This is a clear indication that the turn-initial particle relates the turn it prefaces to what immediately precedes it: if the turn is re-done, the initial particle is no longer appropriate for the new environment. The recycled turn now relates to the repair initiation (Schegloff 2004:101–102).

Turn-initial particles thus deliver important information: they reveal how a speaker has analyzed the prior turn, and they project the shape of the turn to come (Kim and Kuroshida 2013). Yet the *specific* work that a turn-initial particle accomplishes is tied to the sequential position of the turn it is prefacing (see also §2 above). In the following we review the work of turn-initial particles first in sequence-initial turns (§2.2.1), then in responsive turns (§2.2.2), and finally in third position (§2.2.3).

2.2.1 Turn-initial Particles in First Position

Research on turn-initial particles is still in its infancy and a great deal remains to be discovered, particularly in languages other than English. However, the picture that is gradually emerging is that, in first position, turn-initial particles are primarily concerned with conveying the connectedness (or lack of it) between the upcoming turn and prior talk (Heritage 2013b; Heritage and Sorjonen Forthcoming). The rationale behind the work of turn-initial particles in initiating turns has to do with a default assumption in the organization and understanding of conversation, namely that, barring indication to the contrary, next turns will be related to immediately prior turns (Schegloff 2007a:14–15). Turn-initial particles are needed when there is a departure from this "nextness" principle.

Departures from "nextness" occur, for instance, when there is *discontinuity* between adjacent turns at talk. An initiating turn that is not warranted by current sequential or topical development can be marked as misplaced in English with an *oh*-preface: see example (5.22) in Chapter 5 for a case of sequential misplacement. Particle prefaces are also found in the case of topical disjunction: *uh(m)*, for example, is routinely used as a generic pre-beginning or preface for turns introducing first topics (reasons for the call) in English telephone conversation: see example (5.3) in Chapter 5.[27]

Turn-initial particles can, however, also be mobilized to convey *continuity* between an initiating turn and some prior talk if that continuity might not otherwise be expectable. Recall, for instance, the use of *and*-prefacing in a succession of medical interview questions as illustrated in (7.8) in Chapter 7. In this case, although there is little topical relation between a next question and the answer that came immediately before it, prefacing that question with *and* indexes its continuity with the foregoing question and constitutes the turn and its action as part of a larger, agenda-driven activity (Heritage and Sorjonen 1994; Heritage 2013b).

Turn-initial particles can also be used to convey the continuity of a turn introducing a first topic (or in telephone conversation, the reason for the call) if contingencies have led to that turn being sequentially delayed. In English, this can be achieved with turn-initial *so* (Bolden 2008, 2009b). For instance, in the following telephone call, a *so*-preface is used by the called party to solicit a reason for the call after an external contingency has delayed its timely delivery by the caller:

(8.19)   "What's up" (Bolden 2008:312)
((In line 1 Adam is referring to a taped explanation of the protocol of the Call Friend research study, under which the call to his fiancée Berta will be recorded.))

```
1       Ad:    You heard that right,
2       Be:    Hm-hmm,
3              (0.2)
4       Ad:    .hh hhh.hh [hSo:::h
5       Be:               [tk.hh Yup.
6              (2.5)
7       Ad:    °So keep in mind that [this is b-°
8       Be:                          [O(h)h my pho:ne's ringing
9              upstairs now.=too_
10             (0.2)
11      Ad:    Does it matter?
12      Be:    Nope-.
13             (1.8)
14      Be:    I don't care.
15             (.)
16 ->   Be:    ↑So what's up↓ honey.
17      Ad:    {2.0}/{.hhh}
```

---

[27] See Sidnell (2007a) for a study of the disjunctive work that the turn-initial particles *look* and *listen* accomplish in English interaction.

```
18      Ad:   Oh ma:n last night the phone rang, at- three thirty,
19            (.)
20      Be:   In the morning?
21      Ad:   Yeah.
22      Be:   .hhh You're kidding.
```

Once Adam (the caller) has reminded Berta of the research study and its protocol (lines 1–7), it would be incumbent upon him to announce the intended reason for his call, which as it later emerges is to tell her some bad news concerning one of his friends. However, Berta's sudden announcement of an incoming call on another line (lines 8–9) makes it necessary to deal with this contingency first (lines 10–14/15).[28] Berta's next *so*-prefaced turn indexes this delay when she solicits Adam's reason for the call: *So what's up honey* (line 16). In turn-initial position, the particle *so* implies that the upcoming turn is dealing with something that has been projected and is now pending: it construes it as "emerging from incipiency" rather than as coming out of the blue (Bolden 2009b:974).

More generally, the particle *so* can be mobilized as a preface for a wide variety of turns initiating actions such as proffering new topics, making arrangements, and delivering congratulations, if these new actions are treated as something that has been on the speaker's mind for a while (Bolden 2006). In the following extract, for instance, a topic proffer is introduced with *so*:

(8.20)   "Palm Springs" (Bolden 2006:670) (adapted)
((From a get-together hosted by Jim and his wife Leni. Sam is an elderly relative. The talk in line 1 concerns Jim's typewriter.))

```
1       Leni:  Yeah that's (what I'm worrying about)
2       Leni:  (thinking about).
3                    (2.3)
4       ( ):   ((sniff))
5       ( ):   ((grunt))
6  ->   Leni:  So you haven't been out to Palm Springs for awhile.
7              (.)
8              ↓Have you, I can tell you lost your ta:n.
9       Sam:   Not for three weeks (now).
10      Leni:  Yeah, ( ),
11      Sam:   ( [ )
12                [((...))
13      Sam:   I wanna go when it's convenient for me.
```

---

[28] Note the *oh*-prefacing in Berta's turn, which tags it as something disjunctive, a just-now-noticed event (see also Chapter 5 §3.4.1).

In line 6 Leni proffers a new topic, Sam's not having been to Palm Springs, with a B-event statement requesting confirmation. But she prefaces her turn with *so*, effectively construing the matter as having been pending. This implies an "emerging from incipiency" that contributes to continuity rather than discontinuity (out-of-the-blueness) between the new topic proffer and prior talk. By topicalizing the matter this way, Leni also displays other-attentiveness. Indeed, Bolden finds that *so*-prefaced turns launching new conversational topics are in general concerned with the addressee and with issues in the addressee's life world (2006:668).[29]

There is some evidence that construing an otherwise disjunct initiating turn as "connected" by prefacing it with a particle is not only an English practice. A study by Keevallik (2013), for instance, reveals that in Estonian the particle *no(h)* can preface initiating turns in ways that are reminiscent of English *so*. For example, *no(h)* is particularly frequent at the beginning of reason-for-the-call turns (2013:276), as in the following extract:

(8.21)   "Letter" (Keevallik 2013:276) (adapted)
((Phone rings))
```
1    V:   halo
          Hello.
2    H:   kule Indrek siin.
          Listen, it's Indrek.
3    V:   jaa?
          Yeah?
4 -> H:   .hh noh said         kirja       kätte     ve.
              NOH get:IMF:2SG  letter:GEN  hand:ILL  QUES
              NOH did you receive the letter?
5    V:   jaa?
          Yeah?
6    H:   no mis öeldi
          NO what did (it) say?
7    V:   e:i: ei nagu ei lähe kuhugile.
          No, no, (I'm) not going anywhere.
```

After the parties to this call have recognized and/or identified themselves (lines 1–3), caller H moves immediately to his reason for calling: he wants an update concerning a letter that is on its way to the called party V (line 4). H begins his turn with an inbreath and the particle *noh*. As Keevallik notes, H refers to the letter in a way that presupposes that V can identify it and knows that it is due to arrive (line 4). There is thus reason to believe that the parties have already talked about the letter and

---

[29] This creates a striking contrast with topic shifts that are prefaced by *well*: Heritage finds that these are overwhelmingly self-attentive and deal with the speaker's own experiences and concerns (2015:96).

share knowledge of its importance. V's response reveals no problem with these assumptions (line 5). Based on this and numerous similar cases, Keevallik thus concludes that when turns introducing first topics are prefaced by *no(h)*, they invoke a prior topical thread or an earlier interactional trajectory: they imply that the encounter is one in a series of encounters between the two participants (2013:276).

Estonian *no(h)* can also be used to preface topic-proffering turns, especially those that display knowledge of the other's life situation:

(8.22)   "Tests" (Keevallik 2013:279) (adapted)
((E has called her sister K long-distance on the occasion of K's birthday.))

```
1    K:   mts.hh ah nii. m nojah, (.) mul on -
              Oh right.    Well,    (.) I have-
2         .h mul ei ole ka midagi uudist.
              I don't have any news either.
3         (0.3)
4 -> E:   noh, sa teed   arvestusi vä.
              NOH you do:2SG test:PL:PRT QUES
              NOH, you're doing tests or?
5    K:   no meil ei ole arvestusi. mul on
              Well, we don't have any tests.    I have
6         esmaspäev üks eksam. mul on aint neli
              an exam on Monday.    I only have four
7         eksamit. ja kõik.
              exams and that's it.
```

When K professes not to have any news (lines 1–2), E asks whether K is taking tests, using a *noh*-preface for her topic proffer. Since K is a student and it is the time of year for tests and exams, E's query reveals knowledge of, and attentiveness to, her sister's concerns. Keevallik argues that this use of the particle *no(h)*, without being identical to that of turn-initial *so* in English, is nevertheless a similar practice for initiating topics that do not emerge contingently from the prior turn (2013:280).

When particles are used to preface turns in first position, they convey information about how the upcoming turn is related (or not) to what has come before. In English, if the turn is a noticing occasioned by some extra-conversational contingency, an *oh*-preface can be used to indicate its disjunctivity. However, turn-initial particles can also index connectivity, as in the case of *and*-prefacing for questions in a series. *So*-prefacing, for example, of reasons for the call or of topic proffers, indexes a special kind of continuity: it implies that the topic is pending or has been on the speaker's mind for a while. In Estonian, *no(h)*-prefacing in otherwise disjunct reason-for-the-call turns and topic proffers does something similar: it indexes a continuing relationship between the participants.

2.2.2 Turn-initial Particles in Second Position

In responsive turns, turn-initial particles deal with a different set of "nextness" expectations, namely those established by a first pair part. In English, it is the particles *well* and *oh* that have received the most attention in responsive turn beginnings. Both can be used as prefaces in responses to questions and assessments/assertions, yet each does distinctive work in these environments.

Let us look first at *well* in responses to questions. Early conversation analytic research noted that this particle at the beginning of an answer to a question, especially one serving as a vehicle for an invitation or an offer, can foreshadow a dispreferred response, for example, a rejection or refusal (Davidson 1984:109–10): see line 4 in example (B.14) of Online-Chapter B for a case in point. Yet Schegloff and Lerner (2009) furnish evidence that *well* can also preface a preferred (or sequence-conforming) response, as in the following instance:

(8.23)   "Broken my ankle" (Schegloff and Lerner 2009:98) (adapted)
((Ilene and Lisa are making arrangements for Lisa to bring back Ilene's dog Kizzy, who Lisa has been boarding at her kennel.))

```
2        Ile:  Oh well no we:h ↓one of us would be here anywa:y,↓
3              (0.4)
4        Ile:  No cz I'd like to see ↓you:.
5        Lis:  ↓Yes.
6        Ile:  A:nd um then I've just got to go to the hospital trolley,
7              .hh uh: fro: [m two:
8        Lis:              [I think I've broken me a:nkle.
9   ->   Ile:  ((nasal)) Oh:: what've you do:ne,°
10             (0.2)
11  =>   Lis:  We:ll I fell down the step- eh e-haa ↑as (.) a matter of
12             fact it wasn' anything to do with Kizzy, .hhhh I: came ou:t
13             of the ba:throom en down those two little steps in
14             (the [hall) 'n kicked meself on my a:nkle.
15       Ile:       [Mm::,
16       Ile:  Oh:. [(    ).
```

In response to Lisa's out-of-the-blue announcement *I think I've broken me ankle* (line 8), Ilene makes a solicitous inquiry, *Oh what have you done* (line 9), making an informing expectable next. Lisa now provides that informing but prefaces her response with *well* (line 11). As Schegloff and Lerner point out, Lisa's response is sequence-conforming, in the sense that it provides an answer to Ilene's question. In fact, without *well*, it could be taken to be a simple and straightforward answer,

I fell down the step. Yet the *well*-preface implies that the response will not be straightforward, and indeed Lisa continues her turn at some length, first countering the implication that Ilene's dog might have been involved and then providing more detail about the incident (2009:102). The authors conclude that a *well*-preface in response to a *wh*-question, as seen here, serves as an alert that the answer will not be straightforward.

Heritage (2015) examines further types of answers and non-answers to questions, including transformative answers and answers that resist the relevance of the prior question (see Chapter 4 §2.7.2), as well as responses that resist the answerability of the question in the first place (called disclaiming responses here: see Chapter 4 §2.6.3). In all these cases, he finds *well*-prefacing being used when the respondents foreground their own perspectives, interests, or concerns as against those of their interlocutors (2015:95). Heritage concludes that in addition to non-straightforwardness, a turn-initial *well* alerts the interlocutor to an agentive position on the part of the respondent, one that privileges the respondent's perspective or project as opposed to that of the questioner (2015:101).

Answers to questions in English can also be designed with *oh*-prefaces. Recall that we described *oh*-prefacing in response to a polar question as being a means of contesting the fact that the question was asked at all: example (4.28) in Chapter 4 was a case in point. *Oh* treats the prior question as having brought about an attentional change of state; it thus indicates a problem with the question's relevance or appropriateness (Chapter 4 §2.7.2).

Hayashi (2009) attributes similar work to the Japanese turn-initial particle *eh*: it indexes a noticing of something in the talk that departs from the respondent's expectation, orientation, or knowledge. When used in responses to inquiries, *eh* can imply that the question is tangential to the current trajectory of talk, or that it embodies an incongruous presupposition (2009:2122). Here is a case where both interpretations are in play:

(8.24)   "People we know" (Hayashi 2009:2122) (adapted)
((A and B are husband and wife, and C and D are husband and wife, respectively.))

```
1    B:   nanka shitteru hito tte kekkoo.hhh hui ni deta
          Somehow, when we go out, we unexpectedly run into people we
2         toki ni yoku au n desu yo ne.
          know quite often.
3    C:   a::[:::::[:::::
          oh::::::
             [     [
```

```
4      D:         [°u::[::::n°
                   °Yeah::::°
                             [
5      A:         [(    )
                  [
6      B:         [a konaida    mo  oaishimashita mon [ne
                   Oh we ran into each other the other day, too, didn't we.
7      D:                                              [oaishimashita
                                                        We sure
8                 ne::.
                  did.
9      A:    nan no [kaeri] da kke.  ((To B))
              What was it we were coming home from ((when we ran into them))?
                     [    ]
10     B:           [(    )]  ((To D))
11            (0.2)
12  -> B:    eh dakara: kinyoobi ni gohan tabeta ka[eri.
                so      Friday    on  meal  ate   on.the.way.home
              Eh, you kno:w, it was on our way home from the dinner on Friday.
                                                        [
13     A:                                               [aa haa haa haa haa.
                                                         Oh right right right right.
```

B is exclaiming how she often runs into people she knows when taking the bus to the train station and mentions meeting D just recently (line 6). D confirms this in lines 7 and 8. But now A asks his wife B what outing they were on when they met D. B's response (line 12) suggests, through its *eh*-preface, that this question is somewhat irrelevant to the trajectory of talk, and furthermore, through the addition of *dakara* "so/you know", that A should be able to remember anyway. Hayashi concludes that *eh*-prefacing is used in answers to indicate that the question departs from what the respondent expects in terms of its relevance and appropriateness in the local interactional context (2009:2125). See Kim (2013c) for a related use of the turn-initial particle *kulenikka* in Korean.

> In responses to questions, turn-initial particles can be mobilized for at least two jobs: (a) to alert the questioner that the answer will not be straightforward and/or that the action that follows will privilege the respondent's perspective or agenda – in English the particle *well* serves this purpose; and (b) to contest the appropriateness or relevance of a prior question – in English this can be done with *oh*-prefacing, while in Japanese it is accomplished with *eh*-prefacing.

2. Particles

A further means for resisting or sidestepping the constraints of questions, including those of question-word questions, is to deploy the polar negative particle "no" (or its equivalent) as a preface to the response. This practice is attested in English (Raclaw 2013), Estonian (Keevallik 2012), Japanese (Hayashi and Kushida 2013) (see also §2.2.2 in Online-Chapter C), and Korean (Kim 2013a, 2015). Here we focus on Korean, where *ani* is the standard negative response token for denying or disconfirming (i.e., disagreeing with) a positive polar question (Kim 2015:311). However, *ani* can be used to preface a response to a question-word question as well. Here is an extract in which this happens:

(8.25)   "Moving company" (Kim 2015:313) (adapted)
```
1    Jil:   a:: ecekkey ton toy:key manhi sse-ss-e kulayse,
            Ah:: so {I} spent so much money yesterday
2           mak isacim seyntha pwulu-ko mak ile-kwu.
            calling the moving company and things like that.
3    Hee:   e:: com to-wa tal-la kule-ci kulay-ss-e,
            Ye::ah {you} should have asked for help,
4           (0.2)
5    Jil:   nwukwu-hanthey?
            From who?
6->  Hee:   a↑ni:: mwe, namca-tul manh-cahn-a.
            a↑ni:: well,   there are many guys you know.
7           (.)
8    Hee:   ta pappu-n-ka?
            Is everyone busy {perhaps}?
```

Jil's *wh*-question in line 5 ("From who") challenges Hee's just prior suggestion that she should have asked for help. Hee's response to this challenge is prefaced by *ani*: it backs down from her earlier suggestion and resists naming potential helpers. Kim argues that *ani*-prefacing can be used to resist and block challenges implied by *wh*-questions of this sort (2015:316).

But *ani* can also be found as a preface in responses to polar questions – not to deny/disconfirm (or agree/disagree with) the claims they make, but to contest the assumption that the question is confirmable at all, or to resist the way the question is framed. Here is a case in point:

(8.26)   "Australia" (Kim 2015:322) (adapted)
((Jen and Ham are talking about their boyfriends. Ham has just complained that her boyfriend does not seem to care much about her.))
```
4    Jen:   ne-ka hocwu ka-l ke-lase kule-n ke ani-ya?
            It's not because you're going away to Australia?
```

```
5                   (0.4)
6  ->    Ham:       ani:: molu-keyss-e:=
                    ani:: {I} don't know:
7                   =caki-nun nay-ka mwe hocwu ka-ko mwe kule-n ke-lul::,
                    {He} says that he won't care much about me
8                   kunyang sinkyeng an ssu-keyss-tay:=
                    going away to Australia
9                   =ohilye::, kuke-lul kunyang camkkan eti kass-ta-o-nun ke-
                    rather::,    because {it}'s better to think of me as going
10                  la-ko sayngkak-ha-kwu iss-nun key nah-ul ke kath-ayse::,
                    and coming back just in a short time,
```

By proposing an alternative explanation for Ham's boyfriend's behavior in the form of a negative polar question, Jen presupposes that her hypothesis is confirmable or not (line 4). Yet Ham's response, with *ani*-prefacing, contests this assumption: in fact, she claims not to be able to either confirm or disconfirm it (line 6), explicitly blocking the fundamental assumption of the question (2015:325).

> The use of the negative polarity particle ("no") to preface responses to question-word questions is a widespread practice for resisting the assumptions and presuppositions of the question. This practice has been documented with English *no*, Estonian *ei*, Japanese *iya*, and Korean *ani*, and is likely to be found elsewhere. In Korean, the negative polarity particle *ani* can also be deployed as a turn-initial particle in responses to polar questions in order to resist, if not block, their fundamental assumption of confirmability.

In response to assessments and assertions, some of the same particles are used in turn beginnings but the work they do is tailored to an evaluative or descriptive environment. For instance, the particle *well* can be used as a preface in response to assessments and assertions that are on the whole supportive but adopt a "my side" perspective: such responses offer something additional from the respondent's own experience. Recall example (4.79) in Chapter 4, where Edna is complimenting Margy on her recent luncheon: *that was a lovely luncheon* and *it was just delightful* (lines 1 and 2). Margy's response is *well I was glad you came* (lines 3 and 4), where the *well*-preface can be seen as indicating the recipient's own experience or point of view (Heritage 2015:99). This is an aligning response but one that has a "my side" basis.

Responses to assessments and assertions can also be prefaced with the particle *oh* (Heritage 2002a). As observed in §5.5.2 of Chapter 4 and §2.1.1 of Online-Chapter C, *oh*-prefacing in agreeing second assessments allows respondents to convey that they have reached the same conclusion as their interlocutor on epistemically independent grounds. An *oh*-preface can be used to such effect both in cases where the participants share equal access to the assessable, as in example (4.89) in Chapter 4 – A: *it's too depressing.* B: *oh it's terrible* – and in cases where the second speaker has privileged access, as in example (C.3´) in Online-Chapter C – A: *she said it depressed her terribly.* B: *oh it's terribly depressing.* In both cases, the particle *oh* claims epistemic primacy on the part of the respondent, despite the fact that they are assessing from a second, or sequentially subordinate, position.

In Japanese, the particle *eh* is used to preface responses to assessments and assertions that clearly depart from the prior evaluation or opinion. In other words, turn-initial *eh* serves as an alert that what the respondent is about to say will disagree, disalign, or otherwise disaffiliate with what has just been claimed. Here is an example:

(8.27) "Car" (Hayashi 2009:2119) (adapted)
```
1    A:   inaka da kara:: [anmari so-  ] kootsuumoo  hattatsu shitenai.=
          ((My hometown)) is in a rural area, so transportation networks aren't developed much.=
                          [              ]
2    H:                   [°u:::::::n°]
                           °Mhm°
3    N:   =ja    nani basu:?=
          =Then, what, do you take a bus ((to get around))?=
4    A:   =kuruma  kuruma.
          = It's a car, it's a car.
5    H:   eh [kuruma:?]
          Eh you use a car:?
             [        ]
6    A:      [shigoto ] iku no mo kuruma.
             Going to work is also by car.
7         (0.8)
8    H:   ii:: ne:[::::   |ja    ameri]ka mitai janai=
          That's goo::d. It's like America, isn't it, then?=
                  [       |           ]
9 -> A:           [eh ii: | ka na-    ]
                  good  Q   FP
          Eh I wonder if it's good-
10   A:   =juutai demo suru yo::
          =There are traffic jams though.
```

When A explains that in her hometown people use cars to get around and go to work because the transportation system is not well developed, H evaluates this with *ii:: ne::::* "that's good" (line 8). But A now comes in with an *eh*-prefaced response: *eh ii:*

ka na- "I wonder if it's good" that expresses doubt about H's assessment (line 9); in line 10 she proceeds to back up her position with an account: *juutai demo suru yo::* "there are traffic jams though". The *eh*-preface in this sequential position projects that the upcoming turn will not align with the position taken in the prior turn (2009:2120).[30]

> Turn-initial particles in second position work to project how an upcoming response will relate to the prior turn. In the case of first assessments and assertions, they can project that the responsive turn will align with the prior, albeit from the speaker's own perspective (English *well*) or on epistemically independent grounds (English *oh*). But they can also project that the impending turn will disalign with the prior turn, as in the case of Japanese *eh*, which is used to preface divergent or disagreeing responses.

2.2.3 Turn-initial Particles in Third Position

Particles can also be used to preface turns in third position: in this case, since they are produced by the same speaker as the one who delivered the first pair part of the sequence, they convey something about the relationship between these two turns. After a question-answer sequence, for instance, the English particle *well* in turn-initial position can retrospectively cast a prior information-seeking question as *preliminary* to an upcoming action (see also Online-Chapter F §5) and project that the forthcoming turn will be the reason for having asked it (Kim 2013b). Here is a case in point (see also example (C.33) in Online-Chapter C):

(8.28) "Trip to Oxford" (Kim 2013b:126) (adapted)
((Lesley's husband Skip has planned a business trip to Oxford with a colleague of his.))

```
12 ->  Les:    .hhh ↑Where you going to sta↓:y.
13             (0.5)
14 ->  Skip:   ↑Well I don't know whether we're gonna stay or come
15             back yet ehm it c'd be difficult I expect to get a
16             hotel in Oxford at this short not[ice,
17 =>  Les:                                     [.hhhhh Well I was going
18             to say if ↑I ↓came with ↓you perhaps we could stay in
19             ahk- (.) in: Haddenham ↓for the night.↓
20             (.)
```

At the first arrow, Lesley inquires where Skip intends to stay when he goes to Oxford. Note that this question could be taken as a simple request for information:

---

[30] Note that the *eh* in line 5 does not preface a response to an assessment and for this reason is not discussed here. However, it could be said to indicate that the speaker has noticed something in prior talk that departs from pre-existing knowledge, supposition, expectation, or orientation (Hayashi 2009).

there is no indication on its production that it might be doing anything more. Skip responds accordingly at the second arrowed turn, indicating that he does not yet have the information requested, using turn-initial *well* to alert Lesley that his answer will not be straightforward (see §2.2.2 above). Now, in third position, Lesley uses *well* to preface a turn that reveals why she asked the question in the first place: it was done as a preliminary in preparation for a proposal to accompany Skip and spend the night in Haddenham (2013b:133).

As Kim observes, the motivation for using a *well*-preface in this sequential position may be that the purpose of the original question was not immediately clear on its production: it could have been a simple request for information or it could have been a preliminary leading up to something else. *Well* in third position makes it clear that the reason for asking the original question was to prepare the ground for the action that is now about to be delivered.[31]

A *well*-preface in third position can indicate the relevance of a first-position question whose motivation on production may have been indeterminate (for the recipient). It is thus a resource for retroactively disambiguating between a genuine request for information and a (non-type-specific) preliminary leading up to another action.

2.3 Turn-final Particles

We have already encountered turn-final particles at various junctures in this book, primarily in connection with Japanese. For instance, in Chapter 2 §1.2.2 we saw that in Japanese, a Subject-Object-Verb (SOV) language with delayed projectability, final particles such as *ne, yo, sa, ka, no, wa,* and *zo* are one of a number of grammatical resources (others include copulas, nominalizers, and final verb suffixes) that can be used to locate imminent transition-relevance places (TRPs) (Tanaka 2000a:18). And in Online-Chapter C §2.2.1 we see that the Japanese particles *yo* and *ne* are also used to do epistemic work in assessment sequences, claiming either greater access than a co-interlocutor, or equal access, as the case may be, to the assessable (Hayano 2013). But positioning particles in turn-final position is a more widespread practice, documented in many languages. Located "in the interstices of parties' talk" (Tanaka 2000b:1172), turn-final particles have a pivotal role to play in the management of turn transition, as well as in conveying epistemic stance (see, e.g., Enfield et al. 2012).

In the following we review studies of two particular practices with particles in turn-final position: first, the trail-off use of *conjunctionals* (a term introduced by

---

[31] In fact, as Kim shows, type-specific preliminaries such as *what are you doing?*, which project a *specific* type of upcoming action, e.g., an invitation, lack *well*-prefacing when the projected action is then delivered (2013b: 141–142).

Jefferson (1983) to refer to linking elements such as English *so, well, uh, and, but, or,* and the like); and second, the use of tags such as English *right, hunh, eh*[32] in post-completion position of TCUs. We also consider similar practices with turn-final conjunctionals and tags in other languages.

2.3.1 Trail-off Conjunctionals

In Jefferson's terminology, the category of *conjunctional* is broader than that of conjunctions with its subordinating and coordinating subtypes: conjunctionals also include *uh* and diverse other particles (*well, so*), all of which have in common that they come when a speaker is "starting, resuming, or continuing an utterance" and are often followed by a pause (1983:2). Jefferson notes that there are two options for what happens next after a conjunctional + pause: the current speaker continues talking, or another speaker starts up unproblematically. With the second of these options, when there is a "clean" transition to next speaker, the current speaker could be said to be yielding the floor, in which case the conjunctional serves as a turn-final particle. To illustrate this phenomenon, consider the following instances of *so, but,* and *or* where in each case, following a brief pause, there is an unproblematic transition to next speaker:

(8.29)　　"Check deposit" (Jefferson 1983:4) (adapted)
```
1       Bud:    'hh Hadn't been up to get his ch[eck to d]eposit=
2       Emma:                                  [Ya:h,   ]
3 ->    Bud:    =in the ba:nk so
4 ->    Emma:   't' hhhh Okay honey well gee tha:nks for calling...
```

(8.30)　　"Nadine" (Jefferson 1983:4) (adapted)
```
1 ->    Sheila: 'hhhh So uh I haven't uh, hh 'hh met Nadine but, hh
2 ->            (0.3)
3 ->    Erma:   She's a do:ll.
```

(8.31)　　"Thanksgiving turkey" (Jefferson 1983:4) (adapted)
```
1       Emma:   If this THANKSGIVING THING DOESN'T TURN OU::T I'VE GOT
2               THE TURKEY in I'll cook the DA:MN THI:NG?, 'n freeze part
3 ->            of it 'n give you some of it or
4 ->            (1.0)
5 ->    Lottie: Oh:::.
6               (0.7)
7       Lottie: Uh:::, no I don't want any,
```

---

[32] Strictly speaking, tag questions such as English *is he* or *haven't you* are not particles, due to the fact that they are not fixed, uninflected forms. However, tag questions will nevertheless be included here, on the grounds that in turn-final position they work in ways that are similar to particles.

Note that in all of these instances, the conjunctional is produced as the final part of a TCU that has otherwise reached possible syntactic and pragmatic completion; in each case the conjunctional is integrated prosodically with what precedes. Because the transition to next speaker is unproblematic, these conjunctionals could be said to be turn-final particles that constitute recognizable turn endings.

Jefferson (1983) claimed that she was unable to account for how interlocutors know whether a current speaker is planning to continue after a conjunctional + pause or not. But in subsequent research, Local has shown that this is conveyed through prosodic-phonetic delivery: if the conjunctional is followed by a "holding" pause, i.e., one involving a glottal closure that is sustained over a period of time, it will be understood as holding the turn, whereas if the conjunctional is a "trail-off", i.e., if it does not end in glottal closure, has lax and centralized vowels as well as reduced tempo and loudness, and/or is followed by an audible outbreath, it will be treated as yielding the floor (Local and Kelly 1986; Local and Walker 2005) (see also Online-Chapter E §4.2). These findings are corroborated by Walker (2012), who states more generally that trail-off conjunctionals have the same prosodic-phonetic characteristics as other post-accentual words at the end of turns that are designed and treated as possibly complete.[33] Indeed, the conjunctional in each of examples (8.29)–(8.31) above is delivered with "trail-off" prosody.[34]

What are speakers doing interactionally when they end their turn with a trail-off conjunctional? The answer appears to depend on which conjunctional is being used and what its more "standard" use may be. For instance, Raymond (2004) observes that the English word *so* frequently prefaces a TCU that will articulate the upshot of prior talk and indicate the completion of a complex turn or activity (p. 186). When *so* is used with trail-off prosody at the end of a turn, it projects just such an upshot but, because it invites a response from other, it also conveys that the current speaker is not going to produce the upshot (p. 189). Here is an example where we can observe this happening:

(8.32)   "Depressed" (Raymond 2004:189–90) (adapted)
```
11      Mark:   It's a religious: (0.3) thing we're gonna have.
12              (0.3)
13      Mark:   I don't know why:, °but
14              (0.5)
15      Mark:   Uh::m, (·) No- her ex boyfriend's getting married en
16   -＞         she:'s: gonna be depressed so:,
17              (0.8)
```

---

[33] Walker (2012) also examines the visible behavior of speakers around and during the production of trail-off conjunctions and finds that features such as visibly searching for a next speaker or withdrawing gaze also indicate that the turns are transition-ready.

[34] Although not indicated as such in the transcripts for (8.29) and (8.31), the prosodic trail-off is clearly audible in the taped recordings.

Mark's *so* in line 16 projects the upshot of the information he has just provided. But rather than delivering it himself, his trail-off prosody anticipates some response from the interlocutor, implying that the upshot will be left unstated (Raymond 2004:190).[35]

In comparison to *so*, the work that a trail-off conjunctional such as *and* accomplishes in turn-final position is of quite a different nature. Koivisto (2012) has investigated the Finnish equivalent of "and", which is *ja*, as a turn-final particle in the discourse pattern of a general claim + specifying list (Jefferson 1990; Selting 2007; and Online-Chapter F §4). When positioned after a list item in an open list, Finnish *ja* implies that there are other members of the list that could be mentioned but need not be. As Koivisto shows, using a list format with final *ja* is a practice that can be deployed strategically to create the impression that the list has many members, although the turn is potentially complete. Here is a case where this happens:

(8.33)   "School" (Koivisto 2012:1260) (adapted)
((Ella and her grown daughter Mari are trying to decide when Mari and her family will be coming to visit Ella. Mari has just asked if she should call that evening to let her mother know whether she will be coming the next day or the day after.))

```
7       E:    ↓#e#:i se-n oikeestaan sillai sitte, (0.4) #öö#
              ↓it doesn't actually in that way then, (0.4) um
8             sitte väliä o; m- mää e-n niinku sii-hen; (.)
              then matter; I- I can't you know
9             [.hhhhh
10      M:    [nii ei siihen [tar-  ]
              yes one doesn't   ha-
11      E:                    [pysty]    mitään    kummempaa
                               be.able anything strange-COM-PAR
                               can't (say) anything further about that
12 ->         koska (.) mää mene-n aamu-lla   koulu-uj ja; HHHH[HH ((sighs
              because   1SG go-1SG morning-ADE school-ILL and       heavily))
              because (.) I'm going to school in the morning and;
13      M:                                                     [nii joo.
                                                                oh that's right.
14 ->   E:    >mu-1   on< kahteen #koulu# °ja°.
              1SG-ADE be  two-ILL  school  and
              I have school until two °and°.
15      M:    ju:st ↓#joo#. (0.2) .joo (.) [niij ja eihän se, ]
              right.         (0.2)  .yea  (.)  yes and it doesn't you know,
```

---

[35] As studies by Laury and Seppänen (2008) and Koivisto et al. (2011) show, the Finnish conjunction *että* "that/so" can also be used as a particle in turn-final position to project the upshot of the turn but leave it to be inferred.

```
16      E:                              [#sil#°lee°,hh  ]
                                        #like# °that°,
17      M:      ja jos me tullaan niin >me< varmaan tullaan vasta
                and if we do arrive we probably won't arrive until
18              sitten ehkä yheksän mai[ssa.]
                maybe around nine o'clock then ((in the evening))
19      E:                              [Illa]llahan te vasta
                                        you won't arrive
20              tuut[te °sitte°].
                until the evening that's true.
```

In lines 12–14, Ella uses a list format to convey that there are multiple reasons for her not being able to say anything further about the best time for Mari's visit. Actually there is only one reason, namely that she will be at school the next day. But she presents this as a list with several members, "I'm going to school in the morning and" (line 12), with the final *ja* indicating that the list is not exhaustive, although turn transition is possible. The implication is that Ella is very busy and, judging from the heavy sigh (see Online-Chapter E §8) that she produces concomitantly (line 12), that she is also tired. Mari displays understanding in her next turn (line 13), whereupon Ella adds another member to the list: "I have school until two and" (line 14). Again the final *ja* implies that there are more unmentioned members in Ella's list of reasons for not being more specific about the best time for Mari's visit.[36] The general argument, then, is that final *ja* can serve as a resource for creating an open list while at the same time suggesting possible turn completion (Koivisto 2012:1258).[37]

By contrast, the trail-off conjunctional *but* in turn-final position evokes not a list but, *inter alia*, a concessive clause combination as described in Chapter 7 §2.6. Recall that the concessive clause combining pattern involves two steps: first, conceding that an interlocutor's assertion is valid, and second, insisting that a potentially contrasting assertion of one's own also holds. For an example see (7.19) in §2.6 of Chapter 7. The link between these two rhetorically related steps is typically expressed with *but* in English or its equivalent in other languages. Koivisto (2012) examines Finnish *mutta* "but" in this context and observes that when *mutta* is produced turn-finally, it evokes the concessive pattern but only implies the contrasting assertion. Leaving an assertion implicit can be a useful way of dealing with delicate and/or socially problematic matters. Consider, for instance, the following exchange:

---

[36] In contrast to the first list item + *ja* in line 12, the last syllables of the second list item + *ja* are produced with creaky voice and whispery phonation, both of which are prosodic indications of turn yielding in Finnish (Koivisto 2012:1260) (see also Online-Chapter E §6).

[37] Barth-Weingarten (2014) comes to similar conclusions for turn-final *and* in English.

(8.34)   "Phlox" (Koivisto 2012:1264)
((Taina is thanking her friend Ella for some flowers that Ella has sent.))

```
1    T:   ja kiitos ihanista kukista ne ovat niin.h (0.4)
          and thank you for the lovely flowers they were so.
2         niin niin.h loistok#kaat#.
          so so. glamorous.
3    E:   pysykö ne. hh
          did they stay fresh.
4    T:   no py↑:[↓sy. aivan ihanasti.]
          well they did   just wonderfully.
5    E:          [joo. #n- n-# noi - n ]oi taitaa   aika hyvin kestä-ä
                  PRT                  DEM.PL       seem.3SG quite well last-INF
          yeah. I guess they last quite well
6 ->      paitsi floksi              ny vähän vari#se-e# mut.
          except name.of.a.flower    now little shed-3SG  but
          except that phlox sheds (its petals) a little **but**.
7         (.)
8    E:   .HH[HHH
9    T:      [nii:m mutta kuitenki ne oli niil nuppusia.
             yeah but anyway they were so buddy.
10   E:   nii. hyvä. hh ki↑va.
          yeah. good. hh nice.
```

Following Taina's compliment that Ella's flowers stayed wonderfully fresh (line 4), Ella responds by conceding that some of them, in particular the phlox, do not keep well, ending her turn with the particle *mut(ta)* "but" (line 6). This leaves the implied contrasting assertion unstated, namely that the flowers she gave Taina were nevertheless wonderful. By not making this claim overtly, Ella can avoid self-praise (p. 1265). In short, the practice of deploying *mutta* "but" turn-finally serves as a way to avoid producing a socially problematic assertion overtly but imply it nevertheless.[38]

The conjunctional *or*, or its equivalent in other languages, when used as a trail-off in turn-final position, again achieves a different effect. In its standard use as a conjunction, *or* links two alternatives that are generally considered to be exclusive: in the constructed utterance *Are we leaving now or later?*, the alternatives *now* and *later* cannot both be true at the same time (Drake 2015:306). In talk-in-interaction, *or* can be appended to a (polar) question in order to project a contrasting alternative. If it is delivered with trail-off prosody, such an *or* indicates that the alternative will be left unstated. That is, it is hearable as turn yielding, making it relevant for the recipient

---

[38] See Mulder and Thompson (2008) for a discussion of final *but* in English, and Kim and Sohn (2015) for final *kuntey* "but" in Korean (also Chapter 7 §2).

now to confirm or, more tangibly, disconfirm the question. Here is an example from a study of turn-final *or* by Drake (2013, 2015) where we can observe this happening:

(8.35) "Now or" (Drake 2013:92)
((Angela has been telling her friend Eric about a call she just received from a mutual friend named Bobby.))

```
5  ->  Eri:   [Is he still- [is he- has he done a PhD at] U of Y ↑now: ↓or_=
6      Ang:   =no he's just gonna finish his master's. he's student
                teaching
7                this semester and then he's gonna find a job teaching at a
8                high sch[ool,
9      Eri:            [oh okay;
```

Drake argues that the turn-final *or* appended in line 5 to Eric's candidate proposition that Bobby has done a PhD at the university in question projects a contrasting alternative and thus tilts the question toward a negative response. This facilitates a disconfirmation of the original proposition, which is what Angela proceeds to do – immediately and with no sign of dispreference or hesitation (lines 6–8). In other words, turn-final *or* weakens the preference of a positive question for a positive response and makes it just as easy for the recipient to respond negatively (see also Online-Chapter B §1.2).[39] By comparison with a turn-final particle such as *right*, which would imply that Eric is relatively certain of the facts (despite the fact that he is asking), his turn-final *or* indicates instead relative uncertainty (Drake 2015:305).[40]

> Conjunctionals such as English *so*, *and*, *but*, and *or* – if they are delivered with trail-off prosody – can be used as final particles at the end of turns to convey transition-readiness. The same practice is attested with equivalents of these words in other languages when they are produced with whatever counts as turn-final prosody in these languages. The specific work that each conjunctional does as a turn-final particle is related to its more "standard" use in clause combinations: *so* projects an upshot, *and* projects the addition of a similar item, *but* projects a contrast, and *or* projects an alternative. When they are delivered with trail-off prosody, however, these conjunctionals are turn yielding, the implication being that the current speaker will leave the upshot, the next similar item, the contrast, or the alternative unstated. Instead, a response from the recipient is now anticipated. The practice of projecting a matter but leaving it unexpressed can be deployed strategically for a variety of interactional purposes, including the management of socially delicate and/or problematic issues.

---

[39] This observation goes back to Lindström, who states for turn-final *eller* "or" in Swedish inquiries that it "relaxes the preference organization of the turn to allow for a 'no'-type response" (1997:103).
[40] This use of English *or* has much in common with its equivalents in Swedish (*eller*) and in Finnish (*vai*): both of these conjunctions can be deployed as turn-final particles to imply the existence of a contrasting or negative alternative that will, however, remain unstated (Lindström 1997; Koivisto 2017).

2.3.2 Tags

Tags, including what are known as "tag questions", will be understood here as particles (e.g., English *huh?* or *right?*) or particle-like expressions (e.g., English *isn't it?*) that are added on to TCUs that have already been brought to possible syntactic, prosodic, and pragmatic completion. Unlike trail-off conjunctionals, which – as we have seen – are prosodically integrated into their turn, tags come in what is known as "post-possible completion" position (Schegloff 1996b:91). Since the turn has already been brought to possible completion, using a tag is a way for a speaker to re-complete it and select someone else to speak next: the tag serves as a "turn-exit technique" (Sacks et al. 1974:718). Especially when tags have rising intonation, they allow the speaker to mobilize or pursue a response (Stivers and Rossano 2010).[41]

Because of their position in post-possible completion, tags are frequently overlapped by a next speaker orienting to the possible completion of the turn. Here is a case cited by Sacks et al. (1974) attesting to this phenomenon:

(8.36)   "Down here before" (Sacks et al. 1974:707) (adapted)
```
1 ->  A:   Uh you have been down here before [haven't you.
2 ->  B:                                     [Yeh.
```

Jefferson (1981) notes that when a post-positioned tag is overlapped by an incoming response, this is "a sheer, happenstance occurrence" (p. 58). Here is one of her examples:

(8.37)   "Biochemistry" (Jefferson 1981:68)
```
1     Merle:  So your biochemistry is not a part of the medical school
2 ->          it's part of the chemistry depart[ment right?]
3 ->  Royal:                                   [M m h m :.]
```

Here the timing of Royal's response in line 3 is observably oriented to the TRP-projecting accent in *CHEMistry department* (line 2). That the confirmation token happens to overlap Merle's post-positioned *right?* in line 2 is thus an unintentional result of Royal placing the response so as to be well timed with respect to the pacing of prior talk (see also Chapter 2 §3.2 and Online-Chapter E §4.3).

Yet Jefferson (1981) also observes that on occasion tags can be placed *after* a recipient has already begun to respond to the turn to which the tag attaches. In this

---

[41] It should be noted, however, that tags do not invariably have rising intonation, at least not in English (see example (8.36) and Keisanen (2006) for examples of falling-pitch tags). This dimension of tags calls for further research.

position the tag can hardly be pursuing a response, since the tag-producer is likely to have heard the response begin and may even anticipate what its import will be. One of Jefferson's examples of this phenomenon comes from a recording by Bergmann of a German psychiatry intake interview between the doctor, the candidate patient, and her husband. In this case, the tag used is *ist das zutreffend?* ("is that correct?"):

(8.38)   "Doctor Hollmann" (Jefferson 1981:55) (adapted)

```
1      Dr. F.:    (    ) grad Nachricht, (0.8) (   Ihnen) nich
                  (    ) I understand        (0.8) ( that you're) not
2                 ganz gut gu:t geht
                  feeling very well.
3      Frau B.:   Ja:: also das ist [dann die Ansicht  ]
                  Yea::h well that is     the opinion
4 ->   Dr. F.:                      [Is' das zutreffen] d?
                                     Is that correct?
5      Frau B.:   des Herrn Doktor Hollmann
                  of Doctor Hollmann
6      Dr. F.:    A [ja
                  Uh huh
7      Frau B.:     [also meine ist es nicht
                     but it isn't mine.
8      Dr. F.:    Ihre isses nich[t
                  It isn't yours
9      Frau B.:                  [Nei:n
                                  No:
```

Jefferson notes that the psychiatrist Dr. F uses a tag, or response solicitor, *Is' das zutreffend?* "Is that correct?" (line 4) after the patient has already begun to answer with *Ja:: also das ist* "Yea::h well that is" (line 3). A turn that begins with *ja also* "yeah well" – as we have seen in §2.2.2 above – can be heard as foreshadowing a problematic response. Jefferson thus hypothesizes that the doctor's delayed tag may be attempting to "counter, override, interrupt" what is likely to be an "unfavorable" response by ignoring what the recipient has said (p. 54). She calls this practice, tongue-in-cheek, an "abominable", ultimately establishing that it is used not only by Germans and/or psychiatrists, but more generally by the public at large (p. 58).

As the examples above with English *haven't you* and *right* imply, languages can have more than one tag expression in their repertoire. Enfield et al. (2012) list at least nine commonly used tags in Dutch (see Figure 8.1 on next page).

Dutch	Rough translation
..., hè?	..., wouldn't you say?
..., toch?	..., isn't that right?
..., nietwaar?	..., isn't it true?
..., niet?	..., isn't it?
..., ja?	..., yes?
..., OK?	..., OK?
..., zeker?	..., if I'm not mistaken?
..., wedden?	..., wanna bet?
..., wat?	..., what?

Figure 8.1 The most commonly used tag expressions in Dutch conversation (based on Enfield et al. 2012:197)

As might be expected, these tag expressions are not necessarily equivalent or interchangeable with one another. For instance, Enfield et al. explain that *hè?* is used to solicit agreement from the recipient concerning a view or opinion (2012:199), while *toch?* solicits agreement about a factual state of affairs (p. 200). Here is an attested example of *hè?*:

(8.39a) "Shitty weather" (Enfield et al. 2012:203) (adapted)
A: wat een rotweer **hè?**
   what (a) shitty weather hè?

As the authors note, were *hè?* to be replaced here with *toch?*, the effect would be quite different:

(8.39b) "Shitty weather" (Enfield et al. 2012:203) (adapted)
A: wat een rotweer **toch?**
   (something like: what shitty weather, correct?)

In this slightly odd, constructed version, (8.39b), the speaker seems to be inquiring whether the weather is factually bad, whereas in the attested version, (8.39a), the speaker is simply soliciting the recipient's agreement on a personal assessment.

> Tags are particles or particle-like expressions, often – but not invariably – delivered with rising intonation, that occur in post-possible completion position, i.e., after a TRP. In this position they serve as re-completers, allowing the current speaker to exit the turn by selecting another to speak next. Occasionally tags are produced after a next speaker has already begun to respond, in which case they can sequentially delete a projectably unfavorable response. A given language may have a range of tags that can be used as turn-exit devices. In such cases the tags are not necessarily interchangeable but instead may make distinct epistemic claims about the turn they re-complete.

3. Conclusion

As far as we know, all languages have particles that can be used as one-word constructions to build turns at talk and/or to preface or complete TCUs. However, some languages have a larger inventory of particles than others. Particle-rich languages may use separate tokens to make overt distinctions that in particle-poor languages can only be achieved implicitly, for example, through prosodic variation of one and the same token or periphrastically, i.e., with circumlocution. And yet the tasks that can be accomplished with particles in talk-in-interaction are the same across languages. All participants need *minimal* ways of responding to polar questions, of conveying changes of state in response to news and informings, and of acknowledging and/or affiliatively agreeing with assertions. All participants are likely to need ways of displaying a turn's discontinuity, or continuity, with prior talk in first position; of departing from or resisting the constraints imposed by a first turn in second position; and of conveying the relation of a third-positioned turn to the speaker's first. Pre-positioned particles allow them to do this minimally within the TCU. Finally, all participants are likely to need ways of carrying out socially problematic or delicate actions, which trail-off conjunctionals allow them to do, or of pursuing a response, which post-positioned tags achieve. It is thus not surprising that particles are such a widespread resource for the conduct of conversation.

Conclusion

9
Implications for Language Theory

Our survey of how interaction is conducted with linguistic resources (Part I) and how linguistic resources are deployed in interaction (Part II) would be incomplete were we not to consider the implications of these findings for language theory. What characterizes language in this view? What new light can Interactional Linguistics cast on age-old questions concerning language structure, language variation, language diversity, and language universals? These are some of the issues we address in this chapter.

1. Language in an Interactional Linguistic Perspective

For interactional linguists language is above all a form of social behavior. It is an inherently interactional activity observable in social encounters between human beings. It not only exists in the minds of its users but is materialized in their communication with one another. As one means of communication, language in this understanding is deployed along with other resources (visible, haptic, olefactive) in a semiotic ecology for communicative purposes.

As a form of social behavior, language is discoverable through "close looking at the world". This was one of the earliest insights of Sacks (cited in Jefferson 1985:26–27):

Many of the objects we work with would not be accepted as a base for theorizing if they were urged as imagined.

We can then come to see that a warrant for using close looking at the world as a base for theorizing about it is that from close looking at the world we can find things that we couldn't, by imagination, assert were there. One wouldn't know they were "typical".

One might not know that they ever occurred.

Sacks' point is that observable fact is far richer than anything researchers could ever imagine. If we were to present imagined "observations" as findings, we would be constrained by what others consider plausible. But if our observations on language are based on what happens in the real world – and we can point to the conversational record to document them – they are empirical, and no longer constrained by plausibility.

Through "close looking" and with an "analytic" mentality (Chapter 1), interactional linguistic research has found and explicated forms of linguistic orderliness that language scholars have until now ignored or discounted – among these, for example, sound objects such as clicks and aspiration particles (Online-Chapter E §7 and §8), "online" construction types such as dislocations, pivots (Chapter 6 §3.2, §4), and projector frames (Chapter 7 §5.3), lexical items (particles) serving as change-of-state tokens and continuers (Chapter 8 §2.1), etc. That is, the inventory of what are considered linguistic resources has been broadened and the set of operations that can be performed with them opened up, subject only to the limits imposed by observable reality.

> Language in an interactional perspective is a form of social behavior, concrete and observable. It is one semiotic means for communicating in interaction with others, discoverable through "close looking at the world". In this perspective the study of language has broadened to include sound objects, online construction types, and particle-like lexical items hitherto ignored by traditional linguistics, as well as practice-based operations performed with them in the pursuit of communicative goals in talk-in-interaction.

Interactional Linguistics takes the perspective of *interactional constructivism* (Levinson 2005): it sees grammar and social institutions as having been constructed through millennia of interactional encounters. However, rather than attempting to reduce grammar and social institutions to interactional principles alone (*interactional reductionism*), it recognizes the effects of past linguistic development, with its sedimentations and ritualizations, and of social historical institutionalization, both of which in many ways now constrain how interaction and specifically talk-in-interaction are conducted.

2. Design Features of Language

Linguists ever since Hockett (1960) have been concerned with determining which features of human language distinguish it from non-human communication systems, including those observed among animals. Hockett proposed a set of sixteen "design" features of language, including important principles such as displacement, productivity, reflexiveness, and learnability. Interactional linguists would not wish to dispute the validity of many of these features.[1] However, the research done in an interactional linguistic framework has brought to the fore other features of

---

[1] See, however, Wacewicz and Żywiczyński (2015) for a critical view of Hockett's design features from the perspective of evolutionary linguistics.

language which ring truer to its nature as used in social interaction. In the following we review some of the design features of language from an interactional linguistic perspective.

i. *Language is a dynamic process.* Instead of being thought of as a static object consisting of a lexicon and a set of rules for combining lexical units into larger structural units, language in an interactional perspective is viewed as something one *does*. For this reason, many interactional linguists prefer to speak not of language but of *languaging* (Becker 1991; Linell 2009). In the framework presented here, we have opted to speak of language as affording *resources*, which are mobilized as *practices* for the accomplishment of actions in interaction. One outcome of this view is that the boundary between language (resources) and language use (practices) becomes fuzzy: language is manifested in use. In this book Chapters 6–8 and Online-Chapter E discuss different types of linguistic forms as resources for interactional practices, while Online-Chapter F deals with further practices of using language in interaction, for example, for referring, listing, repeating, formulating, etc. Together the resources and the practices, we would claim, constitute language.

ii. *Language is physically embodied.* It is materialized through the human body, specifically through the vocal apparatus. As such it encompasses both single sounds and prosody (Online-Chapter E). In the understanding adopted here, language is primarily a vocal-auditory phenomenon, although its production may have visible effects: smile voice, for instance, is noticeable as spread lips, and articulatory gestures can be seen in lip and jaw positions. Outside of language, but very much a part of the communicative process, are other, freely deployable forms of visible behavior such as gesture, gaze direction, facial expression, body position, and movement. Although we have focused primarily on the linguistic aspects of social interaction here, ideally the whole communicative process – including the interrelation and temporal coordination of all of its semiotic modalities – needs consideration (see, e.g., Streeck et al. 2011). The present volume can be thought of as a contribution to this larger goal.

iii. *Language is publicly displayed.* Language occurs in social interaction, where it contributes to the communicative process. For this it must be accessible, minimally at least, to one's co-interlocutor; typically, however, it is accessible to all co-present parties. The public accessibility of language contributes to its accountability (Heritage 1984b). Participants are held accountable by others for what they say and do not say as reflected in the verbal record of interaction. More tenuous is the accountability of non-verbal but linguistic – i.e., prosodic-phonetic – dimensions of interaction. Although often below the level of conscious awareness, these dimensions – precisely because of their public accessibility – are nevertheless subject to a measure of intersubjective accountability to the extent that they give rise to inferences that steer conversational trajectories.

iv. *Language delivers action.* As a tool for communication in social interaction, language delivers social action (for more on the ontology of action in interaction, see Sidnell and Enfield 2014). These actions are housed in turns at talk (Chapter 4), which themselves are organized into sequences and sequences of sequences (Chapter 5). Language is adapted to its position in specific turns and sequences; in Schegloff's words, it is "positionally sensitive" (1996b:108) (see below). The initial level of granularity at which language is observed (experienced) is thus that of social action. As interactional linguists, we can then describe and analyze it at finer levels of detail.[2]

v. *Language is a set of resources organized syntagmatically and paradigmatically.* The resources of language are organized syntagmatically and paradigmatically for the accomplishment of social action (see also Bybee 2010). The syntagmatic organization of language is reflected in its use in turn construction (Chapter 2) and sequence organization (Chapter 5). Turn-constructional units (TCUs) and turns can be conceptualized as consisting of "positions" (Schegloff 1996b) or, metaphorically, "slots" (Raymond 2013); the same holds *a fortiori* for sequences (Schegloff 2007a). It is in these sequential positions or slots, within the syntagma of turns and sequences, that particular forms of language are mobilized, i.e., produced and comprehended. For each position there are typically alternative ways of filling the slot linguistically. These create a paradigm, or in Schegloff's terms an "organization of practices" (2000c:207), for each position.

vi. *Language unfolds in real time.* Language in social interaction is fundamentally temporal – it emerges in real time, metaphorically speaking "online" (Auer 2009), in the "enchrony" of conversation (Enfield 2011).[3] We have encountered its temporal nature on numerous occasions in this book: not only in the duration and timing of syllables and pauses in turns at talk (Online-Chapter E §4), but also in the positioning of particles within turns (Chapter 8 §2), in the extendability of clauses as reflected in pivots and dislocations, or pre- and post-positionings (Chapter 6 §2.2 and §3), and in the incremental practices of clause combining (Chapter 7 §5). Temporality thus has far-reaching consequences for the nature of language as a communicative tool.

---

[2] On levels of granularity see Schegloff (2000d).
[3] *Enchronic* time has been described as "the move-by-move, normative level of 'interactional time'" (Sidnell and Enfield 2012:310).

2. Design Features of Language

vii. *Language allows for projection.* One of the consequences of the temporality of language is that it must allow for projection. As Auer (2005a) notes, human interaction depends crucially on the possibility of projection: participants must know how actions and action components are sequenced in time in order to be able to anticipate and negotiate their trajectories and their resolution (Auer 2005a:8 and Chapter 2 §1.1). Language facilitates this: as it emerges in time, it foreshadows what will come next through syntagmatically organized structures and patterns. Projectability is found not only in the structure of clauses, where early constituents prefigure later ones with varying degrees of strength (Chapter 6 §1.2), but also in phrases (Chapter 6 §5.1), and even in one-word constructions, where early sounds and prosodies prefigure the ultimate shape of the word (Online-Chapter E §4.4).

viii. *Language allows for extension.* Related to its capacity for permitting projection, language must also allow for the extension of its units in time. This is because participants must be able to modify or add on to their units contingently, in the light of what the other does (Chapter 2 §4). Like projectability, we have encountered extendability on various scales in our survey of linguistic resources as deployed in interaction. Pivots and dislocations (pre- and post-positionings), for instance, are prime examples of internal and external extensions of the clause (Chapter 6 §2.2 and §3), but the phrase is also extendable (Chapter 6 §5.1), and so, to a certain extent, are words (e.g., through lengthenings and aspiration: Online-Chapter E §4 and §8).

ix. *Language allows for repair.* Given the forward orientation of time and its irreversibility, language, which emerges in time, must be repairable (Fox et al. 1996). That is, we must be able to amend, back up and revise, or more generally rework something that has already been said. Language permits this by establishing places for editing, and by furnishing operations through which editing can be achieved and recognized as such (Chapter 3 §2 and Online-Chapter E §4.4).

x. *Language provides for co-participation.* Because language enables projection, is extendable, and happens publicly in interaction, it affords opportunities for co-construction (Lerner 1996a). In fact, as Fox and other researchers have noted, at every moment of their production, utterances in interaction are "temporally unfolding opportunities for co-participation" (Fox 2007:310). This holds in the first instance for turns composed of complex clause combinations (Chapter 7 §6). But it also applies at the level of the simple clause and/or phrase, as C. Goodwin's (1979) study of the interactive construction of a sentence has shown (Chapter 2 §1).

An interactional understanding of language is only partially compatible with a structuralist view such as Hockett's. Hockett (1960), for instance, claims that human language exhibits discreteness, i.e., that linguistic units are perceived categorically, not continuously. This claim reflects the written bias of much of earlier linguistic thinking (Linell 2005). It ignores the role of prosody, whose *modus operandi* involves gradability and whose relevance for interaction is uncontestable (Online-Chapter E). And it wholly ignores the temporality of language in use. Most importantly, however, in contrast to grammatical paradigms in structuralistic descriptions, paradigmatic alternatives in turn and sequence slots are not equivalent with respect to their effects on the interaction; instead, they give rise to different interpretations, inferences, and trajectories of subsequent interaction (Levinson 1983:321 and 367). Yet in many ways the features listed above can be seen to complement those proposed by Hockett: they not only add an interactional dimension to our understanding of language that derives from its use as a means for implementing action in social interaction but also make it clear that language is more than just a structural system in its own right. It is a resource that participants in interaction can make use of actively, as, for example, when they purposely create "deviant" structures in order to engage in meaning-making.

> As a form of social behavior, language in interaction is characterized by a number of "design" features: it is a dynamic process rather than a static entity; it is physically embodied and publicly displayed; it delivers action; its resources are organized as paradigmatic alternatives for specific positions in the syntagma of turns and sequences; it is temporally emergent, allowing for projection, extension, and repair; it is shared and continuously provides for co-participation. This view of language in interaction is only partially compatible with structuralist descriptions.

3. Language Variation and Interaction

Understanding language interactionally has important implications for the way we think about language variation. Language variation refers to the fact that there are often alternating forms for one and the same linguistic unit. The English sound /p/, for instance, is sometimes strongly aspirated and sometimes not. To describe this type of alternation, structural linguists have distinguished between *contextually determined* variation and *free* variation. For instance, whether /p/ is aspirated or not at the beginning of a stressed syllable is said to be *contextually determined*: /p/ is non-aspirated if it follows /s/, otherwise it is aspirated. Thus the word *spin* is pronounced [sp**i**n], but the word *pin* is pronounced [p^h**i**n]. In syllable-final position, on the other hand, the alternation between aspirated and non-aspirated variants of /p/ is said to be *free* variation: nothing in the phonetic context determines whether a speaker who uses, for example, the word *sip* says [sip] or [sipʰ].

Yet interactional linguistic work has shown that aspiration particles can be inserted virtually anywhere in talk for specific interactional purposes. This means that the word *spin* could be said as [sp(ʰ)in] if the speaker wished to flag that word as insufficient or potentially problematic in talk (Online-Chapter E §8). Thus, in talk-in-interaction, what traditional structuralist descriptions classify as contextually determined variants can also be freely chosen for special purposes. Moreover, interactional linguistic research has shown that the choice of what is classified as a free variant can be highly meaningful in interaction. For instance, at points of potential syntactic completion, the use of an aspirated /p/ in syllable-final position can convey the transition-readiness of a turn, while the avoidance of aspiration at that spot can project more same-speaker talk (Online-Chapter E §5.1). This means that so-called "free" variation is not free at all in interaction but is instead sensitive to the sequential context. The structuralist distinction between contextually determined and free variation thus collapses with an interactional view of language. Instead, all linguistic objects are seen as resources or devices that can be freely mobilized in implementing action in interaction.

In the case of syntax, many grammarians have postulated derivational relations between what they see as variants of the same underlying structure. For instance, a clefted sentence is seen as *derived* from a non-clefted one, an extraposed sentence as *derived* from a non-extraposed one. Yet there is little evidence in conversation of a derivational relation between clefted and non-clefted *variants* or between extraposed and non-extraposed *variants* of utterances. Both clefted and extraposed variants are used to manage a range of specific tasks in talk-in-interaction (Chapter 7 §5.1, §5.2); these are quite different from what non-clefted and non-extraposed variants can do. A similar argument holds for so-called *elliptical* variation. After question-word questions, for instance, phrasal answers have long been considered elliptical variants of full-clausal answers. But in reality the two forms of response are used for quite different purposes (Chapter 4 §2.6.1). As with many putative *derivational* variants, interactional linguistic research has found no grounds for assuming a single underlying structure and many grounds for treating the variants as structures in their own right, each used as a resource with its own preferred context(s) of occurrence.

More generally speaking, what interactional linguistic findings such as those reported here imply is that linguistic structures are chosen on the basis of their position in the turn and/or sequence. This insight is captured in Schegloff's notion of "positionally sensitive grammar" (1996b). Positional sensitivity has cropped up on multiple occasions in the preceding chapters. We have seen that, for example, one linguistic object can be appropriate for beginning a sequence (e.g., *uh(m)*:

Chapter 5 §2.2.1), but another appropriate for ending a sequence (e.g., figurative expressions (Chapter 5 §2.2.4)). These two devices are often not interchangeable in the same position. We have also seen that one type of linguistic object can be appropriate for delivering an action in first position (e.g., a clause), but another for delivering an action in second position (e.g., a phrase). Using one where the other would normatively be expected leads to the inference that "more" is being done than normal (Chapter 6 §5.2).

> Taking an interactional linguistic perspective on language means thinking of alternatives in language use not as "variants" of underlying abstract (or more basic) structural units that are distributed in a contextually determined versus free fashion, but rather as resources in their own right, whose selection is normatively appropriate in specific turn and sequence positions. Linguistic alternatives in this view are related to one another when they form paradigmatic choices for the implementation of the same action in talk-in-interaction.

4. Language Diversity and Interaction

Language diversity refers to the incontestable fact that there are many, widely varying languages in the world – in fact, over 7000 according to current counts.[4] Despite Chomskyan claims to the contrary, these languages differ radically from one another at every level of structural description: phonological, morphological, syntactic, and semantic (Evans and Levinson 2009:429; Dryer and Haspelmath 2013). Associated with these languages are radically different cultural practices, which – together with language diversity – can be expected to impinge on the conduct of conversation. It might be thought, then, that conversations throughout the world have little in common. Yet conversation analysts have consistently shown that there is enough similarity in talk-in-interaction across cultures to make comparison meaningful (Moerman 1977; Ford and Mori 1994; Fox et al. 1996; Wells and Peppé 1996; Lerner and Takagi 1999; Luke and Pavlidou 2002; Steensig and Asmuss 2005; Hayashi and Yoon 2006; Ono and Couper-Kuhlen 2007; Sidnell 2007b; Stivers et al. 2007; Fox, Maschler et al. 2009; Fox, Wouk et al. 2009; Stivers et al. 2009; Stivers et al. 2010; Kaimaki 2012; Luke et al. 2012; Enfield et al. 2013; Zinken and Ogiermann 2013; Dingemanse et al. 2014; Floyd et al. Forthcoming).

What appears to ensure the commensurability of conversation across languages and cultures is the existence of a common infrastructure for informal interaction

---

[4] Based on *Ethnologue*, a catalog of the world's languages published by SIL International (www.ethnologue.com).

(Enfield and Levinson 2006; Enfield and Sidnell 2014). As Schegloff (2006) points out, the problems are the same everywhere: how to determine who talks next and when, how to shape turns at talk for the implementation of actions, how to sequence actions so as to form coherent courses of action, how to deal with trouble in speaking, hearing, and understanding, how to formulate talk in a way designed for a particular recipient, how to structure an interactional encounter overall. For each of these concerns there are generic mechanisms, systems of organizational practice, designed to handle them – i.e., turn construction, turn taking, sequence organization, repair, opening/closing routines, etc. – and generic principles such as recipient design (see below) to guide them. What differ across languages and cultures are the specific resources and practices for implementing these organizational systems, their "local inflections" (Sidnell 2007b).

The anthropological literature contains a number of contradictory reports concerning conversational conduct in different cultures, suggesting that what has been described for English and Western European societies may not hold everywhere. For instance, (i) Reisman (1974) claims that in Antigua turn taking is "contrapuntal" and "anarchic", with many voices being heard at the same time, while (ii) Lehtonen and Sajavaara (1985) report that in Finnish conversation there are lengthy silences between turns. Further, (iii) Besnier (1989) claims that in Nukulaelae Tuvaluan candidate understandings are absent, while (iv) Levinson (2005) reports that, on Rossel Island (Papua New Guinea), co-participant guessing is crucial because a taboo prevents speakers from referring to close in-laws and dead relatives by name. Yet careful analysis reveals that in each of these cases the same generic mechanisms and principles are at work as are found in conversation elsewhere. For (i) Sidnell (2001) replicated Reisman's study in the Caribbean using tape-recorded materials and found that participants do monitor each other's talk for possible completion points. In this and all other respects, he argues, the conversations there display the same orderliness as that described by Sacks et al. (1974). For (ii) Stivers et al. (2009) studied transition timing in ten unrelated languages worldwide and established that there is a "target" of minimal gap and overlap between turns across languages, with the range of variation not exceeding a quarter of a second (pp. 10589–90).[5] For (iii) Dingemanse and Floyd (2014) reviewed Besnier's evidence for the lack of candidate understandings in Nukulaelae and found that there are in fact cases of candidate understanding in his data; their absence is noticeable only in gossiping sequences. For (iv) Levinson (2005) shows that despite the indirectness and implicitness of Rossel Island person-referring practices, the preferences, for example, for recognitionals and minimal forms, are

---

[5] Finnish was not included in the study, however; thus, Lehtonen and Sajavaara's (1985) claim has not been challenged.

the same as elsewhere. Moreover, as recognition is being pursued, the same relaxation of the minimization principle is in play (see also Online-Chapter F §1). So far, then, all the evidence suggests that despite the wide diversity of languages and cultures in the world, the same general mechanisms and principles of organization are operating everywhere to constrain the way conversation is conducted.

This does not mean, however, that there is no diversity worthy of interest in conversational interaction across languages and cultures. On the contrary. Where earlier anthropologists sought to establish the influence of diverse linguistic patterning on thought (Whorf 1956) or on socio-cultural relations (Silverstein 1976), now anthropologists are beginning to uncover the telling influence of diverse linguistic practices on action in social interaction. The forerunners of this new approach to linguistic relativity[6] are Sidnell and Enfield (2012): they argue that "different grammatical and lexical patterns of different languages can provide different opportunities for social action" (p. 303).

By way of illustration, Sidnell and Enfield explore one single action type, agreeing with a prior assessment from a position of greater epistemic authority – i.e., a [K+] second assessment (Chapter 4 §5.5.2) – in three different languages. Online-Chapter C §2.2.1 reviews the devices they single out for the implementation of this action type in Caribbean English Creole, Finnish, and Lao. Sidnell and Enfield's argument is that the different resources mobilized in these languages – "if"-prefaced repetition, verb repetition with an overt pronominal subject, and a factive perfective particle – influence the way a [K+] second assessment is effected in each language. Because each of these devices has its own affordances and is used in the respective language for other purposes as well, these affordances and other uses seep into and color the action's implementation in language-specific ways. In the authors' striking comparison, the specific affordances and uses of different linguistic resources bring "collateral effects" into the way the "same" action is accomplished in different linguistic communities, with potentially differing implications for subsequent sequential trajectories. In Caribbean English Creole, for instance, an "if"-prefaced repeat is also used as an interrogative marker in the other-initiation of repair. When it implements an agreeing second assessment, this device treats the first assessment as a polar question, downgrading its epistemic stance and correspondingly upgrading that of the response. Yet in doing agreement, it is closing-implicative: it allows the speaker to have the last word (p. 315). In Finnish, a verb repeat with an overt pronominal subject can be done with two word orders, either as Subject-Verb or as Verb-Subject: both can

---

[6] For a state-of-the-art overview of research on linguistic relativity at the end of the twentieth century see Gumperz and Levinson (1996).

implement [K+] second assessments, yet they have different implications for what happens next. In the case of Verb-Subject, the respondent signals a different perspective on the matter, which can lead to subsequent sequence expansion (p. 317). In Lao, the factive particle *le`q1* is also used in narration to signify completion of an action or event. When it is mobilized to agree with a prior assessment, this particle signals that the speaker has independent knowledge of its truth. At the same time, with its sense of finishedness, it closes down the sequence (p. 318). Thus, the three different devices for the "same" action in three different languages have language-specific added effects, or byproducts, of the means that are selected for accomplishing the action: Sidnell and Enfield describe these byproducts as treating a prior turn as uncertain, foregrounding a different perspective, and introducing a sense of finality (p. 320). More generally speaking, the authors' observations imply that the resources of different languages have different effects on the social actions that are accomplished through them, leading to substantially different "inflections" of a common underlying social order. In their words, "the language you speak makes a difference in the social actions you can perform" (2012:321).

Despite the wide diversity of languages and cultural practices in the world, current research is demonstrating that there is an infrastructure of informal interaction that makes cross-linguistic and cross-cultural comparison possible. This infrastructure consists of a set of generic mechanisms and principles – among others, turn taking, sequence organization, and repair – that have evolved to manage a set of common problems in the conduct of conversation. Yet these generic systems are "inflected" locally in language-specific ways. For instance, the "same" action of an agreeing [K+] second assessment is implemented with three distinct types of linguistic devices in Caribbean English Creole, Finnish, and Lao. Within each language the distinct device has multiple uses and its own affordances, which are swept in, as side effects, when it is mobilized for a [K+] second assessment in that language. In this sense then, *language shapes action*: the affordances and multiple functions of a language's resources influence the nature of what is being done and what its implications are for what happens next.

---

5. Language Universals and Interaction

As we have seen, there is every reason to believe that all languages and cultures share a common infrastructure for informal interaction. The generic systems of organization comprising this infrastructure might be considered "candidate universals" (Schegloff 2006:83) of interaction. But are there any concomitant universal effects on the language or languages for which these systems of organization serve as vehicles?

Interactional linguistic research has recently brought to light one substantive linguistic universal: this is the interjection *huh?*, which has been shown to exist world-wide for open-class other-initiation of repair (Chapter 3 §3.2.1) (Dingemanse et al. 2013; Enfield et al. 2013). Across a wide variety of unrelated languages and cultures, the device that is used in next turn to signal that one has not heard what the other has just said is an open monosyllable consisting of a low front unrounded vowel with at most a glottal consonant [h] or [ʔ] as onset, produced with questioning intonation (Dingemanse et al. 2013:6). Phonetically, the interjection *huh?* is calibrated to some extent with the language system in question: that is, the low front vowel may be more or less low and more or less front; the consonant onset may be present or not depending on the phonemic status of glottal sounds in the language; the intonation may be rising, level, or falling depending on what counts as interrogative prosody in the language. This suggests that the device is to some extent conventionalized and that children must learn to articulate and intone it in accordance with their native language. Yet given the wealth of possibilities for the phonetic-prosodic composition of words across languages, the degree of similarity in the *huh?* interjection cross-linguistically is quite striking. Dingemanse et al. conclude that it is a "universal word" (2013:6). They argue that interlocutors in all languages need a way to let their co-interlocutor know if something has not been heard properly and that *huh?* permits them to do so *quickly*, i.e., with minimal articulatory effort (the articulators do not need to move far from their neutral state), and *effectively* (questioning prosody indicates a knowledge deficit and mobilizes a response) (p. 7). If *huh?* is similar world-wide, they argue, it is because the same selective pressures are in force everywhere and have led to a convergent evolution. Because "conversational infrastructure is part of the evolutionary landscape for words" (p. 7), the authors speculate that there may be yet other universal linguistic items – among them, the continuer *mm/m-hm*, the hesitation marker *uh/um*, and the change-of-state token *oh/ah* – that await discovery (p. 8).

Above and beyond substantive language universals of this sort, Schegloff (2006) has argued that there are abstract principles governing linguistic practice in talk-in-interaction that are universal. One of these is the principle of *nextness*, a relation holding between current position and an immediately following position. This principle is the one behind adjacency pairs, the structural building blocks of interaction (Chapter 4 §1.1). But it has a corollary in language as used in interaction: talk can be thought of as composed of a succession of next elements, for example, words, parts of words, or sounds (Online-Chapter

E §4.4). Talk-in-interaction is processed by reference to nextness: one type of self-initiation of repair, for instance, is located before the next word or next sound of a word (2006:86).

Related to nextness is the principle of *progressivity* (Schegloff 2006:86; also Heritage 2007). Interactants are concerned with the *sequential* progress, or onward movement, of interaction. For instance, they can be observed to technically "prefer" having a question answered by an unaddressed party, moving the sequence forward, over having the person to whom they have addressed the question respond but not provide an answer (Stivers and Robinson 2006). But there is also a preference for *linguistic* progressivity in talk-in-interaction, i.e., for the absence of pauses, cut-offs, inbreaths, and repeats (Schegloff 2006:86). It is the interruption of the production of next sounds, syllables, and words that indicates the initiation of self-repair (Chapter 3 §1.1). Even in the repair process, speakers are concerned with progressivity: each successive attempt at self-repair has been observed to further the progress of the turn under construction (Schegloff 1979). And when a speaker has difficulty finding a next word, co-interlocutors may be observed to provide that word in the interest of progressivity (Goodwin and Goodwin 1986). Thus, participants can be seen to orient not only to sequential progressivity but also to linguistic progressivity in the production of turns at talk. There is good reason to believe this is a similar concern in all societies.

A third universal of linguistic practice in talk-in-interaction is the principle of *minimization* (Schegloff 2006:85; also Levinson 2007). Minimization operates in turn taking (Chapter 2 §1), where initially a speaker has the right to one TCU at a time, and in person reference (Online-Chapter F §1), where there is a preference for using a single referring expression rather than several all at once (Sacks and Schegloff 1979). But it also plays out as an economy of expression, where speakers have been shown to be as economical with words as the situation allows (Levinson 2007:30). The principle of minimization in person reference can be relaxed under certain circumstances, for instance, if recognition must be pursued or if there are local constraints on economical forms such as proper names (Levinson 2007:31). However, the point is that these are special situations interpretable against a universal default principle of minimization (Stivers et al. 2007).

Finally, and perhaps most centrally, there is the universal principle of *recipient design* (Schegloff 2006:89) guiding talk-in-interaction. This principle applies both to what actions a speaker undertakes and to what linguistic resources a speaker mobilizes to implement these actions. In Schegloff's words: "The things one talks about with another are selected and configured for who that other is ... And how one speaks about them – what words, reference forms, and so forth are to be used is also shaped by reference to who the recipient relevantly is at that moment, for this speaker, at this juncture of this interaction" (p. 89). Recipient design as a universal of language use is perhaps most immediately evident in the choice of referring expressions for person, place, and time (Schegloff 1972; Sacks and Schegloff 1979) and indexicals such as T/V forms[7] (Silverstein 1976), but it is by no means restricted to these. It is present in the selection of all linguistic forms for building turns and implementing actions in talk-in-interaction.

Given these universal principles governing language practice, what explanation is there for them? How did they come to be? As Levinson (2006) points out, principles such as these characterize not only talk-in-interaction but human social interaction in general. Interaction – even when no language is involved at all – always involves attributing intentions to another's behavior, taking into account that it will have been produced for a specific other (recipient design). Even non-linguistic interaction has action chains and sequences (nextness); its interactants expect close timing (progressivity); and their communicative intentions are expressed through clues designed to be just sufficient (minimization) (pp. 45–53). The universals of language practice in interaction can thus be thought of as deriving from the universals of interaction in general. As Levinson rightly observes, human interaction does not need language: it can occur in the absence of a shared language or culture and indeed in the absence of conventional language altogether, communication with infants and/or through "home sign" being cases in point (2006:42). Language simply facilitates communication in social interaction and enhances its expressive possibilities. It evolved, in Levinson's words, "*for* something for which there was already a need – that is, for communication in social interaction" (p. 42).[8]

To account for the universality of human interaction, Levinson (2006:44) postulates an "interaction engine", a set of cognitive abilities and behavioral propensities that conspire to make interaction the way it is. The interaction engine, he claims, provides the parameters for variation; its default values account for the commonalities attested across languages and cultures in the way interaction is conducted (p. 62). Whether these commonalities derive from a native endowment, as Levinson implies, or rather constitute the result of

---

[7] T (e.g., French *tu*, German *du*) stands for familiar and informal second-person singular forms of address, V (e.g., French *vous*, German *Sie*) for more distant and formal second-person forms of address, as used in languages making this distinction. Present-day English does not have a T/V contrast and provides only *you* as a second-person address form.
[8] Conceiving of language as an inherently interactional phenomenon thus also goes some way towards explaining the origin and development of language. For studies that take an interactional stance on the phylogenesis and ontogenesis of language see, for instance, Tarplee (1996), Wootton (1997), Tomasello (2003, 2008), Wells and Corrin (2004), and M. H. Goodwin (2006).

congruent cultural evolution, as Dingemanse and Floyd (2014:470) suggest, remains an open question at this time.

> Comparative interactional linguistic research has unearthed at least one concrete linguistic universal: the interjection *huh?*, which appears to be used by recipients across the globe – with local calibration – to indicate a problem in hearing something the other has said (Dingemanse et al. 2013). More items of this sort await discovery. At the level of linguistic practice, Schegloff (2006) has identified four universal principles governing talk-in-interaction: nextness, progressivity, minimization, and – most centrally – recipient design. Yet these principles are not unique to language use in interaction: they characterize human social interaction in general (Levinson 2006). The universals of language practice in talk-in-interaction can thus be traced back to the interactional foundation of human sociality. In this very real sense then, *interaction shapes language*.

Bibliography[1]

Aijmer, Karin. 2007. The interface between grammar and discourse: *the fact is that. Connectives as discourse landmarks*, ed. Agnès Celle and Ruth Huart, 54–72. Amsterdam: Benjamins.

Antaki, Charles. 2008. Formulations in psychotherapy. *Conversation analysis and psychotherapy*, ed. Anssi Peräkylä, Charles Antaki, Sanna Vehviläinen and Ivan Leudar, 26–42. Cambridge: Cambridge University Press.

Antaki, Charles. 2012. Affiliative and disaffiliative candidate understandings. *Discourse Studies* 14:531–47.

Antaki, Charles, Rebecca Barnes and Ivan Leudar. 2005. Diagnostic formulations in psychotherapy. *Discourse Studies* 7:627–47.

Antaki, Charles and Alexandra Kent. 2012. Telling people what to do (and sometimes, why): contingency, entitlement and explanation in staff requests to adults with intellectual impairments. *Journal of Pragmatics* 44:876–89.

Antaki, Charles and Margaret Wetherell. 1999. Show concessions. *Discourse Studies* 1(1):7–27.

Aronsson, Karin and Asta Cekaite. 2011. Activity contracts and directives in everyday family politics. *Discourse and Society* 22:137–54.

Atkinson, J. Maxwell. 1984. Public speaking and audience responses: some techniques for inviting applause. *Structures of social action: studies in conversation analysis*, ed. J. Maxwell Atkinson and John Heritage, 370–409. Cambridge: Cambridge University Press.

Atkinson, J. Maxwell and John Heritage (eds.). 1984. *Structures of social action: studies in conversation analysis*. Cambridge: Cambridge University Press.

Auer, Peter. 1984. Referential problems in conversation. *Journal of Pragmatics* 8:627–48.

Auer, Peter. 1991. Vom Ende deutscher Sätze. *Zeitschrift für germanistische Linguistik (ZGL)* 19:139–57.

Auer, Peter. 1992a. The neverending sentence: rightward expansion in spoken language. *Studies in spoken languages: English, German, Finno-Ugric*, ed. Miklós Kontra and Tamás Váradi, 41–59. Budapest: Linguistics Institute, Hungarian Academy of Sciences.

Auer, Peter. 1992b. Introduction: John Gumperz' approach to contextualization. *The contextualization of language*, ed. Peter Auer and Aldo di Luzio, 1–38. Amsterdam: Benjamins.

Auer, Peter. 1993. Zur Verbspitzenstellung im gesprochenen Deutsch. *Deutsche Sprache* 3:193–222.

---

[1] This bibliography lists the references cited in the book and in the online chapters.

Auer, Peter. 1996a. On the prosody and syntax of turn-continuations. *Prosody in conversation: interactional studies*, ed. Elizabeth Couper-Kuhlen and Margret Selting, 57–100. Cambridge: Cambridge University Press.
Auer, Peter. 1996b. The pre-front field in spoken German and its relevance as a grammaticalization position. *Pragmatics* 6:295–322.
Auer, Peter. 1997. Formen und Funktionen der Vor-Vorfeldbesetzung im gesprochenen Deutsch. *Syntax des gesprochenen Deutsch*, ed. Peter Schlobinski, 55–92. Opladen: Westdeutscher Verlag.
Auer, Peter. 1998. Zwischen Parataxe und Hypotaxe: "abhängige Hauptsätze" im gesprochenen und geschriebenen Deutsch. *Zeitschrift für Germanistische Linguistik* 26:284–307.
Auer, Peter. 2000a. On-line syntax – Oder: was es bedeuten könnte, die Zeitlichkeit der mündlichen Sprache ernst zu nehmen. *Sprache und Literatur* 85(31):43–56.
Auer, Peter. 2000b. Pre- and post-positioning of *wenn*-clauses in spoken and written German. *Cause, condition, concession, contrast: cognitive and discourse perspectives*, ed. Elizabeth Couper-Kuhlen and Bernd Kortmann, 173–204. Berlin: de Gruyter.
Auer, Peter. 2005a. Projection in interaction and projection in grammar. *Text* 25:7–36.
Auer, Peter. 2005b. Delayed self-repairs as a structuring device for complex turns in conversation. *Syntax and lexis in conversation*, ed. Auli Hakulinen and Margret Selting, 75–102. Amsterdam: Benjamins.
Auer, Peter. 2006a. Increments and more: Anmerkungen zur augenblicklichen Diskussion über die Erweiterbarkeit von Turnkonstruktionseinheiten. *Grammatik und Interaktion*, ed. Arnulf Deppermann, Reinhard Fiehler and Thomas Spranz-Fogasy, 279–94. Radolfzell: Verlag für Gesprächsforschung. (www.verlag-gespraechsforschung.de).
Auer, Peter. 2006b. Construction grammar meets conversation: einige Überlegungen am Beispiel von *so*-Konstruktionen. *Konstruktionen in der Interaktion*, ed. Susanne Günthner and Wolfgang Imo, 291–314. Berlin: de Gruyter.
Auer, Peter. 2007a. Syntax als Prozess. *Gespräch als Prozess*, ed. Heiko Hausendorf, 95–124. Tübingen: Narr.
Auer, Peter. 2007b. Why are increments such elusive objects? *Pragmatics* 17:647–58.
Auer, Peter. 2009. Projection and minimalistic syntax in interaction. *Discourse Processes* 46:180–205.
Auer, Peter. 2010. Zum Segmentierungsproblem in der Gesprochenen Sprache. *InLiSt* 49 (www.inlist.unibayreuth.de/issues/49/inlist49.pdf).
Auer, Peter. 2014a. Syntactic structures and their symbiotic guests: notes on analepsis from the perspective of online syntax. *Pragmatics* 24:533–60.
Auer, Peter. 2014b. The temporality of language in interaction: projection and latency. *InLiSt* 54 (www.inlist.uni-bayreuth.de/issues/54/inlist54.pdf).
Auer, Peter, Elizabeth Couper-Kuhlen and Frank Müller. 1999. *Language in time: the rhythm and tempo of spoken interaction*. Oxford: Oxford University Press.
Auer, Peter and Jan K. Lindström. 2011. Verb-first conditionals in German and Swedish: convergence in writing, divergence in speaking. *Constructions: emerging and emergent*, ed. Peter Auer and Stefan Pfänder, 218–62. Berlin: de Gruyter.
Auer, Peter and Jan K. Lindström. 2015. Left/right asymmetries and the grammar of pre- vs. post-positioning in German and Swedish talk-in-interaction. *InLiSt* 56 (www.inlist.uni-bayreuth.de/issues/56/inlist56.pdf).
Auer, Peter and Stefan Pfänder. 2011. Constructions: emergent or emerging? *Constructions: emerging and emergent*, ed. Peter Auer and Stefan Pfänder, 1–21. Berlin: de Gruyter.

Auer, Peter and Susanne Uhmann. 1982. Aspekte der konversationellen Organisation von Bewertungen. *Deutsche Sprache* 1:1–32.
Austin, John L. 1962. *How to do things with words*. London: Oxford University Press.
Barnes, Rebecca K. 2007. Formulations and the facilitation of common agreement in meetings talk. *Text and Talk* 27:273–96.
Barnes, Scott. 2012. On *that's right* and its combination with other tokens. *Journal of Pragmatics* 44:243–60.
Barth, Dagmar. 2000. *That's true, although not really, but still*: expressing concession in spoken English. *Cause, condition, concession, contrast: cognitive and discourse perspectives*, ed. Elizabeth Couper-Kuhlen and Bernd Kortmann, 411–37. Berlin: de Gruyter.
Barth-Weingarten, Dagmar. 2003. *Concession in spoken English: on the realization of a discourse-pragmatic relation*. Tübingen: Narr.
Barth-Weingarten, Dagmar. 2009. Contrasting and turn transition: prosodic projection with parallel-opposition constructions. *Journal of Pragmatics* 41:2271–94.
Barth-Weingarten, Dagmar. 2011a. Double sayings of German *ja*: more observations on their phonetic form and alignment function. *Research on Language and Social Interaction* 44:157–85.
Barth-Weingarten, Dagmar. 2011b. The fuzziness of intonation units: some theoretical considerations and a practical solution. *InLiSt* 51. (www.inlist.uni-bayreuth.de/issues/51/index.htm).
Barth-Weingarten, Dagmar. 2013a. From "intonation units" to cesuring: an alternative approach to the prosodic-phonetic structuring of talk-in-interaction. *Units of talk – units of action*, ed. Beatrice Szczepek Reed and Geoffrey Raymond, 91–124. Amsterdam: Benjamins.
Barth-Weingarten, Dagmar. 2013b. *Cesuring in talk-in-interaction: a parametric approach to "intonation units" and their role in back chaneling, turn-taking, language variation and language change*. Post-doctoral thesis, University of Freiburg, Germany.
Barth-Weingarten, Dagmar. 2014. Dialogism and the emergence of final particles: the case of *and*. *Grammar and dialogism: sequential, syntactic, and prosodic patterns between emergence and sedimentation*, ed. Susanne Günthner, Wolfgang Imo and Jörg Bücker, 335–65. Berlin: de Gruyter.
Barth-Weingarten, Dagmar. 2016. *Intonation units revisited: cesuras in talk-in-interaction*. Amsterdam: Benjamins.
Barth-Weingarten, Dagmar and Elizabeth Couper-Kuhlen. 2002. On the development of final *though*: a case of grammaticalization? *New reflections on grammaticalization*, ed. Ilse Wischer and Gabriele Diewald, 345–61. Amsterdam: Benjamins.
Barth-Weingarten, Dagmar and Elizabeth Couper-Kuhlen. 2011. Action, prosody and emergent constructions: the case of *and*. *Constructions: emerging and emergent*, ed. Peter Auer and Stefan Pfänder, 263–92. Berlin: de Gruyter.
Beach, Wayne A. 1993. Transitional regularities for casual *okay* usages. *Journal of Pragmatics* 19:325–52.
Becker, Alton L. 1991. A short essay on languaging. *Research and reflexivity*, ed. Frederick Steier, 35–41. London: Sage.
Beißwenger, Michael. 2007. *Sprachhandlungskoordination in der Chat-Kommunikation*. Berlin: de Gruyter.
Benjamin, Trevor. 2012. When problems pass us by: using *you mean* to help locate the source of trouble. *Research on Language and Social Interaction* 45:82–109.
Benjamin, Trevor. 2013. *Signaling trouble: on the linguistic design of other-initiation of repair in English conversation*. PhD thesis, University of Groningen.

Benjamin, Trevor and Harrie Mazeland. 2013. Other-initiated repair. *The Encyclopedia of Applied Linguistics*, ed. Carole A. Chapelle. Hoboken, NJ: Wiley-Blackwell (8 pages).

Benjamin, Trevor and Traci Walker. 2013. Managing problems of acceptability through high rise-fall repetitions. *Discourse Processes* 50(2):107–38.

Berger, Peter L. and Thomas Luckmann. 1966. *The social construction of reality: a treatise in the sociology of knowledge*. New York: Doubleday & Co.

Bergmann, Jörg. 1987. *Klatsch: zur Sozialform der diskreten Indiskretion*. Berlin: de Gruyter. (English version: 1993. *Discreet indiscretions: the social organization of gossip*. New York: Aldine de Gruyter).

Besnier, Niko. 1989. Information withholding as a manipulative and collusive strategy in Nukulaelae gossip. *Language in Society* 18(3):315–41.

Betten, Anne. 1976. Ellipsen, Anakoluthe und Parenthesen: Fälle für Grammatik, Stilistik, Sprechakttheorie oder Konversationsanalyse? *Deutsche Sprache* 3:207–30.

Betz, Emma. 2008. *Grammar and interaction: pivots in German conversation*. Amsterdam: Benjamins.

Betz, Emma. 2013. Quote–unquote in one variety of German: two interactional functions of pivot constructions used as frames for quotation in Siebenbürgen Sächsisch. *Journal of Pragmatics* 54:16–34. (Special issue on pivot constructions in talk-in-interaction, ed. Niklas Norén and Per Linell.)

Betz, Emma. 2015a. Indexing epistemic access through different confirmation formats: uses of responsive *(das) stimmt* in German interaction. *Journal of Pragmatics* 87:251–66.

Betz, Emma. 2015b. Recipient design in reference choice: negotiating knowledge, access, and sequential trajectories. *Gesprächsforschung – Online-Zeitschrift zur verbalen Interaktion* 16:137–73 (www.gespraechsforschung-ozs.de).

Betz, Emma and Andrea Golato. 2008. Remembering relevant information and withholding relevant next actions: the German token *achja*. *Research on Language and Social Interaction* 41:58–98.

Biber, Douglas, Stig Johansson, Geoffrey Leech, Susan Conrad and Edward Finegan. 1999. *Longman grammar of spoken and written English*. Harlow: Pearson Education Limited.

Bilmes, Jack. 1988. The concept of preference in conversation analysis. *Language in Society* 17:161–81.

Birkner, Karin. 2007. Semantik und Prosodie von Relativsätzen im gesprochenen Deutsch. *Deutsche Sprache* 35:271–85.

Birkner, Karin. 2008. *Relativ(satz)konstruktionen im gesprochenen Deutsch: syntaktische, prosodische, semantische und pragmatische Aspekte*. Post-doctoral thesis, University of Freiburg, Germany.

Birkner, Karin, Sofie Henricson, Camilla Lindholm and Martin Pfeiffer. 2012. Grammar and self-repair: retraction patterns in German and Swedish prepositional phrases. *Journal of Pragmatics* 44:1413–33.

Blom, Jan-Petter and John J. Gumperz. 1972. Social meaning in linguistic structures: code switching in Northern Norway. *Directions in sociolinguistics: the ethnography of communication*, ed. John J. Gumperz and Dell Hymes, 407–34. New York: Holt, Rinehart, and Winston.

Bohle, Ulrike. 2007. *Das Wort ergreifen – das Wort übergeben: explorative Studie zur Rolle redebegleitender Gesten in der Organisation des Sprecherwechsels*. Berlin: Weidler Buchverlag.

Bolden, Galina. 2003. Multiple modalities in collaborative turn sequences. *Gesture* 3:187–212.

Bolden, Galina. 2004. The quote and beyond: defining boundaries of reported speech in conversational Russian. *Journal of Pragmatics* 36(6):1071–118.

Bolden, Galina. 2006. Little words that matter: discourse markers *so* and *oh* and the doing of other-attentiveness in social interaction. *Journal of Communication* 56:661–88.

Bolden, Galina. 2008. *So what's up?* Using the discourse marker *so* to launch conversational business. *Research on Language and Social Interaction* 41:302–37.

Bolden, Galina. 2009a. Beyond answering: repeat-prefaced responses in conversation. *Communication Monographs* 76:121–43.

Bolden, Galina. 2009b. Implementing incipient actions: the discourse marker *so* in English conversation. *Journal of Pragmatics* 41(5):974–98.

Bolden, Galina. 2009c. Implementing delayed actions. *Conversation analysis: comparative perspectives*, ed. Jack Sidnell, 326–53. Cambridge: Cambridge University Press.

Bolden, Galina. 2010. 'Articulating the unsaid' via *and*-prefaced formulations of other's talk. *Discourse Processes* 12:5–32.

Bolden, Galina. 2016. A simple *da*? Affirming responses to polar questions in Russian conversation. *Journal of Pragmatics* 100:40–58.

Bolden, Galina and Jeffrey D. Robinson. 2011. Soliciting accounts with *why*-interrogatives in conversation. *Journal of Communication* 61(1):94–119.

Brown, Penelope. 1998. Conversational structure and language acquisition: the role of repetition in Tzeltal adult and child speech. *Journal of Linguistic Anthropology* 8:197–221.

Brown, Penelope. 2007. Principles of person reference in Tzeltal conversation. *Person reference in interaction: linguistic, cultural, and social perspectives*, ed. Nick J. Enfield and Tanya Stivers, 172–202. Cambridge: Cambridge University Press.

Bühler, Karl. 1982 [1934]. *Sprachtheorie: die Darstellungsfunktion der Sprache*. Stuttgart: Fischer.

Button, Graham. 1987. Moving out of closings. *Talk and social organisation*, ed. Graham Button and John R. E. Lee, 101–51. Clevedon: Multilingual Matters.

Button, Graham and Neil Casey. 1984. Generating topic: the use of topic-initial elicitors. *Structures of social action: studies in conversation analysis*, ed. J. Maxwell Atkinson and John Heritage, 167–89. Cambridge: Cambridge University Press.

Button, Graham and Neil Casey. 1985. Topic nomination and topic pursuit. *Human Studies* 8:3–55.

Bybee, Joan. 2006. From usage to grammar: the mind's response to repetition. *Language* 82(4):711–33.

Bybee, Joan. 2010. *Language, usage and cognition*. Cambridge: Cambridge University Press.

Chafe, Wallace. 1979. The flow of thought and the flow of language. *Discourse and syntax*, ed. Talmy Givón, 159–81. New York: Academic Press.

Chafe, Wallace (ed.). 1980. *The pear stories: cognitive, cultural, and linguistic aspects of narrative production*. Norwood, NJ: Ablex.

Chafe, Wallace. 1984. How people use adverbial clauses. *Berkeley Linguistics Society* 10:437–49.

Chafe, Wallace. 1988. Linking intonation units in spoken English. *Clause combining in grammar and discourse*, ed. John Haiman and Sandra A. Thompson, 1–27. Amsterdam: Benjamins.

Christmann, Gabriela B. and Susanne Günthner. 1996. Sprache und Affekt: die Inszenierung von Entrüstung im Gespräch. *Deutsche Sprache* 1:1–33.

Clancy, Patricia M., Sandra A. Thompson, Ryoko Suzuki and Hongyin Tao. 1996. The conversational use of reactive tokens in English, Japanese and Mandarin. *Journal of Pragmatics* 26:355–87.

Clark, Herbert H. 1996. *Using language*. Cambridge: Cambridge University Press.

Clark, Herbert H. and Richard J. Gerrig. 1990. Quotations as demonstrations. *Language* 66:764–805.
Clayman, Steven E. 2010. Address terms in the service of other actions: the case of news interview talk. *Discourse & Communication* 4:161–83.
Clayman, Steven E. 2012. Address terms in the organization of turns at talk: the case of pivotal turn extensions. *Journal of Pragmatics* 44:1853–67.
Clayman, Steven E. 2013a. Turn-constructional units and the transition-relevance place. *The handbook of conversation analysis*, ed. Jack Sidnell and Tanya Stivers, 150–66. Chichester: Wiley-Blackwell.
Clayman, Steven E. 2013b. Agency in response: the role of prefatory address terms. *Journal of Pragmatics* 57:290–302.
Clayman, Steven E. and John Heritage. 2002. Questioning presidents: journalistic deference and adversarialness in the press conferences of U.S. Presidents Eisenhower and Reagan. *Journal of Communication* 52:749–75.
Clayman, Steven E. and John Heritage. 2014. Benefactors and beneficiaries: benefactive status and stance in the management of offers and requests. *Requesting in social interaction*, ed. Paul Drew and Elizabeth Couper-Kuhlen, 55–86. Amsterdam: Benjamins.
Clayman, Steven E. and Chase Wesley Raymond. 2015. Modular pivots: a resource for extending turns at talk. *Research on Language and Social Interaction* 48(4):388–405.
Clift, Rebecca. 2001. Meaning in interaction: the case of *actually*. *Language* 77:245–91.
Clift, Rebecca. 2007a. Grammar in time: the non-restrictive *which*-clause as an interactional resource. *Essex Research Reports in Linguistics* 55:51–82.
Clift, Rebecca. 2007b. Getting there first: non-narrative reported speech in interaction. *Reporting talk: reported speech in interaction*, ed. Elizabeth Holt and Rebecca Clift, 120–49. Cambridge: Cambridge University Press.
Collins, Peter C. 1991. *Cleft and pseudo-cleft constructions in English*. London: Routledge.
Cook-Gumperz, Jenny and John Gumperz. 1976. Context in children's speech. *iidem: Papers on language and context.* Working Paper No. 46. Berkeley, CA: Language Behavior Research Laboratory.
Couper-Kuhlen, Elizabeth. 1986. *An introduction to English prosody*. Tübingen: Niemeyer and London: Edward Arnold.
Couper-Kuhlen, Elizabeth. 1993. *English speech rhythm: form and function in everyday verbal interaction*. Amsterdam: Benjamins.
Couper-Kuhlen, Elizabeth. 1995. On the foregrounded progressive in American conversational narrative: a new development? *Anglistentag 1994 Graz*, ed. Wolfgang Riehle and Hugo Keiper, 229–45. Tübingen: Niemeyer.
Couper-Kuhlen, Elizabeth. 1996a. The prosody of repetition: on quoting and mimicry. *Prosody in conversation: interactional studies*, ed. Elizabeth Couper-Kuhlen and Margret Selting, 366–405. Cambridge: Cambridge University Press.
Couper-Kuhlen, Elizabeth. 1996b. Intonation and clause-combining in discourse: the case of *because*. *Pragmatics* 6:389–426.
Couper-Kuhlen, Elizabeth. 1999. Coherent voicing: on prosody in conversational reported speech. *Coherence in spoken and written discourse: how to create it and how to describe it*, ed. Wolfgang Bublitz and Ulla Lenk, 11–32. Amsterdam: Benjamins.
Couper-Kuhlen, Elizabeth. 2001. Interactional prosody: high onsets in reason-for-the-call turns. *Language in Society* 30:29–53.
Couper-Kuhlen, Elizabeth. 2004. Prosody and sequence organization: the case of new beginnings. *Sound patterns in interaction*, ed. Elizabeth Couper-Kuhlen and Cecilia E. Ford, 335–76. Amsterdam: Benjamins.

Couper-Kuhlen, Elizabeth. 2007. Assessing and accounting. *Reporting talk: reported speech in interaction*, ed. Elizabeth Holt and Rebecca Clift, 81–119. Cambridge: Cambridge University Press.

Couper-Kuhlen, Elizabeth. 2009a. A sequential approach to affect: the case of "disappointment". *Talk in interaction – comparative dimensions*, ed. Markku Haakana, Minna Laakso and Jan Lindström, 94–123. Helsinki: Finnish Literature Society (SKS).

Couper-Kuhlen, Elizabeth. 2009b. Relatedness and timing in talk-in-interaction. *Where prosody meets pragmatics*, ed. Dagmar Barth-Weingarten, Nicole Dehé and Anne Wichmann, 257–76. Bingley: Emerald Group Publishing.

Couper-Kuhlen, Elizabeth. 2009c. On combining clauses and actions in interaction. *Virittäjä, Journal of the Society for the Study of Finnish* 113(3):1–15 (http://journal.fi/virittaja/article/view/4206).

Couper-Kuhlen, Elizabeth. 2011. Grammaticalization and conversation. *The Oxford handbook of grammaticalization*, ed. Heiko Narrog and Bernd Heine, 424–37. New York: Oxford University Press.

Couper-Kuhlen, Elizabeth. 2012a. Some truths and untruths about final intonation in conversational questions. *Questions: formal, functional and interactional perspectives*, ed. Jan P. de Ruiter, 123–45. Cambridge: Cambridge University Press.

Couper-Kuhlen, Elizabeth. 2012b. Exploring affiliation in the reception of conversational complaint stories. *Emotion in interaction*, ed. Anssi Peräkylä and Marja-Leena Sorjonen, 113–46. Oxford: Oxford University Press.

Couper-Kuhlen, Elizabeth. 2012c. On affectivity and preference in responses to rejection. *Text and Talk* 32(4):453–76.

Couper-Kuhlen, Elizabeth. 2012d. Turn continuation and clause combinations. *Discourse Processes* 49(3/4):273–99.

Couper-Kuhlen, Elizabeth. 2014a. What does grammar tell us about action? *Pragmatics* 24(3):623–47.

Couper-Kuhlen, Elizabeth. 2014b. Prosody as dialogic interaction. *Prosodie und Phonetik in der Interaktion. Prosody and phonetics in interaction*, ed. Dagmar Barth-Weingarten and Beatrice Szczepek Reed, 221–51. Radolfzell: Verlag für Gesprächsforschung (www.verlag-gespraechsforschung.de).

Couper-Kuhlen, Elizabeth. 2015. Intonation and discourse. *Handbook of discourse analysis* (2nd ed.), ed. Deborah Tannen, Heidi Hamilton and Deborah Schiffrin, 82–104. Chichester: John Wiley & Sons Ltd.

Couper-Kuhlen, Elizabeth and Peter Auer. 1991. On the contextualizing function of speech rhythm in conversation: question-answer sequences. *Levels of linguistic adaptation*, ed. Jeff Verschueren, 1–18. (Selected papers of the 1987 International Pragmatics Conference, vol. 2.) Amsterdam: Benjamins.

Couper-Kuhlen, Elizabeth and Dagmar Barth-Weingarten. 2011. A system for transcribing talk-in-interaction: GAT 2. English translation and adaptation of Selting, Margret et al.: Gesprächsanalytisches Transkriptionssystem 2. *Gesprächsforschung – Online-Zeitschrift zur verbalen Interaktion* 12:1–51 (www.gespraechsforschung-ozs.de).

Couper-Kuhlen, Elizabeth and Marja Etelämäki. 2015. Nominated actions and their targeted agents in Finnish conversational directives. *Journal of Pragmatics* 78:7–24.

Couper-Kuhlen, Elizabeth and Tsuyoshi Ono (eds.). 2007a. Turn continuation in cross-linguistic perspective. *Pragmatics* 17(4), (Special issue).

Couper-Kuhlen, Elizabeth and Tsuyoshi Ono. 2007b. "Incrementing" in conversation: a comparison of practices in English, German and Japanese. *Pragmatics* 17:513–52. (Special issue on turn continuation in cross-linguistic perspective, ed. Elizabeth Couper-Kuhlen and Tsuyoshi Ono.)

Couper-Kuhlen, Elizabeth and Margret Selting (eds.). 1996a. *Prosody in conversation: interactional studies.* Cambridge: Cambridge University Press.

Couper-Kuhlen, Elizabeth and Margret Selting. 1996b. Towards an interactional perspective on prosody and a prosodic perspective on interaction. *Prosody in conversation: interactional studies,* ed. Elizabeth Couper-Kuhlen and Margret Selting, 11–56. Cambridge: Cambridge University Press.

Couper-Kuhlen, Elizabeth and Margret Selting. 2001. Introducing interactional linguistics. *Studies in interactional linguistics,* ed. Margret Selting and Elizabeth Couper-Kuhlen, 1–22. Amsterdam: Benjamins.

Couper-Kuhlen, Elizabeth and Sandra A. Thompson. 2000. Concessive patterns in conversation. *Cause, condition, concession, contrast: cognitive and discourse perspectives,* ed. Elizabeth Couper-Kuhlen and Bernd-Dieter Kortmann, 381–410. Berlin: de Gruyter.

Couper-Kuhlen, Elizabeth and Sandra A. Thompson. 2005. A linguistic practice for retracting overstatements: "concessive repair." *Syntax and lexis in conversation: studies on the use of linguistic resources in talk-in-interaction,* ed. Auli Hakulinen and Margret Selting, 257–88. Amsterdam: Benjamins.

Couper-Kuhlen, Elizabeth and Sandra A. Thompson. 2006. *You know, it's funny*: eine Neubetrachtung der "Extraposition" im Englischen. *Konstruktionen in der Interaktion,* ed. Susanne Günthner and Wolfgang Imo, 23–58. Berlin: de Gruyter.

Couper-Kuhlen, Elizabeth and Sandra A. Thompson. 2008. On assessing situations and events in conversation: "extraposition" and its relatives. *Discourse Studies* 10:443–67.

Craven, Alexandra and Jonathan Potter. 2010. Directives: entitlement and contingency in action. *Discourse Studies* 12:419–42.

Croft, William. 2001. *Radical construction grammar: syntactic theory in typological perspective.* New York: Oxford University Press.

Cruttenden, Alan. 1997. *Intonation* (2nd ed.). Cambridge: Cambridge University Press.

Crystal, David. 1969. *Prosodic systems and intonation in English.* Cambridge: Cambridge University Press.

Curl, Traci S. 2004. "Repetition" repairs: the relationship of phonetic structure and sequence organization. *Sound patterns in interaction: cross-linguistic studies from conversation,* ed. Elizabeth Couper-Kuhlen and Cecilia E. Ford, 273–98. Amsterdam: Benjamins.

Curl, Traci S. 2005. Practices in other-initiated repair resolution: the phonetic differentiation of "repetitions." *Discourse Processes* 39(1):1–44.

Curl, Traci S. 2006. Offers of assistance: constraints on syntactic design. *Journal of Pragmatics* 38:1257–80.

Curl, Traci S. and Paul Drew. 2008. Contingency and action: a comparison of two forms of requesting. *Research on Language and Social Interaction* 41:129–53.

Curl, Traci S., John Local and Gareth Walker. 2006. Repetition and the prosody-pragmatics interface. *Journal of Pragmatics* 38:1721–51.

Davidson, Judy A. 1984. Subsequent versions of invitations, offers, requests, and proposals dealing with potential or actual rejection. *Structures of social action: studies in conversation analysis,* ed. J. Maxwell Atkinson and John Heritage, 102–27. Cambridge: Cambridge University Press.

Davidson, Judy A. 1990. Modifications of invitations, offers and rejections. *Interaction competence,* ed. George Psathas, 149–79. Washington, DC: University Press of America.

Deppermann, Arnulf. 2006. Deontische Infinitivkonstruktionen: Syntax, Semantik, Pragmatik und interaktionale Verwendung. *Konstruktionen in der Interaktion,* ed. Susanne Günthner and Wolfgang Imo, 239–62. Berlin: de Gruyter.

Deppermann, Arnulf. 2007. *Grammatik und Semantik aus gesprächsanalytischer Sicht*. Berlin: de Gruyter.
Deppermann, Arnulf. 2011a. The study of formulations as a key to an interactional semantics. *Human Studies* 34:115–28.
Deppermann, Arnulf. 2011b. Notionalization: the transformation of descriptions into categorizations. *Human Studies* 34:155–81.
Deppermann, Arnulf. 2012. Über Sätze in Gesprächsbeiträgen – wann sie beginnen und wann man sie braucht. *Satzeröffnung*, ed. Colette Cortès, 9–21. Tübingen: Stauffenburg.
Deppermann, Arnulf. 2013. Turn-design at turn-beginnings: multimodal resources to deal with tasks of turn-construction in German. *Journal of Pragmatics* 46:91–121.
Deppermann, Arnulf and Henrike Helmer. 2013. Zur Grammatik des Verstehens im Gespräch: Inferenzen anzeigen und Handlungskonsequezen ziehen mit *also* und *dann*. *Zeitschrift für Sprachwissenschaft* 32:1–39.
Dersley, Ian and Anthony J. Wootton. 2000. Complaint sequences within antagonistic argument. *Research on Language and Social Interaction* 33(4):375–406.
Dersley, Ian and Anthony J. Wootton. 2001. In the heat of the sequence: interactional features preceding walkouts from argumentative talk. *Language in Society* 30:611–38.
De Ruiter, Jan P., Holger Mitterer and Nick J. Enfield. 2006. Projecting the end of a speaker's turn: a cognitive cornerstone of conversation. *Language* 82(3):515–35.
Dingemanse, Mark. 2015. Other-initiated repair in Siwu. *Open Linguistics* 2015(1):232–55.
Dingemanse, Mark, Joe Blythe and Tyko Dirksmeyer. 2014. Formats for the other-initiation of repair across languages: an exercise in pragmatic typology. *Studies in Language* 38:5–43.
Dingemanse, Mark and Nick J. Enfield. 2015. Other-initiated repair across languages: towards a typology of conversational structure. *Open Linguistics* 2015(1):96–118 (doi:10.2478/opli-2014-0007).
Dingemanse, Mark and Simeon Floyd. 2014. Conversation across cultures. *The Cambridge handbook of linguistic anthropology*, ed. Nick J. Enfield, Paul Kockelman and Jack Sidnell, 447–80. Cambridge: Cambridge University Press.
Dingemanse, Mark, Seán G. Roberts, Julija Baranove, Joe Blythe, Paul Drew, Simeon Floyd, Rosa S. Gisladottir, Kobin H. Kendrick, Stephen C. Levinson, Elizabeth Manrique, Giovanni Rossi and Nick J. Enfield. 2015. Universal principles in the repair of communication problems. *PLoS ONE* 10(9):e0136100 (doi:10.1371/journal.pone.0136100).
Dingemanse, Mark, Francisco Torreira and Nick J. Enfield. 2013. Is *huh*? a universal word? Conversational infrastructure and the convergent evolution of linguistic items. *PLoS ONE* 8(11):e78273 (doi:10.1371/journal.pone.0078273).
Di Venanzio, Laura. 2013. Ein Dilemma: der funktionale Kopf in deutschen Selbstreparaturen. *Linguistische Berichte* 233:23–49.
Downing, Pamela A. 1996. Proper names as a referential option in English conversation. *Studies in anaphora*, ed. Barbara A. Fox, 95–144. Amsterdam: Benjamins.
Drake, Anna Veronika. 2013. *Turn-final* or *in English: a conversation analytic perspective*. Unpublished PhD thesis, University of Wisconsin-Madison.
Drake, Veronika. 2015. Indexing uncertainty: the case of turn-final *or*. *Research on Language and Social Interaction* 48(3):301–18.
Drew, Paul. 1984. Speakers' reportings in invitation sequences. *Structures of social action: studies in conversation analysis*, ed. J. Maxwell Atkinson and John Heritage, 129–51. Cambridge: Cambridge University Press.
Drew, Paul. 1997. "Open" class repair initiators in response to sequential sources of troubles in conversation. *Journal of Pragmatics* 28:69–101.

Drew, Paul. 1998. Complaints about transgressions and misconduct. *Research on Language and Social Interaction* 31:295–325.
Drew, Paul. 2003. Comparative analysis of talk-in-interaction in different institutional settings: a sketch. *Studies in language and social interaction*, ed. Phillip Glenn, Curtis D. LeBaron and Jenny Mandelbaum, 293–308. Mahwah, NJ: Erlbaum.
Drew, Paul. 2005. The interactional generation of exaggerated versions in conversations. *Syntax and lexis in conversation: studies on the use of linguistic resources in talk-in-interaction*, ed. Auli Hakulinen and Margret Selting, 233–55. Amsterdam: Benjamins.
Drew, Paul. 2009. Quit talking while I'm interrupting: a comparison between positions of overlap onset in conversation. *Talk in interaction: comparative dimensions*, ed. Markku Haakana, Minna Laakso and Jan Lindström, 70–93. Helsinki: Finnish Literature Society.
Drew, Paul. 2010. *Turn design/form, and the recognition of action – top down or bottom up? Some brief observations*. Nijmegen: Max Planck Institute for Psycholinguistics.
Drew, Paul. 2012. What drives sequences? *Research on Language and Social Interaction* 45(1):61–8.
Drew, Paul. 2013a. Turn design. *The handbook of conversation analysis*, ed. Jack Sidnell and Tanya Stivers, 131–49. Chichester: Wiley-Blackwell.
Drew, Paul. 2013b. Conversation analysis and social action. *Journal of Foreign Languages* 37(3):1–20.
Drew, Paul and Elizabeth Couper-Kuhlen. 2014a. Requesting: from speech act to recruitment. *Requesting in social interaction*, ed. Paul Drew and Elizabeth Couper-Kuhlen, 1–34. Amsterdam: Benjamins.
Drew, Paul and Elizabeth Couper-Kuhlen (eds.). 2014b. *Requesting in social interaction*. Amsterdam: Benjamins.
Drew, Paul and John Heritage (eds.). 1992. *Talk at work: interaction in institutional settings*. Cambridge: Cambridge University Press.
Drew, Paul and Elizabeth Holt. 1988. Complainable matters: the use of idiomatic expressions in making complaints. *Social Problems* 35:398–417.
Drew, Paul and Elizabeth Holt. 1995. Idiomatic expressions and their role in the organization of topic transition in conversation. *Idioms: structural and psychological perspectives*, ed. Martin Everaert, Erik-Jan van der Linden, André Schenk and Rob Schreuder, 117–32. Hillsdale, NJ: Lawrence Erlbaum.
Drew, Paul and Elizabeth Holt. 1998. Figures of speech: figurative expressions and the management of topic transition in conversation. *Language in Society* 27:495–522.
Drew, Paul and Traci Walker. 2009. Going too far: complaining, escalating, and disaffiliating. *Journal of Pragmatics* 41:2400–14.
Drew, Paul, Traci Walker and Richard Ogden. 2013. Self-repair and action construction. *Conversational repair and human understanding*, ed. Makoto Hayashi, Geoffrey Raymond and Jack Sidnell, 71–94. Cambridge: Cambridge University Press.
Dryer, Matthew S. 1997. Are grammatical relations universal? *Essays on language function and language type: dedicated to T. Givon*, ed. Joan Bybee, John Haiman and Sandra Thompson, 115–43. Amsterdam: Benjamins.
Dryer, Matthew S. 2008. Polar questions. *The world atlas of language structures online*, ed. Martin Haspelmath, Matthew S. Dryer, David Gil and Bernard Comrie, chapter 116. Munich: Max Planck Digital Library (http://wals.info/feature/116).
Dryer, Matthew S. 2013. Order of adposition and noun phrase. *The world atlas of language structures online*, ed. Matthew S. Dryer and Martin Haspelmath. Leipzig: Max Planck Institute for Evolutionary Anthropology (http://wals.info/chapter/85).

Dryer, Matthew S. and Martin Haspelmath (eds.). 2013. *The world atlas of language structures online*. Leipzig: Max Planck Institute for Evolutionary Anthropology (http://wals.info).

Du Bois, John W. 1980. Beyond definiteness: the trace of identity in discourse. *The Pear stories: cognitive, cultural and linguistic aspects of narrative production*, ed. Wallace Chafe, 203–74. Norwood, NJ: Ablex.

Du Bois, John W. 1985. Competing motivations. *Iconicity in syntax*, ed. John Haiman, 343–65. Amsterdam: Benjamins.

Du Bois, John W. 1987. The discourse basis of ergativity. *Language* 63:805–55.

Du Bois, John W. 1991. Transcription design principles for spoken discourse research. *Pragmatics* 1:71–106.

Du Bois, John W. 2007. The stance triangle. *Stancetaking in discourse: subjectivity, evaluation, interaction*, ed. Robert Englebretson, 139–182. Amsterdam: Benjamins.

Du Bois, John W. and Elise Kärkkäinen. 2012. Taking a stance on emotion: affect, sequence, and intersubjectivity in dialogic interaction. *Text and Talk* 32(4):433–51.

Du Bois, John W., Stephan Schuetze-Coburn, Susanna Cumming and Danae Paolino. 1993. Outline of discourse transcription. *Talking data: transcription and coding in discourse research*, ed. Jane A. Edwards and Martin D. Lampert, 45–89. Hillsdale, NJ: Lawrence Erlbaum.

Du Bois, John W., Stephan Schuetze-Coburn, Danae Paolino and Susanna Cumming. 1992. Discourse transcription. *Santa Barbara Papers in Linguistics* 4:1–225.

Duden. 2005. *Die Grammatik*. Mannheim: Dudenverlag.

Duncan, Starkey and Donald W. Fiske. 1977. *Face to face interaction: research, methods and theory*. Hillsdale, NJ: Lawrence Erlbaum.

Duranti, Alessandro. 1997. *Linguistic anthropology*. Cambridge: Cambridge University Press.

Duranti, Alessandro (ed.). 2004. *A companion to linguistic anthropology*. Oxford: Wiley-Blackwell.

Duranti, Alessandro and Charles Goodwin (eds.). 1992. *Rethinking context: language as an interactive phenomenon*. Cambridge: Cambridge University Press.

Duranti, Alessandro and Elinor Ochs. 1979. Left-dislocation in Italian conversation. *Syntax and semantics 12: discourse and syntax*, ed. Talmy Givón, 377–418. New York: Academic Press.

Duvallon, Outi and Sara Routarinne. 2005. Parenthesis as a resource in the grammar of conversation. *Syntax and lexis in conversation*, ed. Auli Hakulinen and Margret Selting, 45–74. Amsterdam: Benjamins.

Edwards, Derek. 2000. Extreme case formulations: softeners, investment, and doing nonliteral. *Research on Language and Social Interaction* 33:347–73.

Edwards, Jane A. and Martin D. Lampert (eds.). 1993. *Talking data: transcription and coding in discourse research*. Hillsdale, NJ: Lawrence Erlbaum.

Egbert, Maria. 1996. Context-sensitivity in conversation: eye gaze and the German repair initiator *bitte?*. *Language in Society* 25:587–612.

Egbert, Maria. 1997. Some interactional achievements of other-initiated repair in multi-person conversation. *Journal of Pragmatics* 27:611–34.

Egbert, Maria. 2004. Other-initiated repair and membership categorization: some conversational events that trigger linguistic and regional membership categorization. *Journal of Pragmatics* 36:1467–98.

Egbert, Maria. 2009. *Der Reparatur-Mechanismus in deutschen Gesprächen*. Mannheim: Verlag für Gesprächsforschung (www.verlag-gespraechsforschung.de).

Egbert, Maria. 2017. Selection principles for other-initiated repair turn formats: some indications from positioned questions. *Enabling human conduct: Studies of talk-in-interaction in honor of Emanuel A. Schegloff*, ed. Geoffrey Raymond, Gene Lerner and John Heritage, 167–87. Amsterdam: Benjamins.

Egbert, Maria, Andrea Golato and Jeffrey D. Robinson. 2009. Repairing reference. *Conversation analysis: comparative perspectives*, ed. Jack Sidnell, 104–32. Cambridge: Cambridge University Press.

Egbert, Maria and Monika Vöge. 2008. *Wh*-interrogative formats used for questioning and beyond: German *warum* (why) and *wieso* (why) and English *why*. *Discourse Studies* 10:17–36.

Emmertsen, Sofie and Trine Heinemann. 2010. Realization as a device for remedying problems of affiliation in interaction. *Research on Language and Social Interaction* 43: 109–32.

Enfield, Nick J. 2007. Meaning of the unmarked: how "default" person reference does more than just refer. *Person reference in interaction: linguistic, cultural, and social perspectives*, ed. Nick J. Enfield and Tanya Stivers, 97–120. Cambridge: Cambridge University Press.

Enfield, Nick J. 2009. *The anatomy of meaning: speech, gesture, and composite utterances*. Cambridge: Cambridge University Press.

Enfield, Nick J. 2011. Sources of asymmetry in human interaction: enchrony, status, knowledge and agency. *The morality of knowledge in conversation*, ed. Tanya Stivers, Lorenza Mondada and Jakob Steensig, 285–312. Cambridge: Cambridge University Press.

Enfield, Nick J. 2013. Reference in conversation. *The handbook of conversation analysis*, ed. Jack Sidnell and Tanya Stivers, 433–54. Chichester: Wiley-Blackwell.

Enfield, Nick J. 2015. Other-initiated repair in Lao. *Open Linguistics* 2005(1):119–44.

Enfield, Nick J., Penelope Brown and Jan P. de Ruiter. 2012. Epistemic dimensions of polar questions: sentence-final particles in comparative perspective. *Questions: formal, functional and interactional perspectives*, ed. Jan P. de Ruiter, 193–221. Cambridge: Cambridge University Press.

Enfield, Nick J., Mark Dingemanse, Julija Baranova, Joe Blythe, Penelope Brown, Tyko Dirksmeyer, Paul Drew, Simeon Floyd, Sonja Gipper, Rósa Gísladóttir, Gertie Hoymann, Kobin H. Kendrick, Stephen C. Levinson, Lilla Magyari, Elizabeth Manrique, Giovanni Rossi, Lila San Roque and Francisco Torreira. 2013. Huh? What? – a first survey in twenty-one languages. *Conversational repair and human understanding*, ed. Makoto Hayashi, Geoffrey Raymond and Jack Sidnell, 343–80. Cambridge: Cambridge University Press.

Enfield, Nick J., Paul Kockelman and Jack Sidnell (eds.). 2014. *The Cambridge handbook of linguistic anthropology*. Cambridge: Cambridge University Press.

Enfield, Nick J. and Stephen C. Levinson. 2006. Introduction: human sociality as a new interdisciplinary field. *Roots of human sociality: culture, cognition and interaction*, ed. Nick J. Enfield and Stephen C. Levinson, 1–35. Oxford: Berg.

Enfield, Nick J. and Jack Sidnell. 2014. Language presupposes an enchronic infrastructure for social interaction. *The social origins of language*, ed. Daniel Dor, Chris Knight and Jerome Lewis, 92–104. Oxford: Oxford University Press.

Enfield, Nick J. and Tanya Stivers (eds.). 2007. *Person reference in interaction: linguistic, cultural, and social perspectives*. Cambridge: Cambridge University Press.

Enfield, Nick J., Tanya Stivers and Stephen C. Levinson. 2010. Question-response sequences in conversation across ten languages: an introduction. *Journal of Pragmatics* 42:2615–19.

Englert, Christina. 2010. Questions and responses in Dutch conversations. *Journal of Pragmatics* 42:2666–84.

Erickson, Frederick. 1992. They know all the lines: rhythmic organization and contextualization in a conversational listing routine. *The contextualization of language*, ed. Peter Auer and Aldo di Luzio, 365–97. Amsterdam: Benjamins.

Ervin-Tripp, Susan M. 1976. *Is Sybil there?*: some American English directives. *Language in Society* 5:25–66.

Ervin-Tripp, Susan M. 1981. How to make and understand a request. *Possibilities and limitations of pragmatics*, ed. Herman Parret, Marina Sbisa and Jef Verschueren, 195–210. Amsterdam: Benjamins.

Essen, Otto von. 1964. *Grundzüge der hochdeutschen Satzintonation*. Ratingen: Henn.

Etelämäki, Marja and Laura Visäpää. 2014. Why blend conversation analysis with cognitive grammar? *Pragmatics* 24(3):477–506.

Evans, Nicholas. 2007. Insubordination and its uses. *Finiteness: theoretical and empirical foundations*, ed. Irina Nikolaeva, 366–431. Oxford: Oxford University Press.

Evans, Nicholas and Stephen C. Levinson. 2009. The myth of language universals: language diversity and its importance for cognitive science. *Behavioral and Brain Sciences* 32:429–92.

Fasulo, Alessandra and Chiara Monzoni. 2009. Assessing mutable objects: a multimodal analysis. *Research on Language and Social Interaction* 42:362–76.

Féry, Caroline. 1993. *German intonational patterns*. Tübingen: Niemeyer.

Floyd, Simeon, Giovanni Rossi and Nick J. Enfield (eds.). Forthcoming. *Getting others to do things: a pragmatic typology of recruitments*. Berlin: Language Science Press.

Ford, Cecilia E. 1993. *Grammar in interaction*. Cambridge: Cambridge University Press.

Ford, Cecilia E. 1997. Speaking conditionally: some contexts for *if*-clauses in conversation. *On conditionals again*, ed. Angeliki Athanasiadou and René Dirven, 387–413. Amsterdam: Benjamins.

Ford, Cecilia E. 2000. The treatment of contrasts in interaction. *Cause, condition, concession, contrast: cognitive and discourse perspectives*, ed. Elizabeth Couper-Kuhlen and Bernd Kortmann, 283–311. Berlin: de Gruyter.

Ford, Cecilia E. 2001a. Denial and the construction of conversational turns. *Complex sentences in grammar and discourse*, ed. Joan Bybee and Michael Noonan, 61–78. Amsterdam: Benjamins.

Ford, Cecilia E. 2001b. At the intersection of turn and sequence: negation and what comes next. *Studies in interactional linguistics*, ed. Margret Selting and Elizabeth Couper-Kuhlen, 51–79. Amsterdam: Benjamins.

Ford, Cecilia E. 2004. Contingency and units in interaction. *Discourse Studies* 6:27–52.

Ford, Cecilia E. and Barbara A. Fox. 1996. Interactional motivations for reference formulation: *He had. This guy had, a beautiful, thirty-two o:lds*. *Studies in anaphora*, ed. Barbara A. Fox, 145–68. Amsterdam: Benjamins.

Ford, Cecilia E. and Barbara A. Fox. 2010. Multiple practices for constructing laughables. *Prosody in interaction*, ed. Dagmar Barth-Weingarten, Elisabeth Reber and Margret Selting, 339–68. Amsterdam: Benjamins.

Ford, Cecilia E., Barbara A. Fox and John Hellermann. 2004. Getting past *no*: sequence, action and sound production in the projection of *no*-initiated turns. *Sound patterns in interaction*, ed. Elizabeth Couper-Kuhlen and Cecilia. Ford, 233–69. Amsterdam: Benjamins.

Ford, Cecilia E., Barbara A. Fox and Sandra A. Thompson. 1996. Practices in the construction of turns: the "TCU" revisited. *Pragmatics* 6:427–54.

Ford, Cecilia E., Barbara A. Fox and Sandra A. Thompson. 2002. Constituency and the grammar of turn increments. *The language of turn and sequence*, ed. Cecilia E. Ford, Barbara A. Fox and Sandra A. Thompson, 14–38. Oxford: Oxford University Press.

Ford, Cecilia E., Barbara A. Fox and Sandra A. Thompson. 2013. Units and/or action trajectories? The language of grammatical categories and the language of social action. *Units of talk: units of action*, ed. Beatrice Szczepek Reed and Geoffrey Raymond, 13–55. Amsterdam: Benjamins.

Ford, Cecilia E. and Junko Mori. 1994. Causal markers in Japanese and English conversations: a cross-linguistic study of interactional grammar. *Pragmatics* 4:31–62.

Ford, Cecilia E. and Trini Stickle. 2012. Securing recipiency in workplace meetings: multimodal practices. *Discourse Studies* 14:11–30.

Ford, Cecilia E. and Sandra A. Thompson. 1986. Conditionals in discourse: a text-based study from English. *On conditionals*, ed. Elizabeth C. Traugott, Alice ter Meulen, Judy Snitzer Reilly and Charles A. Ferguson, 353–72. Cambridge: Cambridge University Press.

Ford, Cecilia E. and Sandra A. Thompson. 1996. Interactional units in conversation: syntactic, intonational, and pragmatic resources for the projection of turn completion. *Interaction and grammar*, ed. Elinor Ochs, Emanuel A. Schegloff and Sandra A. Thompson, 134–84. Cambridge: Cambridge University Press.

Ford, Cecilia E., Sandra A. Thompson and Veronika Drake. 2012. Bodily-visual practices and turn-continuation. *Discourse Processes* 49:192–212.

Fox, Barbara A. 1987. *Discourse structure and anaphora*. Cambridge: Cambridge University Press.

Fox, Barbara A. 2001a. An exploration of prosody and turn projection in English conversation. *Studies in interactional linguistics*, ed. Margret Selting and Elizabeth Couper-Kuhlen, 287–315. Amsterdam: Benjamins.

Fox, Barbara A. 2001b. On the embodied nature of grammar. *Complex sentences in grammar and discourse: essays in honor of Sandra A. Thompson*, ed. Joan Bybee and Michael Noonan, 79–100. Amsterdam: Benjamins.

Fox, Barbara A. 2001c. Evidentiality: authority, responsibility, and entitlement in English conversation. *Journal of Linguistic Anthropology* 11:167–92.

Fox, Barbara A. 2007. Principles shaping grammatical practices: an exploration. *Discourse Studies* 9:299–318.

Fox, Barbara A. 2013. Conversation analysis and self-repair. *The encyclopedia of applied linguistics*, ed. Carole A. Chapelle. Hoboken, NJ: Wiley-Blackwell (7 pages).

Fox, Barbara A., 2015. On the notion of pre-request. *Discourse Studies* 17(1):41–63.

Fox, Barbara A., Makoto Hayashi and Robert Jasperson. 1996. Resources and repair: a cross-linguistic study of syntax and repair. *Interaction and grammar*, ed. Elinor Ochs, Emanuel A. Schegloff and Sandra A. Thompson, 185–237. Cambridge: Cambridge University Press.

Fox, Barbara A. and Robert Jasperson. 1995. A syntactic exploration of repair in English conversation. *Alternative linguistics: descriptive and theoretical models*, ed. Philip W. Davis, 77–134. Amsterdam: Benjamins.

Fox, Barbara A., Yael Maschler and Susanne Uhmann. 2009. Morpho-syntactic resources for the organization of same-turn self-repair: cross-linguistic variation in English, German and Hebrew. *Gesprächsforschung – Online-Zeitschrift zur verbalen Interaktion* 10:245–91 (www.gespraechsforschung-ozs.de).

Fox, Barbara A., Yael Maschler and Susanne Uhmann. 2010. A cross-linguistic study of self-repair: evidence from English, German, and Hebrew. *Journal of Pragmatics* 42: 2487–505.

Fox, Barbara A. and Sandra A. Thompson. 1990a. A discourse explanation of the grammar of relative clauses in English conversation. *Language* 66:297–316.
Fox, Barbara A. and Sandra A. Thompson. 1990b. On formulating reference: an interactional approach to relative clauses in English conversation. *IPrA Papers in Pragmatics* 4:183–96.
Fox, Barbara A. and Sandra A. Thompson. 2007. Relative clauses in English conversation: relativizers, frequency and the notion of construction. *Studies in Language* 31:293–326.
Fox, Barbara A. and Sandra A. Thompson. 2010. Responses to *wh*-questions in English conversation. *Research on Language and Social Interaction* 43:133–56.
Fox, Barbara A., Sandra A. Thompson, Cecilia E. Ford and Elizabeth Couper-Kuhlen. 2013. Conversation analysis and linguistics. *The handbook of conversation analysis*, ed. Jack Sidnell and Tanya Stivers, 726–40. Chichester: Wiley-Blackwell.
Fox, Barbara A. and Fay Wouk. Forthcoming. *A cross-linguistic study of self-repair*. Amsterdam: Benjamins.
Fox, Barbara A., Fay Wouk, Makoto Hayashi, Steven Fincke, Liang Tao, Marja-Leena Sorjonen, Minna Laakso and Wilfrido Flores Hernandez. 2009. A cross-linguistic investigation of the site of initiation in same-turn self-repair. *Conversation analysis: comparative perspectives*, ed. Jack Sidnell, 60–103. Cambridge: Cambridge University Press.
Franck, Dorothea. 1985. Sentences in conversational turns: a case of syntactic "double bind". *Dialogue: an interdisciplinary approach*, ed. Marcelo Dascal, 233–45. Amsterdam: Benjamins.
Freed, Alice F. 1994. The form and function of questions in informal dyadic conversation. *Journal of Pragmatics* 21:621–44.
Freese, Jeremy and Douglas W. Maynard. 1998. Prosodic features of bad news and good news in conversation. *Language in Society* 27:195–219.
French, Peter and John Local. 1983. Turn-competitive incomings. *Journal of Pragmatics* 7:17–38.
Gardner, Rod. 1997. The conversation object *mm*: a weak and variable acknowledging token. *Research on Language and Social Interaction* 30(2):131–56.
Gardner, Rod. 1998. Between listening and speaking: the vocalization of understandings. *Applied Linguistics* 19:204–24.
Gardner, Rod. 2001. *When listeners talk: response tokens and listener stance*. Amsterdam: Benjamins.
Gardner, Rod. 2007. The *right* connections: acknowledging epistemic progression in talk. *Language in Society* 36:319–41.
Garfinkel, Harold. 1967. *Studies in ethnomethodology*. Cambridge: Polity Press.
Garfinkel, Harold and Harvey Sacks. 1970. On formal structures of practical actions. *Theoretical sociology*, ed. John C. McKinney and Edward A. Tiryakian, 337–66. New York: Appleton-Century-Crofts.
Geluykens, Ronald. 1992. *From discourse process to grammatical construction: on left-dislocation in English*. Amsterdam: Benjamins.
Geluykens, Ronald. 1994. *The pragmatics of discourse anaphora in English: evidence from conversational repair*. Berlin: de Gruyter.
Giegerich, Heinz J. 1992. *English phonology: an introduction*. Cambridge: Cambridge University Press.
Gilles, Peter. 2005. *Regionale Prosodie im Deutschen: Variabilität in der Intonation von Abschluss und Weiterweisung*. Berlin: de Gruyter.
Gipper, Sonja. 2011. *Evidentiality and intersubjectivity in Yurakaré: an interactional account*. Nijmegen: MPI Series in Psycholinguistics.

Gisladottir, Rosa S. 2015. Other-initiated repair in Icelandic. *Open Linguistics* 2015(1):309–28.
Givón, Talmy. 1979. *On understanding grammar*. New York: Academic Press.
Glenn, Phillip. 2009. *Laughter in interaction*. Cambridge: Cambridge University Press.
Glenn, Phillip and Elizabeth Holt (eds.). 2013. *Studies of laughter in interaction*. London: Bloomsbury Academic.
Goffman, Erving. 1967. *Interaction ritual: essays on face-to-face behavior*. New York: Doubleday Anchor.
Goffman, Erving. 1979. Footing. *Semiotica* 25:1–29.
Goffman, Erving. 1981. *Forms of talk*. Oxford: Basil Blackwell.
Gohl, Christine. 2000. Causal relations in spoken discourse: asyndetic constructions as a means for giving reasons. *Cause, condition, concession, contrast: cognitive and discourse perspectives*, ed. Elizabeth Couper-Kuhlen and Bernd Kortmann, 83–110. Berlin: de Gruyter.
Gohl, Christine. 2006. *Begründen im Gespräch: eine Untersuchung sprachlicher Praktiken zur Realisierung von Begründungen im gesprochenen Deutsch*. Tübingen: Max Niemeyer Verlag.
Golato, Andrea. 2000. An innovative German quotative for reporting on embodied actions: *Und ich so/und er so* "and I'm like/and he's like". *Journal of Pragmatics* 32:29–54.
Golato, Andrea. 2002a. German compliment responses. *Journal of Pragmatics* 34:547–71.
Golato, Andrea. 2002b. Self-quotation in German: reporting on past decisions. *Reported discourse: a meeting ground for different linguistic domains*, ed. Tom Güldemann and Manfred von Roncador, 49–70. Amsterdam: Benjamins.
Golato, Andrea. 2002c. Grammar and interaction: reported discourse and subjunctive in German. *Zeitschrift für Sprachwissenschaft* 22:24–55.
Golato, Andrea. 2005. *Compliments and compliment responses: grammatical structure and sequential organization*. Amsterdam: Benjamins.
Golato, Andrea. 2010. Marking understanding versus receipting information in talk: *achso* and *ach* in German interaction. *Discourse Studies* 12:147–76.
Golato, Andrea. 2012a. Impersonal quotation and hypothetical discourse. *Quotatives: cross-linguistic and cross-disciplinary perspectives*, ed. Isabelle Buchstaller and Ingrid Van Alphen, 3–36. Amsterdam: Benjamins.
Golato, Andrea. 2012b. German *oh*: marking an emotional change of state. *Research on Language and Social Interaction* 45:245–68.
Golato, Andrea. 2013. Reparaturen von Personenreferenzen. *Deutsche Sprache* 41:31–51.
Golato, Andrea and Emma Betz. 2008. German *ach* and *achso* in repair uptake: resources to sustain or remove epistemic asymmetry. *Zeitschrift für Sprachwissenschaft* 27:7–37.
Golato, Andrea and Zsuzsanna Fagyal. 2008. Comparing single and double sayings of the German response token *ja* and the role of prosody: a conversation analytic perspective. *Research on Language and Social Interaction* 41:1–30.
Goldberg, Jo Ann. 1975. A system for the transfer of instructions in natural settings. *Semiotica* 14(3):269–96.
Goldberg, Jo Ann. 1978. Amplitude shift: a mechanism for the affiliation of utterances in conversational interaction. *Studies in the organization of conversational interaction*, ed. Jim Schenkein, 199–218. New York: Academic Press.
Goldberg, Jo Ann. 2004. The amplitude shift mechanism in conversational closing sequences. *Conversation analysis: studies from the first generation*, ed. Gene H. Lerner, 257–97. Amsterdam: John Benjamins.
Goodwin, Charles. 1979. The interactive construction of a sentence in natural conversation. *Everyday language: studies in ethnomethodology*, ed. George Psathas, 97–121. New York: Irvington.

Goodwin, Charles. 1980. Restarts, pauses, and the achievement of a state of mutual gaze at turn-beginnings. *Sociological Inquiry* 50:272–302.
Goodwin, Charles. 1981. *Conversational organization: interaction between speakers and hearers*. New York: Academic Press.
Goodwin, Charles. 1984. Notes on story structure and the organization of participation. *Structures of social action*, ed. J. Maxwell Atkinson and John Heritage, 225–46. Cambridge: Cambridge University Press.
Goodwin, Charles. 1986a. Between and within: alternative sequential treatments of continuers and assessments. *Human Studies* 9:205–17.
Goodwin, Charles. 1986b. Audience diversity, participation and interpretation. *Text* 6:283–316.
Goodwin, Charles. 1995. Sentence construction within. *Aspects of oral communication*, ed. Uta Quasthoff, 198–219. Berlin: de Gruyter.
Goodwin, Charles. 1996. Transparent vision. *Interaction and grammar*, ed. Elinor Ochs, Emanuel A. Schegloff and Sandra A. Thompson, 370–404. Cambridge: Cambridge University Press.
Goodwin, Charles. 2000. Action and embodiment within situated human interaction. *Journal of Pragmatics* 32:1489–522.
Goodwin, Charles. 2002. Recognizing assessable names. *Studies in language and social interaction*, ed. Phillip J. Glenn, Curtis D. LeBaron and Jenny Mandelbaum, 151–61. Mahwah, NJ: Erlbaum.
Goodwin, Charles. 2006. Human sociality as mutual orientation in a rich interactive environment: multimodal utterances and pointing in aphasia. *Roots of human sociality*, ed. Nick J. Enfield and Stephen C. Levinson, 96–125. London: Berg.
Goodwin, Charles. 2007a. Environmentally coupled gestures. *Gesture and the dynamic dimensions of language*, ed. Susan Duncan, Justine Cassel and Elena Levy, 195–212. Amsterdam: Benjamins.
Goodwin, Charles. 2007b. Interactive footing. *Reporting talk: reported speech in interaction*, ed. Elizabeth Holt and Rebecca Clift, 16–46. Cambridge: Cambridge University Press.
Goodwin, Charles and Marjorie Harness Goodwin. 1987. Concurrent operations on talk: notes on the interactive organization of assessments. *IPrA Papers in Pragmatics* 1:1–54.
Goodwin, Charles and Marjorie Harness Goodwin. 1992. Assessment and the construction of context. *Rethinking context: language as an interactive phenomenon*, ed. Alessandro Duranti and Charles Goodwin, 147–90. Cambridge: Cambridge University Press.
Goodwin, Marjorie Harness. 1980. Processes of mutual monitoring implicated in the production of descriptive sequences. *Sociological Inquiry* 50:303–17.
Goodwin, Marjorie Harness. 1990. *He-said-she-said: talk as social organization among black children*. Bloomington, IN: Indiana University Press.
Goodwin, Marjorie Harness. 1997a. Byplay: negotiating evaluation in storytelling. *Towards a social science of language. Vol. 2: Social interaction and discourse structure*, ed. Gregory R. Guy, Crawford Feagin, Deborah Schiffrin and John Baugh, 77–102. Amsterdam: Benjamins.
Goodwin, Marjorie Harness. 1997b. Toward families of stories in context. *Journal of Narrative and Life History* 7:107–12.
Goodwin, Marjorie Harness. 2002. Building power asymmetries in girls' interactions. *Discourse in Society* 13:715–30.
Goodwin, Marjorie Harness. 2006. Participation, affect, and trajectory in family directive/response sequences. *Text & Talk* 26:513–41.

Goodwin, Marjorie Harness. 2007. Participation and embodied action in preadolescent girls' assessment activity. *Research on Language and Social Interaction* 40:353–76.

Goodwin, Marjorie Harness and Asta Cekaite. 2012. Calibration in directive/response sequences in family interaction. *Journal of Pragmatics* 46:122–38.

Goodwin, Marjorie Harness and Asta Cekaite. 2014. Orchestrating directive trajectories in communicative projects in family interaction. *Requesting in social interaction*, ed. Paul Drew and Elizabeth Couper-Kuhlen, 185–214. Amsterdam: Benjamins.

Goodwin, Marjorie Harness, Asta Cekaite and Charles Goodwin. 2012. Emotion as stance. *Emotion in interaction*, ed. Anssi Peräkylä and Marja-Leena Sorjonen, 16–41. New York: Oxford University Press.

Goodwin, Marjorie Harness and Charles Goodwin. 1986. Gesture and coparticipation in the activity of searching for a word. *Semiotica* 62:51–75.

Goodwin, Marjorie Harness and Charles Goodwin. 1987. Children's arguing. *Language, gender, and sex in comparative perspective*, ed. Susan Philips, Susan Steele and Christine Tanz, 200–48. Cambridge: Cambridge University Press.

Goodwin, Marjorie Harness and Charles Goodwin. 2000. Emotion within situated activity. *Linguistic anthropology: a reader*, ed. Alessandro Duranti, 239–57. Oxford: Blackwell.

Grabe, Esther. 1998. *Comparative intonational phonology: English and German*. PhD dissertation, Nijmegen.

Graf, Hans Peter, Eric Cosatto, Volker Strom and Fu Jie Huang. 2002. Visual prosody: facial movements accompanying speech. *Proceedings of the Fifth IEEE International Conference on Automatic Face and Gesture Recognition (FGR2002)* (http://ieeexplore.ieee.org/document/1004186).

Granström, Björn and David House. 2005. Audiovisual representation of prosody in expressive speech communication. *Speech Communication* 46:473–84.

Grønnum, Nina. 2003. Dansk intonation. *Veje til dansk: forskning i sprog og sprogtilegnelse*, ed. Anne Holmen, Esther Glahn and Hanne Ruus, 15–38. Copenhagen: Akademisk Forlag.

Grønnum, Nina and John Tøndering. 2007. Question intonation in non-scripted Danish dialogues. *Proceedings of the XVIth International Congress of Phonetic Sciences 2007*, 1229–32. Saarbrücken: Saarland University.

Gruber, Helmut. 1998. Disagreeing: sequential placement and internal structure of disagreements in conflict episodes. *Text* 18:467–503.

Gülich, Elisabeth and Thomas Kotschi. 1996. Textherstellungsverfahren in mündlicher Kommunikation. *Ebenen der Textstruktur*, ed. Wolfgang Motsch, 37–80. Tübingen: Niemeyer.

Gumperz, John J. 1982. *Discourse strategies*. Cambridge: Cambridge University Press.

Gumperz, John J. and Dell E. Hymes. 1964. The ethnography of communication. *American Anthropologist* 66(6): part II.

Gumperz, John J. and Dell E. Hymes. 1972. *Directions in sociolinguistics: the ethnography of communication*. New York: Holt, Rinehart and Winston.

Gumperz, John J. and Stephen C. Levinson (eds.). 1996. *Rethinking linguistic relativity*. Cambridge: Cambridge University Press.

Günthner, Susanne. 1993. . . . *weil – man kann es ja wissenschaftlich untersuchen*: diskurspragmatische Aspekte der Wortstellung in WEIL-Sätzen. *Linguistische Berichte* 143:37–59.

Günthner, Susanne. 1996a. From subordination to coordination? Verb-second position in German causal and concessive constructions. *Pragmatics* 6(3):323–56.

Günthner, Susanne. 1996b. The prosodic contextualization of moral work: an analysis of reproaches in *why*-formats. *Prosody in conversation: interactional studies*, ed.

Elizabeth Couper-Kuhlen and Margret Selting, 271–302. Cambridge: Cambridge University Press.
Günthner, Susanne. 1997a. Complaint stories: constructing emotional reciprocity among women. *Communicating gender in context*, ed. Helga Kotthoff and Ruth Wodak, 179–218. Amsterdam: Benjamins.
Günthner, Susanne. 1997b. The contextualization of affect in reported dialogues. *The language of emotions*, ed. Susanne Niemeier and René Dirven, 247–75. Amsterdam: Benjamins.
Günthner, Susanne. 1997c. Stilisierungsverfahren in der Redewiedergabe: die "Überlagerung von Stimmen" als Mittel der moralischen Verurteilung in Vorwurfsrekonstruktionen. *Sprech- und Gesprächsstile*, ed. Margret Selting and Barbara Sandig, 94–122. Berlin: de Gruyter.
Günthner, Susanne. 1997d. Direkte und indirekte Rede in Alltagsgesprächen: zur Interaktion von Syntax und Prosodie in der Redewiedergabe. *Syntax des gesprochenen Deutsch*, ed. Peter Schlobinski, 227–62. Opladen: Westdeutscher Verlag.
Günthner, Susanne. 1999a. Polyphony and the "layering of voices" in reported dialogues: an analysis of the use of prosodic devices in everyday reported speech. *Journal of Pragmatics* 31:685–708.
Günthner, Susanne. 1999b. Beschwerdeerzählungen als narrative Hyperbeln. *Kommunikative Konstruktion von Moral*, ed. Jörg Bergmann and Thomas Luckmann, 174–205. Opladen: Westdeutscher Verlag.
Günthner, Susanne. 2000a. *Vorwurfsaktivitäten in der Alltagsinteraktion: grammatische, prosodische, rhetorisch-stilistische und interaktive Verfahren bei der Konstitution kommunikativer Muster und Gattungen*. Tübingen: Niemeyer.
Günthner, Susanne. 2000b. From concessive connector to discourse marker: the use of *obwohl* in everyday German interaction. *Cause, condition, concession, contrast: cognitive and discourse perspectives*, ed. Elizabeth Couper-Kuhlen and Bernd Kortmann, 439–68. Berlin: de Gruyter.
Günthner, Susanne. 2000c. Zwischen direkter und indirekter Rede. *Zeitschrift für Germanistische Linguistik* 28:1–22.
Günthner, Susanne. 2005a. Grammatical constructions in "real life practices": *wo*-constructions in everyday German. *Syntax and lexis in conversation: studies on the use of linguistic resources in talk-in-interaction*, ed. Auli Hakulinen and Margret Selting, 159–84. Amsterdam: Benjamins.
Günthner, Susanne. 2005b. Fremde Rede im Diskurs: Formen und Funktionen der Polyphonie in alltäglichen Redewiedergaben. *Zwischen Literatur und Anthropologie: Diskurse, Medien, Performanzen*, ed. Aleida Assmann, Ulrich Gaier and Gisela Trommsdorff, 339–59. Tübingen: Gunter Narr.
Günthner, Susanne. 2005c. Narrative reconstructions of past experiences: adjustments and modifications in the process of recontextualizing a past experience. *Narrative interaction*, ed. Uta Quasthoff and Tabea Becker, 285–301. Amsterdam: Benjamins.
Günthner, Susanne. 2006a. Grammatische Analysen der kommunikativen Praxis: "Dichte Konstruktionen" in der Interaktion. *Grammatik und Interaktion*, ed. Arnulf Deppermann, Reinhard Fiehler and Thomas Spranz-Fogasy, 95–121. Radolfzell: Verlag für Gesprächsforschung (www.verlag-gespraechsforschung.de).
Günthner, Susanne. 2006b. Was ihn trieb, war vor allem Wanderlust (Hesse: Narziss und Goldmund): Pseudocleft-Konstruktionen im Deutschen. *Konstruktionen in der Interaktion*, ed. Susanne Günthner and Wolfgang Imo, 59–90. Berlin: de Gruyter.

Günthner, Susanne. 2007. Techniken der "Verdichtung" in der alltäglichen Narration. *Sprachliche Kürze*, ed. Jochen A. Bär, Thorsten Roelcke and Anja Steinhauer, 391–411. Berlin: de Gruyter.

Günthner, Susanne. 2008a. Projektorkonstruktionen im Gespräch: Pseudoclefts, *die Sache ist*-Konstruktionen und Extrapositionen mit *es*. *Gesprächsforschung – Online-Zeitschrift zur verbalen Interaktion* 9:86–114.

Günthner, Susanne. 2008b. *Die Sache ist . . .* : eine Projektorkonstruktion im gesprochenen Deutsch. *Zeitschrift für Sprachwissenschaft* 27(1):39–72.

Günthner, Susanne. 2009. Extrapositionen mit *es* im gesprochenen Deutsch. *Zeitschrift für Germanistische Linguistik* 37:15–47.

Günthner, Susanne. 2011a. Between emergence and sedimentation: projecting constructions in German interactions. *Constructions: emerging and emergent*, ed. Peter Auer and Stefan Pfänder, 156–85. Berlin: de Gruyter.

Günthner, Susanne. 2011b. *N be that*-constructions in everyday German conversation: a reanalysis of *die Sache ist/das Ding ist* ("the thing is")-clauses as projector phrases. *Subordination in conversation: a cross-linguistic perspective*, ed. Ritva Laury and Ryoko Suzuki, 11–36. Amsterdam: Benjamins.

Günthner, Susanne. 2011c. The construction of emotional involvement in everyday German narratives: interactive uses of "dense constructions". *Pragmatics* 21:573–92.

Gussenhoven, Carlos. 1984. *On the grammar and semantics of sentence accents*. Dordrecht: Foris.

Haakana, Markku. 2007. Reported thought in complaint stories. *Reporting talk: reported speech in interaction*, ed. Rebecca Clift and Elizabeth Holt, 150–78. Cambridge: Cambridge University Press.

Haakana, Markku. 2010. Laughter and smiling: notes on co-occurrences. *Journal of Pragmatics* 42:1499–512.

Haakana, Markku and Salla Kurhila. 2009. Other-correction in everyday interaction: some comparative aspects. *Talk in interaction: comparative dimensions*, ed. Markku Haakana, Minna Laakso and Jan Lindström, 152–79. Helsinki: Finnish Literature Society.

Haiman, John. 1978. Conditionals are topics. *Language* 54:564–89.

Hakulinen, Auli. 2001. Minimal and non-minimal answers to yes-no questions. *Pragmatics* 11:1–15.

Hakulinen, Auli. 2010a. The relevance of context in the performing of a complaint. *Prosody in interaction*, ed. Dagmar Barth-Weingarten, Elisabeth Reber and Margret Selting, 105–8. Amsterdam: Benjamins.

Hakulinen, Auli. 2010b. *Ingressive speech in Finnish interaction*. Paper read at the International Conference on Conversation Analysis (ICCA) 2010, Mannheim, Germany.

Hakulinen, Auli and Marja-Leena Sorjonen. 2009. Designing utterances for action: verb repeat responses to assessments. *Talk in interaction: comparative dimensions*, ed. Markku Haakana, Minna Laakso and Jan Lindström, 124–51. Helsinki: Finnish Literature Society.

Hakulinen, Auli, Maria Vilkuna, Riitta Korhonen, Vesa Koivisto, Tarja Riitta Heinonen and Irja Alho. 2004. *Iso suomen kielioppi* [Finnish descriptive grammar]. Helsinki: Finnish Literature Society.

Halliday, Michael A. K. 1978. *Language as social semiotic: the social interpretation of language and meaning*. Baltimore, MD: University Park Press.

Halliday, Michael A. K. 1985. *An introduction to functional grammar*. London: Edward Arnold.

Hanks, William F. 1990. *Referential practice: language and lived space among the Maya*. Chicago: University of Chicago Press.

Hanks, William F. 2007. Person reference in Yucatec Maya. *Person reference in interaction: linguistic, cultural, and social perspectives*, ed. Nick J. Enfield and Tanya Stivers, 149–71. Cambridge: Cambridge University Press.

Haspelmath, Martin. 2007. Coordination. *Language typology and syntactic description. Vol. 2: Complex constructions* (2nd ed.), ed. Timothy Shopen, 1–51. Cambridge: Cambridge University Press.

Haspelmath, Martin. 2010. Comparative concepts and descriptive categories in cross-linguistic studies. *Language* 86:663–87.

Haviland, John B. 2007. Person reference in Tzotzil gossip: referring dupliciter. *Person reference in interaction: linguistic, cultural, and social perspectives*, ed. Nick J. Enfield and Tanya Stivers, 226–52. Cambridge: Cambridge University Press.

Hayano, Kaoru. 2011. Claiming epistemic primacy: *yo* marked assessments in Japanese. *The morality of knowledge in conversation*, ed. Tanya Stivers, Lorenza Mondada and Jakob Steensig, 58–81. Cambridge: Cambridge University Press.

Hayano, Kaoru. 2013. *Territories of knowledge in Japanese conversation*. PhD thesis, Radboud University, Nijmegen.

Hayashi, Makoto. 1997. An exploration of sentence-final uses of the quotative particle in Japanese spoken discourse. *Japanese/Korean linguistics*, vol. 6, ed. Ho-min Sohn and John Haig, 565–81. Stanford, CA: Stanford University, Center for the Study of Language and Information.

Hayashi, Makoto. 1999. Where grammar and interaction meet: a study of co-participant completion in Japanese conversation. *Human Studies* 22:475–99.

Hayashi, Makoto. 2001. Postposition-initiated utterances in Japanese conversation: an interactional account of a grammatical practice. *Studies in interactional linguistics*, ed. Margret Selting and Elizabeth Couper-Kuhlen, 317–44. Amsterdam: Benjamins.

Hayashi, Makoto. 2003. *Joint utterance construction in Japanese conversation*. Amsterdam: Benjamins.

Hayashi, Makoto. 2004a. Projection and grammar: notes on the "action-projecting" use of the distal demonstrative *are* in Japanese. *Journal of Pragmatics* 36:1337–74.

Hayashi, Makoto. 2004b. Discourse within a sentence: an exploration of postpositions in Japanese as an interactional resource. *Language in Society* 33:343–76.

Hayashi, Makoto. 2005a. Joint turn construction through language and the body: notes on embodiment in coordinated participation in situated activities. *Semiotica* 156:21–53.

Hayashi, Makoto. 2005b. Referential problems and turn construction: an exploration of an intersection between grammar and interaction. *Text* 25:437–68.

Hayashi, Makoto. 2009. Marking a "noticing of departure" in talk: *eh*-prefaced turns in Japanese conversation. *Journal of Pragmatics* 41:2100–29.

Hayashi, Makoto. 2010. An overview of the question-response system in Japanese. *Journal of Pragmatics* 42:2685–702.

Hayashi, Makoto. 2013. Turn allocation and turn sharing. *The handbook of conversation analysis*, ed. Jack Sidnell and Tanya Stivers, 167–90. Chichester: Wiley-Blackwell.

Hayashi, Makoto and Kaoru Hayano. 2013. Proffering insertable elements: a study of other-initiated repair in Japanese. *Conversational repair and human understanding*, ed. Makoto Hayashi, Geoffrey Raymond and Jack Sidnell, 293–321. Cambridge: Cambridge University Press.

Hayashi, Makoto and Shuya Kushida. 2013. Responding with resistance to *wh*-questions in Japanese talk-in-interaction. *Research on Language and Social Interaction* 45(3): 231–55.

Hayashi, Makoto, Geoffrey Raymond and Jack Sidnell (eds.). 2013. *Conversational repair and human understanding*. Cambridge: Cambridge University Press.

Hayashi, Makoto and Kyung-Eun Yoon. 2006. A cross-linguistic exploration of demonstratives in interaction: with particular reference to the context of word-formulation trouble. *Studies in Language* 30:485–540.

Hayashi, Makoto and Kyung-Eun Yoon. 2009. Negotiating boundaries in talk. *Conversation analysis: comparative perspectives*, ed. Jack Sidnell, 248–76. Cambridge: Cambridge University Press.

Heinemann, Trine. 2005. Where grammar and interaction meet: the preference for matched polarity in responsive turns in Danish. *Syntax and lexis in conversation*, ed. Auli Hakulinen and Margret Selting, 375–402. Amsterdam: Benjamins.

Heinemann, Trine. 2006. *Will you or can't you?*: displaying entitlement in interrogative requests. *Journal of Pragmatics* 38:1081–104.

Heinemann, Trine. 2008. Questions of accountability: yes-no interrogatives that are unanswerable. *Discourse Studies* 10:55–71.

Heinemann, Trine. 2009. Two answers to inapposite inquiries. *Conversation analysis: comparative perspectives*, ed. Jack Sidnell, 159–86. Cambridge: Cambridge University Press.

Heinemann, Trine. 2010. The question-response system of Danish. *Journal of Pragmatics* 42:2703–25.

Heinemann, Trine. 2016. Registering revision: the reduplicated Danish change-of-state token *nå*. *Discourse Studies* 18(1):44–63.

Heinemann, Trine and Aino Koivisto. 2016. Indicating a change-of-state in interaction: cross-linguistic explorations. *Journal of Pragmatics* 104:83–8.

Helasvuo, Marja-Liisa. 2001a. Emerging syntax for interaction: noun phrases and clauses as a syntactic resource for interaction. *Studies in interactional linguistics*, ed. Margret Selting and Elizabeth Couper-Kuhlen, 25–50. Amsterdam: Benjamins.

Helasvuo, Marja-Liisa. 2001b. *Syntax in the making: the emergence of syntactic units in Finnish conversation*. Amsterdam: Benjamins.

Helasvuo, Marja-Liisa, Minna Laakso and Marja-Leena Sorjonen. 2004. Searching for words: syntactic and sequential construction of word search in conversations of Finnish speakers with aphasia. *Research on Language and Social Interaction* 37:1–37.

Hepburn, Alexa. 2004. Crying: notes on description, transcription and interaction. *Research on Language and Social Interaction* 37:251–90.

Hepburn, Alexa and Galina B. Bolden. 2013. The conversation analytic approach to transcription. *The handbook of conversation analysis*, ed. Jack Sidnell and Tanya Stivers, 57–76. Chichester: Wiley-Blackwell.

Hepburn, Alexa and Jonathan Potter. 2007. Crying receipts: time, empathy, and institutional practice. *Research on Language and Social Interaction* 40(1):89–116.

Heritage, John. 1984a. A change-of-state token and aspects of its sequential placement. *Structures of social action: studies in conversation analysis*, ed. J. Maxwell Atkinson and John Heritage, 299–345. Cambridge: Cambridge University Press.

Heritage, John. 1984b. *Garfinkel and ethnomethodology*. Cambridge: Polity Press.

Heritage, John. 1985. Analyzing news interviews: aspects of the production of talk for an overhearing audience. *Handbook of discourse analysis. Vol. 3: Discourse and dialogue*, ed. Teun van Dijk, 95–119. London: Academic Press.

Heritage, John. 1988. Explanations as accounts: a conversation analytic perspective. *Analysing everyday explanation: a casebook of methods*, ed. Charles Antaki, 127–44. London: Sage.

Heritage, John. 1998. *Oh*-prefaced responses to inquiry. *Language in Society* 27:291–334.

Heritage, John. 2002a. *Oh*-prefaced responses to assessments: a method of modifying agreement/disagreement. *The language of turn and sequence*, ed. Cecilia E. Ford,

Barbara A. Fox and Sandra A. Thompson, 196–224. New York: Oxford University Press.
Heritage, John. 2002b. The limits of questioning: negative interrogatives and hostile question content. *Journal of Pragmatics* 34:1427–46.
Heritage, John. 2007. Intersubjectivity and progressivity in person (and place) reference. *Person reference in interaction*, ed. Nick J. Enfield and Tanya Stivers, 255–80. Cambridge: Cambridge University Press.
Heritage, John. 2010a. Questioning in medicine. *"Why do you ask?": the function of questions in institutional discourse*, ed. Alice F. Freed and Susan Ehrlich, 42–68. New York: Oxford University Press.
Heritage, John. 2010b. Conversation analysis: practices and methods. *Qualitative research: theory, method and practice* (3rd ed.), ed. David Silverman, 208–30. London: Sage.
Heritage, John. 2011. Territories of knowledge, territories of experience: empathic moments in interaction. *The morality of knowledge in conversation*, ed. Tanya Stivers, Lorenza Mondada and Jakob Steensig, 159–83. Cambridge: Cambridge University Press.
Heritage, John. 2012a. Epistemics in action: action formation and territories of knowledge. *Research on Language and Social Interaction* 45:1–29.
Heritage, John. 2012b. The epistemic engine: sequence organization and territories of knowledge. *Research on Language and Social Interaction* 45:30–52.
Heritage, John. 2012c. Universal dilemmas and collaterized practices: commentary on Sidnell and Enfield: Language diversity and social action. *Current Anthropology* 53(3):322–3.
Heritage, John. 2013a. Epistemics in conversation. *Handbook of conversation analysis*, ed. Jack Sidnell and Tanya Stivers, 370–94. Chichester: Wiley-Blackwell.
Heritage, John. 2013b. Turn-initial position and some of its occupants. *Journal of Pragmatics* 57:331–7.
Heritage, John. 2015. *Well*-prefaced turns in English conversation: a conversation analytic perspective. *Journal of Pragmatics* 88:88–104.
Heritage, John and Steven Clayman. 2010. *Talk in action: interactions, identities, and institutions*. Malden, MA: Wiley-Blackwell.
Heritage, John and David Greatbatch. 1986. Generating applause: a study of rhetoric and response at party political conferences. *American Journal of Sociology* 92:110–57.
Heritage, John and Geoffrey Raymond. 2005. The terms of agreement: indexing epistemic authority and subordination in assessment sequences. *Social Psychology Quarterly* 68:15–38.
Heritage, John and Geoffrey Raymond. 2012. Navigating epistemic landscapes: acquiescence, agency and resistance in responses to polar questions. *Questions*, ed. Jan P. de Ruiter, 179–92. Cambridge: Cambridge University Press.
Heritage, John and Jeffrey D. Robinson. 2011. "Some" vs "any" medical issues: encouraging patients to reveal their unmet concerns. *Applied conversation analysis: changing institutional practices*, ed. Charles Antaki, 15–31. Basingstoke: Palgrave Macmillan.
Heritage, John, Jeffrey D. Robinson, Marc Elliott, Megan Beckett and Michael Wilkes. 2007. Reducing patients' unmet concerns in primary care: the difference one word can make. *Journal of General Internal Medicine* 22(10):1429–33.
Heritage, John and Andrew L. Roth. 1995. Grammar and institution: questions and questioning in broadcast media. *Research on Language and Social Interaction* 28:1–60.
Heritage, John and Marja-Leena Sorjonen. 1994. Constituting and maintaining activities across sequences: *and*-prefacing as a feature of question design. *Language in Society* 23:1–29.

Heritage, John and Marja-Leena Sorjonen (eds.). Forthcoming. *Turn-initial particles across languages*. Amsterdam: Benjamins.
Heritage, John and D. Rod Watson. 1979. Formulation as conversational objects. *Everyday language: studies in ethnomethodology*, ed. George Psathas, 123–62. New York: Irvington.
Heritage, John and D. Rod Watson. 1980. Aspects of the properties of formulations in natural conversations: some instances analysed. *Semiotica* 30:245–62.
Hochschild, Arlie R. 1979. Emotion work, feeling rules, and social structure. *American Journal of Sociology* 85(3):551–75.
Hockett, Charles F. 1960. The origin of speech. *Scientific American* 203:89–96.
Hoey, Elliott M. 2014. Sighing in interaction: somatic, semiotic, and social. *Research on Language and Social Interaction* 47(2):175–200.
Hoey, Elliott M. 2015. Lapses: how people arrive at, and deal with, discontinuities in talk. *Research on Language and Social Interaction* 48(4):430–53.
Holt, Elizabeth. 1996. Reporting on talk: the use of direct reported speech in conversation. *Research on Language and Social Interaction* 29:219–45.
Holt, Elizabeth. 2000. Reporting and reacting: concurrent responses to reported speech. *Research on Language and Social Interaction* 33:425–54.
Holt, Elizabeth. 2012. Using laugh responses to defuse complaints. *Research on Language and Social Interaction* 45(4):430–48.
Holt, Elizabeth and Rebecca Clift (eds.). 2007. *Reporting talk: reported speech in interaction*. Cambridge: Cambridge University Press.
Holt, Elizabeth and Paul Drew. 2005. Figurative pivots. *Research on Language and Social Interaction* 38:35–61.
Hopper, Paul. 1979. Aspects of foregrounding in discourse. *Discourse and syntax*, ed. Talmy Givón, 213–41. New York: Academic Press.
Hopper, Paul. 1987. Emergent grammar. *Berkeley Linguistic Society* 13:139–57.
Hopper, Paul. 1988. Emergent grammar and the *a priori* grammar postulate. *Linguistics in context*, ed. Deborah Tannen, 117–34. Washington, DC: Georgetown University Press.
Hopper, Paul. 1998. Emergent grammar. *The new psychology of language: cognitive and functional approaches to linguistic structure*, ed. Michael Tomasello, 155–75. Englewood Cliffs, NJ: Erlbaum.
Hopper, Paul. 2001a. Grammatical constructions and their discourse origins: prototype or family resemblance? *Applied cognitive linguistics*, vol. I, ed. Martin Pütz, Susanne Niemeyer and René Dirven, 109–29. Berlin: de Gruyter.
Hopper, Paul. 2001b. Hendiadys and auxiliation in English. *Complex sentences in grammar and discourse*, ed. Joan Bybee and Michael Noonan, 145–73. Amsterdam: Benjamins.
Hopper, Paul. 2004. The openness of grammatical constructions. *Papers from the 40th Regional Meeting of the Chicago Linguistic Society* 40:153–75.
Hopper, Paul. 2011. Emergent grammar and temporality in interactional linguistics. *Constructions: emerging and emergent*, ed. Peter Auer and Stefan Pfänder, 22–44. Berlin: de Gruyter.
Hopper, Paul and Sandra A. Thompson. 1980. Transitivity in grammar and discourse. *Language* 56:251–99.
Hopper, Paul and Sandra A. Thompson. 1984. The discourse basis for lexical categories in universal grammar. *Language* 60(3):703–52.
Hopper, Paul and Sandra A. Thompson. 2008. Projectability and clause combining in interaction. *Crosslinguistic studies of clause combining: the multifunctionality of conjunctions*, ed. Ritva Laury, 99–124. Amsterdam: Benjamins.

Hopper, Paul and Elizabeth Closs Traugott. 1993. *Grammaticalization*. Cambridge: Cambridge University Press.

Horlacher, Anne-Sylvie. 2012. *La dislocation à droite revisitée: une investigation interactionniste*. Unpublished PhD thesis, Université de Neuchâtel.

Horlacher, Anne-Sylvie and Simona Pekarek Doehler. 2014. "Pivotage" in French talk-in-interaction: on the emergent nature of [clause-NP-clause] pivots. *Pragmatics* 24:593–622. (Special issue on approaches to grammar for interactional linguistics, ed. Ritva Laury, Marja Etelämäki and Elizabeth Couper-Kuhlen.)

Houtkoop-Steenstra, Hanneke. 1987. *Establishing agreement: an analysis of proposal–acceptance sequences*. Dordrecht: Foris Publications.

Hutchby, Ian. 2005. "Active listening": formulations and the elicitation of feelings-talk in child counselling. *Research on Language and Social Interaction* 38:303–29.

Imo, Wolfgang. 2009. Die Grenzen von Konstruktionen: Versuch einer granularen Neubestimmung des Konstruktionsbegriffs der Construction Grammar. *Grammatik in der Interaktion* (Gidi Arbeitspapierreihe 24, 11/2009). Universität Münster.

Imo, Wolfgang. 2011. Clines of subordination: constructions with the German "complement-taking predicate" *glauben*. *Subordination in conversation*, ed. Ritva Laury and Ryoko Suzuki, 165–90. Amsterdam: Benjamins.

Iwasaki, Shimako. 2007. Construction of units and interactive turn spaces in Japanese conversation. *Japanese/Korean linguistics*, ed. Naomi Hanaoka McGloin and Junko Mori, 67–80. Stanford, CA: Stanford University, Center for the Study of Language and Information.

Iwasaki, Shimako. 2009. Initiating interactive turn spaces in Japanese conversation: local projection and collaborative action. *Discourse Processes* 46:226–46.

Iwasaki, Shimako. 2011. The multimodal mechanics of collaborative unit construction in Japanese conversation. *Embodied interaction: language and the body in the material world*, ed. Jürgen Streeck, Charles Goodwin and Curtis LeBaron, 106–20. Cambridge: Cambridge University Press.

Iwasaki, Shimako. 2013. Emerging units and emergent forms of participation within a unit in Japanese interaction: local organization at a finer level of granularity. *Units of talk: units of action*, ed. Beatrice Szczepek Reed and Geoffrey Raymond, 243–76. Amsterdam: Benjamins.

Jasperson, Robert. 1998. *Repair after cut-off*. Unpublished PhD thesis, University of Colorado, Boulder, CO.

Jasperson, Robert. 2002. Some linguistic aspects of closure cut-offs. *The language of turn and sequence*, ed. Cecilia E. Ford, Barbara A. Fox and Sandra A. Thompson, 257–86. Oxford: Oxford University Press.

Jefferson, Gail. 1972. Side sequences. *Studies in social interaction*, ed. David Sudnow, 294–337. New York: The Free Press.

Jefferson, Gail. 1973. A case of precision timing in ordinary conversation: overlapping tag-positioned address terms in closing sequences. *Semiotica* 9(1):47–96.

Jefferson, Gail. 1974. Error correction as an interactional resource. *Language in Society* 2:181–99.

Jefferson, Gail. 1978. Sequential aspects of storytelling in conversation. *Studies in the organization of conversational interaction*, ed. Jim Schenkein, 219–48. New York: Academic Press.

Jefferson, Gail. 1979. A technique for inviting laughter and its subsequent acceptance declination. *Everyday language: studies in ethnomethodology*, ed. George Psathas, 79–96. New York: Irvington.

Jefferson, Gail. 1980. On "trouble-premonitory" response to inquiry. *Sociological Inquiry* 50:153–85.
Jefferson, Gail. 1981. The abominable *ne?*: an exploration of post-response pursuit of response. *Dialogforschung*, ed. Peter Schröder and Hugo Steger, 53–88. Düsseldorf: Schwann.
Jefferson, Gail. 1982. On exposed and embedded correction in conversation. *Studium Linguistik* 14:58–68.
Jefferson, Gail. 1983. On a failed hypothesis: "conjunctionals" as overlap-vulnerable. *Tilburg Papers in Language and Literature* 28:1–33.
Jefferson, Gail. 1984a. Notes on some orderliness of overlap onset. *Discourse analysis and natural rhetorics*, ed. Valentina D'Urso and Paolo Leonardi, 11–38. Padova: Cleup.
Jefferson, Gail. 1984b. On the organization of laughter in talk about troubles. *Structures of social action: studies in conversation analysis*, ed. J. Maxwell Atkinson and John Heritage, 346–69. Cambridge: Cambridge University Press.
Jefferson, Gail. 1984c. On stepwise transition from talk about a trouble to inappropriately next-positioned matters. *Structures of social action: studies in conversation analysis*, ed. J. Maxwell Atkinson and John Heritage, 191–222. Cambridge: Cambridge University Press.
Jefferson, Gail. 1984d. Notes on a systematic deployment of the acknowledgement tokens *yeah* and *mm hm*. *Papers in Linguistics* 17:197–216.
Jefferson, Gail. 1985. An exercise in the transcription and analysis of laughter. *Handbook of discourse analysis*, ed. Teun van Dijk, 25–34. London: Academic Press.
Jefferson, Gail. 1986. Notes on "latency" in overlap onset. *Human Studies* 9:153–83. (Special issue on interaction and language use, ed. Graham Button, Paul Drew and John Heritage.)
Jefferson, Gail. 1987. Exposed and embedded corrections. *Talk and social organisation*, ed. Graham Button and John R. E. Lee, 86–100. Clevedon: Multilingual Matters.
Jefferson, Gail. 1988. On the sequential organization of troubles-talk in ordinary conversation. *Social Problems* 35:418–41.
Jefferson, Gail. 1989. Preliminary notes on a possible metric which provides for a "standard maximum" silence of approximately one second in conversation. *Conversation: an interdisciplinary perspective*, ed. Derek Roger and Peter Bull, 166–96. Clevedon: Multilingual Matters.
Jefferson, Gail. 1990. List construction as a task and resource. *Interaction competence*, ed. George Psathas, 63–92. Lanham, MD: University Press of America.
Jefferson, Gail. 1993a. A note on the acknowledgement tokens *mm hm* versus *uh huh*. *Research on Language and Social Interaction* 26:350–1.
Jefferson, Gail. 1993b. Caveat speaker: preliminary notes on recipient topic-shift implicature. *Research on Language and Social Interaction* 26:1–30.
Jefferson, Gail. 2002. Is *no* an acknowledgement token? Comparing American and British uses of (+)/(−) tokens. *Journal of Pragmatics* 34:1345–83.
Jefferson, Gail. 2004a. Glossary of transcript symbols with an introduction. *Conversation analysis: studies from the first generation*, ed. Gene Lerner, 13–31. Amsterdam: Benjamins.
Jefferson, Gail. 2004b. A sketch of some orderly aspects of overlap in natural conversation. *Conversation analysis: studies from the first generation*, ed. Gene H. Lerner, 43–59. Amsterdam: Benjamins.
Jefferson, Gail. 2004c. *At first I thought*: a normalizing device for extraordinary events. *Conversation analysis: studies from the first generation*, ed. Gene H. Lerner, 131–67. Amsterdam: Benjamins.
Jefferson, Gail. 2007. Preliminary notes on abdicated other-correction. *Journal of Pragmatics* 39:445–61.

Jefferson, Gail. 2010. Sometimes a frog in your throat is just a frog in your throat: gutturals as (sometimes) laughter-implicative. *Journal of Pragmatics* 42:1476–84.

Kaimaki, Marianna. 2012. Sequential and prosodic design of English and Greek non-valenced news receipts. *Language and Speech* 55:99–117.

Kamio, Akio. 1997. *Territory of information*. Amsterdam: Benjamins.

Kärkkäinen, Elise. 2003. *Epistemic stance in English conversation: a description of its interactional functions, with a focus on* I think. Amsterdam: Benjamins.

Kärkkäinen, Elise and Tiina Keisanen. 2012. Linguistic and embodied formats for making (concrete) offers. *Discourse Studies* 14:587–611.

Kärkkäinen, Elise, Marja-Leena Sorjonen and Marja-Liisa Helasvuo. 2007. Discourse structure. *Language, typology and syntactic description*, ed. Timothy Shopen, 301–71. Cambridge: Cambridge University Press.

Karlsson, Susanna. 2010. Multimodalitet i listproduktion. *Språk och interaktion* 2, ed. Camilla Lindholm and Jan Lindström, 141–70 (http//:hdl.handle.net/10138/28555).

Kaukomaa, Timo, Anssi Peräkylä and Johanna Ruusuvuori. 2014. Foreshadowing a problem: turn-opening frowns in conversation. *Journal of Pragmatics* 71:132–47.

Keenan, Elinor O. 1977. Making it last: repetition in children's discourse. *Child discourse*, ed. Susan Ervin-Tripp and Claudia Mitchell-Kernan, 125–38. New York: Academic Press.

Keevallik, Leelo. 2010. Minimal answers to *yes/no* questions in the service of sequence organization. *Discourse Studies* 12:283–309.

Keevallik, Leelo. 2011. Interrogative "complements" and question design in Estonian. *Subordination in conversation*, ed. Ritva Laury and Ryoko Suzuki, 37–68. Amsterdam: Benjamins.

Keevallik, Leelo. 2012. Compromising progressivity: *no*-prefacing in Estonian. *Pragmatics* 22:119–46.

Keevallik, Leelo. 2013. Accomplishing continuity across sequences and encounters: *no(h)*-prefaced initiations in Estonian. *Journal of Pragmatics* 57:274–89.

Keisanen, Tiina. 2006. *Patterns of stance taking: negative yes/no interrogatives and tag questions in American English conversation* (Acta Universitatis Ouluensis B Humaniora 71). Oulu: Oulu University Press.

Keisanen, Tiina and Elise Kärkkäinen. 2014. A multi-modal analysis of compliment sequences in everyday English interactions. *Pragmatics* 24(3):649–72.

Keisanen, Tiina and Mirka Rauniomaa. 2012. Organization of participation and contingency in the pre-beginnings of request sequences. *Research on Language and Social Interaction* 45:323–51.

Kelly, John and John Local. 1989. *Doing phonology: observing, recording, interpreting*. Manchester: Manchester University Press.

Kendon, Adam. 1990. *Conducting interaction: patterns of behavior in focused encounters*. Cambridge: Cambridge University Press.

Kendrick, Kobin H. 2015. Other-initiated repair in English. *Open Linguistics* 2015(1): 164–90.

Kendrick, Kobin H., Penelope Brown, Mark Dingemanse, Simeon Floyd, Sonja Gipper, Kaoru Hayano, Elliott Hoey, Gertie Hoymann, Elizabeth Manrique, Giovanni Rossi and Stephen C. Levinson. 2014. Sequence organization: a universal infrastructure for action. Talk presented at the 4th International Conference on Conversation Analysis. University of California, Los Angeles, CA.

Kendrick, Kobin H. and Paul Drew. 2014. The putative preference for offers over requests. *Requesting in social interaction*, ed. Paul Drew and Elizabeth Couper-Kuhlen, 87–113. Amsterdam: Benjamins.

Kendrick, Kobin H. and Paul Drew. 2016. Recruitment: offers, requests, and the organization of assistance in interaction. *Research on Language and Social Interaction* 49(1):1–19.

Kern, Friederike. 2013. *Rhythmus und Kontrast im Türkischdeutschen*. Berlin: de Gruyter.

Kern, Friederike and Margret Selting. 2006a. Einheitenkonstruktion im Türkendeutschen: grammatische und prosodische Aspekte. *Zeitschrift für Sprachwissenschaft* 25:239–72.

Kern, Friederike and Margret Selting. 2006b. Konstruktionen mit Nachstellungen im Türkendeutschen. *Grammatik und Interaktion*, ed. Arnulf Deppermann, Reinhard Fiehler and Thomas Spranz-Fogasy, 319–47. Radolfzell: Verlag für Gesprächsforschung. (www.verlag-gespraechsforschung.de).

Kern, Friederike and Yazgül Şimşek. 2006. Türkendeutsch: Aspekte von Einheitenbildung und Rezeptionsverhalten. *Mehrsprachige Individuen: vielsprachige Gesellschaften*, ed. Dieter Wolff, 101–19. Frankfurt/Main: Lang.

Kim, Hye Ri Stephanie. 2002. The form and function of next-turn repetition in English conversation. *Language Research* 38(1):51–81.

Kim, Hye Ri Stephanie. 2013a. *Ani*-prefaced responses to wh-questions as challenges in Korean. *Japanese/Korean linguistics*, vol. 20, ed. Peter Sells and Bjarke Frellesuig, 381–96. Stanford, CA: Stanford University, Center for the Study of Language and Information.

Kim, Hye Ri Stephanie. 2013b. Retroactive indexing of relevance: the use of *well* in third position. *Research on Language and Social Interaction* 46(2):125–43.

Kim, Hye Ri Stephanie. 2013c. Reshaping the response space with *kulenikka* in beginning to respond to questions in Korean conversation. *Journal of Pragmatics* 57:303–17.

Kim, Hye Ri Stephanie. 2015. Resisting the terms of polar questions through *ani* ("no")-prefacing in Korean conversation. *Discourse Processes* 52(4):311–34.

Kim, Hye Ri Stephanie and Satomi Kuroshima. 2013. Turn beginnings in interaction: an introduction. *Journal of Pragmatics* 57:267–73.

Kim, Hye Ri Stephanie and Sung-Ock Sohn. 2015. Grammar as an emergent response to interactional needs: a study of final *kuntey* "but" in Korean conversation. *Journal of Pragmatics* 83:73–90.

Kim, Kyun-Hun. 1990. *Wh*-clefts in English conversation: an interactional perspective. *Language Research* 26(4):721–43.

Kim, Kyun-Hun. 1993. Other-initiated repairs in Korean conversation as interactional resources. *Japanese/Korean linguistics*, vol. 3, ed. Soonja Choi, 3–18. Palo Alto, CA: Stanford University, Center for the Study of Language and Information.

Kim, Kyu-Hyun. 1999a. Phrasal unit boundaries and organization of turns and sequences in Korean conversation. *Human Studies* 22:425–46.

Kim, Kyu-Hyun. 1999b. Other-initiated repair sequences in Korean conversation: types and functions. *Discourse and Cognition* 6:141–68.

Kim, Kyu-Hyun. 2001. Confirming intersubjectivity through retroactive elaboration: organization of phrasal units in other-initiated repair sequences in Korean conversation. *Studies in interactional linguistics*, ed. Margret Selting and Elizabeth Couper-Kuhlen, 345–72. Amsterdam: Benjamins.

Kim, Kyu-Hyun. 2007. Sequential organization of post-predicate elements in Korean conversation: pursuing uptake and modulating action. *Pragmatics* 17:573–604. (Special issue on turn continuation in cross-linguistic perspective, ed. Elizabeth Couper-Kuhlen and Tsuyoshi Ono.)

Kitzinger, Celia. 2013. Repair. *The handbook of conversation analysis*, ed. Jack Sidnell and Tanya Stivers, 229–56. Chichester: Wiley-Blackwell.

Kitzinger, Celia, Rebecca Shaw and Merran Toerien. 2012. Referring to persons without using a full-form reference: locally initial indexicals in action. *Research on Language and Social Interaction* 45:116–32.

Klewitz, Gabriele and Elizabeth Couper-Kuhlen. 1999. Quote-unquote: the role of prosody in the contextualization of reported speech sequences. *Pragmatics* 9(4):459–85.

Kohler, Klaus J. 1995. *Einführung in die Phonetik des Deutschen*. Berlin: Erich Schmidt Verlag.

Koivisto, Aino. 2012. Discourse patterns for turn-final conjunctions. *Journal of Pragmatics* 44(10):1254–72.

Koivisto, Aino. 2013. On the preference for remembering: acknowledging an answer with Finnish *ai nii(n)* ("oh that's right"). *Research on Language and Social Interaction* 46: 277–97.

Koivisto, Aino. 2015a. Displaying now-understanding: the Finnish change-of-state token *aa*. *Discourse Processes* 52(2):111–48.

Koivisto, Aino. 2015b. Taking an interactional perspective on final particles: the case of Finnish *mutta* ("but"). *Final particles*, ed. Sylvie Hancil, Alexander Haselow and Margje Post, 55–76. Berlin: de Gruyter.

Koivisto, Aino. 2015c. Dealing with ambiguities in informings: Finnish *aijaa* as a "neutral" news receipt. *Research on Language and Social Interaction* 48(4):365–87.

Koivisto, Aino. 2017. On-line emergence of alternative questions in Finnish with the conjunction/particle *vai* "or". *Combining clauses and actions in interaction*, ed. Ritva Laury, Marja Etelämäki and Elizabeth Couper-Kuhlen, 131–50. Helsinki: SKS Finnish Literary Society.

Koivisto, Aino, Ritva Laury and Eeva-Leena Seppänen. 2011. Syntactic and actional characteristics of Finnish *että*-clauses. *Subordination in conversation: a cross-linguistic perspective*, ed. Ritva Laury and Ryoko Suzuki, 69–102. Amsterdam: Benjamins.

Koshik, Irene. 2002. A conversation analytic study of *yes/no* questions which convey reversed polarity assertions. *Journal of Pragmatics* 34:1851–77.

Koshik, Irene. 2003. *Wh*-questions used as challenges. *Discourse Studies* 5(1):51–77.

Koshik, Irene. 2005a. *Beyond rhetorical questions: assertive questions in everyday interaction*. Amsterdam: Benjamins.

Koshik, Irene. 2005b. Alternative questions used in conversational repair. *Discourse Studies* 7:193–211.

Kotthoff, Helga. 1993. Disagreement and concession in disputes: on the context sensitivity of preference structures. *Language in Society* 22:193–216.

Krekoski, Ross. 2012. Clausal continuations in Japanese. *Discourse Processes* 49:300–13.

Kress, Gunther R. (ed.). 1976. *Halliday: system and function in language*. London: Oxford University Press.

Kuno, Susumu. 1973. *The structure of the Japanese language*. Cambridge, MA: MIT Press.

Kupetz, Maxi. 2013. Verstehensdokumentationen in Reaktionen auf Affektdarstellungen am Beispiel von *das glaub ich*. *Deutsche Sprache* 13:72–96.

Kupetz, Maxi. 2014. Empathy displays as interactional achievements: multimodal and sequential aspects. *Journal of Pragmatics* 61:4–34.

Kupetz, Maxi. 2015. *Empathie im Gespräch: eine interaktionslinguistische Perspektive*. Tübingen: Stauffenburg.

Kurtić, Emina, Guy J. Brown and Bill Wells. 2009. Fundamental frequency height as a resource for the management of overlap in talk-in-interaction. *Where prosody meets pragmatics*, ed. Dagmar Barth-Weingarten, Nicole Dehé and Anne Wichmann, 183–204. Bingley: Emerald.

Kurtić, Emina, Guy J. Brown and Bill Wells. 2013. Resources for turn competition in overlapping talk. *Speech Communication* 55:721–43.

Laakso, Minna and Marja-Leena Sorjonen. 2010. Cut-off or particle: devices for initiating self-repair in conversation. *Journal of Pragmatics* 42:1151–72.

Labov, William. 1972. *Sociolinguistic patterns*. Philadelphia, PA: University of Pennsylvania Press.

Labov, William and David Fanshel. 1977. *Therapeutic discourse: psychotherapy as conversation*. New York: Academic Press.

Lampert, Martina. 2013. *Say*, *be like*, *quote (unquote)*, and the air-quotes: interactive quotatives and their multimodal implications. *English Today* 29(4):45–56.

Laury, Ritva. 2012a. Syntactically non-integrated Finnish *jos* (if)-conditional clauses as directives. *Discourse Processes* 49:213–42.

Laury, Ritva, Marja Etelämäki and Elizabeth Couper-Kuhlen (eds.). 2014. Approaches to grammar for interactional linguistics. *Pragmatics* 24(3) (Special issue).

Laury, Ritva and Tsuyoshi Ono. 2014. The limits of grammar: clause combining in Finnish and Japanese conversation. *Pragmatics* 24(3):561–92.

Laury, Ritva and Eeva-Leena Seppänen. 2008. Clause combining, interaction, evidentiality, participation structure, and the conjunction-particle continuum. *Crosslinguistic studies of clause combining: the multifunctionality of conjunctions*, ed. Ritva Laury, 153–78. Amsterdam: Benjamins.

Laury, Ritva, Ryoko Suzuki and Tsuyoshi Ono. Forthcoming. Questioning the clause as a cross-linguistic unit in grammar and interaction. *Studies in Language*.

Lehtonen, Jaakko and Kari Sajavaara. 1985. The silent Finn. *Perspectives on silence*, ed. Deborah Tannen and Muriel Saville-Troike, 193–201. Norwood, NJ: Ablex Publishing Corporation.

Lerner, Gene H. 1991. On the syntax of sentences-in-progress. *Language in Society* 20: 441–58.

Lerner, Gene H. 1992. Assisted storytelling: deploying shared knowledge as a practical matter. *Qualitative Sociology* 15:247–71.

Lerner, Gene H. 1994. Responsive list construction: a conversational resource for accomplishing multifaceted social action. *Journal of Language and Social Psychology* 13:20–33.

Lerner, Gene H. 1995. Turn design and the organization of participation in instructional activities. *Discourse Processes* 19:111–31.

Lerner, Gene H. 1996a. On the "semi-permeable" character of grammatical units in conversation: conditional entry into the turn space of another speaker. *Interaction and grammar*, ed. Elinor Ochs, Emanuel A. Schegloff and Sandra A. Thompson, 238–76. Cambridge: Cambridge University Press.

Lerner, Gene H. 1996b. Finding "face" in the preference structures of talk-in-interaction. *Social Psychology Quarterly* 59:303–21.

Lerner, Gene H. 2003. Selecting next speaker: the context-sensitive operation of a context-free organization. *Language in Society* 32:177–201.

Lerner, Gene H. 2004. On the place of linguistic resources in the organization of talk in interaction: grammar as action in prompting a speaker to elaborate. *Research on Language and Social Interaction* 37:151–84.

Lerner, Gene H. 2013. On the place of hesitating in delicate formulations: a turn-constructional infrastructure for collaborative indiscretion. *Conversational repair and human understanding*, ed. Makoto Hayashi, Geoffrey Raymond and Jack Sidnell, 95–134. Cambridge: Cambridge University Press.

Lerner, Gene H., Galina Bolden, Alexa Hepburn and Jenny Mandelbaum. 2012. Reference recalibration repairs: adjusting the precision of formulations for the task at hand. *Research on Language and Social Interaction* 45:191–212.

Lerner, Gene H. and Celia Kitzinger. 2007. Extraction and aggregation in the repair of individual and collective self-reference. *Discourse Studies* 9:526–57.

Lerner, Gene H. and Tomoyo Takagi. 1999. On the place of linguistic resources in the organization of talk-in-interaction: a co-investigation of English and Japanese grammatical practices. *Journal of Pragmatics* 31:49–75.

Levinson, Stephen C. 1983. *Pragmatics*. Cambridge: Cambridge University Press.

Levinson, Stephen C. 1988. Putting linguistics on a proper footing: explorations in Goffman's concepts of participation. *Erving Goffman: exploring the interaction order*, ed. Paul Drew and Anthony Wootton, 161–227. Cambridge: Polity Press.

Levinson, Stephen C. 2005. Living with Manny's dangerous idea. *Discourse Studies* 7:431–53.

Levinson, Stephen C. 2006. On the human "interaction engine." *Roots of human sociality: culture, cognition and interaction*, ed. Nick J. Enfield and Stephen C. Levinson, 39–69. Oxford: Berg.

Levinson, Stephen C. 2007. Optimizing person reference: perspectives from usage on Rossel Island. *Person reference in interaction: linguistic, cultural, and social perspectives*, ed. Nick J. Enfield and Tanya Stivers, 29–72. Cambridge: Cambridge University Press.

Levinson, Stephen C. 2010. Questions and responses in Yélî Dnye, the Papuan language of Rossel Island. *Journal of Pragmatics* 42:2741–55.

Levinson, Stephen C. 2013a. Recursion in pragmatics. *Language* 89(1):149–62.

Levinson, Stephen C. 2013b. Action formation and ascription. *The handbook of conversation analysis*, ed. Jack Sidnell and Tanya Stivers, 103–30. Chichester: Wiley-Blackwell.

Levinson, Stephen C. and Francisco Torreira. 2015. Timing in turn-taking and its implications for processing models of language. *Frontiers in Psychology* 6(731):10–26.

Levinson, Stephen C. and David P. Wilkins. 2006. *Grammars of space: explorations in cognitive diversity*. Cambridge: Cambridge University Press.

Li, Xiaoting. 2010. Reflections on units in talk-in-interaction: an ICCA10 report. *Gesprächsforschung – Online-Zeitschrift zur verbalen Interaktion* 11:274–82. (www.gespraechsforschung-ozs.de).

Li, Xiaoting. 2013. Language and the body in the construction of units in Mandarin face-to-face interaction. *Units of talk: units of action*, ed. Beatrice Szczepek Reed and Geoffrey Raymond, 343–75. Amsterdam: Benjamins.

Lindström, Anna Karin. 1997. *Designing social actions: grammar, prosody, and interaction in Swedish conversation*. PhD thesis, University of California, Los Angeles, CA.

Lindström, Anna Karin. 1999. *Language as social action: grammar, prosody and interaction in Swedish conversation*. Uppsala: Institutionen för Nordiska Språk vid Uppsala Universitet.

Lindström, Anna Karin. 2005. Language as social action: a study of how senior citizens request assistance with practical tasks in the Swedish home help service. *Syntax and lexis in conversation*, ed. Auli Hakulinen and Margret Selting, 209–33. Amsterdam: Benjamins.

Lindström, Anna Karin. 2009. Projecting nonalignment in conversation. *Conversation analysis: comparative perspectives*, ed. Jack Sidnell, 135–58. Cambridge: Cambridge University Press.

Lindström, Anna Karin. 2017. Accepting remote proposals. *Enabling human conduct: studies of talk-in-interaction in honor of Emanuel A. Schegloff*, ed. Geoffrey Raymond, Gene H. Lerner and John Heritage, 125–43. Amsterdam: Benjamins.

Lindström, Anna Karin and Trine Heinemann. 2009. Good enough: low-grade assessments in caregiving situations. *Research on Language and Social Interaction* 42(4):309–28.
Lindström, Jan. 2006. Grammar in the service of interaction: exploring turn organization in Swedish. *Research on Language and Social Interaction* 39:81–117.
Lindström, Jan. 2013. On the pivot turn construction method in Swedish and Finnish. *Journal of Pragmatics* 54:57–72.
Lindström, Jan and Anne-Marie Londen. 2013. Concession and reassertion: on a dialogic discourse pattern in conversation. *Text and Talk* 33(3):331–52.
Linell, Per. 1998. *Approaching dialogue: talk, interaction and contexts in dialogical perspectives*. Amsterdam: Benjamins.
Linell, Per. 2005. *The written language bias in linguistics: its nature, origins, and transformations*. London: Routledge.
Linell, Per. 2009. *Rethinking language, mind, and world dialogically: interactional and contextual theories of human sense-making*. Charlotte, NC: Information Age Publishing.
Local, John. 1992. Continuing and restarting. *The contextualization of language*, ed. Peter Auer and Aldo di Luzio, 272–96. Amsterdam: Benjamins.
Local, John. 1996. Conversational phonetics: some aspects of news receipts in everyday talk. *Prosody in conversation*, ed. Elizabeth Couper-Kuhlen and Margret Selting, 177–230. Cambridge: Cambridge University Press.
Local, John. 2004. Getting back to prior talk: *and-uh(m)* as a back-connecting device in British and American English. *Sound patterns in interaction*, ed. Elizabeth Couper-Kuhlen and Cecilia E. Ford, 377–400. Amsterdam: Benjamins.
Local, John. 2005. On the interactional and phonetic design of collaborative completions. *A figure of speech: a Festschrift for John Laver*, ed. William J. Hardcastle and Janet Mackenzie Beck, 263–82. Hillsdale, New Jersey: Lawrence Erlbaum.
Local, John, Peter Auer and Paul Drew. 2010. Retrieving, redoing and resuscitating turns in conversation. *Prosody in interaction*, ed. Dagmar Barth-Weingarten, Elisabeth Reber and Margret Selting, 131–59. Amsterdam: Benjamins.
Local, John and John Kelly. 1986. Projection and "silences": notes on phonetic and conversational structure. *Human Studies* 9:185–204.
Local, John, John Kelly and William H. G. Wells. 1986. Towards a phonology of conversation: turn-taking in Tyneside English. *Journal of Linguistics* 22:411–37.
Local, John and Gareth Walker. 2004. Abrupt-joins as a resource for the production of multi-unit, multi-action turns. *Journal of Pragmatics* 36:1375–403.
Local, John and Gareth Walker. 2005. Methodological imperatives for investigating the phonetic organization and phonological structures of spontaneous speech. *Phonetica* 62:120–30.
Local, John and Gareth Walker. 2008. Stance and affect in conversation: on the interplay of sequential and phonetic resources. *Text & Talk* 28:723–47.
Local, John and Gareth Walker. 2012. How phonetic features project more talk. *Journal of the International Phonetic Association* 42:255–80.
Local, John, William H. G. Wells and Mark Sebba. 1985. Phonology for conversation: phonetic aspects of turn delimitation in London Jamaican. *Journal of Pragmatics* 9:309–30.
Londen, Anne-Marie. 1993. Three-partedness as a structural principle in conversation. *Proceedings of the XIVth Scandinavian Conference of Linguistics and the VIIIth Conference of Nordic and General Linguistics, August 16–21, 1993*, ed. Jens Allwood, Bo Ralph, Paula Andersson, Dora Kós-Dienes and Åsa Wengelin, 275–86. Göteborg: Institutionen för lingvistik.

Luke, Kang Kwong. 2012. Dislocation or afterthought? A conversation analytic account of incremental sentences in Chinese. *Discourse Processes* 49:338–65.
Luke, Kang Kwong and Theodossia-Soula Pavlidou. 2002. *Telephone calls: unity and diversity in conversational structure across languages and cultures*. Philadelphia, PA: Benjamins.
Luke, Kang Kwong, Sandra A. Thompson and Tsuyoshi Ono. 2012. Turns and increments: a comparative perspective. *Discourse Processes* 49:155–62.
Luke, Kang Kwong and Wei Zhang. 2007. Retrospective turn continuations in Mandarin Chinese conversation. *Pragmatics* 17:605–35.
Mair, Christian. 1997. Parallel corpora: a real-time approach to the study of language change in progress. *Corpus-based studies in English*, ed. Magnus Ljung, 195–209. Amsterdam: Rodopi.
Mandelbaum, Jenny. 1989. Interpersonal activities in conversational storytelling. *Western Journal of Speech Communication* 53:114–26.
Mandelbaum, Jenny. 2013. Storytelling in conversation. *The handbook of conversation analysis*, ed. Jack Sidnell and Tanya Stivers, 492–507. Chichester: Wiley-Blackwell.
Mathis, Terrie and George Yule. 1994. Zero quotatives. *Discourse Processes* 18:63–76.
Matthiessen, Christian and Sandra A. Thompson. 1988. The structure of discourse and "subordination". *Clause combining in grammar and discourse*, ed. John Haiman and Sandra A. Thompson, 275–329. Amsterdam: Benjamins.
Maynard, Douglas W. 1980. Placement of topic changes in conversation. *Semiotica* 30(3/4):263–90.
Maynard, Douglas W. 1997. The news delivery sequence: bad news and good news in conversational interaction. *Research on Language and Social Interaction* 30:93–130.
Maynard, Douglas W. 2003. *Bad news, good news: conversational order in everyday talk and clinical settings*. Chicago: University of Chicago Press.
Maynard, Douglas W. 2013a. Everyone and no one to turn to: intellectual roots and contexts for conversation analysis. *The handbook of conversation analysis*, ed. Jack Sidnell and Tanya Stivers, 11–31. Chichester: Blackwell.
Maynard, Douglas W. 2013b. Defensive mechanisms: *I-mean* prefaced utterances in complaint and other conversational sequences. *Conversational repair and human understanding*, ed. Makoto Hayashi, Geoffrey Raymond and Jack Sidnell, 198–233. Cambridge: Cambridge University Press.
Maynard, Douglas W. and Jeremy Freese. 2012. Good news, bad news, and affect: practical and temporal "emotion work" in everyday life. *Emotion in interaction*, ed. Anssi Peräkylä and Marja-Leena Sorjonen, 92–112. New York: Oxford University Press.
Maynard, Senko K. 1989. *Japanese conversation: self-contextualization through structure and interactional management*. Norwood, NJ: Ablex.
Mazeland, Harrie. 2007. Parenthetical sequences. *Journal of Pragmatics* 39:1816–69.
Mazeland, Harrie. 2013. Grammar in conversation. *The handbook of conversation analysis*, ed. Jack Sidnell and Tanya Stivers, 475–91. Chichester: Wiley-Blackwell.
Mazeland, Harrie and Mike Huiskes. 2001. Dutch *but* as a sequential conjunction: its use as a resumption marker. *Studies in interactional linguistics*, ed. Margret Selting and Elizabeth Couper-Kuhlen, 141–69. Amsterdam: Benjamins.
Mazeland, Harrie and Leendert Plug. 2010. Doing confirmation with *ja/nee hoor*: sequential and prosodic characteristics of a Dutch discourse particle. *Prosody in interaction*, ed. Dagmar Barth-Weingarten, Elisabeth Reber and Margret Selting, 161–88. Amsterdam: Benjamins.
Mazeland, Harrie and Minna Zaman-Zadeh. 2004. The logic of clarification: some observations about word-clarification repairs in Finnish-as-a-lingua-franca interactions.

Second language conversations, ed. Rod Gardner and Johannes Wagner, 132–56. London: Continuum.
Moerman, Michael. 1977. The preference for self-correction in a Thai conversational corpus. *Language* 53:872–82.
Moerman, Michael. 1988. *Talking culture: ethnography and conversation analysis*. Philadelphia, PA: University of Pennsylvania Press.
Mondada, Lorenza. 2006. Participants' online analysis and multimodal practices: projecting the end of the turn and the closing of the sequence. *Discourse Studies* 8:117–29.
Mondada, Lorenza. 2007. Multimodal resources for turn-taking: pointing and the emergence of possible next speakers. *Discourse Studies* 9:195–226.
Mondada, Lorenza. 2009. The embodied and negotiated production of assessments in instructed actions. *Research on Language and Social Interaction* 42:329–61.
Mondada, Lorenza. 2013. The conversation analytic approach to data collection. *The handbook of conversation analysis*, ed. Jack Sidnell and Tanya Stivers, 32–56. Chichester: Wiley-Blackwell.
Mondada, Lorenza and Florence Oloff. 2011. Gestures in overlap: the situated establishment of speakership. *Integrating gestures*, ed. N. Gale Stam and Mika Ishino, 321–38. Amsterdam: Benjamins.
Mondada, Lorenza and Françoise Zay. 1999. Parenthèses et processus de configuration thématique: vers une redéfinition de la notion de topic. *Pragmatics in 1998: selected papers from the 6th International Pragmatics Conference*, vol. 2, ed. Jef Verschueren, 396–411. Antwerp: IPrA.
Monzoni, Chiara M. 2005. The use of marked syntactic constructions in Italian multi-party conversation. *Syntax and lexis in conversation*, ed. Auli Hakulinen and Margret Selting, 129–57. Amsterdam: Benjamins.
Monzoni, Chiara M. and Paul Drew. 2009. Interactional contexts of story-interventions by non-knowledgeable story recipients in (Italian) multi-person interaction. *Journal of Pragmatics* 41:197–218.
Mori, Junko. 1999a. *Well I may be exaggerating but . . .*: self-qualifying clauses in negotiating of opinions among Japanese speakers. *Human Studies* 22:447–73.
Mori, Junko. 1999b. *Negotiating agreement and disagreement in Japanese: connective expressions and turn construction*. Amsterdam: Benjamins.
Mori, Junko. 2006. The workings of the Japanese token *hee* in informing sequences: an analysis of sequential context, turn shape, and prosody. *Journal of Pragmatics* 38: 1175–1205.
Mulder, Jean and Sandra A. Thompson. 2008. The grammaticization of *but* as a final particle in English conversation. *Crosslinguistic studies of clause combining: the multifunctionality of conjunctions*, ed. Ritva Laury, 179–204. Amsterdam: Benjamins.
Müller, Cornelia. 2003. On the gestural creation of narrative structure: a case study of a story told in a conversation. *Gestures: meaning and use*, ed. Monica Rector, Isabella Poggi and Nadine Trigo, 259–65. Porto: Universidade Fernando Pessoa Press.
Müller, Frank E. 1989. Lautstilistische Muster in Alltagstexten von Süditalienern. *Stil und Stilisierung: Arbeiten zur interpretativen Soziolinguistik*, ed. Volker Hinnenkamp and Margret Selting, 61–82. Tübingen: Niemeyer.
Müller, Frank E. 1996. Affiliating and disaffiliating with continuers: prosodic aspects of recipiency. *Prosody in conversation: interactional studies*, ed. Elizabeth Couper-Kuhlen and Margret Selting, 131–76. Cambridge: Cambridge University Press.
Nakayama, Toshihide. 2002. *Nuuchahnulth (Nootka) morphosyntax*. Oakland, CA: University of California Press.

Neuage, Terrell. 2004. *Conversational analysis of chatroom talk*. PhD thesis, University of South Australia.

Niemelä, Maarit. 2010. The reporting space in conversational storytelling: orchestrating all semiotic channels for taking a stance. *Journal of Pragmatics* 42:3258–70.

Niemi, Jarkko. 2014. Two *yeah but* formats in Finnish: the prior action engaging *nii mut* and the disengaging *joo mut* utterances. *Journal of Pragmatics* 60:54–74.

Noonan, Michael. 2007. Complementation. *Language typology and syntactic description. Vol. 2: Complex constructions* (2nd ed.), ed. Timothy Shopen, 52–150. Cambridge: Cambridge University Press.

Norén, Kerstin and Per Linell. 2007. Meaning potentials and the interaction between lexis and contexts: an empirical substantiation. *Pragmatics* 17:387–416.

Norén, Niklas. 2007. *Apokoinou in Swedish talk-in-interaction: a family of methods for grammatical construction and the resolving of local communicative projects*. Linköping: Linköping University.

Ochs, Elinor. 1979. Transcription as theory. *Developmental pragmatics*, ed. Elinor Ochs and Bambi B. Schieffelin, 43–72. New York: Academic Press.

Ochs, Elinor. 1996. Linguistic resources for socializing humanity. *Rethinking linguistic relativity*, ed. John J. Gumperz and Stephen C. Levinson, 407–38. Cambridge: Cambridge University Press.

Ochs, Elinor, Emanuel A. Schegloff and Sandra A. Thompson (eds.). 1996. *Interaction and grammar*. Cambridge: Cambridge University Press.

Ochs, Elinor and Bambi B. Schieffelin. 1976. Foregrounding referents: a reconsideration of left dislocation in discourse. *Proceedings of the second annual meeting of the Berkeley Linguistics Society*, 240–57. Berkeley, CA.

Ochs, Elinor and Bambi B. Schieffelin. 1983. Foregrounding referents: a reconsideration of left dislocation in discourse. *Acquiring conversational competence*, ed. Elinor Ochs and Bambi B. Schieffelin, 158–74. Boston, MA: Routledge & Kegan Paul.

Ochs, Elinor and Bambi B. Schieffelin. 1989. Language has a heart. *Text* 9:7–25.

Ogden, Richard. 2001. Turn transition, creak and glottal stop in Finnish talk-in-interaction. *Journal of the International Phonetic Association* 31:139–52.

Ogden, Richard. 2004. Non-modal voice quality and turn-taking in Finnish. *Sound patterns in interaction*, ed. Elizabeth Couper-Kuhlen and Cecilia E. Ford, 29–62. Amsterdam: Benjamins.

Ogden, Richard. 2006. Phonetics and social action in agreements and disagreements. *Journal of Pragmatics* 38:1752–75.

Ogden, Richard. 2010. Prosodic constructions in making complaints. *Prosody in interaction*, ed. Dagmar Barth-Weingarten, Elisabeth Reber and Margret Selting, 81–103. Amsterdam: Benjamins.

Ogden, Richard. 2012a. The phonetics of talk-in-interaction: introduction to the special issue. *Language and Speech* 55(1):3–11.

Ogden, Richard. 2012b. Making sense of outliers. *Phonetica* 69:48–67.

Ogden, Richard. 2013. Clicks and percussives in English conversation. *Journal of the International Phonetic Association* 43:299–320.

Ogden, Richard. 2014. *Extending phonetics: spoken and musical interaction*. Paper read at the International Conference on Conversation Analysis (ICCA) 2014, Los Angeles, CA.

Ogden, Richard and Sara Routarinne. 2005. The communicative function of final rises in Finnish intonation. *Phonetica* 62:160–75.

Ogden, Richard and Traci Walker. 2013. Phonetic resources in the construction of social actions. *Units of talk: units of action*, ed. Beatrice Szczepek Reed and Geoffrey Raymond, 217–312. Amsterdam: Benjamins.

Oh, Sun-Young. 2005. English zero-anaphora as an interactional resource. *Research on Language and Social Interaction* 38:267–302.
Oh, Sun-Young. 2006. English zero anaphora as an interactional resource II. *Discourse Studies* 8:817–46.
Oh, Sun-Young. 2007. The interactional meanings of quasi-pronouns in Korean conversation. *Person reference in interaction: linguistic, cultural, and social perspectives*, ed. Nick J. Enfield and Tanya Stivers, 203–25. Cambridge: Cambridge University Press.
Ono, Tsuyoshi and Elizabeth Couper-Kuhlen. 2007. Increments in cross-linguistic perspective: introductory remarks. *Pragmatics* 17(4):505–12.
Ono, Tsuyoshi and Sandra A. Thompson. 1994. Unattached NPs in English conversation. *Berkeley Linguistics Society* 20:402–19.
Ono, Tsuyoshi and Sandra A. Thompson. 1995. What can conversation tell us about syntax? *Alternative linguistics: descriptive and theoretical modes*, ed. Philip W. Davis, 213–71. Amsterdam: Benjamins.
Ono, Tsuyoshi and Sandra A. Thompson. 1997. Deconstructing "zero anaphora". *Berkeley Linguistics Society* 23:481–91.
Ono, Tsuyoshi, Sandra A. Thompson and Yumi Sasaki. 2012. Japanese negotiation through emerging final particles in everyday talk. *Discourse Processes* 49:243–72.
Pekarek Doehler, Simona. 2011a. Emergent grammar for all practical purposes: the on-line formatting of left and right dislocations in French conversation. *Constructions: emerging and emergent*, ed. Peter Auer and Stefan Pfänder, 45–87. Berlin: de Gruyter.
Pekarek Doehler, Simona. 2011b. Clause-combining and the sequencing of actions: projector constructions in French conversation. *Subordination in conversation: a cross-linguistic perspective*, ed. Ritva Laury and Ryoko Suzuki, 103–48. Amsterdam: Benjamins.
Pekarek Doehler, Simona, Elwys De Stefani and Anne-Sylvie Horlacher. 2015. *Time and emergence in grammar: dislocation, topicalization and hanging topic in French talk-in-interaction*. Amsterdam: Benjamins.
Pekarek Doehler, Simona and Anne-Sylvie Horlacher. 2013. The patching-together of pivots in talk-in-interaction: on "double dislocations" in French. *Journal of Pragmatics* 54:92–108. (Special issue on pivot constructions in talk-in-interaction, ed. Niklas Norén and Per Linell).
Peräkylä, Anssi and Johanna Ruusuvuori. 2006. Facial expression in an assessment. *Video analysis: methodology and methods*, ed. Hubert Knoblauch, Bernt Schnettler, Jürgen Raab and Hans-Georg Soeffner, 127–42. Peter Lang: Frankfurt.
Peräkylä, Anssi and Marja-Leena Sorjonen (eds.). 2012. *Emotion in interaction*. New York: Oxford University Press.
Persson, Rasmus. 2013. Intonation and sequential organization: formulations in French talk-in-interaction. *Journal of Pragmatics* 57:19–38.
Persson, Rasmus. 2014. *Ressources linguistiques pour la gestion de l'intersubjectivité dans la parole en interaction: analyses conversationnelles et phonétiques*. PhD dissertation, Lund: Lund University.
Persson, Rasmus. 2015. Registering and repair-initiating repeats in French talk-in-interaction. *Discourse Studies* 17(5):583–608.
Pfeiffer, Martin C. 2010. Zur syntaktischen Struktur von Selbstreparaturen im Deutschen. *Gesprächsforschung – Online-Zeitschift zur verbalen Interaktion* 11:183–207. (www.gespraechsforschung-ozs.de).
Pfeiffer, Martin C. 2015. *Selbstreparaturen im Deutschen: syntaktische und interaktionale Analysen*. Berlin: de Gruyter.

Pike, Kenneth L. 1945. *The intonation of American English*. Ann Arbor: University of Michigan Publications.

Plug, Leendert. 2014. On (or not on) the "upgrading-downgrading continuum": the case of "prosodic marking" in self-repair. *Prosodie und Phonetik in der Interaktion. Prosody and phonetics in interaction*, ed. Dagmar Barth-Weingarten and Beatrice Szczepek Reed, 70–85. Radolfzell: Verlag für Gesprächsforschung (www.verlag-gespraechsforschung.de).

Podesva, Robert J. 2007. Phonation type as a stylistic variable: the use of falsetto in constructing a persona. *Journal of Sociolinguistics* 11(4):478–504.

Pomerantz, Anita. 1978a. Compliment responses: notes on the co-operation of multiple constraints. *Studies in the organization of conversational interaction*, ed. Jim Schenkein, 79–112. New York: Academic Press.

Pomerantz, Anita. 1978b. Attributions of responsibilities: blamings. *Sociology* 12:115–21.

Pomerantz, Anita. 1980. Telling my side: "limited access" as a "fishing" device. *Sociological Inquiry* 50:186–98.

Pomerantz, Anita. 1984a. Agreeing and disagreeing with assessments: some features of preferred/dispreferred turn shapes. *Structures of social action: studies in conversation analysis*, ed. J. Maxwell Atkinson and John Heritage, 57–101. Cambridge: Cambridge University Press.

Pomerantz, Anita. 1984b. Pursuing a response. *Structures of social action: studies in conversation analysis*, ed. J. Maxwell Atkinson and John Heritage, 152–63. Cambridge: Cambridge University Press.

Pomerantz, Anita. 1986. Extreme case formulations: a way of legitimizing claims. *Human Studies* 9:219–29.

Pomerantz, Anita. 1988. Offering a candidate answer: an information seeking strategy. *Communication Monographs* 55(1):360–73.

Pope, Emily. 1976. *Questions and answers in English*. The Hague: Mouton.

Potter, Jonathan and Alexa Hepburn. 2010. Putting aspiration into words: "laugh particles", managing descriptive trouble and modulating action. *Journal of Pragmatics* 42:1543–55.

Quasthoff, Uta M. 2001. Erzählen als interaktive Gesprächsstruktur. *Text- und Gesprächslinguistik*. HSK 16. Vol. 2: *Gesprächslinguistik*, ed. Klaus Brinker et al., 1293–1309. Berlin: de Gruyter.

Quirk, Randolph, Sidney Greenbaum, Geoffrey Leech and Jan Svartvik. 1985. *A comprehensive grammar of the English language*. London: Longmans.

Raclaw, Joshua. 2013. *Indexing inferables and organizational shifts: no-prefaces in English conversation*. PhD thesis, Department of Linguistics, University of Colorado, Boulder, CO.

Rauniomaa, Mirka and Tiina Keisanen. 2012. Two multimodal formats for responding to requests. *Journal of Pragmatics* 44:829–42.

Raymond, Geoffrey. 2000. *The structure of responding*. Unpublished PhD thesis, University of California, Los Angeles, CA.

Raymond, Geoffrey. 2003. Grammar and social organization: *yes/no* interrogatives and the structure of responding. *American Sociological Review* 68:939–67.

Raymond, Geoffrey. 2004. Prompting action: the stand-alone *so* in ordinary conversation. *Research on Language and Social Interaction* 37:185–218.

Raymond, Geoffrey. 2010. Prosodic variation in responses: the case of type-conforming responses to *yes/no* interrogatives. *Prosody in interaction*, ed. Dagmar Barth-Weingarten, Elisabeth Reber and Margret Selting, 109–29. Amsterdam: Benjamins.

Raymond, Geoffrey. 2013. At the intersection of turn and sequence organization: on the relevance of "slots" in type-conforming responses to polar interrogatives. *Units of talk:*

units of action, ed. Beatrice Szczepek Reed and Geoffrey Raymond, 169–206. Amsterdam: Benjamins.

Raymond, Geoffrey and John Heritage. 2006. The epistemics of social relationships: owning grandchildren. *Language in Society* 35:677–705.

Raymond, Geoffrey and John Heritage. 2013. One question after another: same-turn-repair in the formation of *yes/no* type initiating actions. *Conversational repair and human understanding*, ed. Makoto Hayashi, Geoffrey Raymond and Jack Sidnell, 135–71. Cambridge: Cambridge University Press.

Reber, Elisabeth. 2012. *Affectivity in interaction: sound objects in English*. Amsterdam: Benjamins.

Reber, Elisabeth and Elizabeth Couper-Kuhlen. 2010. Interjektionen zwischen Lexikon und Vokalität: Lexem oder Lautobjekt? *Sprache intermedial: Stimme und Schrift, Bild und Ton* (Jahrbuch 2009 des Instituts für Deutsche Sprache), ed. Arnulf Deppermann and Angelika Linke, 69–96. Berlin: de Gruyter.

Reisman, Karl. 1974. Contrapuntal conversations in an Antiguan village. *Explorations in the ethnography of speaking*, ed. Richard Bauman and Joel Sherzer, 110–24. London: Cambridge University Press.

Rendle-Short, Johanna. 2007. *Catherine, you're wasting your time*: address terms within the Australian political interview. *Journal of Pragmatics* 39:1503–25.

Rendle-Short, Johanna. 2010. *Mate* as a term of address in ordinary interaction. *Journal of Pragmatics* 42:1201–18.

Rieger, Caroline. 2003. Repetitions as self-repair strategies in English and German conversations. *Journal of Pragmatics* 35:47–69.

Robinson, Jeffrey D. 2006. Managing trouble responsibility and relationship during conversational repair. *Communication Monographs* 73:137–61.

Robinson, Jeffrey D. 2013. Epistemics, action formation, and other-initiation of repair: the case of partial questioning repeats. *Conversational repair and human understanding*, ed. Makoto Hayashi, Geoffrey Raymond and Jack Sidnell, 261–92. Cambridge: Cambridge University Press.

Robinson, Jeffrey D. and John Heritage. 2005. The structure of patients' presenting concerns: the completion relevance of current symptoms. *Social Science and Medicine* 61:481–93.

Robinson, Jeffrey D. and Heidi Kevoe-Feldman. 2010. Using full repeats to initiate repair on others' questions. *Research on Language and Social Interaction* 43(3):232–59.

Rossano, Federico. 2010. Questioning and responding in Italian. *Journal of Pragmatics* 42:2756–71.

Rossano, Federico. 2013. Gaze in conversation. *The handbook of conversation analysis*, ed. Jack Sidnell and Tanya Stivers, 308–29. Chichester: Wiley-Blackwell.

Rossano, Federico and Katja Liebal. 2014. "Requests" and "offers" in orangutans and human infants. *Requesting in social interaction*, ed. Paul Drew and Elizabeth Couper-Kuhlen, 335–64. Amsterdam: Benjamins.

Rossi, Giovanni. 2012. Bilateral and unilateral requests: the use of imperatives and *mi X?* interrogatives in Italian. *Discourse Processes* 49:426–58.

Rossi, Giovanni. 2014. When do people not use language to make requests? *Requesting in social interaction*, ed. Paul Drew and Elizabeth Couper-Kuhlen, 303–34. Amsterdam: Benjamins.

Ruusuvuori, Johanna. 2007. Managing affect: integration of empathy and problem-solving in health care encounters. *Discourse Studies* 9:597–622.

Ruusuvuori, Johanna. 2013. Emotion, affect and conversation. *The handbook of conversation analysis*, ed. Jack Sidnell and Tanya Stivers, 330–49. Chichester: Wiley-Blackwell.

Ryave, Alan L. 1978. On the achievement of a series of stories. *Studies in the organization of conversational interaction*, ed. Jim Schenkein, 113–32. New York: Academic Press.

Sacks, Harvey. 1971. Das Erzählen von Geschichten innerhalb von Unterhaltungen. *Zur Soziologie der Sprache*, ed. Rolf Kjolseth and Fritz Sack, 307–14. Opladen: Westdeutscher Verlag.

Sacks, Harvey. 1974. An analysis of the course of a joke's telling in conversation. *Explorations in the ethnography of speaking*, ed. Richard Baumann and Joel Sherzer, 337–53. Cambridge: Cambridge University Press.

Sacks, Harvey. 1984. Notes on methodology. *Structures of social action: studies in conversation analysis*, ed. J. Maxwell Atkinson and John Heritage, 21–7. Cambridge: Cambridge University Press.

Sacks, Harvey. 1986. Some considerations of a story told in ordinary conversation. *Poetics* 15:127–38.

Sacks, Harvey. 1987. On the preference for agreement and contiguity in sequences in conversation. *Talk and social organization*, ed. Graham Button and John R. E. Lee, 56–69. Bristol: Multilingual Matters.

Sacks, Harvey. 1992a. *Lectures on conversation*, vol. 1, ed. Gail Jefferson. Oxford: Blackwell.

Sacks, Harvey. 1992b. *Lectures on conversation*, vol. 2, ed. Gail Jefferson. Oxford: Blackwell.

Sacks, Harvey and Emanuel A. Schegloff. 1979. Two preferences in the organization of reference to persons in conversation and their interaction. *Everyday language: studies in ethnomethodology*, ed. George Psathas, 15–21. New York: Irvington.

Sacks, Harvey, Emanuel A. Schegloff and Gail Jefferson. 1974. A simplest systematics for the organization of turn-taking for conversation. *Language* 50:696–735.

Sadock, Jerrold M. and Arnold Zwicky. 1985. Speech act distinctions in syntax. *Language typology and syntactic description.* Vol. 1: *Clause structure*, ed. Timothy Shopen, 115–96. Cambridge: Cambridge University Press.

Sánchez-Ayala, Ivo. 2003. Constructions as resources for interaction: lists in English and Spanish conversation. *Discourse Studies* 5:323–49.

Schegloff, Emanuel A. 1968. Sequencing in conversational openings. *American Anthropologist* 70:1075–95.

Schegloff, Emanuel A. 1972. Notes on a conversational practice: formulating place. *Studies in social interaction*, ed. David Sudnow, 75–119. New York: The Free Press.

Schegloff, Emanuel A. 1979. The relevance of repair to syntax-for-conversation. *Discourse syntax*, ed. Talmy Givón, 261–86. New York: Academic Press.

Schegloff, Emanuel A. 1980. Preliminaries to preliminaries: *can I ask you a question?*. *Sociological Inquiry* 50:104–52.

Schegloff, Emanuel A. 1982. Discourse as an interactional achievement: some uses of *uh huh* and other things that come between sentences. *Analyzing discourse: text and talk*, ed. Deborah Tannen, 71–93. Washington, DC: Georgetown University Press.

Schegloff, Emanuel A. 1984. On some questions and ambiguities in conversation. *Structures of social action: studies in conversation analysis*, ed. J. Maxwell Atkinson and John Heritage, 28–52. Cambridge: Cambridge University Press.

Schegloff, Emanuel A. 1987a. Recycled turn beginnings: a precise repair mechanism in conversation's turn-taking organisation. *Talk and social organisation*, ed. Graham Button and John R. E. Lee, 70–85. Clevedon: Multilingual Matters.

Schegloff, Emanuel A. 1987b. Analyzing single episodes of interaction: an exercise in conversation analysis. *Social Psychological Quarterly* 50:101–14.

Schegloff, Emanuel A. 1987c. Some sources of misunderstanding in talk-in-interaction. *Linguistics* 25:201–18.

Schegloff, Emanuel A. 1987d. Between micro and macro: contexts and other connections. *The micro-macro link*, ed. Jeffrey C. Alexander et al., 207–34. Berkeley, CA: University of California Press.

Schegloff, Emanuel A. 1988a. Discourse as an interactional achievement II: an exercise in conversation analysis. *Linguistics in context: connecting observation and understanding*, ed. Deborah Tannen, 135–58. Norwood, NJ: Ablex.

Schegloff, Emanuel A. 1988b. Presequences and indirection: applying speech act theory to ordinary conversation. *Journal of Pragmatics* 12:55–62.

Schegloff, Emanuel A. 1988c. On an actual virtual servo-mechanism for guessing bad news: a single case conjecture. *Social Problems* 35:442–57.

Schegloff, Emanuel A. 1990. On the organization of sequences as a source of "coherence" in talk-in-interaction. *Conversational organization and its development*, ed. Bruce Dorval, 51–77. Norwood, NJ: Ablex.

Schegloff, Emanuel A. 1991. Issues of relevance for discourse analysis: contingency in action, interaction, and co-participant context. *Computational and conversational discourse*, ed. Eduard H. Hovy and Donia R. Scott, 3–35. Berlin: Springer-Verlag.

Schegloff, Emanuel A. 1992. Repair after next turn: the last structurally provided defense of intersubjectivity in conversation. *American Journal of Sociology* 97:1295–345.

Schegloff, Emanuel A. 1996a. Confirming allusions: towards an empirical account of actions. *American Journal of Sociology* 102:161–216.

Schegloff, Emanuel A. 1996b. Turn organization: one intersection of grammar and interaction. *Interaction and grammar*, ed. Elinor Ochs, Emanuel A. Schegloff and Sandra A. Thompson, 52–133. Cambridge: Cambridge University Press.

Schegloff, Emanuel A. 1996c. Some practices for referring to persons in talk-in-interaction: a partial sketch of a systematics. *Studies in anaphora*, ed. Barbara A. Fox, 437–85. Amsterdam: Benjamins.

Schegloff, Emanuel A. 1997a. Practices and actions: boundary cases of other-initiated repair. *Discourse Processes* 23:499–545.

Schegloff, Emanuel A. 1997b. Third turn repair. *Towards a social science of language: papers in honor of William Labov.* Vol. 2: *Social interaction and discourse structures*, ed. Gregory R. Guy, Feagin Crawford, Deborah Schiffrin and John Baugh, 31–40. Amsterdam: Benjamins.

Schegloff, Emanuel A. 1997c. "Narrative analysis" thirty years later. *Journal of Narrative and Life History* 7:97–106.

Schegloff, Emanuel A. 1998. Reflections on studying prosody in talk-in-interaction. *Language and Speech* 41:235–63.

Schegloff, Emanuel A. 2000a. On turns' possible completion, more or less: increments and trail-offs. Paper read at the EuroConference on Interactional Linguistics 2000, Spa, Belgium.

Schegloff, Emanuel A. 2000b. Overlapping talk and the organization of turn-taking for conversation. *Language in Society* 29:1–63.

Schegloff, Emanuel A. 2000c. When others initiate repair. *Applied Linguistics* 21:205–43.

Schegloff, Emanuel A. 2000d. On granularity. *Annual Review of Sociology* 26:715–20.

Schegloff, Emanuel A. 2001. Conversation analysis: a project in process: "increments". Forum Lecture, LSA Linguistics Institute, University of California, Santa Barbara, CA.

Schegloff, Emanuel A. 2004. On dispensability. *Research on Language and Social Interaction* 37:95–149.

Schegloff, Emanuel A. 2006. Interaction: the infrastructure for social institutions, the natural ecological niche for language, and the arena in which culture is enacted. *Roots of human sociality: culture, cognition and interaction*, ed. Nick J. Enfield and Stephen C. Levinson, 70–96. Oxford: Berg.

Schegloff, Emanuel A. 2007a. *Sequence organization in interaction: a primer in conversation analysis*. Cambridge: Cambridge University Press.

Schegloff, Emanuel A. 2007b. Conveying who you are: the presentation of self, strictly speaking. *Person reference in interaction: linguistic, cultural, and social perspectives*, ed. Nick J. Enfield and Tanya Stivers, 123–48. Cambridge: Cambridge University Press.

Schegloff, Emanuel A. 2009a. One perspective on conversation analysis: comparative perspectives. *Conversation analysis: comparative perspectives*, ed. Jack Sidnell, 257–406. Cambridge: Cambridge University Press.

Schegloff, Emanuel A. 2009b. A practice for (re-)exiting a sequence: *and/but/so* + *uh(m)* + silence. *Language in life, and a life in language: Jacob Mey – a Festschrift*, ed. Bruce Fraser and Ken Turner, 365–74. Leiden: BRILL.

Schegloff, Emanuel A. 2010. Some other *uh(m)*s. *Discourse Processes* 47:130–74.

Schegloff, Emanuel A. 2013. Ten operations in self-initiated, same-turn repair. *Conversational repair and human understanding*, ed. Makoto Hayashi, Geoffrey Raymond and Jack Sidnell, 41–70. Cambridge: Cambridge University Press.

Schegloff, Emanuel A., Gail Jefferson and Harvey Sacks. 1977. The preference for self-correction in the organization of repair in conversation. *Language* 53: 361–82.

Schegloff, Emanuel A. and Gene H. Lerner. 2009. Beginning to respond: *well*-prefaced responses to *wh*-questions. *Research on Language and Social Interaction* 42:91–115.

Schegloff, Emanuel A., Elinor Ochs and Sandra A. Thompson. 1996. Introduction. *Interaction and grammar*, ed. Elinor Ochs, Emanuel A. Schegloff and Sandra A. Thompson, 1–51. Cambridge: Cambridge University Press.

Schegloff, Emanuel A. and Harvey Sacks. 1973. Opening up closings. *Semiotica* 8:289–327.

Scheutz, Hannes. 1992. Apokoinukonstruktionen: gegenwartssprachliche Erscheinungsformen und Aspekte ihrer historischen Entwicklung. *Dialekte im Wandel*, ed. Andreas Weiss, 243–64. Göppingen: Kümmerle.

Scheutz, Hannes. 1997. Satzinitiale Voranstellung im gesprochenen Deutsch als Mittel der Themensteuerung und Referenzkonstitution. *Syntax des gesprochenen Deutsch*, ed. Peter Schlobinski, 27–54. Opladen: Westdeutscher Verlag.

Scheutz, Hannes. 2005. Pivot constructions in spoken German. *Syntax and lexis in conversation*, ed. Auli Hakulinen and Margret Selting, 103–28. Amsterdam: Benjamins.

Schieffelin, Bambi B. and Elinor Ochs (eds.). 1986. *Language socialization across cultures*. Cambridge: Cambridge University Press.

Schiffrin, Deborah. 1994. Making a list. *Discourse Processes* 17:377–406.

Schönfeldt, Juliane and Andrea Golato. 2003. Repair in chats: a conversation analytic approach. *Research on Language and Social Interaction* 36:241–84.

Schönherr, Beatrix. 1993. Prosodische und nonverbale Signale für Parenthesen: "Parasyntax" in Fernsehdiskussionen. *Deutsche Sprache* 21:223–43.

Schönherr, Beatrix. 1997. *Syntax – Prosodie – nonverbale Kommunikation: empirische Untersuchungen zur Interaktion sprachlicher und parasprachlicher Ausdrucksmittel im Gespräch*. Tübingen: Niemeyer.

Schröder, Ulrike, Thomas Johnen, Mariana Carneiro Mendes, Caroline Caputo Pires, Diogo Henrique Alves da Silva, Thiago da Cunha Nascimento and Flavia Fidelis de

Paula. 2016. Um sistema para transcrever fala-em-interação: GAT 2. Portuguese translation and adaptation of Selting, Margret et al.: Gesprächsanalytisches Transkriptionssystem 2. *Veredas atemática* 20(2):6–61.
Schubiger, Maria. 1958. *English intonation: its form and function.* Tübingen: Niemeyer.
Schuetze-Coburn, Stephen, Marian Shapley and Elizabeth G. Weber. 1991. Units of intonation in discourse: a comparison of acoustic and auditory analyses. *Language and Speech* 34(3):207–34.
Schulze-Wenck, Stephanie. 2005. Form and function of "first verbs" in talk-in-interaction. *Syntax and lexis in conversation*, ed. Auli Hakulinen and Margret Selting, 319–48. Amsterdam: Benjamins.
Schwitalla, Johannes. 2012. *Gesprochenes Deutsch: eine Einführung* (4th ed., revised and extended). Berlin: Erich Schmidt Verlag.
Scollon, Ron. 1976. *Conversations with a one year old: a case study of the developmental foundation of syntax.* Honolulu: University of Hawai'i Press.
Searle, John R. 1969. *Speech acts: an essay in the philosophy of language.* Cambridge: Cambridge University Press.
Searle, John R. 1976. A classification of illocutionary acts. *Language in Society* 5:1–23.
Selting, Margret. 1987a. *Verständigungsprobleme.* Tübingen: Niemeyer.
Selting, Margret. 1987b. Reparaturen und lokale Verstehensprobleme – oder: zur Binnenstruktur von Reparatursequenzen. *Linguistische Berichte* 108:128–49.
Selting, Margret. 1987c. Fremdkorrekturen als Manifestationsformen von Verständigungsproblemen. *Zeitschrift für Sprachwissenschaft* 6:37–58.
Selting, Margret. 1988. The role of intonation in the organization of repair and problem handling sequences in conversation. *Journal of Pragmatics* 12:293–322.
Selting, Margret. 1992. Intonation as a contextualization device: case studies on the role of prosody, especially intonation, in contextualizing storytelling in conversation. *The contextualization of language*, ed. Peter Auer and Aldo di Luzio, 233–58. Amsterdam: Benjamins.
Selting, Margret. 1993. Voranstellungen vor den Satz: zur grammatischen Form und interaktiven Funktion von Linksversetzung und Freiem Thema im Deutschen. *Zeitschrift für Germanistische Linguistik* 21:291–319.
Selting, Margret. 1994a. Konstruktionen am Satzrand als interaktive Ressource in natürlichen Gesprächen. *Was determiniert Wortstellungsvariation? Studien zu einem Interaktionsfeld von Grammatik, Pragmatik und Sprachtypologie*, ed. Brigitte Haftka, 299–318. Opladen: Westdeutscher Verlag.
Selting, Margret. 1994b. Emphatic speech style: with special focus on the prosodic signalling of heightened emotive involvement in conversation. *Journal of Pragmatics* 22:375–408.
Selting, Margret. 1994c. Question intonation revisited. *Proceedings of the 7th International Phonology Meeting Phonologica 1992*, ed. Wolfgang Dressler, Martin Prinzhorn and John R. Rennison, 243–56. Torino: Rosenberg & Sellier.
Selting, Margret. 1995a. *Prosodie im Gespräch: Aspekte einer interaktionalen Phonologie der Konversation.* Tübingen: Niemeyer.
Selting, Margret. 1995b. Der "mögliche Satz" als interaktiv relevante syntaktische Kategorie. *Linguistische Berichte* 158:298–325.
Selting, Margret. 1995c. Sprechstile als Kontextualisierungshinweise: die sprechstilistische Kontextualisierung konversationeller Aktivitäten, am Beispiel mündlicher Erzählungen in Gesprächen. *Stilfragen: Jahrbuch 1994 des Instituts für deutsche Sprache*, ed. Gerhard Stickel, 225–56. Berlin: de Gruyter.

Selting, Margret. 1996a. On the interplay of syntax and prosody in the constitution of turn-constructional units and turns in conversation. *Pragmatics* 6:357–88.

Selting, Margret. 1996b. Prosody as an activity-type distinctive cue in conversation: the case of so-called "astonished" questions in repair. *Prosody in conversation: interactional studies*, ed. Elizabeth Couper-Kuhlen and Margret Selting, 231–70. Cambridge: Cambridge University Press.

Selting, Margret. 1997a. Sogenannte Ellipsen als interaktiv relevante Konstruktionen? Ein neuer Versuch über die Reichweite und Grenzen des Ellipsenbegriffs für die Analyse gesprochener Sprache in Interaktionen. *Syntax des gesprochenen Deutsch*, ed. Peter Schlobinski, 117–56. Opladen: Westdeutscher Verlag.

Selting, Margret. 1997b. Interaktionale Stilistik: methodologische Aspekte der Analyse von Sprechstilen. *Sprech- und Gesprächsstile*, ed. Margret Selting and Barbara Sandig, 9–43. Berlin: de Gruyter.

Selting, Margret. 1999a. Communicative style. *Handbook of pragmatics*, ed. Jef Verschueren, Jan-Ola Östman, Jan Blommaert and Chris Bulcaen, 1–24. Amsterdam: Benjamins.

Selting, Margret. 1999b. Kontinuität und Wandel der Verbstellung von ahd. *wanta* bis gwd. *weil*: zur historischen und vergleichenden Syntax der *weil*-Konstruktionen. *Zeitschrift für Germanistische Linguistik* 27:167–204.

Selting, Margret. 2000. The construction of units in conversational talk. *Language in Society* 29:477–517.

Selting, Margret. 2001a. Fragments of units as deviant cases of unit-production in conversational talk. *Studies in interactional linguistics*, ed. Margret Selting and Elizabeth Couper-Kuhlen, 229–58. Amsterdam: Benjamins.

Selting, Margret. 2001b. Probleme der Transkription verbalen und paraverbalen/prosodischen Verhaltens. *Text- und Gesprächslinguistik: ein internationales Handbuch zeitgenössischer Forschung. Vol. 2: Gesprächslinguistik*, ed. Klaus Brinker, Gerd Antos, Wolfgang Heinemann and Sven F. Sager, 1059–68. Berlin: de Gruyter.

Selting, Margret. 2004a. Regionalized intonation in its conversational context. *Regional variation in intonation*, ed. Peter Gilles and Jörg Peters, 49–73. Tübingen: Niemeyer.

Selting, Margret. 2004b. Listen: sequenzielle und prosodische Struktur einer kommunikativen Praktik – eine Untersuchung im Rahmen der Interaktionalen Linguistik. *Zeitschrift für Sprachwissenschaft* 23:1–46.

Selting, Margret. 2005. Syntax and prosody as methods for the construction and identification of turn-constructional units in conversation. *Syntax and lexis in conversation*, ed. Auli Hakulinen and Margret Selting, 17–44. Amsterdam: Benjamins.

Selting, Margret. 2007. Lists as embedded structures and the prosody of list construction as an interactional resource. *Journal of Pragmatics* 39:483–526.

Selting, Margret. 2008. Interactional stylistics and style as a contextualization cue. *Rhetorik und Stilistik. Rhetoric and stylistics: an international handbook of historical and systematic research*, ed. Ulla Fix and Andreas Gardt, 1038–53. Berlin: de Gruyter.

Selting, Margret. 2009. Communicative style. *The pragmatics of interaction*, ed. Sigurd D'hondt, Jan-Ola Östman and Jef Verschueren, 20–39. Amsterdam: Benjamins.

Selting, Margret. 2010. Affectivity in conversational storytelling: an analysis of displays of anger or indignation in complaint stories. *Pragmatics* 20:229–77.

Selting, Margret. 2012. Complaint stories and subsequent complaint stories with affect displays. *Journal of Pragmatics* 44:387–415.

Selting, Margret. 2013. Verbal, vocal, and visual practices in conversational interaction. *Body – language – communication: an international handbook on multimodality in*

human interaction, ed. Cornelia Müller, Alan Cienki, Ellen Fricke, Silva H. Ladewig, David McNeill and Sedinha Teßendorf, 589–609. Berlin: de Gruyter.
Selting, Margret. 2016. Praktiken des Sprechens und Interagierens im Gespräch aus der Sicht von Konversationsanalyse und Interaktionaler Linguistik. *Sprachliche und kommunikative Praktiken*. Jahrbuch 2015 des IDS, ed. Arnulf Deppermann, Helmuth Feilke and Angelika Linke, 27–56. Berlin: de Gruyter.
Selting, Margret, Peter Auer, Birgit Barden, Jörg Bergmann, Elizabeth Couper-Kuhlen, Susanne Günthner, Uta Quasthoff, Christoph Meier, Peter Schlobinski and Susanne Uhmann. 1998. Gesprächsanalytisches Transkriptionssystem (GAT). *Linguistische Berichte* 173:91–122.
Selting, Margret, Peter Auer, Dagmar Barth-Weingarten, Jörg Bergmann, Pia Bergmann, Karin Birkner, Elizabeth Couper-Kuhlen, Arnulf Deppermann, Peter Gilles, Susanne Günthner, Martin Hartung, Friederike Kern, Christine Mertzlufft, Christian Meyer, Miriam Morek, Frank Oberzaucher, Jörg Peters, Uta Quasthoff, Wilfried Schütte, Anja Stukenbrock and Susanne Uhmann. 2009. Gesprächsanalytisches Transkriptionssystem 2 (GAT 2). *Gesprächsforschung – Online-Zeitschrift zur verbalen Interaktion* 10:353–402, (www.gespraechsforschung-ozs.de).
Selting, Margret and Elizabeth Couper-Kuhlen. 2000. Argumente für die Entwicklung einer interaktionalen Linguistik. *Gesprächsforschung – Online-Zeitschrift zur verbalen Interaktion* 1:76–95 (www.gespraechsforschung-ozs.de).
Selting, Margret and Elizabeth Couper-Kuhlen (eds.). 2001a. *Studies in interactional linguistics*. Amsterdam: Benjamins.
Selting, Margret and Elizabeth Couper-Kuhlen. 2001b. Forschungsprogramm "Interaktionale Linguistik". *Linguistische Berichte* 187:257–87.
Seppänen, Eeva-Leena and Ritva Laury. 2007. Complement clauses as turn continuations: the Finnish *et(tä)*-clause. *Pragmatics* 17(4):553–72.
Shaw, Rebecca and Celia Kitzinger. 2012. Compliments on a home birth helpline. *Research on Language and Social Interaction* 45(3):213–44.
Sicoli, Mark A. 2010. Shifting voices with participant roles: voice qualities and speech registers in Mesoamerica. *Language in Society* 39:521–53.
Sidnell, Jack. 2001. Conversational turn-taking in a Caribbean English Creole. *Journal of Pragmatics* 33(8):1263–90.
Sidnell, Jack. 2006. Coordinating gesture, gaze and talk in re-enactments. *Research on Language and Social Interaction* 39:377–409.
Sidnell, Jack. 2007a. *Look*-prefaced turns in first and second position: launching, interceding and redirecting action. *Discourse Studies* 9:387–408.
Sidnell, Jack. 2007b. Comparative studies in conversation analysis. *Annual Review of Anthropology* 36:229–44.
Sidnell, Jack. 2007c. Repairing person reference in a small Carribean community. *Person reference in interaction: linguistic, cultural, and social perspectives*, ed. Nick J. Enfield and Tanya Stivers, 281–308. Cambridge: Cambridge University Press.
Sidnell, Jack (ed.). 2009. *Conversation analysis: comparative perspectives*. Cambridge: Cambridge University Press.
Sidnell, Jack. 2010. *Conversation analysis: an introduction*. Oxford: Wiley-Blackwell.
Sidnell, Jack. 2012. Turn-continuation by self and by other. *Discourse Processes* 49: 314–37.
Sidnell, Jack and Rebecca Barnes. 2013. Alternative, subsequent descriptions. *Conversational repair and human understanding*, ed. Makoto Hayashi, Geoffrey Raymond and Jack Sidnell, 322–42. Cambridge: Cambridge University Press.

Sidnell, Jack and Nick J. Enfield. 2012. Language diversity and social action: a third locus of linguistic relativity. *Current Anthropology* 53:302–33.

Sidnell, Jack and Nick J. Enfield. 2014. The ontology of action, in interaction. *The Cambridge handbook of linguistic anthropology*, ed. Nick J. Enfield, Paul Kockelman and Jack Sidnell, 423–46. Cambridge: Cambridge University Press.

Sidnell, Jack and Tanya Stivers (eds.). 2013. *The handbook of conversation analysis*. Chichester: Wiley-Blackwell.

Silverstein, Michael. 1976. Shifters, linguistic categories, and cultural description. *Meaning in anthropology*, ed. Keith Basso and Henry A. Selby, 11–55. Albuquerque, NM: University of New Mexico Press.

Silverstein, Michael. 2001. The limits of awareness. *Linguistic anthropology: a reader*, ed. Alessandro Duranti, 382–401. Malden: Blackwell.

Şimşek, Yazgül. 2012. *Sequenzielle und prosodische Aspekte der Sprecher-Hörer-Interaktion im Türkendeutschen*. Münster: Waxmann.

Sorjonen, Marja-Leena. 1996. On repeats and responses in Finnish conversations. *Interaction and grammar*, ed. Elinor Ochs, Emanuel A. Schegloff and Sandra A. Thompson, 277–327. Cambridge: Cambridge University Press.

Sorjonen, Marja-Leena. 2001a. *Responding in conversation: a study of response particles in Finnish*. Amsterdam: Benjamins.

Sorjonen, Marja-Leena. 2001b. Simple answers to polar questions. *Studies in interactional linguistics*, ed. Margret Selting and Elizabeth Couper-Kuhlen, 405–31. Amsterdam: Benjamins.

Sorjonen, Marja-Leena and Auli Hakulinen. 2009. Alternative responses to assessments. *Conversation analysis: comparative perspectives*, ed. Jack Sidnell, 281–303. Cambridge: Cambridge University Press.

Sorjonen, Marja-Leena and Anssi Peräkylä. 2012. Introduction. *Emotion in interaction*, ed. Anssi Peräkylä and Marja-Leena Sorjonen, 3–15. New York: Oxford University Press.

Sorjonen, Marja-Leena and Liisa Raevaara. 2014. On the grammatical form of requests at the convenience store: requesting as embodied action. *Requesting in social interaction*, ed. Paul Drew and Elizabeth Couper-Kuhlen, 243–68. Amsterdam: Benjamins.

Steensig, Jakob. 2001. Notes on turn construction methods in Danish and Turkish conversations. *Studies in interactional linguistics*, ed. Margret Selting and Elizabeth Couper-Kuhlen, 259–86. Amsterdam: Benjamins.

Steensig, Jakob and Birte Asmuss. 2005. Notes on disaligning *yes but* initiated utterances in German and Danish conversations: two construction types for dispreferred responses. *Syntax and lexis in conversation*, ed. Auli Hakulinen and Margret Selting, 349–73. Amsterdam: Benjamins.

Steensig, Jakob and Trine Heinemann. 2013. When *yes* is not enough – as an answer to a *yes/no* question. *Units of talk: units of action*, ed. Beatrice Szczepek Reed and Geoffrey Raymond, 207–41. Amsterdam: Benjamins.

Steensig, Jakob and Trine Heinemann. 2014. The social and moral work of modal constructions in granting remote requests. *Requesting in social interaction*, ed. Paul Drew and Elizabeth Couper-Kuhlen, 145–70. Amsterdam: Benjamins.

Steensig, Jakob and Tine Larsen. 2008. Affiliative and disaffiliative uses of *you say x* questions. *Discourse Studies* 10:113–33.

Stevanovic, Melisa and Anssi Peräkylä. 2012. Deontic authority in interaction: the right to announce, propose, and decide. *Research on Language and Social Interaction* 45:297–321.

Stevanovic, Melisa and Jan Svennevig. 2015. Epistemics and deontics in conversational directives. *Journal of Pragmatics* 78:1–6.

Stivers, Tanya. 2004. *No no no* and other types of multiple sayings in social interaction. *Human Communication Research* 30(2):260–93.

Stivers, Tanya. 2005. Modified repeats: one method for asserting primary rights from second position. *Research on Language and Social Interaction* 38:131–58.

Stivers, Tanya. 2007. Alternative recognitionals in initial references to persons. *Person reference in interaction: linguistic, cultural, and social perspectives*, ed. Nick J. Enfield and Tanya Stivers, 73–96. Cambridge: Cambridge University Press.

Stivers, Tanya. 2008. Stance, alignment, and affiliation during storytelling: when nodding is a token of affiliation. *Research on Language and Social Interaction* 41:31–57.

Stivers, Tanya. 2010. An overview of the question-response system in American English conversation. *Journal of Pragmatics* 42:2772–81.

Stivers, Tanya. 2011. Morality and question design: *of course* as contesting a presupposition of askability. *The morality of knowledge in conversation*, ed. Tanya Stivers, Lorenza Mondada and Jakob Steensig, 82–106. Cambridge: Cambridge University Press.

Stivers, Tanya. 2013. Sequence organization. *The handbook of conversation analysis*, ed. Jack Sidnell and Tanya Stivers, 191–209. Chichester: Wiley-Blackwell.

Stivers, Tanya, Nick J. Enfield, Penelope Brown, Christina Englert, Makoto Hayashi, Trine Heinemann, Gertie Hoymann, Federico Rossano, Jan P. De Ruiter, Kyung-Eun Yoon and Stephen C. Levinson. 2009. Universals and cultural variation in turn-taking in conversation. *Proceedings of the National Academy of Sciences of the United States of America (PNAS)* 106:10587–92.

Stivers, Tanya, Nick J. Enfield and Stephen C. Levinson. 2007. Person reference in interaction. *Person reference in interaction: linguistic, cultural, and social perspectives*, ed. Nick J. Enfield and Tanya Stivers, 1–20. Cambridge: Cambridge University Press.

Stivers, Tanya, Nick J. Enfield and Stephen C. Levinson. 2010. Question-response sequences in conversation across ten languages. *Journal of Pragmatics* 42:2615–860.

Stivers, Tanya and Makoto Hayashi. 2010. Transformative answers: one way to resist a question's constraints. *Language in Society* 39:1–25.

Stivers, Tanya and Jeffrey D. Robinson. 2006. A preference for progressivity in interaction. *Language in Society* 35:367–92.

Stivers, Tanya and Federico Rossano. 2010. Mobilizing response. *Research on Language and Social Interaction* 43:3–31.

Stivers, Tanya and Jack Sidnell. 2005. Introduction: multimodal interaction. *Semiotica* 156(1/4):1–20.

Stoltenburg, Benjamin. 2002. Parenthesen im gesprochenen Deutsch. *InLiSt* 34 (www.inlist.uni-bayreuth.de/issues/34/index.htm).

Stoltenburg, Benjamin. 2007. Wenn Sätze in die Auszeit gehen . . . *Zugänge zur Grammatik der gesprochenen Sprache*, ed. Vilmos Ágel and Mathilde Hennig, 137–76. Tübingen: Niemeyer.

Streeck, Jürgen. 2002. Grammars, words, and embodied meanings: on the uses and evolution of *so* and *like*. *Journal of Communication* 52:581–96.

Streeck, Jürgen. 2009. Forward-gesturing. *Discourse Processes* 46:161–79.

Streeck, Jürgen, Charles Goodwin and Curtis LeBaron (eds.). 2011. *Embodied interaction: language and body in the material world*. Cambridge: Cambridge University Press.

Streeck, Jürgen and Ulrike Hartge. 1992. Previews: gestures at the transition place. *The contextualization of language*, ed. Peter Auer and Aldo di Luzio, 135–57. Amsterdam: Benjamins.

Svennevig, Jan. 2008. Trying the easiest solution first in other-initiation of repair. *Journal of Pragmatics* 40:333–48.

Szczepek Reed, Beatrice. 2006. *Prosodic orientation in English conversation*. London: Palgrave Macmillan.
Szczepek Reed, Beatrice. 2010. Intonation phrases in natural conversation: a participants' category? *Prosody in interaction*, ed. Dagmar Barth-Weingarten, Elisabeth Reber and Margret Selting, 191–212. Amsterdam: Benjamins.
Szczepek Reed, Beatrice. 2014. Phonetic practices for action formation: glottalization versus linking of TCU-initial vowels in German. *Journal of Pragmatics* 62:13–29.
Taleghani-Nikazm, Carmen. 2005. Contingent requests: their sequential organization and turn shape. *Research on Language and Social Interaction* 38:159–79.
Taleghani-Nikazm, Carmen. 2006. *Request sequences: the intersection of grammar, interaction and social context*. Amsterdam: Benjamins.
Tanaka, Hiroko. 1999. *Turn-taking in Japanese conversation: a study in grammar and interaction*. Amsterdam: Benjamins.
Tanaka, Hiroko. 2000a. Turn-projection in Japanese talk-in-interaction. *Research on Language and Social Interaction* 33:1–38.
Tanaka, Hiroko. 2000b. The particle *ne* as a turn-management device in Japanese conversation. *Journal of Pragmatics* 32(8):1135–76.
Tanaka, Hiroko. 2001. The implementation of possible cognitive shifts in Japanese conversation: complementizers as pivotal devices. *Studies in interactional linguistics*, ed. Margret Selting and Elizabeth Couper-Kuhlen, 81–110. Amsterdam: Benjamins.
Tanaka, Hiroko. 2004. Prosody for marking transition-relevance places in Japanese conversation: the case of turns unmarked by utterance-final objects. *Sound patterns in interaction*, ed. Elizabeth Couper-Kuhlen and Cecilia E. Ford, 63–96. Amsterdam: Benjamins.
Tanaka, Hiroko. 2005. Grammar and the timing of social action: word order and preference organization in Japanese. *Language in Society* 34:389–430.
Tanaka, Hiroko. 2008. Grammatical resources for delaying dispreferred responses in English: from a Japanese perspective. *Language in Society* 37(4):487–513.
Tanaka, Hiroko. 2010. Multimodal expressivity of the Japanese response particle *huun*: displaying involvement without topical engagement. *Prosody in interaction*, ed. Dagmar Barth-Weingarten, Elisabeth Reber and Margret Selting, 303–32. Amsterdam: Benjamins.
Tannen, Deborah. 1984. *Conversational style: analyzing talk among friends*. Norwood, NJ: Ablex.
Tannen, Deborah. 1989. *Talking voices*. Cambridge: Cambridge University Press.
Tao, Hongyin. 1996. *Units in Mandarin conversation*. Amsterdam: Benjamins.
Tao, Hongyin and Michael J. McCarthy. 2001. Understanding non-relative *which* clauses in spoken English, which is not an easy thing. *Language Sciences* 23:651–77.
Tarplee, Clare. 1996. Working on young children's utterances: prosodic aspects of repetition during picture labelling. *Prosody in conversation*, ed. Elizabeth Couper-Kuhlen and Margret Selting, 406–35. Cambridge: Cambridge University Press.
Terasaki, Alene K. 1976. *Pre-announcement sequences in conversation*. Social Science Working Paper 99. School of Social Science, University of California, Irvine, CA. (Published as Terasaki 2004: see below.)
Terasaki, Alene K. 2004. Pre-announcement sequences in conversation. *Conversation analysis: studies from the first generation*, ed. Gene H. Lerner, 171–223. Amsterdam: Benjamins. (First appeared as Social Science Working Paper 99, School of Social Sciences, Irvine, CA, 1976.)
Thompson, Sandra A. 2002. "Object complements" and conversation: towards a realistic account. *Studies in Language* 26:125–64.

Thompson, Sandra A. Forthcoming. Understanding "clause" as an emergent "unit": special issue on units. *Studies in language*, ed. Ritva Laury, Ryoko Suzuki and Tsuyoshi Ono.

Thompson, Sandra A. and Elizabeth Couper-Kuhlen. 2005. The clause as a locus of grammar and interaction. *Discourse Studies* 7: 481–505. (Also in *Language and Linguistics* 6:807–37.)

Thompson, Sandra A., Barbara A. Fox and Elizabeth Couper-Kuhlen. 2015. *Grammar and everyday talk: building responsive actions*. Cambridge: Cambridge University Press.

Thompson, Sandra A., Robert E. Longacre and Shin Ja J. Hwang. 2007. Adverbial clauses. *Language typology and syntactic description.* Vol. 2: *Complex constructions* (2nd ed.), ed. Timothy Shopen, 237–300. Cambridge: Cambridge University Press.

Thompson, Sandra A. and Anthony Mulac. 1991a. A quantitative perspective on the grammaticization of epistemic parentheticals in English. *Approaches to grammaticalization.* Vol. 2: *Focus on types of grammatical markers*, ed. Elizabeth Traugott and Bernd Heine, 313–29. Amsterdam: Benjamins.

Thompson, Sandra A. and Anthony Mulac. 1991b. The discourse conditions for the use of complementizer that in conversational English. *Journal of Pragmatics* 15:237–51.

Thompson, Sandra A. and Ryoko Suzuki. 2014. Reenactments in conversation: gaze and recipiency. *Discourse Studies* 16(6):816–46.

Thumm, Markus. 2000. The contextualization of paratactic conditionals. *InLiSt* 20 (www.uni-potsdam.de/u/inlist/issues/20/index.htm).

Tomasello, Michael. 2003. *Constructing a language: a usage-based theory of language acquisition*. Cambridge, MA: Harvard University Press.

Tomasello, Michael. 2008. *Origins of human communication*. Cambridge, MA: MIT Press.

Uhmann, Susanne. 1992. Contextualizing relevance: on some forms and functions of speech rate changes in everyday conversation. *The contextualization of language*, ed. Peter Auer and Aldo di Luzio, 297–336. Amsterdam: Benjamins.

Uhmann, Susanne. 1996. On rhythm in everyday German conversation: beat clashes in assessment utterances. *Prosody in conversation: interactional studies*, ed. Elizabeth Couper-Kuhlen and Margret Selting, 303–65. Cambridge: Cambridge University Press.

Uhmann, Susanne. 2001. Some arguments for the relevance of syntax to same-sentence self-repair in everyday German conversation. *Studies in interactional linguistics*, ed. Margret Selting and Elizabeth Couper-Kuhlen, 373–404. Amsterdam: Benjamins.

Uhmann, Susanne. 2006. Grammatik und Interaktion: Form follows function? – Function follows form? *Grammatik und Interaktion*, ed. Arnulf Deppermann, Reinhard Fiehler and Thomas Spranz-Fogasy, 179–202. Radolfzell: Verlag für Gesprächsforschung (www.verlag-gespraechsforschung.de).

Van der Goot, Marloes H., Michael Tomasello and Ulf Liszkowski. 2014. Differences in the nonverbal requests of great apes and human infants. *Child Development* 85:444–55.

Vásquez, Camilla. 2010. Examining two explicit formulations in university discourse. *Text & Talk* 30:749–71.

Vatanen, Anna. 2014. *Responding in overlap: agency, epistemicity and social action in conversation*. PhD thesis, Department of Finnish, Finno-Ugric and Scandinavian Studies, University of Helsinki.

Vinkhuyzen, Erik and Margaret H. Szymanski. 2005. *Would you like to do it yourself?* Service requests and their non-granting responses. *Applying conversation analysis*, ed. Keith Richards and Paul Seedhouse, 91–106. Basingstoke: Palgrave Macmillan.

Vorreiter, Susanne. 2003. Turn continuations: towards a cross-linguistic classification. *InLiSt* 39 (www.inlist.uni-bayreuth.de).

Wacewicz, Sławomir and Przemysław Żywiczyński. 2015. Language evolution: why Hockett's design features are a non-starter. *Biosemiotics* 8:29–46.
Walker, Gareth. 2001. *A phonetic approach to talk-in-interaction: increments in conversation*. MA dissertation, University of York.
Walker, Gareth. 2004a. *The phonetic design of turn endings, beginnings, and continuations in conversation*. PhD thesis, Department of Language and Linguistic Science, University of York.
Walker, Gareth. 2004b. On some interactional and phonetic properties of increments to turns in talk-in-interaction. *Sound patterns in interaction*, ed. Elizabeth Couper-Kuhlen and Cecilia E. Ford, 147–70. Amsterdam: Benjamins.
Walker, Gareth. 2007. On the design and use of pivots in everyday English conversation. *Journal of Pragmatics* 39:2217–43.
Walker, Gareth. 2010. The phonetic constitution of a turn-holding practice: rush-throughs in English talk-in-interaction. *Prosody in interaction*, ed. Dagmar Barth-Weingarten, Elisabeth Reber and Margret Selting, 51–72. Amsterdam: Benjamins.
Walker, Gareth. 2012. Coordination and interpretation of vocal and visible resources: "trail-off" conjunctions. *Language and Speech* 55:141–63.
Walker, Gareth. 2013. Phonetics and prosody in conversation. *The handbook of conversation analysis*, ed. Jack Sidnell and Tanya Stivers, 455–74. Chichester: Wiley-Blackwell.
Walker, Traci, Paul Drew and John Local. 2011. Responding indirectly. *Journal of Pragmatics* 43:2434–51.
Weber, Elizabeth. 1993. *Varieties of questions in English conversation*. Amsterdam: Benjamins.
Weidner, Matylda. 2016. Aha-moments in interaction: indexing a change of state in Polish. *Journal of Pragmatics* 104:193–206.
Weiste, Elina and Anssi Peräkylä. 2013. A comparative conversation analytic study of formulations in psychoanalysis and cognitive psychotherapy. *Research on Language and Social Interaction* 46:299–321.
Wells, Bill and Juliette Corrin. 2004. Prosodic resources, turn-taking and overlap in children's talk-in-interaction. *Sound patterns in interaction*, ed. Elizabeth Couper-Kuhlen and Cecilia E. Ford, 119–44. Amsterdam: Benjamins.
Wells, Bill and Sarah Macfarlane. 1998. Prosody as an interactional resource: turn-projection and overlap. *Language and Speech* 41(3–4):265–94.
Wells, Bill and Sue Peppé. 1996. Ending up in Ulster: prosody and turn-taking in English dialects. *Prosody in conversation: interactional studies*, ed. Elizabeth Couper-Kuhlen and Margret Selting, 101–30. Cambridge: Cambridge University Press.
Whalen, Jack and Don H. Zimmerman. 1998. Observations on the display and management of emotion in naturally occurring activities: the case of "hysteria" in calls to 9–1–1. *Social Psychology Quarterly* 61(2):141–59.
White, Anne and Chase Raymond. 2014. *Time reference in the service of social action*. Paper read at the International Conference on Conversation Analysis (ICCA) 2014, Los Angeles, CA.
Whorf, Benjamin Lee. 1956. *Language, thought, and reality: selected writings of Benjamin Lee Whorf*, ed. John B. Carroll. Cambridge, MA: MIT Press.
Wichmann, Anne. 2000. *Intonation in text and discourse*. London: Longman.
Wichmann, Anne. 2001. Spoken parentheticals. *A wealth of English*, ed. Karin Aijmer, 177–93. Gothenburg: University Press.
Wiggins, Sally and Jonathan Potter. 2003. Attitudes and evaluative properties: category vs. item and subjective vs. objective constructions in everyday food assessments. *British Journal of Social Psychology* 42:513–31.

Wilkinson, Sue and Celia Kitzinger. 2006. Surprise as an interactional achievement: reaction tokens in conversation. *Social Psychology Quarterly* 69(2):150–82.

Wilkinson, Sue and Ann Weatherall. 2011. Insertion repair. *Research on Language and Social Interaction* 44:65–91.

Wootton, Anthony J. 1981a. Two request forms of four year olds. *Journal of Pragmatics* 5:511–23.

Wootton, Anthony J. 1981b. The management of grantings and rejections by parents in request sequences. *Semiotica* 37:59–89.

Wootton, Anthony J. 1989. Remarks on the methodology of conversation analysis. *Conversation: an interdisciplinary perspective*, ed. Derek Roger and Peter Bull, 238–58. Clevedon: Multilingual Matters.

Wootton, Anthony J. 1997. *Interaction and the development of the mind*. Cambridge: Cambridge University Press.

Wootton, Anthony J. 2005. Interactional and sequential features informing request format selection in children's speech. *Syntax and lexis in conversation*, ed. Auli Hakulinen and Margret Selting, 185–207. Amsterdam: Benjamins.

Wouk, Fay. 2005. The syntax of repair in Indonesian. *Discourse Studies* 7:237–58.

Wright, Melissa. 2005. *Studies of the phonetics–interaction interface: clicks and interactional structures in English conversation*. PhD thesis, University of York.

Wright, Melissa. 2011a. The phonetics–interaction interface in the initiation of closings in everyday English telephone calls. *Journal of Pragmatics* 43(4):1080–99.

Wright, Melissa. 2011b. On clicks in English talk-in-interaction. *Journal of the International Phonetic Association* 41(2):207–29.

Wu, Ruey-Jiuan Regina. 2004. *Stance in talk: a conversation analysis of Mandarin final particles*. Amsterdam: Benjamins.

Wu, Ruey-Jiuan Regina. 2006. Initiating repair and beyond: the use of two repeat-formatted repair initiations in Mandarin conversation. *Discourse Processes* 41:67–109.

Wu, Ruey-Jiuan Regina. 2009. Repetition in the initiation of repair. *Conversation analysis: comparative perspectives*, ed. Jack Sidnell, 31–59. Cambridge: Cambridge University Press.

Wu, Ruey-Jiuan Regina. 2011. A conversation analysis of self-praising in everyday Mandarin interaction. *Journal of Pragmatics* 43(13):3152–76.

Yoon, Kyung-Eun. 2010. Questions and responses in Korean conversation. *Journal of Pragmatics* 42:2782–98.

Zhang, Wei. 2012. Latching/rush-through as a turn-holding device and its functions in retrospectively oriented pre-emptive turn continuation: findings from Mandarin Chinese. *Discourse Processes* 49:163–91.

Zinken, Jörg. 2013. Reanimating responsibility: the *weź*-V2 (take-V2) double imperative in Polish interaction. *Approaches to Slavic interaction*, ed. Nadine Thielemann and Peter Kosta, 35–61. Amsterdam: Benjamins.

Zinken, Jörg and Eva Ogiermann. 2011. How to propose an action as objectively necessary: the case of Polish *trzeba x* ("one needs to x"). *Research on Language and Social Interaction* 44:263–87.

Zinken, Jörg and Eva Ogiermann. 2013. Responsibility and action: invariants and diversity in requests for objects in British English and Polish interaction. *Research on Language and Social Interaction* 46(3):256–76.

Appendix

Transcription Systems

Most examples in the chapters of this book are given in transcript form using one of the following two transcription systems:

i. the CA system, originally devised by Gail Jefferson and subsequently revised by CA scholars (see, e.g., Jefferson 2004a; Hepburn and Bolden 2013)
ii. the GAT system, originally developed and subsequently revised by a group of German interactional linguists and conversation analysts (Selting et al. 1998, 2009).

While the two transcription systems use many of the same conventions, the GAT system aims for greater explicitness and clarity in the representation of prosodic and paralinguistic features in talk-in-interaction.

The main transcription symbols used in each system are listed here:

CA Transcription Symbols

(Abbreviated representation following Schegloff 2007a:265–69; see also Sidnell 2010:ix–x.)

Temporal and Sequential Relationships

[[	point of onset of overlap
]]	end of overlap
//	point of overlap (in older transcripts)
*	end of overlap (in older transcripts)
=	latching
(0.5)	silence in tenths of a second
(.)	micropause, ordinarily less than 0.2 second

Symbols Used to Represent Aspects of Speech Delivery

Punctuation marks indicate intonation, not grammatical function.

.	falling, or final, intonation contour
?	rising intonation
,	continuing intonation
?, or ¿	rise stronger than a comma but weaker than question mark
: ::	sound prolongation or stretching; the more colons, the longer the stretching

Underlining to indicate stress or emphasis

<u>w</u>ord <u>word</u> WOrd w<u>O</u>rd	"Underlining is used to indicate some form of stress or emphasis, either by increased loudness or higher pitch. The more underlining, the greater the emphasis. Therefore, underlining sometimes is placed under the first letter or two of a word, rather than under the letters which are actually raised in pitch or volume. Especially loud talk may be indicated by upper case; again, the louder, the more upper case. And, in extreme cases, upper case may be underlined." (Schegloff 2007a:267)

Combinations of underlining and colons used to indicate intonation contours:

_:	falling intonation contour
:̲	rising intonation contour
↑ ↓ ↑ or ^	sharper intonation rises and falls than would be indicated by combinations of colons and underlining; or a whole shift, or resetting, of the pitch register
°	following talk markedly quiet or soft
° °	talk between degree signs markedly softer than the talk around it
> <	talk between the "more than" and "less than" symbols is compressed or rushed
< >	talk between the "less than" and "more than" symbols is slowed or drawn out
<	immediately following talk is "jump-started", i.e., sounds like it is started with rush
hhh	hearable aspiration; the more "h"s, the more aspiration; may represent
(hh)	breathing, laughter, etc.
.hh or .hh	inhalation
{}	surrounds alternative transcriptions separated by /
-	after a word or part of a word: cut-off or self-interruption

Other markings

(( ))	transcriber's description of events
(word)	uncertain transcription
( )	unidentified syllables or segments or speakers
(a)/(uh)	alternative hearings

GAT Transcription Symbols

(Overview as summarized in Couper-Kuhlen and Barth-Weingarten 2011:37–39; see also Selting et al. 2009.)

Minimal Transcript

Sequential structure
[ ]   overlap and simultaneous talk
[ ]

In- and outbreaths
°h / h°   in- / outbreaths of appr. 0.2-0.5 sec. duration
°hh / hh°   in- / outbreaths of appr. 0.5-0.8 sec. duration
°hhh / hhh°   in- / outbreaths of appr. 0.8-1.0 sec. duration

Pauses
(.)   micro pause, estimated, up to appr. 0.2 sec. duration
(-)   short estimated pause of appr. 0.2-0.5 sec. duration
(--)   intermediary estimated pause of appr. 0.5-0.8 sec. duration
(---)   longer estimated pause of appr. 0.8-1.0 sec. duration
(0.5)/(2.0)   measured pause of appr. 0.5 / 2.0 sec. duration (to tenth of a second)

Other segmental conventions
and_uh   cliticizations within units
uh, uhm, etc. hesitation signals, so-called "filled pauses"

Laughter and crying
haha hehe hihi   syllabic laughter
((laughs)) ((cries))   description of laughter or crying
<<laughing> >   laughter particles accompanying speech with indication of scope
<<:-)> so>   smile voice with indication of scope

Continuers and response takens
hm, yes, no, yeah   monosyllabic signals
hm_hm, ye_es,   ⎫   bi-syllabic signals
no_o   ⎭
?hm?hm,   with glottal closure, often negating

Other conventions
((coughs))   ⎫   non-verbal vocal actions and
<<coughing> >   ⎭   events with indication of scope

(cont.)

( )	unintelligible passage
(xxx), (xxx xxx)	one or two unintelligible syllables
(may i)	assumed wording
(may i say/let us say)	possible alternatives
((unintelligible, appr. 3 sec))	unintelligible passage with indication of duration
((...))	omission in transcript
->	refers to a line of transcript relevant in the argument

Basic Transcript

<u>Sequential structure</u>	
=	fast, immediate continuation by a new turn or segment (latching)
<u>Other segmental conventions</u>	
:	lengthening, by about 0.2–0.5 sec.
::	lengthening, by about 0.5–0.8 sec.
:::	lengthening, by about 0.8–1.0 sec.
?	cut-off by glottal closure
<u>Accentuation</u>	
SYLlable	focus accent
!SYL!lable	extra strong accent
<u>Final pitch movements of intonation phrases</u>	
?	rising to high
,	rising to mid
–	level
;	falling to mid
.	falling to low
<u>Other conventions</u>	
<<surprised> >	interpretive comment with indication of length

Fine Transcript

```
Accentuation
SYLlable            focus accent
sYllable            secondary accent
!SYL!lable          extra strong accent

Pitch jumps
↑                   smaller pitch upstep
↓                   smaller pitch downstep
↑↑                  larger pitch upstep
↓↓                  larger pitch downstep

Changes in pitch register, with scope
<<l>       >        lower pitch register
<<h>       >        higher pitch register

Intralinear notation of accent pitch movements
`SO                 falling
´SO                 rising
⁻SO                 level
^SO                 rising-falling
ˇSO                 falling-rising

↑`                  small pitch upstep to the peak of the accented
                        syllable
↓´                  small pitch downstep to the valley of the
                        accented syllable
↑⁻SO or ↓⁻SO        pitch jumps to higher or lower level accented
                        syllables
↑↑`SO or ↓↓´SO      larger pitch upsteps or downsteps to the peak
                        or valley of the accented syllable

Loudness and tempo changes, with scope
<<f>       >        forte, loud
<<ff>      >        fortissimo, very loud
<<p>       >        piano, soft
<<pp>      >        pianissimo, very soft
<<all>     >        allegro, fast
<<len>     >        lento, slow
<<cresc>   >        crescendo, increasingly louder
<<dim>     >        diminuendo, increasingly softer
<<acc>     >        accelerando, increasingly faster
<<rall>    >        rallentando, increasingly slower

Changes in voice quality and articulation, with scope
<<creaky>   >       glottalized
<<whispery> >       examples of change in voice quality as stated
```

Index

abrupt join, 90, 94
accent
   non-TRP projecting, 92, 94
   possible turn-final, 83
   TRP-projecting, 75
accent-timed language, 70
accentuation, 69
acceptance of offer, 259, 260
account, 443, 454
   by design vs. on demand, 456
accountable, 454
acknowledgment vs. affiliation, 506
   American English, 506
   British English, 507
   Finnish, 509
action, 27, 28
   ascription, 210
   context-shaped vs. context-renewing, 6
   double-barrelled, 213
   formation, 210
   responsive, 230, 497
   type, 212
activity, 28
actually, 321
adjacency pair, 212, 552
   base, 329
A-event, 509
affirmation, 238
affirming/confirming but resisting, 241
agreeing but asserting epistemic independence, 300, 302
agreement with assessment, 294, 295
alright, 326
"although", 443, 460
although, 460
analysis
   bottom-up, 217
   top-down, 216
and, 429
   prefacing, 436, 516
"and", 435
   as turn-final particle, 530

and uh(m), 351
answer, 218
   transformative, 242
answering system, 498
antecedent of relative clause, 469
apokoinou construction, 381, 383
argument omission, 411
aspiration particle, 542, 547
assertion, 506
assessment, 283, 514
   downgraded, 289, 296
   extended telling, 285, 337
   first-position, 287
   linguistic design, 288
   second-position, 294
   sequence-closing, 286, 336
   sequential environment, 285
   upgraded, 289, 295

back-connecting, 346, 438
   as resumption, 348
   recycling with prosodic continuation, 346
   recycling with prosodic restart, 346
   with *and uh(m)*, 351
   with Russian *-to*, 352
"because", 440, 454
B-event, 220, 227, 320, 509
but, 430
   turn-final, 431
"but", 436
   as turn-final particle, 531

Caribbean Creole English, 158, 167, 168, 303, 550
categorize/categorization, 116, 139, 142, 196
change-of-state particle, 542, 552
   Danish, 503
   Finnish, 503
   German, 502, 503, 505
   Japanese, 503, 505
Chinese (Mandarin), 89, 91, 119, 173, 193, 201, 366, 411

611

clause, 23, 355, 359, 361, 365, 378, 380, 424
　adverbial, 449
　causal, 450
　complement, 462, 463, 466, 467, 487
　conditional, 450, 457
　conditional freestanding, 458
　curtailed, 410
　non-finite, 391
　postposed circumstantial, 450, 451
　pre-posed circumstantial, 450, 453
　relative, 462, 469
　verb-first conditional, 457
clause combination, 426
　additive, 429
　adversative, 443
　alternative, 439
　asyndetic, 428, 442
　bipartite, 489, 491
　circumstantial, 440, 449
　concessive, 444, 445
　contrastive, 430
　hendiadic, 432, 433
　hypotactic, 440, 443, 449
　paratactic, 429, 440, 443
　reason, 440
　subordinate, 462
cleft construction, 475
　pseudo, 475
click, 333, 542
co-construction (*see also* turn, collaborative
　　construction), 369, 545
collaborative completion, 38
collateral effects of means for accomplishing an
　　action, 550
comparative concept, 355
complaint, 222, 435, 449
complement
　-taking predicate, 462, 466, 467, 492
　type, 462
complementizer, 462, 467
Complex Transition Relevance Place
　　(CTRP), 51
compliance with request, 259, 260, 261
compliment, 292
compound turn-constructional unit (TCU), 59, 453
concession, 445
　show, 446
confirmation, 238
　overt in English, 240
confirming an allusion, 214
conjunctional, 528
　as turn-final particle, 528
　trail-off, 529
connective (*see also* connector)
　as turn preface, 348
connector
　concessive, 443, 461
　detached, 431, 439

construction, 363
　with subject omission, 424
contextualization, 9
　cues, 8, 9
　theory, 8
contingency
　in requesting, 254
　of situated interaction, 22
continuer, 497, 511, 542, 552
　vs. acknowledgment token, 512
　vs. assessment token, 513
contrast (to something previously said), 63
contrastive focus, 68
Conversation Analysis, 5, 7, 16
　methodological tools, 7, 13
　vs. Interactional linguistics, 17
coordination, 426
　clausal, 426
correction, 113, 114
　embedded, 202
　exposed, 202
cut-off, 109, 117, 125, 126
　closure, 125

Danish, 53, 263, 279, 281, 300, 445, 503
data, 19, 20, 23, 26
delayed-projection language, 40, 42, 46, 53, 56,
　　62, 368
delaying device, 117
denial, 238, 245
dense construction, 412, 416, 424
deviant case, 25
dialogical character
　of spoken language, 363
directive, 253
disagreement with assessment, 296, 297, 305
disclaiming, 232, 236
disconfirmation, 238, 245, 247
discontinuity marker, 346
dislocation, 542
dispreference, 207
double saying, 235, 336, 341
Dutch, 57, 58, 59, 226, 348, 436, 501, 535

early-projection language, 46, 53, 367, 368
embedding, 426
emergent, 22
emergent grammar, 364, 365
enchrony of conversation, 544
end field, 376, 378
entitlement in requesting, 254
epistemic
　gradient, 230
　parenthetical, 463
　phrase, 463, 464
　stance, 238
Estonian, 104, 466, 499, 518, 523
expansion, 95, 394

Index

extension, 95, 424
　clausal, 394, 409
　of sentences and clauses, 370
　of units in time, 545
extraposition, 475, 482, 491
　integrated, 486
　non-integrated, 485

face, 444
figurative expression, 324
finiteness, 389
Finnish, 59, 70, 78, 104, 117, 119, 134, 135, 137, 138, 204, 227, 251, 262, 273, 355, 371, 378, 431, 432, 460, 495, 530, 549, 550
　acknowledgment vs. affiliation, 509
　affirmation vs. confirmation, 238
　agreement with first assessment, 299, 550
　authoritative agreement with first assessment, 303
　change-of-state particle, 279, 281, 503, 505
　complementizer *että* "that", 467
　denial vs. disconfirmation, 245
　echo answering system, 499
　freestanding *jos* "if" clause, 257, 458
　infinitive construction, 392, 393
　lexical repair initiator *eiku*, 126
　maximal response to polar interrogative, 242
　morphological repair, 134
　noun phrase (NP), 417, 419
　other correction, 205, 206, 207
　self-repair, 126, 132
　self-repair initiation device, 201
　turn holding, 55, 69, 94
　turn yielding, 70, 87, 531
　turn-final particle, 432, 530, 531, 533
　"yes … but" construction, 305, 307, 445
first-verb construction, 62, 447
form, 28, 29
format, 28, 29, 113
　tying, 306
formulation, 339
　closure-relevant, 335, 339
　expansion-relevant, 339
fragment, 108
free
　(phrasal) constituent (*see also* phrase, free(standing)), 421
　constituent (e.g., free NP), 95, 99, 420
French, 59, 70, 75, 77, 88, 409, 460, 499, 554
　disconfirmation of negative polar interrogative, 248
　left dislocation construction, 397, 398, 401
　pivot construction, 386, 388
　pseudocleft construction, 481
　right dislocation construction, 405
　tag, 225
　upgraded second assessment, 300
front field, 376, 378
functional head, 131

German, 41, 42, 47, 51, 56, 58, 59, 61, 70, 72, 77, 91, 95, 97, 100, 101, 107, 117, 120, 136, 137, 138, 148, 154, 158, 160, 162, 165, 166, 168, 171, 173, 179, 181, 182, 184, 186, 189, 190, 193, 257, 355, 360, 363, 366, 372, 375, 380, 391, 393, 396, 400, 401, 403, 420, 424, 445, 451, 498, 506, 554
　"although", 443, 460, 461
　because, 88
　"because", 441
　breaking and/or abandoning talk, 109
　change-of-state particle, 502, 503
　clause extension, 407, 408
　complementation, 464
　compliment response, 309
　denial/disconfirmation of negative polar interrogative, 248
　dense construction, 412, 416
　early projection, 40, 46, 367, 368
　extraposition structure, 483, 484
　intonation phrase, 50
　news receipt, 279, 282
　oh response to informing, 505
　parataxis vs. hypotaxis, 440
　phrase structure, 422
　pivot, 382, 385
　position of circumstantial clause, 450
　projection, 11, 42, 69, 88, 430
　projector construction, 487
　pseudocleft construction, 476, 480
　relative clause, 471
　reproach with "why", 222
　second assessment, 299
　self-repair initiation device, 201
　sentence brace, 41, 100, 378, 407
　syntax of self-repair, 130, 132
　tag, 225, 432, 535
　turn holding, 55, 69, 92, 94
　turn yielding, 81, 84
　verb-first construction, 293, 430, 457
　word/constituent order, 41, 360, 363, 378, 409, 450
glue-on, 99
Greek, 279

hanging topic, 394, 396
Hebrew, 136, 137
hendiadys, 432, 433
hesitation marker, 552
holding
　pause/silence, 55, 89
hypotaxis, 428

Icelandic, 146
"if", 450, 458
if-clause, 253, 492
inbreath, 333
incoming
　competitive, 106
　non-competitive, 106

increment/incrementation, 95, 101, 102, 363, 474, 490, 491
Indonesian, 119
infinitive construction, 393
informing, 232, 266, 269
    but resisting, 234
    linguistic design, 273
infrastructure for interaction (*see also* interaction, infrastructure for), 551
initiation of repair, 113, 147
insertable, 99
insertion repair, 128
interaction
    engine, 554
    focused vs. non-focused, 19
    infrastructure for, 548
interactional achievement, 22
Interactional Linguistics, 12, 14, 16, 26
    audio vs. video data, 20
    context-sensitive analysis, 22, 26
    data-grounded categories, 23,
    everyday vs. institutional data, 19
    mediated data, 20
    methodology, 14, 15
    online perspective, 22, 26
    principles of work, 18
interactive turn spaces, 46
interrogative
    negative, 304
    polar, 218, 224, 320
    question-word, 218, 220, 232
interrogativity, 218, 321
interruption, 104, 107, 108
intonation phrase, 50
invitation, 223
Italian, 78, 88, 221, 225, 256, 397, 401, 460, 499, 506

Japanese, 11, 42, 54, 56, 60, 62, 78, 97, 100, 101, 117, 133, 134, 138, 176, 179, 180, 355, 369, 418, 419, 527
    (turn-)final particle, 527
    agree-disagree answering system, 498
    change of state, 279, 505
    clause combining, 426
    contrastive marker, 432
    delayed projection, 40, 42, 46, 53, 63, 88, 368
    eh-response to assessment/assertion, 525
    eh-response to inquiry, 521
    news receipt, 282, 503
    placeholder repair, 119, 120, 123
    postpositional particle, 45
    question word, 220
    resisting a question with "no", 523
    second assessment, 299
    self-repair, 132
    self-repair initiation device, 201
    topic closure, 328
    turn expansion, 370
    turn yielding, 70, 84, 87
    unexpressed constituents, 45, 411
    upgraded first assessment, 291
    upgraded second assessment, 303
    verb-final, 42, 362
joint utterance completion, 369

K+/K−, 218
Korean, 46, 56, 63, 102, 119, 143, 147, 148, 150, 168, 177, 409, 411, 523, 532
    agree-disagree answering system, 499
    candidate understanding, 56, 177
    clausal extension, 409
    delayed projection, 42, 53, 63
    increment, 101
    indexical expression, 168
    "no" response to question-word question, 523
    strategy of "upshot-first-and-details-later", 63
    topic closure, 328
    turn-initial particle to resist a question, 522, 523, 524
    word order, 63, 362

language
    accountability of, 544
    as languaging, 543
    as positionally sensitive, 544
    as social behavior, 541
    design features, 542
    diversity, 548, 550
    functional theories of, 4
    paradigm of use, 544, 546
    universal, 551
    variation, 546
language and temporality, 544
Lao, 150, 303, 550, 551
left dislocation (construction), 372, 394, 396, 397, 400
left-headed, 423
Linguistic Anthropology, 10
linguistic relativity, 10, 550
linguistic resource, 320, 356
location of/locating the repairable or trouble source, 117, 127, 139
London Jamaican, 73, 75

macro-projection, 39
micro-projection, 39, 69
middle field, 376, 378
minimization principle of linguistic practice, 553, 554
misplacement, 515
    downgraded repetition repair, 345
    lexical marker, 342
morphological
    bonding, 136
    repair, 133
morpho-syntactic organization of languages, 137
multimodal, 35
multi-turn unit, 61
multi-unit turn, 34

Murrinh-Patha, 146, 148, 168
"my-side" telling, 229

narrow focus, 68
news delivery, 266
   distinguished from informing, 268, 269
   good vs. bad, 271, 279
   linguistic design, 270
news receipt, 275, 502
   German, 279, 281, 282
   Japanese, 282
   oh, 235, 276
newsmark, 276, 278
next turn repair initiation (NTRI), 114, 139
nextness principle of linguistic practice, 552, 554
next-turn onset, 366
"no" preface in response to question, 523
non-add-on, 97
non-finiteness (*see also* infinitive construction), 391
Norwegian, 142, 148
noun phrase (NP)
   full, 333

of course, 244
offer, 249
   action template for, 251
   linguistic design, 249
   preferred over request, 249
oh
   as turn preface, 243, 300
   extra high and pointed, 278
   falling pitch, 277
   rising pitch, 277
oh-preface
   in response to assessment/assertion, 524
   in response to question, 521
okay, 326
online syntax, 363
open class initiator (of repair), 140
opportunity space(s), 114
"or", 438, 532
   as turn-final particle, 532
other-correction, 201
   abdicated, 203
other-initiation
   formats, 144
   of other-repair (correction), 201
   of repair, 113, 138, 552
   of self-repair, 139
other-repair, 113
outcome (of repair), 113
overlap/overlapping talk, 103, 104, 105, 108
   resolution device, 105

parallel-opposition construction, 68
parataxis, 428
parenthetical insert, 56
parenthetical sequence, 57

particle, 493, 495, 542
   change-of-state (*see also* change-of-state particle), 502
   for minimal affiliation, 506
   for minimum acknowledgment, 506
   freestanding, 494, 497, 514
   position in sequence/turn, 43, 496
   positive and negative, 498
   prosodic-phonetic configuration, 495, 499
   reiterated, 495
   turn-final, 53, 54, 70, 84, 87, 100, 494, 495, 527
   turn-initial, 494, 495, 514
   upgraded, 501
pause/silence
   holding, 54, 55
   TCU-internal, 54
   trail-off, 55
phrase, 23, 101, 361, 416, 419, 424
   free(standing), 423
pitch onset
   high, 318, 331
pivot, 381, 383, 385, 388, 542
placeholder repair, 119
positionally sensitive grammar, 547
possible completion point, 37
possible last accent, 72, 81
possible syntactic completion (of a sentence or clause), 377
post-completion extension, 452
post-framing, 127
post-positioned, 117
post-possible completion, 534
practice, 27, 29, 216, 356, 543
pre-announcement, 268
preference
   action-related, 231
   for less severe over more severe types of repair, 142
   for stronger over weaker other-initiations of repair, 140
   hierarchy, 142, 143
   organization/structure, 446
   structures for repair, 115, 208
pre-framing, 127
preliminary, 526
prepositional phrase, 418
pre-sequence (*see also* sequence, pre-expansion), 313
problem
   of expectation/acceptability, 188
   of hearing, 147
   of hearing, localized, 156
   of hearing, non-localized, 147
   of hearing, specified, 156
   of hearing, unspecified, 147
   of reference, 162
   of understanding, 170
   treatment, 146
   type, 196
pro-drop, 411

progressivity, 112, 113, 114
  principle of linguistic practice, 553, 554
project, 215
projectable/projectability, 31
projection, 37, 39, 61, 368, 377, 545
  early (*see also* early-projection language), 40
projector construction, 481, 487, 492, 542
prosodic packaging, 371
prosodically
  integrated, 372
  marked, 85, 88, 191, 193
  non-salient, 191
  salient, 191
  separate, 372
pseudocleft construction, 476
  French, 481
  German, 480
pseudocleft piece, 478, 492

question, 217
  declarative, 228, 320
  rhetorical, 223
  specifying, 232
  telling, 232
question word
  category-specific, 140
  class-specific, 156
  class-unspecific, 156

reason for the call, 316, 331, 516, 518
recategorization (of trouble sources or problems), 116, 142, 154
recipient design principle of linguistic practice, 553, 554
recycle/recycling, 130, 132
  scope of, 130, 134
reference, 471, 472
  to person, 553
refusal of request, 259, 263, 265
rejection of offer, 259, 263, 265
relative clause, 356
  adnominal, 470, 474
  non-restrictive, 470, 471, 472
  restrictive, 470, 471
  sentential, 470, 474
relative construction
  biclausal, 470
  monoclausal, 469
relativizer, 469
repair, 112, 113, 116, 545
  initiation format, 196
  initiation opportunity space, 114
  initiator, 116
  mechanism, 112
  operation, 113, 116, 128, 146, 196
  post-positioned self-initiation, 123
  pre-positioned self-initiation, 118
  proper, 116
  self-initiation of, 116
  sequence, 114
  third-position, 114, 479
repairable, 113, 114
  types of, 127
repairer, 116
repetition, modified, 301, 302
replacement, 98
request, 249
  bilateral, 256
  linguistic design, 253
  mascarading as offer, 257
  unilateral, 256
request for
  action, 212
  confirmation, 218, 226
  information, 218, 225
  permission, 212
resource, 28, 29
  linguistic, 211, 356, 543
response
  repetitional, 241
  to compliment, English, 294, 307
  to compliment, German, 309
  to self-deprecation, 310
rhythm, 77, 80
rhythmic coordination, 78
right dislocation (construction), 402, 405
right-headed, 423
rush through, 89, 94
Russian, 119, 242, 352, 498, 500

self-deprecation, 287, 310
self-initiation of repair, 113, 553
self-repair, 113, 132
  same-sentence, 130
sentence, 23, 359, 361, 365, 424
  brace (*Satzklammer*), 378
sequence, 28, 215, 328
  beginning, 330
  closing, 335, 339
  insert expansion, 329
  misplaced, 342
  organization, 64, 328
  post-expansion, 330
  pre-expansion, 329
  type, 215
sequence-closing third, 330
sequentiality, 312, 328
skip-connecting (*see also* back-connecting), 436
smile voice, 543
so, 516, 529
  preface, 517
  trail-off, 529
social actions, 212
sound object, 542
Spanish, 78, 88
Speech Act Theory, 213

spoken language, 359
stopping or abandoning a turn, 108
structuration, 364
subject omission, 411, 412, 416
subordination, 426, 428
   clausal, 426
subsequent version, 438
summary assessment, 324, 335, 336, 486
surprise, 271
Swedish, 263, 465
   clause, 376, 377, 378
   conditional "if" clause, 457, 458
   pivot (*apokoinou*) construction, 382, 383, 385
   projection, 53
   self-repair, 132
   syntax, 363
   TCU, 375, 377, 380
   turn-final particle, 533
   upgraded second assessment, 300
   verb-first construction, 430, 457
   word/constituent order (fields), 376, 377, 380, 450
   "yes ... but" construction, 445
syllable-timed language, 70
syntagma of turn/sequence, 544
syntax of self-repair, 129, 130

tag, 224, 304, 534
   "abominable," 535
   Dutch, 226, 536
talk-in-interaction, 6
TCU, 39
   structural organization, 375
   tasks to be dealt with in, 375
   types of continuation, 98
temporal reference, 389
tense, 389, 391
Thai, 116, 176, 411
thinking face, 122
timing, 77
topic
   change, disjunctive, 315, 322, 515
   closing, 324, 326, 486
   first, 315, 316, 516
   initiation, 467
   management, 315
   proffer, 233, 320
   resumption, 436
   shift, stepwise, 314, 315, 321, 325, 332, 478
   transition, 325, 327
topicality, 314
   distinguished from sequentiality, 312, 354
topicalization, 379
topological field models, 363
traditional grammatical and prosodic units, 23

trail-off silence, 55, 109
transcription, 21
transition relevance space, 69, 70, 71, 72
transition-relevance place (TRP), 31, 70
truncated turn, 53, 54, 85
Turkish, 53, 70, 75, 363
turn, 22, 34
   collaborative construction (*see also* co-construction), 444, 454, 490
   design, 216
   effective beginning, 514
   ending, phonetic features, 73
   expansion, 94
   holding, 88
   yielding, 72, 88
turn-constructional unit (*see also* TCU), 22, 31, 34, 51, 52, 377, 380
turn-initial particle
   in first position, 515
   in second position, 520
   in third position, 526
types
   of evidence, 24
   of other-initiated repair, 197
typological word order models, 362

uh(m), 316
unexpressed constituents (*see also* zero anaphora), 45, 46, 410
universals of interaction, 554

validation, 26
variation
   contextually determined, 547
   elliptical, 547
   free, 547
verb repeat, 499, 550
verb-final (languages, clauses), 42, 102, 362
verb-second (languages, clauses), 362
voice quality, non-modal, 87

well, 518
   as turn preface, 236
well-preface
   in response to assessment/assertion, 524
   in response to question, 520, 521
Welsh, 499
word order, 42, 46, 136, 375, 377
word search, 118

Yélî Dnye, 167, 220
"*yes ... but*" construction, 305, 446

zero anaphora (*see also* unexpressed constituents), 411